The Integrated Model of Literacy

The integrated model of literacy is the only model that considers reading, writing, and spelling development and highlights the **synchrony**, or integrated relationships and connections among these areas. (This model is also called the synchrony model of literacy development; this text uses the terms *integrated* and *synchrony* synonymously in talking about the model.) For example, you may observe a child who might be considered a beginning reader, pretending to read a story using the illustrations rather than reading the words on the page. Observing further, you also note that the child uses scribbling or random letters and numerals to represent ideas. Based on those observations, you can use the integrated model of literacy development seen in both Table 3.1 as a flexible framework to help you identify students' behaviors at various phases of literacy development. Table 3.1 is organized by phase and presents characteristics and behaviors that pertain to each phase. Figure 3.1 presents the same information but in a more dynamic manner. Together they will help you understand what to look for and how to u~~se this information when you work with your students.~~

As you scan acro~~ss~~ ~~3.1 you will notice the synchrony, or~~
connections, betwee~~n~~ ~~ick walk-through~~
will help you conside~~r~~
phase.

Orthographic knowledge, a term used in Table 3.1, refers to the knowledge students have about how words are constructed and used (sometimes called *word knowledge*).

Spelling and orthographic knowledge are linked because students put their orthographic knowledge into action when they spell words, and it is the act of spelling that most readily reveals their level of word knowledge. But students also use orthographic knowledge when they make sound-symbol correspondences and recognize words as they read. Thus orthographic knowledge is a part of all areas of literacy: reading, writing, and spelling (Gill, 1992; Henderson & Templeton, 1986).

This model of literacy lays out distinct points of reference along a continuum of literacy development. As you will see in many examples in this text, students' reading behaviors predict how they spell, and students' spelling predicts how they read. As you look at the model, you will notice that constellations of reading, writing, and spelling behaviors grow increasingly complex as students exhibit more sophisticated development.

The constellations of literacy behaviors have fuzzy boundaries. As students move from one developmental phase to another, they often carry over behaviors associated with a previous phase as they move to more complex understandings. To compare the phases to grade levels consider these ranges. Some of the aspects of development follow:

Phase	*Range of Grade Levels for Each Phase*
Emergent	Pre-k to middle of 1
Beginning	K to middle of 2
Transitional	1 to middle of 4
Intermediate	3 to 8
Advanced	5 to 12

Developing Literacy

Developing Literacy
An Integrated Approach
to Assessment and Instruction

Donald R. Bear
University of Nevada, Reno

Diane Barone
University of Nevada, Reno

Houghton Mifflin Company

Boston   New York

Senior sponsoring editor: *Loretta Wolozin*
Associate editor: *Lisa Mafrici*
Senior project editor: *Rosemary Winfield*
Senior production/design coordinator: *Carol Merrigan*
Senior manufacturing coordinator: *Priscilla Bailey*
Marketing manager: *Pamela Laskey*

Cover design: *Cathy Hawkes; cover image: Sol LeWitt, Arcs from Four Corners in Four Colors, 1996, courtesy of the artist; photo: Woodruff/Brown Photography.*

Photo credits: page 7, Elizabeth Crews; page 30, Elizabeth Crews; page 50, Jean Claude LeJeune; page 84, Karen Preuss/The Image Works; page 111, Jean Claude LeJeune; page 147, Elizabeth Crews; page 177, Jean Claude LeJeune; page 195, Jean Claude LeJeune; page 209, Elizabeth Crews; page 223, Elizabeth Crews; page 282, Elizabeth Crews; page 284, Elizabeth Crews; page 313, Jean Claude LeJeune; page 360, Elizabeth Crews; page 398, Elizabeth Crews; page 426, Elizabeth Crews; page 435, Elizabeth Crews; page 464, Jeffrey Dunn/Stock Boston.

Credits continue on page C-1, which constitutes an extension of the copyright page.

Printed in the U.S.A.

Library of Congress Catalog Card Number: 97-72441

ISBN: 0-395-62176-3

123456789-DH-01 00 99 98 97

To the students and children we teach:
Thank-you for sharing and inspiring.

Brief Contents

Contents   xv
Preface   ix

PART ONE   Foundations of Assessment and Literacy Development   1

  1   What Is the Integrated Process of Assessment and Instruction?   3
  2   Essential Elements of Literacy   26
  3   How Literacy Develops: An Integrated Model of Literacy Development   61

PART TWO   Approaches to Informal Literacy Assessment   91

  4   Individual Literacy Assessments   93
  5   Whole-Group and Small-Group Informal Assessment   138

PART THREE   Classroom Instruction Integrated with Assessment   169

  6   Emergent Literacy   171
  7   Beginning Literacy   206

Children's Voices: What Children and Their Teachers Say About Literacy Learning   249

  8   Diversity in Literacy Learning   265
  9   Transitional Literacy Development   301
  10   Intermediate and Advanced Literacy   339

PART FOUR   Supporting Readers Within and Beyond the Classroom   381

  11   Understanding the Range of Reading and Writing Difficulties   383
  12   Formal Literacy Testing and Measurement   408
  13   Teaching Learners Who Experience Difficulties   431
  14   Epilogue: Building a Community of Learners   460

Glossary   G-1
Children's References   R-1
References   R-5
Credits   C-1
Name Index   I-1
Subject Index   I-7

Contents

Brief Contents vii

Preface x

PART ONE Foundations of Assessment and Literacy Development 1

1 What Is the Integrated Process of Assessment and Instruction? 3

What You Know About Assessment at This Time: The No-Book DRTA 4

TAKING A CLOSER LOOK:
Create Your Own No-Book DRTA 5

Our View of Assessment 5

TAKING A CLOSER LOOK:
A No-Book DRTA on Assessment as Brainstormed by a Group 6

The Integrated Process of Assessment and Instruction 7

Seven Essential Themes 8

TAKING A CLOSER LOOK:
Word Study on Terms Related to Assessment 11

The Activities of Assessment 12

TAKING A CLOSER LOOK:
Questions to Guide Self-Evaluation 15

Assessing Your Teaching 15

Special Times to Assess 16

Building a Personal Philosophy of Literacy Instruction: Four Guidelines for Teaching and Learning Literacy 17

Have Confidence in a Few Basic Principles of Literacy Development 18

Know That Teaching Is Not Telling 21

Teach with Vigor, and Use Common Sense 22

Develop Effective Management Skills 22

2 Essential Elements of Literacy 26

Three Worlds of Experience 27

The Social World 29

The Ecology of Language and Literacy Learning 29

The Social Importance of Literacy 36

Suggestions for Effective Instruction in the Social World 38

The Psychological World 41

The Mind, Language, and Literacy 41

Constructing Meaning in Literacy 42

Perception in Literacy 47

TAKING A CLOSER LOOK:
Extending the Text 48

Attitude and Sense of Self 48

STUDENT STUDY:
Seven First-Graders Learn to Read, One Doesn't 51

Suggestions for Effective Instruction in the Psychological World 52

The Physical World 53

The Biology of Language 53

TAKING A CLOSER LOOK:
Extending the Text 55

The Physical Acts of Reading and Writing 54

Health 56

Suggestions for Effective Instruction in the
Physical World 57

TAKING A CLOSER LOOK:
The Many Facets of Integration 58

3 How Literacy Develops: An Integrated Model of Literacy Development 61

The Integrated Model of Literacy 62

TAKING A CLOSER LOOK:
Why Synchrony? Why Development? 65

Emergent Readers and Writers 66

Reading 67

Spelling and Orthographic Knowledge 70

Writing 71

Beginning Readers and Writers 71

Reading 72

TAKING A CLOSER LOOK:
Try Reading Like a Beginner 74

Spelling and Orthographic Knowledge 75

Writing 79

Transitional Readers and Writers 80

Reading 81

Spelling and Orthographic Knowledge 82

Writing 83

Intermediate and Advanced Readers and Writers 85

Reading 86

Spelling and Orthographic Knowledge 87

Writing 89

PART TWO Approaches to Informal Literacy Assessment 91

4 Individual Literacy Assessments 93

Why Have Individual Assessments? 94

How to Describe Students' Literacy: Functional and Developmental Expressions 95

Functional Expressions of Literacy 96

Developmental Expressions of Literacy 103

Assessing Individuals with Informal, Qualitative Inventories 104

Getting Started 106

Introductory "Get to Know You"
Interview 106

Informal Reading Inventory 108

STUDENT STUDY:
Steve's Word Recognition 110

TAKING A CLOSER LOOK:
Marking Oral Reading 116

Spelling Assessment 120

Writing Together 120

STUDENT STUDY:
Lois 128

Interpretation and Evaluation 128

5 **Whole-Class and Small-Group Informal Assessment**   138

Links Between Individual and Whole-Class or Small-Group Assessment   140

The Assessment Process: Observation, Documentation, and Interpretation   141

Whole-Class Assessment Strategies   141

Small-Group Assessment Strategies   145

Using Whole-Class and Small-Group Instructional Events for Assessment   148

Pulling Together Your Assessment Information   154

STUDENT STUDY:
David's Literacy Biography   155

The Assessment Process: Evaluation and Planning   159

Using Portfolios for Evaluation   161

Other Means of Evaluation   164

Planning for Instruction   165

PART THREE   **Classroom Instruction Integrated with Assessment**   169

6 **Emergent Literacy**   171

Who Are Emergent Readers and Writers?   173

Early Literacy Knowledge   175

Knowledge of Language   175

Knowledge of Books and Reading   176

TAKING A CLOSER LOOK:
Excursions   178

Knowledge of Print   178

Informal Assessment of Emergent Literacy Knowledge   179

Book Knowledge   182

Knowledge of Print   185

Portfolios   192

Integrated Instruction for Emergent Readers and Writers   194

Reading   194

Storytelling   197

Writing   199

Letter Knowledge   201

7 **Beginning Literacy**   206

Who Are Beginning Readers and Writers?   207

Reading Instruction Integrated with Assessment   209

Reading to Students   209

Reading with Students   212

TAKING A CLOSER LOOK:
Related Center Activities   217

TAKING A CLOSER LOOK:
The Dictation Cycle   219

Reading on Their Own: Cooperative and Independent Activities   221

Learning on Their Own: Independent Reading Activities   222

Writing Instruction Integrated with
Assessment 224

Writing with Students: Support Activities for
Composing Together 224

Writing on Their Own: Cooperative and
Independent Activities 232

Word Study and Spelling Instruction Integrated
with Assessment 235

Word Study in the Semiphonemic Phase 237

Word Study in the Letter-Name Phase 242

TAKING A CLOSER LOOK:
Principles of Word Study 244

Coordinating Spelling with Word Study 244

Children's Voices: What Children and Their Teachers Say About Literacy Learning 249

 8 Diversity in Literacy Learning 265

Language Diversity 268

Learning a New Language 269

Assessment of Students Whose First Language
Is Not English 272

TAKING A CLOSER LOOK:
Learning a Second Language 274

Instruction for Students Whose First Language Is Not English 276

Cultural, Racial, and Socioeconomic Diversity 283

Assessment of Students with Diverse
Backgrounds 287

Instruction for Students with Diverse
Backgrounds 291

TAKING A CLOSER LOOK:
Criteria for Multicultural Book Selection 292

TAKING A CLOSER LOOK:
Stereotypes 293

Students Who Require Additional
Academic Support 294

Assessment for Students Who Require
Additional Academic Support 294

TAKING A CLOSER LOOK:
The Dilemma of Retention 296

Instruction for Students Who Require
Additional Academic Support 296

 9 Transitional Literacy Development 301

Who Are Transitional Readers and Writers? 303

Three Important Issues of the Transitional
Phase 304

Reading Instruction Integrated with
Assessment 305

Reading to Students 305

Reading with Students 305

TAKING A CLOSER LOOK:
The Issue of Word Calling 310

STUDENT STUDY:
Organizing Ideas 323

Reading on Their Own: Cooperative and Independent Activities 324

Writing Instruction Integrated with
Assessment 326

Writing with Students: Guided Writing
Activities 327

Writing on Their Own: Cooperative and
Independent Activities 330

Word Study and Spelling Instruction Integrated
with Assessment 332

Word Study in the Within-Word Pattern
Phase 333

Coordinating Spelling with Word Study 337

10 **Intermediate and Advanced Literacy** 339

Who Are Intermediate and Advanced Readers and Writers? 340

Reading Instruction Integrated with Assessment 343

Reading to Students 343

Reading with Students 344

Reading on Their Own: Cooperative and Independent Reading Activities 353

Writing Instruction Integrated with Assessment 356

Writing with Students: Support Activities for Composing Together 356

TAKING A CLOSER LOOK:
Weighing the Role of Mechanics in Writing 359

Writing on Their Own: Cooperative and Independent Activities 360

Word Study and Spelling Instruction Integrated with Assessment 362

STUDENT STUDY:
Marika Shows What She Knows 363

Word Study in the Syllable-Juncture Phase 365

Word Study in the Derivational-Constancy Phase 374

Coordinating Spelling with Word Study 376

TAKING A CLOSER LOOK:
Students' Role in Planning and Assessment 378

PART FOUR Supporting Readers Within and Beyond the Classroom 381

11 **Understanding the Range of Reading Difficulties** 383

The Developmental Continuum: A Model That Emphasizes Delay, Not Deficit or Difference 384

Recognizing a Student Who Is Experiencing Literacy Difficulties 386

Identifying and Understanding Sources of Students' Difficulties 388

Special Literacy Needs Within the Developmental Continuum 389

TAKING A CLOSER LOOK:
What Do We Know About Vision and Reading Difficulties? 392

STUDENT STUDY:
Why Can't Jack Read? 396

Students Beyond the Continuum 399

TAKING A CLOSER LOOK:
Dyslexia 400

TAKING A CLOSER LOOK:
Teaching Children with Severe or Profound Hearing Losses 402

How Understanding the Causes of Literacy Difficulties Helps the Classroom Teacher 403

Locate Special Services When Necessary and Appropriate 403

12 **Formal Literacy Testing and Measurement** 408

Standardized or Norm-Referenced Tests 409

Norm-Referenced Test Characteristics 411

Interpreting Norm-Referenced Test Results 411

TAKING A CLOSER LOOK:
Testing Terms 412

Individual Testing 416

TAKING A CLOSER LOOK:
First Grade Takes a Test 417

Diagnostic Norm-Referenced Tests 417

Criterion-Referenced Tests   421

Formal Testing Within the Overall Assessment Framework   423

Pros and Cons of Norm-Referenced Tests and Measures   425

   Pros   426

   Cons   427

13   Teaching Learners Who Experience Difficulties   431

Planning Instruction for Students with Difficulties   433

   Finding Ways for Students to Enjoy Reading and Writing   433

   Planning for Change: Set Priorities and Understand What Can Be Achieved   433

   Considering Resources   434

   Meeting to Plan   434

   Assess the Effectiveness of Instruction   437

   Develop Meaningful Goals and Objectives   438

   Special Services and Programs   439

   Inclusion, Integration, and Coordination   441

STUDENT STUDY:
Jack's Educational Plan   442

Literacy Instruction for Students with Difficulties   443

   Start by Reading to Students   444

   Reading with Students   444

   Writing   448

   Word Study Activities   449

STUDENT STUDY:
Michael Learns to Write   450

   Success in the Content Areas: Perseverance and Coping   453

Special Instructional Methods   455

14   Epilogue: Building a Community of Learners   460

Families, Schools, and Literacy   461

   Including Families in Literacy and Learning   461

   School as a Community for Learning   463

Growing as a Professional   466

   Extending Your Knowledge of Teaching and Learning on Your Own   467

   Extending Your Knowledge of Teaching and Learning with Support from Others   468

Glossary   G-1

Children's References   R-1

References   R-5

Credits   C-1

Name Index   I-1

Subject Index   I-7

Preface

Developing Literacy: An Integrated Approach to Assessment and Instruction is a comprehensive exploration of how to teach children to read and write. It integrates instruction and assessment. Assessment is grounded in literacy instruction in the classroom, and this instruction is informed by what teachers learn through informal assessment during instruction. It also examines literacy instruction, especially for students with difficulties, from a developmental perspective. That is, we approach the study of reading instruction and assessment by emphasizing the relationship between literacy and child development. This perspective is needed given the variations in literacy development in classrooms today.

Audience and Purpose

This book was written primarily for use in a second course in literacy for preservice teachers and in a variety of upper-level literacy assessment and foundations courses in which professional teachers, as part of their graduate work, study literacy development and apply assessment practices in the classroom. *Developing Literacy* is an ideal companion for site-based coursework as well as a resource for practicing teachers in daily instruction.

Perhaps the greatest strength of this text is its emphasis on the *classroom*. For instance, it includes classroom adaptations of assessment activities that have a long history in literacy instruction and are now made part of all teachers' repertoires. Literacy assessment is the province of all teachers, regular and specialized. In addition, throughout *Developing Literacy*, you can hear the distinct voices of children and youth that help to bring the classroom setting alive. Real children are highlighted through many examples and student studies, and a special insert—"Children's Voices: What Students and Their Teachers Say About Literacy Learning"—introduces you to ten children who talk about what they like to read and how they are learning to read and write. This orientation to literacy learners helps clarify how teachers can and must involve children in meaningful ways in the assessment process.

In *Developing Literacy*, students' instructional activities are provided in reading, writing, and word study across the spectrum of development. You will see that classrooms are composed of children who are at different phases in their development and therefore must be taught in ways that address these developmental differences.

Content and Organization

Developing Literacy consists of fourteen chapters divided into four parts. Part I, *Foundations of Assessment and Literacy Development,* consists of three chapters that lay the foundation for literacy instruction and assessment. Chapter 1 introduces literacy and assessment and shows how the two are integrated. Chapter 2 presents literacy essentials through a prism of three worlds of experience—social, psychological, and physical. Chapter 3 concisely describes development through a discussion of the emergent, beginning, transitional, intermediate, and advanced phases of literacy development.

The two chapters in Part II, *Approaches to Informal Literacy Assessment,* cover practices you can use to assess children individually and in small groups. Chapter 4 focuses on ways to assess children's reading, writing, and spelling through informal assessments, including assessments that are part of traditional informal reading inventories. Chapter 5 demonstrates how these informal assessments are adapted in small-group settings within a classroom—the context in which most teachers conduct their assessments.

Part III, *Classroom Instruction Integrated with Assessment,* is the heart of the book and draws on the first two parts of the text into the classroom. Students learn to build on children's social, psychological, and physical worlds, and to integrate assessment into daily instruction. These chapters discuss reading, writing, and word study instruction by phase of literacy development. You can refer to specific chapters to plan your own instruction in a developmental way. In Chapter 6, the emergent phases of literacy development are explored, emphasizing the role of families in learning to read and write. Chapter 7 considers the beginning phases of literacy development and includes a detailed discussion of support reading. The focus of Chapter 8 is on teaching children from diverse languages, cultures, and socioeconomic backgrounds. This chapter is placed between Chapters 7 and 9 (on beginning and transitional phases of literacy, respectively) because these two phases represent a critical period of instruction for students from diverse backgrounds. Chapter 9 provides a discussion of the transitional phase, the period when children gain some independence as they read simple chapter books and write lengthy stories. Chapter 10 examines reading, writing, and word study activities for students in the intermediate and advanced phases.

Part IV, *Supporting Readers Within and Beyond the Classroom,* focuses on students who experience difficulties learning to read and write. By studying how teachers work with children who have difficulties, you can refine and apply what you have learned about literacy instruction and assessment. Chapter 11 provides the information that classroom teachers need to know about identification and definitions of reading problems from dyslexia to developmental delays. Chapter 12 contains information on literacy testing and measurement and provides tools that can help you to interpret the results of formal tests. Chapter 13 explores alternative learning options and remedial activities that make it possible for students to grow as readers and writers in spite of variations in their development. Throughout these chapters the developmental perspective provides the grounding to plan instruction in the classroom even for students with difficulties. Finally, Chapter 14 helps students encourage teachers to build a community of learners with families as well as a community of teachers.

Special Pedagogic Features

The many special features of *Developing Literacy* aid students in understanding new concepts and vocabulary and encourage mastery of the material in the text. Nine features are particularly noteworthy:

- *Conversations* These brief conversations are derived from roundtable discussions held by practicing teachers and our students who have taken literacy instruction courses. These items pique interest as student-readers recognize some conversation issues and concerns as their own.

- *Guide Questions* Following the conversations, four or five guide questions urge students to think about what they already know about the concepts presented in the chapter *and* help students anticipate the concepts to be learned in the chapter.

- *Taking a Closer Look* There are times we want to provide just a bit more coverage and a few more examples on a subject to introduce new concepts and teaching practices. These close looks explore important issues and present specific guidelines for teaching, thereby providing the depth you need to understand challenging topics.

- *Student Study* Each *Study* tells a story about an individual or shows interaction among a small group of students. These studies introduce students to the types of children they eventually may encounter in their classrooms. By thinking through the examples, they can learn to apply this same type of thinking with their own students.

- *Children's Voices: What Children and Their Teachers Say About Literacy Learning* In this special insert, ten elementary school students are interviewed and talk about how they learned to read and write. The insert includes fascinating student writings and drawings as well as the voices of two teachers, Adine Petrulli and Becky Schneider, as they describe how these children were active learners in their classrooms. This feature links the children's and teachers' accounts to an exciting overview of the phases of literacy development and key text concepts.

- *Key Terms* The end of each chapter lists key terms that students need to know. In reviewing these lists, students identify the terms they understand as well as those they need to reexamine.

- *Study Notes* Each chapter also ends with a series of Study Notes that remind students of what concepts and activities are important. These brief statements lead students to complete the guide questions presented at the beginning of each chapter.

- *Follow-Up Activities* Suggested activities at the end of each chapter give readers the opportunity to extend their knowledge by conducting specific activities with individual and small groups of elementary school students. Readers explore related resources in the community and visit schools to observe instruction and interview teachers.

- *Glossary* The glossary is available for students to use to check their knowledge of vocabulary that has been highlighted throughout *Developing Literacy*.

Ancillaries That Accompany This Text

Accompanying *Developing Literacy* is an Instructor's Resource Manual with Test Items. The manual contains an abundance of assessment activities and materials for students to use in their teaching and preservice practicums. Model syllabi show a few ways you can use *Developing Literacy* with your students. Annotated lecture outlines of each text chapter mesh the instructor's ideas and examples with the key concepts of the text. Examples of how students are involved in instruction and assessment can be used in class discussions and lectures. A variety of charts can be used as handouts or overhead transparencies to guide students in developing activities. Finally, the manual contains test items that test students' comprehension and ability to apply what they have learned in the context on classroom situations and activities.

Acknowledgments

This preface would be as long as the book if we could thank everyone who has helped us. First, then, we gratefully acknowledge the teachers who shared the wonderful ways they teach children to think, read, and write.

Second to none are our families. Writing this text took time away from family activities, and we dedicate to you this book for teachers and children.

The conversations at the beginning of each chapter set the tone of this book by bringing children's and teachers' voices to learning. Many other conversations have gone into making this book, and many educators shared their friendship and their conversations. We want to thank our fellow teachers who participated in the conversations: Tamara Baren, Rob Bray, Carol Caserta-Henry, Sharon Cathey, Brian Crosby, Carol Curtis, Leslie Doukas, Willie Edwards, Syna Erb, Steve Howe, Sandy Madura, Francine Mayfield, Karen McVeigh, Shari Nielson, Diane Olds, Sherry Paladino, Adine Petrulli, Melissa Pruyn, Claudia Rossi, Rebecca Schneider, Lynn Terry, and Sandy Whellams.

Colleagues at other colleges and universities also joined us in conversations that are woven into this text: Mary Abouzeid, Ron Cramer, Ann Fordham, Tom Gill, Dorsey Hammond, Marcia Invernizzi, Darrell Morris, Brenda Sabey, Bob Schlagal, Helen Shen, Charles Temple, Frank Vellutino, and Jerry Zutell. We also want to thank faculty members at the University of Nevada, Reno and Las Vegas, who gave their support and understanding to produce this text: Vern Luft, Meggin McIntosh, Marilyn McKinney, Maria Meyerson, Rebecca Mills, and Mike Warner.

Reviewers of the manuscript gave important feedback that we tried our best to understand and incorporate into this text. We thank them for their guidance:

Diane D. Allen, University of North Texas

Christopher Baker

Eugene H. Cramer, The University of Illinois at Chicago

Mariam Jean Dreher, University of Maryland–College Park

Robert Gaskins, University of Kentucky

Douglas K. Hartman, University of Pittsburgh

Peter Hasselriis, University of Missouri–Columbia

Valerie Helgren-Lempesis

Carol Lauritzen, Eastern Oregon State College

Susan K. Leone, Clarion University of Pennsylvania

Charles A. Perfetti, University of Pittsburgh

Suzanne Robbins, West Liberty State College

Mary F. Roe, University of Delaware

Mark Sadoski, Texas A & M University

Linda L. Ekman Simmons, Fort Lewis College

Dixie Lee Spiegel, The University of North Carolina at Chapel Hill

Steven A. Stahl, The University of Georgia

Robin Steed, Brigham Young University

Rebecca Swearingen, Southwest Missouri State University

Yvonne L. Turner, California State Polytechnic University–Pomona

Constance Ulmer, Appalachian State University

The support of our publisher has been immense. Loretta Wolozin, senior sponsoring editor, represented the publisher's commitment to writing a book that reflects what we know about literacy development, instruction, and child-centered approaches to teaching. Merryl Maleska Wilbur, developmental editor, contributed to the growth and structure of this text, and we find ourselves grateful for her contributions to our personal growth as teacher educators. We also want to thank Rosemary Winfield, senior project editor, and Jean Zielinski De-Mayo, editorial assistant, for their keen and kind attention to details and clarity throughout.

Finally, among the family, children, students, and teachers who have helped us write this book, we want to make a special acknowledgment to Edmund Henderson and Shane Templeton, our closest professional mentors and friends.

D.B.
D.B.

Developing Literacy

PART ONE

Foundations of Assessment and Literacy Development

Contents

1 What Is the Integrated Process of Assessment and Instruction?

2 Essential Elements of Literacy

3 How Literacy Develops: An Integrated Model of Literacy Development

1 What Is the Integrated Process of Assessment and Instruction?

Conversation

Sharon: What is assessment? That is where we have to start. As an administrator, I visit classrooms, and I watch all the time to see if assessment is being used as an ongoing tool. I've found that for years and years it was the piece that had been left out.

Carol: As a classroom teacher, assessment has become a real issue for me. It's become critical. What am I actually doing with these children? I have them only 180 days a year. I used to think that was a lot, but it's not, especially when you work with at-risk children.

Steve: As a first-year teacher, I wonder how we can assess learning and still provide grades and whether assessing and learning can go together. That was my charge last year. In many cases, I don't think I met that charge. I think I provided grades and was still trying to assess learning. If we're going to know about learning, we've got to know our students, not just what we are teaching. So my big focus in assessment this year is trying to meet the twofold need: grades and learning.

Sharon: One of the hardest things for beginning teachers is that you are so busy making plans and planning activities that you look at the class as a whole. It is hard to take the time to look at the individuals and then the word *assessment* on top of that.

Some of the best learning—and teaching—comes about through conversations between interested professionals. Each chapter of *Developing Literacy* begins with excerpts from conversations we have had with teachers, preservice teachers, and principals about instruction and assessment. In this brief discussion, Sharon, a principal, and two new teachers explore the issue of assessment.

In this first conversation, you can see that these teachers are working hard to make assessment a meaningful process. All three value assessment, especially as it guides instruction. They also note that sometimes assessment is moved from the forefront of their instruction process as they worry about grades and planning for instruction. Sharon comments that new teachers, as they try to balance all the expectations of their new role, find it is easy to lose sight of the individual students in their class as they focus on the class as a whole. In this book, you will learn how to facilitate your global understanding of your students as a class as you simultaneously consider the unique literacy strengths of each student.

Guide Questions for Chapter 1

The guide questions at the beginning of each chapter introduce the fundamental ideas presented in the chapter. If, after reading this chapter, you can answer the following questions in detail, then you have begun the important process of making this knowledge your own.

- What is the integrated process of assessment and instruction?
- Describe the seven key themes associated with assessment.
- Describe the four activities of assessment.
- Discuss the times that assessment occurs during an academic year.
- What are the four principles of teaching and learning in literacy?

What You Already Know About Assessment at This Time: The No-Book DRTA

As you begin this exploration into assessment and instruction, reflect on what you already know about assessment. When your mind is primed or prepared to think about a topic, it is easier to remember and organize new information (Raphael, 1986). By asking yourself what you already know about assessment, you will activate your background knowledge and be ready to incorporate it into learning new information more actively and thoroughly (Anderson & Pearson, 1984; Neisser, 1976).

Let's prime our thinking about assessment with a **no-book directed reading thinking activity** (DRTA) (Bear & McIntosh, 1991; Gill & Bear, 1988). This and other prereading brainstorming activities help you to determine what elementary students already know about a topic they are beginning to study. A no-book DRTA, similar to the one presented here, can also be quite rewarding at the end of a study project to see what students have learned.

····· TAKING A ·····
CLOSER LOOK **Create Your Own No-Book DRTA**

1. List *everything* you can think of that might be in this book: *Developing Literacy: An Integrated Approach to Assessment and Instruction.*

2. Arrange your listed items into groups. The items in each group should be connected to each other in some way.

3. Name each group. In what order would these items be arranged if this were a table of contents?

Several students followed the steps in the no-book DRTA to brainstorm the following terms related to assessment. They asked themselves these two questions:

What do I know about assessment and instruction?

What do I think will be in this book?

They made individual lists for two minutes; then they pooled ideas and organized them under headings as shown in this Taking a Closer Look. Try this exercise yourself and compare your ideas to theirs.

Our View of Assessment

The following discussion includes seven perspectives on assessment that we value and hope will enhance your growth as a teacher of literacy.

You may be using this book in a reading and language arts methods course. In other courses, you learn about human development and discover that people learn best when they are active and motivated. You have or will most likely spend time with preschool, elementary, or intermediate students as part of a practicum (in-school) experience or a job and, of course, perhaps as a parent. In this book, you will build on your personal knowledge and experience to focus on *how children learn* to read and write, and *what classroom teachers do* to guide children's growth. If you have recently taken a course in literacy, you know that the area of assessment has changed tremendously. There has been a surge of interest in authentic and student-centered assessments. Numerous articles, entire journals, and books have been dedicated to studying new ways to assess students' learning and growth (Ballard, 1992; Bouffler, 1993; Calfee & Perfumo, 1993; Taylor, 1991; Tierney, Carter & Desai, 1991; Valencia, Hiebert & Afflerbach, 1994).

In the past, teachers learned about the assessment process in diagnosis courses, as if assessment was something apart from teaching and learning. This instruction centered on teacher-made spelling tests, math drills, multiple-choice tests, short-answer tests, and an occasional project, such as a book report, a report of a state, or a biography. Diagnosis courses emphasized standardized group

····· TAKING A ·····
CLOSER LOOK

A No-Book DRTA on Assessment as Brainstormed by a Group

Informal assessments

Informal inventories
Authentic assessment
Portfolios
Projects
Hands-on activities
Pictures
Oral presentations
Reflections in journal
Self-evaluation
Conferences
Holistic scoring
Checklists

Reading and writing behaviors and development

Developmental levels
Instructional levels
Reading fluency
Writing fluency
Reading comprehension
Concept of word
Spelling development
Word recognition

Instruction

Comprehension
Identifying words
Finding materials
Reading, writing, and spelling instruction
Supporting all students

Testing and grading

Teacher-made tests
Commercial tests
Exams
Multiple-choice and essay tests
Standardized tests
Norm-referenced tests
Standard deviations
Standard error of measurement
Advantages and disadvantages of testing
Percentiles, stanine, and grade level scores
Bell curve, raw score
Reliability and validity

Formal tests

Intelligence tests
End-of-year tests

Other information

Previous assessments
Psychologist's report
Medical information
Language, listening, and talking
Auditory and visual information

Why assess?

Planning for instruction
Evaluation
Deciding placement
Determining levels
Redirecting teaching

tests and individual intelligence tests, but they did not discuss ways to sit beside children and learn about literacy by watching and talking to the student as he or she worked.

Today, assessment is an essential part of teaching, and ongoing, informal assessment helps to guide instruction. In fact, it is such a basic and guiding teaching process that it is interwoven with instruction in an ongoing cycle that we refer to as the integrated process of assessment and instruction.

Students read, write, and talk together as they create their own stories.

The Integrated Process of Assessment and Instruction

The *integrated process of assessment and instruction* grounds all discussion in this book. Figure 1.1 provides an overview of the integrated process of assessment and instruction. As you can see by examining the diagram, the assessment process involves four components: *observation, documentation, interpretation,* and *evaluation and planning.* This process leads to an understanding of the strengths and needs of students in literacy learning, and its results inform instruction. Teachers continue this process on an ongoing basis as they informally assess students during instruction. As a result, as teachers learn more about students, they can constantly revise the content and process of instruction. This process fosters

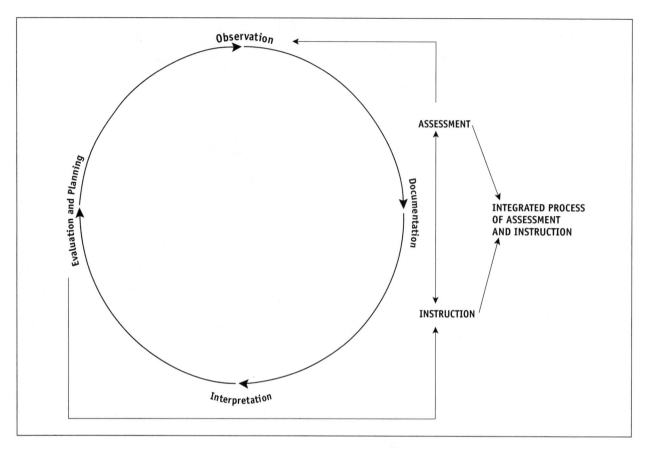

Figure 1.1
The integrated process of
assessment and
instruction

the development of teachers who constantly reflect about students, instruction, and assessment.

Within the integrated process of assessment and instruction, we have identified seven themes that are essential to this process and that are interwoven throughout our discussion.

Seven Essential Themes

1. *Assessment is interwoven with instruction in an ongoing, integrated process.* The teaching and learning context in this book is always the classroom and how you as a classroom teacher can facilitate each student's growth. In this book you will explore a variety of ways to observe students in all literacy events, to use daily instruction to assess students' literacy development, and then to plan further instruction (Hiebert, Valencia & Afflerbach, 1994; Morrow, 1993; Stayter & Johnston, 1990). In this way, you'll learn to integrate assessment into all your instruction. You'll see that assessment is broader than teacher-made, end-of-chapter, or standardized tests: it also involves observing

students' growth in the normal course of classroom activities, projects, units of study, and special programs.

2. *Students, teachers, and parents are involved in the integrated process of assessment and instruction.* Today, teachers use assessment techniques and measures that are managed by students and teachers as they work together in meaningful activities. Instead of focusing solely on standardized measures of reading achievement, teachers create partnerships with students, parents, and communities (Ueland, 1992) that support the integrated process of assessment and instruction. In this way, what students learn and do is valued by a larger audience, and in many cases, the quality of students' work rises (Goldenburg, 1992; Hansen, 1992; Heath, 1983). Parents are not seen as intruders in the classroom but as valued colleagues, and students' social life outside school is welcomed (Comer, 1988; Dyson, 1993; Fine, 1990). This linking of assessment and instruction integrates two student communities—home and school (Kornhaber & Gardner, 1993)—and places learning goals solidly in the context of students' lives.

3. *Assessment and instruction are not about problems but about abilities.* Assessment and instruction often are thought of in terms of difficulties or problems—what a student cannot do. In this text, though, assessment and instruction are viewed from the opposite perspective—what students *can do* and how their current understandings can be enriched. We believe that all students have learning strengths and that teachers can find ways to help them discover and extend these strengths. Accomplishing this goal involves using intuition, wonder, risk-taking, and responsibility (Dewey, 1938). During assessment, teachers *sit beside* students to observe them, document their work, and guide them as they learn to think and communicate. During instruction, teachers are facilitators of instruction, which is guided by students' current understanding of literacy.

4. *Assessment and instructional planning examine the synchrony or integration of literacy development.* This book uses a model of literacy development that shows you constellations of literacy behaviors. The integrated aspect of the model looks across all literacy areas—including reading, writing, spelling, and vocabulary—for signs of development and growth (Henderson, 1990). For example, as you look at students' writing development, think also about their reading. The synchrony model identifies reading behaviors that relate to observed writing behaviors.

Most important, the developmental model of literacy is based on the understanding that all development is a process. Although formal tests have a place in the assessment process, most assessment practices described in this book are linked to instruction in a dynamic process of literacy development. Literacy growth is not linear; it "usually occurs in fits and starts, some upward or forward progress, then backsliding or consolidation" (Patton, 1990, p. 114). Most formal testing will show where you start and finish but will miss the important details of the journey.

This model is a valuable part of the integrated assessment and instruction process and will help you observe students in action. Its general framework and your knowledge of your students' experimentations will lead you to understand their development. The Russian psychologist Vygotsky made the same point when he described how instruction that is within a student's zone of proximal development can lead development. For instruction to be useful, it must move ahead of a child's development and be a model for imitation and experimentation. Through practice, students imitate your modeling and experiment with new ways to read, write, and spell. The place to aim instruction is on what Vygotsky called "the maturing functions" (Vygotsky, 1987, pp. 210–211). Additionally, this model provides a vocabulary for ongoing conversations about students' growth.

5. *Assessment and instruction influence affect and attitude.* Motivation is a crucial component of learning. Motivated students strive to understand and comprehend what they do (Guthrie, Van Meter, McCann, Wigfield, Bennett, Poundstone, Rice, Faibisch, Hunt & Mitchell, 1996). They want to make sense of what they read and what they write. We believe strongly that to create the rich social and healthy psychological settings that foster positive attitudes about learning, instruction must be interesting, student-centered, and targeted to students' language and literacy development (Au & Kawakami, 1984; Palinscar, 1986; Rogoff, 1990). The learning environment needs to satisfy these affective, cognitive, and linguistic demands.

In learner-centered assessments, students share what is important to them about learning, including the content and the context of learning. This text describes schools that use a collaborative orientation to learning and have classroom settings that are cooperative and often multiaged (organized to include two or three grade levels, where children stay for multiple years and instruction focuses on students' learning strengths).

6. *Assessment and instruction are about groups and individuals.* Assessment and instruction are as much about a classroom and building a productive learning environment as they are about individuals and helping each student to become literate. You can assess the class's ability to work together, as well as assess your own effectiveness in teaching. Teaching students to take responsibility for the health and comfort of the learning environment is one important goal (Noddings, 1992). Beyond this focus on the classroom as a whole, this text provides a close look at students as individual literacy learners. It also details ways for you to assess and document the literacy development of each student in your classroom as individuals and in small-group and whole-group settings.

7. *Assessment and instruction must respect students' diversity.* Teachers can find a variety of ways for students to show what they know (Au, 1993). Unfortunately, when assessment and instruction are too narrow, they can penalize students or treat them unfairly. For students who come to school with different language strengths and backgrounds, assessment and instruction are not fair when students are expected to take tests developed for English-speaking students and to learn solely through materials written in English. Beyond language issues, tests are fair when they are a coherent part of a multidimensional assessment process. Tests that are fragmented from the curriculum or are unidimensional may require only one type of skill, such as the ability to read and answer questions, while they are thought to test subject area knowledge and understanding of content and concepts. For example, many criterion-referenced tests and

···· TAKING A ····
CLOSER LOOK

Word Study on Terms Related to Assessment

This word study highlights important concepts related to the key terms in this chapter.

assess *Assess* is derived from the Latin word *assidere* "to sit beside." The assessment process is one of sitting beside students to guide their growth.

observe This is an old idea that comes fairly directly from the Latin *observare*. Its definitions capture the intended meaning quite well: "to perceive or notice," "to watch attentively," "to make a systematic or scientific observation of," "to say by way of comment or remark" (from *The American Heritage Dictionary*).

document The *doc* part of *document* is derived from "to teach." Documentation is a part of teaching. The process of documenting involves creating some sort of evidence, some physical record.

interpret This word comes from the Latin word *interpres*, "a negotiator." In many ways, you are a negotiator when you explain to others what you have observed and documented. You may interpret students' work differently than parents and other teachers do. For example, where you may see dynamic expression, fluency, good length, and complexity in a student's journal writing, a parent may see sloppy handwriting, bad grammar, and poor mechanics. As you interpret, you may search for a common understanding of students' work: you may explain to parents the developmental nature of invented spelling to show them that correctness is not the only standard, and explain that correct punctuation evolves as students practice writing.

evaluate Perhaps the most interesting derivations are for the word *evaluate*. The term that is most closely associated with grading is rooted in the Latin word *plantare*, "to plant." Evaluation is valuing what students have learned and therefore is a preliminary step to grading. But evaluation requires more purpose than grading: it involves planning what we do with our students—and not in the punitive, gatekeeping way that grading can imply.

diagnosis Diagnosis is what teachers once studied to understand students' special needs. *Diagnosis* is an old word derived from Greek and primarily related to the identification of disease. Today diagnosis is felt to reflect a medical model that identifies learning problems rather than learning strengths.

placement tests designed for content areas often are largely reading comprehension tests.

The assessment process should include student input in terms of how they will be assessed and what will be assessed. Unfortunately, few students know how assessments are used and how much teacher-made tests will count toward their grades (IRA/NCTE Joint Task Force on Assessments, 1994; Johnston, 1992). In this text, students have an active role in the assessment process, from the first steps of observing progress to the final steps of instructional planning.

The Activities of Assessment

Within the overall assessment-instruction process illustrated in Figure 1.1, a smaller cycle illustrates the four components or activities of assessment itself—observation, documentation, interpretation, and evaluation and planning. Although their connection to instruction gives them meaning and context, these four components can nonetheless be defined and discussed individually. Assessment is a process that begins with observation and leads to evaluation and planning. Evaluation and planning guide instruction and bring the assessment process back to observation.

Observation

Teachers who make assessment part of their daily teaching are careful observers. They are like actors whose eyes become trained to observe humanity so that they more fully understand their roles. *Good teachers observe how students respond to instruction and how students progress.*

How do teachers learn to observe? First, they make time to *reflect.* Reflection goes on while you teach, when you're at home, and when you meet with colleagues. In the classroom, with students clamoring for assistance, it is often difficult to simply watch and reflect on what is going on. When teachers take time to reflect on what they see, their thinking becomes *metacognitive.* This metacognitive activity helps them to grow as professionals and to develop informed decisions about what to teach and how to organize instruction.

What do teachers look for when they observe? Observation, like assessment in general, goes on when teachers lead instruction as well as when students work independently or in small groups. Teachers observe students' work, their attitudes, their verbal interactions, and much more. In addition to observing students, teachers observe their own teaching. They see how students respond to what they say and use the materials they have placed in a center, and they observe the overall climate of the classroom.

You can develop your own observation skills. Instead of skimming over the activity in the classroom, slow down and concentrate on individuals. If you take the time to observe your students and your teaching carefully, not only will you become an expert kidwatcher (Goodman & Goodman, 1989), but you will open new avenues for instruction. You'll understand your role as a teacher more fully and grow to be more aware of learning strengths and appropriate instruction.

Documentation

Documentation is an important part of the assessment process. Documentation is the physical evidence that you and your students collect to show what they have done and what they have learned. These documents support your observations and show parents and administrators what you and your students have accomplished. As you develop methods to document students' learning and growth, you'll be able to show parents what their child has done in your classroom and what kind of progress the student has made. These documents also remind you and your students of their accomplishments.

The kinds of documentation are quite varied and should include materials collected by students, parents, and teachers. Collections might include districtwide achievement test results, samples of daily class work selected by students, and writing or reading samples that a parent selects. Often, documentation is verbal and written (Csikszentmihalyi, 1990): for example, students may express why they have chosen to put specific work samples into a portfolio.

Teachers today try to balance the type of documentation they collect. Teachers might include anecdotal records, students might contribute their projects, and parents might provide letters and notes. In this part of the assessment process, there should be no secrets or hidden documents. Students and parents should have equal access to the documentation. At some point, teachers, parents, and students share with each other the materials they think serve to document a student's growth in literacy.

The challenge for students and teachers is to find interesting and meaningful ways to document what has been learned. For example, performances of understanding (Gardner, 1991) "require an individual to apply facts, skills, and principles to complex problems in domains not previously encountered" (Kornhaber & Gardner, 1993, p. 18).

There are many ways to document the literacy growth of students in your classroom:

artwork	peer evaluations
reports	work contracts
copies of letters	teacher-made and student-made tests
drafts of stories	movies
journals	interviews
response and learning logs	outside evaluations
copies of letters	exhibitions
teacher's anecdotal records	performances
self-evaluations	

For most students, documentation is a source of enormous pride as it reflects hard work and personal accomplishment.

Interpretation

Interpretation is the process of ordering and making sense of observations. Interpretation uses documentation to show, in concrete terms, how students have grown and what they can do now that they could not do before.

The relative nature of interpretation needs to be stressed. Because no two students come to your classroom with the same knowledge or at the same point developmentally, each student's documentation must be interpreted relative to her or his starting point. Similarly, teachers do not expect students to develop at the same pace and to learn the same information at the same time. Therefore, it is important that interpretations provide a longitudinal profile of students' growth and development.

As a first step, teachers review the documentation to ensure that a fair and representative sample of students' work has been collected. Occasionally, holes in the documentation can occur—as when samples of students' work are missing, one area is overrepresented with samples, or another area has little documentation.

Then, once confident that the documentation presents a fair and accurate record, teachers look for patterns in students' reading, writing, and spelling. In the developmental model presented in Chapter 3, you will see that certain patterns of literacy behaviors will help you place students' growth along a developmental continuum from the emergent to an advanced stage of literacy development (Morrow, 1993).

Evaluation and Planning

Evaluation is a time to value students' activity and to plan instruction. Evaluation is a metacognitive activity in which teachers and students reflect on the personal value of their work. It is an opportunity to consider educational needs and interests and to make concrete plans and resolve for the future.

Students are evaluating when they pause to count how many pages of a difficult book they have read. Evaluation can also occur at the conclusion of a body of work—for example, when students exhibit documentation, perform, or enjoy their exhibits as an aesthetic experience. Evaluation is a time to congratulate students for their accomplishments, to brainstorm about what can be learned next, and to show and exhibit documentation for feedback from others. Students join in the parent-teacher conferences to show parents their documentation.

What part does grading play in evaluation? Grading is a part of evaluation and is designed to *quantify* students' documentation. Grades can become the primary focus in evaluation and, unfortunately, often are based on too narrow a slice of students' work. Grading can be destructive when students' work is boiled down to one number or is based only on high-stake testing (quizzes, tests, exams). Instead of relying on a few test scores, teachers now base grades on broader and richer samples of students' documentation. Students often are included in this process and are invited to select pieces of work that should be considered for grading.

Self-evaluation helps students become independent learners. When students are taught to evaluate their growth and development by examining their documentation, they also can evaluate the goals they established for themselves for the period they are considering. In fact, many teachers do not evaluate students

····· **TAKING A** ·····
CLOSER LOOK

Questions to Guide Self-evaluation

We ask three questions when we teach students to reflect on the quality of their work (Henderson, 1990). After an extended period of independent or small group activity, try asking students to take five or ten minutes to reflect on these questions:

1. Did you do the best you could?

2. Did you finish your work?

3. What did you do when you were through?

These questions can guide students to plan and organize instruction. For example, during one evaluation period, students at an art center were frustrated that they didn't have enough time to complete their work. They solved their problem by scheduling return visits to the easels and by finding places to store unfinished paintings.

These questions are an important part of teaching students to evaluate their learning and to be productive during learning episodes.

until students evaluate themselves because they want them to take an active role in the assessment process.

Evaluations, and particularly self-evaluations, naturally lead students to set short- and long-term goals for the future. As students, parents, and teachers reflect, "Now that these things have been accomplished, what is next?" they move into a period when students and teachers plan instruction and perhaps even develop units of study.

Assessing Your Teaching

Instruction improves when teachers assess their own teaching. From observation to self-evaluation, this self-assessment is a way for teachers to be accountable and to demonstrate that they have accomplished what they were hired to do. As an ongoing process, self-assessment is practiced throughout entire teaching careers: teachers continue to learn more about teaching and learning, to be open to constructive critiques of their teaching, and to place student learning in the forefront of their thinking.

In documenting your own effectiveness as a teacher, start with the positive. What do you like about your teaching? What activities work well and why? Some teachers make a list of successful activities and lessons. What makes an activity effective? Is it the way the students are grouped, the way that materials are used, or the way that work is introduced? Review your instructional strategies and materials and student preferences and choices with an eye to identifying what is successful.

Now that you have identified some positive experiences, consider your expectations for teaching. Sometimes, especially at the beginning of a career, it is impossible to succeed in all aspects of teaching. New teachers often become discouraged when they try a new teaching routine or activity, but it is unreasonable to expect a new teaching activity to work perfectly the first time. You may try a new small-group activity and find that students fail to work well together. Many factors could have led to this unpleasant result. Was the work too difficult? If these students had never before worked in a small group, were they clear about your expectations for them? Identify a specific aspect of the activity to work on the next time so that you are more pleased with the results.

This type of self-evaluation calls for honest self-reflection, an assessment of one's knowledge base, and the discipline to set goals for professional growth. To maintain your vision of good teaching, try closing your eyes to imagine what the successful class activity might look like: students are working in small groups, some are seated on the floor, some are crouched over a table helping each other with their writing, and other students are seated at various centers working alone or with a partner. Do not lose sight of the hum of purposeful activity. Through self-evaluation, teachers find the resolve to try new activities, to focus on new areas of interest, to talk to colleagues about what they are doing in their teaching, and to survey colleagues for new resources.

Assessment of teaching is an essential part of being a professional who stays in touch with ongoing developments in the teaching profession. The assessment process will help you to be a happier teacher, and ultimately, students' happiness and growth will increase with your own (Atwell, 1987; Goswami & Stillman, 1987; Heath, 1991; Sarason, 1993).

Special Times to Assess

Although as a classroom teacher you will most frequently engage in assessments that are ongoing, cyclical, and integrally interwoven with the daily activities of classroom instruction, you will need to focus on assessment at three other special times: (1) at the beginning of the year, (2) when a student is not making adequate progress, and (3) at the end of the year. These are times when assessments are conducted in a more deliberate manner.

At the beginning of the year, or whenever a new student enters a class, teachers assess students' development and their language and literacy levels. As teachers assess development, they also look at students' affect to determine whether students are confident about their reading and writing and to note how students involve themselves in classroom activities. During the first few weeks, students need to learn how classroom activities are organized and to get to know and trust their new teacher. At the beginning of the year, it is also helpful for the teacher to know something about the students' families, especially those family conditions that may affect students' learning.

Later in the year, teachers reassess students who have not made adequate progress in learning. Students may experience developmental delays, language differences that make it difficult for them to read and write English at grade level, or severe or primary learning problems uniquely related to language and literacy. To understand these students more fully, teachers conduct individual assessments and enlist the help of specialists employed by the school district.

At the end of the year, teachers assess students again in various ways. Most school districts require students to take a standardized test a few months before the end of the year to show the achievement levels of students in particular schools. In addition to districtwide testing, teachers conduct a variety of other, more useful year-end assessments (Pearson, 1994). Many teachers finalize the ongoing assessment process for students by completing individual records or profiles of reading, writing, and spelling development. Within these accounts, teachers may include records of oral reading fluency, samples of students' first-draft writing, informal spelling inventories, teachers' written comments, checklists, student portfolios or folders, response and learning logs, and goal-setting interviews with students, teachers, and parents. Many new and exciting ways to record student growth have been developed recently, and we shall share them throughout this text.

At the end of the year, students can review their portfolios and the curriculum guides for that grade level and write summaries of what they learned over the year. They can prepare a profile for their next-year teachers of what they have learned during the year and also write letters to students who will have their current teacher next year. These letters serve as introductions to the following year's new students.

Building a Personal Philosophy of Literacy Instruction: Four Guidelines for Teaching and Learning Literacy

Influenced by our own personal teaching experiences and the work of others, we have formulated four principles for teaching students to read and write. As you develop your own personal philosophy about teaching and learning, particularly teaching and learning centered on literacy, consider adopting and adapting these principles to meet your students' needs. As you read this section, you'll notice that the word *assessment* is not used explicitly. Our focus here is on the development of literacy and the attitudes and efforts that guide teachers in helping students achieve their fullest development. Each principle presented here, however, underlies the assessment activities you have already learned about in this chapter. After you read the discussion once, you might review each principle and identify how assessment practices reflect these teaching principles. The four principles are listed here:

1. Have confidence in a few basic principles of literacy development.

2. Know that teaching is not telling.

3. Teach with vigor, and use common sense.

4. Develop effective management skills.

These principles apply to all teaching and learning and are critical to successful and sustained teaching on your part and successful and sustained learning on the part of your students.

Have Confidence in a Few Basic Principles of Literacy Development.

Your understanding of literacy development will grow when your classroom experiences mesh with your personal experiences, courses, reading about literacy, and knowledge of students. As you observe in your own classroom and reflect on the experiences that you and your students have shared, you will build rich understandings of literacy development.

To facilitate your reflection and growing knowledge of literacy development, we would like to share a few basic principles of teaching and learning literacy.

Students Learn to Read by Reading and to Write by Writing.

The principle that children learn to read by reading and to write by writing may seem silly, but not long ago beginning instruction in reading and writing involved little authentic reading or writing. Children spent most of their time in classrooms practicing forming letters and learning their corresponding sounds. Teachers read to students, but students rarely were asked to interact with books or to compose stories (Morrow, 1993; Teale, 1982).

As researchers explored the homes of children who learned to read and write before entry to school, they discovered that these children had many experiences with books and with paper and pencils (Clark, 1976; Durkin 1966; Morrow, 1983; Teale 1978). In addition, Hansen (1969) discovered that although the parents of these children represented all educational, occupational, and socioeconomic levels, they all found it important and enjoyable to create literacy-rich environments in their homes by providing their children with books, paper, crayons, and pencils. With easy access to these materials, children found reading and writing to be pleasurable activities, became familiar with the language used in books, and understood written language conventions (Smith, 1971).

Researchers (Heath, 1982; Ninio & Bruner, 1978) then began to investigate the transactions that occurred between parent and child. They observed how children asked questions and how parents built on those comments and modeled more complex ways of responding to the text. For instance, the child might comment on a dog in the illustration by saying, "Doggie." The parent might then respond, "Yes, you see the dog going through the fence. See, he's going to have to squeeze to get through."

Teachers have borrowed from the exemplary practices of parents (Holdaway, 1979). They are now incorporating opportunities for children to read and write consistently in their classrooms, and they are scaffolding—rephrasing or modeling dialogue—in their own instruction in response to students' learning. When you enter most classrooms, you will notice library corners that invite students to read. You will hear teachers talk to students about their reading and students talking to other students about their reading and writing. You will see teachers expecting young children, even children in preschool, to write freely as they learn about the conventions of written language (Temple, Nathan, Temple & Burris, 1993). These teachers believe that students need time to read and write as they learn about reading and writing, and they have structured their classrooms to give students this time.

If you look and listen closely, you also will observe that these teachers build on the knowledge that students share, similarly to how parents dialog with their children. For instance, a child who is composing a story about an elephant writes the letter *L* for elephant. When the teacher sits next to the child and asks him or her to share what has been written, the child says that the story is about an elephant and that so far the word *elephant* has been written. The teacher compliments the effort and the child's attempt to write important ideas on paper. The teacher also might explore other ideas that the child plans to include in the story. Following this discussion, focused on meaning, the teacher then narrows to the word that the child has already represented, perhaps by saying that you can certainly hear the letter *L* in elephant and by helping the child to decipher other important letter sounds. Much of the scaffolded instruction that you provide to your students will be equally informal and important in nudging them to new understandings about literacy.

It's equally important to provide this scaffolding or support to students when they are engaged in more advanced literacy activities and to allow students the freedom to take chances with their reading and writing. Finding a balance between intervening and staying away will allow your students to experiment successfully with their new literacy learning.

Children Make Interesting Errors as They Develop as Readers and Writers.

Goodman (1969) and Clay (1972) highlighted the approximations that students made as they tried to read through text. For example, a child might read *mother* for *she*. Initially, these interesting errors raised concern that the child was unaware of the sound/symbol relationship, but further study made it apparent that the child focused more on meaning than on sound/symbol relationships. As children develop as readers and writers, this focus often shifts (Marsh, Friedman, Welsh & Desberg, 1981).

In the past, teachers and researchers were unaware of the importance of children's scribbling. Now we know that children distinguish between writing and drawing as early as age three, although their writing and drawing are still considered scribbling (Harste, Woodward & Burke, 1984). Early scribblings take on characteristics of the culture. For instance, children scribbling in the United States use a circular movement that looks a bit like their parents' writing, whereas children in Saudi Arabia include symbol shapes that resemble conventional writing in their language.

As shown in the example described above where the child tried to represent the word *elephant,* children use important letters in words to represent whole words. As children become more proficient as readers and writers, they include more letters until most of their writing is considered conventional (Henderson, 1990).

As a teacher, you'll need to support children in their efforts so that they do not become discouraged. Expecting children to turn in perfect projects each time will certainly limit their willingness to take chances with their new literacy learnings. Equally important, share your knowledge of children's development with parents to help them understand the importance of their children's interesting "errors." This will answer their concerns that these errors will become permanent and their child will never attain conventional knowledge about reading or writing.

All Children Learn to Read and Write in Pretty Much the Same Way.

As shown by the studies of children who learned to read before they began formal schooling, children must have plenty of books, paper, and writing tools, as well as someone to interact with. In addition to these essential ingredients, children also need time and support to investigate books and writing. They need to be engaged in experiences that allow them to read and write on a daily basis. Once children arrive at school, they engage in reading and writing by responding to a variety of formal instructional strategies, yet there are commonalities in their development (these will be detailed in Chapter 3). This fact highlights another important observation: *teaching and learning are not the same.*

Children do not always learn what teachers teach. Maximum learning occurs when teachers match children's development with teaching strategies. If teachers teach beyond students' abilities, students may learn ways to cope with the instruction but most likely will not be able to make this knowledge their own. When teachers teach below students' abilities, students may show signs of boredom as the lesson continues. A brief example will clarify this point. Imagine that you have decided to teach the class about the initial consonant *b* with words like *big, ball,* and *boy.* Many children participate in the lesson and generate other words that begin with *b.* These children have been using initial consonants to represent words in their journals (for example, *m* for *mother).* Other students listen to you but never volunteer a word. When given a follow-up worksheet, they randomly color in words. In their journals, these students use random letters and numerals to represent words (for example, *7* for *mother).* The remaining children listen to you a bit and often blurt out answers. They hastily color in the worksheet and then move to other activities. These children include vowels in words in their writing and clearly understand sound/symbol relationships for initial consonants (for example, *MOTHR* for *mother).* If you had assessed their literacy development, you might have changed your instruction to better meet students' learning needs. Certainly, the children who were using random letters and numerals in their writing were not ready to formally explore initial consonant *b.* In this text, we will focus on the matches that should occur between instruction and children's development, as noted during ongoing, informal assessment.

Literacy Cannot Be Broken Up into a Set of Discrete Skills.

Modern literacy research (Clay, 1979; Valencia, Pearson, Peters & Wixson, 1989) has shown that the whole of literacy is greater than the sum of its parts. One mistake that teachers made in the 1940s and beyond was to try to break literacy into a set of skills that could be taught discretely (Stallman & Pearson, 1990). Some diligent principals had charts with every child's achievement identified in a sequence of two hundred essential literacy skills. We remember entering schools in the 1970s where principals showed off these charts before allowing us to visit their schools. The charts were thought to be important documentation of the literacy growth of students within the school, and children were expected to be fluent readers and writers once they had mastered these skills. Unfortunately, children mastered the skills but often did not connect these skills with real reading and writing. From the very beginnings of instruction, students need to work in an active and rich classroom context, join in discussions centered on meaning in both reading and writing, and succeed in these literacy excursions.

Know That Teaching Is Not Telling.

We have already discussed this principle briefly in the preceding section, particularly through the example of trying to teach a class of students about the correspondence between the letter *b* and sound. You may have experienced similar events in your own education, such as being told what to understand about a poem in a literature class. These experiences generally silence students and lead them to wait for the teacher's words of wisdom so that they know what to memorize for a quiz or exam. Compare these personal memories to the more active way of involving students in learning discussed below.

The change to more active learning contexts developed from research done in early childhood development, social interaction theory, and cooperative learning. Pestalozzi (Rusk & Scotland, 1979), Froebel (1974), and Dewey (1966) emphasized the importance of play to learning and involved children in learning situations where they talked to teachers and other children as they manipulated objects and materials. Hands-on math and science learning have their roots with these early childhood educators. Piaget (Piaget & Inhelder, 1969) and Vygotsky (1978) noted the importance of the social context for learning, particularly when the child's learning was being scaffolded by a more proficient person, whether another student or adult. Vygotsky described the *zone of proximal development,* where learning is best supported by an individual or a group that is slightly above the child's cognitive development. Here children can perform above their present levels because they are supported by others who are more proficient. Other language researchers (Cazden, 1972; Chomsky, 1965; Halliday, 1975) talk about the benefits of environments that are rich in language and have supportive adults to facilitate language development. These environments allow children to talk about their learnings and to interact in discussions about learning with teachers and other students on an equal basis. Finally, newer research into the strength of learning in cooperative groups rather than competitive groups (Johnson & Johnson, 1987;

Slavin, 1990) has supported active learning. Students share questions and project responsibilities as they work in groups with their peers.

The classroom implications of this research have led teachers to initiate workshops where students work together on their reading and writing. Teachers may assign students to work in groups and choose among writing, drawing, acting, or other ways to share their reading. Overall, these classrooms are busy places where children interact with other children and the teacher about their reading and writing activities.

Teach with Vigor, and Use Common Sense.

In order to continue enjoying teaching, you will need to balance vigor and common sense. We wish that we had valued this principle at the beginning of our teaching careers. Often, as new teachers and also as experienced teachers, we feel that we should read each and every piece that each child writes, create a new learning center for our students today, or revise our entire literacy curriculum by tomorrow. These goals are commendable but not practical. For example, staying up all night to read every piece of writing composed by your students may lead you to feel satisfied that you have responded to each student and are aware of each student's work. But when you face your class for another full day of teaching, you will be exhausted and probably not able to provide your best support to students. In addition, by responding to all the pieces, you have taken away from students their responsibility to learn how to respond to other students' work. Here is where vigor needs to be balanced with common sense. Try some problem solving about other ways that you might meet this need to respond.

A second example focuses more on using common sense to balance vigor. We can remember teaching students about a particular skill day in and day out and wondering why several students were not learning. The goal was to teach the children about the short *a* sound, as in *bat*. Each day for two weeks the children made creations that had the short *a* sound in them, ate food that had the short *a* sound, sang songs with this sound, read books that featured this sound, and so on. Nowhere in all of this teaching and planning were the developmental levels of the students considered. Reflecting on this teaching, one might wonder what happened to common sense. Teachers often find themselves in similar situations. Although they certainly have the vigor to continue with such unproductive teaching, common sense dictates a change of strategy. The discussion about children's development in Chapter 3 provides guidelines to help you in your reflections about common sense and vigor.

Develop Effective Management Skills.

Finding effective ways to manage a literacy program within your classroom takes time and experience. Perhaps the most important aspects of establishing effective management skills are (1) learning about each student's development at the beginning of the school year and (2) introducing and developing routines with students. As you read this book, you will discover numerous ways to analyze each student's literacy development, many of which are informal assessments that are conducted as you interact in routine teaching with your students. You will learn to use this information to plan instruction using flexible grouping patterns. For example, as you carefully observe your students during the first days of the school year, you will discover how they approach text and go about making sense of it. You will be able to use the strategies that they already have developed to move them to new levels of understanding. You will discover some students who might work well together for some small-group directed instruction because of their similar developmental needs and other students who want to conduct a project to share their similar interests.

Simultaneously with observing students' literacy development, you will be establishing routines in your classroom. Although some teachers are afraid to establish routines for fear that students will be bored by them, most teachers and students welcome familiar routines so that they can invest their energy in learning rather than trying to figure out what happens next. After years of research, Atwell (1987) and Calkins (1986) finally concluded that routine allows children to focus on their learning. Early in their careers, they believed that introducing new activities and routines made their classrooms more exciting to students. Eventually, however, they discovered that students waited for them to orchestrate classroom learning and found it hard to be independent in their learning when the classroom context was constantly changing.

As you consider potential routines for your classroom, think about the active learning that will occur there. You will need places in your room for students to think, talk, read, and write. This type of learning often requires longer blocks of time than teachers anticipate. Some teachers use the entire morning for reading and writing workshop. With these longer blocks of time, children can become quite involved in projects, particularly those that take more than one day to complete. As you plan, consider which of these projects might work with your students, how students will be able to interact with them, and where they will store them until tomorrow. Some teachers are uncomfortable with this idea of unfinished work, but they soon discover the benefits of work in progress: children are excited about it and become more independent in their learning when engaged in it.

These four principles of literacy instruction reappear throughout this text. You will ponder classroom management, for instance, when we discuss the complexity of reading and writing workshops. You might explore vigor when we talk about certain strategies that seem labor-intensive. Remember your personal experiences, your previous and current coursework, your knowledge of students, and your learning as you move through this text. They will all help you develop your own personal philosophy of literacy instruction.

Conclusion and Study Notes

These are exciting times in educational assessment. Numerous professional groups have challenged educators to rethink how children are assessed (National Coalition of Advocates for Students, 1992; IRA/NCTE Joint Task Force on Assessment, 1994). The aim is to make assessment a meaningful activity that is much more than administering a standardized test at the end of the school year. Teachers are on the front line of instruction and are being asked to develop their own methods to assess students' development and progress (Chittenden & Courtney, 1989).

This chapter has laid the foundations for literacy assessment and established that assessment and instruction are integral parts of teachers' daily activities. The following study notes include the major points discussed in this chapter. As you study these notes, see what details you can add.

What Are Integrated Assessment and Instruction?

1. Assessment is interwoven with instruction in an ongoing, integrated process.
2. Assessment and instruction involve students and parents.
3. Assessment and instruction are centered on students' abilities.
4. Assessment and instruction reflect the synchrony of literacy development.
5. Assessment and instruction include affective and attitudinal aspects.
6. Assessment and instruction are about groups and individuals.
7. Assessment and instruction respect diversity.

Aspects of Ongoing Assessment

1. Observe students, class dynamics, and your instruction.
2. Document student and class activities.
3. Interpret students developmentally and in terms of what they can do.
4. Evaluate the progress, appreciate the learning, and plan instruction together.

When to Assess

1. At the beginning of the year
2. Ongoing
3. When a student has difficulty developing as a reader and writer
4. At the end of the year

Four Principles for Teaching

1. Have confidence in a few basic principles of literacy development.
2. Know that teaching is not telling.
3. Teach with vigor, and use common sense.
4. Develop effective management skills.

Key Terms

The following specialized vocabulary was presented in this chapter. Review these terms and go back to reread about any you are unsure of.

Assessment	Informal testing
Observation	Formal testing
Interpretation	No-book DRTA
Planning and organization	

Follow-Up Activities

1. Observation is a skill that develops with practice and experience. Visit a classroom and practice your observation skills. Try each of the strategies listed below.

   Two Running Columns: Draw a line down the center of a blank sheet of paper. On the left side make a list of the activities you observe and the times of the observations. Write down what the teacher and students are doing. Note relevant facts and materials. On the right side write comments, ideas, questions, and quotes.

   Five-Minute Concentrated Looks: Find a quiet place in the room to sit with your notebook and take notes. Note when you began your observation, and simply spend five to seven minutes sitting, observing, and writing.

2. The assessment process is a part of daily teaching. Select a sample of student writing and drawing. Consider the sample carefully and write down what you discover about this child's literacy as revealed in this sample. You may want to share your discoveries with the child's teacher to see what else might be revealed.

2 Essential Elements of Literacy

Conversation

Carol: My school district's mission statement contains three little but important words: "individualized, personalized program" for every student. We can do this. We can individualize and personalize learning.

Sharon: We started to personalize our programs by talking to parents. When we asked, all parents, no matter what language they spoke, could tell us what their children ought to learn this year.

Leslie: In our school, we started to have more conversations about what we really want for kids. We got a lot of ideas and support from parents. For example, our parent advisory group looked at the district's achievement tests and decided they wanted more realistic assessments.

Steve: I spend a lot of time individualizing instruction. Students come in with such varied backgrounds and skills, but it always comes back to getting to know the students. In my sixth-grade class last year, I had one student who would not write and would not participate in the classroom. For years he avoided getting involved. He just sat back and said, "Fail me." I suspected he thought he couldn't write well, so I said, "I don't care how you write—this is what we are going to do. You write the assignment before class and give me the paper. Nobody will see it except you and I. We'll take two recess times per week to go over your folder and talk about how to make your writing better." He would bring in three or four pages of writing. Sometimes he would copy right out of the book, and I would have to stop him. He would write things about the ghetto you can only see on television, but he knew that I wasn't sharing it with anyone. We made a start and began to build from there.

These teachers, like many others, are searching for ways to understand their students as individuals. Carol noted that we can individualize and personalize instruction. Leslie found that parents wanted to have a role in how their children were assessed. Steve gave personalized and individual attention to a student who had given up, and made a difference. In his first year of teaching, Steve learned to move into the community and develop ways to understand students' families, school histories, language, motivation, and experience.

This chapter presents the essential elements that students must have in place for literacy to grow. Teachers see that literacy and language grow in three worlds: social, psychological, and physical worlds. You will see in this chapter how teachers learn about these worlds to understand their students and plan instruction.

Guide Questions for Chapter 2

- What social influences affect how students learn to read and write?

- What are the psychological aspects of reading and writing?

- How do readers and writers construct meaning?

- How does our students' physical health relate to learning to read and write?

- Why is language so important to literacy?

Three Worlds of Experience

Much of individualizing literacy education comes down to building trust with students. Another big part of knowing students is to understand their worlds of experience. Students' lives can be described in three dimensions, contexts, or worlds of experience: social, psychological, and physical (Eccles, 1975). By studying these three worlds, we can make multidimensional observations of students' literacy and learning that reflect their health and personal settings and the forces from outside the classroom that influence learning and instruction (Heath, 1991).

In Figure 2.1, the three worlds and some of their essential elements are presented as embedded circles. The physical world of the learner includes everything from students' health to their physical environments. The psychological world is the world of information, meaning, and personal motivation. Communities are constructed in the social world, which supports the other worlds like a basket. The psychological and the physical worlds are nested in this outer, social world (Bronfenbrenner, 1981; Kuglemass, 1990), and so there we will begin our exploration in this chapter.

Figure 2.2 presents another way to visualize these relationships. In this case, the three overlapping worlds of existence have the word *language* at their center. It is a broad term that includes the two subcategories of spoken/oral language and written language/literacy.

Figure 2.1
Three Worlds of Experience

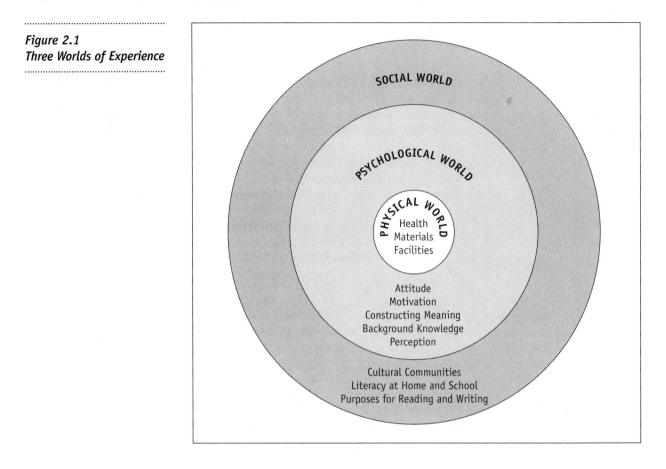

Literacy belongs at the core of our study. We will be exploring its essential elements in this chapter. But the discussion will also branch out to include spoken language because the two are intimately connected. In fact, literacy itself depends on and stems from our basic human capacity to use language.

Language is a unique part of our human physical, psychological, and social lives: As a species we are *physically* "wired" to talk and learn language. Through *psychological* processes we organize language in our minds, and use complex language activity to expand our abilities to think and act. Language is driven by the *social* world in which we use language to communicate. This chapter discusses the central role of language—in both its spoken and written forms. In it, you will begin to learn a recurrent theme in this book—that in our assessments, we must teach ourselves to observe both forms of language as they operate in these three worlds. The discussion of the three worlds in this chapter forms a foundation for Chapter 3's discussion of how literacy develops from birth onward. You will see that literacy learning arises out of a complex interaction among these three worlds. Individual and group development are complementary processes that occur in a milieu of social, psychological, and physical worlds of experience. The social world, because of its importance to the other two worlds, is a good place to start the discussion.

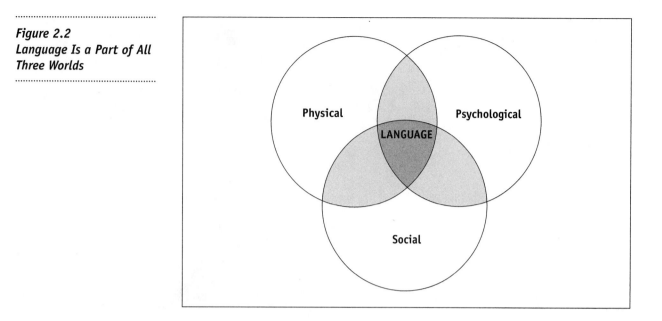

Figure 2.2
Language Is a Part of All Three Worlds

The Social World

A classroom of elementary students contains a marvelous mix of social backgrounds. Students' social world is probably the most influential aspect of learning to be literate (Dyson, 1993). The social world is like a basket for the development of the physical and psychological worlds. In the social world, through the company of others, our students define themselves. Through their explorations in the social world, they develop ideas and beliefs about themselves and the world (Neisser, 1976, p. 193).

Literacy flourishes where reading and writing are strong social habits; it seems natural to say that children learn about literacy where others in their world read and write. Because literacy is found in an ecology of meaningful social situations and contexts, the contexts themselves are defined first, and then certain social contexts are examined in greater detail. We consider how home and school and the interrelationship between these settings affect children's language and literacy learning. You will see how classrooms and communities have become increasingly multicultural and bilingual. Then, to gain a greater perspective on how literate society has become, we will briefly examine the history of literacy and explore the role of literacy in our modern society. Finally—as we do for each of the three worlds in this chapter—we will offer some specific teaching suggestions that address the particular world of experience.

The Ecology of Language and Literacy Learning

Now more than ever before, teachers must educate the whole child and make school and studies relevant to students' lives and interests. To do this, teachers know they must understand the social world of their students. This social world has an ecology, a relationship between its environments and the people who populate them.

Certain distinct social settings, or environments, can be associated with, say, schooling, shopping, child care, restaurants, religion, medical care, sports and recreation, telephoning, and watching television. By examining the social world, look at how families, schools, students, and teachers create partnerships for learning. Teachers must know the ecology of the social environment if they are going to help students develop and maintain the habits of being literate.

Concentric Circles of the Social World

In mapping the ecology of social situations, think of three circles of involvement (Bronfenbrenner, 1981; Kuglemass, 1990). As shown in Figure 2.3, the global (macro) sphere includes society's values, ideologies, and beliefs, including community attitudes and beliefs about knowledge and schooling. This global level also includes the influences of political and regulatory institutions.

The next sphere of experience is the circle of institutions and matters outside of the classroom or individual. These facilities and services affect the activities of individuals and classrooms. For example, if the community tax base for schooling falls apart, elementary class sizes may rise from twenty-six students to thirty or funding for field trips and materials might get cut.

The core (micro) level is the immediate level of individual or classroom activity. Figure 2.3 shows the broad range of personal social settings for the individual. School time occupies a large part of students' lives. Students and teachers spend six hours together, five days a week, perhaps two hundred days a year (six

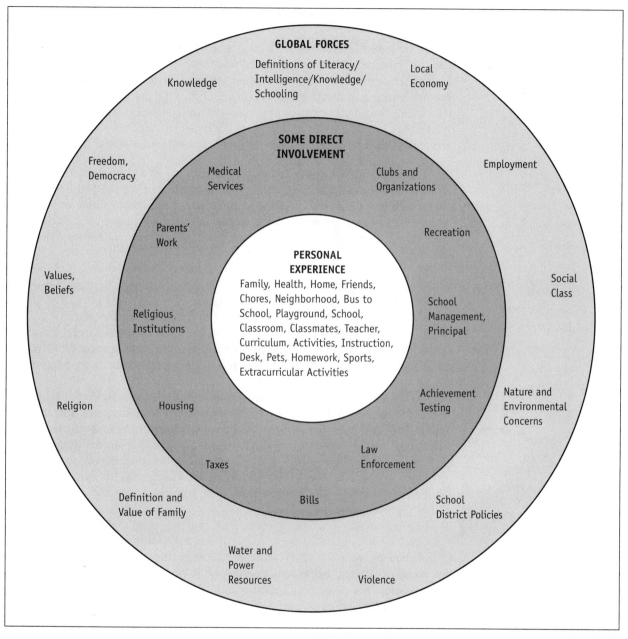

GLOBAL FORCES

Knowledge

Definitions of Literacy/
Intelligence/Knowledge/
Schooling

Local
Economy

Freedom,
Democracy

Employment

**SOME DIRECT
INVOLVEMENT**

Medical
Services

Clubs and
Organizations

Values,
Beliefs

Parents'
Work

Recreation

Social
Class

**PERSONAL
EXPERIENCE**
Family, Health, Home, Friends,
Chores, Neighborhood, Bus to
School, Playground, School,
Classroom, Classmates, Teacher,
Curriculum, Activities, Instruction,
Desk, Pets, Homework, Sports,
Extracurricular Activities

Religious
Institutions

School
Management,
Principal

Religion

Housing

Achievement
Testing

Nature and
Environmental
Concerns

Taxes

Law
Enforcement

Definition and
Value of Family

Bills

School
District Policies

Water and
Power
Resources

Violence

Figure 2.3
Circles of Experience

thousand hours). Inside the classroom, students and teachers construct a culture
in which students are comfortable to share and participate and where they take
risks in their activity. Throughout the day, students create other social settings as
they gather into groups on the playground, in the music room, and the cafeteria.

Learning at Home and Learning at School Build on Each Other

At the micro level in the ecological map, the players in the learning environment include parents, fellow students, and teachers. Prior to formal instruction, the home, neighborhood, and child care settings provide the primary social contexts for learning oral and written language. From the earliest moment that children make sounds, they use language for some social purpose or intention. Before they learn to write and read, children learn through oral language how language is used in various social situations. Literacy builds on this knowledge.

Oral Language Repertoires   Language grows in a culture and is nurtured by the languages and dialects students use at home and school. Studies of when and how children use oral language in social situations show us that in some environments children are active verbally, and in others they are silent. Such differences relate to the structure of social situations and environments (Bloom & Lahey, 1978).

Early on, children develop repertoires of language styles, which they change with some regularity as social situations change. These repertoires include different dialects and accents, as well as global changes in voice and pitch. The choice of speaking style depends on the role they choose and what they want to say. For example, students talk more formally to people in authority—a parent, a teacher, a principal, a boss—than they do to their friends. Listen to students' talk on the playground, on the bus and in the classroom. You will see how their speech styles change from one setting to another.

Studies of students' verbal interaction and repertories in the social milieu have exploded cultural stereotypes and prejudices about language and thinking (Labov, 1972). All languages are equally complex and rich, and no dialects are better than others; dialect merely reflects linguistic background. When students are free to talk in the ways they are most comfortable, they become more active language participants. Teachers who succeed best in getting students to become active language users at school are those who recognize, respect, and encourage students' natural language styles.

Through their world experiences with oral language and reading, students build expectations of how people in particular roles will talk and behave. By the end of their elementary years, when students read a novel they expect certain characters to talk and behave in certain ways. When they read a murder mystery, they may expect a detective to appear and ask particular types of questions that help find out who committed the crime.

Home Is a Natural Place to Learn About Literacy   The home has long been recognized as the most natural place to learn about literacy (Huey 1908/1968). Literacy is a positive habit that we can learn from parents. At home, literacy activities include watching others read and write, hearing about books and writing at work, being read to, buying books, reading the television schedule, and reading well enough to complete homework. When literacy activity is plentiful at home, children observe how literacy can be used and imitate their models accordingly. As a beginning reader and writer, a daughter will imitate her mother by making project lists and writing notes. If parents read and write at home, children will, too. If parents make shopping lists, children will, too.

You can see the significance of literacy at home when you know that

- Approximately 4 percent of our children are early readers who learn how to read without formal instruction before they enter school.

- One of the best predictors of reading success at the end of first grade is whether or not a child is read to at home.

- You can predict how well a student will write by knowing how many books they have at home.

Facts such as these show us that literacy at home is important to help students learn to read. Children who are read to and are around people who read and write learn the role of literacy in their community. For example, parents who read to their children and write at home show them how to match the forms of written language with particular *purposes* and functions. Children learn, for example, that holiday cards often rhyme and that lists remind us what we need to buy at the store. They may come to expect a newspaper at the table and regular trips to the library and bookstore.

Home Talk and School Talk How we talk is a part of how we present ourselves (Goffman, 1981), and it reflects our culture and background. Students and teachers show fairly distinct differences between the ways they talk at home and at school.

Students who do not attend some sort of preschool classes or "play school" with an older friend before kindergarten can experience a devastating clash between home language and school language that can make adjustments to school difficult. Gee argues that "a change in style can amount to a change in social identity" (Gee, 1989, p. 299). When they first come to school, children try the language styles they used at home. When teachers ask children to connect with the language of school, they may at the same time unconsciously ask children to connect "with another culture's mode of expression, presentation of self, and way of making sense." This abrupt change may also highlight cultural values differences between home and school (Gee, 1989, p. 299).

When you compare home talk to school talk, you'll notice some startling differences not of sophistication or complexity, but rather of character and blend. For example, at home, parents and children ask about the same number of questions. At school, however, teachers ask more questions than parents, and children may ask two-thirds fewer questions at school than they do at home (Wells, 1986). In the classroom, teachers often structure discussions to save time and to help students understand a particular point. This leaves children little room to elaborate or stray from the topic (Simons & Murphy, 1986, p. 202). Gordon Wells has observed that although teachers' intentions are good, classroom discourse is often restrictive and leaves few opportunities for students to "exploit the linguistic resources they show evidence of possessing in their interactions with adults at home" (Wells, 1986, p. 89).

Multiculturalism and Bilingualism

In this era of **multiculturalism,** our schools are becoming an increasingly diverse social environment as students come from many cultural and linguistic backgrounds and bring those cultures and languages with them into the classroom. Many of them are or will become **bilingual** (have proficiency in two languages); monolinguals understand and use only one. Monolingual speakers, readers, and writers will soon be in a minority. Thus, it is important for you as a classroom teacher to understand the interaction between second language learning and learning to read and write; most of Chapter 8 covers this topic. But let's take an initial look at the subject now, especially with an eye toward a social context.

There is no universal agreement on how best to provide language and literacy instruction for non–English-speaking students, nor is it possible to develop such universal and steadfast policy. No one idea pleases everyone, and as you may have observed in your local newspaper editorials, discussions can become politicized and emotional in socially diverse communities. In large part, the establishment of second-language education will take place at regional levels.

What *is* clear throughout the studies on second-language learning is that it is undesirable and unrealistic to expect students to abandon their primary languages for English. Instead, many teachers believe that students must obtain a proficiency in English that allows them to be active learners and active in commerce while retaining their native language.

Resources where you teach will probably be scarce, so it is best to set priorities for language education and focus on the most efficient use of these limited resources. As a teacher, you may get valuable information about community language needs from some of the many local groups, such as community leaders, teachers, and social service and health care workers who are in regular contact with a culturally pluralistic clientele. Professionals among these groups can work together to guide the community in the most effective use of limited resources to meet students' goals and needs and parents' expectations.

To develop an effective learning environment in their classrooms, teachers need to learn about students' diverse cultural backgrounds, including their languages. They must create a variety of concrete, meaningful social activities that are contextualized in their students' lives, but are not language dependent. Students then explore a variety of verbal and nonverbal ways to communicate what they have learned. Through these positive social experiences, teachers learn to appreciate and even speak various languages. If you are open about learning your students' languages, they will become interested in English. In oral language instruction teachers help students learn English and provide opportunities for students to maintain their native tongues and to become *bilingual.* Grosjean cautions us not to use monolingualism as the "yardstick" to measure language proficiency. Unfortunately, "even bilinguals hold themselves to monolingual norms, and still others hide their knowledge of their 'weaker' language" (Grosjean, 1989, p. 5). This makes it even more important for the elementary teacher to understand students' language development and their knowledge of various languages.

Bilingualism, as a developmental process, differs somewhat from learning just one language. For example, children often mix **vocabularies** and switch between languages. This mixing is good evidence and a positive sign that children are learning two languages.

Often non–English-speaking parents are unsure of how they can help their children to learn a second language: They want to know if they should speak only English at home, and if they should try to talk to their children in English if they are just learning themselves. Speaking only English at home would invite students to abandon one language for another, a mistake to avoid. Still, students need a certain amount of exposure to learn this second language, and because younger children have an easier time learning a second language, home is a good place to begin learning.

These are some of the issues faced by parents who do not speak English. Parents can be shown ways to blend their own literacy with their children's by reading to their children and listening to them read. Parents find time for children to be around spoken English, and they encourage success in school through the development of study habits and pride in achievement.

We have everything to gain by having students read in their native language at the same time they are trying to learn English. Some teachers have observed that denying students use of their language in school drives a wedge between home and school, and reduces the needed interaction of languages and communication. If we want to make education relevant to students, it needs a rich mix of materials of interest to students and a permeable curriculum that permits flow between the world in and outside of the classroom.

In the president's column to the membership of the International Reading Association, Marie Clay highlighted the need to encourage language development of all kinds at a young age, and the earlier the better. Literacy instruction, she wrote, should be included in the mix of language instruction because

> Failure in literacy learning during the first years of school can limit all school achievement. . . . If we pay too little attention to what is done in school programs, it can lead to increased numbers of adult illiterates. . . . [C]hildren use what they learn in the preschool years in their later literacy learning. They learn a great deal about the language of books by hearing stories told and books read. There are many situations around the world where that one piece of information could be applied with good results (Clay, 1992).

Literacy can come in all languages, wherever there is a reason to write and read in that language. Many educators have discovered that literacy activity and schooling in all of a student's social settings relate closely to success in learning to read and write in English, no matter what the language.

As you will see in Chapter 7, reading and writing support oral language development. When educators provide reading materials for bilingual students that help them to maintain their native languages, students learn about commonalties across all written and spoken languages. This reflection on language advances the students' understanding of themselves and their culture.

The important factor is access. Let's consider briefly an historical and a modern look at how access to schooling and literacy has evolved.

The Social Importance of Literacy

What is the social importance of literacy? Do we need to be literate in to-day's society in order to be successful? To answer these questions, we must examine how literacy was used in the past and how it is used today. Throughout this discussion, think about the ways in which we use written language.

A Brief Social History of Literacy

Literacy has had a short life relative to speech: Speech developed 150,000 years ago, and written language is slightly more than 5,000 years old. Both speech and writing are tools that humans use for social purposes. Written language serves the same social purposes and functions as oral language (Egan, 1987). But written text adds a level of explicitness that is unique in language and may be perhaps the reason that writing developed. Writing was first used in many cultures to record gifts, and today we still use it to chronicle our social interactions and to keep written accounts of events, inventories, directions, family histories, and contracts.

Writing quickly became associated with religion. In Europe in the Middle Ages, the clergy were one of the few literate groups, and they read the holy texts to conduct souls from this life to the next. In Western cultures, until about the middle of the fifteenth century, literacy was limited to the wealthy upper classes. For example, in Florence in 1339, only 10 percent of the total population learned to read (Graff, 1987).

In ancient China, literacy was reserved for the upper class. Applicants for low-level civil service positions had to memorize passages for the exams. The examiner recited a text, and the applicant had to pick up where the examiner left off. Only applicants for top government positions had an opportunity to interpret what they read. Literacy was used for record keeping and for social and civil activities.

In the early days of reading, readers focused on recitation and memorization. Critical thinking was neither expected nor necessarily desired. Many religions relied heavily on recitation and rereading rhythmic phrases. Even the name of the Islamic holy book, the Koran, means "to recite." Literacy was a public activity and a social tool, closely connected with oral language. Because text was scarce, for most of the history of literacy, reading has been something that one does aloud. Beginning in the 1400s, reading became something that one did silently.

The spread of literacy in Western cultures during the fifteenth century is largely attributed to technological advances in printing. For example, moveable type in 1453 brought the Gutenberg Bible into the hands of many more people. These technological advances supported a democratization of literacy, thought, and social activity.

Child labor laws have helped ensure education and literacy as almost universal rights. In the United States, libraries and public schools have given a broad base of the general population access to literacy and education. As late as the 1940s, the high school drop-out rate was 60 percent. Today, the high school drop-out rate is more like 30 percent, and technological advances and changing economies require higher and higher levels of literacy and education for full employment.

Until the 1950s, we measured children's literacy achievement by their ability to read words. Since then, teachers have become more interested in comprehension and in developing critical thinking and the higher layers of **understanding.** With these increased expectations for literacy, and with the general spread of literacy and education in our society, more people are reading better today than ever before. In a recent national study, 80 percent of high school students read at a fourth-grade level (Applebee, Langer & Mullis, 1987).

If more people are reading better today than ever before, why do newspaper and magazine headlines decry our lack of success? One reason is that many adults still lack basic literacy skills. For example, more than 13 percent of American adults cannot read a cash register receipt or read well enough to complete social service forms unassisted. Another reason is that we need to read better today than ever before. A fourth-grade reading level does not suffice in the modern world. Standards for participation have risen rapidly, and the demands for literacy have never been greater. We have come a long way from the days when literacy was measured by the ability to sign your name, read words, memorize, and recite! Today, workers spend approximately forty minutes reading at work each day (Venezky, 1991). Nearly half of all adult Americans read too poorly to use literacy to advance in their jobs. Within the near future, most working people will need to read material written at an eleventh-grade level (Chall, 1983) and use what they learn to think and solve problems.

Learning, Literacy, and Educational Opportunities in Our Modern Society

From a philosophical point of view, literacy is part of freedom. Literacy gives citizens access to information. Although education is a right in many countries, politics, economics, and social structures affect the quality of instruction and exposure to literacy that students receive (Kozol, 1991; Shannon, 1992).

Serious disparities exist in the quality of education and the literacy achievement among children in our schools. You can probably visit two first grades from different parts of any town and find large differences in how well students read and write. In one town, we have observed an eight-month difference in the average achievement of first graders from two schools—one located in an affluent, upper-middle-income neighborhood and another in a low-income area of town. At the secondary level, the drop-out rate in a middle-income high school is less than that in a low-income school. The economically advantaged children are not smarter; they have had opportunities to handle books, talk about and listen to stories, and be a part of or observer of literate activity at home.

Part of the problem lies in how schools are funded. Funding inequalities within communities make it difficult to provide comparable literacy experiences in school. Middle- and upper-income districts can spend $12,000 per student, up to three times as much as inner-city and poorer districts (Taylor & Piché,

1991). The richer districts can afford to pay their teachers better, they offer more professional experiences such as field trips and funding for conferences, their buildings are in better shape, class sizes are smaller, and they have fewer needy children to drain financial and emotional resources.

These "savage inequalities," as Kozol (1991) described them, also exist at home. For many students, financial difficulties may manifest themselves as a transient life style, a shortage of food, poor health, and inadequate medical care. These are serious problems, and it is intolerable that any child should suffer them. Financial difficulties at home also influence children's experience with books. In an Australian study discussed by Connell (1994) high-income couples spent almost nine dollars a week on literacy materials compared to two dollars a week by single-parent families who received social services (Whiteford, Bradbury & Sauders, 1989).

Literacy, however, does not relate absolutely to economic or physical advantage. Many fine readers emerge from economically poor homes, and many parents, regardless of economic disadvantage, read regularly to their children and make literacy an important part of home life (Snow, Barnes, Chandler, Goodman & Hemphill, 1991). But when we consider that in the United States, 17 percent of the people buy 90 percent of the books (R. West, Graham Lecture, April, 1994), the lack of access to opportunities and resources for learning to read and write in many socioeconomic settings is troubling. How can the social world provide the necessary experiences to promote literacy under such circumstances?

Suggestions for Effective Instruction in the Social World

We can do many things to make our schools richer settings for literate behaviors to grow. The following are suggested ways to bridge the gap between home and school and ways to restructure instruction to foster literacy.

1. *Make literacy a part of the social life in the classroom.* Literacy is a social habit, and students need to be involved in literacy socially. Some children come to school with very little time spent listening to stories (Allington, 1994).

Children need plenty of exposure to the entertaining and useful ways written language is used in their communities. They need to know about folk tales, lists, advertisements, poetry, picture books, rhymes, score cards, chapter books, short stories, comic books, and magazines.

Sometimes, teachers feel pressured to cover the curriculum. In concentrating on teaching separate skills, they forget to pay attention to some of the more global activities, like simply reading to students and talking about books. They forget to look at where the students are starting from and how much experience they have had with literacy.

2. *Pay attention to the quality of the verbal interaction in the classroom.* Literacy instruction works best if teachers change the verbal patterns of interaction during literacy instruction. Many teachers teach with a "Big T" nearly all of the time. Big T teachers talk, lecture, and explain, and their students listen. Au and Kawakami (1984) caution against too much teacher-directed, Big T teaching.

Just as we teach students to show, not just tell, in their writing, teachers need to show and not just tell in their teaching. They need to *model* and *demonstrate*, and help students work with each other (Stremmel & Ru, 1993).

If you were to tape record the verbal interactions in an elementary classroom, you would hear that the great majority of the verbal interaction is procedural, and in the form of directives such as "Turn to page 16," "Come, let's line up for lunch," and "Read a neighbor's story and then tell him or her what you liked about the story." All of these statements are direct requests, and all are initiated by the teacher. Far fewer questions are asked, and most of those are also procedural: "What is the answer to the third question?" "When do we go to music?" This type of teacher-dominated interaction occurs when teachers concentrate on covering the curriculum and forget the needs of the students (Wells, 1986). When you find a classroom in which students talk to each other and ask substantive questions, spend time observing this teacher as she guides student discussions, interactions, and questions.

3. *Find ways for students to be active learners.* Students bring many capabilities to school, and as Wells has observed, outside of school they are "already active, self-directed learners." Effective teachers find out more about the particular interests and abilities of individual pupils by listening to what they have to say and by encouraging them to ask the questions they want to ask (Wells, 1986, p. 92). If you give students more choice in what they read and write, they will feel a greater sense of ownership in the learning process (Giroux, 1992; Langer & Applebee, 1986).

"Little t" teaching is one way to involve students in their own education. "Little t" teachers give students an active role in planning instruction. They work with students to plan units of study, choose reading materials, and work through the writing process. To expand student involvement, these teachers are willing to move beyond the textbooks and to address curricular goals by using activities that may not look the same each year (Collins, 1986). Students in pursuit of their interests bring vitality and novelty to curriculum organization. If you are open to what your students read and write about, if you can find practices for student-directed activities and ways for your students to express themselves, you will improve both your literacy instruction and their learning.

4. *Close the gap between home and school.* Children are more successful when their parents accompany them to school (Bronfenbrenner, 1981). But some students feel like they live two lives, and the two do not meet: They do not talk about home at school, and school does not come home.

Often, this distance between home and school keeps parents and teachers from understanding each other. Some schools have waiting lists of parents who want to help the teacher on a field trip, but they are exceptions. Too few parents can take the time during the day to come to school. Still, many employers understand this need to link home, work, and school. The U.S. Department of Education, for example, allows parents to spend up to four hours each pay period at their children's schools. Throughout this text, we shall discuss other ways to have students involve their families in learning.

5. *Move assignments into the community.* Literacy education intersects the social world in a meaningful way when you work with students to create units of

study with active, permeable curricula and activities that make homes, peer groups, and school environments part of students' learning to read and write (Dyson, 1993).

How do we help children to reach into their own communities and also share their home culture to enrich the school setting? There are many ways to encourage students to look within their culture. For example, some teachers begin investigations of a new topic by asking students to explore their cultures for information. Students may create an "I Search" paper that explores what they and others in their community know about a topic.

A local context, a community connection, gives fuller context to what students read and write in class. If your fourth-grade students are studying the state's history, you can invite local experts, including parents, from the community as speakers.

In many classrooms, students and teachers incorporate local culture with the broader curricular goals. Students might write a family history, for example, that meets language arts as well as social studies goals and objectives. Teachers who are committed to literacy instruction that builds a democratic culture find that this type of student control helps to bridge the gap between home and school (Tyack & Tobin, 1994).

6. *Develop a caring class environment.* Let students know that you value their working together and helping each other. Respond to what is going on in students' lives, showing that you care for them. To care for students, you will need to understand their physical, psychological and social needs (Noddings, 1992).

7. *Develop a cooperative learning environment in which students form a community of partners.* Students work in various partnerships. They might have a partner for word study, a buddy reader, a math partner, a friend to write a story with, a small group to work on a science project, an outside team for basketball, and on and on. Students learn how to form partnerships to get things done in the classroom, the school, and in the community as a whole. Partnerships teach students important problem-solving lessons. They learn that together we work through life's lessons; we look at each other's strengths, and we know each other's failings and kindnesses. Cooperative learning activities build social settings in which students are comfortable to risk and share ideas; they help students to become active, social learners (Gibbs, 1987; Johnson & Johnson 1982, 1984).

When we encourage children to work in small groups, they develop partnerships in which they can accomplish greater things than if they had worked alone (Moll & Greenberg, 1990; Stremmel & Ru, 1993). These partnerships provide instruction within what Vygotsky calls the *zone of proximal development* (Vygotsky, 1978). Instruction within a student's zone of proximal development contains activities and concepts that are neither too difficult nor too easy. Students learn new information and skills best when instruction is within the zone of proximal development. Proximal partnerships form among classmates who are at similar skill levels and allow students to teach each other. Proximal partners may be slightly ahead of another, at about the same place, or a bit behind.

8. *Network for professional development.* You will find educators who support the development of integrated curricula in teacher groups, local and national professional organizations, colleges, and universities. Chapter 14 includes a list of national professional organizations. Most of these groups have local associations.

The Psychological World

Where is the psychological world? It is in our minds or psyches. The brain is physical, but the mind is composed of a variety of mental talents that bring meaning, sense, and direction to our lives. Through our experiences, we construct ideas and thoughts about the world. We develop some of these concepts consciously, as when we choose to learn a skill. Others we absorb without direct instruction or conscious reflection.

The psychological aspects that underlie literacy include what we think about; what we see, perceive, and organize for memory and understanding; and our motivations and attitudes. For example, to understand a written idea, readers use their knowledge of written language to read the words and their remembered experiences to make sense of and think about the ideas. Students' interests in literacy and their attitudes about themselves as literate and thinking individuals are crucial, motivating parts of the psychological world of literacy.

In the following section, we will take a look at the mind's relationship to language and literacy. In the subsequent three sections, we will examine each of the three psychological aspects of language and literacy: cognition, perception, and attitude.

The Mind, Language, and Literacy

Language plays a special role in our minds. Humans are uniquely equipped to talk, and through language we advance our thinking. Language is a unique psychological tool because it gives humans the ability to describe our world and to "accumulate observations of our ancestors" (Gibson, 1979, p. 263). Language allows us to talk about past events and people no longer with us, and about existing people, events, and objects elsewhere. In conversations, people find some common ground or *shared context* and can then share new information.

Young children have difficulty creating this shared context of people not present or events in the past, which can make it tricky to have a phone conversation with a child who does not put the whole message into words. Their immediate world and personal experiences provide the context, and young children assume that you, the listener, are inside that same immediate circle. Piaget used the term *egocentrism* to emphasize, in part, the young child's inability to take the perspective of the listener to know how much to communicate. Gradually, children acquire the skill to put an entire message into words so that the entire meaning can be gathered from just the words (Cook-Gumperz, 1986; Simons & Murphy, 1986).

Human ability to put an entire message in words is an important topic in the study of written language development. It is one of the key ways in which the psychological and linguistic processes of spoken language form the foundation for written language. Although many similarities exist between the mind's ability to use spoken language and written language as tools to understanding, some critical differences also exist. For instance, writing must convey the basic meaning and the sense of ideas without the aid of the human voice, eye contact, body language, and so forth (Cook-Gumperz, 1977; Ricard & Snow, 1990).

In fact, it can be argued that reading and writing are the most sophisticated of human mental activities. Reading draws on all that students know about language, as well as on their background experiences, to understand what they read as they *construct* meaning from the text. In the next three sections, you will learn more about this meaning construction process and about how the information from the page reaches and is stored in our brains. You will also see that literacy involves motivation and the desire to make sense of what we read and write. Without this motivation, literacy does not thrive.

Constructing Meaning in Literacy

Comprehension is in the mind. Students construct meaning while they read and write. They base their comprehension and the ideas they want to express on their own background and experiences. Their language and experience also influence the understanding they acquire when they read. Figure 2.4 uses the illustration of pages in a book to display our different ways of understanding what we read and to show the multidimensional characteristics of what we call understanding. As we read, we move from basic, lower-level understanding of the structure of the language, to middle-level putting together the meaning, and higher-level use of the information in the text to solve problems.

The first pages of Figure 2.4 show that when students begin to read, they work to orchestrate their knowledge of language and literacy. Psychological processes that are heavily language dependent include making sound–symbol correspondences, reading words, and holding the words together by understanding the grammar or syntax.

The middle pages of Figure 2.4 represent the more traditional ways in which we define understanding. This is the level of making basic sense—if students can retell or answer questions about what they read, they have a middle-level understanding of it. These middle layers of understanding meet the requirements of most comprehension tests. However, understanding does not stop there.

At its best, understanding focuses on thoughts and ideas. When students read with higher-level understanding, they build on what they read to develop new ideas. They add new information to existing vocabularies, schemas, and ways of thinking. Their understanding becomes increasingly regulated by thought and less by language. In authentic assessments that reflect higher-level understanding, students create drawings and models as nonverbal ways of showing what they know.

Higher-level thinking is the most advanced form of understanding. It begins with the role of critical thinking and is brought to action in the creation of new ideas and knowledge.

Figure 2.4
Types of Understanding
in Literacy

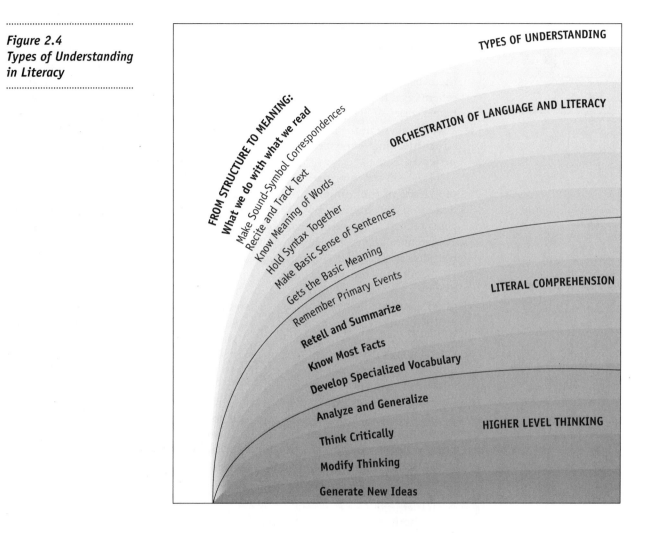

Students do not always have to formulate new ideas when they read, but they must move beyond making sense of language and memorizing and reciting facts. You can guide your students to critical thinking through specific activities conducted mostly in small groups. When students think critically, they learn facts in a broader context, learn them more easily, and use them more effectively. Your goal in teaching students to understand is for each student to think critically and to become, as Shirley Brice Heath observed, "an individualist, a reflective skeptic, a questioner, a doubter, an arguer, and an observing bystander" (1991, p. 12).

Observing students' literacy in terms of these types of understanding is important in assessment. Teachers observe how language and psychological processes interact, and they look and listen for various indications of experience and proficiency with each of these types of understanding.

Below are four important building blocks that students need to utilize in constructing meaning as they read.

Schemas for Thinking

As students strive to understand what they read, they use their knowledge of the world. Their memories of past experiences guide their thinking and give them expectations. These expectations for the world are called **schemas.** A schema can be described as a plan, a framework that makes it possible to anticipate a series of events or attitudes—for example, students have a framework for how to behave in the library—and it is through these schemas that students construct meaning. Schemas change with experience and are influenced by the experiences in the social world (Neisser, 1976; Pichert & Anderson, 1977).

It is as if the information gathered from exploration in the world is stored in the closet of the mind. In the closet are hangers on which hang related and matching information. For example, there may be a series of hangers for concepts related to sports or ideas about religion. When students aim to understand experiences and new ideas, they bring related hangers forward. Choosing the right hangers calls for students' active attention.

When students are not actively involved in what they are learning, or when the information is mostly new and no hangers are readily available, the information falls to the floor. On the other hand, when teachers help students to anticipate learning and have schemas ready, students bring a variety of hangers to the information and they learn new information more efficiently.

Students use schemas to group or chunk information and to maximize the amount of information they can efficiently remember. Existing schemas help students shape new memories and store new information.

Some schemas are organized as episodes in long-term memories. Other schemas or plans help learners to chunk information that is less episodic, such as telephone numbers and words. For example, you may look at a telephone number such as 247-1492 and chunk the seven digits into two groups. The 1492 can be remembered as the year Columbus set sail. The dialing prefix, 247, might correspond to an area of your town.

Schemas in Written Language

Readers develop schemas for special writing forms as well. Reading a detective novel requires a different set of schemas than does the expository writing in a textbook. Acquiring schemas for these new forms is like learning to like a new food. Readers acquire a taste for various writing forms through exposure and good experiences.

Students use schemas to construct meaning in their reading and writing. The schemas for various written forms can be grouped into three modes, as shown in the three columns in Table 2.1. James Britton studied these written forms as well as the schemas readers and writers develop when they read or write (Britton, 1994). His work helps us to look at the schemas students will use in reading and writing.

Expository writing, in the left column, is written in a transactional mode. Writing in the **transactional mode** focuses on factual information. Newspapers, legal documents, directions, and textbooks are just a few examples. Read-

	Transactional Mode	Expressive Mode	Poetic Mode
Table 2.1 **Linguistic Forms and Roles**	**EXPOSITORY** newspaper advertisement court document job application essay textbook **Participant Role**	**PERSONAL** diary journal autobiography letter	**FICTION** poem folk and fairy tales short stories and novels drama dramatic reading acting **Spectator Role**

ers and writers play a **participant role** when they consider the truth value of the facts in the text. Poetry and fairy tales are written in the **poetic mode.** Here the reader plays a **spectator role** and adopts the muse, experiences the emotional content of the work, but watches the story "go by." When Cinderella's carriage turns back into a pumpkin, for example, the reader is surprised but does not stop the story to question the truth value of the event. Readers know that these are abnormal events, but they maintain a willingness to keep on imagining and watching.

In between the poetic and transactional modes is the **expressive mode.** The reader or writer's personal life is central to the expressive mode, and the schemas called on have a personal orientation. The written forms in this mode— diaries, autobiographies, letters—have a factual orientation, as does the transactional mode, but also offer an emotional component that is apparent in the poetic mode and not in the transactional mode.

Readers are not fully participants or totally spectators, but instead rely on the expressive mode when they lack schemas for information and ideas they read in either the transactional or poetic mode. In the expressive mode they can reformulate the information in terms of their personal experience, internalize the plot, and assimilate the ideas. Children play in the expressive mode when they act out stories they have heard. On the playground, they chase each other to Cinderella's ball to dance with the prince, and they turn into Ninja Turtles, jumping from rock to rock to avoid the torments of their archrival, Rocksteady. By integrating the story into their lives, children own the stories and develop more elaborated schemas of written language forms to use whenever they read and write.

Students move from the transactional mode to the expressive mode to compare information they have read with what they know from past experiences.

Concept of Story

In addition to familiarity with the three modes, students need to develop a special schema for how stories work, which we call **concept of story.** Students with a full concept of story recognize that stories—whether they be oral folk tales or written chapter books—share some critical defining elements including beginnings, middles, and ends, and events connected over time to a central theme, hero, or moral that depicts and expresses beliefs and feelings. In the most fundamental sense, concept of story is simply a special way of organizing information.

Writing based in the poetic mode is usually rich in story structures. Students who get plenty of exposure to material in this mode can easily learn the fundamentals of telling stories in writing and develop a concept of story (Applebee, 1978). As children expand their knowledge and develop schemas of "how stories go" by listening to stories, and through independent reading and writing, they find it easier to predict story outcomes, to understand what they read, and to create stories of their own.

Students come to school with the stories they have heard at home. Story structure and storytelling can vary from home to home, from home to school, and one culture to another. To help students develop a broader sense of how stories go, we begin with their own stories, and stories from their own cultures. And then, primarily by reading to students, we introduce a broad range of storytelling styles.

The concept of story is not limited to the poetic mode, however. Many writers of informational books embed the facts in a story. Biography is an example of a written form that incorporates both the transactional and story modes. Biographies work well in teaching history because they use story devices from the poetic mode to make the facts interesting and memorable.

As you assess students, you will want to learn what written forms they have experienced. Many second- and third-grade readers who are behind in their reading come to reading with little experience listening to stories and, consequently, with poorly developed concepts of story.

As students become more proficient readers their story schemas become more sophisticated. You will want to trace their development of different schemas for various writing forms or genres throughout the school year. You can track how your students are developing various schemas by examining their oral retellings, written responses to stories, small group discussions, and their own stories and reports.

Metacognitive Strategies

When students construct meaning, they use metacognitive processes or strategies. These strategies are like schemas for reading and writing particular types of texts. They provide the scaffolding or support students need to become mature readers and writers with a repertoire of strategies and reading styles to fit different reading and writing purposes.

Teachers sometimes introduce specific metacognitive strategies to help students gather information while they read, allocate their time for effective studying, and adjust reading rates. The no-book directed-reading thinking activity (DRTA) in Taking a Closer Look on page 5 is an example of such a metacognitive strategy. In this case, students learn a metacognitive strategy to study a textbook and to "study smart."

Metacognitive strategies are equally important in writing. In writing instruction, students learn the *process* of writing and a specialized vocabulary and strategies to guide them from prereading to publication. They use metacognitive strategies when they discuss what they might do in their next drafts and when they talk about character development, chapter titles, and layout. Listen to students as they use metacognitive strategies to help each other in small groups. The language they use to talk about editing and revision reflects their knowledge of metacognitive strategies for writing.

Perception in Literacy

Perception is the second area of the psychological world. The perceptual system is made up of psychological processes that help us to make sense of what we see and hear. We gather our perceptions, largely unconsciously, through our activity and exploration.

When we talked about concept of story, we said that students have a sense of how stories go. This sense starts with perception of patterns in how words are organized. Hearing, or audition, and vision are important perceptual systems in reading and writing. Perceiving oral language and perceiving the patterns of written words are the crucial perceptual literacy activities.

"Perceiving is a stream" (J. J. Gibson, 1979, p. 240). It is not a snapshot from the bank, but more like a movie taken by someone moving with the stream. When students jump in and move in a stream of language and literacy activities, they begin to perceive aural and visual patterns in language and literacy.

Literacy experiences build on each other, and with more experience reading and writing students build their perceptions into new knowledge (Gibson, 1979, p. 258). This is particularly evident in how students use their knowledge of the spelling system, the *orthography* (Bear, 1992; Cummins, 1984; Juel & Leavell, 1988; Tunmer, 1989). During reading, students constantly balance what they see on the page with what they know about how words are spelled, the orthography of written language. As their eyes move across the page, readers use their orthographic knowledge to divide the letter strings into words and then to group the words into meaningful phrases and sentences.

As students' orthographic knowledge becomes more detailed, they acquire fluency in their reading and writing. With this fluency in the perceptual system, students have more time to think about the meaning of what they read, and this is when we see real fluency in students' reading.

Attitude and Sense of Self

The third facet to the psychology of literacy development and education relates to self-concept, personality, and affect. Students' psychological well-being—their attitudes, motivations, and interests—influence learning in general. If you are to understand how best to help students learn literacy skills, you must consider their attitudes about themselves as learners, readers, and writers, and their motivations and interests in the material they are reading and writing.

····· TAKING A ·····
CLOSER LOOK   ## Extending the Text

When we discuss the letter reversals children make in writing and reading, visual perception is at issue. Although some people say that children reverse *b* and *d* because they see the letters backwards, this is probably not the case. Nearly all children see these letters correctly, but children who make reversals usually lack the knowledge and experience to recognize the distinctive features of these letters. Children need plenty of experience reading and writing words before they can figure out the visual differences among the letters of the alphabet. To master the differences between *b* and *d,* for example, children need to acquire enough sight words that begin with each of those letters to distinguish between them.

Even mature readers can have difficulty remembering the distinctive features of individual letters. Try a little experiment: As quickly as you can, write one of those fancy lower case *g*s, the *g* with the two funny circles. Those of us who do not write our *g*s this way find it a challenge at first, but experience and development lead to learning.

Psychological Health

It is extremely difficult to motivate students to learn when they are preoccupied with emotional issues in their lives. Sometimes, parents have difficulty realizing that their children have psychological problems. One family visited school to see if their son had a problem learning to read. Indeed, this third-grader was behind in his reading achievement, but he was also misbehaving in fairly tragic ways at home. In the parent interview, the parents revealed that their son had set fire to their bed. Although teachers could work with the child to help him become a better reader, clearly, the family needed to attend to his emotional needs before he would have the energy to attend to learning in school.

Situations at home need not be as dramatic as this to upset students' learning. Still, changing schedules, family economics, conflict, divorce, and other disruptions distract and upset children, making it difficult to pay attention to school tasks. In a class of twenty-five children it is likely that at least a few come to school upset by what has been going on at home. As you can see in the writing below, Jennie's journal told us a good deal about her life and the things that were important to her.

An entry from Jennie's journal.
by Jennie, March 14
I wish we hade
Lots and lots uf
money. And I
wish we get
Free Food. And
I wish we

hade Lots Lots
of babeys. And
I wish no one
cane be meane
to use nevuy
nevery [never, never].

The classroom teacher responded to Jennie's journal entry by writing and reading this note to her the next day:

Those are really thoughtful wishes.
I can tell you took some time to write this entry!

How would this message shape your impressions of this child? How would you have responded to this journal entry? What would you write back? In this case, the teacher praised Jennie for her thoughtfulness and effort, but the teacher was also anxious about Jennie's health. If families are lucky, they can find help when they need it.

It is difficult but not uncommon to have troubled children in an elementary classroom. Teachers must be prepared to help these children in extra ways. Will your school provide breakfasts? Should you talk to your principal? How might the family be approached? What community resources might you think about tapping? We will discuss these questions and others in later chapters. For now, it is enough to be mindful that psychological well-being is an important issue in learning.

Motivation to Read and Write

Difficulties in learning to read and write create their own problems and pressures. Such problems affect students' attitudes in negative ways and can create a cycle of literacy learning failure: Students experience difficulty, they become frustrated, and, caught in a vicious cycle of failure and frustration, they may find ways to avoid literacy activities (Taylor, 1991).

Sometimes these students lose their nerve and their willingness to try and learn to read. They may find other ways to participate in schooling, positive or disruptive. Many students who create discipline problems also have problems reading.

This is a common situation for students in the upper elementary grades. Consider the fifth-grader who reads more like a second- or third-grader and cannot read the words in the fifth-grade texts and stories with sufficient accuracy to achieve basic understanding. When students fall that far behind, they find it difficult to feel motivated to read and, without regular success, difficult to be cooperative. Unless teachers take special steps to find materials that are interesting, meaningful, and readable, such a student is unlikely to be interested or progress in learning to read and write.

What is the profile of a motivated student? Although not an exhaustive list, here are some traits of motivated students: Motivated students see themselves as readers and writers. They spend plenty of time reading and writing, and literacy is a regular activity and habit, as strong a habit as watching television.

Motivated students have a "can do" attitude about activities that involve finding and recording information. They volunteer to look up topics, and they enjoy writing down information. Motivated students also are risk takers; for example, they'll try to read a challenging book, spell unfamiliar words, and use a new writing style. Motivated readers listen to stories, they have favorite books, and they talk to others about what they read. Motivated readers know where to find books, and motivated writers have audiences for their work (including themselves).

Motivated students like to "construct joint or group solutions to problems" with peers, and they want to share meaning with classmates when they work in groups or as a class (Tudge, 1990, p. 168). Such motivations to read and write have a deep sociological base in home and school. Teachers work with students and parents to create a culture of caring and sharing that rewards and cherishes literacy. They take a large step toward motivation by understanding students' literacy development and by creating literacy activities students will find meaningful and achievable.

Suggestions for Effective Instruction in the Psychological World

You can use the instructional material in Part 3 to help students construct meaning and expand their orthographic knowledge. Here we'll concentrate on the third aspect of the psychological world—that of building motivation. Below are some classroom-level ways in which successful teachers motivate students to read and write.

STUDENT STUDY

Seven First-Graders Learn to Read, One Doesn't

To consider the role of motivation in learning to read, let's examine the writings of several students in the eighth month of their first-grade year. On this day, students were asked to write on this question: "How are you learning to read?"

As you read through their written responses, you can see that children see themselves as learning in various ways. The children say they learned to read in many different ways. Betty learned *abc* sounds, and her dad "tot me the vowels." Betsy got started because she saw her mom and dad reading. Samantha wrote that she learned from a television program. Michael looked at foreign money, and David memorized words. Although these children say they were *taught* in different ways, you will see many commonalities in how they *learned*.

How I Learned to Read
First-Graders—May

Clarissa
I was in kindugardin. After school my mom red me a Book. Then in a flash! I red the hol Book. My mom was so hapy she dancestu (danced). I was so good at reading!

Dave
see I first sownded words out and then I memorized them and now I no How to read

Michael
I Learned to Read dy reading Groop and dy Mr. Bear and by spelling at howm and I Lookt at foron mony and Red the words

Betsy
I saw mom, and dad reading all the time. So I started trying and before I new it I could read then I read really hard Books and now I'm a really good reader.

Samantha
I sounded out things and I watched the electric company then I got better and read harder words and when I was five I read our bedtime story! And when was six I read!

Robert
My mom and dad wud read me a book and I look at the wrad as they say it and I mamaris it

Betty
First I learned abc sounds. And then I learned how to read cat. And Then dog. Then other words. My dad tot me the vowels And now I can read a lot harder words.

Evelyn
I bo not no hw to Read. bo Susn no.

Some of these children were personally motivated to read and write and were encouraged at home. As we have discussed in this section, children must be willing to take risks, and must see themselves as successful readers and writers. Evelyn is an unfortunate example of someone who is not motivated to read. Evelyn had repeated first grade, and at the end of her second year in first grade she still did not see herself as a reader. If Evelyn was to learn to read and write, her teachers needed to address this issue first. They assessed her development by looking at her writing and then generated activities and materials that she could read with interest and fair ease. As Evelyn began to see what she could do, she began to see herself as a reader.

1. *Be a model.* Successful teachers share their positive attitudes about themselves as readers and writers. Students see them read and write and check out books from the library. They talk about what they are reading and writing.

2. *Give students positive feedback about themselves as readers and writers.* Successful teachers learn a great deal about students' development by studying their mistakes and inventions, but they spend little time correcting students. They know that students learn the most when they spend plenty of time reading and writing; they compliment students often and use students' assessments to plan instruction.

3. *Spend plenty of time reading and writing with students.* Successful teachers read to students stories they are not able to read themselves. They dedicate extended periods of time to reading and process writing. Students read to themselves for twenty-five minutes each day, and they write for an equal period of time. Teachers develop writing workshops aimed at helping students publish their writing. Their students work in pairs and small groups to talk about what they are reading and writing.

4. *Help students formulate goals for their studies and literacy development.* Successful teachers talk to students about their goals and interests and offer guidance as requested.

5. *Teach developmentally.* Because students lose interest in learning when they experience little success, successful teachers know students' development and provide literacy activities in which they can be successful.

6. *Spend extra time with students who are troubled.* There is a saying, "teachers always have their one," their one student who is hurting and who needs some special attention. Student behaviors and attitudes can indicate that they are upset by events at school or elsewhere. Successful teachers find ways to give these students a little more attention than they would under normal circumstances.

7. *Recognize students' talents.* Each student has talents; often these show up in small-group activities. A successful teacher looks for and recognizes these wide-ranging talents (Kornhaber & Gardner, 1993). Talents are what make us shine as individuals. Some people can, with little training or practice, carry a tune, paint a picture, or hit a ball, and others cannot. Yet with good instruction and the will, we can learn to be fairly decent singers, painters, or ballplayers. The same is true for literacy. Nearly all of us have the capability to become fine readers and writers.

The Physical World

Reading and writing are activities of the mind that occur within a social context. They are also physical activities. In discussing the physical world of literacy we will first examine the biological foundations of literacy. Humans are born ready to learn language, and on this foundation, literacy builds. Language is organized as a rhythmic activity, and we will discuss how the rhythm of oral language is also found in written language.

In the second part of this section, we will examine the physical characteristics of reading and writing, primarily what we do with our eyes when we read and our hands as we write.

It is no coincidence that a healthy body, mind, and home life are imperatives for a democratic and literate society (Havelock, 1976). We will examine the influence of physical health on students as they learn to read and write and offer suggestions for developing a positive physical world for literacy.

The Biology of Language

No matter where on Earth we were born, we arrived ready to unravel and learn the language of our parents. We are "wired" to be language users. In these ways, language and language learning are part of human biology.

Language Development

The first years of life form a critical period of language development, particularly the first five years, and, depending on how the critical period is defined, this stretches up to ten years. During this critical period of language development children learn language most naturally. Children who are deprived of language during the critical period, by hearing impairment, for example, may not develop language adequately. The critical period of language development also reminds parents and teachers how important the first five years can be in the education of their children and students (Lenneberg, 1967).

Babies hear sounds. Very early they learn to discriminate human sounds from nonhuman sounds, to recognize how various caregivers talk, and to recognize the meaning of the different melodies in peoples' voices. Babies and infants love to play with sounds, and they soon begin to imitate the language around them. You can hear babies cooing in their cribs just before they go to sleep or just after they wake up. There they play with the sounds their mouths can make. They work hard to coordinate bursts of air through the vocal tract, mouth, around the tongue, and through the shape of the lips. Later, children mix their own soft sounds into melodies that sound like phrases. Gradually, they mold sounds into words, and these one-word sentences grow into phrases and sentences (Crystal, 1987).

Language, Breathing, and Rhythm

Just as literacy is built on language, language in its own way is adapted to breathing. Over time, the way we breathe has shaped the way we talk.

The combination of speech and breathing creates a **rhythm of language.** Rhythm is considered a fundamental property of language, which consists of patterns of sound organized in rhythmic combinations (Lea, 1980). Researchers have observed that the rhythm of language is matched to the rhythms of the human body, including the rhythm of our breathing and the rhythm of the electrical energy in our brains (Lashley, 1951; Lenneberg, 1967). There is good evidence that young children come to literacy with a powerful natural understanding of the rhythmic structures of spoken language (Read & Schrieber, 1981).

The rhythm of language corresponds to phrasal structures usually six or seven syllables in length. If you listen to someone talking or reading aloud, you will hear pauses between phrases and sentences. Our speech rhythms correspond to phrases. Sometimes these speech rhythms are called speech envelopes or breath groups. This natural length of a breath dictates how speech is divided and grammar or syntax develops.

Written language builds on the rhythms of oral language (Egan, 1987; Havelock, 1976). In writing, these rhythms are organized as phrase boundaries and often are punctuated with commas and periods. Punctuation marks cue readers to the rhythmic structures and grammatical boundaries within and between sentences. Punctuation also marks conceptual units as well as places to pause when reading aloud. For example, mature oral readers pause, on average, one and a quarter seconds between sentences.

Children build on their knowledge of the rhythmic structure of language when they first learn to read and write. Teachers capitalize on this knowledge by using rhymes, ditties, poems, and pattern books in which powerful phrase structures capture some of the basic rhythms of language. Children find it easy to memorize the patterned language of these simple stories and to make the connection between spoken and written language (Cathey, 1991).

The Physical Acts of Reading and Writing

Reading and writing are physical activities that involve the eyes and the hand.

Eye Movements and Reading Rates

One of the major merits of reading is that we can read faster than we talk; silent reading can save us time. Eye movements are guided by the way we chunk the text to construct meaning.

In reading English, readers first orient to the top left of the page and they make a *fixation*. Fixations are short pauses in the movement of the eyes. Fixations of mature readers last about 270 milliseconds, or a little more than a quarter of a second—about as long as it takes to start and stop a stopwatch.

In one fixation, a reader usually sees seven to nine character spaces within focused vision. Other objects might appear in a blur on the periphery. Immediately, readers try to make some basic sense of what they have seen (Rayner & Pollatsek, 1989).

After the fixation, readers aim down the line of text, and in twenty to thirty milliseconds the eyes make a small, rapid, jerky movement, a *saccade,* to the next group of letters and spaces. At the end of the line, readers make a return sweep to the left and orient to the left margin of the next line. A reader who is not skimming a text reads every word in this way. Most of the time, we see more than just one word and, as fast as we can, we connect words into phrases and sentences.

Mature readers mostly read at 200 to 350 words per minute (wpm), although fluency varies quite a bit. For example, when we read difficult material that contains new concepts and vocabulary, the whole process slows down: fixations become longer, we make more regressions to reread material, and our overall rate decreases.

Mature readers also vary fluency and reading rates to suit particular tasks. For example, reading rates for studying and taking notes are six times slower (fifty words per minute) than reading an easy novel, a page-turner. Readers skim text to obtain an overview or to scan for specific information at 1,000 to 2,000 wpm.

····· TAKING A ·····
CLOSER LOOK   ## Extending the Text

The rhythmic structure of language forms the foundation for all other language forms. You can observe children using rhythmic structures by singing with them. They experiment with the rhythm of language as they learn new songs. Ask a four-year-old to sing *The Wheels on the Bus* with you. Take her through a few verses of the song:

> (1) The driver on the bus says, "Move on back,
> Move on back, Move on back."
> The driver on the bus says, "Move on back,"
> All around the town.

> (2) The driver on the bus says, "Clap your hands,
> Clap your hands, Clap your hands."
> The driver on the bus says, "Clap your hands,
> All around the town."

Many four-year-olds master this rhythmic song with ease. However, they may have difficulty changing the beat of the song. Change the rhythmic structure slightly by adding an extra word to what the bus driver says. Ask the child to repeat and sing with you on the following verse; she likely will have difficulty changing the beat.

> (3) The driver on the bus says, "Jump down the steps,
> Jump down the steps, Jump down the steps."
> The driver on the bus says, "Jump down the steps,"
> All around the town.

The change from a three-beat rhythm to a four-beat calls for a manipulation that three- and four-year-olds find more difficult than do older children.

Beginning readers lack the flexibility to adjust reading fluency. They have not acquired a basic mastery that would permit them to process text rapidly. The whole process is slower for beginning readers; their fixations last longer and include fewer characters. They need more time to identify what they see as words. As a result, their reading rates may hover around forty wpm. The more they read and the more sight words they learn, the faster they read.

Physical Aspects of Writing

Most writers pay little attention to the physical act of handwriting. They don't have to think about how to form the letters. Handwriting is influenced by two aspects of development: (1) the student's physical development, and (2) the student's orthographic knowledge. Children's physical development and coordination vary. Early on, their grip on the pencil is awkward and their writing is large and difficult to read. As fine motor skills improve, an easy grip of the first two fingers against the thumb seems to be most efficient, and the writing becomes easier and neater.

The second aspect that influences students' writing fluency and speed is orthographic knowledge, the knowledge students have about how words are spelled. (Bear, 1991). Beginning readers and writers, for example, write much more slowly than more advanced learners. When they copy, students in a beginning level of literacy development copy disfluently, letter by letter.

It is important for teachers to place handwriting and letter formation in proper perspective relative to the entire writing process. Getting started with ideas and purpose are far more important issues than teaching young students to spell correctly and to write neatly. The last thing you want is for the physical aspects of writing to interfere with children's productivity. A major part of teaching writing is helping students to recognize their ideas, and their needs for written expression. Of course, do not ignore the importance of grip, posture, and letter formation to legibility and fluency. Provide directed lessons in which you demonstrate and have students practice their handwriting, but keep lessons that focus on the mechanics of writing separate from the time students spend in the writing process.

Computer use will continue to grow in our society; many students have computers at home. At school, a good computer with a good printer is like having a learning center and a printing press in the classroom. IBM-compatible operating systems such as Microsoft Windows, as well as Macintosh operating systems, have made software manageable for students. Preschool children learn to point and click to steer themselves through the software. For third-graders and up, software teaches keyboarding skills. Avoid using software that is simply a set of worksheets on computer.

CD-ROM software is very exciting for literacy learning. CD programs can tell a story that moves smoothly back and forth from graphics to text and is interactive because the students choose where they go. The hardware moves the software quickly enough to retrieve vast amounts of interesting information and details in a short period of time. Programs such as The Oregon Trail, Civilization, and SimCity allow students to take the journey, build the civilization, city, or colony, and save what they have done for another day. CD-ROM drives allow classrooms to use full encyclopedia and reference book sets that support the printed word with video and audio clips and hypertext buttons that take the reader to related topics in dictionaries, biographical dictionaries, thesauruses, atlases, and books of quotations.

With a modest collection of books on CD, you can scan by various features and make printed copies for small-group reading activities. More software is becoming available that can be controlled developmentally. Texts will be able to branch in a number of directions for reading and conceptual difficulty.

A classroom that has access to a phone or cable can be connected to the world through the Internet and World Wide Web. It is impressive how much reading and writing goes on when students talk to each other around the world.

For the next several years, students will have most access to computers and computer services such as America Online, CompuServe, and Prodigy at home. Because most classrooms offer limited access to computers, such projects offer a golden opportunity for students to work together cooperatively and to teach each other what they know both about the subject they are investigating and the software they are using.

Health

Students' health affects how well they are able to learn. Far too often, students come to school hungry or in poor health. The problem is clear: Students who are ill have a harder time learning. If children's bodies are malnourished, their brains cannot develop in a healthy way. Hungry children or children in pain cannot focus on learning to read and write. In 1991, 14 million children lived in poverty (U.S. Bureau of the Census, 1992). Many of these children lack the basic health and life stability to fit into traditional schooling models. Poverty has a severe impact on education (Connell, 1994).

In addition to basic health and nutrition needs, which affect children's attention and actual brain development, we must also consider children's hearing, sight, and speech. Ear infections, for example, are common during childhood and can keep children from hearing and, in turn, from learning language easily.

As the classroom teacher, you will be the primary link between the child and the school. You will find breakfast programs and special funds that provide food and clothing for children. Also, you will make referrals to school and district health workers to find medical services for children, including dental, vision, and hearing screening. Most urban school districts have special programs for homeless children, and many districts have programs for highly transient children, particularly children of migrant workers.

Suggestions for Effective Instruction in the Physical World

Teachers learn about students' experience in the physical world and work to bring health and resources to the classroom. Here are a few ways teachers make the classroom a receptive and productive place for literacy and learning.

1. *Learn about children's language.* Literacy builds on a strong oral language. You will want to know something about each child's language development and background. Listen for times when students are most vocal to assess their language structures and vocabulary. You may want to listen to the language children use when they play together. You can also assess what rhymes and songs students can memorize. Children who can repeat language patterns will later use those patterns in their speech.

You will want to assess the language children use at home and at school. Talk with students about the languages they hear and use at home. Many students limit their use of English to school or to when they translate from another language for their parents. Ask your students how they help their parents communicate, and you will hear them talk about trips to stores and phone calls where they have served as translators.

Some students have worked with speech and language specialists. Examine their permanent folders to see what their language and speech goals and objectives have been. Look to see what further work was recommended.

As a precursor to literacy, you can enrich the oral language of your students by singing and reciting rhymes together and by encouraging students to do plenty of talking. Be sure to read and tell them plenty of stories.

2. *Help students to be comfortable with their handwriting.* You will observe that some students are uncomfortable when they write. They struggle to spell the

The Many Facets of Integration

Each of the three worlds that we have discussed—the social world, the psychological world, and the physical world—is connected to, or *integrated* with, the other two. For example, student motivation to read and write is fostered in the social world. Similarly, children's physical health and psychological health influence their social interactions.

Another kind of *integration* will occur as you make your classroom into a dynamic learning center, its own minicommunity of learners. Each learner will bring a unique perspective to the minicommunity of your classroom and change the whole by doing so.

Teachers find many ways to make learning relevant for students and to provide more effective literacy instruction. Integration is an important concept in the drive for relevancy and effective teaching. One recent analysis came up with five applications of the concept of integration (Templeton, 1997). Take another look at Figure 1.1, The Integrated Process of Assessment and Instruction, on page 8, and reflect on the integration of the social, psychological, and physical worlds of experience.

1. *Integrate subject areas*: Find ways to integrate various subject areas into a theme so that, for example, students study math as part of their broader studies in American colonial history.
2. *Integrate roles*: Create an integration of teacher and student roles and responsibilities so that teachers and students share management deci-sions and are active partners as they research subjects together. This sort of integration implies that, except for some "givens" or "bottom lines," teachers and students play on an even playing field.
3. *Integrate development*: Learning in one area influences development in another. In their ongoing assessments, teachers look across reading, writing, and spelling and see comparable progress across these three areas. When they understand and recognize development, they can conceptualize a series of instructional possibilities.
4. *Integrate literacy instruction*: For many years, teachers have separated the language arts into separate categories and taught them as separate subjects using reading basals, spelling books, and language arts textbooks. Writing had been taught mechanically as part of grammar lessons. But instruction in one area of language arts influences growth in another. When you teach word study, you will also teach reading, and in particular, word recognition.
5. *Integrate into a larger community*: Literacy activities become more meaningful when literacy serves a larger purpose and community. By integrating literacy into the many social circles in which your students live, you will help them find rich contexts and many purposes for reading and writing.

words, and they are so uptight about writing correctly that they have a death grip on their pencils. In small-group and whole-class discussions, discuss with students how they feel about handwriting. Reduce the pressures to write correctly and neatly by conducting lessons on how to invent spellings and by conducting separate handwriting lessons in which you show students how to form letters, and to write so they can reread what they have written. Younger writers can make their writing more readable by placing a finger between each word for sufficient spacing.

It's good for students to take pride in penmanship, but they should not be overly concerned with neatness and correct spelling when they are writing their first drafts. As Henderson observed: "We want the idea to feed the pen and not the pen to interfere with the ideas." Deemphasize neatness when students revise. Encourage them to cross out text and to note places where they want to make insertions.

3. *When you visit a school, observe how computers are used in the classroom.* Each school has its own strategy for using computers. Some schools have a computer room that children visit once or twice a week. Other schools disperse computers among the classrooms. Some schools are lucky enough to have two or more computers in each classroom *and* frequent access to computer rooms. Most teachers want to work with computers and have studied how to use computers in the classroom. It is a reasonable goal to start with one computer and printer and to make sure that they are up and running and that students are comfortable using them. Often the most effective computer teachers are the students themselves.

4. *Know the policy for reporting health and safety concerns.* Classroom teachers are advocates for students' welfare. Sadly, some students live in desperate situations. You may at times have to make some unpleasant decisions. By law, you must call social services when you can document abuse or mistreatment. Your school district will follow state and federal laws for reporting suspected child abuse. Check with the principal and school district office for a written policy that you are to follow.

Conclusion and Study Notes

In this chapter you have seen how teachers must have a good understanding of their students' lives. You have also seen how important language is to learning to read and write. To integrate instruction, the three worlds of the student are integrated so that each child brings a personal interest to reading and writing.

- The psychological and physical worlds of experience are nested and nurtured in the social world.

- Language development is central to students' learning to read and write.

- Literacy flourishes where reading and writing are strong social habits.

- Language is a part of each student's social identity.

- In the social world, students need access to books from an early age.

- There are many types of understanding. An important goal of literacy is to enhance higher level thinking.

- Students bring their knowledge of the social world to understand what they read.

- Readers develop schemas for different genres.

- Students take on different roles as they interact with the text. Readers are spectators and participants as they read to construct meaning.

- Students' concept of story deepens as they become more familiar with different story styles and develop an understanding of how stories are told.

- Three parts of the psychological world to affect language and literacy are cognition, perception, and attitude.

- Motivated students believe that they will be successful when they read and write.

- Language development involves the brain and the body physically.

- There is a critical period of language development during the first five years of life.

- Children bring their knowledge of rhythmic structures to literacy.

- Assessment and instruction are integrated activities that include observations of students' three worlds of experience.

Key Terms

As a mature reader, you are acquiring terms in this specialized area we call literacy instruction. Here is a list of the specialized vocabulary presented in this chapter. Can you explain these terms?

multiculturalism	participant role	concept of story
bilingualism	poetic mode	understanding
schemas	spectator role	vocabulary
transactional mode	expressive mode	rhythm of language

Follow-Up Activities

1. In this chapter, we have seen how second language learning and bilingualism are embedded in the social worlds of our students. The English as a Second Language (ESL) teacher can serve as an important resource about the languages and cultures among students. Interview an ESL teacher and ask her to tell you about the second language learning among her students. Is there a silent period? Is development gradual? Ask her about the languages in her school. How many different languages are spoken? (You may be surprised by how many languages are spoken in a local school.) When is literacy instruction introduced?

2. Interview first- or second-graders and ask them how they learned and are learning to read and write. Ask them to respond in writing, perhaps as a journal entry.

3. Talk to a small group of students and ask them what their favorite stories are. Write down stories as they call them out. You can organize the stories by genre as you write them on a chart.

   Try this out with different age groups. Ask them about being read to at home. Describe your own experience in being read to or reading to your children, and ask them to describe their experiences. What are their attitudes about reading and writing?

4. Visit a first-grade or kindergarten classroom several months after school begins and ask the students and teachers about the songs they know and about the songs and rhymes they like. Listen for the rhythm of their singing. Write one of their songs out on a chart and describe the rhythmic structure of the text.

3 How Literacy Develops: An Integrated Model of Literacy Development

Conversation

Steve: When you first start teaching, all of a sudden you're in the classroom, and you are the professional—right now. You don't want to cross the hall and ask that other teacher to come in and do your assessment because he can't leave. Where do you start?

Carol: Fortunately, with the training I've been getting, I can assess these children in class. I figure out where they are in their developmental reading, spelling, and writing, and then I can work with each of them at their developmental level.

Steve: An important part of the assessment is to know where you're starting from with the individual students. That's a dilemma for any teacher.

Leslie: I spend a lot of time telling my students that this assessment is only for me. It is not for a grade. They say, "Oh, now I know why," and then they go for it a lot more.

Steve: I want to be the guy who helps them become better than they are. Some students work in baby steps, and others take giant steps. I'm an educator: I'm there to give everybody that step up.

Leslie: I've found that my students have multiple growing speeds. They grow really slow for awhile, and then they take a major developmental leap, and you say, "You can do that now? You couldn't do that a month ago." I love to say that to kids. They are really tickled.

This chapter's conversation is centered on the assessment process that teachers engage in as they first meet their students. These teachers are voicing concerns and opinions that many teachers share about assessing students, especially at the beginning of the year. Steve, a first-year teacher, is worried that he may not know how to figure out where his students are academically. When he talks about student growth as being represented by "baby steps" and "giant steps," he's acknowledging that his students will not learn at an even rate. Carol, who has just finished a master's program in literacy and has practiced assessing students, seems more comfortable in her beginning-of-the-year assessment. Leslie comments on the importance of bringing students into the assessment process. She reduces their anxiety by telling them the purpose of this up-front assessment.

This chapter builds on your knowledge of students' literacy learning and expands this knowledge by sharing a model that integrates students' development in reading, writing, and spelling. This integrated literacy model, which is considered a *flexible framework,* can be used as a guide when assessing students.

Guide Questions for Chapter 3

- What is the purpose of the integrated model of literacy?

- How does the integrated literacy model facilitate a match between assessment and instruction?

- Describe the major characteristics of the emergent, beginning, transitional, intermediate, and advanced phases of literacy development in readers and writers.

The Integrated Model of Literacy

The **integrated model of literacy** is the only model that considers reading, writing, and spelling development and highlights the **synchrony,** or integrated relationships and connections, among these areas. (This model is also called the synchrony model of literacy development; this text uses the terms *integrated* and *synchrony* synonymously in talking about the model.) For example, you may observe a child who might be considered a beginning reader pretending to read a story using the illustrations rather than reading the words on the page. Observing further, you also note that the child uses scribbling or random letters and numerals to represent ideas. Based on those observations, you can use the integrated model of literacy development seen in both Table 3.1 and Figure 3.1 as a flexible framework to help you identify students' behaviors at various phases of literacy development. Table 3.1 is organized by phase and presents the characteristics and behaviors that pertain to each phase. Figure 3.1 presents the same information but in a more dynamic manner. Together, they will help you understand what to look for and how to use this information when you work with your students.

As you scan across the top of Figure 3.1, you will notice the synchrony, or connections, between literacy knowledge and behaviors. A quick walk-through

Table 3.1 Integrated model of reading, writing, and spelling development

READING

	Emergent	Beginning	Transitional	Intermediate/Advanced
Behaviors and characteristics	Directionality	Disfluency Reads aloud Fingerpoints	Silent reading predominates	Familiarity with different styles and genres
	No concept of word	Rudimentary–functional concept of word	Approaching fluency in oral and silent reading	Fluent, with expression and dramatic presence in oral and silent reading
Response to literature and meaning construction	Drawings and some writing	Retellings	Retellings and summaries, analysis	Analysis and generalization

SPELLING AND ORTHOGRAPHIC KNOWLEDGE

Prephonemic	Semiphonemic	Letter Name	Within Word	Syllable Juncture/ Derivational Constancy
Scribbling random letters or numerals	Initial and final consonants	Vowels included Full phonological awareness	Abstract and relational Long and irregular vowels	Morphological analysis How syllables fit together External/inflectional: junctures and affixes Internal/derivational: bases and roots

Examples:

bed	MMS7	b, bd	bad	bed	bed
chain	FKJL	c, cn	can, chan	chrane	chain
battle	90LS	b, bl, btl	batl	batel, batle	battel, battle
commotion	EKMSK	c, cm	cumshn	comoshun	commosion, commotion
reversible	CLXSN	r, rb	rafrbl	revrsebl	reversable, reversible

WRITING

Pretend	Beginning	Transitional	Intermediate/Advanced
Situational	Disfluency Letter by letter	Approaching fluency Focus on meaning	Experience with different writing styles and genres Building expression and voice

Source: Adapted from Henderson (1990).

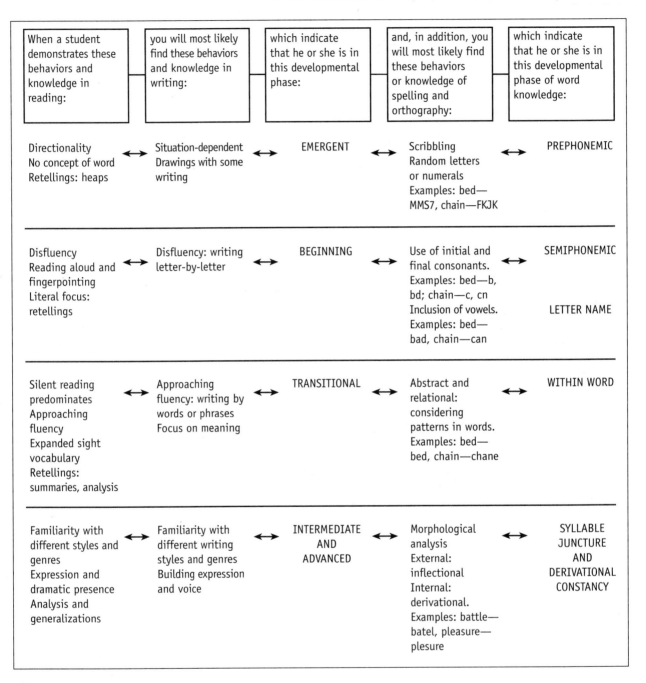

When a student demonstrates these behaviors and knowledge in reading:		you will most likely find these behaviors and knowledge in writing:		which indicate that he or she is in this developmental phase:		and, in addition, you will most likely find these behaviors or knowledge of spelling and orthography:		which indicate that he or she is in this developmental phase of word knowledge:
Directionality No concept of word Retellings: heaps	↔	Situation-dependent Drawings with some writing	↔	EMERGENT	↔	Scribbling Random letters or numerals Examples: bed— MMS7, chain—FKJK	↔	PREPHONEMIC
Disfluency Reading aloud and fingerpointing Literal focus: retellings	↔	Disfluency: writing letter-by-letter	↔	BEGINNING	↔	Use of initial and final consonants. Examples: bed—b, bd; chain—c, cn Inclusion of vowels. Examples: bed— bad, chain—can	↔	SEMIPHONEMIC LETTER NAME
Silent reading predominates Approaching fluency Expanded sight vocabulary Retellings: summaries, analysis	↔	Approaching fluency: writing by words or phrases Focus on meaning	↔	TRANSITIONAL	↔	Abstract and relational: considering patterns in words. Examples: bed— bed, chain—chane	↔	WITHIN WORD
Familiarity with different styles and genres Expression and dramatic presence Analysis and generalizations	↔	Familiarity with different writing styles and genres Building expression and voice	↔	INTERMEDIATE AND ADVANCED	↔	Morphological analysis External: inflectional Internal: derivational. Examples: battle— batel, pleasure— plesure	↔	SYLLABLE JUNCTURE AND DERIVATIONAL CONSTANCY

Figure 3.1.
The Model in Action

····· TAKING A ····· CLOSER LOOK

Why Synchrony? Why Development?

The synchrony model demonstrates that children can develop as readers and writers in an orderly and natural fashion if educators effectively match instructional strategies and activities to students' development. This integration of children's literacy development and instruction means that teachers aim to understand students' development as an aid to planning instruction.

You can be sure that your students' development is a natural unfolding by combining an understanding of development with effective teaching practices. The synchrony model helps you do this. Once you know where a student is developmentally, a host of literacy activities suggest themselves. In effect, your students provide leads for instruction, and you can in turn find the teachable moments when it makes sense to talk about various aspects of literacy. For example, discussing how writers use quotation marks makes sense only when students are experimenting with quotations in their reading and writing.

Why Synchrony?

When teachers consider the synchrony, or relationships, among literacy behaviors instead of focusing on just one aspect, they can predict that when they see x (for example, writing), they can expect y (for example, reading strategies). This critical ability allows teachers to note when one aspect of literacy development is out of balance with another.

Why Development?

When you understand children's typical literacy development and know what knowledge children use to reach to new literacy understandings, you can observe each child in class and recognize that child's strengths and needs as a literacy learner. This knowledge of literacy development allows you to

- know what to look for in assessment,
- flexibly group students for instruction based on developmental needs, and
- foster and facilitate students' learning by capitalizing on the appropriate developmental moment in their knowledge growth.

will help you consider constellations of literacy behaviors at each developmental phase. An emergent reader, for example, will understand directionality and that text moves from left to right, but be unable to read isolated words in text. If asked to tell about a story that was read, he or she would most likely recall some of the important events but in no particular order. He or she would usually represent words through scribbling and if asked to write a story would most likely include drawings with some writing.

Orthographic knowledge, a term used in Table 3.1, refers to the knowledge students have about how words are constructed and used (sometimes called *word knowledge*).

Spelling and orthographic knowledge are linked because students put their orthographic knowledge into action when they spell words, and it is the act of spelling that most readily reveals their level of word knowledge. But students also use orthographic knowledge when they make sound–symbol correspondences and recognize words as they read. Thus, orthographic knowledge is part of all areas of literacy: reading, writing, and spelling (Gill, 1992; Henderson & Templeton, 1986).

This model of literacy lays out distinct points of reference along a continuum of literacy development. As you will see in many examples in this text, students' reading behaviors predict how they spell, and students' spelling predicts how they read. As you look at the model, you will notice that constellations of reading, writing, and spelling behaviors grow increasingly complex as students exhibit more sophisticated development.

The constellations of literacy behaviors have fuzzy boundaries. As students move from one developmental phase to another, they often carry over behaviors associated with a previous phase as they move to more complex understandings. To compare the phases to grade levels, consider these ranges:

Phase	*Range of Grade Levels for Each Phase*
Emergent	Pre-K to middle of 1
Beginning	K to middle of 2
Transitional	1 to middle of 4
Intermediate	3 to 8
Advanced	5 to 12

For example, a child who can focus on meaning in reading stories and read relatively fluently, both transitional traits, may still represent words by confusing the short vowel, a beginning trait.

The first phase of literacy development is that of emergent readers and writers.

■ *Emergent Readers and Writers*

This phase of literacy development was in the past considered a time of *reading readiness*. Teachers and parents believed that children needed to reach a certain level of maturity before they were ready to learn to read. Children were not considered ready to learn to read until they had mastered auditory discrimination (recognition of sounds), visual discrimination (recognition of shapes and letters), left-to-right progression of text, visual motor skills (cutting on a line), and gross motor skills (skipping and hopping) (Morrow, 1993).

In the past ten years the term *readiness* has been replaced with a new term, **emergent literacy.** This small change in terms reflects a large change in beliefs about how children develop in literacy. Teachers and parents now believe that learning to read and write starts at birth or before. Parents have an important role in the earliest part of the process of learning to read and write as they read to the children and encourage them to write messages on paper. Teachers then build on this knowledge as they engage children in reading and writing activities in the classroom (Clay, 1972).

Children who exhibit literacy behaviors at the emergent phase pretend to read, write, and spell. They are becoming familiar with literacy in a global way. As you watch a young child read, you may see the child hold a book backwards and fumble through turning the pages. Often you will hear the child commenting on the illustrations while perusing the book. This child, if asked to write, will likely produce pages of writing, usually composed of scribbles or random letters and numerals. Although in the past researchers ignored much of this development, many today recognize and have narrowed their focus to this exciting time of literacy development (Durkin, 1966; Holdaway, 1979; Morrow, 1983; Taylor, 1983; Teale, 1984).

Reading

Awareness of Book

Children learn about literacy by watching those people closest to them read and write. By sharing reading and writing experiences, parents teach their children the pleasure and meaningfulness associated with reading and writing.

Preschoolers who are frequently read to associate particular times of the day with story time. These young children usually start the reading growth process by handling chubby books and plastic bath-time books. They enjoy hearing the illustrations identified, and they respond by imitating the labels that their parents attach to the pictures. These simple books often are counting books, concept books, or contain simple rhymes.

Other preschooler books offer an interactive component. The text may, for example, encourage the child to find some particular item on a page. Richard Scarry's books provide an excellent example of this type of book. Many of his books include a character named Lowly Worm. The child and parent search each page to find Lowly Worm in a plane or riding a bus. The conversation between the child and parent might sound like the following:

> Parent: Do you see Lowly Worm?
>
> Child: (Points to Lowly Worm.)
>
> Parent: What is Lowly Worm doing?
>
> Child: Plane!

This type of book makes it easy for parents to interact with their child while they read. In some interactive favorites, children do something to the book. *Pat the Bunny* (Kundhardt, 1940), which has endured for more than fifty years with touchable surfaces such as a father's sandpaper beard and a soft flannel bunny, asks, "Can you pat the bunny?"

Environmental Print

In addition to enjoying books and poems, young children begin to explore the text they see in their world. Children first learn these words in context. For instance, they can read the word *STOP* as long as it is on a stop sign, and they soon learn to recognize the word *McDonald's* on seeing the golden arches (Harste, Woodward, & Burke, 1984). In such situations, the child reads the logo as a whole, including the shape of the sign. At first, the young child attends to the logo as a whole and processes it as a picture, perhaps focusing on the shapes or colors, but not the text. They may say "toothpaste" when they see a tube of Crest toothpaste, or call Cheerios merely "cereal" (Adams, 1990). As young children become aware of letters, they begin to attend to the print and can then read a word out of its usual context (Ehri, 1987).

Knowledge of Print

In their explorations with text, children learn about print and how books are put together. They find out, by watching their parents turn a book over and around, where the top and front of the book are. Children at this level pay close attention to illustrations. They learn that illustrators take three-dimensional objects and represent them in two-dimensional space. They also learn that each page can contain a separate illustration. For example, one young child, observing the illustrations in *Goodnight Moon* (Brown, 1947), wanted to know why there were so many moons in the book. A brief discussion about how each picture was a separate drawing of the night sky did not clarify matters for her, but further reading experience did, and soon she began to understand how illustrators represent events in stories.

If parents focus attention on the words on a page in addition to the illustrations, children begin to notice print's directionality. Early on, young children learn that text is written and read from left to right, and it makes a return sweep at the end of a line (Clay, 1972). If you watch closely, you may even see a child sweep a finger under the words in a story in a left-to-right motion.

Other concepts about print that children begin to understand as they explore books and written material include

- A book has a front and back.
- A book has a top and bottom.
- Print is arranged left to right.
- Oral language can be represented in written words.
- Words are composed of letters.
- Sounds and letters have a relationship.
- The alphabet contains letters and sounds (Clay, 1975).

Listening to Stories

One of the most important skills that young children learn during this level is to listen to stories. A favorite informal assessment, reading a story to a preschool or kindergarten class, quickly reveals which children have experienced many hours of listening to stories. Some children, particularly those who have been read to from an early age, will sit still and listen attentively, often voicing comments about the story. Other children, including those who have had fewer reading experiences, may begin squirming and wiggling after listening to only a few pages of text.

Early Reading Experiences

Figure 3.1 shows that emergent readers do not yet have a **concept of word,** the ability to match spoken words with words in text. A young child at this level may run a finger under the words on a printed page but in most cases will create a text grounded in the illustrations. For example, the text may be, "The dog was hiding under the fence." The emergent reader might read, "I see the dog by the fence." Gaining the ability to match speech to print allows students to independently read text (Morris, 1981; 1983). Concept of word is a crucial skill that allows emergent readers to develop into beginning readers and writers.

Emergent readers mainly point to pictures and name them. They do this from page to page and do not create a story as they comment on the illustrations. Each page is, in essence, a separate reading event. If an adult is sitting with them as they read, they often engage the adult in a conversation about the pictures. Each page becomes an interesting detour focused on the picture, not on any meaning central to the story (Sulzby, 1985).

As children gain experience with books, they begin to form a story by linking their comments on the illustrations from page to page. As they read, they sound as if they are storytelling or carrying on a conversation with the listener. They choose words typical of oral conversations, and they do not use the intonation associated with reading a book.

Eventually, children combine the above storytelling strategy with more book-like reading. You might hear them incorporate words from a book and then move to storytelling (Sulzby, 1985). In a book such as *Brown Bear* (Martin, Jr., 1983), you might hear them read, "Brown bear, what do you see?" and then they might say, "Do you see the bird on this page? It's red. Let's peek and see what is on the next page. Red bird, what do you see?" They might continue in this fashion as they move through the book.

These types of reading experiences set the stage for what we call *conventional reading.* As children join parents and teachers in interacting with books in informal settings, they learn about the conventions of print and the pleasure of being involved with books, and they develop strategies for reading books.

Response to Literature and Meaning Construction

Emergent readers and writers who are asked to write or tell about the stories that have been read to them often retell the most important events first, in no particular order. In fact, they appear unable to retell a story from beginning to middle and end. Applebee (1978) has called these rather random collections of the most important events *heaps.*

Children's understandings of how stories are constructed grow from the stories they hear at home and school. To help children create this story knowledge, teachers read to students every day for extended periods. As they read, they draw students into discussions about story characters and about story events and how they flow from one to another.

Spelling and Orthographic Knowledge

Early in the emergent level, children recognize a difference between drawing and writing (Harste, Woodward & Burke, 1984). Children may use scribbling for both, but their scribbling for a picture, for instance, is usually larger than the tight scribble that they might use to represent their name. Figure 3.2 shows the clear difference between a three-year-old's scribble used to represent mom and the tighter scribble used for a signature.

Spelling at this phase is primarily pretend spelling. It can be called *prephonemic* (*pre,* before, and *phonemic,* pertaining to the smallest units of sound) because the child does not represent words using sound/symbol strategies and cannot reread written text. Children's spellings move gradually from a picture/scribble strategy to using letters that they know.

Students in the prephonemic phase often learn the alphabet by singing the alphabet song and then by learning the letters in their names and writing their names. They may be able to represent the letters in their name but cannot use this knowledge to compare the first letter in their name with the first letter in another word. In Figure 3.3, David represents his name accurately and then goes on to write about his illustration using random letters to represent his ideas. Notice that the letters do not correspond to the letters in the words that he was trying to spell. These are just letters with which he is familiar.

Figure 3.2. A three-year-old's scribbled drawing and signature Source: Adapted from D. Barone (1996, p. 283).

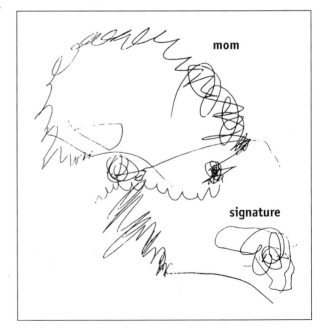

Figure 3.3. David's signature and random letters *Source: Adapted from D. Barone (1993, p. 32).*

Writing

Students in the emergent phase do plenty of play writing in the same way that they play in reading. They are experimenting with ways to write down their ideas. Although you may not be able to read what they have written, they will gladly tell you their ideas. Don't be surprised if their ideas are much more involved than what they have written. On some occasions, children will write down a few letters and then spend almost a half hour talking about what they have written. Frequently, they will start their writing with a picture, and their text will expand on what they have represented in the drawing. Young students often write about the events in their lives, but unless you know their experiences, you may not be able to understand what the child has written. The writings are situation-dependent, and the children assume that you are as familiar with the events being represented as they are.

Later in this phase, children may copy from bulletin boards, books, or the chalkboard. But because they still lack concept of word, they may copy letters backwards, leave out letters, or run one word into another. Sometimes adults get concerned when children make such errors, but until children develop the ability to match speech to text, they will not always make letters correctly or follow a left to right progression.

Beginning Readers and Writers

Many teachers and parents consider the beginning reading and writing phase the most exciting time of literacy development, perhaps because the signs of growth are so visible. Children begin to read independently, they can read and write words, and they can read reliably from their own writing.

Some teachers describe this phase as the time when children *crack the code* of the reading and spelling system (Chall, 1983; Weaver, 1988). Indeed, children do use the alphabet to separate word sounds (Clarke, 1988; Walsh, Price & Gillingham, 1986). They begin to make conventional matches between sounds and letters; to understand the *alphabetic principle* of English (Templeton, 1986). Emergent readers are unable to match the first letter in their name to a similar first letter in another word, but beginning readers and writers can easily match up words that begin with the same consonant. They use the alphabet to spell by using the **letter-name** strategy, that is, they use names of alphabet letters to help them spell words. Let's examine the reading, writing, and spelling and orthographic knowledge of students at this phase of literacy development.

Reading

Three predominant reading behaviors are associated with beginning reading:

1. Beginning readers tend to read aloud to themselves.

2. Beginning readers fingerpoint as they read.

3. Beginning readers are disfluent and inexpressive in their reading; they read word by word.

These are not taught behaviors; rather, it seems that no matter how children are taught, if they are beginning readers, they will display these behaviors. Teachers and parents who recognize these behaviors as typical of beginning readers also see them as positive signs of development.

Reading Aloud and Fingerpointing

Many kindergarten and first-grade classrooms have quiet reading time, sometimes called *silent sustained reading* (SSR). During this reading time, you can hear a steady hum of voices, often from beginning readers. Even when they read silently, you can hear them pronounce the words. Sometimes parents and teachers giggle as they hear a child loudly reading a word for emphasis. The child is usually unaware of the volume of his or her *silent* reading.

Beginning readers also tend to fingerpoint when they read. Like the reading-aloud strategy, using their fingers helps children keep their place and provides another source of support as they read. Before it was understood that fingerpointing is a natural part of beginning reading, teachers would ask students to stop pointing as they read or to use a card as a marker. Now, students continue fingerpointing until evidence suggests that they have moved beyond this phase and should discard this behavior. Usually, as readers develop in proficiency, they drop fingerpointing and use it only when the reading material gets difficult and they need the additional support.

Fluency

Beginning readers and writers are disfluent in their reading, even when they are fluent in their natural speech (Bear, 1989; 1991; Carver, 1992). Just as **flu-**

ency is characterized by smooth, quick reading, **disfluency** is a slow reading rate (at least half the average adult rate) accompanied by a general hesitancy and a lack of phrasing. Disfluency is also called *word-by-word reading* because beginners frequently pause as long as one second between words. Their reading often lacks expression and is monotone, which makes the reading sound choppy and unnatural.

Disfluency relates directly to the students' knowledge of orthography. Beginning readers and writers make a tradeoff between speed and accuracy. Their orthographic knowledge, in this case their knowledge of how the alphabet represents sound, is not rich enough for them to move through text quickly and easily. They will become fluent readers only when they know more about spelling and can easily read and write many frequently occurring words (Perfetti, 1985).

Another way to think about disfluent reading is to imagine yourself reading a technical journal article about, say, immunology. Our guess is that you would be unfamiliar with the language, the concepts, and the vocabulary related to immunology. As you read this article, you would expend great cognitive energy in pronouncing the words in an attempt to gain meaning. The pronunciation problems would affect your comprehension. You might begin to read disfluently, perhaps to fingerpoint, and you might even start reading the text aloud. The Taking a Closer Look exercise will remind you of what it is like to read disfluently.

These three reading behaviors provide you with indicators of when beginning reading ends and transitional reading begins. In most cases, they drop away as readers become more proficient.

Concept of Word

Concept of word, the ability to match speech with text, is considered a benchmark in literacy development (Morris, 1980; 1981; 1983). Emergent readers and writers have not reached this phase; beginning readers and writers have either a rudimentary or full understanding of concept of word.

Children's reading behaviors at different points in acquiring concept of word can be assessed by using a chant such as "Crackers and Crumbs" (Dunn & Pamenter, 1990, p. 37):

Crackers and crumbs
Crackers and crumbs
These are my fingers
These are my thumbs
These are my eyes
These are my ears
They'll all grow big
In the next ten years.

First, have students memorize this chant. Once a child has it memorized, sit next to the child and write the first four lines, saying the chant as you write it. Read the first four lines again, pointing to each word as you read. Following this step, take the child's hand and model this reading and pointing. Then let the child read the first four lines of the chant alone.

····· TAKING A ·····
CLOSER LOOK   Try Reading Like a Beginner

It has been many years since you experienced what it is like to read as slowly as a beginner. For this exercise you will need a watch with a second hand or a stopwatch. First, time yourself reading the passage below at a normal pace.

> Paul Bissex began his writing at age five with an indignant note to his mother, who, busy talking with friends, had not noticed that the child was trying to ask her something. After trying a few times to get her attention he went away, but soon returned with this message printed on a piece of paper: *RUDF.* Luckily for him, his mother was perceptive enough to decode this note ("Are you deaf?"), understand its importance, and quickly give the boy the attention he had been asking for.
>
> As the boy began to explore written English, his mother paid steady attention to the ways in which he was doing it.

Check your watch for your time. This passage is 109 words long (*John Holt, Learning All the Time,* Reading, MA: Addison-Wesley, 1989). Now find your reading rate in the following chart:

words/seconds × 60 = words per minute (wpm)

109/120 × 60 = 55 wpm
109/90 × 60 = 73
109/60 × 60 = 109
109/40 × 60 = 164
109/30 × 60 = 218
109/20 × 60 = 327
109/15 × 60 = 436

Reading this passage in twenty to thirty seconds translates as a reading rate of between two hundred and three hundred words per minute.

Now give yourself a full two minutes to read this same passage. Read more slowly. Fingerpoint, start moving your lips, pretend that you are having difficulty reading some words, make a few regressions (go back to the beginning of the line or sentence). Reading so slowly is harder than it seems. You can see how it might be hard to comprehend a text when reading at this speed. Beginning readers need to experience fluency as often as possible. Pattern books, familiar rhymes, and dictations can give them this practice.

A child who has rudimentary concept of word will point to most words accurately, but will lose accuracy with two-syllable words. The first word in this chant, "crackers," will cause difficulty for children with a rudimentary concept of word. They may point to the word "and" when they say the second syllable in "crackers"—"ers." On the third line, children who almost have concept of word will point accurately to the first three words, "These are my," but then fall off track in pointing to "fingers." You will see them looking for the next word as they say the second syllable in "fingers"—"ers." Children who have a full understanding of concept of word point accurately and with some speed as they provide two beats for two-syllable words such as "crackers."

To fully assess whether a child has a full or rudimentary understanding of concept of word, you might ask students to find words in the middle of the text. For example, in "Crackers and Crumbs," ask children to find "my" in sentences such as: "These are my fingers" or "These are my thumbs." Children who can point to words *immediately* have acquired a full concept of word. Children who can identify only the easier words or words at the beginning or end of sentences, or who need to read through text from the beginning to the word in the middle of a sentence, have acquired a rudimentary understanding of concept of word.

Response to Literature and Meaning Construction

Beginning readers and writers most often respond to stories with retellings and in some cases summaries of what they have read. For example, after reading the book *Caps for Sale* (Slobodkina, 1976), students Aamir and Dylan wrote about the story in response notebooks. The two boys included what they considered the most important events of the story and excluded others. As seen in their summaries below, they were most interested in the man who was selling the caps (Barone, 1992, p.91).

> Aamir: A guy had 17 caps and he can't sell them. He was sad; very, very sad. So he slept on a tree and 17 monkeys took the hats.
> Dylan: A guy had 17 caps and he could not sell any caps. He napped. So these monkeys took his caps and he woke up. He saw the monkeys and they copied him.

Beginning readers and writers like Aamir and Dylan are most involved with the literal events of stories. They enjoy writing about what happened. Although when they talk about stories they frequently include their personal opinions, these personal opinions rarely appear in their writings about stories (Barone, 1992).

Spelling and Orthographic Knowledge

Beginning readers often use one of two strategies to spell words (Henderson, 1990; Henderson & Templeton, 1986). During what is called *semiphonemic* spelling or orthographic knowledge, students use the initial and perhaps final consonant to represent words. They can spell some (semi) of the sounds (phonemes) present in words. As students begin to represent the vowels in words in addition to the initial and final consonants, we call them letter-name spellers. These children can use the letters of the alphabet to help them spell, and can represent each sound (phoneme) that they hear in a word. For example, letter-name spellers can identify letter names in *bat* and represent each sound they hear, although they may often confuse the vowel representation.

Semiphonemic Spelling

Semiphonemic spellers map the sound of the initial consonant to the letter in the alphabet. For consonants, the match between the letter name and the sound the letter makes is fairly close, so a child who wants to spell *pat* might write *P* or *PT*. A few of the letters, particularly *c, g, h,* and *w,* do not provide much help. Consequently, children may spell *water* as *Y, YT,* or *YTR.* The *t* and the *r* are clear enough, but can you see why they might spell *w* with a *y?* Say the letter name *W.* It starts with a /d/ sound. The letter name *Y,* however, is pretty close to the /w/ sound as you can hear and feel when you say *y.*

As students move beyond the prephonemic spelling strategies they used as emerging spellers, they begin by representing the initial consonant and then begin to represent the last sounds they hear and feel when they say a word as they write it. Figure 3.4 shows a first-grade student's journal entry. This child has used the beginning consonant for each word that he chose to write. Try to read his writing; his illustration will clue you in to his message: "I like to make a house."

In spelling, children sometimes represent word sounds by the way the letters sound or feel. Students glean spelling information by checking how word sounds "feel" when they pronounce them. Linguists (Read, 1975) call the way sounds are made in the mouth **manner and point of articulation.** Try the *Y* substitution for the *W* again. As you say the letter name *Y,* you should be able to feel the air coming out to make the /w/ sound.

How semiphonemic spellers spell *dragon* provides another opportunity to understand how sounds feel in the mouth. Students often spell *dragon* as *J* or *G* or perhaps *JR* or *GR.* To compare the similarities between the *dr* and *jr* sounds, say *dragon* and then say *jragon.* Similarly, students may at first spell *train CH* and later *CHN.* Say *chrain* and *train* and feel how alike they are in the mouth.

Young readers at this semiphonemic phase can recognize some single-syllable words. Their sight vocabularies are growing gradually. They are picking up these words from real reading and writing contexts, not by memorizing word lists, an important point highlighted throughout this book.

Letter-Name Spelling

As skills improve, children add vowels for each major syllable. The **long vowels** are easy to represent, because the letter name and the long vowel are one and the same. A child who uses a letter-name strategy might spell the word *road* as *ROD.* You can see that the child hasn't used the conventional *oa* to represent this sound in this word, but has simplified the vowel representation by using the letter with the long vowel sound. Students who use letter-name strategies don't yet know the long vowel patterns, as seen in the word *road.* They may be able to read words with long vowels patterns, but they will write a one-to-one correspondence between the number of sounds in a word and the number of letters—one letter for each sound (phoneme) that they hear.

Mario's spelling example, seen in Figure 3.5, clearly shows this one-to-one correspondence between sound and letter. Mario was asked to spell words in a

developmental spelling list as part of an informal assessment. Notice that Mario used the alphabet letter to represent the long vowel in his spelling of *drive*. For consonant sounds, Mario did not write *ship*, for instance, with two letters for the digraph *sh* because this digraph conveys only one sound, which Mario chose to represent with an *R*. He used this same strategy by writing a *W* to represent the *wh* digraph in the word *when*.

The **short vowel,** such as the sound *a* makes in *bat*, provides the most interesting aspect of the letter-name phase. Children spell short vowels depending on how they hear and feel the sounds. They do not have the alphabet names of the letters to rely on because there are no letter names that represent the sounds that short vowels make. The letter name for *a* in *bake* is easy, but what letter should be used to represent the *e* sound in *red*? Research shows that children unconsciously choose the vowel closest in point of articulation to the short vowel they are trying to spell (Read, 1975; Templeton & Bear, 1992).

To test this for yourself, suppose you were a letter-name phase speller and you wanted to write *bed*. What letter is closest to the short *e* sound? Try this: Say the short *e* and then the long *e* . . . /eh/—/ee/. Feel where each is made in the mouth relative to the other. Do you feel the long *e* toward the front of your mouth? Now try feeling the contrast between the short *e* and the long *a* /eh/ as

**Figure 3.5. Mario's
first-grade spelling**
Source: Adapted from D.
Barone (1997).

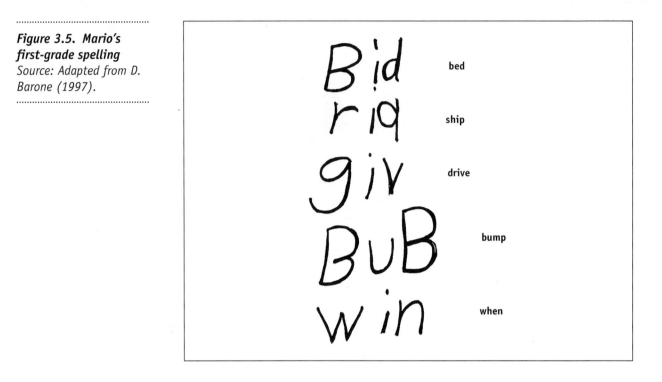

in *bed* and /ay/ as in *hay*. Say these two pairs a few times to get a feel for their positions in your mouth. Which letter is closer to the short *e* sound—*a* or *e*? The answer is the long *a*, and this is the choice that you would make if you were using a letter-name strategy. You would spell *bed* as *BAD*.

Here is another example: What letter will students use to represent the short *i* in *stick*? Let's try two contrasts with the short *i* as in *fish*. Practice saying the /ih/ as in *fit* and the /i/ as in *find*. Then practice saying the /ih/ as in *fit* and the /e/ as in *feet*. Again, say each pair several times and compare the relative positions. The long *e* feels closer to the short *i*, and in fact, letter-name spellers often spell *stick* as *STEK*.

The following chart will help you keep track of the possible long vowel substitutions for short vowels.

Word to be spelled $\rightarrow$ ***How the short vowel is represented***

bad	BAD
bed	BAD
bit	BET
pot	PIT
but	BOT

As you can see, the substitutions go to the previous long vowel: Starting from *but, u* goes to *o, o* goes to *i, i* goes to *e,* and *e* goes to *a.*

Another distinguishing feature of the letter-name spelling phase has to do with a feature called the **preconsonantal nasal.** Letter-name spellers leave out the *n* or *m* that occurs before another consonant. Here are some examples.

Word to be spelled ⟶ *How the word is represented*

bump	BOP, BUP
stand	SAD, STAD
shrimp	SEP, SHRIP
pink	PEK, PIK

In Figure 3.5 Mario spells *bump* by eliminating the preconsonantal nasal. This is significant: Students who *include* the preconsonantal nasal in their writing are at the end of the letter-name phase and will soon move to a new phase of understanding about words.

Students' spelling abilities parallel their reading abilities. Letter-name-level students' orthographic knowledge enables them to read a variety of single-syllable words. Over the course of this phase, students master short vowel patterns, and they learn to read most single-syllable words, including words that follow regular and frequent short and long vowel patterns.

Writing

Now that students are experimenting with initial and final consonants and short and long vowels, their writing becomes easier for them and for others. Their knowledge of concept of word and the alphabet improves their writing. They can write down any idea that comes to mind and can reread it in the same way each time.

Children in this writing phase are limited somewhat by the physical act of writing. Beginning writers parallel beginning readers in that they are somewhat disfluent. They don't know how to spell many words and so must spend time and thought on inventing most of the words that they write. You and I write mostly without pause, whereas these children spend time thinking about the ideas that they want to express and concentrating on spelling each word letter-by-letter.

Children who use semiphonemic writing strategies and have a rudimentary understanding of concept of word may write a word or two, up to a few sentences, but rarely much more. As shown in Figure 3.4 on page 77, this writing can create a reading challenge for teachers and parents. Teachers often ask students to reread what they have written. Illustrations help students and teachers remember a topic (Dyson, 1989).

Students who have a full understanding of concept of word and use letter-name writing strategies may still experience occasional difficulty in rereading what they have written, but the vowel in each major syllable helps. The following example shows how greater orthographic detail reduces the ambiguity of the message.

S

SP

SEP

SLEP

Accompanied by other linguistic clues and perhaps a picture, you would have no difficulty recognizing *SLEP* as *sleep*, whereas *S* is a good deal more difficult to decipher.

Beginning writers often over- or underestimate when allocating space for words. They frequently start a word on one line and then put the letters that would not fit on the next line. Sometimes they start these words at the beginning of the next line, and other times they may start in the right margin and write to the left.

You will also notice that, as children develop concept of word, they begin to leave spaces between their words. At first, some children find leaving this space quite difficult. Kindergarten and first-grade teachers will tell you about children who use dots or lines to mark the spaces between words.

It is always interesting to look beyond the form of children's writings to their content. We sometimes search so carefully for structural nuance that we forget to just enjoy the topics of their writing. As you recall, during the emergent literacy phase of development, much of what children write is situational. Often, these children believe that we know all about what has happened to them and therefore know all the background about their writing. Students act as informers of their writing by reading it to us and by filling in our lacking background knowledge. Beginning readers and writers still most often choose to write about themselves (Calkins, 1986). Often they enrich their ideas with illustrations.

The next developmental level, transitional readers and writers, are more flexible in their use of reading and writing strategies. For example, they move away from the literal emphasis on stories to a more inferential understanding. They also begin to experiment with different types of writing such as stories, poems, and nonfiction pieces.

Transitional Readers and Writers

The transitional nature of students' growth highlights this third constellation of literacy behaviors. Students begin to acquire mature literacy behaviors: they begin to read silently and read and write more fluently, and many of their invented spellings look more conventional. They no longer require as much support from adults or more proficient peers as when they were beginning readers and writers. They can read independently as long as they can easily comprehend the text. These materials they read fluently and can read orally with expression where appropriate. These students are more fluent in their writing and produce longer text that focuses more on meaning (Henderson, 1990).

Transitional readers move into a world of books (Newkirk, 1987). They begin to explore independently many of the books that were read to them. They also begin to explore nonfiction books as they gain an interest in the world around them.

These students read single-syllable words well, and they read most familiar two-syllable words with increasing accuracy and fluency. Their orthographic knowledge allows them to easily read most words and to focus their remaining cognitive energy on comprehension.

Reading

Transitional readers have the following predominant characteristics:

1. They begin to read silently.

2. They read with greater fluency and accuracy.

3. They are more focused on the meaning of what they read.

Silent Reading Predominates

Silent reading becomes the predominant mode for reading. These students can read and comprehend without the oral support of saying the words out loud. Silent reading becomes faster than oral reading.

Fluency and Accuracy

These students read at a more rapid pace than beginning readers and writers. The term used to describe their growth in fluency is *approaching fluency* (Carver, 1992). They tend to read almost twice as fast as they did as beginning readers, approaching 120 words per minute in easy materials.

Transitional readers read with expression and enthusiasm. They can adjust their pitch and volume, place emphasis on particular words to express meaning, and shape their phrasing to lead smoothly from one phrase to another. They can do this on the first reading of easy material, and they are more proficient if they have had a chance to reread the material before an oral presentation.

Sight Vocabulary Expands

One of the most important developments is the transitional student's expanded knowledge of words. Students can read almost all single- and two-syllable words. They are busy acquiring a stable sight vocabulary. As they try to pick up speed and read more in phrases rather than in single words, they may misread a number of function words such as *then, who, what,* and so on. In most cases, these words do not interfere with constructing meaning from the text. This trait diminishes as students move to the end of the transitional phase.

Reading Choices

Now the universe of what students read widens vastly. They begin to reread their favorite picture books. At this point in a student's development, the child can truly appreciate the beauty of the illustrations, along with the ability to easily read the text in most of these old favorites.

Picture adventure stories are also quite appealing to students. The Magic School Bus series by Joanna Cole (Scholastic Publishers) is popular. In particular, second- through approximately fourth-grade students like these information books and their irreverent and yet flattering adventures of a teacher and her field trips. Students use the extensive illustrations to elaborate the text meaning. These books are a nice transition from more familiar picture books to nonfiction material.

These students find simple chapter books particularly pleasing and use their ability to read them as a measure of their own growth as readers. Easy chapter books such as Ann Cameron's Julian stories and Beverly Cleary's Ramona books provide students with success as they move into this genre. Such books deal with children in situations familiar to students, and readers need only adjust to the longer narrative text.

Sometimes teachers are concerned when more mature readers spend most of their reading time with picture books or with series of books known more for their number than their name. This easy, familiar reading allows students to develop fluency as readers and to practice reading as their teachers and parents have modeled for them. This is an important time for transitional readers as they practice and consolidate previous knowledge.

Response to Literature and Meaning Construction

Transitional writers still retell and summarize the events and main ideas of stories they have read, but they begin to experiment more with analytical responses. Sometimes students begin their responses with a brief summary and then shift to an analysis of what they think is important about the story. Figure 3.6 shows a student's response that utilizes a *double-entry draft* (DED) framework. In a double-entry draft, students copy an important word, phrase, or sentence from a book and then discuss why they have chosen this piece of text (Barone, 1989). In this response to a book called *Ramona Quimby, Age 8* (Cleary, 1981), the student makes a personal connection between the text and her own experiences. The teacher then continues the dialogue about the book by commenting on the student's response.

Whereas young students, even preschoolers, interpret books through personal connections, transitional readers and writers begin to routinely explore deeper understandings in their conversations and writing about books. Transitional students really begin to enjoy responding to stories and then hearing comments by other students about the same story. They begin to understand that stories can have multiple interpretations and to appreciate the multiple understandings possible within a single story.

Spelling and Orthographic Knowledge

When students have become comfortable representing short-vowel sounds accurately they begin experimenting with how to represent long-vowel sounds. They begin using *within-word pattern* strategies to determine increasingly abstract and complex spellings. For example, they may now need to use two letters

Figure 3.6. A student's response using a double-entry draft (DED)
Source: Adapted from D. Barone (1990, p. 52).

Sunday mornint ramona and Beezus were still resolved to be perfect until dinner time.	I know why they were trying to do that. They didn't want to make dinner. that's why. Don't you think Ramona and Beezus are a little tricky?
My comment:	I think they are a lot tricky. I wonder if they will get out of cooking dinner?

to represent one sound, as with the *o* and *a* in the word *road.* They no longer represent long-vowel sounds by using an alphabet letter strategy. They have learned enough about the short vowels that, when they edit, you will hear them say, "That's not 'time,' that's 'Tim.'"

The most common long-vowel patterns these students begin to examine include

CVCe—silent *e* as in *same, Pete, line,* and *hope*

CVVC—vowel digraphs as in *nail, peel,* and *coat*

CVV—vowel digraphs as in *hay, tea,* and *toe*

In each case, the vowel sound is marked or represented with two vowels. Students observe the middles of words and look for long-vowel patterns. They also begin to settle on the spelling of most *r*-influenced vowels as in *shark, fire, forest, girl, fur,* and *her.*

Within-word pattern spellings look correct, and the words could be written in this way. For example, *TIEM* for *time, CLEEN* for *clean,* and *WAIGHT* for *weight* make sense and are readable. The student is using his or her knowledge of sounds and letters, but the words just don't happen to be spelled this way.

As in reading, transitional spellers solidify their orthographic knowledge of single-syllable words. They consolidate their knowledge of how to represent short and long vowels in single-syllable words and, unlike beginning readers and writers, can more easily represent the words they wish to write. They no longer need to write their most familiar words letter-by-letter but write some words as wholes and others as groups of letters. They might write *school* without a pause, but they may write *letter* by first writing *let* and then *ter.* As you might guess, they produce longer pieces of writing because they are spending less time and energy writing each word. Although we don't recommend having children copy from the board, these children can do so without much difficulty (Henderson, 1990; Henderson & Templeton, 1986).

Writing

The most noticeable feature of writing during this developmental phase is the length of the written pieces. Their ability to represent single-syllable words makes it easy for students to fill a page with text.

A student writes about the ideas she is exploring in her reading.

They continue to write narratives in sequences and at first may be exhausting in their detail. Some write quite long sentences with plenty of *and then*s. Gradually, throughout this phase, students focus on the bigger picture—what the story is about and what message they want to get across (Calkins, 1986).

Unlike students in earlier phases of development, transitional students' writing is not situational: the reader can get its meaning without background information. Transitional writers also become more purposeful in their writing and more conscious of possible readers. They want their readers to understand what they have written, they want to convey meaning, and they want to entertain. The entire meaning is conveyed in the words. In addition, they generally are more interested in dialogue and punctuation in their writing and like to experiment with quotation and exclamation marks.

In addition to writing narratives, students begin to experiment with nonfiction writing. They may create text that imitates the nonfiction books they are reading and show concern about getting the details correct. Loren's wolf report in Figure 3.7 and its many specific facts about wolves demonstrate his need to be careful about details.

Figure 3.7. Loren's wolf report *Source: Adapted from D. Barone (1994, p. 286).*

> THE WOLF
>
> BY LOREN
>
> The wolf lives everywhere but deserts and forests. It lives in sparsley populated regions like wilderness regions.
>
> Wolves weigh 150 to 170 pounds. THEY are 5-6 feet long and 2 1/2 feet tall.
>
> The wolf's fur can be gray, white, or black.
>
> Wolves eat anything they can catch. They eat rabbits, cows, bulls, and the moose. Farmers get angry. They shoot them!
>
> Wolves run very fast. They run 40 miles a day. They can run 35 miles in one hour.
>
> I like wolves because they can run fast.

Students begin to explore a variety of genres in their writing, which may include plays, reports, books for younger students, poems, recipes, and new scripts. They enjoy trying on these new genres as they move beyond familiar story writing. Although they are willing to experiment with writing, they can also become frustrated when their actual writing fails to meet their expectations. You may see many false starts on exciting projects at this time (Calkins, 1986).

Intermediate and Advanced Readers and Writers

In these final and most sophisticated phases of literacy development, students become familiar with a variety of genres and different styles of authors. It is a time when students become flexible in their reading and can use a variety of styles from careful reading to skimming, depending on the genre and purpose of reading. Students develop confidence and comfort in their skills as readers and writers. They learn that reading and writing serve many functions, and many such students discover the enjoyment that goes with being a proficient reader and writer.

By the end of the intermediate phase of literacy development, students can read almost anything put before them and, if given enough time, can pronounce even difficult new vocabulary. Like you and me, if intermediate readers know a lot about a topic, their reading will be accurate and fluent, and they will fit the new information in with what they already know and think about the topic. On the other hand, if the topic is new, they will read more slowly, with a few more hesitations in reading some vocabulary words, and they will take in information on a literal level. This is a time when students make more use of expository materials and develop study habits for their work in textbooks and nonstory materials (McGee & Richgels, 1985).

As students move into the final stage of advanced reading, they develop a repertoire of reading and writing styles. These students enjoy exploring new subjects in depth. As they enter a new field of study, they learn its particular vocabulary, learn to read the visual presentations, such as charts and tables, that accompany text, and learn to understand the style of writing associated with the topic. This is a time when students begin to consider themselves experts in certain areas. It is also a time when students begin to express their dislikes of certain topics. For instance, a student who has had bad experiences with mathematics or science may avoid reading about those subjects.

Reading

Intermediate Readers

Intermediate readers acquire real confidence in their reading, and for the first time reading takes over as a major tool for learning new vocabulary (Bear, Invernizzi & Templeton, 1996; Templeton, 1989). They learn to use careful reading for studying and textbook reading and faster pleasure reading for magazines and such.

Intermediate readers continue to prefer silent reading because it is much faster than oral reading. Silent reading also supports comprehension and fluency, so there is little need for students to read orally.

When students reach this phase of literacy development, content reading takes on new importance. Reading nonfiction helps students begin to develop skills in studying, note taking, skimming, and scanning, and they benefit from any instruction that makes reading nonfiction easier.

The intermediate phase is also a time when students *read to learn*. Reading to learn focuses on gathering information from textbook-type materials. When students use all of their reading time reading to learn information, they begin to read almost exclusively in textbooks and their love of learning is not nurtured. Students who read only because they have to read are at risk of developing what is known as *aliteracy*. Aliteracy is a term applied to students who can read but choose not to. They read only when an assignment is given, and they express no joy at the possibility of reading or writing. Students need the opportunity to read from a wide variety of genres, and they need to be able to choose the materials that they read. This wide reading and personal choice should help develop readers who can read and enjoy it, too.

Advanced Readers

As students build on their experiences with a variety of genres, they begin to explore new subjects in depth. Advanced readers adjust their reading styles based on the purpose and the genre that they are reading. Their reading styles change dramatically when they read newspapers, novels, poems, cartoons, catalogues, driving manuals, song books, magazines, advertisements, and picture books.

As a student in higher education, you have probably learned to adjust your reading rate and style as you move through various forms of information. For example, you use one reading style when reading a book for a children's literature class, a different style when rereading your notes, and perhaps your most careful reading style for a textbook or article. This flexibility has come with experience. On the topic of literacy, for example, you are becoming an experienced specialized reader who is quite familiar with the literacy vocabulary. When you first started to read in this area, terms such as emergent literacy and orthographic knowledge were unfamiliar. But experience with the specialized vocabulary has made reading easier.

In most materials, advanced readers read between 250 and 350 words per minute (Carver, 1992). When a reader is familiar with a writing style and the content of the material, reading rates may increase to five hundred or six hundred words per minute. Advanced readers can be quite good at fast reading, also known as skimming and scanning, which implies that readers skip text to obtain an overview or to find particular information. This type of inspectional reading is a powerful tool for reading some expository materials.

Response to Literature and Meaning Construction

These students truly enjoy responding to what they read. In most instances, they move beyond the literal events of what they are reading to interpretive responses. They make connections between events in books, in their lives, and events in other books. They also write about the themes of books and how considering such themes help them understand the human condition (Barone, 1992).

A fifth-grade student wrote the following response to the book *The Butter Battle Book* (Seuss, 1984; Barone, 1993b). He generalizes about the book's meaning and extends this meaning to the world in general.

> The story was about the things that bigotry can start. This story shows how foolish people can be. I think what the author was trying to say is that people shouldn't solve their differences by warfare alone. They should discuss their differences instead of having a war.

Students at previous phases of development can also make such responses, but the greater cognitive energy they expend in the reading process tends to leave less energy for responses at these more abstract levels.

Spelling and Orthographic Knowledge

Intermediate and advanced readers and writers have a stable understanding of how to spell single-syllable words. For example, they show no hesitation reading and spelling *hop* and *hope*. Students who are at the **syllable juncture** phase show confusion in how to add affixes (prefixes or suffixes) to words. They may spell *popping* as *POPING*. As they discover how to add affixes to words, they begin to explore the structure of words through an investigation of word roots. Students who are exploring this aspect of words are at the **derivational constancy** phase. Let's examine each of these phases of orthographic development.

Syllable Juncture

Much of spelling focuses on how to spell polysyllabic words, especially on how syllables come together—the juncture between the syllables. One of the earliest and most important orthographic features studied is the consonant doubling pattern and principle, which students master during this phase. Now that students know that *hope* is HOPE and *hop* is HOP, they begin to understand how the second syllables of *hoping* and *hopping* affect the previous syllables. They begin to double the preceding consonant when adding a second syllable to some short vowel words that follow the CVC (consonant-vowel-consonant) pattern.

hop	hopping	versus	hope	hoping
clam	clamming	versus	claim	claiming

Throughout this phase, students work with how syllables are added to words. With their knowledge of how short and long vowels connect with other syllables, they learn that the *b* in *rabbit* and the *g* in *struggle* are doubled, and that the *t* in *hotel* and the *p* in *maple* are not. You can see their experimentation with affixes in their invented spellings of *table* as *TABEL,* *label* as *LABLE,* and *maple* as *MAPEL.*

As students learn how syllables are combined, they begin to make spelling–meaning connections (Templeton, 1989). They learn that the affixes they add to words affect the meaning of the word and additionally can change its syntactic function. For instance, *distrustful* begins with a prefix *dis* that means negation and a suffix *ful* that changes the noun into an adjective. The focus on meaning during this phase is on the *external* parts of words, the parts that are added either to the beginning or to the end of a word.

Derivational Constancy

As you would expect, students begin this phase with a thorough understanding of the basic principles of adding affixes onto words. Students build on this knowledge as they explore the *internal* structure of words, the morphology, particularly the roots.

As students look at the meaning patterns in words, they develop an eye for how words look. They begin to recognize distinctive patterns in words that mark their meaning. They see that although the sound changes in words like *please* and *pleasure,* the spelling remains constant.

Students now have enough facility with words to extract meaning patterns. For instance, *medicine, medicinal,* and *medic* are variations on the root *med,* but they can see that the root stays the same in spite of changes in sound. Although they may not be explicitly aware that these words share the same Latin root, they can see the constancy in meaning.

Also, students learn that some sound interactions influence spelling. For example, the *in* in *insensitive* has the same meaning as the *il* in *illogical.* But *inlogical* doesn't sound right, so the *in* prefix turned into *il.* Another example is evident when we try to say *adtract.* It is difficult to say, and became *attract.*

The best teachers help students develop a curiosity about words and their structures. This curiosity about words leads students to explore word structure, foreign borrowings, and the classical roots of the orthography in the words they encounter in their reading as orthographic knowledge and vocabulary develop simultaneously.

Writing

Intermediate and advanced writers have learned to convey the entire meaning in words, and they discover their own writing voice as well. At first, they may write with a particular audience in mind, such as other students in the class. They may purposefully choose words that they hope convey their ideas.

In addition to voice, these students are in control of their writing. They choose among more and less formal styles for the best form for each piece (Bereiter, 1980). They know, for instance, when using a report form makes more sense than using a narrative structure.

Conclusion and Study Notes

The synchrony model provides a schema for literacy development. The ultimate goal of such a model is to help teachers plan instruction that matches children's literacy development. The integrated model of literacy development provides a gauge to observe students as they use literacy in authentic ways. By looking at students' reading, writing, and spelling in developmental terms, you will be able to describe their progress.

You can work with students to develop authentic assessment instruments. These assessments will allow you to move beyond the rigid standardized test score measures of grade-level equivalencies. You will be able to show students how they can document their development as the two of you collect samples of work through the year. Then, in turn, you and the student will be able to explain to parents how literacy is developing.

A keen understanding of literacy development is crucial to developing meaningful assessment techniques. Forthcoming chapters will discuss each phase of development in more detail and will provide authentic assessments of literacy that match student development.

In this chapter, we have considered the following main points:

- The integrated model of literacy is unique in that it looks across reading, writing, and spelling development and highlights the synchrony, or integrated relationships and connections, among these areas.

- Orthographic knowledge is a general term for the knowledge students have about words.

- Emergent literacy is a philosophy that values children's learning from birth or before. This philosophy replaces the idea of reading readiness.

- Concept of word is considered a benchmark in literacy development.

- Students who can read and choose not to read may develop what is known as aliteracy.

Key Terms

Below is some of the specialized vocabulary that you encountered throughout this chapter. Define each term and think of examples that will help you remember what each term means.

integrated model of literacy

synchrony

orthographic knowledge

emergent literacy

concept of word

fluency/disfluency

manner and point of articulation

long vowels and short vowels
preconsonantal nasals

Follow-Up Activities

1. Interview a teacher about his or her understanding of models of literacy development. How does this teacher describe and assess development? Does the teacher use a model similar to the synchrony model?

2. Observe in a classroom with special education students. Look for developmental patterns among the students. If these students regularly write in a journal, try to sit with a student and have him or her share several entries. See if you can determine an approximate phase of development from these entries.

3. Visit several classrooms during silent sustained reading. Record behaviors that you see as students read.

PART TWO

Approaches to Informal Literacy Assessments

Contents

4 Individual Literacy Assessments

5 Whole-Class and Small-Group Informal Assessment

4 Individual Literacy Assessments

Sherry: How do I know where to begin with a student? I just started tutoring a child, and I don't know what I should work on. I don't know what materials and activities I should use.

Jill: I have the same question about when I am in the classroom. How will I assess students? When do I assess students?

Amanda: Remind me what the difference is between assessment and testing. Aren't we required to give tests at the end of the year? We also had weekly or regular tests in class.

Mark: But we're trying to get more than test scores. I want to know more about assessing students who are having problems learning to read and write.

Sharon: We need to let parents know at the beginning of the year that we are going to be assessing their children. And then we need to follow up by sharing what we learn and including them in planning.

Carol: I think that someday we'll create individual educational plans for all students, not just the students in special education.

Dawn: Yes, I make time at the beginning of the year to spend some individual time with students. I want them to talk to me in individual conferences. They show me what they are learning, reading, and writing.

Mark: I want to get back to Jill's question: What is the difference between assessment and testing? I remember when I was in fourth grade they said that I should go off into this room to work with a teacher. I don't know why they sent me, but

I guess they thought I had a reading problem. We did a lot of testing in there. Do we have to do so much testing? What has this got to do with teaching in the classroom?

These students want to know more about the differences between assessing and testing. Mark wants to know where to start instruction and how to assess in a way that answers questions about teaching. This chapter and the next chapter provide answers to those questions by focusing on ways to assess students as individuals and in small classroom groups.

This is a chapter in which you apply what you learned about development in the previous chapter to understand the literacy of an individual student. It provides you with the tools teachers use to assess how students read and write and at what developmental level they perform. You will learn many practices to assess students' literacy including measures of comprehension, reading accuracy and rate, narrative and expository writing, and spelling development. This assessment process is useful when you need to look closely at one child, and these assessment activities are easily adapted to practices that are a part of your literacy instruction in the classroom.

Guide Questions for Chapter 4

- What aspects of reading, writing, and spelling are examined in informal literacy assessments?

- How are reading and listening comprehension assessed?

- What can be learned by marking a student's oral reading?

- What are functional reading levels? What are grade-level descriptions of reading?

- How is a developmental level of literacy determined?

▌ *Why Have Individual Assessments?*

What you learn here about individual assessment will provide a model for your work with groups of students. For instance, you will learn in this chapter how to listen closely to and make a **qualitative analysis of a child's oral reading.** The assessment skills you apply to one child are the same as those you will apply in various classroom settings and groupings.

Many teachers meet with students periodically for individual conferences to have a short period of time together, one-on-one, to talk and share (Atwell, 1986; Graves, 1983). These conferences can occur during independent and small-group activity times. Some teachers use sustained silent reading periods and times when students are writing with each other to meet with individuals. Beginning in the second grade, some teachers set aside one time of day, two days a week, for individual meetings. Students can sign up for a meeting, or the teacher can ask a student to come to a conference center or station to meet.

Teachers conduct individual conferences for many reasons. Here is a brief list of the types of discussions and activities that are part of individual conferences:

Getting-to-know-you conferences

How's-it-going? meetings

Sharing what the student is reading

Informal reading, writing, and spelling inventories

Writing conferences

Reviews of the curriculum and goal setting

Planning sessions for student-directed group activities

Thematic meetings to discuss projects and self-assessments

During the first two weeks of school, conferences focus on getting to know each other. Throughout the year, individual conferences address immediate needs, such as discussing projects and student-directed activities.

Although some conferences take place where a student is working, the conference center is a little more private, and you can keep papers and files that you use in conferences at hand. The ideal spot is one where you have a bit of personal space but can continue to see into the class.

A few times a year you will need to use the entire informal process described here with individual students whose circumstances call for in-depth assessments of literacy. You may sense that a child is not progressing satisfactorily, or a parent may say, "I notice that my child doesn't read as well as other third-graders. Do you think there's a problem?" At such times you will want to double-check your daily observations in instruction and then conduct an entire informal literacy assessment. Informal assessments create the documentation you and others need to plan instruction and to show the progress you observe. If you are tutoring or enrolled in a practicum, this assessment process will help you know where to begin working with a child and to track your progress together.

As we described in Chapter 1, assessment is the process of sitting beside a student to observe what he knows. The informal assessment methods presented in this chapter ask you to sit beside a student, to confer and to listen and describe how a student reads, writes, and thinks.

■ *How to Describe Students' Literacy: Functional and Developmental Expressions*

How do we describe the literacy of our students? It is not enough to say that a student is a *good* reader or is *behind* the other students. Teachers are more descriptive about their students' work.

You can describe students' literacy in two ways: **functional** and **developmental expressions.** Functional expressions are about reading and writing in the real world of school, home, and, eventually, work. Developmental expressions describe a student's advances from one phase to another, as we discussed in Chapter 3. To think about how students *function*, ask, "Do I know what students can do?" To assess function, take a close look at what students can read and understand and what and how they write. To consider *development*, ask, "Do I know where they are along the developmental spectrum?" Let's start with a close examination of functional expressions of literacy.

Functional Expressions of Literacy

The idea of functional reading levels has been a part of literacy assessment throughout the twentieth century (Johns & Luhn, 1983). Students' ability to function has been divided into three gradations or reading levels (Betts, 1957): independent, instructional, and frustration reading levels.

Independent Levels

A student's **independent level** is the level at which the student can read comfortably and easily. The student reads with fine accuracy and excellent comprehension. No support from a teacher or reading buddy is necessary for independent-level functioning.

Instructional Levels

A student's **instructional level** is the level at which the student can read with good accuracy and moderate fluency. Comprehension is adequate, and the student can get the main idea of what was read. The guidance of a teacher and the support of partners helps students to read difficult words and to understand what was read.

Frustration Levels

No matter how much support a student may receive, materials that are at a student's **frustration level** are too difficult to read carefully, especially if the student is trying to understand the text in detail. Students may at times be especially motivated to read frustration-level materials. On a limited basis this is fine, and you can show them how to scan for key information. But when students spend too much time reading and writing at a frustration level, all kinds of learning and behavioral problems crop up. For students to learn about literacy and to experience fluent and extended reading, they must have plenty of experience reading at an instructional or independent level. There are ways to observe and document students' instructional and independent levels so that they avoid the hazards of working at length at a frustration level.

The boundaries between functional levels are not meant to be rigid. For example, Teacher A may find that what she calls independent-level reading material another teacher would call instructional. It helps to consider functional levels along a continuum. With a little discussion and by sharing examples of actual texts, Teachers A and B may find that they are closer than they thought.

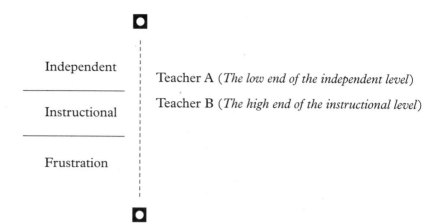

Independent

Teacher A (*The low end of the independent level*)

Instructional

Teacher B (*The high end of the instructional level*)

Frustration

Each of these levels possesses a range so that a student may be described as at the high end or low end of a functional reading level. As in all assessments, the labels are less important and useful than the descriptions of what students actually do when they read and write.

Table 4.1 presents criteria teachers commonly use to determine functional reading levels. The numbers placed in parentheses in this figure are not absolute scores, but they describe a range of behaviors to establish parameters for the

Table 4.1 Functional Reading Levels

Functional Levels (Comfort Level)	Criteria for Functional Levels	Instructional Reading Activities
Independent level (easy)	Excellent reading comprehension (~90% accuracy) Fluent reading rate and good oral reading expression Few oral reading errors (~3 errors per hundred words)	Pleasure reading Sustained silent reading When students work independently
Instructional level (comfortable)	Good comprehension (~70%) A fairly fluent reading rate and some oral reading expression Good accuracy in oral reading (~5 errors per 100 words)	Teacher support Small-group activities Partner reading
Frustration level (too difficult)	Poor comprehension (~50%) Disfluent, slow reading rate, hesitant and unexpressive Numerous reading errors (~10 errors per 100 words)	For overviews and figures Skimming and scanning Only when interest is strong

three functional reading levels. These levels are defined broadly. For example, at the instructional level, comprehension is said to be "good," and at the frustration level, comprehension is characterized as "poor."

The criteria for beginning readers are a little different. Beginning readers are naturally disfluent in their reading. Also, the error rate of 10 words in 100 is acceptable for beginning readers for new materials in instructional-level reading.

The final column in Table 4.1 presents a range of instructional activities for each functional level. Most activities should be at students' independent and instructional levels. When you listen to students read, and when you talk with them about what they have read, think about these criteria to determine what reading materials they might find useful.

Grade-Level and Contextual Expressions of Reading

We can describe students' functional reading levels and their literacy capabilities in two ways. We can (1) describe how well students read graded passages and then say that they can read a range of specific grade levels or (2) describe how students function in their daily lives in authentic texts and contexts—describe the actual texts they read and the literacy activities they engage in, in school and elsewhere.

There is a rough correspondence between the grade levels and the texts students can read at an instructional level. For example, a transitional reader may function in these ways:

Functional Levels	*Grade-Level Difficulty*	*Types of Books*
Independent	2	Complex pattern books up to simple chapter books such as *Amelia Bedelia*
Instructional	3	Easy chapter books such as the *Box Car Children* series
Frustration	4	Chapter books up to two hundred pages, such as the *Goosebumps* books

First, let's look at grade-level expressions and then at contextual descriptions of students' reading.

Grade-Level Expressions

Functional reading levels have traditionally been expressed by grade-level measures of readability. The readability formulas used to determine grade-level measures take into account the difficulty of the reading vocabulary and the complexity of the sentences.

A student's functional reading levels often fall in a row, or within a range:

Independent	2
Instructional	3
Frustration	4

A slightly more advanced student may report a range of instructional levels:

Independent	2
Instructional	3–4
Frustration	5

When a student's functional level is reported by grade level, it means that the student reads at the middle of that grade level. The more advanced student above can read third-grade and many fourth-grade materials at an instructional level.

A student's functional grade level is determined by how well she reads graded passages according to the criteria in Table 4.1. The procedures for marking and scoring the reading accuracy, fluency, expression, and comprehension are discussed below.

Contextual Expressions

The best way to overcome the difficulties of using grade-level expressions in assessment is to include authentic texts and daily instructional contexts. Contextual expressions use actual examples from students' reading to describe independent, instructional, and frustration levels. Just as a teacher might say, "My students really enjoyed hearing this book, but many of them found it a little tough reading," contextual expressions describe specific texts that students can read at independent, instructional, and frustration levels. A teacher might say, "Mary found *Charlotte's Web* a little tough, and she could read *Madeline* comfortably, with good accuracy, modest fluency, and good comprehension. *Madeline* is interesting, instructional-level material for Mary."

It is better to give examples of specific materials at students' instructional levels than to say that a student can read second-grade books. Specific examples of texts students read over the year provide the documentation to say, "In September, John read the books listed here, and now, in May, he can read these more difficult materials." Figure 4.1 presents an example of materials that have been used successfully with children at the different phases of development discussed in the previous chapter. Notice the differences among these texts. *Henry and Mudge* has been classified as a book for transitional readers, whereas *Fudge-a-Mania* is an instructional-level book for midlevel intermediate readers. In conferences, teachers can show parents these reading materials arranged by developmental level to give them a sense of the types of books their children are reading and will be expected to read during the year.

Functional Spelling and Writing Levels

Teachers can apply the concept of functional levels to determine what types of spelling and writing activities are easy, comfortable, or too difficult. Criteria for functional spelling and writing levels are presented in Table 4.2.

Henry gave Mudge
a tight hug,
then he went inside,
biting his fingernails.
When he was washed
and in bed,
Henry lay in the dark.
His eyes were big.
His heart was pounding.
His knees were shaking.

Then
WISH! FLOP!

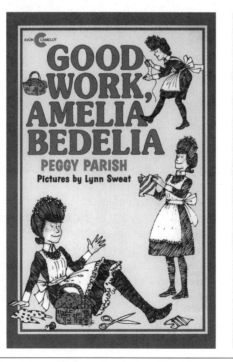

Figure 4.1
***Examples of Instructional-
Level Texts for Students in
Different Phases of Reading
Development*** *Source:
Middle transitional—Rylant
(1991) and Parish (1963);
middle intermediate—Blume
(1990).*

Amelia Bedelia put a little of this
and some of that into a bowl.
She mixed and mixed.
"Now for that sponge," she said.
Amelia Bedelia got a sponge.
She snipped it into small pieces.
"There," she said.
"Into the cake you go."

◆23◆

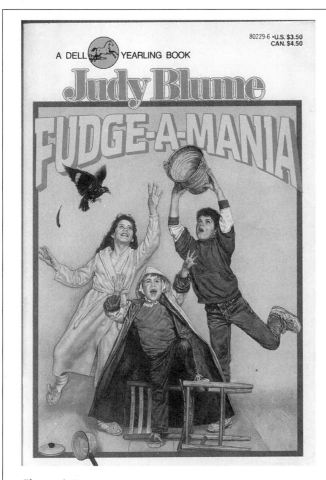

The I.S.A.F. Club

Fudge was counting his Cheerios when Jimmy and I came down to breakfast the next day. As soon as we sat down Sheila waltzed in, wearing her fuzzy pink robe and her bunny slippers, as usual. Jimmy took one look and doubled over. Sheila poured herself a glass of juice, then made herself comfortable at the table between Buzzy Senior and Fudge. "Good morning, sweetheart," Buzzy Senior said, kissing her cheek.

"Good morning, honey," Fudge said, kissing her other cheek.

94

Figure 4.1
Continued

Table 4.2   Functional Spelling and Writing Levels

Functional Levels	Criteria for Functional Levels		Activities	
	Spelling	**Writing**	**Spelling**	**Writing**
Independent level (easy)	Spelling accurate	Fluency in writing and effective communication of ideas	Words to look for when editing	Fully engaged in the writing process
Instructional level (comfortable)	Developmentally predictable invented spellings that can be reread	Fair writing fluency, ideas presented clearly	Word study instruction involves features students are experimenting with	Focus on a few composing and mechanical skills; work with partners for revising and editing
Frustration level (too difficult)	Invented spellings not developmental, many cannot be reread	Writing labored, slow, hesitant; ideas not communicated effectively and lack clarity	Encourage invented spelling; frustration-level spelling words not part of word study and spelling activities	Give support and find easier writing tasks; revise and edit selected aspects

Functional Spelling Levels Functional spelling levels help teachers think about appropriate word study activities for students at different developmental levels. Several graded spelling lists have been developed to determine functional and developmental phases or stages of spelling (Bear, Invernizzi & Templeton, 1996; Ganske, 1994; Schlagal, 1992; Henderson, 1990).

Instructional-level spelling activity in word study relates to development. On spelling lists such as the word lists in spelling books, students will spell between 40 and 50 percent of the words correctly (Morris, Blanton & Blanton, 1995). At the instructional level, students experiment with various spelling patterns, and they benefit from spelling and word study activities that include support from the teacher and fellow students. At the frustration level, the child's concern for accuracy in spelling interferes with getting ideas down on the page. Spelling activities become frustrating when the words in focus are beyond students' developmental levels. When words are too tough, students may use a brute force memorization strategy and, as a result, may not be able to see the patterns that underlie the spellings.

Functional Writing Levels No particular set of criteria to determine graded writing levels has been widely accepted in literacy assessments. However, many school districts make qualitative, holistic assessments of students' writing. You most likely have had your own writing evaluated in the same way as part of the teacher certification process—for example, in the Preprofessional Skills Test (PPST). Many school districts have a writing curriculum guide for each grade level, and through an analysis of students' writing, teachers can say that students have or have not achieved expected learning levels for a particular grade level. Most curriculum guides suggest a balance between composing skills and the mastery of mechanics. This chapter includes a developmental and qualitative inventory for narrative and expository writing. In both guides, students' writing is assessed for ideas as well as structure.

A student at the independent writing level can write with ease and present ideas clearly through written language. A student at the instructional writing level can successfully communicate ideas in writing, although some support will be helpful. At the frustration level of writing, the demands are so great that the student is unable to develop and communicate ideas.

You will need to be sensitive to students' instructional levels as you plan activities. The third column in Table 4.2 illustrates the relationship between the functional levels and literacy activities. Activities at the frustration level of functioning focus on encouraging experimentation and on readjusting activities to a more productive level.

Developmental Expressions of Literacy

Developmental expressions of literacy are based on the sequence of phases described in Chapter 3. It works best to discuss students' development versus their grade level. To review some of the relevant aspects of development from the previous chapter, recall the age ranges for the phases of development:

Phase	*Range of Grade Levels for Each Phase*
Emergent	Pre-K to middle of 1
Beginning	K to middle of 2
Transitional	1 to middle of 4
Intermediate	3 to 8
Advanced	5 to 12

You know a student has reached a given developmental level when you observe a general integration of development in reading, spelling, and writing.

Table 4.3 elaborates on the model of development from Table 3.1 on page 63.

As you work with a student, use Table 4.3 to find consistency across reading, writing, and spelling behaviors. Look for a configuration of behaviors that place the student along this continuum from emergent to advanced phases of literacy development.

Table 4.3   Specific Literacy Behaviors by Phase of Development

| Literacy Behaviors | Phases of Literacy Development | | | | |
	Emergent	Beginning	Transitional	Intermediate	Advanced
Reading:					
Fluency	In a storybook voice, mimics a reader	Disfluent, word-by-word, one- to three-word phrasing Prefers oral reading	Approaching fluency Often quite phrasal Reads silently	Fluent Entirely phrasal in reading Reads silently	Fluent
Rate	In a story-reading voice or at a conversational rate	40–80 wpm	70–140 wpm	120–250 wpm, skimming	140–350 wpm, skimming
Expression	Rhythmic phrases	Monotonic but reads a few words and phrases expressively	Some expression and emphasis	Develops a repertoire of reading styles	
Comprehension	Can retell the gist of a story they've heard	Sequential retellings and summaries	Analysis and generalizing	Problem solving and personal reflection	

Assessing Individuals with Informal, Qualitative Inventories

This section provides directions for specific informal literacy assessments that allow you to analyze a student's literacy qualitatively to form functional and developmental expressions. The individual assessment activities will uncover valuable information about a student's development and functional levels. Individual assessments use four basic activities:

Introductory, "Get to know you" interview

Informal reading inventory

Continued

Phases of Literacy Development

Literacy Behaviors	Emergent	Beginning	Transitional	Intermediate	Advanced
Writing:					
Fluency and production	Draws and colors with ease	Writes at least three sentences with ease	Writes a paragraph with ease	Writes three paragraphs about any familiar topic	
Expression	Talks expressively while drawing	Writes large letters and occasional punctuation, underlines, repeats for expression	Uses semantic focus and some punctuation	Develops styles for unique purposes Broad stylistic growth (for example, dialect usage, changing voice)	
Spelling:	*Prephonemic*	*Semiphonemic– letter name*	*Within-word pattern*	*Syllable juncture*	*Derivational constancy*
Phrase and orthographic knowledge	Draws and begins to use graphics	Uses consonants and advances to experiment with short vowels	Spells short vowels correctly Eperiments with long-vowel patterns	Spells single-syllable words correctly Experiments with two-syllable word patterns Begins to study the spelling and meaning connections	Spells most words correctly Examines derivations and roots

Spelling assessment

Writing together

The assessments discussed below are a natural part of individual conferences. In the rest of this chapter, we show you how to use them to determine functional and developmental expressions of a student's learning. You can obtain a good deal of information in two individual, fifteen-minute assessment sessions. We include some suggestions for making economical use of your time when you conduct individual assessments, and you will also pick and choose what parts to administer. Chapter 5 explains how to conduct these activities in a small group.

Getting Started

You can begin to talk with your students about individual assessment when you introduce the concept of conferences and where conferences fit into the daily schedule. In the morning, when the class goes over the daily schedule, explain that in a conference, students and teachers read, write, and talk together, one-on-one.

In individual conferences, sit *next* to your student. Sitting next to the student is less formal and less intimidating than sitting across a table. The student should sit to your left if you are right-handed and on the right if you are left-handed. In this way, your notes are off to the side and not in the center between you and the student.

As you practice these and similar individual assessment activities, remember to take notes when you work with students. At first, a student may wonder and ask, "What are you writing?" A simple explanation is best: "These notes help me to remember what we did today." After the student returns to his or her desk, take a moment to complete writing notes. Be sure to write the student's name on the notes and date them.

Most students are comfortable reading and writing with a teacher. They are cooperative and seem to enjoy the individual work. If a student does not want to participate or seems to freeze up, consider what adaptations make sense. Stopping is always an option. Keep work at the frustration level to a minimum. Make notes and use the opportunity to think about what the student's behavior may mean when she takes tests or is working independently in the classroom.

Finally, consider using an audio recorder. Depending on each student's comfort, you might turn the recorder on and leave it running or collect a recording of just one activity, particularly the oral reading and comprehension check. Be sure to check the equipment before each session.

When you ask a student to participate in one of these assessment activities you should take a moment to explain why you are working together. You may explain that these activities will help you to be an effective teacher. You can say to the student that the activity will "help me learn more about how you are learning to read and write."

Introductory "Get to Know You" Interview

The interview schedule is designed to last ten minutes and helps you to get to know the student. Pick and choose the questions you want to ask. Be flexible in how you use the interview. With an older student, you may want to spend more time learning about his school and learning history. The questions in Figure 4.2 will guide you through a brief "get to know you" interview. To establish an informal mood during the interview, you may want to hold your writing pad in your lap.

Each question can tell you something about the student. Even a simple question such as, "What is your name?" may provide some insight into a student's language and communication. Some children tell you their full names, in-

*Figure 4.2
Student Interview
Schedule*

Student Interview Schedule

Name _____

Teacher _____ Date _____

Name _____ How old are you? _____

Date of birth _____ Grade _____

How many people are in your family? _____

Interest Inventory

What sports do you play? _____

Are you in any clubs? Do you collect anything? _____

What do you like to do with your best friends? (Note ages/grades) _____

_____

What are your favorite T.V. programs? _____

What do you do after school? _____

School Experiences and Learning to Read and Write

How are you learning to read and write? _____

What are your favorite books? _____

What do you like to read and write about? _____

What have been the favorite things you have written? _____

Do you read and write at home? _____

Who reads to you at home? _____

Do you go to the library? _____

What do you want to learn this year? _____

What do you want to study? _____

Do you know what you are supposed to learn in school this year? _____

---

cluding a middle name, and other students say just their first names. Most likely, one response won't tell you much, but when you add it to many other responses, you will begin to form hypotheses about a student's development. After you ask a question, give time for the student to answer. If the question was misinterpreted, ask follow-up questions. Try to write down quotes as you can; the specific language will document language development.

In part, the goal of the initial interview is to help you understand the student's daily routines. You may be able to use the questions about television and what the student does after school to open a discussion of the student's daily schedule. For example, a student may say that he comes home after school and watches television, has dinner, then returns for more television, and after a few favorite shows, may go to bed. The television question may tell you about the role literacy and homework play at home. Certainly, children who watch four or more hours of television each day are at risk of not doing well in school (Neuman & Roskos, 1993).

The last several questions ask the student to reflect on how he is learning. This can clue you in to the student's success and interest in reading and writing. The questions about school can also help you to understand what the student wants to learn.

The interview will give you a good deal of preliminary information to consider as you develop an instructional program. Later during the year you will make more use of open-ended questions such as, "How's it going?" and specific questions about the student's activities, such as, "Where are you in constructing your report?"

Informal Reading Inventory

Following the "get to know you" interview, the teacher selects passages to read together and selects a way to assess the student's word knowledge. The assessment activities, which examine many aspects of how the student reads these passages, including oral reading and comprehension, are known collectively as *informal reading inventories*.

Informal reading inventories have been a part of individual, informal assessments since 1915 (Johns & Luhn, 1983). Educators use informal reading inventories to determine students' developmental and functional reading levels by analyzing how students read from a collection of brief reading passages and graded word lists. As noted earlier, classroom teachers might conduct a complete informal reading inventory just a few times a year, to help assess a student's reading difficulties. Most of the time, teachers shorten and adapt these procedures for individual conferences and small group activities. We'll discuss some adaptations that teachers make throughout this and the next chapter.

Word Recognition in Isolation

We can examine a student's **orthographic knowledge** and her store of sight words by looking at how she reads words in isolation—without assistance from other students or the teacher. In this individual assessment activity, a student is asked to read lists of words. Each list usually contains twenty words that are typical of words used at various grade levels. Most commercial informal reading inventories have graded word lists from the preprimer level to the twelfth grade and include alternate forms.

The words in these lists progress in difficulty: the word structures become more complex and the words occur less frequently. Following are sample words from four levels. Notice that the words in the fourth-grade list are substantially more complex than the words on the third-grade list. Fourth-grade lists generally contain many more two- and three-syllable words.

Graded Word Lists for Word Recognition in Isolation

Preprimer	Grade 2	Grade 3	Grade 4
and	another	carry	assembly
look	change	family	jewel
get	first	half	nervous
little	sleep	together	cartridge
be	these	clean	captive
you	men	morning	prairie

Source: Burns/Roe Informal Reading Inventory, Form B.

How the student reads from these graded word lists shows you what the student knows about the structure of words, her orthographic knowledge. In a qualitative look, the teacher considers how many words a student reads quickly and easily, as well as the quality of the incorrect attempts. Accuracy or correctness *and* fluency or automaticity are key factors. Two students who have the same accuracy score may still be quite different in their orthographic knowledge when fluency and automaticity are considered. Scoring is straightforward: On a twenty-word list, each word is worth five points. The functional levels for **word recognition in isolation** are

Independent   90%

Instructional 70

Frustration   50 or below.

Students who are emergent and early beginning readers will not recognize the words on the first list, the preprimer word list. When this happens, move on to assess emergent literacy, concept of word, concept of story, and early word knowledge as discussed in Chapter 6.

Reading Passages

During individual conferences, teachers ask students to read with them to examine their **reading comprehension,** accuracy, fluency, and expression. Teachers must consider first which passages a student should read and then how best to examine the student's comprehension, reading accuracy, fluency, and expression.

Passage Selection Graded passages can be drawn from *commercial informal reading inventories,* or the teacher can pull a passage from classroom texts. Teachers use commercial informal inventories most often to conduct more thorough informal reading assessments. They pull passages from classroom texts for regular progress checks at the beginning, middle, and end of the year.

Many teachers use commercial informal reading inventories to determine functional reading levels. Such inventories include passages that have been

STUDENT STUDY

Steve's Word Recognition

In this student study you will get a feel for how to administer and interpret an informal test of word recognition in isolation.

Here is a record of how Steve read several of the words from the preprimer list when he was in his sixth month of second grade. He knew the words *ball, go, book, and, red,* and *are* immediately at sight. He read *day* as *boy,* a *b–d* reversal that is expected of children at this developmental level, and then he used some sounding-out strategies for a few words:

Word	Response
hurry	hazard, help
try	tail, t, ter, tree
hope	hall, h-p, hobby

He has many strategies for using his knowledge of orthography to figure out words. He begins with a strong knowledge of initial consonants and moves from there.

As part of this word recognition, Steve participated in a little word study to see if he would benefit from some guided instruction on these points. After trying to read *all,* Steve was shown *tall* and *hall,* and then he was asked, "If this is *tall* and the second word is *hall,* what is this word?" He could not make the generalization to *all.* This suggests that his knowledge of word families is not as strong as it might be given his word recognition of other words.

Overall, Steve had 35 percent word recognition in isolation for this preprimer list. At this frustration level, he would have difficulty reading stories that used these words unless he had plenty of support from the teacher and contextual support from the text's language patterns and pictures.

Steve's comments gave us a sense of how he believes he is learning words. For example, when he read *with,* he called it *was* and *were* and commented, "I used to have that word. When, what, winter—they're the only words I know begins with a *w* and has a *h.*" Then, when he seemed frustrated, he called the word *egg* as *roar* and commented, "Never learned that word."

Steve's performance raises two concerns: (1) Steve may be trying to sound words out letter by letter, trying to make the orthography more regular than it is. The teacher would want to see if he sounds out to the exclusion of using other language systems. (2) Steve may think that he has to memorize words and that he has to wait until the words are assigned before he can read them. Steve was a bit uptight when he made errors, and his worrying might be a real concern if it is a pattern.

In individual sessions, teachers explore students' reading comprehension through recalls and comprehension questions.

checked for readability from preprimer level (PP) up to grade thirteen. Some inventories end with eighth-grade passages.

Commercial informal reading inventories come with detailed directions for administration. In most, the student reads successively more difficult graded passages, alternating between reading orally and silently, and then either retells or answers comprehension questions.

If the teacher has conducted an informal assessment of word recognition in isolation, then reading begins at the last grade level where the student scored 90 percent or above in word recognition. More routine progress checks may not include a word recognition in isolation assessment. In that case, the teacher may choose a passage that is one or two grade levels below the student's grade placement.

In cases where the results of a spelling analysis are available, then, given the synchrony between reading and spelling, the teacher may be able to base choices of reading material on the student's spelling abilities. For example, if a teacher learned that a student was in the within-word pattern phase of spelling, then the student could start by reading beginning-level materials, which would probably be at an easy, independent level. The student would continue to read until he or she had difficulty understanding the passages or reading the words. Some of the many published informal reading inventories are listed on page R-5.

You will also develop your own selection of four to six favorite and tried passages to use in individual conferences. *Teacher-made inventories* are especially useful when you want to see how a new student will read the materials that are part of regular classroom activities and units of study.

For your teacher-made inventories, you can select passages from your current classroom reading program and science and social studies texts. Selections in basals and literature-based elementary reading programs are arranged by grade level. Stories at the beginning of many basal readers are written at a lower readability level than stories at the end. Generally, students find the stories at the beginning of a reader easier to read than stories at the end. As you become familiar with the reading program materials, you can select passages that are representative of the reading that students do during the year.

Books that report grade-level readability provide another source of materials for an informal reading inventory. Many of the paperbacks that students read list the reading level on the back cover. The abbreviation *RL* stands for reading level, and the number following is the grade-level readability. RLs are reported in tenths, as in RL4.2. The determination of grade levels is not such a fine skill that there is much difference between RL4.2 and 4.3, but clearly students will find a 4.2 book easier to read than a 6.2 book.

When you choose an excerpt, think about whether or not the passage makes sense by itself. You might need to give the student some orientation or a reading goal: "Read this story to find out what happens when Judith is at the grocery store." Think, too, about how best you can explore the student's comprehension. Commercial reading inventories use comprehension questions and **retelling** to assess a student's understanding, and so can you. The passages you select should offer opportunities to ask questions to determine what information the student acquires as well as to explore the student's inferential thinking—the student's ability to read between the lines—and an opportunity to observe what routes to comprehension the student has developed.

Passage length will be a factor to consider at different levels of reading. For early beginning readers, passages between forty and eighty words in length are sufficient. For beginning readers in first through third grades, passages may range from eighty to one hundred twenty words. For transitional readers beginning in second grade, passages are 120 to 150 words in length. Intermediate passages range from 150 to 300 words, and passages for advanced readers may range from 300 to 450 words.

You may find another source of material in what the student is reading at the time of your conference. Although in small group discussions you may obtain a general sense of what and how well a student is reading, in individual conferences you can focus a bit more. Ask the student to share the book she is reading during independent reading time, as in sustained silent reading period. In an individual conference you may ask a student, "Read a little bit of the book you are reading on your own." Or you may ask the student to read a particular passage. "Read a paragraph or two to show me what the book is about."

Introducing the Reading After choosing a passage, you might introduce it by giving the student an overview. For example, in a passage about worms, you might comment, "This is a passage about what worms do in the garden." When you ask a student to read, be sure the student knows that afterward the two of you will discuss what he or she read: "After you read a passage, I will ask you to tell me about what you read." Except for beginning readers, who prefer to read orally, students can read a few passages orally and a few silently.

After each reading and comprehension check, choose whether or not to move on to a more difficult passage. Stop when the student experiences a good deal of inaccuracy, a very slow reading rate, or when comprehension is very low. Avoid having the student read frustration-level materials. When you use passages that the student has selected from her independent reading, you will want to observe the self-selected reading materials on a few more occasions. If the student habitually chooses materials that are too difficult, you should conduct a few lessons on how and why to select easier texts.

Analyzing Passage Reading As you assess passage reading you will be asking yourself, "Given the student's accuracy, fluency and expression, and comprehension, is this material at an independent, instructional, or frustration level?" Before you listen to a student read, decide how general or specific your documentation must be. Teachers use general measures for functional assessments on a day-to-day basis, but a combination of general and specific measures is useful.

Below are some general and specific measures to assess passage reading.

Comprehension. To assess comprehension, you must get students to express what they learned from the reading. Some students are eager to talk about what they read, and you can simply ask them to retell the passage. Others hesitate to summarize or reflect on what they learned. You will need to ask probing, open-ended questions to see if they know more than they are able to articulate.

Teachers explore comprehension in several ways. Working individually, many teachers have students retell or respond orally to comprehension questions. Transitional, intermediate, and advanced students can respond in writing. In retelling, teachers ask students to tell about what they read. Retelling gives a student an opportunity to organize the information. Younger students tend to pour out the facts, and older students tend to organize the retellings in a sequence. This growth in organization matches the developmental sequence of written response presented in Table 3.1.

As you listen to a student's retelling, write down as much as possible of what the student says. If necessary, follow up the retelling with questions that encourage the student to elaborate and recall more details. The retelling can be rated with three or four gradations:

excellent = $\sqrt{++}$
very good = $\sqrt{+}$
satisfactory = $\sqrt{}$
poor = $\sqrt{-}$.

Here is a list of qualities to consider when you examine a student's retelling. These qualities are listed in developmental order (Barone, 1992; Brown & Cambourne, 1987). For example, a beginning reader will present a concrete sequence, whereas an intermediate reader will more likely include an interpretation of the passage as part of the retelling.

Quality of Retelling

Presents events in sequence

Retells concretely

Recollects facts in order

Retells a summary

Is literal

Elaborates points: none, some, lots

Recalls events or feelings

Analyzes

Comments on or evaluates what was read

Interprets passage

Makes generalizations

Uses detail or inferences to substantiate ideas

Comments on the form and style of the passage

Although we prefer retellings because they may provide a richer picture of the student's language and thinking, teachers sometimes ask the student to answer comprehension questions. Most commercial inventories provide between eight and ten questions to answer. Questions are quick and easy to score, and this format gives an indication of how the student might do with similar tests and assignments.

Comprehension questions are usually one of three types: **factual, vocabulary,** and **inferential,** but some other possibilities include main idea, detail, sequence, vocabulary, and cause-and-effect questions.

Factual, main idea and detail questions call for exact responses to see if after reading a passage the student can identify the major events. Sometimes a question calls for two or three responses or items. You can score such responses as partially correct if you wish.

Vocabulary questions ask the student to use the information from the text to define a word or phrase in the passage. For example, in a commercial reading inventory a vocabulary question asks, "What does the word *nurses* mean in the sentence 'All this time the mother nurses them?'" (Burns & Roe, 1989, p. 144). The student may know one meaning of *nurse* but not this one, and this lack of experience may influence the child's understanding of what was read.

Inferential questions call for the student to interpret the story because the answer is not explicitly stated in the text. Inferential questions are not opinion questions. The answer is inferred from the text if the student "reads between the lines."

It's important to, on a regular basis, write down exactly what the student says so that you can have a sample of the child's oral language. Some students answer in a relaxed style using their own language. Others answer verbatim from the text. Some students are quick to make "don't know" responses. In such cases, you might rephrase the question or turn to retelling.

When you want to know more about the reasoning behind a student's answer, you may want to ask, "What in the story makes you say that?" This encourages the student to recall specific parts of the text to support a comment.

You can give partial credit for answers to questions, particularly if the answer has multiple parts or you ask additional related questions. The following criteria are used for functional levels for comprehension:

Functional Level	*Comprehension Questions Answered Correctly*
Independent	90%
Instructional	70
Frustration	<50

When a student scores between levels on the comprehension questions, you can use other indicators to help you to determine the overall functional levels.

Oral reading accuracy. Analyzing oral reading in great detail can be time-consuming work. Still, you will be more skilled in the general ratings if you practice the detailed analyses first. Therefore, we begin with general ratings that teachers use in regular progress checks and then discuss the more detailed procedures for analyzing oral reading.

You make a general rating of **oral reading accuracy** when you note the name of the book, the page, and make a general reading rate where excellent is marked as a $\sqrt{++}$, very good as $\sqrt{+}$, satisfactory as a $\sqrt{}$, and poor as $\sqrt{-}$.

You can also make anecdotal records of a student's reading. You may photocopy the passage from the book the child read and include this page in your portfolio records for that child. For example, here is an anecdotal record on Sean from the beginning of the year:

September 8: Sean read the worm passage.
Comment: *Miscued on functor words: with for when, to for in.*

To provide a detailed rating of oral reading, photocopy the passage, then mark and score it for specific oral reading miscues. Four types of reading miscues are counted as reading errors: substitutions, omissions, additions, and each time the teacher tells the student a word. In the Taking a Closer Look that follows, notice the marks that do not count as miscues or errors but help you to remember how a student read. Reading pauses (/ marks) are interesting to analyze given their location. Consider if there are pauses at grammatical boundaries, with pauses at the ends of sentences and shorter pauses at phrase boundaries. Many pauses are related to reading accuracy as the passages become more difficult. Also look at intonation and word emphasis marks as they reflect the student's expression and deeper understanding of the writing.

Words that are mispronounced multiple times are counted only once as errors. Miscues of proper nouns are not counted as errors. Dialect can also

····· TAKING A ·····
CLOSER LOOK

Marking Oral Reading

The goal of marking oral reading is to create a clear picture of how the student read. To determine a reading accuracy score, the first four categories of miscues are counted as reading errors.

Miscue	How to Mark
1. Omissions	Circle words or parts of words omitted. Do not count the same errors more than once.
	We had (fun) running.
2. Substitutions	Write substitution above the word.
	with
	when
3. Additions	Use a caret (^) and write in additions.
	big
	The ^ dog
4. With help	Write *WH* above the word when the student has been told the word
	WH
	We ate ///fruit

The following miscues are not counted as errors.

5. Self-corrections	Make a check mark (√) above self-corrections.
	first √
	forest
6. Pauses	Draw a slash mark (/) for each one-second pause.
	Continue to draw slashes for one-second pauses.
	He / wasn't
	After three pause marks (///), tell the student the word and mark *WH* above it.
	WH
	The ///jacket

7. Repetitions	Draw a wavy line (~) underneath words and phrases that a student repeats.
	It has old buildings.
8. Intonation and word emphasis	Mark rising and falling intonation contours at the end of a phrase with arrows (↑↓). Write an *e* over words that are emphasized.
	e
	Will he be at the store?↑
9. Omitted punctuation	Circle punctuation that is ignored.
	train ⊙ The family
10. Word inversion	Use an inversion sign (∿) to show word reversals.
	(said ⌣ Bobby).

Abbreviations for Margin Notes

Following is a list of behaviors to look for when a student reads. Mark in the margin where the behavior starts and ends. For example, you may notice that fingerpointing (*FP*) starts as the student begins having difficulty reading the text.

Word-by-word reading *WxW*

Head movement *HM*

Lip movement *LM*

Fingerpointing *FP*

Slight vocalization or whispering (silent reading) *SV* Rate in words per minute = words in passage × 60 seconds to read

influence certain errors. As noted in Chapter 2, we all have our own dialects, and in some dialects words sound as if the ends are dropped off. For example, many students drop *ing* in their oral reading. Dialectical miscues are not counted as errors, but rather as differences in speaking.

Determine a percentage-based reading accuracy score by dividing the number of words read correctly by the number of words in the passage. If the percentage of words read correctly is 90 percent or less, then the material is probably too difficult for that student. For transitional and intermediate readers, consider the following oral reading accuracy rate.

Functional Level	*Accuracy*
Independent	97% (97/100 words read correctly)
Instructional	95
Frustration	≤90

Using this scale, a student who makes three or fewer errors per hundred words is reading at an independent level, and a student who makes ten or more miscues is reading frustration-level material. A few more errors are acceptable for primary students in instructional-level reading. This is because beginning readers doing instructional-level work in the classroom read and reread familiar materials with teacher support.

As you reflect on the student's oral reading, consider whether or not the student read for meaning. Did the student attempt to make sense of the text? If so, some of the word substitutions will be similar in orthographic structure and in meaning. Meaning errors predominate during the emergent and beginning phases of literacy development. Orthographic errors begin to dominate by the middle of the beginning phase. In the transitional phase, there is a blend of these two types of miscues (Bear, 1992; Biemiller, 1970).

Many miscues that count as oral reading errors are minor and do not distort meaning. For example, if a student read *The call is **for** you* as "The call is **to** you," this change would not likely disrupt meaning. However, other changes make quite a difference. For example, the student who read *The frog **was** the smallest pet in the store* as "The frog **water** small pet in the store." made a significant change in meaning. Orthographically, you can see that the student was working with the *w*, and the word *water* disrupts the syntax and the meaning of the text.

When a student makes miscues that change the meaning of the text, make note of whether the student went back to reread the sentence or pushed on in spite of disruptions in meaning. Students who insist on making sense of what they read are thinking as they read, and that is good. However, some students read without worrying about whether or not they are making sense of what they read, and both their reading miscues and their comprehension will reflect this.

Reading fluency and expression. **Reading rate** is a specific measure that is calculated by:

$$\frac{\text{Words in passage}}{\text{seconds}} \times 60 = \text{Words per minute}$$

Table 4.4 relates functional reading rates to developmental phases. You will notice that functional reading rates for beginning readers are quite different from those for intermediate and advanced readers. Notice also the oral and silent reading rates of transitional readers. At the instructional level, oral and silent reading rates are the same. In independent materials, however, silent reading rates begin to exceed oral reading rates. When students know enough about the words to read them quickly and easily, silent reading begins to outpace oral reading. These rates are an extrapolation from several sources (Bear, 1992; Biemiller, 1970; Lipson & Wixson, 1991; Sabin, Clemmer, O'Connell & Kowal, 1979).

You can use a general rating system to document a student's fluency and expression. The following ten-point general scoring system for rating fluency and expression is a useful tool (1=very confident, 5=not confident). It includes two questions in each of two steps.

Fluency:

1. Was the student's reading fluent or disfluent? Fluent Disfluent

2. How confident are you of your assessment? 1 2 3 4 5 1 2 3 4 5

Total fluency score: 1 2 3 4 5 6 7 8 9 10

Expression:

1. Was the student's reading expressive? Expressive Unexpressive

2. How confident are you of your assessment? 1 2 3 4 5 1 2 3 4 5

Total expression score: 1 2 3 4 5 6 7 8 9 10

In the course of listening to several students read the same passage, you will develop a good sense for this scaling.

Other Behaviors. You can note a host of other behaviors in your assessment. In addition to fingerpointing and lip movement (LM) during silent reading, make observations that will help you to answer these questions:

What is the student doing while reading?

Is the student comfortable?

Is the student squirming? Are legs folding and unfolding underneath the seat?

Does the student move his or her face close to the page?

Does the student move closer to the page as difficulties increase?

Is the student tense? Is there lip biting? Too relaxed?

Does the student look over to you when difficulties are encountered?

Does the student refer to pictures, if any, when the reading becomes difficult?

These questions help you assess the student's development, motivation, and affect when reading. Students who fingerpoint, for example, are likely to be in the

Table 4.4 Oral and Silent Reading Rates

| | Functional Reading Levels | | | | | |
| | Independent | | Instructional | | Frustration | |
Phase of Development	Oral	(Silent)	Oral	(Silent)	Oral	(Silent)
Emergent	In a story-reading voice, mimicking a reader					
Beginning	60–80	(Not applicable)	40–70	(Not applicable)	20–35	(Not applicable)
Transitional	80–130	(90–140)	70–120	(70–120)	40–60	(40–60)
Intermediate	130–140	(140–250)	120–150	(120–200)	<80	(<100)
Advanced	50–160	(250–500)	40–160	(200–250)	<100	(<120)

beginning phase of development. When a student is tense or uninterested, you can begin to look more deeply at the student's motivation and feelings of success surrounding literacy.

Listening Comprehension

You use the same assessment techniques to explore listening comprehension as you would reading comprehension, but in this case you read to the student. Begin by selecting a passage that the student may have a little difficulty reading but that you think is within the student's range of understanding.

In a general way, listening comprehension gives you a sense of a student's verbal potential. Often, a student who can understand a story at a particular level has the potential to read at that level. Students who listen to graded passages generally are expected to understand what they hear to at least one year ahead of the grade placement. Sometimes listening comprehension will help clarify whether a student is experiencing a reading problem or a problem more broadly related to language facility. As you will see in Figures 4.6 and 4.8, Karla is just such a student.

You can use these general and specific scoring criteria to see patterns in how a student reads different passages. The criteria can be summarized in this way:

Functional Level	Comprehension	Oral Reading Accuracy	Oral Reading Fluency and Expression
Independent	Excellent (90%)	High (97%)	Fluent, phrasal, and expressive
Instructional	Good (70)	Good (95)	Modest fluency and some expression
Frustration	Poor (50)	Medium–low (90)	Disfluent and unexpressive

Listening comprehension = 70%

Spelling Assessment

The goal of spelling assessment is to discover a student's phase of development. In routine progress checks, teachers usually forgo the assessment of word recognition in isolation and look at the student's orthographic knowledge through the student's spelling.

You can determine a student's spelling phase when you have accumulated several writing samples. If you are short on samples, you may want to ask the student to spell words from one of the qualitative spelling inventories. When you are working with new students or want a more systematic assessment over time and across students, you can use a spelling inventory found in word study books and articles (Bear & Barone, 1989; Bear, Invernizzi & Templeton, 1996; Templeton, 1997).

Identifying a student's spelling phase can help you confirm a student's developmental level, for there is usually a relationship between reading and spelling phases. For example, a student in the within-word-pattern phase of spelling begins to read with some fluency and, as a transitional-phase reader, can automatically identify most single-syllable words.

Some spelling inventories are designed to focus on the upper levels of spelling (Bear, Templeton & Warner, 1991), whereas others focus within a developmental level (Ganske, 1994; Schlagal, 1992). Elementary school teachers will find the spelling inventory in Figure 4.3 useful.

Invented spellings give you a window into what students know about orthography. For example, a student who spells *THROTE* for *throat* is experimenting with how long vowel patterns are spelled. You can use this information to plan word study instruction. Table 4.5 can be a guide to development level when you interpret a student's invented spelling. Circle the spelling errors that you see and note if they fall within a range of development. You should see a pattern to the errors. Choose one phase that reflects the invented spellings and then determine if the student is in the early, middle, or late part of that phase.

As you can see, the directions suggest that words be administered in groups of five. When a student spells most of the words correctly, refer to the next group or more difficult spelling lists. If a student's spelling is not on the chart, use your knowledge of developmental spelling to place the invented spelling on the continuum of spelling errors.

Writing Together

In this final assessment activity, the student writes on a subject of interest. The goal of writing together is to observe and assess the student writing. The initial writing assessment focuses on choosing a writing topic and writing a first draft. This type of writing is called *freewriting*. Be sure to observe closely to ensure that children are able to start the writing process independently.

Begin the activity by explaining that you would like the student to write for a while about anything: "I'd like to ask you to write something. What would you like to write about? What has happened in your life that you would like to write about?"

Figure 4.3
Elementary Qualitative
Spelling Inventory
Source: Adapted from Bear,
Invernizzi, and Templeton
(1996).

Elementary Qualitative Spelling Inventory

Instructions: Let the student know that you are administering this inventory to learn about how he or she spells. Here's a possible script: "I am going to ask you to spell some words. Try to spell them the best you can. Some of the words will be easy to spell. Some will be more difficult. When you do not know how to spell a word, spell it the best you can. Write down all the sounds you feel and hear."

Say the word once. If you wish, read the word in the sentence, and then say the word again.

First Five Words

1. bed   I hopped out of *bed* this morning.   bed
2. ship   The *ship* sailed around the island.   ship
3. drive   I learned to *drive* a car.   drive
4. bump   That is quite a *bump* you have on your head.   bump
5. when   *When* will you come back?   when

Second Five Words

6. train   I rode the *train* to the next town.   train
7. closet   I put the clothes in the *closet*.   closet
8. chase   We can play run and *chase* with the cats.   chase
9. float   I can *float* on the water with my new raft.   float
10. beaches   The sandy *beaches* are crowded in the summer.   beaches

Third Five Words

11. preparing   I am *preparing* for the big game.   preparing
12. popping   We are *popping* popcorn to eat at the movies.   popping
13. cattle   The cowboy rounded up the *cattle*.   cattle
14. caught   I *caught* the ball.   caught
15. inspection   The soldiers polished their shoes for *inspection*.   inspection

Fourth Five Words

16. puncture   I had a *puncture* in my bicycle tire.   puncture
17. cellar   I went down to the *cellar* for the can of paint.   cellar
18. pleasure   It was a *pleasure* to listen to the choir sing.   pleasure
19. squirrel   We found the tree where the *squirrel* lives.   squirrel
20. fortunate   It was *fortunate* that the driver had snow tires during the snowstorm.   fortunate

Fifth Five Words

21. confident   I am *confident* that we can win the game.   confident
22. civilize   They had the idea that they could *civilize* the forest people.   civilize
23. flexible   She was so *flexible* that she could cross her legs behind her head.   flexible
24. opposition   The coach said the *opposition* would give us a tough game.   opposition
25. emphasize   In conclusion, I want to *emphasize* the most important points.   emphasize

An alternate spelling list has been developed and can be used in place of the first 20 words: net, trip, crime, dump, then, chain, forest, trail, soap, reaches, comparing, topping, battle, fought, intention, rupture, stellar, treasure, confident, tempest.

Table 4.5   Error Guide for Developmental Spelling List

Phases	Semi-phonemic	Letter Name	Within-Word Pattern
1. bed	b bd	bad	bed
2. ship	s sp shp	sep shep	sip ship
3. drive	jrv drv	griv driv	drieve draive drive
4. bump	b bp bmp	bop bomp bup	bump
5. when	w yn wn	wan whan	wen when
6. train	j t trn	jran chran tan tran	teran traen trane train
7. closet	k cs kt clst	clast clost clozt	clozit closet
8. chase	j jass cs	tas cas chas chass	case chais chase
9. float	f vt ft flt	fot flot flott	flowt floaut flote float
10. beaches	b bs bcs	bechs becis behis	bechise beches beeches beaches

Phases	Syllable Juncture		Derivational Constancy
11. preparing	preparng preypering		praparing prepairing preparing
12. popping	popin poping		popping
13. cattle	catl cadol		catel catle cattel cattle
14. caught	cot cote cout cought caught		
15. inspection	inspshn inspechin		inspecshun inspecsion inspection
16. puncture	pucshr pungchr puncker		punksher punture puncture
17. cellar	salr selr celr seler		seller sellar celler cellar
18. pleasure	plasr plager plejer pleser plesher		plesour plesure pleasure
19. squirrel	scrl skwel skwerl		scqoril sqrarel squirle squirrel

Reflection on Writing Fluency

Some students have a hard time getting started. You can ask the student how you might be able to help. To be sure, if a student is terribly hesitant to write, you might suggest possible writing topics. Your knowledge of the student's interests may lead to suggestions such as, "You might want to write about what you and your friends do together or about your baseball team." During these freewriting activities, remind students not to worry about spelling everything correctly and that it is more important to get ideas written down. You can ask students to draw a picture to go with the writing. Drawing before writing can encourage a hesitant writer, especially one in the emergent phase of development.

Many teachers write with their students when they meet in individual conferences. If the teacher writes with the student, the student is less likely to ask how to spell. In addition, students are more interested in sharing when they see the teacher participating.

Continued

Phases	Within-Word Pattern	Syllable Juncture	Derivational Constancy
20. **fortunate**	forhnat frehnit foohinit	forchenut fochininte fortunet	fortunate
21. **confident**		confadent confedint confedent confadent conphident confiadent confedent confendent confodent confident	
22. **civilize**		sivils sevelies sivilicse cifillazas sivelize sivalize civalise civilise civilize	
23. **flexible**		flecksibl flexobil fleckuble flecible flexeble flexibel flaxable flexibal flexable flexible	
24. **opposition**	opasion opasishan opozcison opishien opasitian	opasition oppasishion oppisition oposision oposition opposition	
25. **emphasize**		infaside infacize emfesize emfisize imfasize ephacise empasize emphasise emphisize emphasize	

Source: Adapted from Bear and Barone (1989).

Note: The prephonemic phase is not presented here.

You can ask the student to reread the finished writing. It helps to look at the writing together and, if you cannot read some of the words, to make notes for future reference. See what the student does when she reads an incomplete text.

Some aspects to consider are how easy or difficult it was to get the student started, how concerned the student was with neatness and correctness, and how willing the student was to use different language forms. Some students seem constrained by what they can spell correctly. Some are overly concerned with getting things right or with neatness and correctness. You will also want to observe writing mechanics, including how the student holds the pencil, how letters are formed, how fluently the student writes, and how well the student uses punctuation.

Guidelines for Evaluating Writing

You will be evaluating numerous features in your students' writing. Figure 4.4 presents two checklists of writing standards developed by Cramer (1982). One assesses narrative writing, and the second assesses expository writing. These guidelines take us through a variety of standards for good writing and rates them into high, middle, and low levels.

Standards for Evaluating Composing Skills for *Narrative* Writing

Circle the appropriate level.

Story Structure

Low: No identifiable beginning, middle, or end. Story problem unclear. Action and characters not developed or related. Essential details missing or confusing. Story problem not solved, or resolution unrelated to events.

Middle: Beginning, middle, and end present, but not always identifiable. Story problem presented, but not completely developed. Some conversational or descriptive details included. End may not show logical resolution of problem.

High: Identifiable beginning, middle, and end. Characters introduced and problem presented. Characters and problem well developed with appropriate conversational or descriptive detail. Story ends with believable resolution of problem.

Story Setting

Low: Setting of story not identifiable. Details inappropriate and confusing.

Middle: Time and place of story are hinted at, but uncertain. Further references to setting may be inconsistent with original time or place.

High: Time and place of story clearly set. Specific details related to setting given in appropriate context. Setting consistent throughout.

Story Characters

Low: Characters not believable. Details related to character development are inconsistent, inappropriate, or missing. Difficult to distinguish one character from another. Action of characters unrelated to problem.

Middle: Characters are somewhat believable. Some descriptive or conversational details given. Details may not develop character personality. Action of characters not always related to problem. Major and minor characters not clearly discernible.

High: Characters believable. Descriptive or conversational detail develops character personality. Action of characters relates to problem. Major characters more fully developed than minor ones.

Story Conversation

Low: Conversation among characters haphazard, incomplete, or muddled. Much of the conversation inappropriate to circumstances and to personality of story characters. Conversation seems unrelated to story being told.

Middle: Conversation sometimes appropriate to circumstances and to characters. Conversation may reveal character personality or relationships among characters. Conversation sometimes not clearly related to story.

High: Conversation appropriate to story circumstances and to personality of each character. Conversation used to reveal character and develop interrelationships among characters. Conversation clearly relates to story.

Story Idea

Low: Story idea is trite or otherwise uninteresting. Story lacks plot or plot is vague. Story ends abruptly or reaches no definite conclusion.

Middle: Story idea is interesting. Idea may lack freshness or imaginativeness. Story has a plot. Plot may not be well developed or entirely consistent. Story ending may not be satisfying or interesting.

High: Story idea is fresh or imaginative. Story plot is well developed, is consistent, and comes to a satisfying, surprising, or otherwise highly effective ending.

Figure 4.4
Guidelines for Evaluating Composing Skills for Expository & Normative Writing Source: Adapted from Cramer (1982).

·······································

Language in Writing

You will want to examine the student's language use in writing. Although language can reflect how the student speaks, it also can be constrained by the writing task itself.

The student's writing will reveal the student's knowledge of language forms. An examination of the language systems may provide some evidence of language

---

Standards for Evaluating Composing Skills for *Expository* Writing

Circle the appropriate level.

Quality of Ideas

Low: Most ideas vague, incoherent, inaccurate, underdeveloped, or incomplete. Details often unrelated to topic. Nothing imaginative or thoughtful about the ideas.

Middle: Unevenness in completeness and development of ideas. Most ideas related to topic; a few unrelated. Sound, but unimaginative ideas.

High: Ideas relevant to the topic, fully developed, rich in thought and imagination, and clearly presented.

Quality of Organization

Low: Introduction, development, and conclusion unclear. Emphasis of major and minor points indistinguishable. Sentences and paragraphs seldom related by transitions. Overall lack of coherence and forward movement.

Middle: Introduction, development, or conclusion not easily identified. Emphasis on major or minor points sometimes not well balanced. Transitions between sentences and paragraphs used but without consistency. Forward movement variable.

High: Introduction, development, and conclusion well structured, complete, and easily identified. Emphasis of major and minor points well balanced. Sentences and paragraphs clearly related by transitions. Logical forward movement.

Selection of Words

Low: Word selection inexact, immature, and limited. Figurative language seldom used.

Middle: Word selection usually suitable and accurate. Overused words and clichés somewhat common. Figurative language lacks freshness when used.

High: Facility and flair in word selection. Writer experiments with words in unusual and pleasing ways. Figurative language used often in interesting and imaginative ways.

Structure of Sentences

Low: No variety in sentence structure; often only simple sentences are used. Transitions limited to such words as *then*, conjunctions to *and*. Awkward and puzzling sentences and fragments often appear.

Middle: Some variety in sentence length and structure. Transitions used when necessary. Few sentence constructions awkward and puzzling. Run-on sentences and sentence fragments appear but do not predominate.

High: Sentence length and structure varied. Sentences consistently well formed. Smooth flow from sentence to sentence. Run-on sentences and sentence fragments rarely appear.

Structure of Paragraphs

Low: Topic sentences seldom used. Irrelevancies common. Order of details haphazard. Little or no command of the four common paragraph types (narrative, explanatory, descriptive, persuasive).

Middle: Topic sentences usually stated. Irrelevancies uncommon. Order of details usually suitable. Limited ability to use the four common paragraph types.

High: Topic sentences stated and supported with relevant details. Appropriate variety used in ordering details (chronological, logical, spatial, climactic). Four types of paragraphs used when appropriate.

Figure 4.4
Continued
....

differences and difficulties. Following is a list of the language systems with questions to cue your evaluation:

- *Orthographic system.* What does the spelling tell you about orthographic development? What words does the student spell correctly? Are the invented spellings indicative of a phase of development?

- *Syntactic system.* What is the structure of the language? Can you reread it and understand the arrangement of the words and the grammatical structure? Are the sentence structures complex and diverse?

Standards for Evaluating *Mechanical Skills* for Narrative or Expository Materials

Circle the appropriate level.

Grammar and Usage

Low: Frequent errors in the use of nouns, pronouns, modifiers, and verbs.

Middle: Grammatical conventions of inflections, functions, modifiers, nouns, pronouns, and verbs usually observed. Grammatical errors sometimes occur.

High: Grammatical conventions of inflections, functions, modifiers, nouns, pronouns, and verbs observed. Grammatical errors infrequent.

Punctuation

Low: End punctuation often used incorrectly. Internal punctuation seldom used. Uncommon punctuation is almost never used correctly.

Middle: Sentences usually end with appropriate punctuation. Internal punctuation used with occasional errors. Uncommon punctuation sometimes used, but often inaccurately.

High: Sentences consistently end with appropriate punctuation. Internal punctuation and other less common punctuation usually correctly used.

Capitalization

Low: First word of sentence often not capitalized. Pronoun *I* often a small letter. Proper nouns seldom capitalized. Other capitalization rules usually ignored.

Middle: First word of sentences nearly always capitalized. *I* always capitalized. Well-known proper nouns capitalized. Other capitalization rules used, but not consistently.

High: First word of a sentence and the pronoun *I* always capitalized. Well-known proper nouns nearly always capitalized. Good command of other capitalization rules regarding titles, languages, religions, and so on.

Handwriting/Neatness

Low: Handwriting difficult or impossible to read. Letters and words crowded. Formation of letters inconsistent. Writing often illegible.

Middle: Handwriting usually readable, but some words and letters difficult to recognize. Some crowding of letters and words.

High: Handwriting clear, neat, and consistent. Forms all letters legibly with consistent spacing between letters and words.

Figure 4.4
Continued
....

- *Semantic system.* What vocabulary does the student use in the writing? Is there a wide choice of words?

- *Pragmatic system.* What is the purpose of the writing? How are the ideas organized?

- *Prosodic system.* How are the phrases structured? Is there punctuation to indicate sentence and phrase breaks?

You will be able to see the relative sophistication of a child's language in the complexity of usage of these five language systems. For example, a student who writes in complex sentences with a rich vocabulary may have the same strengths in oral language as a classmate who writes in simple sentences with a rudimentary vocabulary.

Functional and Developmental Expressions of Writing

After considering Cramer's guidelines, reflect on the student's functional writing level: Was the writing easy for the student? Was the student comfortable, or was writing a difficult experience? Review the writing behaviors in Table 4.2 that are associated with independent, instructional, and frustration levels.

For a developmental expression of writing, you can refer to the developmental model to discern what reading behaviors describe students in the writing phases. Teachers expect beginning writers to write slowly somewhere along a continuum of laborious letter-by-letter writing to a more confident writing style that yields one or two paragraphs within a fifteen-minute writing period. Note in Table 4.3 that transitional writers begin to take off; they write with some fluency and they begin to play with expression in their writing. They begin to analyze their writing and make generalizations from one piece of writing to another. The transitional writer's stories are more elaborate and often focus on a main character.

Intermediate and advanced writers develop a repertoire of writing styles according to the needs and purposes they have experienced. Their writing continues to grow conceptually and can focus on themes in stories and on issues and problem solving in expository writing. These students experience significant growth in stylistic usage, and their language structures grow in complexity. For example, you will notice that sentence length increases dramatically as a student explores combining phrases and ideas in new ways.

After you understand the student's functional and developmental levels, and you have a sense of how the student approaches composition, you can turn to other aspects of the writing process. To assess a student's ability to edit for clarity and correctness, the student can show you multiple drafts of a piece of writing that he is preparing for publication, the final step of the writing process. You will be able to see what editing skills the student has acquired and check them off that student's list of curricular goals. In Chapters 7, 8, and 10 you will see how students work with guidelines for writing to assess how they use the writing process.

Before we turn to the interpretation and evaluation of an informal literacy assessment, let us see how the process worked in the following study of a student's writing.

Summaries and Profile Guides

Summaries of important observations and results complement the samples of students' reading and writing in the student's portfolio. Two ways to summarize what you have learned in the individual assessment are presented: (1) the summary sheet and (2) the profile guide. Teachers keep individual assessments, summaries, and profile guides in a teacher's portfolio. The teacher's portfolio contains individual files on each child as well as a collection of materials that reflects work from the class.

Summary Sheets Teachers create summary tables to describe each student. For a complete, informal reading assessment, a summary sheet like the one for Karla in Figure 4.6 can be used. The summary sheet has three sections. The top section is labeled Orthographic Knowledge and includes word recognition and **spelling assessments.** The next section summarizes passage reading. The section at the bottom summarizes the student's functional and developmental

STUDENT STUDY

Lois

In the following writing about Halloween (Figure 4.5), Lois, a fourth-grader, displays the range of features you can look for in a student's writing.

First, we observed that Lois wrote with interest and with modest fluency. She presented a clear sequence of events with good detail. Although the summary is organized, the piece has no title, introduction, generalization, or analysis of the experience.

In Lois's writing, the phrases begin with a first-person pronoun and are connected with *and*s and a *then*. The seven lines were written as three sentences, with punctuation missing at the end of the second sentence. She uses a mix of cursive and manuscript writing. Many words are spelled correctly including *family, watched, went,* and *house.* She spelled *trick or treat* as *treac'otreat* without capitalization. You can see at the top of the page that she erased HO. She erased her title after pausing to think of the third letter in *Halloween.*

Lois spells short-vowel words mostly correctly, and she is experimenting with long-vowel spellings, as in *staid* for *stayed.* Without prompting, she went back through her writing to read for correctness and changed some spellings including *whent* for *went.*

Lois drew a pencil sketch of her living room that shows her sitting on a couch watching *Beetle Juice.* It was Lois's idea to include a drawing. Based on this information and interpretation, we could hypothesize from this sample that she is in a transitional phase of literacy development.

Interpretation and Evaluation

Two questions can guide your thinking about interpretation and evaluation: How do teachers summarize their findings? How do these functional and developmental expressions lead to planning instruction?

levels and includes information related to the student's learning to read and write.

Look for patterns in the summary sheet. See if the scores for reading accuracy in passage reading and word recognition are at similar functional grade levels. What patterns in synchrony can you detect in the student's reading, writing, and spelling development? You may want to refer to Table 3.1 to look for these matches between reading, writing, and spelling.

In this study of Karla, a fifth-grader, you can see how a case summary sheet is a collection of observations that leads to developmental and functional assessments. Beginning at the bottom of the summary sheet in Figure 4.6, it is important to note that Karla is learning English as a second language. Just above the comments are summaries of the functional and developmental levels. It was

Figure 4.5
Lois's Writing Sample

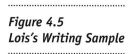

I went around the block with my family and we went to to my friends house. and I when treat:treat with her. I was a clown then I went home and watched Bedle Juce I staid up sintill 12:00.

determined that her functional grade levels were independent 2, instructional 2–3, and frustration 3. It was also determined that she was an early transitional reader and writer. Here, the developmental level is probably more useful than the functional grade levels. Karla is in fifth grade, and it will be important to find her interesting materials that are written at an easy level. Repeated reading of easy rhythmic texts in preparation for a presentation to others would be helpful for Karla.

By comparing the word recognition scores with the reading comprehension scores you can see that Karla had learned to read many words but was having

SUMMARY SHEET: Individual Literacy Assessment

Student's Name: _Karla_

Teacher: _R. Chamberlain_

Date: _3-29-96_

ORTHOGRAPHIC KNOWLEDGE

Informal Test of Word Recognition

Form: _Woods & Moe Informal Reading Inventory_

Level		
PP	_100%_	Early beginning assessment activities:
P	_95_	_____ No concept of word
1	_90_	_____ Rudimentary concept of word
2	_60_	_____ Full concept of word
3	_70_	Alphabet naming:
4	_50_	Individual dictation:
5	_____	
6	_____	
7	_____	

Informal Spelling Inventory

Form: _Elementary Qualitative Spelling Inventory (Bear, 1992)_

Phase: _Middle-within word pattern_

Representative Spellings:

chese	_chase_	
flote	_float_	
quien	_when_	_(in Spanish means "who")_
poping	_popping_	
catle	_cattle_	
inpesen	_inspection_	

INFORMAL READING INVENTORY

Form: _Woods & Moe_

Level or Name of Passage	Reading Accuracy (% words correct)	Level	Oral	Comprehension Check Silent	Comprehension Check Listening	Rate (WPM) Oral	Rate (WPM) Silent
P _____	_____	P	_____	_____	_____	_____	_____
1 _____	_____	1	_____	_____	_____	_____	_____
2 _____	_____	2	_____	_____	_____	_____	_____
3 _____	_98%_	3	_25%_	_____	_67%_	_94%_	_____
4 _____	_97_	4	_38_	_37%_	_____	_88_	_109_
5 _____	_93 FP_	5	_57_	_25_	_____	_63_	_70_
6 _____	_____	6	_____	_____	_____	_____	_____
7 _____	_____	7	_____	_____	_____	_____	_____

Figure 4.6
Karla's Summary Sheet

Grade: _____5_____   Age: _____11_____

Summary of Functional Grade Levels: Circle Phase of Literacy Development:

Independent   _____1_____   (Early)   I.   Emergent

Instructional   _____2–3_____   Middle   II. Beginning

Frustration   _____3_____   Late   III. (Transitional)

Listening Comprehension _____2_____   IV. Intermediate

                                                      V.   Advanced

WRITING Functional Level by Phase: _Transitional_____

Observations and recommendations: _Primary language is Spanish. Orthographic knowledge is ahead of English language and_

comprehension. Motivated. Needs plenty of reading to, and support to learn English. Look at Spanish conversation and experiences

reading and writing in Spanish. Dramatic reading, content dictation for fluency.

Figure 4.6
Continued

difficulty expressing her ideas in the comprehension checks. She had never attained an instructional level for comprehension. This discrepancy in achievement calls for a closer analysis of her retellings and her answers to the comprehension questions.

We returned to our marking of oral reading to see that Karla's reading accuracy is high but there are many self-corrections and dialectical omissions. While these are not counted as reading accuracy errors, these behaviors indicate that Karla does not read fluently and with ease. For example, on the third-grade passage she made six self-corrections, which disrupted fluency. In addition, she made repeated dialectical miscues in which suffixes were omitted—for example, dropping -*ing* and -*ly*.

In reading passages, Karla scored at a frustration level in comprehension of the third-grade passage. Normally, passage reading would stop at this point. Since Karla was in fifth grade and had such strong word recognition skills, passage reading was continued. In the comprehension checks, Karla started with retellings of what she remembered, and then we asked her questions. This provided a good sample of Karla's oral language patterns. Karla's retellings were primarily sequential; she told the facts with some analysis and no generalizations. She hesitated over vocabulary questions but often was correct in her understanding of the vocabulary. She missed the major points or the surprise ending on two stories, in spite of knowing the basic facts. Karla's listening comprehension was well below her grade placement.

At this point, it is clear that Karla did not understand what she read as fully as she might. The implications for instruction and schooling were profound. Karla's orthographic knowledge, observed and documented in word recognition and spelling, had outpaced her ability to understand text. Karla could not understand easy stories with a basic English vocabulary. As noted at the bottom of the summary sheet, her literacy achievement would rely primarily on language development and instruction.

Profile Guide The profile guide presented in Figure 4.7 is another way to summarize your observations. The profile provides a detailed, qualitative list of literacy behaviors to summarize individual assessment.

Sharing What You Learned

It is important to find ways to share your assessment findings with parents and the student. More than grades, which we discuss later, discussions with parents and students about how students are learning helps you to teach and plan for the future. Throughout this book, we show you ways to involve students, parents and other educators in the assessment process. The focus here is on sharing what you learned in the individual assessment.

In individual conferences, show the parent and child some of what you did together. You can talk about the passages the student read, the level of comprehension, the spelling, and the writing.

Do not use too many specialized terms, and define any terms that you use. Instead of talking about scores, interpret the scores in terms of functional levels and developmental phases. Define and explain what the student's independent, instructional, and frustration levels are. Talk about how the student's instructional level compares to materials used in the student's current grade level or educational setting. As we discussed earlier, it's useful to produce the samples of materials arranged by developmental level in Figure 4.1.

Talk about literacy development. Using a condensed version of Table 3.1, we show parents where their child is along the continuum. With this chart of development before you, outline a few of the reading, writing, and spelling behaviors you see at this point in the student's performance.

This is a good time to describe how this assessment relates to the student's success in school. For example, explain to the parent that the student should be able to read the school materials comfortably if that student is reading on grade level and is at an acceptable phase of development for that grade level. Parents of a student who is well behind the present grade placement need to know this and start long-term planning accordingly. Planning for students with difficulties is discussed in Part 4.

When you sit with parents, you can relate the assessment to what the student and parents think about a child's development. You may ask questions that have the student reflect on how she is learning: "What can you do now that you couldn't before?" and "How have you grown over the year?"

You can discuss literacy development with parents and students in individual meetings that are interactive and student-directed. As you develop a portfolio system and a way for students to exhibit their work, ask students to show how they have grown and how they are learning to read and write. After some modeling from the teacher, students can take some leadership in assessments by inviting the parents to attend and can then lead the discussion by sharing samples of their work.

Reading

Phase of Development (circle): *Emergent, Beginning, Transitional, Intermediate, Advanced? Early, Middle, Late?*

For Emergent and Beginning Readers:
___ No concept of word   ___ Full concept of word
___ Rudimentary   ___ Needs support
    concept of word   materials

Oral Reading:
___ Accuracy score   ___ Expression
___ Rate and fluency   ___ Reads for meaning
___ Substitutes with real   ___ Self-corrects
    words

Reading and Thinking:
___ Answers comprehension questions
    ___ Main idea   ___ Inferential
    ___ Factual knowledge   ___ Critical
    ___ Vocabulary
___ Retelling (from Y. Goodman & C. Burke, 1972)
    ___ Characters   ___ Theme
    ___ Character development ___ Generalizations
    ___ Events   ___ Major concepts
    ___ Plot
___ Guided reading thinking activity
    ___ Makes predictions   ___ Reflects on
    ___ Proves predictions   information and ideas
                              ___ Skims expository texts

Listening Comprehension:
___ Adequate for grade level

Orthographic Knowledge

In Reading:
Reads most
___ Initial   ___ Short vowel patterns
___ Final   ___ Long vowel patterns
___ Consonant blends and   ___ Two-syllable words
    digraphs   ___ Polysyllabic words

For beginners:
___ Learns sight words from dictations
___ Size of word bank: _____

In Spelling:
Phase of Spelling (circle): *Early, Middle, Late (Prephonemic, Semiphonemic, Letter Name, Within-Word Pattern, Syllable Juncture, Derivational Constancy)*

Spells most
___ Initial consonants   ___ Preconsonantal nasals
___ Final consonants   ___ Long vowel patterns
___ Consonant blends   ___ Two-syllable words
    and digraphs   ___ Polysyllabic words
___ Short vowel patterns

Writing

Phase of Development (circle): *Early, Middle, Late*
___ Writing is in synchrony with reading and spelling

Cramer's Guidelines: *(Low, Middle, High)*
___ Quality of ideas   ___ Grammar and usage
___ Quality of organization   ___ Punctuation
___ Selection of words   ___ Capitalization
___ Structure of sentences   ___ Handwriting/neatness
___ Structure of paragraphs

Written Fluency:
___ Fluent   ___ Disfluent
___ Approaching fluency

Meaning and Personal Style:
___ Situational   ___ Personal expression
___ Episodes and stories   and voice
___ Conveyed meaning

Written Response to Ideas and Events:
___ Heaps   ___ Analyzing and
___ Retelling   generalizing
___ Summary   ___ Personal reflection and
                                  problem solving

Language
___ Development is   ___ Interactive
    age appropriate   ___ Shares ideas and
___ Production is clear   interests
___ Expansive   ___ Leadership style
___ Vocabulary

Strengths and Interests:
_____
_____
_____
_____

Figure 4.7
An Individual Assessment Profile Guide
....

Coding:(optional)   **0 = Outstanding**   **VG = Very good, above average**   **S = Satisfactory**
P = Problematic   **? = Needs to be studied further**

STUDENT: _____ Karla _____   DATE(S): _____ 4-19-96 _____

Guide questions for rationale: Why are you doing this activity? What about this student's development makes this activity worthwhile? Consider questions like: Why did you choose that reading? Why is this a good writing activity for this student? What do you expect will happen?

Notes for presenting the activities: Number activities showing the order of presentation. Note how long is scheduled for each activity. List the steps to each activity. You may want to include guide questions, stopping points, and transitions to the next activity.

Read to	Read with	Write with	Word Study and Miscellaneous
Rationale	Rationale	Rationale	Rationale
Teacher reads—models fluency; helps student develop listening comprehension. Literal responses can lead to inferences. Student practices explaining situation in own words. Must draw on previous information about characters to make inferences. Students also make prediction about future of characters.	Readers Theater—develops reading fluency, expression; provides opportunities for repeated readings. Hope this activity will encourage more group sharing. If all can agree, present to rest of class next week.	Journal—student practices writing skills, creativity. Promotes writing, thinking fluency. Purpose is production —as much writing as possible in 10 minutes. Rule review—Karla has asked for help before. She's beginning to check for errors in writing.	Chit Chat—catch up on activities. Time to share interests. Word Study—Karla has asked about spelling of contractions. Also, I have spotted misspellings of contractions in writing.
Activity	Activity	Activity	Activity
5 Read *Pinballs* together: Chapter 10 (10–15 minutes) Recall—comprehension questions: – Where is Thomas going? – Why do you think Mr. Mason went with him? – What was Thomas thinking about during his visit with the Bensen twins? – Why didn't he ask them about how they found him? – What do you think will happen now?	7 Readers Theater—practice with Francesco and Scott (15 minutes). Move to a different area.	2 Review rules for capitaliz-ation and punctuation (2–3 minutes). 3 Journal—topic: write about your week without school (10 minutes). 6 Finish *Sarah Plain and Tall,* writing/drawing from previous sessions. Make copies. (5–10 minutes).	1 Chit Chat—discuss activities of the past week (5 minutes). 4 Word Study (10–15 minutes) —List word combinations that make contractions. —Discuss reasons for using them. —Write list in word study notebook

Figure 4.8
Lesson Plan for Karla

....

Planning Instruction

Specific plans for instruction must be practical and at the same time incorporate the goals created by the student and parents. You can call on a basic repertoire of activities, which vary according to a student's development and incorporate the student's interests and areas of study:

TEACHER: _____ *Rose Chamberlain* _____   ASSESSMENT

Questions for Reflection: What happened? What did the student(s) do? Write down some of what students said or wrote. Did the activity accomplish what you wanted? Did the student perform in the manner you expected? Was the work at the right developmental level? How will this activity change what you do in the future? How will what you did be reflected in your next lesson?

Read to	Read with	Write with	Word Study and Miscellaneous
Karla finished coloring her last illustration from <u>Sarah</u>, while I read <u>Pinballs</u>. She listened and answered questions about where Thomas J. went (the hospital). After some leading discussion, she said that Thomas J. was trying to find out about the Bensens' finding him.	*We practiced the play <u>Captain Bumble</u> during the last 15 minutes of class. Karla read the part of the 1st mate. Her voice was soft, but she was making some effort. The group plans to share the play with the rest of the class next week. We will work on expression on Wednesday and perhaps raise projection.*	*Karla wrote in her journal about visiting her relatives. Karla still has trouble with capitalization and periods. I hesitate to correct her journal so I suggested that she read it and see if anything needed a period or capital letter. I noticed later that she added commas and periods in a variety of places.*	*I noticed that students use contractions but misspell them, so today we brainstormed contractions, noting the 2 words that are combined. ex: do not→ don't, is not → isn't. We talked about substituting an apostrophe for the o in <u>not</u>. Karla said she had done this before. It was a good review.*

Figure 4.8 Continued

....

- Reading with the student
- Reading to the student
- Writing with the student
- Word study

If you present these four types of activities at each student's functional and developmental level, you will have an extremely successful literacy program with your students. Part 3 presents classroom activities in developmental order for each of these components.

If you are working with a child individually you can use a **lesson plan** format like the one in Figure 4.8. You can see that Karla's tutor, Rose, incorporated many of the recommendations noted in the summary sheet in Figure 4.6. For example, Rose used readers theater as a dramatic reading activity. In addition, each lesson, she read to and talked with Karla to provide more experience with English. This sample plan includes the four fundamental literacy activities.

Three headings are used to plan and describe these activities: **rationale** for the activity, a brief description of the activity, and an assessment of the activity. In examining the rationale for an activity, plan for developmental needs and interests. To conduct an activity because it is a fun activity is an insufficient reason. The work has to be meaningful and performable.

The procedures for an activity are listed in the activity section, and the assessment part of the lesson plan leads to evaluating the effectiveness of instruction and planning subsequent lessons.

Conclusion and Study Notes

This chapter has taken you through the process of conducting an individual assessment. In the classroom, we incorporate the assessments into individual conferences. Given the little time teachers have to dedicate to individual conferences, some of these assessment activities are conducted in small groups, saving the most pertinent assessments for individual meetings. Teachers use these fuller versions of these assessments individually, a few times a year, with students who appear to have difficulties.

A student's literacy can be described functionally and developmentally. Functional grade-level descriptions are complemented by developmental descriptions. With them, you can plan literacy instruction in a context that is interesting and meaningful to the student.

As a classroom teacher you will adapt these activities to small group sessions that are a regular part of classroom instruction. These small group activities will help you to plan instruction throughout the year and are the focus of Chapter 5.

- Informal literacy assessments provide qualitative looks at students' literacy.

- Developmental levels correspond to the phases of literacy described in Chapter 3.

- Functional reading levels are expressed by describing the actual materials students can read, and by describing a range of grade levels for a student's independent, instructional, and frustration reading levels.

- Reading comprehension and listening comprehension are measured by examining the quality of the student's retelling or ability to answer comprehension questions.

- By marking a student's oral reading, teachers have a record of oral reading fluency and reading strategies.

- Omissions, substitutions, additions, and "with help" from the teacher are considered oral reading miscues.

- Corrections, repetitions, and marginal notes for fingerpointing and word-by-word reading are noted but are not scored.

- Reading rate is a measure of fluency, and is calculated in this way: words/seconds x 60 = words per minute (wpm).

- Look at the pause structure and expression of a student's oral reading to see if there was enough fluency for the student to pause at major syntactic boundaries.

- All of these assessment practices are easily adapted to the classroom setting and small group meetings with students.

Key Terms

Many of the terms in this chapter describe assessment activities that are a part of individual assessments. Can you recall what the procedures were for these activities?

functional descriptions of literacy

independent, instructional, and
  frustration levels

developmental descriptions

phases of reading, writing and
  spelling development

reading comprehension

retelling as a way to examine
comprehension

factual, vocabulary, literal, and
inferential comprehension
questions

orthographic knowledge

spelling assessments

word recognition in isolation

oral reading accuracy

qualitative analysis of oral reading

reading rate

lesson plan activities

rationale for an activity

Follow-Up Activities

1. Conduct an individual assessment with a student. You can use one of the commercial inventories or develop your own. Then, with the proper permission, conduct an informal literacy assessment as described in this chapter. Summarize your findings with a profile guide or a summary sheet.

2. Conduct one assessment activity with several children, either individually or in a small group. For example, you could conduct an interview and then a writing activity with three different students. In each case, summarize what you learned about the student. Suggest developmental and functional levels. List activities that would motivate and be developmentally appropriate for the students.

5 Whole-Class and Small-Group Informal Assessment

Conversation

Diane: How do you—or you and the kids—start figuring out and letting the kids know what their strengths are?

Steve: This is a dilemma for any teacher. When you walk into any classroom of thirty students, you better have something for most of them to do while you assess a few of them.

Sherry: But what exactly do you do to assess students?

Amy: I just began studying to be a teacher in January, and I want to know how you start teaching. I don't know where teachers start.

Britta: I think I'd start by giving them the spelling-by-stage assessment and see how they do on that. Then I'd assign them to small groups.

Sherry: I'm confused about how you start. I'm just afraid.

Amanda: Do you just give them a book? No, I think you would start with a word sort and dictations.

Mark: What do you expect of first-graders at the beginning of the year? And what do you expect of them at the end of the year?

Dawn: Well, at the beginning of the year, some will already know about words in books, some will know how to read, and some won't even be able to make a letter.

Mark: How do you figure out who knows what?

Dawn: I'll probably give them a writing journal. Some of them won't know what they're writing. They might copy words off the wall. Some of them will only write their names. But I'm going to see their different levels. There's going to be a lot of diversity.

Sara: At the end of first grade, not all the children are at the second-grade, first-month level. Can't you use a portfolio system to track their progress? That way you don't necessarily test them, but you'll be able to see their growth.

Dawn: If I were to assess my students in groups, I could find materials they could read at an independent level or at an instructional level.

Denise: You have to know your students as a class and also as individuals before you can assess them. You need to know their background and observe them socially.

Paula: Where do you start? I've learned about all kinds of assessment, but I won't really understand it until I am in the classroom and trying it—from the first day of school.

These preservice and beginning teachers are sharing their concerns and questions about being a new teacher. They realize that their students will come to school with different strengths. Their issues—how to assess students and what to do with the class while they assess a few students—are issues that teachers grapple with each year as they start to work with a new classroom of students.

The concepts in this chapter build on those you explored in Chapter 4. In this chapter you will move from considering one child at a time to determining ways to assess whole classrooms of students. In particular, you will examine ways of adapting assessment strategies designed for individual students to practical classroom use. Many of the assessment strategies will require you to work with a small group of students while your remaining students are engaged in other activities. We have some suggestions of productive ways to engage other students while you work with small groups.

Guide Questions for Chapter 5

- How would you involve parents in the informal assessment of your students?

- Describe the recommended strategies for whole-class assessment. What would you learn from implementing these strategies?

- Describe the recommended strategies for small-group assessment. What would you learn from implementing these strategies?

- How does assessing students in instructional settings enhance your knowledge of students' literacy?

- Why is it important to synthesize the information that you gather during informal classroom assessment? How might you organize this information?

The beginning of a school year is a teacher's busiest time. Teachers who anticipate building a productive school year often start off the year by establishing classroom behavioral expectations and routines and by assessing students' academic strengths. Teachers begin the year with little background knowledge of the students in their care. They must constantly observe how students work in groups, work alone, approach a reading or writing activity, and so on. As efficiently as possible, each teacher tries to become comfortable with a new group of students, just as the students are getting comfortable in this new classroom.

Students are busy figuring out the culture of the class. First, they explore to see which friends are with them this year. They examine the physical organization of the classroom for clues to what might be expected of them. They watch and listen to the teacher to learn about the teacher's new sets of expectations. They are also a bit wary about this new environment as they have not yet learned to trust this teacher. Often students who have experienced difficult learning situations in school take the longest to become comfortable in a new classroom setting. They worry that the teacher might disapprove of their reading or writing skills.

This somewhat anxious time presents a perfect opportunity for students and teachers to become better acquainted. Students need to be assured that early assessments are specifically designed for planning instruction and not for blaming students for their academic shortcomings. The closeness of the assessment process allows students to build trust in the teacher and this new classroom environment. Additionally, many informal assessments provide students with an authentic voice in helping build a joint curriculum. Parents, too, play a part in this important foundation-setting time of the year. After all, they know the most about their child and can provide important information to make their child's school year successful.

Links Between Individual and Whole-Class or Small-Group Assessment

Chapter 4 discussed many ways to informally assess a child's strengths as a reader and writer. By starting with individual assessment, you now have a clear model of how to work with a student from observation, to documentation, to interpretation, and finally to evaluation and planning for instruction. As you might guess, the process of assessment becomes a bit more complicated when considering twenty-five or thirty students.

The most exciting and challenging part of classroom informal assessment is evaluation and planning—considering the strengths and needs of individual students for actual instruction. Your teaching will reflect this complexity as you organize your students into a variety of group situations.

Many assessment strategies use either small-group or whole-class settings. Few of the strategies are unusual in any way. At its best, informal assessment is not overly cumbersome or time-intensive; it is an essential part of teaching and learning. As you continue to observe your students throughout the school day, you will see how the distinctions between teaching and informal assessment are blurred and how each teaching event presents the teacher and students with a time for assessment.

Based on discussion in Chapters 1 through 4, select a grade level that you anticipate teaching or are teaching, and jot down some information about your students that might be valuable to know. Review the conversation at the beginning of the chapter and its recurring question, "How do I start?" A good place to start is to determine what you need to know about your students to plan instruction. Save your notes and look back at them when you have completed this chapter.

The Assessment Process: Observation, Documentation, and Interpretation

Our discussion of assessment strategies that can be administered to the whole class or in small groups will focus on the beginning of the year when you are establishing your instructional goals, but you will also use many of these strategies throughout the year and especially at the close of the year to document student growth.

Whole-Class Assessment Strategies

Bridges to the Community

Teachers, especially new teachers, sometimes are more focused on setting up their classroom and preparing the academic curriculum than on talking to parents. But parents can provide important information about students during the initial assessment process. Here are some simple ways to draw parents into the initial assessment process.

Letters Home A few weeks before school begins many teachers take time to write a short letter home to the parents of their soon-to-be students. They may share a bit of their personal lives such as a few details about their families. Then they discuss a few of their plans for the upcoming school year. The letter usually ends with a request for the family to share important information about their child. In addition, some teachers request the child to write to the teacher about important information and ideas they have for the school year. These letters are a warm way to meet your new students and gather important information. And they create a bridge to the families of your students.

Autobiographies You may want to begin the year by having each student write an autobiography. Autobiographies will help you find out what is important to your students and help students learn about each other as individuals.

Young students may create autobiographies that are mostly drawings. Some teachers have young students tape record their autobiography as they share the important events or important people in their lives. Other teachers take dictation as the young students tell them their autobiography.

Autobiographies take on an added dimension when parents contribute information. Students learn about interviewing as they talk to their parents about their childhood. Parents may even be willing to share baby books, photo albums, early drawings, and other milestone information to enrich the autobiography.

Getting to Know Your Students

Learning Interviews In learning interviews, students talk to you about their previous in-school and out-of-school learning experiences. Learning interviews help you identify students who love to read and those who avoid it. They provide some knowledge about those students who have had many writing experiences and those who have had few or none. If you ask students about how they have learned to read or write, some might focus on the exact process. They might include statements about parents or grandparents who read to them or special books shared by teachers. Some students find it more difficult to talk about learning to write than about learning to read because they confuse talking about handwriting with talking about writing.

Teachers sometimes record students' responses to direct questions in a daily journal. The answers help teachers plan teaching for the year. When students can write these comments, they gain experience in writing their own ideas.

Interest Interviews A journal entry may be the best place to discover your students' reading and writing interests. You can ask students to write about the types of books that they like to read, their hobbies, or what they do in their free time. Although you will want to broaden their reading and writing interests as the school year progresses, you can make students comfortable at the beginning of the year by discussing books and magazines that relate to their interests. These materials allow your students to share their expertise and become comfortable in the new classroom setting.

Planning and Goal Setting The journal is an appropriate place for your students to write about the academic curriculum. Have them brainstorm possible topics for exploration or books that they want to read. Following this writing, convene for a whole-class exploration of some of the areas you have planned and discuss how to incorporate topics of importance to students.

In a separate journal entry, students can plan their goals for the year. At first you may see students write, "I want to read better." As students gain experience at setting goals, you will notice that the goals become more specific. For example, they may write, "I want to get better at reading, so I am going to read three books in the next six weeks." This student goal setting allows you to see what your students consider important as they plan their learning future. You may want to broaden this goal setting to include parents' goals. Parents, after all, have expectations for their children, and teachers need to be aware of these goals as they plan their curricula.

Getting to Know the Literacy Strengths of Your Students

Whole-Class Guided Listening-Thinking Activity (GLTA) In the *whole-class guided-listening thinking activity,* developed by Stauffer (1980), the teacher reads a story to the class and determines student involvement and comprehension.

How to Go About a GLTA

1. Select either a picture book or a chapter book that has a strong plot and many possible conclusions.

2. Read the book to find a series of several stopping places to ask students what they think will happen next.

3. Ask students to examine the book cover or chapter title and decide what the book or chapter may be about.

4. Begin reading and continue until your first stopping place. Ask students what might happen next. Return to earlier predictions to revise or eliminate some. Then continue reading to your next stopping place. Continue this procedure until you complete the book or chapter.

5. When you have finished reading, revisit earlier predictions and talk about the book in general.

What to Consider. As you work with your whole class, first note those students who participate most actively in this procedure. Note also those students who participate but make predictions that do not seem to relate to the story. Document those students who seem to be listening but never participate. And finally, note those students who seem never to engage with the activity.

Form small groups of six or seven students who provided unusual responses, who were reluctant to participate, or who were not a part of the activity, and repeat the GLTA with them. By reducing the size of the group, you can focus more closely on just these students to determine if they are familiar with story form and if they enjoy listening to stories.

Ten-Minute Write You will choose the topic for this ten-minute writing assessment. Be sure to choose topics that are familiar to students and allow them flexibility in their writing. Engage students in discussion prior to writing to stimulate their prior knowledge and prime them for writing. When they are ready, tell them that they have ten minutes to write and that they should produce their best effort. Let them know that you are not worried about spelling on this first-draft effort. You might tell older students that they will have a few minutes at the end for editing.

While students are writing, find a location that allows you to observe all the students in your class. Note students who have an easy or difficult time getting started, who start and stop a lot, and who use the entire time without a break. These important writing rhythms influence other classroom writing work. For example, slow starters require longer writing sessions. If you provide them with only fifteen minutes for writing, they might never begin.

When the ten minutes are up, give your students time to share. Note those students who feel comfortable sharing their work and those who hold back. As the final step in the assessment, collect the papers and makes notes of each as to whether the piece makes sense and how the student has structured the writing. Does the writing clearly share the writer's ideas? Does it have a clear beginning, middle, and end? How much did the student produce? You can count the number of words and use this as a baseline for comparison with other ten-minute writing samples. Finally, look at the correctness of the work. Note how many of the words represented were spelled correctly. Consider other grammatical elements such as subject–verb agreement and punctuation, particularly if you allowed time for editing.

The directions and brainstorming for Nicole's ten-minute write, shown in Figure 5.1, focused on an exciting time with her family. Nicole, a second grader, chose to write about when her brother fell off the monkey bars and broke his arm and when he broke his leg skiing. She ends her piece by stating that she heard about these accidents from her mother, but did not see them herself.

In evaluating the content of Nicole's writing, we see that it certainly makes sense. She has told about two separate events in her brother's life and made a

Figure 5.1
Nicole's Ten-Minute
Writing Sample

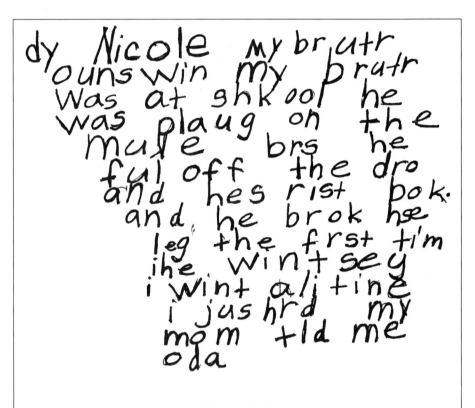

Translation
Once when my brother was at school he was playing on the monkey bars. He fell off the bar and his wrist broke. And he broke his leg the first time he went skiing. I went (not clear). I just heard my mom told me (not clear).

connecting theme of the broken bones. She has even used the word *once* to entice us into her recount of these events.

In evaluating her writing form, we see that Nicole writes in one long paragraph. She has written forty-six words in this composition, including a title, and has used only one punctuation mark—at the end of *broke*. Her writing is easier to read at the beginning of her story. Toward the end, as she grows tired, her spelling is more invented and difficult to read.

In her spelling, Nicole attempts many words that she is unsure of spelling but that are important to the telling of her story. For instance, she spells *brother* as *brutr*, *school* as *shkool*, and *playing* as *plaug*. She correctly spells other words such as *my, was, he*, and *off*. Examine her writing closely to see what else you can discover.

Small-Group Assessment Strategies

Managing the Classroom During Small-Group Assessment

Small-group assessment strategies are a bit more complicated than whole-class strategies. Small groups of seven or eight students usually work well, and early groups will include a mix of students. While you work with the small group, however, your other students must be engaged in meaningful projects that they can accomplish without teacher support. Such projects are more difficult to develop at the beginning of the year, when students are still becoming comfortable in their new classroom setting. The best projects are simple and structured so that all students can succeed. Here are a few suggestions for initial projects:

1. Have the students read a book and then draw and write about it. You might have students select several books so that they don't wander in search of a better book.

2. Have students complete a self-portrait that will accompany their autobiography.

3. Have students design a cover for their writing folder, portfolio, or any other storage folder.

4. Have students work on their autobiography, learning history, or any other aspect of the informal assessment process.

5. Have small groups of students listen to a story on tape and then draw and write about it.

When you have assembled your small group and the remaining students understand what they are to do while you work with the small group, you are ready to begin.

Following are descriptions of the spelling-by-stage assessment, small-group guided listening-thinking activities and **guided reading-thinking activities**, and the informal reading inventory (IRI) as modified for classroom use. You can vary the order of small-group assessment strategies, although you might want to leave the IRI for last. The IRI is the most test-like activity and may raise student anxiety levels.

Spelling-by-Stage Assessment

The spelling-by-stage assessment determines a student's ability to represent single-syllable to multisyllabic words. It uses the developmental spelling list that appears in Chapter 4 and is adapted here for small-group administration.

Administering the Spelling-by-Stage Assessment If you are working with first-graders and perhaps second-graders, ask your students to spell only the first five words. Older students can write the first ten words. Remind them that the words may become difficult to spell. Then say each word, use it in a sentence, and then say it again. For example: "*Bed*, I sleep in a bed. *Bed.* Please write *bed.*" When you have finished the last word, it is time to dismiss these students and call another group of students. Continue assessing small groups until the whole class has participated.

Analyze each spelling sample to determine which students are at the prephonemic, semiphonemic, or letter-name phase of orthographic development. Call any students who are not at these phases of development to another small-group session and ask them to spell the next five words in the qualitative spelling inventory. Analyze the results. The only students who will need to be called again are those students who are potentially at the derivational constancy phase of development.

What to Consider After you have analyzed all the spelling samples, you are ready to create groups for your initial word study activities. *These groups will constantly change* as students refine their understandings of the orthographic representation of words.

Small-Group Guided Listening-Thinking Activity (GLTA) and Guided Reading-Thinking Activity (GRTA)

The guided listening-thinking activity (GLTA), discussed above as a whole-class informal assessment, needs to be repeated in small groups for older students who refused to participate in the whole-class activity, whose predictions seemed off base, or whose reading levels still puzzle you. For primary students, you may want to continue with small-group GLTAs to better understand your students' prediction and comprehension strengths.

Older students and students who can read independently are ready for small-group guided reading-thinking activities (GRTA). This activity proceeds just as the GLTA did, except that students read independently. In general, authentic children's literature works well for GRTAs. But unless you are sure of each book's reading level, you may want to use basal stories for initial GRTAs. Basal stories are usually short, matched to grade level, and provide easy-to-find stopping points to engage your students in discussion about previous and new predictions.

Small-group GRTAs usually begin with material written at grade level. By using this material, you can determine which students find grade-level material easy or difficult and which students process text slowly or fluently.

When you have completed a GRTA or GLTA with one group, jot down any important information that you discovered and then move on to another group. When you have worked with the entire class, form new groups based on the knowledge that you have gathered. Repeat the process using a lower-level pas-

A teacher informally assesses children's comprehension.

sage with students who found the grade-level passage difficult. With students who read the text easily but comprehended with difficulty, you may want to try again with a more familiar story structure—a fairy tale, perhaps—and note their ease or difficulty with comprehension. When you complete the GRTAs and GLTAs, you will have discovered who is reading at or below grade level, but you will not have learned much about those students who are reading above grade level. The informal reading inventories will provide this information.

Informal Reading Inventory (IRI)

As you learned in Chapter 4, conducting an IRI, even with a single student, can be a lengthy process. Small-group IRIs are shortened to save time but therefore provide less information. For example, in our modified IRI process, students read silently, and you will not be able to glean how they attempt to figure out unknown words. We believe that the rich database acquired from the other aspects of informal assessment make this an appropriate trade-off. Some teachers decide that small-group IRIs are unnecessary if the information gathered during the GLTAs or GRTAs is sufficient to plan instruction. They might do IRIs individually only with students who have reading and writing difficulties.

How to Administer an IRI Published IRIs allow you to make copies for student assessment. You need to copy the passages that are one grade level below, at grade level, and one grade level above the grade that you teach. Each student will need a copy of the grade-level passage and the accompanying questions. Be sure to delete the answers that are provided to the test administrators.

In each small group of seven or eight students, hand out the passage and ask students to read it silently. To see how rapidly they read, have students start reading at the same time. As each student finishes, write down the time. Later, calculate how long each student took and how many words they were able to read in a minute. (All IRIs include directions for these calculations in the manual.) When students finish, have them turn over the passage. Give them the questions about the passage, which then are answered independently.

When all students have taken the IRI and you have determined which students read the passage at an instructional, independent, or frustration level, create a second round of groups. Students who read the passage at the instructional level can work with grade-level material and do not need to be reassessed at this time. Students who had difficulty with the passage should be reassessed with a passage at one grade level lower. Continue this process with these students until you discover each student's instructional level. For students who read the passage at an independent level, repeat the process with passages that are one grade level above their current placement. Continue this process until you have discovered each student's instructional level.

What to Consider. This assessment strategy will help you determine each student's reading instructional level and fluency rate. With this information you can find material that students can read with you, their parents, or a peer as well as material that students can read independently. You will also know which students need instruction to strengthen their reading rate.

Using Whole-Class and Small-Group Instructional Events for Assessment

In addition to the specific assessment strategies discussed above, teachers observe students during regular instructional events. This type of observation might stretch your observation skills at first. In addition to teaching and classroom management, you will add looking at students as they are involved with instruction. A good place to start is scanning the class for management issues. For instance, after you give directions for a project, note those students who begin immediately and those students who take a while to engage. By making such observations, you will develop a deeper understanding of the rhythms of your students.

After observing general behavior patterns, move in and observe instructional rhythms. Find larger blocks of time to see how students begin work, manage their time, and draw their work to closure. Free-choice reading, reading and writing workshops, and word study offer a wealth of opportunities for observation.

Free-Choice Reading

Observation possibilities are rich during free-choice reading. You will observe some children who are in love with books. They surround themselves with books and appear to tune out the classroom as they read. Other students want to be involved with reading but sometimes need help in finding the right book. Still others avoid reading altogether and spend the whole free reading time looking for the right book and a comfortable place to read.

If you observe less desirable behavior patterns, you can help change them. Ohlhausen and Jepson (1992) offer directions for helping children learn to select books. They offer the *Goldilocks plan,* in which students learn to decide which books are too easy, just right, or too hard for them. Too easy books are those they have read before and can read every word in. Just right books are new and have a few words they do not know. Too hard books have many words they do not know and a story that is hard to follow. Students are invited to try these books again in a few months. When students have gained strategies for selecting free-choice books, see if some formerly reluctant readers are now more willing to engage with books. Other students may have broadened their interests in reading and begun selecting books that they rejected earlier.

Reading Workshop

Some teachers make free-choice reading and reading workshop the same event. Reading workshop, however, usually includes independent reading, small-group reading, and a combination of whole-group, small-group, or individual instruction with the teacher. During reading workshop, students talk about books, write about books, draw about books, perform drama in relation to books, and so on.

During reading workshop, focus on how students interact with books. Through your routine instruction, you are able to determine the ease or difficulty students have in comprehending or understanding books. Use some of the following ways to explore student comprehension or understanding.

Retellings A retelling allows you to gather information about a student's comprehension (Goodman, Watson, & Burke, 1987; Johnston, 1983). When you ask younger students to retell a story, see if they remember the key events in the plot. Do they retell the story in a systematic way with events in correct order?

During the reading workshop, you might sit beside a student who has just finished reading a book and ask him or her to tell you about the story. If the student struggles with parts of the retelling, you can ask some probing questions: "Tell me more about . . ." "Can you help me understand what happened after. . . ?" or "What did the characters do after. . . ?"

A more teacher-directed strategy for retelling is to give a student a book that you have already read and that you know is at the student's instructional reading level. Ask the student to read the book and then tell you about the important parts of the story. As the student retells the story, you can check off each event mentioned on a retelling guide that you have prepared in advance. A retelling guide includes the important events and characters in the story. For example, in

"Jack and the Beanstalk" your list of characters would include Jack, his mother, the giant, and the giant's wife. Your list of events might include the following:

1. Mother sends Jack to sell the cow.

2. Jack sells cow for seeds.

3. Jack plants seeds.

4. Jack climbs beanstalk and finds giant's house.

5. Jack steals gold.

6. Giant's wife hides Jack when giant arrives.

7. Jack runs out and climbs down the beanstalk.

8. Giant follows Jack.

9. Jack cuts down beanstalk and giant is killed.

10. Jack's family is happy.

Brown and Cambourne (1987) list several different forms for retelling similar to or variations of the one we have discussed:

1. *Oral-to-oral retelling.* The teacher reads a story out loud and the student orally retells it. This form is best for emergent readers and writers.

2. *Oral-to-written retelling.* The teacher reads a story out loud and the student retells the story in writing, emergent readers and writers by drawing.

3. *Written-to-oral retelling.* The student reads the text and orally retells it to the teacher.

4. *Written-to-written retelling.* The student reads the text and retells it through writing.

Retelling activities help you gain a knowledge of student comprehension. If a student predominantly focuses on the literal comprehension of a story, you nudge them to explore it on a more inferential level. To explore the inferential or personal meaning a student attaches to a story, you might ask the student why the giant's wife helped Jack. This type of question could engage the both of you as there is no clear answer. You might also share stories that you think about when you read about Jack and then ask what connections the student makes to other stories. And finally, you might explore personal connections that the student makes with this story.

Response to Literature Response to literature can be as simple as having students talk about the story that they or you just read or as complex as having students create a mural or perform a play. When students participate in a variety of activities that follow reading, they share, expand, and express their comprehension and understanding of stories. Dyson (1987) suggests that response-to-literature events are an essential part of meaning making. Through them, students actively engage in understanding the complex ideas shared in books. Rosenblatt (1978) described responses in terms of **aesthetic** and **efferent** stances. The best way to think about these stances is on a continuum. When students respond using the efferent stance, they focus on the elements of the story or the plot—the literal aspects of the story. When students respond using the aesthetic stance, they focus on the personal aspects of the story—the personal connections. Students often respond using a combination of the aesthetic and efferent stances.

Drama. Students enjoy acting out stories. Paley (1981), Collins (1992), and Jett-Simpson (1978), among others, detail students' drama activities in the classroom. Through drama activities, small groups of students put a personal touch to their understanding of the characters and plot of the story, and the remaining students in the class enjoy being the audience. The drama form provides a different lens for observing and documenting your students' literacy strengths.

Art. Students enjoy drawing in response to the stories they read. Their drawings indicate the part of the story or the character in the story that was most important to them. The artwork and discussion provide another lens for viewing students' aesthetic responses to stories.

Drawing gives you a window into the inferences that students make about people and places as they read. For instance, when Barone (Lovell, 1992) asked her students to draw a picture of the caravan (trailer) that Danny lived in in *Danny, the Champion of the World* (Dahl, 1978), two students responded in totally different ways. Mary Martha drew the caravan exactly as described in the book, while Michael added things that he might expect to see in a home—a television set, for example. By viewing the drawings, as shown in Figure 5.2, you can tell that Mary Martha is very close to the text and her drawing might be considered efferent. Michael, on the other hand, made a more aesthetic response, in that he represented the caravan and then added his personal touches to the drawing.

Writing. Students enjoy writing about what they read. If you allow students to respond openly, without structure, you will notice a variety of responses. Barone (1992) and Atwell (1987) have described the writings that students produce after reading. Students may focus on the literal aspects of a text and write a retelling of a story or a summary. At other times, students write about the inferential or personal aspects of a story. They may write about a personal connection between the story and their life, or they may write about the theme or abstract quality of a story.

Student writings provide you with a window into their understandings, their periods of confusion, and their times of insight during reading. You will discover students who focus on the literal elements of what they read and students who consider the abstract or personal qualities of a story.

Talk. The simplest way to discover what students comprehend or understand about stories is to sit next to them and chat. You do not have to prepare any questions for this talk: you just need to be interested and willing to listen to your students talk about a book.

Eeds and Wells (1989) explored discussions among small groups of students about the books they read. They discovered that some students retold the story,

Figure 5.2
Mary Martha's and
Michael's Drawings of
Danny's Caravan Source:
Lovell (1992, pp. 15–32).

Mary Martha's drawing of Danny's caravan

Michael's drawing of Danny's caravan

others talked about personal connections to the story, and some students voiced criticism about the author as a writer. Either they liked the way this person wrote or they didn't, and they offered reasons why. In a more current piece, Wells (1995) provides strategies for teachers to use as they lead "grand conversations" with students. He cautions teachers to engage in a genuine dialogue with students and not a "gentle inquisition" (p. 132).

As you sit with a small group of students, observe what students say about their reading. Some students use the group as a vehicle to gain understanding of a story. They may ask their fellow students about the meaning of a word, the feelings of a character, or a particularly confusing part of the plot.

Writing Workshop

A writing workshop, unlike the ten-minute write, allows you to observe your students as they write about their own topics. It provides an extended writing time during which you can see how your students select a topic and proceed to write about it. You will notice which students actually complete a writing based on a topic and which students begin but never seem to finish. Consider, too, how students go about choosing ideas. Some students talk to other students, some students read or watch television, and other students draw or create a brainstorming web.

Once students have ideas to write about, observe how they draft, revise, and edit their pieces. Students who have had extensive experience with writing know that drafts are full of errors that can be corrected later; they are most focused on getting their ideas down. They also know about the publishing process and the sharing of their work with others. They look forward to this time and often have specific ideas about how the audience should respond to their work.

When you have observed the process of writing, move to a micro level and observe the content and form of a student product. Just as you did with the ten-minute writing sample, see if the student was able to write a cohesive piece. Then note how well the student revised and edited this piece. Look at the feedback the author received from other students, parents, or yourself and determine how well the author incorporated these suggestions into the text.

As you can see, the writing workshop provides a window into more than just a student's writing product. It lets you observe the academic and social process of writing.

Word Study

Small word-study groups provide opportunities to see how well your students can categorize pictures or words. For instance, when you work with letter-name phase students, note which ones easily generate words that have an *a* in them, like *cat*. When enough words are generated for sorting, focus in on how students generate categories and how accurate they are in placing words in categories. In addition to observing students who may have difficulty with sorting, note students who find the sorting easy. They may be ready to study the more complex aspects of a word's orthography.

Pulling Together Your Assessment Information

When you have completed the informal assessment process with each of the students in your classroom, you are ready to synthesize the information you have collected. In this section, we first consider a broad perspective of the whole class and then narrow the focus to individual student profiles. Finally, we discuss student- and teacher-centered portfolios.

A Whole-Class Perspective

The first step in pulling together assessment data is to build profile sheets of your whole class. Chart students' reading and spelling levels and what you learned through students' written and oral retellings. And you certainly will want to include information that you discovered about students' literacy during reading and writing workshops.

Each teacher must experiment with this process and find the recording system that works best. You may want to consolidate all of the literacy information about students into a class chart. The chart would certainly need to reflect the aspects of literacy development you find most important in planning instruction. Table 5.1 shows a sample chart.

Profiling Individual Students

Denny Taylor (1993) writes about assessing children's literacy growth within instructional settings and stresses moving away from formal testing. As part of assessment, she recommends writing a descriptive **literacy biography** for each student that begins with a summary of the student's reading and writing strengths, interests, and literacy history, as well as the parents' and student's goals, and so on. Literacy biographies provide a way to share this explicit knowledge with parents at conferences or in written reports. An example of a literacy profile is provided in the following Student Study. This profile was written by David's teacher at the beginning of third grade. In her entry she consolidated the information that she discovered about David and began to plan for instruction that built on David's literacy strengths.

Table 5.1 **Chart of Literacy Learning**

Name	IRI/phase	Comprehension	Book Choice	Retelling	Writing	Spelling
Jerry	3rd/tran-sitional	Literal, beginning to grasp inferential	Easily able to make a selection, likes mysteries best, esp. *Nate the Great*	Beginning to include more writing, making personal connections to stories	Uses clusters for prewriting, working on a mystery story; focuses on getting ideas down	Within-word pattern

David's Literacy Biography

September 11, 1995

Goals

David's parents say that he loves to read at home. He has lots of books, especially books about animals. They read to him every night. They want him to be a better writer this year. They are worried that he spells words wrong. They aren't sure how to help him with his spelling.

David says that he wants to get along with his friends better. He had lots of fights last year, especially on the playground. He wants to write a report about snakes. He is worried about spelling so many words, though. Spelling can be hard.

Literacy Background

David was in a combined first- and second-grade room where he was able to choose the books that he wanted to read. He talked about picking books that were about animals. He liked reading books with pictures. He said that sometimes he wrote book reports. When David talked about writing, he said that his teachers wrote his stories for him and then he copied them. He said that in second grade he wrote a story about his friends and the games they played.

David says that he learned to read by reading a lot of books. He says that he isn't sure about writing. It is hard work to get it all right.

Reading

In the GLTA activity, David was always willing to predict what might happen, and he always tied it to the text of the story. He seemed to stay close to the text and rarely offered ideas that were not directly stated.

On the IRI, David was able to read third-grade material. He answered eight questions correctly, and the questions he missed related to vocabulary. He is a transitional reader.

Writing and Spelling

David spends a lot of time looking for an idea. On the ten-minute write, he took almost seven minutes before he began to write. He would stop and start a lot, and he really used his eraser. During writing workshop, he was always asking a friend for an idea. He has started to write with Mark about snakes. This joint venture writing may keep him more focused.

David is in the letter-name phase of development. He writes each word letter-by-letter. During the word-sorting activities, David was initially confused and just watched the other children. On the second sorting activity, he started to generate some words, although he was reluctant to provide sorting categories.

Evaluation and Instruction

1. Build on David's love of books.

2. Try art and writing response activities to move him beyond a literal understanding of stories.

3. Support David as he becomes more confident about his writing. Have him write every day and with a friend.

4. Spelling will develop from much reading and writing and continued focus on short vowels in his sorting activities.

This initial entry provides a place to synthesize information about a student. It serves as a benchmark as you work with this student throughout a year. David's teacher discovered his love of books, and she will use this strength as she builds on his present knowledge of writing and spelling. His enjoyment in working with other students will be supported and should nurture his confidence to take more risks with his writing and spelling.

Portfolios

Teachers have been experimenting with **portfolios** for several years in a multitude of ways. You may have had experience building your own portfolio as you moved through your education courses (Mosenthal, Daniels, & Mekkelsen, 1994). You may have collected evidence of how you were developing as a teacher in a portfolio that reflected your goals as a preservice teacher.

Teacher-Centered Portfolios Stewart and Paradis (1994) discovered that the first portfolios were highly teacher-centered. The teacher decided how they would be organized and what would be included. As teachers worked with portfolios over time, they relinquished their authority, and the portfolios became more student-centered. As you begin the portfolio process with students, create portfolios with at least two major sections: a teacher-organized and a student-organized section.

It is important to balance the information that you include in your teacher-centered portfolio to reflect all areas of literacy: listening, speaking, reading, and writing. Begin with the initial literacy biographic entry and the supporting documentation, and add notes and student samples as you extend and refine your initial assessment. For example, if a student moves from drawing as the sole medium of response to including writing, photocopy this sample, date it, and place it into the portfolio.

Teacher-centered portfolios document literacy growth. This documentation can be as simple as a note regarding a literacy event that you observed to a paper written by a student that demonstrates his or her use of the writing process. Share the portfolio with the student and parents. In fact, with your documentation in evidence, portfolios make it easier to talk to a parent about an observation.

Student-Centered Portfolios Students organize their portfolios in many ways—expandable folders, three-ring binders, or oversized envelopes. Teachers sometimes limit the form of the portfolio due to space constraints for storage. You may want to set up ground rules for students. For instance, you may ask students to have sections in their portfolio that will demonstrate how they have grown as readers and writers, how they have grown in their mathematics understanding, how they have learned to get along with others, and so on. The most important part of the portfolio process is for you and your students to document why each item is included. When asked to explain why they included, for instance, a piece of writing, students sometimes seem surprised at the question. One child resolved this situation by saying, for each item, that he liked it. Later in the year, he was able to explain more specifically why he included an item.

As students create their portfolios, it is important that they include samples that demonstrate both the processes and products of literacy. Tierney, Carter, and Desai (1991, pp. 72–74) suggest many possibilities for documenting reading and writing for portfolios:

1. Projects, surveys, reports, and units from reading and writing

2. Favorite poems, songs, letters, comments

3. Finished samples that illustrate wide writing (persuasive, letters, poetry, information, stories)

4. Examples of writing across the curriculum (reports, journals, literature logs)

5. Literature extensions (scripts, visual arts, written forms, webs, charts, time lines)

6. Student records of books read

7. Audio tapes of reading

8. Writing that illustrates critical thinking about reading

9. Notes from reading and writing conferences

10. Writing that shows growth in usage of traits (self-correction, punctuation, spelling, grammar, form)

11. Samples that show the writing process and how ideas were modified

12. Self-evaluation

You and your students will undoubtedly come up with many more ideas.

One Exemplar Portfolio In Mrs. Schneider's (formerly Ms. Barone) school, portfolios are begun in kindergarten and move with the students as they progress through the grades. The following exemplar portfolio belongs to Heather, who has taken longer than other students to develop in literacy. She is starting third grade and is considered a beginning reader and writer. A small selection of samples have been selected to represent many of the artifacts included in her portfolio.

In the teacher/parent category of her portfolio, Heather's teacher kept a sample of her early writing—a story about her teacher—from initial brainstorm for ideas through to final draft. She saved Heather's initial spelling-by-stage assessment and her first IRI.

In the initial cluster in Figure 5.3, Heather views her teacher in three major categories: pals, personality, and what she eats. This brainstorming activity shows that Heather organizes her thinking before she begins to write and that she is willing to write words that she doesn't know how to spell.

Heather's first draft of her story appears in Figure 5.4. Her draft closely follows her cluster in organization. When she completed her draft, Heather met with two other students who helped her revise her story as seen in Figure 5.5. These friends suggested that she find additional information and write more. They also helped her with editing by circling some misspelled words and helping her fix them.

In addition to this story and other writing samples, Mrs. Schneider kept records of all informal assessment pertaining to Heather. Included here are three samples: a journal entry, the IRI, and the spelling inventory.

Figure 5.3
Brainstorm for a Story
About a Teacher

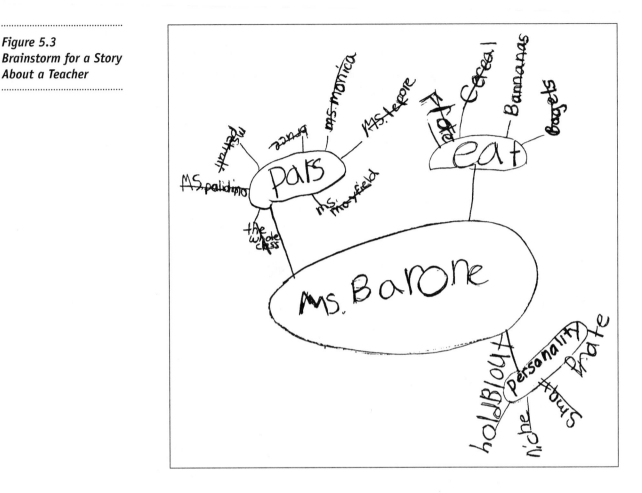

In her early journal entry in Figure 5.6, Heather shows that she likes cats and dogs, indicates that she is eight years old, and asks her teacher several questions, including how old she is. Heather's message for the most part is clear. On one line we can guess some words but not the meaning, and in the last line Heather uses *me* for *am.* This entry and the previous writing sample indicate that Heather can communicate through writing, although some of the words and meaning may be difficult to decipher.

In the IRI sample (Figure 5.7), Heather was asked to read independently and to answer the questions by herself. Heather was certainly willing to answer the questions; however, her teacher realized that this passage and questions were too hard for her.

The final teacher-selected sample is the spelling inventory (Figure 5.8). Based on this sample, Heather's teacher noted that she was able to represent most initial consonants and placed her at a letter-name phase.

Heather chose to include three stories that she had written during the school year. One of the stories was about pigs, another about a dinosaur, and

Figure 5.4
*Draft with Suggestions
from Peer*

a third about her friend. In addition to her stories, she had a list of some of the books she read and a few journal entries. Heather wrote that she included each of these samples because she liked them and she worked hard on them. Figure 5.9 shows one cluster, and Figure 5.10 shows the first draft of her pig story.

Look through these samples to discover Heather's literacy strengths. Balance what you see in Heather's folder with the samples kept by the teacher. Take a few moments to list Heather's literacy strengths and needs.

The Assessment Process: Evaluation and Planning

When you have completed informal assessment at the beginning of your school year and have started student and teacher portfolios, you are ready to begin evaluation and planning for instruction. The information you have gathered

Figure 5.5
Response Form: A
Student's Response to
Heather's Story

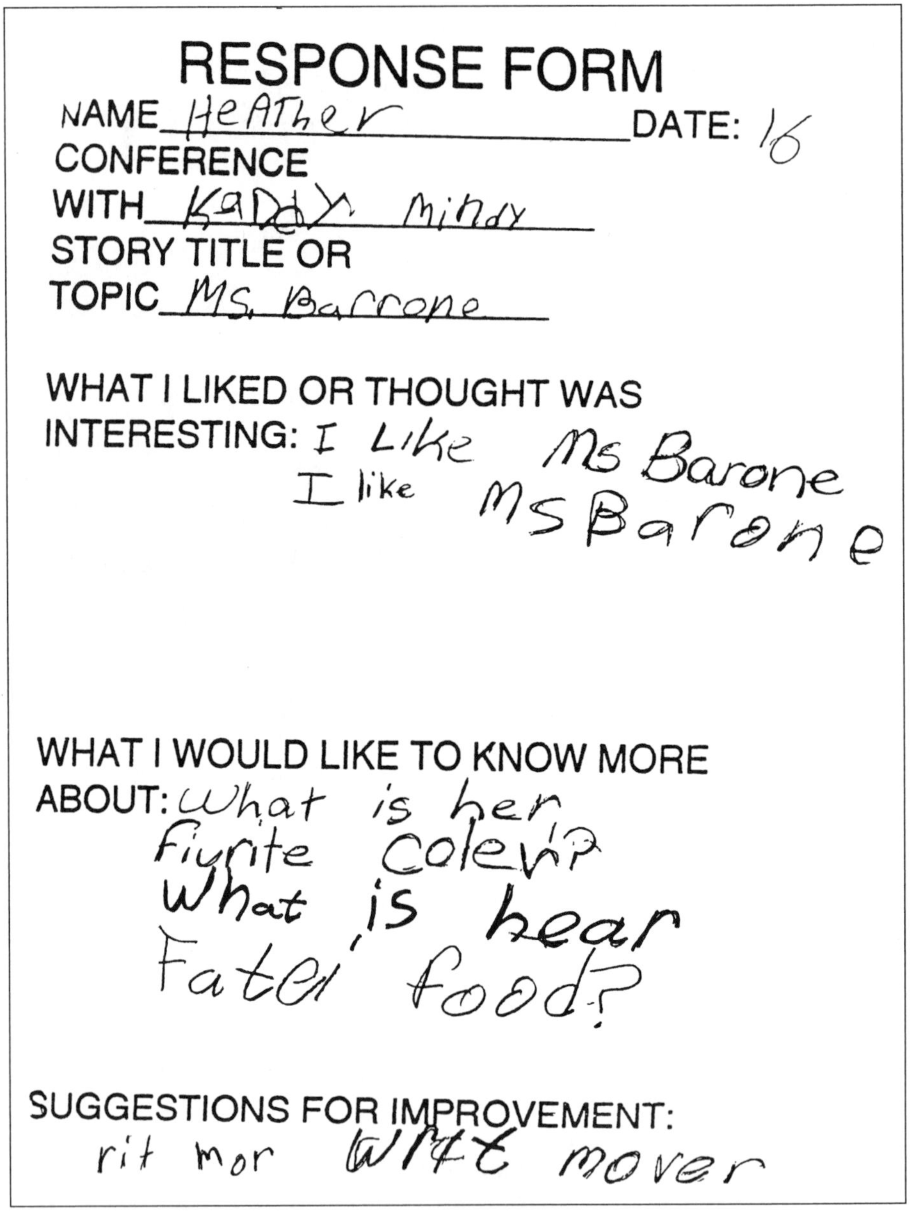

RESPONSE FORM

NAME _Heather_ DATE: _16_

CONFERENCE
WITH _Kathy mindy_

STORY TITLE OR
TOPIC _Ms. Barrone_

WHAT I LIKED OR THOUGHT WAS
INTERESTING: I Like Ms Barone
I like MsBarone

WHAT I WOULD LIKE TO KNOW MORE
ABOUT: What is her fiyrite colev?
What is hear Fater food?

SUGGESTIONS FOR IMPROVEMENT:
rit mor WI4E mover

about each student and your class in general gives you a rich, multifaceted view of the literacy strengths and needs of your students as individuals and of your class as a whole.

At this point, teachers stop to compare what they know about their students with the general curricular expectations of their school district or state. In some cases, the class may have already mastered a particular concept or skill. Or students may display a beginning understanding of a concept. Some students might

require a lot of foundational work before they are ready to work at their grade level. Teachers expect that all classes have students at various levels of literacy development.

The following sections take another look at portfolios as they are used for evaluation. We then consider other ways of evaluating students and end with following the assessment cycle toward instruction.

Using Portfolios for Evaluation

Portfolios are not just collections. They are a means for assessing literacy growth. As portfolios build, teachers, students, and parents can see the record of growth throughout the year. Portfolio entries should be gathered for a specific purpose, and every time a child places writing samples in a portfolio, he or she should be able to document why. For example, the child might wish to include an attempt at revision because it was different from previous attempts.

In matters of evaluation, teachers and parents often are concerned with grades. We recommend that portfolios not be graded. Portfolios reflect the individuality and uniqueness of the student; they are not meant to be standardized. Rather, students should describe the effort put into an entry and what the entry demonstrates to the reader about the student's literacy. However, if they are graded, then follow the advice of Tierney, Carter, and Desai (1991, p. 147), who advocate "multiple grades differentiating a variety of aspects of student achievement, effort, and goals. Ideally, we prefer narrative comments that capture the individual and what he or she has done and is doing."

Student Self-Evaluations and Reflections

As the portfolio begins, you might want to encourage conversation with the student about personal goals and parents' goals. These goals can form a

Figure 5.7
Third-Grade-Level IRI
Questions and Answers

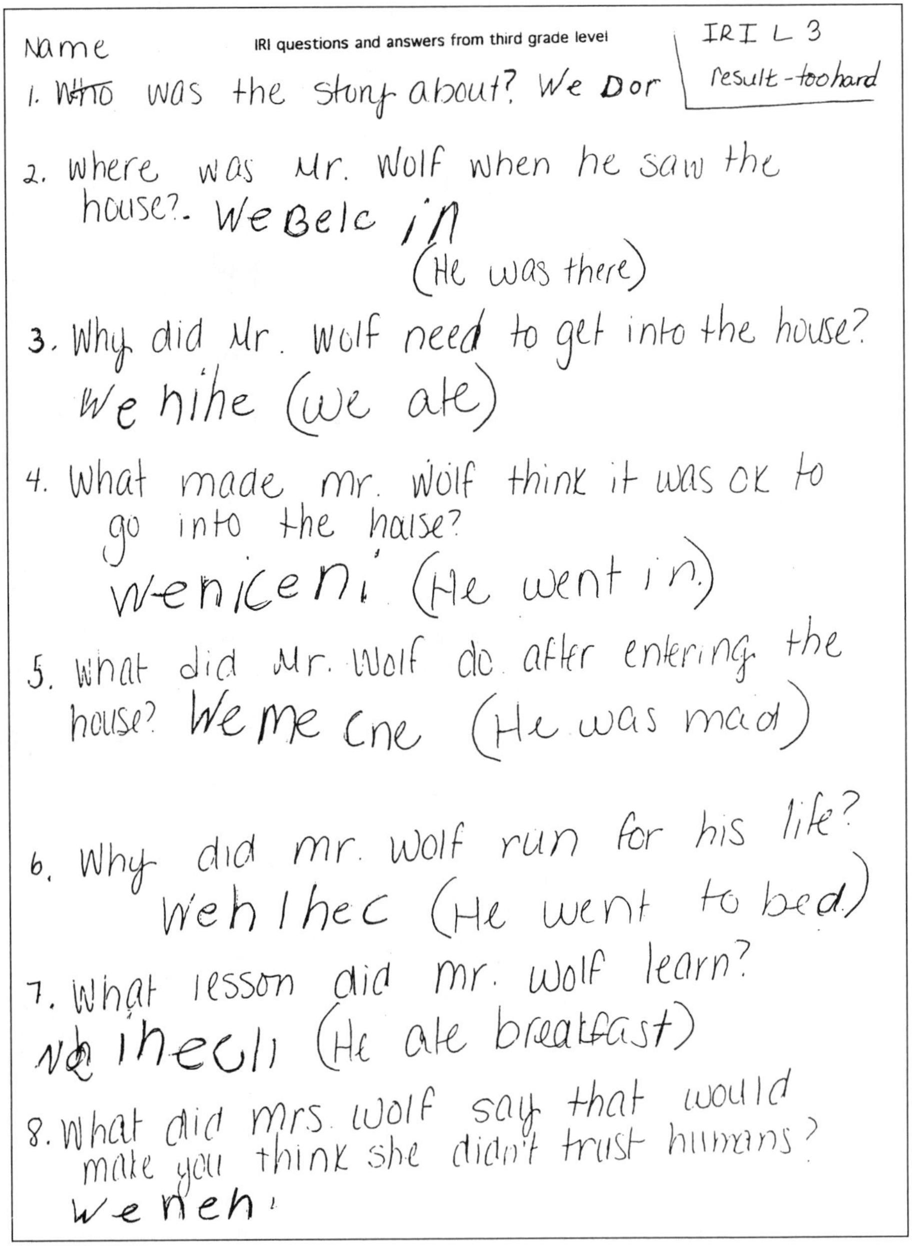

Name ____ IRI questions and answers from third grade level   IRI L 3
result—too hard

1. Who was the story about? We Dor

2. Where was Mr. Wolf when he saw the house?. We Belc in
(He was there)

3. Why did Mr. wolf need to get into the house? We hihe (We ate)

4. What made Mr. Wolf think it was ok to go into the house?
weniceni (He went in.)

5. what did Mr. Wolf do after entering the house? We Me cne (He was mad)

6. Why did mr. wolf run for his life? weh Ihec (He went to bed.)

7. What lesson did mr. wolf learn?
No ineoli (He ate breakfast)

8. What did mrs. wolf say that would make you think she didn't trust humans?
we neh.

framework for the portfolio as the student collects samples and reflects on his or her academic work in general and the portfolio in particular to determine his or her success in meeting the established goals. This process is not easy. It often takes time for students to learn to reflect on their work and note how it documents their success at achieving a goal.

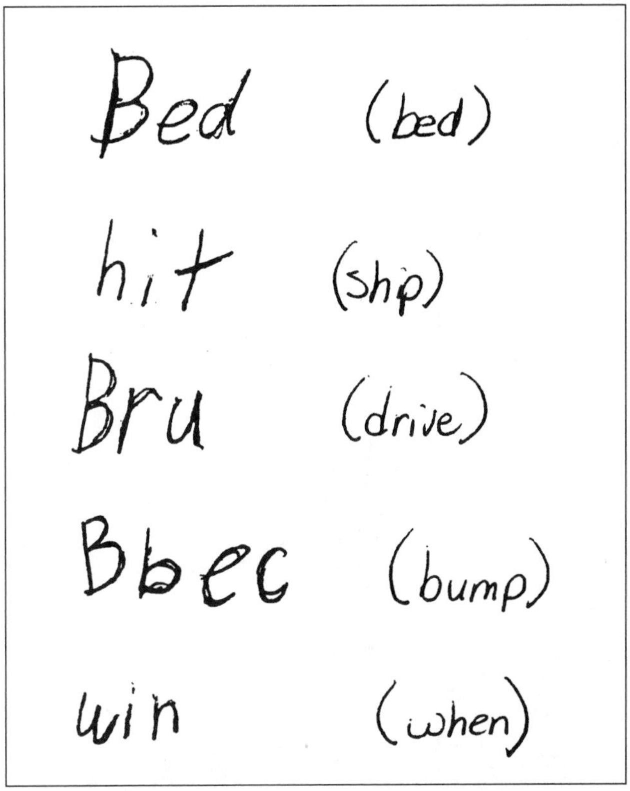

Bed   (bed)

hit   (ship)

Bru   (drive)

Bbec   (bump)

win   (when)

**Figure 5.8
Spelling-by-Stage
Inventory**

Teacher Evaluations

Teacher evaluations should also be grounded in the student's, parents', and teacher's goals for students. As anecdotal notes and samples of student work are collected and added to the student's portfolio, you can compare these samples to the predetermined goals and reflect on the student's success in achieving these goals. As you have guessed, this process is based on individual student goals, strengths, and needs.

You may be thinking, "But what about grades?" Well, we very much believe in teaching students so that they are successful, which means that students will not always experience grade-level curricula and sometimes they will work beyond grade-level expectations. How, then, is it possible to grade students on grade-level curricular expectations? One method is to test students on grade-level curriculum only when they can succeed. With this approach, testing is never a whole-class endeavor. A second method is to provide a rubric to your students before you grade a major assignment. For example, if you expect your students to be able to write a fairy tale after exploring fairy tales in reading, you and your students would list the criteria that detail how the assignment will be graded. For the fairy tale, the students would identify several good and bad characters, a

Figure 5.9
Brainstorm About a Pig
Story

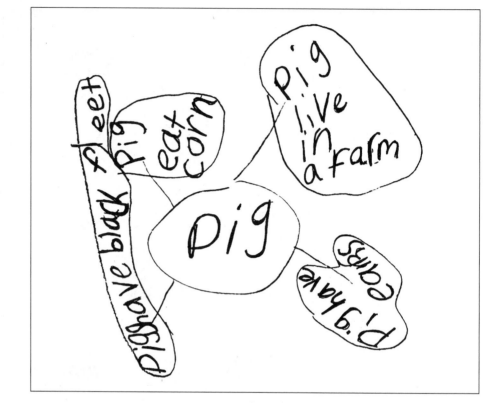

series based on three, a problem to be resolved, and so on. You also can establish the assignment format so that students know they are to use paragraphs, correct spelling, good grammar, and such. Then there are no surprises: students know exactly how an assignment will be graded before they turn in their work. Be willing to open up conversations about grading in your school and to encourage open discussion of the dilemmas relating to grading and supporting students as individuals.

Teachers also need to keep a personal log that reflects on the act of teaching. By taking a few moments to jot down when a lesson went particularly well or poorly, a teacher can assess what contributed to its success or failure and take that valuable insight into planning future activities.

Other Means of Evaluation

In addition to the already described informal assessment, teachers use other means to evaluate students. Teacher-created tests, for example, help determine if students understand a concept or skill that has been taught. These test grades are often used to generate grades for report cards.

Formal standardized tests are often administered to students not only to evaluate individual performance but to let parents and other interested parties

Figure 5.10
Final Draft Without Illustrations

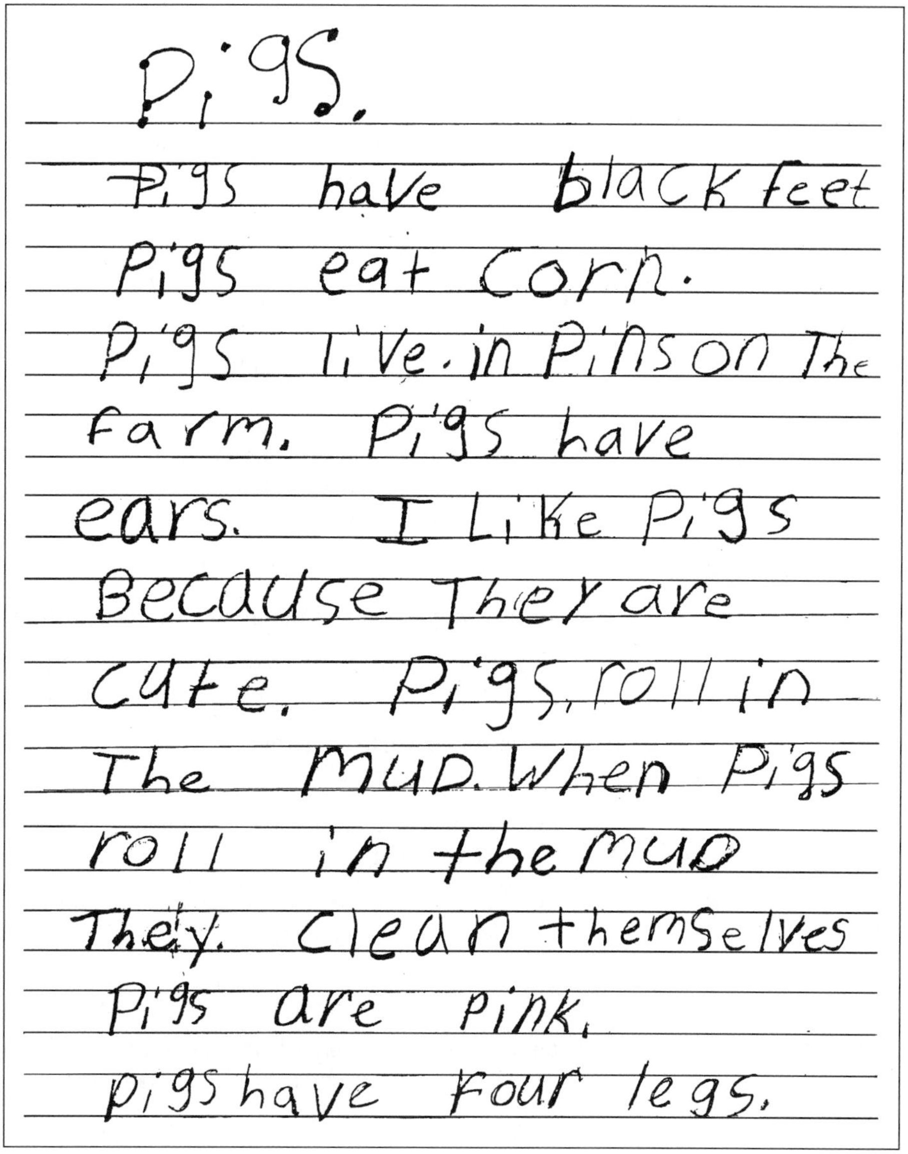

Pigs.

Pigs have black feet
Pigs eat corn.
Pigs live in pins on the
farm. Pigs have
ears. I like pigs
because they are
cute. Pigs, roll in
the mud. When pigs
roll in the mud
they. clean themselves
Pigs are pink,
pigs have four legs.

know how a school district is doing in relation to other schools in the state or in the nation. Chapter 12 discusses formal testing in depth.

Planning for Instruction

After the assessment process is complete, the important question you face is how you will use this information to provide instructional support for each of your students. This is both the most difficult and most exciting part of teaching.

Sometimes whole-class instruction is the most beneficial. Other times, you will want to group students in general or specific small groups. Students sometimes need to work with a partner or alone. The following chapters consider instructional strategies for children all along the literacy continuum. In each of these chapters, we explore instructional situations and strategies that support students at their level of literacy development.

Conclusion and Study Notes

This chapter has focused on ways to adapt assessment to a classroom of students. The chapter began by exploring ways of inviting parents to help broaden a teacher's knowledge of students through letters and autobiographies. It then moved into the classroom to consider strategies for informally assessing students' literacy strengths in whole-class and small-group settings. The chapter concluded with an examination of the evaluation and instruction components of the assessment process, including literacy biographies and portfolios.

In this chapter we have considered the following main points:

- Adapting individual assessment strategies for use in classroom settings,

- Involving parents in the integrated assessment and instruction process,

- Implementing strategies to understand students' literacy strengths, including the GLTA, ten-minute writes, and spelling-by-stage assessment,

- Observing students during routine instruction to gain relevant information about their literacy development,

- Using the Goldilocks Plan, which helps children select books at appropriate reading levels, and

- Creating teacher-centered and student-centered portfolios as documentation of students' literacy growth.

Key Terms

Consider each of the terms below and try to think of examples for each term. You may want to talk to other students in your class as you work through the list.

guided reading-thinking activity	aesthetic reading
ten-minute write	literacy biography
interest inventory	portfolio
efferent reading	

Follow-Up Activities

1. Visit a teacher at the beginning of the year and work with this teacher on informal literacy assessment. Talk to the teacher about what he or she considers important to know about students. Ask the teacher how this information is used.

2. If you have never created a portfolio, start one. Create a portfolio about you. How would you show someone what is important to know about you? Now create a section that shows your interests in teaching. Think about what you included and why.

3. Talk to a student about what this student wants to learn in school. Notice if the student has established goals or never thought about them before. Ask about this student's reading and writing histories. What did you learn by talking to this student?

4. If you have never had a chance to write or draw about a story you have read, find a favorite book and explore this type of response. You may be surprised at what you choose to write or draw about.

PART THREE

Classroom Instruction Integrated with Assessment

Contents

6   Emergent Literacy

7   Beginning Literacy

8   Diversity in Literacy Learning

9   Transitional Literacy

10 Intermediate and Advanced Literacy Development

6

Emergent Literacy

Denise: I don't remember learning how to read. I don't remember being taught. I just know that when I went to kindergarten, I knew how to read. My mom read to me a lot, but I don't remember actually having instruction.

Amanda: I remember it being important to do it fast. If I could read fast, then I was a good reader.

Britta: I remember sitting in rows, and the person in front of me would read a paragraph and then I would read a paragraph. It was embarrassing. I hated it.

Keith: We had to read until we made a mistake. If you made a mistake right away, you sat down.

Susan: I remember the *Dick and Jane* reading series.

John: You remember being read to when you were young, but did you do any writing before school?

Sherry: I remember I had papers. I was always scribbling or doodling.

Marie: I remember that when I was really young, I turned my room into a haunted house for Halloween. I remember sitting at my desk trying to figure out how to spell *blood*. I knew it wasn't *BLUD* because I could picture the word in my head. But I couldn't remember what letters made that *oo* sound.

John: What do you think kids coming into first grade will be like?

Sherry: You're going to have every kind of kid. Some people, like my sister-in-law, start reading to the baby when it's in the womb. Other people don't read a word to their kids. Some kids don't even go to kindergarten. Some children come into first grade never having held a book. That's why your first job will be to assess where they are and what experiences they've had. You'll need to give everyone as much experience as you can by modeling and reading to them. Have them look at picture books and magazines.

Britta: There are lots of books out there. Pattern books like *Brown Bear,* let them learn a couple of sight words, follow along, and feel what it's like to read. You model reading for them, and they start to get it.

Keith: I saw something interesting in a primary classroom. One of the kids read from her journal. She made words with combinations of letters that I've never seen before, and yet she knew exactly what it said. She read right along without a mistake.

Nancy: I find that emergent readers who are least resistant to working with me are from classrooms with a lot of print all over the place and a teacher who always reads to them.

Amanda: I think that's major. If people around you read, then you're going to learn to read.

The students in the above dialogue were discussing literacy teaching and learning for emergent readers and writers. Their reflections might recall experiences you had when you first learned to read and write. Then they began to discuss the diversity of experiences their future students will have and how this diversity will influence their instruction. They recognized the importance of reading to children as a way of fostering literacy development. They considered which materials might be appropriate for emergent readers and writers, and some suggested finding plenty of books that are written in patterns. Interwoven throughout their conversation was the importance of parents to the process of learning to read and write.

As we move into our examination of emergent readers and writers, take a few moments to jot down how you learned to read and write. The greatest recent changes in literacy instruction have occurred at this phase of development, so our discussion in this chapter may vary considerably from your personal early reading and writing experiences. And yet, as teachers, we often revert to what was done to us in moments of stress (Clandinin & Connelly, 1986). As we discuss strategies for emergent readers and writers, compare these strategies to those that were used when you were an emergent reader and writer.

Guide Questions for Chapter 6

- Describe the literacy knowledge of a child who is considered an emergent reader and writer.

- How can a teacher effectively assess a child's knowledge of books and reading?

- How can a teacher effectively assess a child's knowledge of print?

- What strategies can a teacher employ to build a child's literacy knowledge?

- How can a teacher tailor a portfolio to reflect the growth and needs of a child who is an emergent reader and writer?

Who Are Emergent Readers and Writers?

Children as young as newborns are considered **emergent readers and writers.** Literacy learning, research has determined, begins at birth or before (Clay, 1991). This idea that children acquire literacy at such a young age is new to many people. It was long believed that literacy learning did not begin until children entered school. But, in fact, children go through a long and gradual process of acquiring literacy that begins at home and continues at school (Teale & Sulzby, 1986). Based on this new view of literacy, the curriculum provided to preschool and kindergarten youngsters has changed so that, instead of assuming that children enter school naive about reading and writing, teachers build on the literacy knowledge children have gained in their home environments (Clay, 1991).

Table 6.1 summarizes some of the literacy behaviors you might observe among emergent readers and writers. Keep them in mind as we further discuss emergent readers and writers.

Table 6.1
Overview of Emergent Literacy Behaviors

Reading

- The child cannot yet easily memorize a short poem.

- The child focuses on the illustrations when engaged in reading.

- The child often loses his or her place when tracking print.

Spelling and Orthographic Knowledge

- The child mixes scribbles, letters, and numerals when writing.

- The child does not yet understand the correspondence between letters and their sounds.

- The child can recognize environmental print in its context.

Writing

- The child uses drawings to express ideas.

- The child is not yet consistently able to read his or her writing.

- The child usually uses illustrations to retell a story.

You may be surprised that these behaviors are even considered part of literacy development. When you were young, your parents and teachers may have dismissed these behaviors because they were not considered conventional or did not resemble adult reading or writing. They may have thrown away your early scribblings and saved only your first successful attempt to write your name. Today, those early behaviors are considered part of the progress toward conventional literacy. These efforts are viewed as evidence of what children can do and not as failed attempts.

In response to this new view of children's literacy development, several professional educational organizations have developed new teaching and learning rationales. These rationales provide the framework for many preschool and kindergarten programs. The following rationale was developed by the International Reading Association (IRA) (1985). IRA's rationale encompasses childhood literacy, parent responsibility, and classroom instruction:

1. Literacy begins in infancy.

2. Parents need to provide a rich literacy environment to help children acquire literacy skills.

3. School personnel need to be aware that children come to school with prior knowledge of oral and written language.

4. Early reading and writing experiences at school should build upon that existing knowledge.

5. Learning requires a supportive environment that builds positive feelings about self as well as about literacy activities.

6. Adults need to serve as models of literacy behavior by demonstrating an interest in books and print.

7. During literacy experiences, children need to interact within a social context so that they can share information and learn from each other.

8. Early literacy experiences should be meaningful and concrete and should actively involve the child.

9. A literacy development program should focus on holistic approaches, utilizing functional experience that include the use of language, listening, writing, and reading.

10. Differences in cultural and language backgrounds need to be acknowledged and addressed.

Much of this chapter's discussion is based on the points highlighted in the International Reading Association's rationale.

■ *Early Literacy Knowledge*

Knowledge of Language

> Language is a complex, specialized skill, which develops in the child spontaneously without conscious effort or formal instruction, is deployed without awareness of its underlying logic, is qualitatively the same in every individual, and is distinct from more general abilities to process information or behave intelligently (Pinker, 1994, p. 18).

Most children easily acquire language as they interact with their parents or other significant persons, as when parents reward a child's earliest cooing with a smile. However, even in communities where adults do not routinely talk to children until they are able to converse with adults, children acquire language (Heath, 1983). It is the children who are busy learning the language of their parents (Pinker, 1994).

Young children create language just for the pleasure of hearing it. This type of language is known as **noncommunicative speech** (Stone & Church, 1984). Noncommunicative speech can take three forms: *repetition, monologue,* and *dual* or *collective monologue.* In repetition, the child repeats words or phrases. At about seven or eight months of age, babies start babbling real syllables such as *ba-ba* (Pinker, 1994). This behavior continues as children mature. You may hear a young child repeating a phrase from a poem over and over. For example, a child may sit holding a doll and repeating, "Rock-a-bye baby." Monologues are repeated sounds or phrases that resemble a one-person conversation. In classrooms, you might notice a child engaged in a monologue while painting or writing. Often, a child will carry out a full conversation with no particular audience in mind. Finally, a dual or collective monologue occurs when more than one child is playing in the same area and each child carries out a monologue with no expectation that the other child will respond.

Not all children's language is noncommunicative. The greater portion of children's language is focused on **communicative speech.** Near a baby's first birthday, the child begins to communicate using single words. These single words are most often labels for familiar objects—*eyes, nose, bottle, mama, dada*— or they represent routines or actions—*bye, hi, look* (Pinker, 1994).

At about eighteen months, language growth explodes. Children begin to amass a vocabulary at the rate of a new word almost every two hours (Morrow, 1993). They also begin to discover the syntactical order of our language—that phrases of two or more words have a proper order. For example, a child will say, "See baby," not "Baby see." A child of three can usually produce fluent conversation that is grammatically correct. During this time, you may hear a child create some interesting, logical speech errors. A child may use *goed* for the past tense of *go* or *tooths* for the plural of *tooth.* Pinker (1994, p. 276) describes the three-year-old as "a grammatical genius-master of most constructions, obeying the rules far more often than flouting them, respecting language universals, erring in sensible, adultlike ways, and avoiding many kinds of errors altogether." This development continues, and by the time children are seven or eight years old, they have developed a grammar similar to an adult's and they understand more than three thousand words (Morrow, 1993).

Children arrive at school capable of using oral language to communicate. In school this knowledge must expand in three distinct ways. First, the child must learn to communicate with different speakers in an unfamiliar environment. Each child learns to be more flexible in language use as he or she attempts to communicate with teachers, other parents, and fellow students. This adjustment requires little effort where there is a close match between the home language and school language. But imagine a child who enters preschool with a dialect quite different from that of the teacher and the effort each must make to understand the other. Second, the child's home language is refined and extended within the school setting. A child discovers new meanings for familiar words and extends his or her vocabulary with new words. Third, the child becomes more familiar with the language used in books and aware of the differences between oral language and book language (Clay, 1991).

Knowledge of Books and Reading

Young children learn both about the pleasure of reading and about the content of stories as parents, older siblings, or other caretakers read to them. First books are quite simple in format. Often these books, mostly known as concept books, consist of a few cardboard or fabric pages. Infants tend to chew on their earliest books, so publishers usually create them in a resilient format. Books such as *What Do Babies Do?* (Slier, 1985) allow parents to engage very young children in a discussion about routine events in the day of a baby. Other favorite books that parents frequently read to young children may be familiar to you, such as *The Three Little Kittens* (Cauley, 1982), *The Real Mother Goose* (Wright, 1916), or *Goodnight Moon* (Brown, 1947).

As young children read at home or in preschool, they begin to identify objects in illustrations, talk about characters and events, become comfortable with book language, and become familiar with how books are organized. Children enjoy pointing to objects in pictures and asking, "What's that?" Parents then enter the game and name the object. In this way, children expand their knowledge of the world. For example, when a young child named Michael listened to *Eating the Alphabet* (Ehlert, 1989), he went through the book systematically asking the name of each fruit or vegetable represented. Then, he sorted them into yummy or yucky foods based on his previous eating experiences.

Children enjoy talking about the characters and events within books. These discussions help children understand that books or stories convey meaning. McGee and Richgels (1990) recall Kristen, who commented that the picture of the old rabbit in *Goodnight Moon* looked "just like Mommy" (p. 127). Children who talk about the characters in books and try to decide if they are good or bad are attempting to make personal connections to the stories and characters as they gain meaning.

Emergent readers and writers explore a story together.

As parents lead children into storybooks, common word elements in stories become familiar. Children learn about "once upon a time" and "lived happily ever after." They become enamored with some of the unusual words or phrases in books. One young child threatened to send everyone he knew to Australia after hearing *Alexander and the Terrible, Horrible, No Good, Very Bad Day* (Viorst, 1972). Other children repeat novel words that they hear in books, such as *impossible* or *sensational,* just for the pleasure of saying and hearing them.

Children also learn about the way books are organized. They discover where books begin and end. They learn about pages and how to turn them. They realize that pages have illustrations and words, although they may not be able to point to a word (Snow & Ninio, 1986). They understand the routines that go with reading. For instance, when reading is going to begin, they quickly get into a comfortable spot. Then someone reads, and during pauses discussion occurs. This pattern repeats to the end of the story.

Children who have frequently been read to enter school with a repertoire of knowledge about books. This knowledge serves them well as they develop in literacy. Children who have had few experiences with book reading must acquire this fundamental knowledge of books before they can move into more complex understandings of literacy.

····· **TAKING A** ·····
CLOSER LOOK   **Excursions**

Children come to school with variable literacy experiences in their homes. But even children who have few book-reading experiences with their parents or caregivers encounter home literacy activities. Anderson and Stokes (1984) described families in which major literacy experiences for young children involved watching parents read magazines or mail. Pelligrini, Perlmutter, Galda, and Brophy (1990) observed children being read cartoons or advertisements as their primary home literacy experiences. Finally, Purcell-Gates (1996) noted that low-income families primarily engaged in reading for entertainment (reading television guides or magazines) or for daily living routines such as cleaning or shopping.

An important point is that some of these routines directly support literacy instruction in school and others do not. Children who have experienced thousands of hours of book reading at home are certainly ready to participate in book reading experiences in school. Those who have not will need to become familiar with books in school.

As a teacher, especially a preschool or kindergarten teacher, your awareness of your young students' different literacy experiences will be important to their academic futures. Unfortunately, many low-income children get placed in low-ability reading groups. In these groups, children frequently experience low-level reading tasks that focus on decoding or literal comprehension (Allington, 1983; Cazden, 1986; Hiebert, 1983). You may choose more success-oriented learning strategies such as placing reading and writing in familiar contexts (valuing home literacy events in the classroom) (Heath, 1983), using flexible groups for instruction (Hart, 1982), and using scaffolded instruction through peer and cross-age tutoring (Greenfield, 1984).

Knowledge of Print

Children have early encounters with print in their home and community as parents talk about the places that children are visiting. Often these places are connected with a familiar logo for a supermarket, fast-food chain, or a gas station. Although children may see a specific logo, such as Exxon, they may just call it the gas place. Masonheimer, Drum, and Ehri (1984) discovered that young children recognize the appearance of the logo or its context, not the words in it. So, a child who is shown the Pepsi logo, even with the word *Pepsi* distorted, would still call it *Pepsi* or *soda*. Eventually, children acquire knowledge of letters and their corresponding sounds and then begin to distinguish both the context and the words associated with an object. Even though children are reading the context of a sign, not its words, parents take special pride in hearing their young child "read" a word such as *STOP* upon seeing a stop sign.

Children who use books soon learn that words differ from illustrations. Following from this knowledge, they discover that print has **directionality** (Clay, 1975). As parents write, or as they point while reading English, for example, children notice that the text tracks from left to right. They also begin to learn about other aspects of print. For example, as parents read, alphabet books in particular, and as children experiment with writing their name, children discover that letters are important, too.

If, in addition to books, children have access to paper and pencils, they begin to experiment with print. At first they use illustrations or scribbles to represent what they want to say. At about age three, children begin to distinguish drawing and writing (Harste, Woodward, & Burke, 1984). As experience accumulates, they begin to include letters and letter-like characters with their illustrations. In Figure 6.1, a preschool child drew two trees and a vehicle. At the bottom of the sheet he included letters, written from left to right. The eyes within some of the letters were in imitation of the smiling faces his teacher drew in some of the words that she wrote to her students. His sample shows how he has recognized that illustrations can be accompanied by words and that they are different.

As children continue to experiment with writing, they learn about two important principles described by Clay (1975)—the **recurring** principle and the **generativity** principle. In the recurring principle, children learn that a limited amount of letters appear again and again. In Figure 6.2, Joey has learned that repeating the same letters results in different words. Joey has decided that *o, e,* and *y* (letters from his name) can be repeated to form a variety of words. His understanding of combining and recombining the letters to generate many new words represents the generativity principle.

As you look at his writing, you will notice that Joey has discovered that printed words have spaces on either side of them. He has begun to discover knowledge about the **concept of word in print.** The concept of word in print is defined as the match between oral and written language, and the knowledge that words are recorded with spaces between them (Morris, 1980).

When children enter preschools or kindergartens, they bring considerable literacy knowledge with them. Teachers are now encouraged to build upon this knowledge as they move children to conventional reading and writing. The next section of the chapter deals with informally assessing the literacy knowledge that children bring from home.

Informal Assessment of Emergent Literacy Knowledge

Today, most preschool and kindergarten teachers encourage children to engage in reading and writing activities. Teachers and parents know that young children will produce approximations of what we consider conventional reading and writing behaviors. When you walk into one of these classrooms, you may see children writing down a food order in a play restaurant, reading a book to a friend, or writing in a journal. These children are learning about literacy as they perform *authentic literacy activities*—activities that are grounded in real reading and writing.

Figure 6.1
A Preschooler's Writing

In contrast, in past years young children spent much time in learning to correctly write their names and the letters of the alphabet. Teachers read to children but did not encourage children to use books. Children were getting ready for real reading and writing, which would begin in first grade. One holdover from these skill-oriented classrooms that you may still see in many kindergartens is the letter-of-the-week instruction. Teachers who use this as their sole curriculum have organized their instruction around an alphabet letter and its sound. They still see

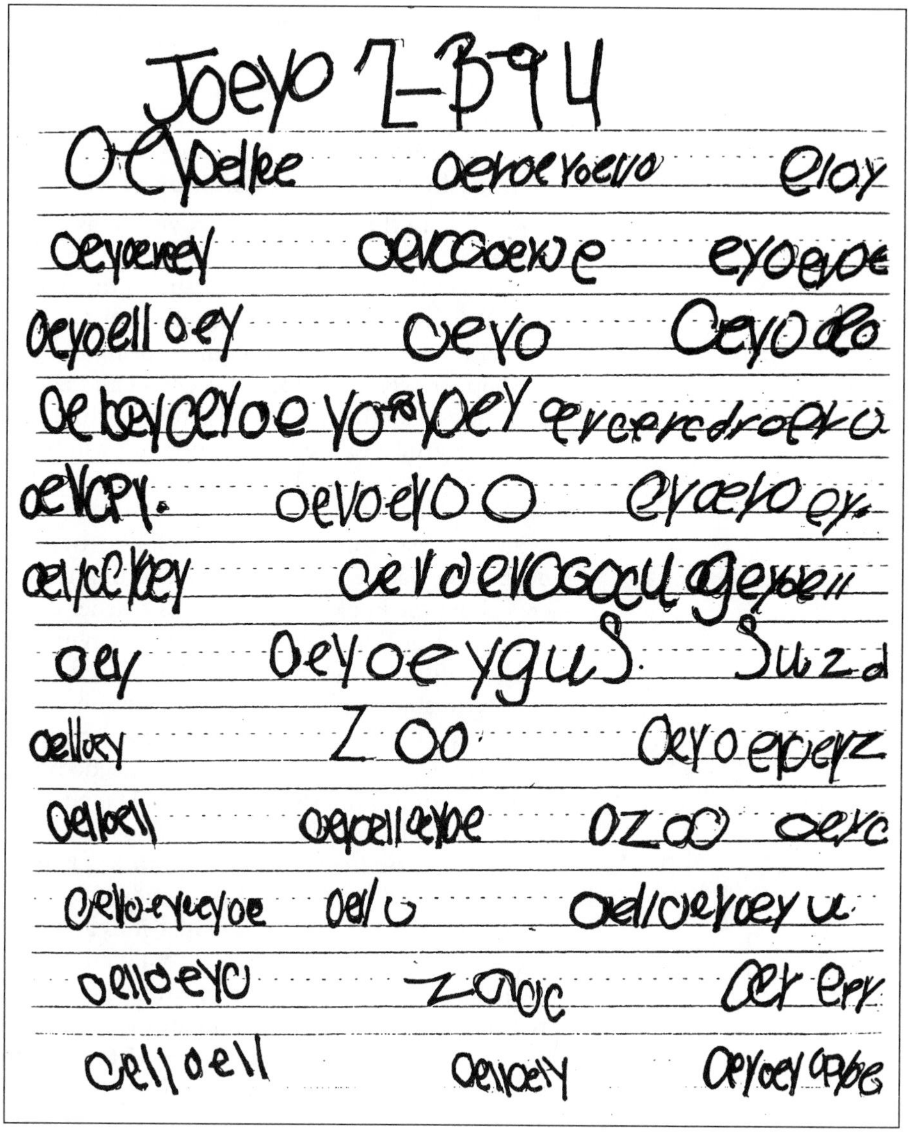

Figure 6.2
Writing That Shows the
Generativity Principle

early reading instruction as grounded in specific skills that eventually lead to reading and writing. Although we certainly consider individual skills during the assessment process, these skills are documented as children engage in authentic reading and writing activities that reflect our current understandings of the development of literacy.

Preschool and kindergarten teachers can gather most of their assessment information by observing children in routine instructional activities. We will highlight some of the observations that you may want to make to discover individual students' literacy development. Some of the observations work best one-on-one.

Book Knowledge

Assessing Children's Familiarity with Stories

Reading to the class is a quick way to assess which students have had previous experiences with books. Children who have had many encounters with books usually are eager to participate in these activities. They tend to make predictions and offer insights about the story. Children who have had fewer experiences with books may remain quiet during these activities, move to the fringe of the group, or even leave the group. If a child consistently leaves the group as you are reading, take the time to read to this child in a one-on-one situation. By reducing the group to the two of you, you will be able to learn if the child enjoys stories but is put off by the group size or if the child just is not familiar with storybook reading.

Such assessments call for common sense. In one classroom, a child always moved to the back of the group, seemed uninterested, and never offered any comments about the book being read. His teacher discovered by talking to his parents that he was learning English as a second language. He was able to converse quite well in English, but he was unfamiliar with stories. His parents used his primary language to share more factual information with him. When the teacher read a story to him, one-on-one, in his primary language, he readily commented about the story. This teacher learned that he needed time to become comfortable with stories written in English. She provided taped stories written in his first language to serve as a bridge to his understanding of stories written in English.

This scenario highlights one of our key beliefs about assessment: *observe the child in a variety of situations before making decisions about a child's literacy knowledge.* Remember to look at the similarities and differences across observations as you form interpretations about a child's development. In observing a child's knowledge of books, you are also finding out about print knowledge. The same is true for other informal assessments. Compare what you see to the overview of emergent literacy behaviors in Table 6.1 to note similarities and differences from this benchmark list.

Assessing Knowledge of Book Structure

Clay (1972) developed an assessment, *Concepts about Print Test,* that deals with many aspects of books. Specifically, this test assesses children's knowledge of the following concepts of books:

1. Book orientation,

2. Differences between illustrations and print,

3. Directionality of print,

4. Book terminology such as word, letter, top or bottom of page, and

5. Beginning and end.

Assessing print knowledge works best in a one-on-one situation. To begin this assessment, select a simple, short **predictable text** (about eight pages). Many of the books for young readers published by the Wright Group are perfect for this evaluation. Clay has developed special books for this assessment (*Sand* and *Stones*), but others work just as well. Many teachers have found that a child appreciates hearing the story before you begin the assessment procedure. Figure 6.3 provides a checklist to record the observations that you make. Here is the assessment procedure and the concepts it studies:

- *Book orientation.* Give the child the book. Have the child point out the front and back of the book. Have the child point out the title of the book. If the child can point to the title, ask, "What is its purpose?"

- *Differences between illustrations and print.* Open the book to the first page. Ask the child to point to the illustrations and then to the print. Following this, ask the child to point to where you should begin reading.

- *Directionality of print.* Ask the child to point to the first line of text. After the child has pointed to this line, ask where you should read next. The child should show the sweep that is made as you read, starting at the left, through the line, and then to the beginning of the next line.

- *Beginning and end.* Ask the child to point to the beginning and end of the book. If the child is able to point to the beginning and end of the book, ask the child to point to the beginning and end of the story on a page of text.

- *Book terminology such as word, letter, and top or bottom of page.* Ask the child to point to the top and bottom of a page. Ask the child to point to a word. If the child can point to a word, ask the child to point to a word that you identify. For example, "Point to the word that says *brown.*" If the child points to a word, ask the child to point to a letter. Then ask the child to point to a specific letter. You might want to discover at this point if the child is aware of upper- and lowercase letters. After you have finished looking at words and letters, ask the child to identify end punctuation.

Assessing Facility with Reading and Sense of Story Structure

You can assess children's reading abilities and sense of story structure by observing them as they interact with and respond to books in the classroom or in a one-on-one story session. In a one-on-one setting, select a simple, predictable story, similar to the one you used to assess knowledge of books. Tell the child that first you are going to read the story and then you'll listen as the child reads the story to you. If the child is worried about not knowing how to read yet, offer to help if needed. Read the story to the child. You might even want to talk about it a bit when you are done, but this talking should be spontaneous and friendly, not a series of comprehension questions. When this process is complete, ask the child to read the story to you. Here, you need to listen carefully. You may even want to tape record the child's "reading." When the child has finished, analyze what you have observed to discover what strategy the child used. Sulzby (1985) described the progression of emergent story reading from least sophisticated to most sophisticated:

Figure 6.3
Concept of Book
Assessments

Name _____ Date _____

CONCEPT OF BOOK ASSESSMENT

Book Orientation Knowledge

_____ Able to point to front of the book

_____ Able to point to back of the book

_____ Able to point to title

_____ Able to identify the purpose of a title

Differences Between Illustrations and Print

_____ Able to point to illustrations

_____ Able to point to print

_____ Able to point to place where reading should begin

Directionality of Print

_____ Able to show the directionality of print on a page

Knowledge of Beginning and End

_____ Able to point to the beginning of the story

_____ Able to point to the end of the story

_____ Able to point to the beginning of the story on a page

_____ Able to point to the end of the story on a page

Understanding of Book Terminology, Such as Word, Letter, Top or Bottom of Page

_____ Able to identify the top and bottom of a page

_____ Able to point to a word

_____ Able to point to a specific word that has been identified

_____ Able to point to a letter

_____ Able to point to a specific letter that has been identified

_____ Able to point to a lowercase letter

_____ Able to point to an uppercase letter

_____ Able to identify a period

_____ Able to identify an exclamation mark

_____ Able to identify a question mark

1. *Attending to pictures, not forming a story.* The child "reads" by identifying the illustrations on each page. There is no story connection from one page to another.

2. *Attending to pictures, forming an oral story.* The child connects the story from one illustration to another. The child recounts an oral story, and the story sounds like a conversation.

3. *Attending to pictures, forming an oral and book-language story.* The child connects the story from one illustration to another. The child recounts the story using oral or storytelling language and some book language. For instance, the child will tell the story with a storyteller's cadence and then shift to a rhythm in keeping with book reading.

4. *Attending to pictures, forming a book language story.* The child's speech and intonation sound as though the child is reading in a conventional sense. The listener does not need to see the illustrations to make sense of the reading.

5. *Attending to print.* The child's attention moves away from the illustrations to the text and conventional reading begins. Four patterns may be observed here:

    a. *refusal:* refuses to read because, "I don't know how to read,"

    b. *aspectual:* reads text that is known and pretends on the rest,

    c. *holistic:* emphasizes getting the words right, with little focus on the meaning of the story,

    d. *independent:* has the ability to read the words in the text.

After this process is complete and you have discovered how a child approaches a text, you may want to ask the child to retell, not recite, the story with the book closed. During this process, find out if a child is able to recall the beginning, middle, and end of a story. This remembering is easier for children who have listened to many stories. They tacitly know the structure of stories and remember key parts or events. Retellings are discussed in detail in Chapter 5.

Knowledge of Print

The easiest way to discover what children know about print is to ask them to write. Many teachers, even teachers working with preschoolers, ask their students to write each day in a journal or at a writing center. From these writings, you can discover if a child feels comfortable with the idea of writing. Some children refuse to write at first because they want it to be right or they just haven't had any experience with writing. Other children begin writing as soon as they receive the materials. Make note if a child is scribbling to represent writing or is using letters or even words.

As you consider the following samples of children's writing from preschool classrooms, think about the way each child is representing ideas. In Figure 6.4, a child chose to draw an apple to represent writing. Although the child cannot

Figure 6.4
Journal Writing in a
Preschool Classroom

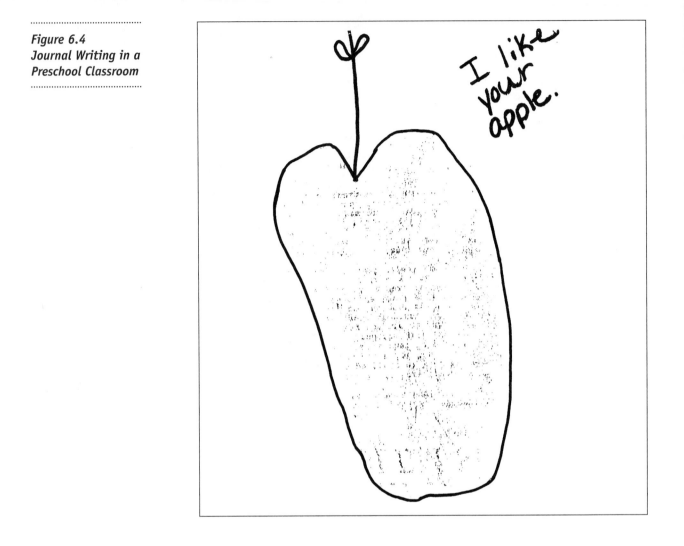

conventionally read or write yet, the teacher has modeled communication through writing by writing back, "I like your apple." In Figure 6.5, Drew decided to write his name. Drew used interesting shapes to represent the letters in his name. His teacher, too, responded in writing: "Look at your name!" This teacher supported his attempts to learn to write his name and did not focus on how his effort failed to match a conventional representation of his name. Drew will most likely continue this practice, especially because his teacher conveyed her pleasure at his efforts.

In Figure 6.6, a preschool child has included a single letter to accompany or explain his happy face drawing. In Figure 6.7, John has decided to write his name and a few other words. Notice that John wrote his name conventionally. He has his name writing all figured out. Although his name is correct, however,

Figure 6.5
Preschooler's Attempt at
Writing His Name

his words are composed of random letters. He sometimes begins on the left and writes to the right. When his letters appear backwards, he has written from the right to the left. Teachers and parents sometimes worry that writing similar to John's indicates that a child is dyslexic and will have serious difficulty learning to read and write. For most children, this is not the case; John just has not yet mastered left-to-right directionality and the form of letters. As he matures in his literacy understandings, he will become more conventional in their use.

Another way to investigate knowledge of print is to observe how children write at a writing center or in a dramatic play center. This type of observation is less formal than that described above. Many teachers provide a variety of writing materials in both locations. Children may use memo writing as they pretend to take a message over the phone or use lists to remember the orders of their play restaurant guests (Rybczynski & Troy, 1995). Teachers who allow

Figure 6.6
Preschooler's Use of
a Single Letter for
Writing

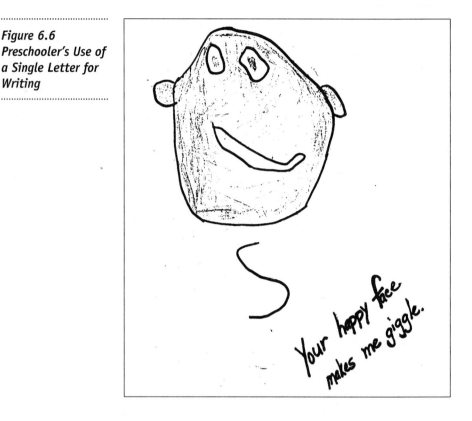

for this type of writing note that children quickly become aware of the power of labels. They notice the labels around the classroom, and they want labels placed on areas of the room that they want left alone. Children will solicit the help of a teacher to write a label or sign that warns other children to leave their block creations alone.

A benchmark in children's writing is the ability to spell their name with conventional writing. This is a truly important moment to the child and parents. Children begin to get interested in letters when they can write their name (Barone, 1994). At first, they are surprised that another person's name might have the same first letter as their name. Following this discovery, they begin to explore the letters in books in general and in alphabet books in particular. Now the structure of an alphabet book begins to make sense to these young children.

You can observe this development of name writing through the signatures that your students affix to their work. Some teachers expect children to sign into the classroom each day, and this signing in provides another opportunity to observe children's name writing ability and development (McGee & Richgels, 1996).

The form in Figure 6.8 provides a way to record the writing development of children as they learn about print, but you may want to revise it so that it better fits your needs.

Figure 6.7
John's Writing Showing
Left-to-Right and Right-
to-Left Orientation

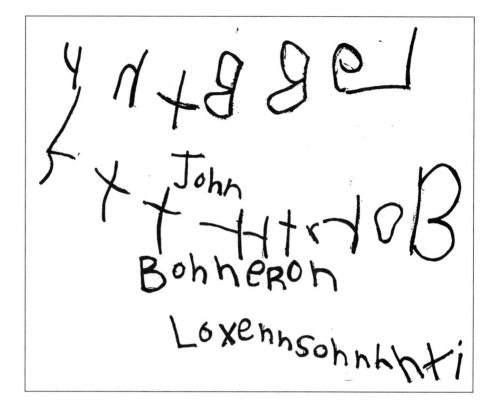

Knowledge of Concept of Word in Print

Most preschool and kindergarten children still lack knowledge of a concept of word in print—the connection between a spoken word and the word in print, and the knowledge that words are separated by spaces. Still, it is important for you to know if any of your students do have an understanding of the concept of word in print. These children possess more sophisticated knowledge of reading, writing, and the orthographic representation of words. In fact, they are considered beginning readers and writers, not emergent readers and writers.

To assess the concept of word in print (Morris, 1980, 1993), teach the children in your class a short poem or nursery rhyme. Nursery rhymes work very well. You will want the poem to have at least one two-syllable word. A familiar nursery rhyme such as "One, two, buckle my shoe" works quite well. Teach the children at least the first two lines of this rhyme orally until they have no difficulty saying it. When the children in your classroom have mastered this poem, plan to meet with each child separately. Prepare multiple copies of the poem so that you are able to record the reading behaviors of each child, similar to the markings you did on a running record.

As you sit next to the child, ask the child to say the first two lines of the poem to you. Once the child has repeated these lines, write the poem for the child. When writing the poem, say each word as you record it:

Figure 6.8
Writing Development-
Knowledge of Print

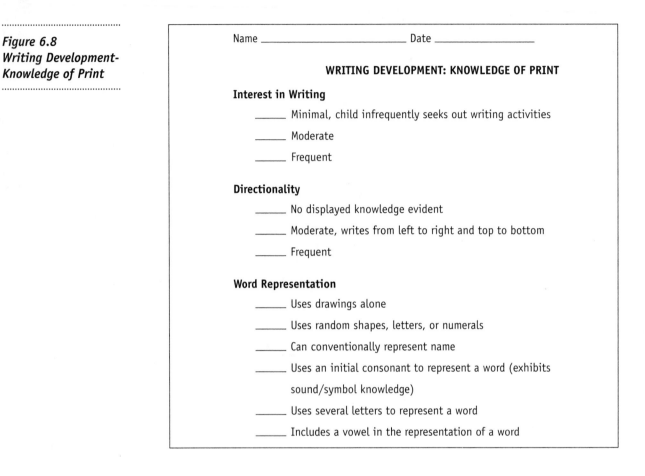

Name _____ Date _____

WRITING DEVELOPMENT: KNOWLEDGE OF PRINT

Interest in Writing

_____ Minimal, child infrequently seeks out writing activities

_____ Moderate

_____ Frequent

Directionality

_____ No displayed knowledge evident

_____ Moderate, writes from left to right and top to bottom

_____ Frequent

Word Representation

_____ Uses drawings alone

_____ Uses random shapes, letters, or numerals

_____ Can conventionally represent name

_____ Uses an initial consonant to represent a word (exhibits sound/symbol knowledge)

_____ Uses several letters to represent a word

_____ Includes a vowel in the representation of a word

One, two, buckle my shoe
Three, four, shut the door

When the poem is recorded on paper, read the poem to the child, pointing to each word as you read it. Then take the child's hand in yours and repeat the reading process. After these two reading episodes, ask the child to read the poem pointing to the words. As the child reads, you will record on your copy of the poem the reading behaviors that you observe. For instance, if the child says *kle* and points to *my,* you will write *kle* above the word *my.* After the child has read the entire poem, you might ask him or her to point to specific words such as *two, shoe, three,* and *shut.* Figure 6.9 shows a model form for recording the behaviors that you observe.

Generally, when children participate in a concept of word in print assessment, you will observe three patterns of response.

• *No concept of word.* A child who does not understand the concept of word in print cannot track the print during reading. The child is unable to point to the words that are being read. If the child points accurately to a word, it is a chance occurrence.

Figure 6.9
Concept of Word in Print

Name _____ Date _____

CONCEPT OF WORD IN PRINT

One, two, buckle my shoe

Three, four, shut the door

buckle _____

shoe   _____

shut   _____

three   _____

Results

_____ Full or functional concept of word

_____ Rudimentary concept of word

_____ No concept of word

- *Rudimentary concept of word.* A child with a rudimentary concept of word is using the principle that there is one word for each syllable. The child can track print while reading, but a two-syllable word such as *buckle* may cause difficulty. The child is becoming familiar with letters and their sounds and may self-correct when pointing to *my* and saying *-kle.* A student who self-corrects will usually go back to the beginning of the line and start the reading and pointing process again. When you ask this child to point out specific words, he or she will often go back to the beginning of the poem to identify each word that you request.

- *Full or functional concept of word.* A child who can track print and read the words with no difficulty is said to have full or functional concept of word. This child can point to specific words without going back to the beginning of the text.

Knowing your students' concept of word in print will help you understand their reading and writing behaviors. Children who lack a concept of word in print will have difficulty when instruction focuses on alphabet letters, for instance. They still aren't sure where words begin and end or what letter a word might begin with. Children with a rudimentary concept of word can make sense of this letter instruction because they are beginning to explore the relationships between sound and symbols. Children with a full concept of word would find letter instruction redundant; they have already figured out sound-to-symbol relationships.

When you have assessed concept of word in print in this more formal way, you will not need to repeat the process. You can listen in as a child reads a simple text to see if a match is made between the word reading and pointing. In writing, observe the form of the composition to determine if a child has acquired a concept of word in print. In Figure 6.10, a kindergarten child has written in his journal. He used some letter-like forms to represent his writing and provided no spaces between any of his words. One word flows into the next. In Figure 6.11, you can see that when this young child wrote about Freddie Krueger, he included spaces and dots to mark the space between words. Often, as young children discover concept of word in print, they find it difficult to leave spaces between words. They will use dots and lines at first until they become more comfortable leaving space. Assessing concept of word in print provides a good opportunity to look at reading and writing behaviors and see parallel literacy development.

Portfolios

The most successful portfolios for students at emergent phases of development are those that are organized into three large compartments. The first compartment contains samples of a child's literacy collected by the parents. When parents interact in the classroom or come for conferences, they bring literacy products that their child has produced at home. Some of these samples might include environmental print that the child has identified, lists that the child has created when going to the store, drawings, and so on. When you include parents in the portfolio process, they become keen observers of their own child's literacy development.

The next compartment consists of samples that the child has decided belong in the portfolio. This part of the portfolio provides a window into what the child sees as important to his or her own literacy development. The child gets to con-

Figure 6.10
Writing Showing No
Concept of Word
Development

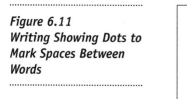

Figure 6.11
Writing Showing Dots to
Mark Spaces Between
Words

sider work done at home or at school and periodically may have a chance to revise the selections that have been made and add or delete materials in the portfolio. Most teachers also ask the child to discuss why a particular item has been
included. At this point in a child's literacy development, the teacher usually
records the child's reasoning on a piece of paper attached to the work.

The third section contains the teacher's important observations and docu-
mentations of literacy. In this section, you include any samples of work and
checklists that you used to determine a child's phase of literacy development.
You also assess the child's growth systematically at least three times a year—at
the beginning of the year, the middle of the year, and the end of the year. In addition, you systematically review at least three times a year data gathered from
day-to-day observations. In this way, you will create a rich picture of a child's literacy development that allows the parents, child, and you to see the child's literacy growth over a school year.

As you have most likely already surmised, these portfolios become the cen-
terpiece for conferences about a child. Working together on the portfolio has
made the parents, teacher, and child true collaborators. Each participant will
have important observations to share, and all will feel valued in this process.

▉ *Integrated Instruction for Emergent Readers and Writers*

All good instruction is imbued with and informed by assessment. By this we mean that everything you observe and learn about your students' learning processes and the products they create must in turn influence and direct all of your teaching. In the unified cycle of teaching, as discussed in Chapter 1, each learning event provides you with additional information about a child's literacy knowledge to use in further teaching.

This section includes specific teaching strategies to encourage literacy development in your emergent readers and writers, most of whom will be in preschool and kindergarten. However, you may at any grade level encounter a student who is considered an emergent reader and writer. These strategies are equally useful for older students if you make accommodations for their age and interests. For instance, a third- or fourth-grader may not appreciate working with the book *Brown Bear,* unless, for example, the student is preparing this text to read to a younger student. Successful teachers stay aware of the needs and attitudes of their older students as they prepare lessons that build on that child's literacy strengths.

Reading

Reading to Your Students

The most important part of your role as a literacy teacher is to read to your students frequently. As you expose your students to a variety of books and repeat favorites, your main emphasis should be the meaning of the story. Encouraging your students to make predictions about what they think will happen in a story will keep the meaning in focus (Harste et al., 1984).

It can be frustrating when you are reading to a large group of young students and one of them calls out something irrelevant. For example, "My mom is picking me up after school." Neuman and Roskos (1993) offer some suggestions to keep students on track with shared reading.

1. *Choose predictable books for shared reading.* Predictable books are written with rhythm, rhyme, and repetition in mind. Phrases and words repeat often so that children get actively involved in a story. For instance, in *Hattie and the Fox* (Fox, 1986), the phrase "Goodness gracious me!" repeats several times. In addition, the story follows a cumulative pattern in which one new line of text is added on alternate pages. Read a few pages of this book and see how children can easily become involved with the story:

> Hattie was a big black hen.
> One morning she looked up and said,
> "Goodness gracious me!
> I can see a nose in the bushes."
>
> "Good grief!" said the goose.
> "Well, well!" said the pig.

A teacher shares a book with emergent readers and writers.

"Who cares?" said the sheep.
"What next?" said the cow.

And Hattie said,
"Goodness gracious me!
I can see a nose
and two eyes in the bushes!"

"Good grief!" said the goose.
"Well, well!" said the pig.
"Who cares?" said the sheep.
"What next?" said the cow.

And Hattie said,
"Goodness gracious me!
I can see a nose, two eyes,
and two ears in the bushes!"

Predictable books usually follow one of four patterns. The first pattern uses *repetition*. As in *Hattie and the Fox*, phrases or sentences are repeated over and over. A second pattern is a *cumulative sequence*. This pattern builds on repetition with repeated and expanded phrases or sentences. A third pattern is *rhyme and rhythm*. This pattern uses a strong beat and rhythm, which is usually punctuated at the end of a line. The fourth pattern is a *sequential* pattern. These books are organized around seasons, the days of the week, the alphabet, or counting (Rhodes, 1979).

2. *Engage in shared book reading by selecting big books.* Big books are just that: big. Publishers have taken stories such as *Hattie and the Fox* and printed them in a large book format with large text. When you share a big book, children can see the illustrations better, which helps them stay interested in the story. Children can also see the text, especially if you point to the words while reading. This simple activity highlights the importance of words in a text and helps students develop their concept of word in print. Holdaway (1979) describes this process of reading with children as a *shared book experience*. During this process, teachers focus on the meaning of a story and in addition, highlight important vocabulary or phonics principles.

Tompkins and Hoskisson (1995) suggest six steps for a shared book experience:

1. *Introducing the book.* The teacher talks about the topic of the book or engages the children in the book by using the cover to encourage predictions.

2. *Reading the book.* The teacher reads the book aloud with the children following along. The children are encouraged to chime in when they know a phrase or word.

3. *Responding to the book.* Children respond to the book by talking or writing or drawing about the book.

4. *Repeated readings.* The teacher rereads the book to the children and the children are encouraged to read the book independently.

5. *Exploring the text.* The teacher uses the book for minilessons that focus on letters, words, or sentences. The teacher may also focus on reading strategies during these lessons.

6. *Extending the interpretation.* Students extend their understanding of the book through talking, drama, writing, or art projects.

You will also want to enlist parents, grandparents, older students, and anyone else who is willing to read to your students. These volunteers can read to the class as a whole, and then they can read to students one-on-one. Such reading pairs are important, especially for young children who have had few story reading opportunities at home. The pair can engage in extensive discussions about the book that just aren't possible in larger settings (Morrow & Smith, 1990).

Wordless books provide another genre useful with young children. These books are most often composed solely of illustrations, although some have a few words. In each case, however, the story line is carried by the illustrations. These books allow children to exercise their ability to pay attention to illustrations. In doing so, they get to create their own story to go with the illustrations. Some teachers tape each child's story so that other children can listen to the various versions.

Students Reading

In addition to sharing books that teachers choose, students need many opportunities to explore books on their own. Even in preschool, children should have time to select books they want to explore. These book exploration and sharing times are social events for young children and can be noisy. The children do not read silently; their pretend reading is often at conversation level. They also like to share an important discovery with a friend.

If you are to give children the opportunity to select books, you need to organize the books into a library where children can reach them. In many preschools and kindergartens, you will see bookcases that consist of only two shelves, which are placed on the floor. Although the books are below the height of most adults, they are perfectly placed for children's viewing. Children tend to make most of their book selections based on the cover (Morrow, 1993). Store books so that children can easily see their covers, perhaps in racks or filed in small tubs so that children can sort through them.

Storytelling

Creating Stories for Dramatic Play

Paley (1990) describes her kindergarten class's storytelling experiences. Children, on a daily basis, created stories that Paley recorded. The storytelling process did not stop here, though. The children used their stories to create classroom plays. They chose actors and rehearsed the play, and revisions occurred as the children asked the author questions. Through this process the children began to understand the nature of revision and the power of storytelling.

Joseph, a student in Paley's kindergarten, created the following story (Paley, 1990, p. 24):

> Once when snake was sleeping and he was hearing noises bump, bump, bump that was his friend alligator. That's Simon. Then there was a bang dong, ding, dong. Do you like that, Simon? And then snake said to alligator, "I want something to eat," and alligator said, "Come to my house." Then the mother snake comes. Katie, you're the mother snake. and she has six babies. Then a lion comes and the lion tries to get into the dream but he can't. So he goes away.

Paley's approach gave the children a golden opportunity to see their words come down into print. They began to understand how speech maps to print and to see the power of their words as enacted in a play.

Language Experience Approach

Another way for children to create stories is through the **language experience approach** (Allen, 1976; Stauffer, 1980). This is another strategy for allowing children to see their speech converted into print. The strength of the language experience approach is that it builds literacy knowledge based on students' current oral language. Teachers use oral discussions to form a story or text. In this strategy, working with a small group of students allows each child more opportunity to engage in conversation.

Typically, teachers begin a language experience activity by sharing a discussion stimulus with the students. Students love to talk about real things, and teachers who have used fish, insects, and other animals have had no difficulty motivating children to talk about them. If live creatures are not possible, simple science experiments encourage discussion, and collections of interesting things such as shells are also engaging.

When the talking slackens, it is time to put the stimulus away and take a dictation from the students, to get their thoughts down. Be sure to put the stimulus out of sight, or you will have great difficulty getting them to focus on the creation of a text.

When the stimulus is put away, encourage the children to come up with a topic or title for the writing. If this is their first dictation, you may need to model by suggesting a topic or title. Narrowing in on a topic or title helps children focus on the content of the text. Next, encourage students to contribute ideas. You might use the exact words of one child or combine one child's words with another's and form a single sentence. For emergent readers and writers, we recommend keeping the text simple and somewhat structured to help your students read the text independently. You might begin a sentence with the name of the child who contributed the idea: *Kelly said, "The spider is black,"* so that children can find their names and read their contributions.

Say each word as you record it for your students. Reading as you write helps to bring children's attention to the speech–print match (concept of word in print). Once the entire text or story is recorded, read it in its entirety to the students while pointing to the words. Encourage this rereading several times as you encourage the children to memorize this text. This memorization will allow students to feel what it is like to read fluently and to develop concept of word in print.

The following text was created by a group of kindergarten children. Their teacher brought in a spider for them to watch and talk about. Following the discussion, the students created this text:

The Spider

Kelly said, "The spider is black."
John said, "I think the spider is scary."
Jamal said, "I had a nightmare about a spider."
Anna said, "I remember the Itsy Bitsy Spider."
Mike said, "That spider is big."

This teacher used the strategy of including the children's names in the text as a supportive help for the children's independent reading. She also kept the text relatively short. Long texts are too difficult for young children to track or to memorize. You will also notice that, although we say the children are creating stories, these early attempts are more like lists than stories.

When this teacher wrote the children's story, she chose to record it on an overhead projector. By using the overhead instead of a paper chart or chalkboard, she could keep eye contact with the students. As a timesaving bonus, she could take the dictation straight from the transparency and make copies of the text for each student.

The children then finished that day's work on the story by illustrating their copies of the text. Illustration helps the child remember the content of the story.

On the next day, the teacher asked the children to reread their story about the spider. She led the first reading, but eventually the children took over the reading. The children kept their copies of the story in a folder or personal reader to return to on other occasions.

This is about all you need to accomplish in a language experience activity with emergent readers and writers: the children learn to express themselves and discover the importance of communication, they see their words form a story, and they gain experience with reading the story. As children move into becoming beginning readers and writers, the language experience activity can provide other instruction in how to locate words, illustrate individual sentences, and engage in word study.

Another variation of the language experience approach is to place labels or charts in the room. If a center requires directions, you and the children can create a chart with the directions. These charts often include illustrations to help children remember the message. These labeling activities let children discover the importance of written communication.

Writing

In Play Centers

Thanks to the work of Neuman and Roskos (1991), among others, we now recognize the importance of including reading and writing materials in play centers. The goal here is to incorporate any reading or writing materials that would naturally occur in such settings. For instance, the play store should have signs for the merchandise, forms for recording a sale, and so on. By including such items, literacy becomes an integral part of the children's creative play.

Neuman and Roskos (1993, p. 224) offer suggestions on how to select literacy props for a play setting:

1. The material must be *appropriate* and safe for the use of young children. For instance, paper would be appropriate and safe, but what about a stapler? Evaluate items based on safety issues, including location and supervision.

2. The material should be authentic to the environment. An old real phone would be a better choice than a toy phone, for example.

3. The material must serve a function that children recognize. Props that relate to a certain area, such as the kitchen, are placed together, so that children become familiar with novel items.

The authors also recommend that just a few literacy items be included at first. As the children become comfortable with these, additional items can be added.

In Journals

As we have mentioned earlier, it is important for young children to write in journals on a daily basis. Through this activity, they come to realize the importance of written communication. At first, most preschoolers and kindergartners will convey a message with a drawing. Their early journals are often filled with drawings. Later, they will include scribbling, letter-like forms, and eventually letters and words. A journal provides an exceptional place to watch this development.

In Response to Books

Children, even emergent readers and writers, need opportunities to write or draw about the books they are reading or hearing. For example, Figure 6.12

Figure 6.12
Child's Writing in Response to a Dinosaur Book

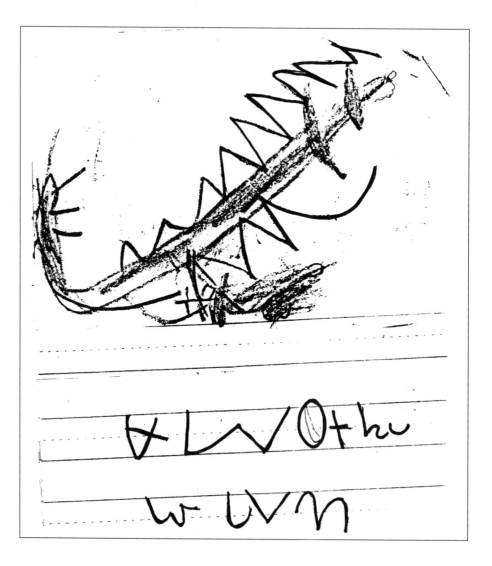

shows a preschool child's response to a book about dinosaurs, which his teacher read to the class. He has chosen to draw pictures of the mother and baby dinosaur. He then included some letter-like shapes that he read as "the mother and baby dinosaur." Clearly this child understands the relationship between an illustration and the text that explains it.

Letter Knowledge

Phonemic Awareness

Important research (Adams, 1990) has documented the value of children being aware of sound–symbol relationships. Children need to hear the sounds in words to be able to read, write, and spell (McGee & Richgels, 1996). They need to recognize word sounds as individual phonemes and then match each sound with its corresponding symbol. For example, in order to read or write the word *frog,* a child must be able to detect from the sound at the beginning of the word that it begins with the *fr* blend. This child then needs to understand the short *o* sound and hear the *g* sound at the end of the word.

Although the importance of phonemic awareness to reading and writing has been well documented, the instructional approach to help this knowledge develop has been riddled with controversy. At first glance, isolated sound–symbol instruction appears to support phonemic awareness learning for young children. In the past, teachers provided large, routine blocks of time for this isolated practice. However, Adams (1990) and other researchers have noted that children who have considerable book-reading experience usually acquire knowledge of sound–symbol relationships. They learn about letters and their sounds as they build knowledge about books and the words within them. Morrow (1993) recommends that teachers select books that focus on language play to give children experiences with real books and draw attention to sound–symbol relationships. Shared book experiences with books not necessarily focused on language play can also draw attention to the story and to the important sound–symbol relationships. As you see, the new suggestions for instruction at this developmental phase include a carefully balanced instructional program that uses authentic book experiences to explore how words are constructed, especially sound–symbol relationships.

Exploring Letters

Young children, especially after they recognize their names, enjoy exploring letters. They find magnetic letters particularly fun to manipulate. They also enjoy most alphabet books. As you choose alphabet books to explore, be careful to choose ones that are basic in format. Some more complex alphabet books work better with older students.

Children will focus on the letter names first. The sound–symbol relationship is a quite abstract concept for children. Although learning this concept is important for reading (Adams, 1990), children acquire their knowledge of letters and sounds as they are read to and in their writing. We recommend that formal study on initial consonants not begin until children are talking about and representing

Figure 6.13
Picture Sort

initial consonants in their writing. This waiting may seem strange, but instruction before this time is often meaningless to children.

This is not to say that letters are ignored. Certainly, as a teacher you will engage these children with alphabet books and draw their attention to the letters. Rather, initial consonant instruction should be informal until a child demonstrates knowledge of the abstract principles of sound–symbol relationships.

Concept Sorts

Although it is inappropriate to teach children about beginning consonants before they are representing initial consonants in their writing, you can lay a foundation for this instruction by using pictures. Invite children to sort a small group of about nine to twelve pictures into categories, for example. We call this sorting of pictures **concept sorts.** Sorting allows children to form generalizations about how pictures may be classified. Eventually, they will use this same thinking to sort words by phonic principles, meaning principles, syntax, and so on.

Figure 6.14
Book Facsimiles *Source: Stone (1990).*

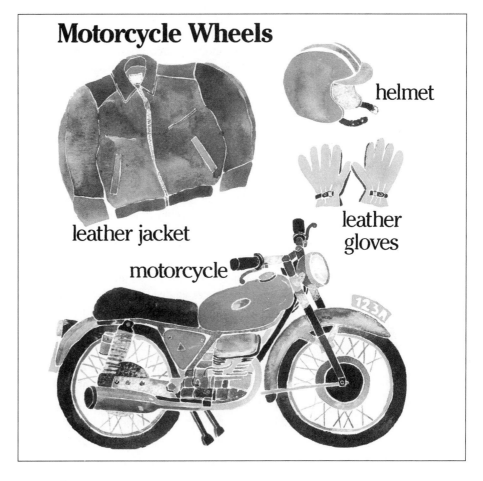

Motorcycle Wheels

helmet

leather jacket

leather gloves

motorcycle

Gillet and Temple describe two types of sorting (1990). The first type is called a **closed sort.** In a closed sort, the teacher defines the category. You may ask the children to find all of the pictures that show clothing. An **open sort** allows children to define the category and group pictures by categories that are apparent to them.

For each sorting activity, ask the children to sort the same pictures numerous times to show that similar objects can be sorted in various ways. For instance, consider the pictures in Figure 6.13. You might start with a closed sort and ask the children to find all the pictures of vehicles. Once the boat, taxi, and airplane are identified, ask how else they are alike. The children might say that people can ride in them, people make them, they use gas to move, and so on. Then ask the children how some of the other pictures are alike. You have moved from a closed to an open sort in which the children might group the clothes or the building materials. Following this sorting activity, you might provide the children with a pile of magazines. The children could then continue to find pictures of other vehicles, clothing, or building materials depending on your directions.

To parallel sorting by concepts, you may want to explore books that are organized around concepts. For instance, in *Wheels* (Shone, 1990), the author has organized each page around a different kind of wheel. Figure 6.14 shows the "Motorcycle Wheels" page from this book. Children might want to create their own concept books as individuals or as a class. They could find or draw pictures related to a concept. These pictures could be glued into a booklet. Then the teacher or a volunteer could label each page for the student. Students will want to reread these books.

Conclusion and Study Notes

This chapter considered the literacy development of emergent readers and writers. We began the chapter by looking at the literacy knowledge that children can bring from home to school. We then explored strategies to informally assess a child's emergent literacy knowledge. Following from these strategies, we revisited the concept of portfolios and what they might look like for emergent readers and writers. Finally, we detailed integrated classroom instruction that builds on the literacy strengths that children bring from home. It is important to remember that, although it is easy to envision emergent readers and writers as preschoolers and kindergartners, many times in your teaching experiences you will meet a youngster who is not in a primary grade and yet is considered an emergent reader and writer. In these cases, you will need to modify the instructional activities presented in this chapter to support your older student.

In this chapter we have considered the following main points:

- Children as young as newborns can be considered emergent readers and writers. Literacy learning is now considered to begin at or before birth.

- Children's language can be noncommunicative or communicative. In noncommunicative language, children create language just for the pleasure of hearing it. In communicative language, children try to interact with another person.

- Children learn that print has directionality. They also learn about the recurring and generativity principles.

- Children learn that in books there are differences between illustrations and text. They learn that books have a beginning and an end, a top and bottom of pages, and words and letters.

- In the process of acquiring a concept of word in print, children may have no concept of word, rudimentary concept of word, or full concept of word.

- Predictable text and language experience are recommended for emergent readers.

- Emergent readers engage in writing through journals, story writing, and in response to books.

Key Terms

In this chapter, we have encountered terms that may or may not have been familiar to you. Think about each of the terms listed and come up with examples that will help add these terms to your own personal knowledge.

emergent readers and writers   concept of word in print

noncommunicative speech   predictable text

communicative speech   language experience approach

directionality of print   concept sort

recurring principle   closed sort

generativity principle   open sort

Follow-Up Activities

1. Talk to a preschool teacher or a kindergarten teacher about how this teacher organizes the curriculum. Ask the teacher to show you some of the literacy materials that will be used in the class.

2. Read a story to a young child. Talk about the story and ask the child to read the story to you. Think about the strategy the child is using to read the story.

3. Practice the concept of word in print assessment with several young children in a single classroom. What did you discover about each child's concept of word in print? How will this knowledge influence your instruction?

4. Have a child write a letter to you. What did you discover about this child's knowledge of print?

5. Practice the concepts of book assessment. What did your student understand about a book's organization?

7 Beginning Literacy

Stacy: I subbed in a first-grade class a couple of weeks ago, and that school used the district's reading program along with another book, something like *Dick and Jane,* except it was called *Stan and Nan!* Students were grouped in high, middle, and low reading groups.

Donald: And what do you think?

Stacy: I was amazed. I haven't been in such a traditional classroom since I was in that grade. Most classrooms have all moved away from having perfectly straight rows of desks and chairs.

Dawn: Did students have time during the day to read anything on their own?

Stacy: No, *Stan and Nan* was it.

Britta: I've been subbing a lot in first grades, but just the second half of the year. I want to know how you *start* teaching first grade. Do students need to know the alphabet first? In one first-grade class I had them point to words on a chart; only one kid in the whole class could do it perfectly.

Wendy: What could the rest do?

Britta: They could follow along as we read together. That one child, though, could read on his own. I'm confused. How do you start at the beginning of the year?

Donald: If you don't have *Stan and Nan,* where do you go? What do you think?

Shari: There are lots of books out there—pattern books like *Brown Bear, Brown Bear* and other books—where students can pick out a few sight words and then learn the pattern of the story. They follow along and get the whole feeling of what it's like to read and what they're supposed to be doing. As you model reading, they start to understand what it is you are doing, and they start to get it.

Shari is in her third year of teaching. She is right: most first-graders do "get it." Shari also answers Britta's question about where to begin: We model reading and make sure they have plenty of practice following familiar text.

Guide Questions for Chapter 7

- What reading behaviors are characteristic of the beginning reader?
- How does concept of word progress throughout beginning literacy?
- What are support activities and support materials?
- How are beginning writers involved in the writing process?

Beginning reading is the first time that children understand that letters are used to represent sounds in words. Having acquired a concept of word, beginners read and write in conventional ways: they can read brief rhymes and stories, and they can write stories. As you read, you will learn about the range of literacy activities to teach beginners. You will see that support reading and writing activities are essential for beginners. You will also see how word study and spelling are integrated into literacy instruction.

▧ *Who Are Beginning Readers and Writers?*

Many teachers say that first grade is their favorite because they see so many students begin to read. Most children pass through the beginning phase during first and second grades. This is a period of beginnings during which many students acquire the ability to read and reread simple texts accurately (Juel, 1991). The same is true for writing. Beginning writers use letters to represent word sounds, they use the alphabetic system, and now others can read and reread what they write.

As you can see in Table 7.1, which describes the behaviors and characteristics of beginning reading and writing, there is a good deal of hesitancy in these first efforts. Reading and writing naturally go slowly for beginners, in large part because they must put a lot of concentration into reading and writing the words (Perfetti, 1985).

Beginning readers have a **rudimentary concept of word** that over the course of this phase develops into a **full concept of word.** Students with a rudimentary concept of word successfully read and reread relatively short passages, such as rhymes and dictations that are just a sentence or two long. The range of instructional level materials for beginning readers covers easy pattern books and

Table 7.1
Overview of Beginning
Readers and Writers

Reading

Behaviors and Characteristics

1. Disfluency when reading aloud
2. Fingerpoint during reading
3. Rudimentary to full concept of word in print

Responses to Literature and Meaning Connection

- Literal focus—retellings and summaries

Spelling and Orthographic Knowledge

1. Semiphonemic spelling strategies
   - Use of initial and final consonants
2. Letter-name spelling strategies
   - Includes short vowels

Spelling Examples	*Semiphonemic Strategies*	*Letter-Name Strategies*
bed	b, bd	bad, bed
chain	cn, chn	can, chan
battle	b, bl, btl	batl
commotion	c, cm	cumshn
reversible	r, rfb	rafrbl

Writing

- Disfluency when writing

brief dictations to easy chapter books. When students develop a full concept of word, the length of texts that they can reread increases substantially from a few sentences to several paragraphs. Students' reading and writing tend to be disfluent. Their lack of orthographic knowledge limits word identification in reading, spelling, and writing. Fluency improves as orthographic knowledge increases (Bear, 1991b).

Table 7.1 also shows the type of invented spelling you will see as students grow from the **semiphonemic** to the **letter-name** phase of development. Spelling and word study during the semiphonemic phase focus on initial and final consonants, and on short-vowel patterns during the letter-name phase. This shift corresponds to the growth from rudimentary to full concept of word. When you have identified which students are beginning readers, the next question is, What materials and activities match their instructional level? This chapter addresses that question.

Beginning readers read together in their classroom library.

▨ *Reading Instruction Integrated with Assessment*

You can make assessment part of reading when you (1) read to students and (2) read with students and when (3) students read on their own. Reading to and reading with students are familiar essential literacy activities discussed in Chapter 4. You can also observe students during cooperative and independent reading activities.

Reading to Students

Observing students is a natural part of reading to them. You have probably already noticed differences among children as they sit and listen to you read. Students who have been read to regularly develop a rich concept of how stories are structured and told, and they listen carefully (Morrow, 1993). These are the children in the front row with backs comfortably bent, necks held forward, and faces set on where you hold the page. Other children may move around and appear not to listen carefully. Over several weeks, or maybe a few months, you will see most of these young children settle in and be more active listeners. Shortening the length of the reading sessions and introducing some beginning creative dramatics help draw students into listening to stories (Siks, 1977; Stewig, 1983). Try some characterization while reading (for example, "Can you pretend you are stirring the soup?").

Teachers guide students' reading by planning approximately twenty-five minutes each day during which the beginning readers listen to someone read to them. Practice in short periods is crucial for students learning how to listen to stories. It is far better to stop a story reading session too soon than to go on for too long. Gradually, you can increase the amount of time that you read to your students. Following are some activities to help students understand and enjoy the times they are read to.

Read Alouds

To plan a read aloud, read the material or story first, and take time to think about how best to present the story or information. Consider the following points when you plan a read aloud from either narrative or expository materials.

What do I read to students? Choose books that complement thematic studies or units. Choose stories and information books because they are well written and a pleasure to listen to and read. Start with stories that are short and to the point and that you enjoy. Professional journals regularly carry updated lists of good books to read to beginning readers (see Chapter 14). Several annotated collections of books to read to students, such as *The New Read-Aloud Handbook* (Trelease, 1989) and *Eyeopeners* (Kobrin, 1988), are available as well. Students may ask you to read their favorites in class. To be safe, choose a few books to share, even if you read only one. It is disappointing to find out that a story doesn't work well when you have no backup in hand.

What do students know about what I am reading? Use informal discussions and clustering around a topic to assess what students know about a story or topic. Consider students' background knowledge and vocabulary. What do they know about when and where the story takes place? Does the story have key ideas or terms that you need to explain?

How do I read to students? To prepare, read the story aloud a few times to locate stopping points for discussion. Plan the reading by making notes of good stopping points. You can jot down open-ended, predictive questions on sticky notes. Plan where you will sit with the group so that everyone can see. You can sit on an adult chair or stool to read to a large group; the floor or a child's chair brings you close to a small group of students.

Introduce the book to the students. Without giving away too much of the story, let them know why you like the book. Hold the book so that all students can see the pictures and at a slant forward from the top to avoid glare from the lights. Some teachers hold books in front of them and read upside down, a hard thing to do with longer texts and big books. A good method is to hold the book at arm's length for wide viewing. You can read big books well from an easel, either a small tabletop easel or a painting easel.

What discussion do I anticipate? The discussion will most likely cover what you consider the big issues and important ideas and what the students consider the big issues and most important ideas. Ask them to identify the most memorable event and most emotive passages. Find out what associations students make with this story or information and of what they are reminded as they listen. Consider how well students will be able to understand this text after hearing it for the first time. Will they understand the events? Will they enjoy the way the story was told? Will they enjoy listening to you read? They will if you share your genuine pleasure in reading to them through your expression, the tone of your voice, and eye contact with each student (Templeton, 1995).

Guided Listening to Stories

A guided listening-thinking activity (GLTA) is more focused than a read aloud. As you may recall from Chapter 5, the guided listening cycle has four steps. The first three are predict, listen, and check predictions (Templeton, 1995). This cycle of predict-listen-check predictions repeats to the end of the reading. The fourth step is resolution, when students reflect on the story. The stories used in a guided listening activity are between fifteen and twenty-five minutes long. Picture books work well in the first guided lessons with beginning readers because they show students how books are understood by reading the pictures.

In guided reading and listening activities, teachers help students to have big questions (Clifford & Friesen, 1993). Prediction is the key to a guided listening activity. Often, beginning readers are unaccustomed to "What do you think will happen?" questions. They may say, "I haven't heard this story before, so I don't know what will happen," or "Turn the page so that I can see the picture. Then I'll know what will happen next." This is your cue to encourage their development by replying, "I know you don't know, but what do you *think* is going to happen next?" It takes time to show students that you are serious about this question. You may have some long pauses waiting for students to make predictions.

When students are hesitant, you can start the discussion with a vote on just a few predictions. You may read two or three stories before students make predictions easily, but it is worth the investment, for the predictions help students to think as they listen and read. To document students' thoughts, write their predictions on a pad or chart.

Guided Listening to Exposition

Expository, or nonfiction, texts provide information, facts, and descriptions of how things work. In reading expository text, teachers encourage discussion among students and help them find the books and expository materials that will answer questions and entertain. These inquiries give purpose to literacy activity.

An important part of your instruction is an initial assessment to help you understand students' conceptual backgrounds. Encourage students to talk about a subject so that you can learn what they know. Three good questions to ask as you begin reading an expository text to students are *"What do you know (about the topic)? What do you think you know? What do you want to find out?"* (Stauffer, 1980). Not only will you find out what students know, but by wondering about what they want to learn, your students will become more interested in the subject and will listen with greater purpose.

Charting Ideas

Chart what students say when they are thinking out loud as a group. These charts document students' understanding of stories and expository texts. You can post the charts or keep them on a chart pad for reference when groups come back together or when you want to review students' ideas. Not only are discussions enhanced when you chart students' ideas, but students use what they learn about charting to brainstorm and organize ideas for writing.

Clustering, webbing, and mapping are three ways to make a verbal display of ideas. As shown in Figure 7.1, each of them starts with the central idea placed in the center of the diagram as a thematic base or core concept. In *clustering,* ideas are organized around a main idea. Rather like free association, students call out ideas related to a topic or story. Students often create clusters before writing similar to the cluster in Figure 7.1, which a child created before writing about kittens. Like a cluster, a *web* has a center, but a web is more complex, with strands organized around a core concept. A few of the many types of webs are literature, concept, and feeling webs (Bromley, 1991). Note in the web in Figure 7.1 that subordinate or supporting information extends from the strands. You can color-code items within webs for easier reading. Teachers and students use webbing to plan thematic and literature studies (Pappas, Kiefer & Levstik, 1995). As you web with students on a topic, you will learn what students know about a subject, and together you can think about the important ingredients for a particular unit of study. Like a web or a cluster, a *map* is a schematic. Maps, however, present the events and directions in a logical sequence. Students can compare maps and see commonalities in how stories are organized.

Reading with Students

Teachers provide reading support to beginning readers through **choral reading** and through **support reading materials** that include familiar patterns, rhymes, and language experience dictations. The support beginning readers need varies with their development and the difficulty of the materials. You can document students' growth throughout this phase of reading development by observing several behaviors. Figure 7.2 summarizes the observations to focus on when you read with beginning readers. Based on your observations, you can supply support materials and activities until students have plenty of books that they can read on their own with accuracy and fluency.

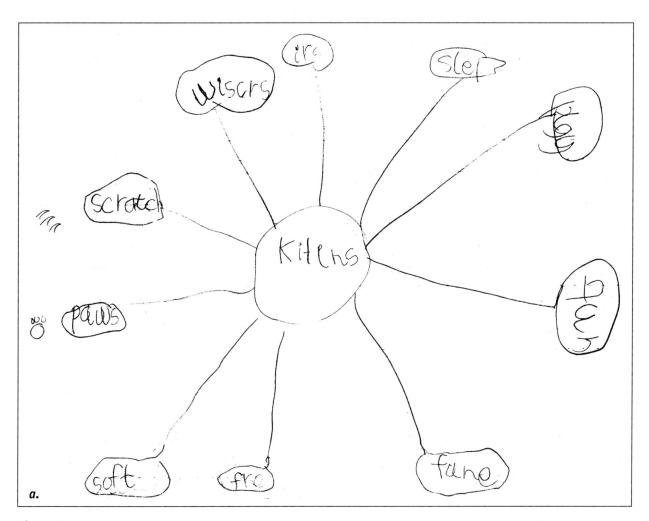

Figure 7.1
Idea Cluster, Web, and
Story Map
a. Cluster of Kittens by a
First-Grader

Choral Reading

In **choral reading,** the teacher's voice supports students (Tompkins & Hoskisson, 1995). You and your students read out loud together. You decrease your voice volume as students read more smoothly on their own. If they hesitate, you can take the lead and read slightly ahead of them:

(teacher) ————————➤

(student) ————➤

When you read a little ahead, students can hold the phrases together as they read.

Some teachers express concern that by providing support, they encourage students to memorize and recite without reading. It is true that to read students

b.

Geography

Nevada — desert
Brazil — rainforest
Rockies — mountains

Weather

Watercycle
precipitation
condensation
evaporation

Climate
dry
humid
wet
ice cold

Types
Hurricanes
tornadoes
clouds
sun

3 forms of matter
solid ——— ice
liquid — rocks
gas   rain
       lakes
       rivers
clouds
steam

c.

The Very Quiet Cricket

sees a she cricket
Boy cricket
Meets big cricket,
Rub wings,
No sound

sees a moth
Boy Chirps!

meets cricket,
No sound

meets mosquitoes,
No sound

meets dragonfly,
No sound

meets bumble bee,
No sound

meets Cicada, No sound

meets locust,
No sound

meets praying mantis, No sound

meets worm,
no sound

meets spittle bug,
no sound

Figure 7.1 (Continued)
b. Web of Weather to Plan a Unit of Study
c. Story Map to Summarize Story Events

must look at the page. Therefore, as you support read with students, be sure that they look at the text and follow along.

Aim for students to reread several familiar texts twice a day. Rereading familiar materials regularly rejuvenates the memory and allows students to practice reading at an independent or instructional level. By reading and rereading support materials, students also learn words as they read. Most students need

Figure 7.2
Checklist for Observing
Beginning Readers

BEGINNING READER CHECKLIST

Student's Interest in Materials

_____ Discusses the stimulus or story in a small group

_____ Follows along in rereading

_____ Dictates with little prompting after stimulus

_____ Reads in personal reader twice a day

_____ Reads personal readers in sustained silent reading

Length of Patterns, Rhymes, and Dictation

Books:

_____ Easy pattern

_____ Medium pattern

_____ Lengthy pattern

Sentences:

_____ 1

_____ 2

_____ 3

Paragraphs:

_____ 1

_____ 2

_____ 3

Concept of Word in Print

_____ Rudimentary:

_____ Mostly accurate

_____ Needs a running start to find some words

_____ Always accurate

_____ Collect 2 to 6 sight words

_____ Full:

_____ Accurate

_____ Find words in context easily

_____ Fluently

_____ Collect many sight words

Fluency

_____ Disfluent

_____ Some fluency

_____ Fluent

Reads Aloud During SSR

_____ Always

_____ Occasionally

_____ Reads silently

Fingerpoint Read

_____ Always

_____ Occasionally

_____ Does not fingerpoint

Do students find instructional and independent books to read?

_____ No

_____ Occasionally

_____ Can find plenty

Will students benefit from further use of support materials and activities?

_____

_____

_____

between four and twelve meaningful exposures to learn a word (McKeown et al., 1985), and beginning readers need closer to twelve exposures.

Personal Readers

Personal readers are individual collections of all of the materials that beginning readers practice rereading (Bear, Invernizzi & Templeton, 1996). Personal readers contain copies of songs, rhymes, easy pattern stories, group experience charts, and individual dictations, with each entry dated or numbered for future reference (see Figure 7.3). A review of these personal readers provides a clear view of students' literacy growth. Over time, the length of the materials in the entries increases and students read them with greater fluency and expression.

Shared Reading of Patterns and Rhymes

Shared reading materials include **pattern stories,** rhymes, and simple songs or ditties. The materials are memorable and usually have a predictable rhythm and repeated lines. You often will introduce these materials in whole-class settings and then have your students reread them regularly in small groups. Small changes in presentation can make a big difference in keeping students interested in rereading these familiar texts: you can rewrite the rhyme that is on a chart and reread it from an overhead, or you can type the text of a big book and have students illustrate it and enter it in their personal readers.

Big Books   Your grandparents may have used big books as their first readers in the 1930s. Now big books have reemerged as materials to support beginning readers. Placed on an easel, big books are easy to see for children in small groups and whole classes.

The texts in big books vary; early beginning readers do best with texts that have just a few sentences on a page. When the text is more complicated, you can read the long pages and have your students focus on repetitive individual sentences or words.

Figure 7.3
Personal Reader with
Short- and Long-Term
Word Banks

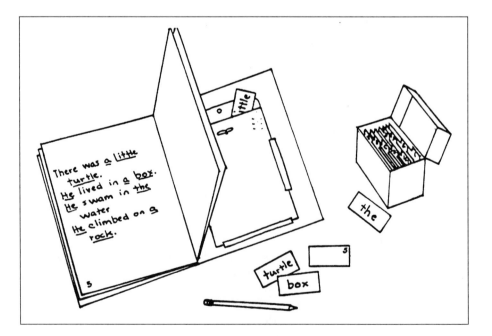

····· TAKING A ·····
CLOSER LOOK   **Related Center Activities**

Many productive center activities can accompany pattern and support reading. Following are some activities for reading and rereading shared reading materials. After you introduce these activities to students in small group meetings, you can set them up in centers.

1. *Listening center:* Students listen to tape recordings of the rhymes, ditties, and patterns, as they follow along in the text.

2. *Putting sentence strips in order:* Students arrange sentence strips of the story in proper order.

3. *Picture drawing:* Students draw pictures to accompany the rhymes and patterns.

4. *Library center:* Students reread commercial and class pattern books.

5. *Tracking with a pointer:* With a partner, students reread various charts that are posted around the room.

Simple Patterns The choices among simple patterns range from simple books found in the library or in collections such as *The Story Box Series* to districtwide reading programs. Look for the popular and predictable *Brown Bear, Brown Bear* (Martin, 1967) and many others, such as *Houses* (Cowley, 1983), which reads: "In the red house, there is, . . . a blue house. And in the blue house there is, . . . a pink house . . . a yellow house . . . a green house . . ." Only one word changes, and with the supporting pictures, the text is quite easy to read.

Spanish-language simple pattern books are especially good materials for students who are native Spanish speakers. As is examined in Chapter 8, until students speak relatively fluent English, their primary reading materials are pattern books and individual dictations in their first language. Simple patterns like the one in ¡*Vete!*(Cowley, 1986) can also help English speakers learn a little Spanish. Support from the pictures makes it easy to learn a pattern such as: "¡Vete! La vaca se fue. La oveja se fue. El cerdo se fue."

Easy Rhymes Rhymes are easy to remember. Many students come to school knowing rhymes that you will be using in shared reading. Remember to slow down the reading if students do not follow the text as they recite.

Children learn less familiar rhymes more quickly when they chant them to the beat of more familiar ones (Dunn & Pamenter, 1987; 1990). Notice that the rhythm of "Five little monkeys" applies to this rhyme: "Five little hot dogs / frying in a pan. / Grease got hot / and one went bam!" "John Jacob Jingleheimer Schmidt" is an example of a rhyme better known as a song (Lipman, 1994). You will also find songs written into easy pattern books, including many of the songs written or performed by Raffi, such as *Oh Mister Sun* (Raffi, 1980) and *Down by the Bay* (Raffi, 1987).

Longer Pattern Books As beginning readers progress, they read longer texts. Toward the end of the beginning reading stage, students can read texts that are several lines long and fairly complicated. *It Didn't Frighten Me* (Goss, Harste, & Romney, 1984) is a longer pattern text that students at the end of the beginning phase can read with fair ease: "One pitch black, very dark night, Right after Mom turned off the light, I looked out my window only to see, An orange alligator up in my tree! But . . . that orange alligator didn't frighten me." This pattern continues throughout the book, and the only thing that changes is what he sees in his tree.

Language Experiences

Every child has stories to tell, and **language experiences** use students' language and ideas to create reading materials. Students dictate to their teacher what they want written down, and this text serves as material for reading and rereading. Reading their own words and ideas makes learning to read easier for the beginning reader, much as reading the patterned language in rhymes and pattern books does.

Language experience activities begin with a memorable experience—the more concrete the better. For example, a raccoon skull is more memorable than a photograph of a skull. The physical object makes for a richer experience and stimulates students to use more memorable language in their dictations. Sometimes, students try to tell stories to go along with an experience. Instead, ask students to describe the experience—what the animal looks like rather than a story about the animal.

Observe the students' styles of dictating. Beginning readers who know little about written language dictate to you as if they were telling you a story. You will need to slow them down. Write one sentence or phrase at a time, even though you may remember more, and have them observe what you are writing. Students who have a deeper understanding of text will dictate to you as if you were a secretary, pausing for you to write (Henderson, 1981).

You can generate language experience texts in two ways: group experience charts and individual dictations.

Group Experience Charts These charts begin their usefulness with emergent readers and continue to provide important reading material in the first part of beginning reading. The texts generated in **group experience charts** are among the first to enter the personal readers. They can be perfect for use with students who have a rudimentary concept of word and who are in the semiphonemic phase of spelling. For dictations longer than a sentence or two, teachers move to individual dictations.

Individual Dictations Students who can reread their one- or two-sentence dictations with good accuracy over several days and who have a solid rudimentary concept of word begin to replace group experience charts with **individual dictations.** A new individual dictation is collected every seven days or so.

····· TAKING A ·····
CLOSER LOOK   The Dictation Cycle

The dictation cycle proceeds in the following way:

Day 1
Have the experience and discuss it.
Take a dictation.
Obtain a title.
Reread dictation to the student.
(Make any changes or additions requested by the
   student.)
Reread dictation with student.
Student draws a picture or brings a photograph.
Type dictation for the student.

Day 2
Reread dictation to student.
Reread dictation *with* student.
Harvest known words.
Reread dictation with student.

Days 3–7
Student rereads dictation.
Point randomly to underlined words.
Make word cards of known words.

The following dictation by Travis is a good example of a short, descriptive, and clearly organized dictation. This dictation was easy for him to read:

The Pumpkin (#3)

October 14

The pumpkin is a dog.
It has two eyes, two teeth
and two ears. It has a vine
sticking out. I like it.

The steps to collecting individual dictations are organized into five activities over several days: an experience, a discussion of the experience, collecting a dictation, rereading the dictation, and harvesting known words.

In a twenty-five-minute small-group meeting (usually no more than ten students in a class will benefit from individual dictations), you can collect three or four individual dictations while other students in the small group draw. When finished, students can reread their new dictations to a partner. Over the course of two or three days, it is possible to collect an individual dictation from all students in the small group. Aides and parents can be taught to take dictations, which can speed the process.

Ideally, dictations are typed. The word processor is a wonderful resource for taking students' dictations. Enlist help from willing parents, older students, partners in education, and secretaries. As with all materials that go in students' personal readers, make several copies of the dictations.

Students identify words they know so that they can be collected or harvested as sight words. Have them underline or circle sight words in their dictations, and then point to these words in random order to see which ones students still know at sight. Write the sight words on small cards for use in word study activities like the ones presented below.

Combining Shared Reading and Language Experience Materials

Students enjoy dictating or writing their own versions of favorite pattern stories and songs. For example, after reading *Down by the Bay* (Raffi, 1987), John dictated his own version and illustrated it, as shown in Figure 7.4. You can also compose simple songs to complement the experiences that are the basis for group experience charts. For example, after making popcorn and developing a group experience chart with a group of primary children, a teacher may compose a jig like: "Pop, pop, pop, I can't stop," thereby creating another familiar text for students to reread.

Down by the bay, where the watermelons grow
Back to my home I dare not go.
For if I do my mother will say,

"Did you ever see a duck driving a truck,
Down by the bay?"

Figure 7.4
John's Version of "Down by the Bay"

Reading on Their Own: Cooperative and Independent Reading Activities

Beginning readers have a new skill to share with classmates. They find joy in being able to read dictations, rhymes, and simple songs to classmates in cooperative activities. To prepare students to work independently and cooperatively, practice partner and independent reading with them in small groups. During periods of independent and cooperative activity, walk around the room and make notes of what students are doing. These observation notes can help you guide a discussion of how students worked together.

Reading Workshop

Reading workshop is a time for students to work cooperatively at reading and discussing what they read (Atwell, 1987). During a typical twenty-minute workshop, beginning readers read in pairs. They share their pattern books and dictations, and when they read from their personal readers, students put a check mark at the bottom of each page they have reread together.

Students enjoy walking around the room with partners and using the pointer to read the posted experience charts and patterns. You can also equip areas of the room with easels and big books so that small groups can comfortably congregate to reread familiar big books.

You have an opportunity to assess student interest, involvement, and motivation as you plan how you expect students to work cooperatively. As you assess reading workshops, consider social interaction as well as the specific materials students are reading.

Students find partners: Are they able to find partners?

Character of the partnerships: Are the partnerships working?

Materials: Do they find materials to read?

Support: Do they have the support they need and want?

Personal readers: Do beginning readers read from personal readers? Do beginning readers add to their personal readers?

Practice: Is there enough instructional level reading? Do beginning readers read during the majority of reading workshop time?

Creative and Cooperative Responses

Students' creative responses are an important part of the assessment process because they reveal and document their understanding, thinking, and talents. Too often students show what they learn by answering questions or by simply summarizing what they read. But many wonderful, creative small-group discussions spring up when students choose what and how they respond to what they have read. Creative responses give students a way to exercise personal talents. When you plan for creative responses, consider the range of activities and resources your students can manage independently at the time. Children will need some guided practice, for example, before they learn to manage the paint and easel station.

Also consider how easily your students think up ideas and methods for responding. To generate more response ideas, have students share their ideas and perhaps chart some possibilities. Add in some ways you can respond to stories, too. When you draw or paint a favorite character, you provide a wonderful model for the children.

Painting murals on a six- by three-foot piece of butcher or chart paper spread on the floor is a good way for several students to chronicle a story they have read. They are sharing some positive, small-group interaction and problem solving as they work together to plan their drawing and painting. Students in the beginning phase often depict the main characters. If a group has read a book together, each group member can choose one character to draw or paint. Similarly, if the whole class has read a book, each group can be responsible for depicting one scene. Later, students can share their thinking when they introduce and display their mural.

Young students enjoy reenacting stories with hand and finger puppets. You can set up sock puppets as a center activity, and together two students can practice their favorite parts, play-act the characters, or practice a particular scene to share with others. For long-term projects, students can develop their own plays and pursue staging and set design. Gradually, these activities turn into writing activities similar to those below.

Learning on Their Own: Independent Reading Activities

It is true that students learn to read by reading. Ironically, in some classrooms, children may spend as few as six minutes a day reading (Anderson, Hiebert, Scott & Wilkinson, 1985). As you engage students in activities like the following, you will want to make adjustments according to your assessment of how productively students read together and independently.

Sustained Silent Reading

Sustained silent reading (SSR), also known as DEAR time (drop everything and read), is as important as any other reading time. Some beginning readers will need practice before they are able to sustain independent reading. Within a month, you will be pleased by the steady hum of voices during SSR with beginning readers. This is a good sign, for as you know, beginning readers tend to read aloud to themselves. An SSR period of ten to fifteen minutes is a fine length for beginning readers.

You can arrange four or five desks as a cluster or seat students at a table with a basket of books placed in the center. When you start SSR, students choose a book from the basket to read, or they can turn to their personal readers. You might ask beginning readers to reread three of the latest entries in their personal readers during this time.

Support Reading at Home

Recreational reading is an activity to encourage both in the classroom and at home. You will know you are succeeding in developing readers when students

*Big books are read
individually for practice
in fluency.*

want to take books home to read and parents report that their children read on
their own. You can invite students to take home copies of their personal readers,
pattern books, and the books they write themselves to read to their loved ones.
When they are at home, children benefit from having someone next to them for
support as they read.

Parents have a lot of questions about how they can help their children read:
"Do I have my child sound out the words, or do I tell the words?" "How do I
know if a book is too difficult for my child?" Show parents how to read with their
children by providing one-page guide sheets for children to take home. You can
also teach students to show others how to read with them. For example, students
can say, "I'll tap you on the shoulder when I want you to help me with a word.
I'll tap twice if I want you to read." Consider making a brief videotape demonstration of you reading with a student and of children reading together. You can
show the tape to parents at school meetings or conferences and let students take
it home if they have VCRs.

One important message to parents is that children should not struggle when they read. The three-second-wait rule discussed in Chapter 4 also applies here: If a child pauses for three seconds, tell the child the word.

◼ *Writing Instruction Integrated with Assessment*

Teachers of beginning writers help students focus first on getting their ideas down on the page and then on sharing what they have written with others. Beginning writers write in whatever way helps them reread what they have written (Temple, Nathan & Temple, 1988). At first, beginning writers must work hard to translate their ideas and language into writing. Their frequent halts to make letter-sound correspondences keep their writing disfluent and only a few words in length. As they progress through this stage, you'll see their writing fluency and production increase (Bear, 1991a).

Writing with Students: Support Activities for Composing Together

Beginning writers benefit from a good deal of support from their teachers and peers. Many of the books and rhymes you use in support reading provide good support for beginning writers. Students model their writing on the themes and language patterns they hear in children's literature.

As you write with students in small groups, you will see how they grow in independence during the beginning phase of writing development. Look for and encourage the behaviors outlined for beginning writers in Figure 7.5. If you emphasize the initial parts of the writing process—prewriting and writing, or composing—you will help students develop a love for writing that instills a desire to revise and edit.

Pattern Writing Activities

Borrowing patterns in writing gives students an easy entry into writing and even producing their own books. Beginning writers start by being quite involved in getting the letters down for the sounds they hear. After rereading a pattern story several times, have your students write their own versions. Encourage them to observe and then imitate repeated patterns. In addition to pattern or predictable books, beginning readers continue to read alphabet and number books at an independent level and to use them as models for writing their own alphabet, number, and concept books.

Imitations of *Brown Bear, Brown Bear, Houses,* and *Down by the Bay* are popular. Some patterns are even easier, as in Figure 7.6, where Sarah inserted one word in a simple pattern book. This sample also documents Sarah's orthographic development and her use of the bubble for dialogue. Using art to support their stories, as Sarah did, is an important part of early writing efforts for these students. You will want to save samples of students' writing to document many aspects of students' development.

Figure 7.5
Checklist for Observing
Beginning Writers

BEGINNING WRITER CHECKLIST

Drawing

_____ Draws pictures most of the time   _____ Draws pictures to go with the writing

Composing/Writing

_____ Rereads what was written   _____ Uses patterns for writing

_____ Thinks of ideas for writing   _____ Uses models as themes in stories

Length

_____ One- or two-word patterns   _____ Two to four lines

_____ Easy pattern books   _____ Two to four paragraphs

_____ Chapter books

Fluency

_____ Disfluent   _____ Fluent

_____ Some fluency

Writing Process

_____ Prewrites   _____ Gives feedback to others

_____ Reads writing to others   _____ Makes changes based on feedback

1 = Generally no   2 = Usually   3 = Nearly always

Will students benefit from further use of support materials and activities?

_____

Kenneth Koch's book, *Wishes, Lies, and Dreams* (1970), provides many wonderful patterns for children to follow. The poems are particularly powerful because they are written by children throughout the elementary grades. One versatile pattern is the "I wish" pattern, which can be completed with one or several words. Other patterns allow you to assess students' relational thinking. An easy pattern is a two-clause pairing of "First, then." For example, one child wrote:

First I do my spaling
Then I do my math.

First I look for Estort eags
Then I pek tham up in my baskit.

Figure 7.6
"A Cat Can . . .": Simple Pattern for Writing

First I jump rop by mysalf
Then I jump rop with my frans.

First I eit loch
Then I go out for resus.

Students exercise what they know about a subject through their pattern writing. For example, in a unit of study on the senses, Mrs. Gray had her class think of their favorite animals and plants and their five senses. As a whole class, the children brainstormed some favorites, and then they were ready to write and draw. In Figure 7.7, Sarah used the "My favorite" pattern to write and draw about her favorite thing to touch and her favorite sound.

My favrite thing to touch in my cat figaro.

My favrite sound is a chom birds bozing. Bozz

Figure 7.7
"My Favorite" is an easy pattern for writing.

Pattern writing is an instructional-level activity for beginning writers that builds on the patterns students discover when they read. Students develop a bounty of new reading materials in the patterns they write and share.

Models for Writing

Beginning writers will begin to imitate the rhythmic structures and the descriptive detail in books beyond simple patterns. For example, students enjoy using *Cloudy with a Chance of Meatballs* (Barrett, 1978) as a model for writing weather reports of the things that fall from their skies. You can assemble class books from each student's version of the model.

Students enjoy writing stories about princesses and princes, and they enjoy taking language and themes from familiar folk and fairy tales and using them in their writing. For example, Connie used several motifs in a wonderful eleven-page story with accompanying pictures about a pretty princess and prince who met, married, and had ten children. Unfortunately, the king had to go to war, and "he didt kom bak in a log time. The Kwin was vary sad." In this sample from her book, in Figure 7.8, the foundation of marriage among nobility is present. Indeed, many tales talk about finding a mate over the ocean.

Figure 7.8
Page from Connie's Story,
"The Prins and the
Pinsasas"

Expository texts also provide models for writing. Students can use guided listening activities and discussions to generate ideas and examples in writing. In Figure 7.9 Shila has used a model from the book *Melting* (Bolton, 1986) to present an example of something that melts and then summarize an experiment on melting.

Guiding Students Through the Writing Process

Students encounter the writing process when they are beginning readers and writers. They experience what authors do when they write, and they begin to obtain feedback from classmates and rewrite a few first drafts for publication (Calkins, 1986; Graves, 1983, 1991; Harste, Short & Burke, 1989).

Based on current research, the writing process can be summarized in five stages: prewriting, writing, rewriting, editing, and postwriting (Lapp & Flood, 1993). The process does not unfold with these stages in a strictly prescribed sequence; rather, the parts interact. For example, a student may return to rewriting after receiving further feedback from classmates in a postwriting activity.

Beginning writers concentrate on the prewriting, writing, and postwriting stages of the writing process (Calkins, 1986). When you plan which writing skills to focus on, look at what students bring to writing. Meet with students in small groups or individual conferences to discuss what they know about the writing process. Talk with them about how they write their stories. Let students know they will write regularly, that they have choice in what they write about, and that they will be able to work with others to discuss and share their writing.

Prewriting The prewriting stage begins with helping students find something to say. Often, students generate writing ideas directly from their personal experiences. At other times they write their own versions of a particular story.

In small groups, guide your students in thinking of what they want to write about. Brainstorm ideas on a chart. The fewer ideas you offer, the better, and the more writing topics will spring from student ideas and discussions. Have your students reserve the first few pages in their journals to record possible writing topics from these brainstorming sessions.

**Figure 7.9
"Wat Melt's": A
Beginning Writer
Describes Melting**

Wat Melt's by Shila to me Shila Shila have you ever wibdred wat melting was? I have and hers a few thing 's that bo and don't you eat your popSicol out side and let it melt I bon't. Now we will try a icsparomet take a ice cude. and a plat. pot the ice cude on a plat leve the ice cude on the plat. leve the plat out side for a harf howr you will have a plat of water bot no ice cude. The sun meltid it.	What Melts? by Shila Have you ever wondered what melting was? I have and here's a few things that do and don't. You eat your popcicle outside and let it melt. I don't. Now we will try a experiment. Take a ice cube and a plate. Put the ice cube or a plate. Leave the ice cube on the plate. Leave the plate outside for a half hour. You will have a plate of water but no ice cube. The sun melted it.

When you and the students have explored some topics, you can pick one and model idea clustering. Other prewriting and brainstorming activities include drawing pictures, looking through books, and simply talking about ideas with classmates. Although time to talk may on the surface seem a waste of time, ensuring plenty of time for students to talk with each other about their ideas and experiences is probably the most important thing you can do to help students to get ready to write. The talk provides a valuable rehearsal for what they write.

Writing Beginning writers are slow, laborious writers, and they need plenty of time to write, both cooperatively and independently. Many teachers schedule a daily block of time for writing workshop.

Beginning writers often write one-word stories. In Figure 7.10 you can see that Veronica has an interest in dance. Her picture shows happy people singing, and her word *DANS (dance)* tells another part of her story.

You can use small groups or individual meetings to assist children as they work to get their ideas down on paper. You will find that many beginning writers are hesitant because they cannot spell the words they want to write. Some students become so concerned with correct spelling that they write only words they know how to spell. This problem can limit expression to such a great extent that their writing becomes stilted and does not represent their ideas.

Encourage students to get their ideas down on the page before worrying about spelling words correctly. You can help students to overcome their hesitancy by showing them how to invent their spelling. In a small group, give your students a difficult word and then have them brainstorm and chart a few possible spellings. One small group of beginning writers came up with these possibilities for *vacation: VASN, VAKASHUN, FKA, VACASN, VAKASN, VA*. The teacher said that these were all possible invented or temporary spellings, and all good ways to spell *vacation*. Then the teacher explained that the important thing was that students could reread their spelling. One lesson on this subject will not suffice.

You can learn a lot about students' ability to write freely by walking around the room while they write. And as you observe, you can also take the time to help beginning writers when they get stuck or cannot reread what they wrote.

Many beginning writers string their words together without spaces. As you walk around, suggest that these students put a finger space between words. This will make a big difference in making their writing readable.

Rewriting In rewriting, the revision part of the writing process, students work toward clarity. After a month of writing, have your students look back through what they have written and select one piece of writing that they would like to revise for publication. Ask them to reread their writing to see if there is anything they want to change or add.

When students revise, notice what they have chosen to change, or if they were even interested in making changes. Are they concerned with ideas or with editing and correctness?

Using your own writing, show students how to reread a piece of writing to see if the ideas make sense. Encourage them to use a caret ^ to insert, to draw lines to connect insertions, and to scratch through words rather than to spend time erasing.

Editing Students discover many places to change grammar and punctuation as they rewrite and revise. For example, when a classmate cannot read what was written, the student makes spelling and punctuation changes to make the piece easier to read.

The time to teach students about some editing features is when they are already experimenting with them. For example, a good time for a lesson on periods is when students use them occasionally, perhaps in unconventional ways such as between words. Similarly, when you focus on correcting spelling, base your choice of what invented spellings to correct on your students' developmental level: beginning writers in the semiphonemic phase can spell the beginnings and ends of words correctly; students in the letter-name phase begin to work on short-vowel patterns in their editing for spelling.

Explain the writing process, and particularly the editing stage, to parents. Some parents do not understand why teachers do not correct children's writing, and will ask, "How can they learn if you do not correct them?" During parent meetings and in notes home, show parents samples of children's reading, writing, and spelling that represent the developmental phases. Let parents know that you are studying their children's development and progress carefully and that you time your spelling and mechanics lessons based on students' developmental readiness.

Postwriting Students can share what they have written in a multitude of postwriting activities, including the following:

- Response groups
- Writing workshops
- Author's chair (Graves & Hansen, 1983)
- Author bulletin boards
- Programs for guests
- Student books
- Class books

- Reading to students in other classrooms

- Class newspapers

Students need positive feedback for their hard work. In small groups, you can show students how to share their writing. You and your students can work together to establish guidelines to avoid put-downs and an overemphasis on writing mechanics such as spelling, punctuation, and even grammar. Show students how to start with the positive: "After Eva reads, tell her some things you like about her writing." Model ways to give positive feedback and how to be specific. Classmates learn to tell the author one thing they like about the writing. After students note what they liked, they ask the author questions, which may lead the author to a discussion about possible additions. Students often are eager to revise their stories based on student comments.

Publication brings closure to the writing cycle and gives students a great sense of accomplishment in their writing. When students decide to publish their work, consult with them about what form they would like their work to take. You can equip classroom publishing centers with materials to make books and art work. A word processor is also a handy tool to develop a polished piece. Beginning writers use word processors ably with simple directions and the help of a partner, parent, or teacher. As students develop their publications, show them how to include title pages, dedications, and brief biographies. Students also enjoy writing mock reviews of their books and pasting the reviews onto the back cover.

Writing on Their Own: Cooperative and Independent Activities

Students need to write for extended periods nearly every day, and they will get the most out of this time when they have a clear purpose and can work cooperatively and independently in a relaxed manner. You will need to assess how students interact in writing times, much as you did in reading on their own:

Partners: Do students work well in partnerships?

Rereading: Can students reread what they have written?

Practice: Are there enough writing workshops each week? Do students write at home?

Sharing: Are students effective in sharing what they write? Are there sufficient opportunities to share?

Materials: Do students find their folders and journals efficiently? Are writing, drawing, and publishing materials available?

Word processing: Do students work with a partner in word processing?

Track how long students work independently and cooperatively. You can help students lengthen the time they work independently by writing with them in small groups. By watching you and practicing, they will build a repertoire of writing styles and practices to use when they write on their own. You, in turn, will find specific areas to focus on as the class moves back and forth between writing with others and on their own.

Writing Workshops: Students Helping Students

Writing workshop is a favorite time of day when students work with class-mates to write. As you introduce writing workshops, review ways to work to-gether and ground rules for how and where students work. When students are working purposefully, they move around the room without disrupting others.

Writing workshops for beginning writers last from fifteen to thirty minutes. In most writing workshops, students choose partners. You might limit groups to two or at most three students in a group.

Occasionally, teachers assign writing partners, particularly when one student needs help getting ideas down on the page. For example, in a multigrade class-room beginning writers might be paired with transitional writers. One ground rule is that all students are responsible for writing and drawing. Transitional writers can take dictations from beginning writers when the beginning writers grow tired. Daniel, a transitional writer, commented on the process of working together: "He asks me to write it. We both come up with ideas."

It is wonderful to see what ideas writing partners pursue. Beginning writers enjoy making maps and video game routines; they label their diagrams and write descriptions and write stories about their games. Some partners develop special rules for their out-of-classroom clubs.

Independent Writing Activities

Many types of independent activities give beginning writers the time they need to work and practice independently without interruptions.

Sustained Silent Writing (SSW)   During sustained silent writing (SSW) the entire class works independently. Often, after students are comfortable with sustained silent reading (SSR), teachers turn this independent reading time into an independent writing period (SSW) and schedule SSR later in the morning. As in the SSR period, SSW is scheduled at a specific time, three times a week. Writing periods begin with just a minute or two of writing and extend to fifteen minutes.

After you show students how to conference with each other, the independ-ent writing period can be followed by a small group sharing time. One student is the leader and guides the sharing. For example, leaders are taught to ask for comments about the writing before another person shares. As beginning writers' production increases, groups may not have enough time for everyone to share what they have written. In response to this good problem, you can encourage students to develop rules for sharing. They might, for example, limit sharing to one page. When the same problem arose in one classroom, students decided to rotate the sharing over a three-day period. In this way, authors were able to share extended passages. Some teachers use the SSW as a preparatory activity for the writing workshops discussed above.

Beginning writers learn organizational skills as they learn to put their writ-ing in folders instead of jamming it into desks. Your students can keep manila folders they have decorated in baskets, in cubbies, or on a bookshelf near the class library. Except for journals or learning logs, students should keep all of their work, including first and second drafts, in writing folders. These folders are invaluable during student and parent conferences. Periodically, perhaps monthly or at the end of each grading period, students should clean out these folders. They can save some of their pieces for portfolios and take some work home.

Journals and Learning Logs In many primary classrooms, students write daily in their **journals.** Students use their journals like an artist's sketchbook: the journal is where students try out ideas and skills. Beginning writers often include drawings with journal entries.

Learning logs are a type of journal in which students respond to what they learn. Logs provide excellent documentation of what students learn. Children like to make lists and draw pictures of what they learn. Journals and learning logs may be corrected for content but not for mechanics and spelling. Most teachers give students the option of not sharing their entries; they can fold the pages in their spiral notebooks in half if they do not want the teacher to read something.

As you can see in some of the writing samples in this chapter, rereading what students have written in their journals can be a challenge. You may want to sit with beginning writers as they finish writing and ask them to read what they have written. Many teachers use a light pencil at the bottom of a page to make an unobtrusive note of what students write. These notes do not seem to bother students, and when they ask what you are doing you can explain that the notes help you to remember what they have written.

Students find teachers' responses to their journals immensely satisfying. When students leave for the day or during a break in the day, take a few minutes to respond to their journal entries. The next day, at the beginning of the sustained silent writing period, walk around the room and, if they ask you, read what you have written to them. Your daily response to their efforts will help you get to know them and will encourage them to write to you. A month or two after the school year begins, you can limit your responses to eight to ten journals daily so that each student hears from you every second or third day. Your responses should be nonjudgmental and supportive and should focus on *what,* not *how* students write. Figures 7.11 and 7.12 show responses from an experienced teacher.

Response Logs Reading **response logs** also offer students a place to respond to what they are reading and learning. When beginning writers respond to what they read and learn, they tend to write retellings and summaries (Barone, 1992). They might retell the most important or favorite parts of a story.

Letter Writing Letter writing expands the range of choices in postwriting activities. When you make a post office center a regular part of the classroom, you can help students learn the process of writing and sending letters to relatives, other teachers, older students, and authors.

Writing activities and topics for beginning writers readily cross over from other classroom subjects, such as science and social studies, and from many areas of student interest. Regardless of the topic, however, students write better and enjoy it more when their writing entwines itself into meaningful study themes and their own experiences.

Figure 7.11
Sample of Student's
Journal and the Teacher's
Response (lettering)

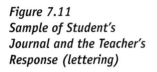

> I Like want I G#to Go To My DADs
>
> *I Know your dad must like seeing*
> *you too.*

Word Study and Spelling Instruction Integrated with Assessment

Word study and spelling instruction help students examine words. Word study activities include word identification activities (strategies for reading and sight word recognition), word sorts, and word study games. In word study, students learn how words are structured and use this knowledge to improve as readers (Adams, 1990; Lundberg & Hoien, 1991). Spelling instruction is discussed separately because schools often have a distinct spelling curriculum and program. However, spelling and word study instruction do blend.

We divide the discussion of word study and spelling instruction into two parts because students who are in the beginning reading and writing phase pass through two phases of spelling: the semiphonemic phase and the letter-name phase. You will base word study and spelling instruction on informal assessment of students' spelling development as described in Chapters 4 and 5. You will usually introduce word study and spelling activities in small group meetings. When students understand the activity, they will repeat it and similar activities independently or with a partner.

To assess the effectiveness of your word study and spelling programs, examine how your students participate in word identification activities, word sorts, word study games, and spelling activities. Figure 7.13 summarizes the key points to consider.

Word Study in the Semiphonemic Phase

Semiphonemic spellers usually have a rudimentary concept of word. They spell the first sound and, later, the final sound of each word and exclude vowels

Figure 7.12
Sample of Student's Journal and the Teacher's Response (drawing with lettering)

in most words. They are in the early beginning reading phase, and at a tacit level they use their knowledge of initial and final consonants to help them identify words. In word study and spelling, they examine initial consonants and consonant blends and digraphs. They collect a few sight words from the pattern stories, rhymes, and dictations in their personal readers and keep them in individual word banks (see below).

*Figure 7.13
Checklist for Observing
Word Study and Spelling
Among Semiphonemic
and Letter-Name Spellers*

BEGINNING SPELLER CHECKLIST

Identification of Words in Context: How does the student figure out words in context?

_____ Goes back to the beginning

_____ Looks at pictures

_____ Tries sounding it out

_____ Starts with first sound   _____ Just right   _____ Too labored

Collecting Sight Words: Does the student collect sight words from what he or she reads?

_____ One or two words   _____ Three or four words   _____ Many words

Word Banks: How large is the student's word bank?

_____ Small (20–40)   _____ Medium (50–100)   _____ Large (150–250)

Picture and Word Sorts and Games

_____ Explain sorts: Can the student explain why he or she sorted words or pictures the way it was done?

_____ Development: Is word study instruction developmental?

_____ Accuracy: Is there good accuracy in the student's sorts?

_____ Fluency: Does the student sort with greater speed once there is accuracy?

_____ Sorting: Can the student sort pictures and words independently?

_____ Word study options: Does the student know how to play word study games?

Spelling in Writing: What is the role of spelling correctness in the student's writing?

_____ Invents spellings when needed

_____ Writes with spaces between words

_____ Student's concern for correctness in spelling:

        _____ Limited vocabulary and expression of ideas

        _____ Appropriate concerns about correctness

        _____ Writing is difficult to read

Spelling Lists and Tests: How does the student study spelling lists and take tests?

_____ Studies words in lists that match developmental spelling assessments

_____ Finds words that match the pattern of his or her spelling words

_____ Has 50% accuracy on Monday pretests

_____ Has high accuracy rate on final tests

_____ Is not upset by these tests

_____ Recognizes words that he or she misspells

Identifying Words in Context

Students grow familiar with words as they read familiar rhymes, pattern books, and dictations. You can use rhymes, patterns, and dictations to show students word identification strategies and to find and collect sight words for use in word study activities.

Sometimes while rereading shared reading and language experience materials, students will get stumped by a word: they don't remember it, and their orthographic knowledge is too limited to help figure out the spelling. You can use these opportunities to show students how to identify words in context. Show them how to look at pictures or the other words in the sentence and to think about the story when they are stuck (Nessel & Jones, 1981). Students in the semiphonemic phase benefit from learning how to go back and reread from the beginning of a phrase, sentence, or story. Getting a running start often helps students identify words they had difficulty reading before.

When semiphonemic students identify words in familiar pattern books and dictations one word will become a power word—usually because it is most important or because it is unusually long. For example, in the following rhyme (Lee, 1975), the word *alligator* is often identified before other words:

Alligator pie, alligator pie,
If I don't get some I think I'm going to die.
Take away the green grass, take away the sky,
But please don't take away my alligator pie.

Students find it most easy to identify words at the beginning of a line. The second easiest words are those at the end of lines, and the most difficult are those in the middle. For example, when Brian was asked to find *alligator* in the above rhyme, he pointed to the word instantly. When he was asked to find *away*, he had to go back to the beginning of the poem to reread it until he found the word. Students who go back to identify words in context have a rudimentary concept of word, whereas students who can immediately recognize words in context have a full concept of word. Brian, for example, was close to having a full concept of word. By showing students how to read beyond an unknown word and to go back to reread in context, you will help them learn how to identify words on their own.

Another way to show beginning readers how to identify words is to call out words and ask students to point them out in big books or pattern stories written on chart paper. Reciprocally, students can call words out for you to find, and you can demonstrate finding the words by going back to reread or by finding the word from the initial consonant sound.

Another way to practice word identification processes is to make word cards of selected words and ask students to find the words in the text. In a whole group setting, teachers use plastic hanging pocket charts which display sentence strips. Students are given large cards with individual words from the sentence. They take the cards and place them in the pocket underneath the word in the sentence.

Collecting Sight Words for Word Banks

Students can harvest words for word study out of shared reading and language experience materials. On the second or third day of working with a new personal reader entry, have your students underline words that they *really* know. Students may at first have difficulty figuring out which words they really do know, but you can help them identify which words they can read in isolation and without having to go back into the text. For example, *alligator* would have been such a word for Brian.

Write the underlined words on word cards that have been cut from blank index cards to a size of one by two inches. On the back of the cards, students write their initials and the number or date of the story. The initials identify the owner so that words can be returned after children sort or play word study games.

The words from the current week's shared reading or dictation are placed in a short-term **word bank.** Figure 7.3 on page 216 shows an example of a short-term word bank—an envelope or small plastic bag taped or stapled to the back of each student's personal reader. Short-term word banks hold words that the students know from the new stories and rhymes they are practicing that week.

As you might guess, there is also a long-term word bank. The long-term word bank is a collection of words from previous readings. Students can collect these words in a small box, perhaps a card file box, but a potato chip tube or a small tin with a plastic cover will do. They will use words from the long-term word bank in word study activities such as the ones presented below.

Have your students review their words on a regular basis. Words they cannot read easily are discarded. However, for some words, show students how to figure out a word from context. Have them turn in their personal readers to the story number as noted on the back of the word card. Students can either start at the beginning of the story or at the beginning of the sentence the word came from and read. Usually, students are able to read the word correctly when they return to the story. In this way they learn how to use context to read difficult words.

Students in the semiphonemic phase of spelling acquire words slowly. At first, these students collect just one or two words from their support reading texts. Students need to collect twenty or more words before they are ready to begin word sorts. Until then, they sort pictures by initial consonant sounds.

Picture and Word Sorts

Students in the semiphonemic phase use easily recognized picture cards of a uniform size to sort by initial consonant sound. One-by-two-inch cards are small enough for several pictures to fit in three columns as students work on the floor or on their desks. Numerous commercial picture card packages are available to use for picture sorts (Bear, Invernizzi & Templeton, 1996). In addition, many reading programs include picture cards.

You can introduce your students to picture sorts by showing them the sorting categories. Ask students to say the names of the pictures as they sort. In this way they will hear and feel the similarities in sound. In the example in Figure 7.14, the three picture headings are pictures of a box, a man, and a rake. The

Figure 7.14
Picture Sort by
Initial Consonant

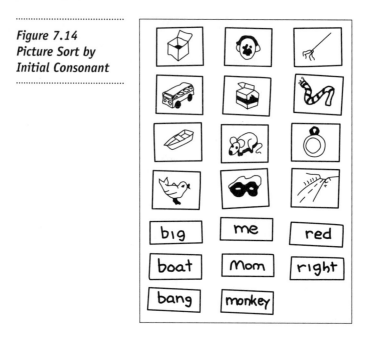

students would sort a picture of a bus by saying "bus-box, bus-man, bus-rake" and then put the picture of the bus underneath the picture of the box.

After students sort, they read through each column to check their sorts, making corrections as they go. Many sorts include a leftover, or oddball, pile column for pictures that fail to fit other categories, to keep students on their toes.

In word sorts, students place known words into different categories (Morris, 1982; Schlagal & Schlagal, 1992). Word sorts can be extensions of picture sorts. For example, a follow-up activity to the picture sort in Figure 7.14 is for students to look through their word banks for words that begin with the same sounds as *box, man,* and *rake.*

Initial Consonant Picture and Word Sorts Edmund Henderson and Betty Lee, a first-grade teacher, suggested a sequence to use to study initial consonants (Henderson, 1981, 1990): bmrs, pntg, cfdg, and jklw. Students begin with picture sorts in which they compare and contrast pictures gradually, contrasting b with m, then b and m with r, then b, m, and r with s, before moving to the next set of initial consonants. Students spend more time covering the first four initial consonants than the other sets while they learn how to examine words and compare them by their initial sounds.

Consonant Blend and Digraph Picture and Word Sorts When you can see by their word sorts and first-draft writings that your students have mastered initial consonants, they are ready to begin studying consonant blends and digraphs, two-letter combinations that make one sound, such as *ph* in *graph*. Picture sorts are a useful format for contrasting initial consonants with consonant blends and digraphs. For example, students compare words that begin with the same sound as *bell* with words that begin with the same sound as *blanket*.

After sorting pictures, students search through their word banks for words that begin with the same initial consonants and consonant blends and digraphs. Word bank words won't contain many blends or digraphs at first. Therefore, don't expect students to master consonant blends and digraphs in spelling until the middle or end of the letter-name phase (Bear, 1992).

Your goal in having your students examine consonant blends and digraphs is to teach them to see blends and digraphs as one unit. For example, *sh* is two letters that function as a unit at the beginning of a word. This sets the stage for the letter-name phase, when students examine short-vowel patterns.

Hunting and Drawing Pictures Students who can find pictures of words that sound alike at the beginning are applying their knowledge of initial consonants. This is considered a more difficult task than picture sorts. In these hunts, students look through magazine pages for pictures of objects that begin like *bell*. To save confusion, be sure to limit the magazine page choices to pages that you know have pictures of the consonant under consideration.

A still more difficult task is to draw pictures of same-sound words. Children who can independently generate several drawings are ready for another series of consonants. Students enjoy working individually or in small groups to make initial consonant books using pictures they have drawn or cut and pasted. After students cut and paste or draw their pictures, they write the word beside their entry. They write the initial consonant and draw a line. As you review this work with students, show them the rest of the word.

Alphabetizing When students have studied twelve of the initial consonants, they are ready to sort their word bank words into alphabetical order. By this time, students have collected approximately forty words. You can make a center activity in which they work with a large alphabet strip on the floor. Ask your students to place the word bank words on the alphabet strip and then stack the words in alphabetical order. When students alphabetize, they can use a card file box to help keep their words in order.

Word Study Games

Practice is the name of the game when students play word study games. Among numerous choices that give students practice in examining the patterns and features you have introduced, some perennial favorites include concentration, tic-tac-toe, and bingo (Bear, Invernizzi & Templeton, 1996).

Any board game can be made into a word study game by placing either picture or word cards on the squares, or using them as cards students draw for their hands. Students look for matches to the squares they land on or for the card they draw. During this phase you can use pictures with words from word banks mixed in.

Word Study in the Letter-Name Phase

Students who have a full concept of word are busy collecting many sight words. They include vowels in spelling syllables, and they can accurately spell initial and final consonants. They examine short-vowel patterns, and in word study activities they begin with sound discriminations between short and long-vowel sounds. Later, they study short-vowel patterns that are colored by vowel-like consonants (*ball, bark, cow, crawl*) and preconsonantal nasals (*bump, stand*).

Word Study in Context

Students in the middle and later part of the beginning reading phase use their orthographic knowledge of short-vowel patterns to identify the middle sounds of some words. For example, Vicky had trouble reading the word *clothes* in a dictation sentence. The rest of the sentence, "They have clothes," didn't help with meaning, nor did the surrounding sentences. She looked at the picture and still could not identify the word. Then she put her orthographic knowledge to use and quietly mouthed, "cuh, cull, oh, clothes."

You will still be showing students at this level how to help themselves when they are stuck. During the letter-name phase, they will do a little more sounding out (Biemiller, 1970). Some students do too much sounding out, letter by letter. Encourage students to read to the end of the sentence to see if they can make sense of the words. If not, they should reexamine the text and look at the pictures for context clues.

Picture and Word Sorts

The process of differentiating between long and short vowels begins with students sorting pictures. Next, they focus on one short vowel at a time. You can guide word study in small-group lessons and then have your students follow up by working together and independently to explore these patterns further in sorts, word hunts, and word study games.

Sorting for Vowel Families Begin your study of vowel families with **short-vowel word families.** Although many teachers start with short ă, you can begin with any short vowel. The important point is that your students study short-vowel patterns before they study long vowels.

You may spend four weeks studying the first short vowel, but the time invested will shorten your study of the other short vowels because all short vowels operate on the same principles. When students study the first short vowel, they are learning about all short-vowel patterns. If you begin with the short ă, focus on the word families, the unambiguous short ă patterns first; that is, *at* and *an*. Avoid short ă words that end with *ll* or *r* at this time.

Beginning with picture sorts, have your students compare pictures that have the same short vowel but differ in their ending—for example, *net* and *bed*. After these picture sorts, ask students to search through their word banks for words that fit these sound patterns. You can record their brainstorming of other words that sound the same in the middle and then show them the patterns.

Students will add many more words to their word banks during the letter-name phase. Students who know the word *sat* can add words such as *rat, hat,* and even *sack.* They can create word wheels and flip books much like the letter books they made during the semiphonemic phase.

After your students demonstrate in their reading, spelling, and word study that they understand the short-vowel pattern for the first vowel, they are ready to study a second vowel. Some teachers study the short ŏ next because it is substantially different from the short ă.

Consonant-Vowel-Consonant Patterns As students examine two short vowels, they will begin to understand the general structure of short vowels. Show students that the words they have studied follow the **consonant-vowel-consonant** pattern (CVC). When you work with students in small group activities comparing and contrasting short-vowel patterns, they begin to see the similarities across vowels—that, for example, *Ben* and *rat* are both CVC patterns. From the earlier study of consonant blends and digraphs, students see that words such as *black, stem, sick, shot,* and even *grump* follow a CVC pattern.

Other Short-Vowel Patterns As sight vocabularies and word banks grow, students are sure to start noticing words that contain exceptions. When students present exceptions, students can find other words that help them to see the original word, not as an exception but as part of a pattern. For example, when studying short ŏ in a small group, your students may wonder how they should sort words that sound and look like *cow* in the middle. As you help students to brainstorm words that look like and sound like *cow,* they will see that some words look and sound the same (*now, how, bow*) and other words look like *cow* but sound different (*low, tow, mow*).

At the end of the letter-name phase, students' word banks become too large and cumbersome to manage. Their sight vocabularies are extensive, and teachers can begin to make up sorts that are composed of twenty known word cards.

Word Study Games

Word study games can now focus on short-vowel patterns. Students continue to enjoy tic-tac-toe, bingo, and concentration, and when you are sure that students can read the words that you use in word study games, you are ready to introduce games such as word-study go fish and follow-the-path board games. You can make your own game boards, paste them onto manila folders, and then laminate them. Once laminated, you can use erasable ink markers to fill in the spaces on the board with patterns you want students to match during the board game. You can introduce these games in small groups. Your students should play them cooperatively, mostly in pairs. They are practicing games and should be played quickly without great concern for who wins. If time permits, your students can add words from the game into their word study notebooks.

Coordinating Spelling with Word Study

Just as with word study programs, you will plan a spelling program, including spelling lists and exercises according to students' development. Given the

····· TAKING A ····· CLOSE LOOK   Principles of Word Study

Keep the following few principles of word study in mind as you plan activities. They apply to word sorts throughout the letter-name and within-word pattern phases of spelling:

1. *Base each word study on the current phase of spelling development.* Students understand orthographic patterns when they are already experimenting with them (Invernizzi, Abouzeid & Gill, 1994).

2. *Word study activities help students to examine words.* A subtle distinction exists between teaching students words and teaching them how to examine words. Students learn words by doing plenty of reading and writing (Adams, 1990; Templeton & Bear, 1992). Word study contributes to growth in spelling and in word identification in reading.

3. *Look for both accuracy and fluency in students' sorting.* If the student makes three or four errors, then take a step backward and focus on easier word study activities that produce greater accuracy.

4. *Use known words in word study.* Word study is too difficult when students use unknown words. Only use words that they can easily read out of context.

5. *Sort words by their similarities and by their differences.* Provide word study activities in which students can see these similarities and contrasts.

range of development in any classroom, you can expect to need three spelling lists and related activities.

An appropriate spelling list is one that matches the patterns students need to study. As you have seen already, students in the semiphonemic phase study initial consonants and consonant blends and digraphs, and letter-name spellers study short-vowel patterns. On an appropriate spelling list, students will score 50 percent on the pretest and obtain good accuracy in spelling with reasonable practice (Morris, Blanton, Blanton & Perney, 1995).

Semiphonemic Spellers

Spelling lists in which the words must be spelled correctly often put semiphonemic spellers at their frustration levels. You will achieve greater learning if instead you focus their spelling tests on spelling the first sounds correctly. For example, students who have studied the letter *b* should be able to spell correctly the beginning of words that begin with a *b,* but should not have to spell the entire words correctly.

Letter-Name Spellers

Spelling lists for students in the letter-name phase are based on the vowels they examine in word study activities. For example, students who are examining short *ĕ* families would have a spelling list that includes these families. Most spelling series include four exercises and a bonus activity for each week's spelling list. You can replace many of these spelling activities with word study activities, which give more practice in examining patterns. Letter-name spellers can add to or develop their own spelling lists by finding words that sound or look like the spelling words. Have students bring two or three words each to their word study groups. They can examine the words and create a ten- to fifteen-word list. In one classroom, a group of students studying the basic CVC families generated this list: *fad, mad, sad, bat, rat, cat, clap, fall, ball,* and *call.* They agreed to write each word three times and to take a practice test on Wednesday or Thursday. In contrast, a group of students who were at the end of the letter-name phase agreed on the following list: *sketch, lent, left, yet, me, bless, nest, crept, slept,* and *west.*

In spelling tests, students can call the words to each other. They review their work for changes they want to make. After correction, they write each misspelled word three times. A student who misses more than 30 percent of the words on the final spelling test probably needs to back up to an easier list. It is important to remember that you should never expect students to spell words that they cannot read (Gill & Scharer, 1996; Templeton, 1991).

Conclusion and Study Notes

This chapter has presented ways to work with students in the beginning phase of literacy. It has emphasized providing the support that students need to experience success in reading and to see themselves as readers and writers. Writing activities, also designed to provide support, are in most cases extensions of support reading activities. Students first work through the writing process during the beginning phase. In word study and spelling, students in the semiphonemic phase examine beginning consonants, and as they progress to the letter-name phase, they concentrate on short-vowel sounds and patterns.

Students experience many new activities during this beginning phase of development, and they have a host of supporting materials: personal readers, word banks, and journals. They are becoming the students they thought they would become when they entered first grade, and they are excited because they begin to read easy books and write in a conventional way that others can reread.

- Concept of word, described as the ability to reread familiar text accurately, distinguishes emergent from beginning readers.

- Beginning readers and writers read disfluently, they read aloud, and they often point to the words as they read.

- Beginning readers are in either the semiphonemic or letter-name stage of spelling.

- Students' listening comprehension is developed through GLTAs, charting, clusters, and webs.

- This is a time of support for beginning readers. Teachers support students by reading together chorally.

- Personal readers contain copies of rhymes, pattern stories, group experience charts, and individual dictations that students reread. Big books are used in shared reading experiences.

- In reading workshops, students read in pairs; they read to each other familiar pattern books and dictations, and they read new materials together.

- Beginning readers begin sustained silent reading periods each day.

- In the writing process beginning writers concentrate on prewriting, writing, and postwriting. Rewriting and editing are introduced, but they are minor aspects of the writing process for beginners.

- In writing workshops, students write together, and they help each other with revision and editing.

- There are many postwriting activities that include response groups, author's chair, and class books.

- Independent, beginning writing activities include learning and response logs as well as letter writing.

- Beginning readers collect known words from their familiar books and stories to create word banks. They use these known words in word sorts.

- Word study for semiphonemic spellers focuses on initial and ending consonants. Consonant blends and digraphs are introduced.

- Word study for letter-name spellers begins with word families and then focuses on the consonant-vowel-consonant patterns.

- There are many picture and word sorts and word study games to introduce to beginning readers.

Key Terms

rudimentary and full concept of word	group experience charts
semiphonemic spelling	individual dictations
letter-name spelling	reading workshops
support reading materials	writing workshops
choral reading	journals, logs, and response logs
personal readers	word banks
shared reading	short-vowel word families
pattern books	consonant-vowel-consonant
language experiences	

Follow-Up Activities

1. Work with a small group of beginning readers to develop and reread a group experience chart. Begin with an experience and plenty of talking, and then chart what students say, using the format, "Child said, '. . .'" Have children come to the chart individually to point to the words as they read. Determine if they have a rudimentary or full concept of word and how they identify words in context. See if the children can collect sight words, and ask them to draw pictures to go with the chart.

2. Teach a group of fifth- or sixth-graders to read one-on-one with beginning readers. Once a week, have the older students come prepared to read a particular book, and, in turn, have beginning readers share their favorite selections from their personal readers. Show the older students the kinds of books the younger ones enjoy.

3. Make a collection of rhymes, poems, and songs that beginners can reread and use in their writing. The materials can range in difficulty and length from two-line poems to entire songs.

4. Observe beginning writers during writing workshop. Determine where the children are in the writing process. Use Figure 7.5 to guide your observations of students while they write.

Children's ■ VOICES ■

What Children and Their Teachers Say about Literacy Learning

Throughout this book, you can hear the voices of university students, teachers, Donald Bear, and Diane Barone. In this special section, listen to children talking about how they have learned to read and write. Their teachers describe them in the classroom, so you can understand each child in his or her classroom context.

Above: Children reading together in Becky Schneider's classroom.

Left: A small-group learning activity with Becky Schneider.

About Whitney Elementary School— Las Vegas, Nevada

The children who are introduced here are all members of a K–5 urban school in Las Vegas, Nevada, called Whitney Elementary. Principal Francine Mayfield helped found a program where students have enough time with a teacher so that school feels like a family. In addition to multiaged classrooms divided into primary and intermediate levels, classrooms are organized into families of students who attend assemblies, eat lunch, have recess, and take field trips together. Primary students move into intermediate classes within their family.

The philosophy of this school is that all students can be successful learners, and to help them achieve success, teachers teach to students' strengths. Flexible grouping, themed instruction, process writing, literature groups, peer and cross-age tutoring, and other innovative instruction practices are common in all the classrooms within the school.

Children writing in journals in Adine Petrulli's classroom.

Top: Three children read together in a library area.

Below: A child works alone with an interactive learning machine.

The Primary and Intermediate Classrooms of Whitney Elementary: A Closer Look

Two classrooms within this school served as the sites for this interviewing project. The first classroom is a primary class of first- and second-graders led by Adine Petrulli. Adine has been teaching at Whitney for five years and student taught there before she joined the staff. Adine's goals for her students and herself are centered on developing a love of learning, independence, and confidence in making decisions and on fostering meaningful learning endeavors. This year in Adine's classroom, the children are focusing on teamwork. The classroom has been transformed into a baseball playing field to establish this theme.

The second classroom is an intermediate classroom of third-, fourth-, and fifth-graders led by Becky Schneider. Becky has been a teacher at Whitney for four years and before coming to Whitney taught four- and five-year-olds in a preschool setting. She believes that her students should have choice in what they learn,

*Children gather facts as
they prepare to write a
group report.*

problem solve independently, and have enthusiasm for learning. The theme for her classroom this year is roots. Students have explored their own backgrounds and are studying the foundations of our country.

These teachers believe in teaching to students' strengths and allowing student choice in the reading and writing curriculum. They also use portfolios to help students, teachers, and parents understand each student's development. Each teacher has developed a year-long theme that guides instruction.

The Background of Students at Whitney Elementary

While you may think that the children who attend this school come from middle-income backgrounds, 54 percent of the children receive free or reduced lunch, and 33 percent are homeless. There is a rich diversity of students within this school: the student population is 10 percent Hispanic, 3 percent African-American, 1 percent Asian, and 86 percent Caucasian.

The children interviewed represent all phases of literacy development. From Adine Petrulli's classroom, emergent and beginner readers and writers were selected. From Becky Schneider's classroom, beginner, transitional, and advanced readers and writers were selected. Additionally, one child is learning English as a second language, and two other children receive special education support once a day within the regular classroom from the special education teacher.

Interviewing the Children and Their Teachers

Throughout this book, we have emphasized that knowing your students helps you build instruction that lets them grow as readers and writers. In this section, you can hear what children say about how they learned to read and write and about what they select as some of their favorite books and authors. You also can observe how children at different levels of literacy development think about the process of reading and writing.

Diane Barone has been working with Whitney Elementary for five years; she knows the children and the teachers, and they know her. In the fall of 1996, Diane interviewed children from Adine's and Becky's classrooms and talked to each child individually. They all were asked the same questions:

How did you learn to read?

What are some of your favorite books or authors?

How did you learn to write?

What do you like to write about?

What do you read and write at home?

At the end of the interview (each lasted about a half-hour), each child drew a picture of himself or herself reading or writing.

Each page of this section contains the words of children representing all phases of literacy development as they talk about how they learned to read and write. You see their self-portraits and hear their teachers talk about these students as readers and writers in the classroom. After you see how the children represent literacy and its role in their worlds, we conclude this special section with some key themes expressed by their thoughts and work. Not surprisingly, you encounter these themes throughout this text.

Celia
An Emergent Literacy Learner

Adine Petrulli Talking About Celia

❝You always know where Celia is in the room because she's the first one to answer any question. She is shy when meeting new people. But, once she feels comfortable with you, she tries her best to show you how much she is learning.

Celia reads constantly at home and at school. She can often be found reading a book out loud to a pretend audience. She loves illustrations and recognizes great detail in them. She takes pride in discovering new words and sharing her knowledge with other classmates.

Journal writing is another love of Celia's. She enjoys writing about her family and her dog. She reads any responses to her writing aloud to emphasize her pride in her work.❞

My dad read to me. I like books with easy words. I like Adventures of Toy Story. There are lots of easy words. I don't know about an author. I have lots of books at home. I have lots. Winnie the Pooh is special. He falls out of the honey tree a lot.

My dad taught me to write. He writes so I could copy it. That's how I started to be a good writer. I write stories.

Focus on Celia's Literacy Learning

- Reads at home and school
- Writes with Dad
- Enjoys journal writing
- Reads books and journal responses aloud
- Knows words at prephonemic level

Ashley
An Emergent Second Language Literacy Learner

I learned how to read. My mom taught me. She helped me with words I didn't know. She read them to me. I like <u>Harriet the Spy</u>. I bought it. I found it in the library. They gave it for free. I tell my mom what books I want. "Mom, I want <u>Harriet the Spy</u>." I never read it. I read the back of it, and I see the cover. I like to read in my room. I like the books and papers my mom gives me. She gets books for me. I have my own bookshelf with lots of books.

My mom helped me learn to write. She got the pencil. She put my hand on the pencil. Then I wrote by myself. I write pictures and in my journal. My mom tells me what to write. I could think what I could do.

Adine Petrulli Talking About Ashley

❝Ashley loves working in the hallway. She says that it helps her concentrate. Her older brother and mom help her with her homework, but Ashley tries to be very independent.

As an emergent reader, Ashley has a lot of confidence. She focuses on her strengths, sharing what she does know. Using new information gained from word study activities, she recognizes similarities in words like the initial consonant sound. She loves rhyming texts, sometimes reading them aloud as a song.

Ashley enjoys writing about her friends and family. You can always find her writing about a new adventure that she and her older sister have been on. Ashley's confidence in her ability can be seen in her writing as she uses her imagination to write about myriad people and places.❞

Focus on Ashley's Literacy Learning

- Reads with Mom
- Visits library
- Writes in journal
- Loves rhyming texts
- Writes imaginative family adventures
- Recognizes words with similar initial consonants sounds; semi-phonemic level

Kurt
A Beginning Reader

Adine Petrulli Talking About Kurt

"When I think of Kurt, I think of energy. He can never stay in one place very long to work, so it helps that he has the freedom to move around the room. Even though he is active, he does his best to remain focused.

Kurt loves to read with others. He spends a great deal of his free time reading and loves to go to the library. As an early reader, he uses contextual support and visual cues to aid in identifying difficult words. He is willing to ask for help when he needs it and is excited to continue the story.

He enjoys writing in his dialogue journal about the books he reads, retelling the stories and making adaptations to them. We write to one another about favorite books and parts of stories. He uses inventive spelling to help with difficult words so that he can share his ideas. "

Focus on Kurt's Literacy Learning

- Practices reading at home
- Mom and Dad help with unknown words
- Writes small and stays in lines
- Writes about interests (basketball)
- Visits library
- Reads frequently during free time
- Identifies difficult words with contextual and visual cues
- Enjoys dialogue journal writing
- Retells (with adaptations) stories
- Uses inventive spelling and is experimenting with short vowels; letter name level

I learn to read by I keep on practicing at home. I read a lot at home. I'm not a very good reader. There are some words I don't know. My mom or my dad help. I like 101 Dalmatians. It's about a lot of dogs, and I like dogs. I like What a Bad Dream by Mercer Mayer. If I pick an easy book, I can read them myself. There are a lot of words I know. I read it. I read before dinner, so it's not very late, late. I'm cranky in the morning.

I was here for first grade, and I was writing pretty big until I turned seven. Then I wrote smaller and stayed in the lines. I write about things that I like—basketball. I'm learning at it. Last time in p.e. I made one shot. I just write what happens every-day. What I do.

Brittney
Beginning Reader Receiving Special Education Support

I learned to read at school. My teacher read to me, and then I read the words after her. I like to read chapter books. I read them at home too. I like Mrs. Schneider, my teacher, to pick out books for me to read. If she tells me to pick out a book to read by myself, I look at one of the pages and read it. If there are five words that are too hard on a page, then I know it is too hard for me. I remember reading Arthur's Babysitter a lot of times. I really liked it. I don't have a favorite author or illustrator yet.

I learned to write at school. When I was in kindergarten, the teacher would spell words on the board, and I would copy them. Now, when I write, I brainstorm about what I want to write about. When you think about what you're going to write, it helps. I ask other people in my class questions about my topic too. They always give me ideas.

Focus on Brittney's Literacy Learning

- Reads chapter books
- Screens book pages for difficulty
- Knows words at letter name phase
- Brainstorms prior to writing
- Queries peers for writing topics
- Rereads stories for comprehension
- Uses peers for reading support
- Uses interviewing to collect information
- Writes biographies about friends
- Uses writing process

Becky Schneider Talking About Brittney

66 When I think of a sweet, honest, and hardworking student, Brittney comes to mind. Brittney will help anyone who needs it without a qualm. She is supported by her peers and often turns to them for assistance. Socially, she hangs out with students in our room who are above grade level academically.

Brittney is a beginning reader. Reading is difficult, yet she will reread a story until she understands what it is about and is able to read it fluently. While reading, you can find Brittney next to her friends who can help her out if needed. She likes reading mysteries and will challenge herself to find clues within the mystery. Our goal is to have her reading a Ramona book by the end of the year.

Writing is an easier process for Brittney. Because we take our writing through the writing process, it is not threatening to her. She writes many biographies about her friends. She uses interviewing to collect information and will somehow include all of the information in her writing. She enjoys being with her friends and will write about their experiences in her stories. 99

Valerie
Transitional Reader Receiving Special Education Support

I don't know how I learned to read. I like Dr. Seuss books, and I read poetry at home. My favorite book at home is Where the Sidewalk Ends. When I find a book to read, I look at the words and see if they are easy. I like to read books with easy words. I don't have any favorite authors or illustrators. I like the book I Love You Forever. I read that one lots of times.

I learned to write by just writing. I just started writing, and then I started writing good. I like to write stories.

Becky Schneider Talking About Valerie

❝Valerie is a little girl with big brown eyes and pigtails. She is tiny in stature and is always being taken care of by other students. Valerie comes from a family with two children. She is the oldest. Her family has set high expectations for her and will go above and beyond to help her be successful.

Valerie is becoming a fluent reader. She is determined to become a dynamic reader. She sits by her peers who are fluent readers so they can support her when needed. She likes being read to and frequently is seen chorally reading with other students. Valerie talks about characters in her books and will retell the problems they faced. She often relates her own experiences if they are similar.

By choosing topics she is familiar with, Valerie writes detailed stories. She writes nonfiction and will choose topics such as animals, friends, and family. She is excited about publishing her work so she can participate in authors' chair. Her involved illustrations are always the focus of our authors' chair discussions.❞

Focus on Valerie's Literacy Learning

- Reads poetry
- Screens book pages for level of difficulty
- Knows word patterns
- Learned writing through practice
- Retells character problems
- Support from peers while reading
- Writes nonfiction, detailed stories
- Makes detailed illustrations

Amanda
Beginning Reader

I learned to read because my mom read a book with me. She told me the words, and I got used to them. Now I like to read big novels like <u>Matilda</u>. It is a good book. The book is not like the movie. I read the <u>Stinky Cheese Man</u>, and I have read the <u>Really Ugly Duckling</u>. It is a good book too. I still read at home, but now I sometimes read to my mom. I read to her until she goes to sleep, and then I ask my dad if I can go outside. When I pick out a book to read, I look through it to see if it looks like a good book. If it looks good, then I read it. I like to read Goosebumps books because they are good. I don't really have a favorite author.

I learned to write in school. When I first started school, I used to write, and then I got used to it more and more. I like to read, but I love, love, love, love, love, love to write! I like to write books best. I write in my reading response journal and in my journal, too. When I write, I just think of things that I did, and then a couple of days later I write about what happened. Sometimes at home, I make a little book for my mom with a whole bunch of pages. She likes those.

Becky Schneider Talking About Amanda

66 Amanda is one of the happiest students I know. She always has a grin on her face and laughs all of the time. She is not hesitant to help out her peers, but if they aren't cooperative, she will move on to someone who is. Amanda has great family support in reading and writing, which enables her to be successful.

Amanda came to me at grade level in reading and writing. Because she is determined to understand the stories she reads, she has slowly moved beyond her grade-level expectations. She enjoys humorous stories and likes Roald Dahl as an author. She frequently reads alone to ensure she gets a lot accomplished, and she can reread if she wants. She also enjoys reading to other students and is often surrounded by others listening to her.

Amanda picks topics to write on that are familiar to her. She writes about her pets and will include lively descriptions of their personalities. Her writing is complete in that her audience rarely has a question about it. She is enthusiastic about her writing and loves to share in authors' chair. 99

Focus on Amanda's Literacy Learning

- Learned reading with Mom
- Reads to Mom now
- Screens books for quality and interest
- Learned writing at school
- Writes in reading response journal
- Knows word patterns
- Has tremendous family support
- Enjoys humor
- Reads to peers and alone
- Writes comprehensively about familiar topics
- Shares writing with peers

Cody
Transitional Reader

Becky Schneider Talking About Cody

"Cody has always been considered the class clown. Where there are willing ears, Cody is by them entertaining. Cody comes from a family with four children. His blond spiky hair and toothless smile always seem to work for him when he gets into trouble.

Cody came to this class at grade level in reading and writing. Family support and motivation have allowed him to surpass his grade level during the past two years. He loves reading comic books. He can always be found in the corner on a bean bag discussing the plot and animation of his comics.

When he writes, I am always amazed at his creativity. He usually writes fictional stories dealing with other imaginary worlds. His characters come to life because of the humorous descriptions and antics they get into. Cody is one of the few students who constantly seeks a conversational answer in his journal. In the month of December, we dialogued about how we would catch Santa this year. He is still waiting for my promised photo to prove Santa exists."

Focus on Cody's Literacy Learning

- Learned reading and writing with teacher, Mom, and Dad
- Repeated words they read
- Copied words they wrote
- Knows word patterns
- Brainstorms prior to writing
- Writes letters
- Writes in journal (enjoys conversational style)
- Tremendous family support
- Enjoys reading comic books
- Discusses plot and animation of comics
- Writes creative, fictional stories

I got taught to read by my teachers and my mom and dad. They, like, read me a word, and I would repeat it, and I got used to reading. I like to read the Goosebumps books and mysteries and scary stories. I love to read! I really don't read books over again. I like to read the comics over and over. My favorite author is R.L. Stine. When I pick other books, I find one I think I will like, and I read through a few pages, and I see if I'm interested.

I got taught to write by my mom and dad and teachers. They, like, write something down like a letter, and I would write it after them. I like to make books, write letters, and write to my teacher in my journal. When I write a book, I like think of something. I do a brainstorm to see if I will have enough ideas to make a book. I don't write much at home—just my homework and letters.

Jered
Advanced Reader

Becky Schneider Talking About Jered

66 Jered is a sweet, soft-spoken boy most of the time but will defi-
nitely let you know his opinion on things. Jered is a leader in our class
and usually organizes our groups when working cooperatively. Jered is
supported in reading and writing by his family. He visits the library frequently and has daily assistance with any homework or projects. He is
very social and loves to work cooperatively, but only if he can pick his
group.

Jered has made tremendous progress in reading. He came to me at
grade level and is now one of our top readers. He likes to read biographies on athletes, especially basketball players and football players.
Jered discusses his books continuously with his friends. In fact, Jered
has a reserved place on the couch that everyone leaves just for him.

Jered uses his friends to support his writing. His friends become
his characters in some sort of plot about sports. He uses a lot of dialogue in his writing to let his characters really come alive. As with
reading, Jered always writes near his friends. He bounces ideas back
and forth and will not put anything in his stories that his friends do
not approve of. 99

Focus on Jered's Literacy Learning

- **Learned to read with Mom**
- **Screens back cover to determine level of difficulty**
- **Reads books multiple times for understanding**
- **Identifies letter patterns with words; syllable juncture phase**
- **Writes short poems**
- **Visits library frequently**
- **Reads athlete biographies**
- **Discusses books with peers**
- **Uses peers for writing support and ideas**
- **Uses dialogue in writing**

My mom taught me to read. She got books from the library.
She even ordered me <u>Highlights</u>. I really like reading the
Goosebumps books. They are not scary, but I like to read
them. When I pick a book to read, I like to read the back. If I
miss ten words, it's hard. Then if it's not hard, I can read it if
it's in my ability. I read books over again if I don't understand
them. I read the <u>Phantom Toll Booth</u> over again. I read it in
third grade and fourth grade. Now I understand it better. I'm
like my friends. I like books by R.L. Stine, and I like Judy Blume,
too.

I learned to write by first learning the ABCs. I look at
words to see patterns. I look to see if they are alike, like
sheep and deep. That helps me spell. I like to write. I write
about things I like to do. At home, I write short poems.

Buster
Advanced Reader

Becky Schneider Talking About Buster

"The leader of our class is Buster. Wherever Buster is, a group of students will be found awaiting his approval. The slicked back hair and baggy jeans are a fad started by Buster. He demands respect by all those who come in contact with him. His strong personality outweighs his tiny body frame, enabling him to maintain his leadership role.

Buster is above grade level in both reading and writing. His comprehension is unbelievable in the minute details he can recall. He usually winds up reading with his buddies, sharing and discussing almost any genre. He likes science information books and biographies on athletes best. He will never admit he likes to read, but I have caught him numerous times so engrossed in a book that he is oblivious to his surroundings.

Buster never wrote a thing until he could write an entire word. Lizard, he tells me, was the first thing he wrote. Because he wants his writing to be flawless, writing takes longer. When he does finish a story, it is told as though you are in the story. He writes about fictional characters that usually have humorous character traits, often similar to the traits of his friends. Buster loves to involve his friends in everything that he does."

My grandma taught me to read. She just, like, taught me to sound it out and stuff. She would read a sentence and tell me to repeat it. I like to read mysteries. They, like, got action. I don't read books again. I have only read one book three times. It was Keep the Light Burning Abby. I like it. She was, like, living in the White House. Stephen King is probably my favorite author. He writes scary stories.

I don't know how I learned to write. I wouldn't write until I could write a whole word. My first word was lizard. I spelled it all right. I'm not sure that I always like writing workshop. I just think of something in my head, and then I write about it.

Focus on Buster's Literacy Learning

- Learned to read with Grandma
- Sounds out and repeats words; syllable juncture phase
- Has favorite author, Stephen King
- Likes mysteries
- Has excellent comprehension
- Reads, shares, and discusses with peers
- Uses humorous, fictional characters in writing

Conrad
Advanced Reader

Becky Schneider Talking About Conrad

"When I think of Conrad, I see a determined, talkative, and intelligent student. Conrad is eleven years old and has a younger sibling. He has big eyes, brown hair and wears baggy shorts and an oversized jacket. His family supports Conrad in reading and writing and has a house full of books.

Conrad came to me in third grade. He was above grade level in reading and writing and has continued to remain so. Conrad's determination helps him get through difficult books. He continuously asks questions about his book and isn't satisfied until an answer meets his approval. He has a tremendous vocabulary and uses words from his books in his reading and writing. Conrad is often curled up on the couch reading science fiction. He is one of the students who add words to our tough word chart. He likes to read a book he can discuss with a friend.

Conrad uses a variety of styles in his writing. He likes to be the narrator so that he can introduce the characters and settings and insert his opinion throughout the story. He loves to write advice books and uses interviewing to collect information. Conrad is able to sift through this information and demonstrate his abilities as a dynamic writer. "

Focus on Conrad's Literacy Learning

- Learned writing by watching others
- Writes nonfiction
- Writes at home (grocery and birthday lists)
- Asks continuous questions about books he's reading
- Has tremendous vocabulary
- Knows words at derivational constancy phase
- Writes advice books
- Uses interviewing to collect information
- Prefers to narrate stories (introduces characters and setting)

I learned to read by reading a lot. Before I got to school, my mom read me a lot of books, and I used to sound them out. I still read a lot at home. I like to read the comics and my mom's books. I like to read books by R.L. Stine—not his books for kids but his books for adults, like Girlfriend and Boyfriend. I love the books by J.R.R. Tolkien, especially The Hobbit. My friend Chandler got me reading them. When I pick books that aren't by Roald Dahl, R.L. Stine, J.R.R. Tolkien, or Elizabeth Winthrop, my favorite authors, I don't read the first page. I look at the cover, and if I like it, I read a chapter. I like thick books. They give me more to read. I check the theme of the book. I like comedy and drama books the best. One book that I have read over and over is 911 Emergency Rescue. It's kind of funny. I like the theme; it has comedy and drama.

I learned to write by usually watching people write. I learned from that. My mom had me in a class when I was four. I talked sentences when I was two. That's when I learned to write. I like to write nonfiction and stories. I write anything that pops into my head. After the idea pops into my mind, I think about what I know to see if I have enough. If I am writing with someone, I ask them for information. My mom has me write a ton at home too. I write the grocery list and what I want for my birthday. That's important because my birthday is next week.

What Do the Children Teach Us?

The thoughts shared by these children and their teachers reflect some important aspects of learning to read and write.

- **Parents are important.** Both children and teachers talk about how parents support their child's literacy development and help them learn to value literacy. This support is provided on a routine basis by families, in many cases poor families, who often are not credited with providing this type of support.

- **Learning to read and write is a social activity.** These children often choose to read or write with friends.

- **Students seek response from other students, parents, and teachers.** The children often ask other children for help with reading and writing.

- **Students enjoy selecting the books they want to read and the topics for stories to write.** The students can cite their favorite authors and books and also talk about strategies for selecting books that they can read successfully.

- **Students and teachers build on strengths.** Both students and teachers can articulate what students do well with reading and writing and what they need to improve. Learning develops from instruction based on these strengths.

- **Children use and create their own strategies.** The students find ways, such as partner reading and writing, to support their own personal reading and writing excursions.

- **Literacy learning is an integrative process.** The process of literacy involves listening, reading, writing, speaking, dramatizing, drawing, laughing, and physically reaching for books.

8 Diversity in Literacy Learning

Mark: We did a pilot program at my school in which parents, students, and teachers met at the beginning of the year to discuss the students' strengths.

Sharon: At my at-risk school, I never heard teachers say that parents sat and said nothing. They do really care. They just don't always know what to do.

Diane: How do you encourage parents to be part of the educational team? And how do you talk to parents who don't speak English as their first language?

Sharon: We made it a priority to reach every parent. We called, we visited homes, we knocked on doors. We went the extra mile to go out into the neighborhood. We arranged conferences around their time schedules. We noted what days parents were off work and when they were sleeping. The parents were much more able and willing to come to school after these initial contacts. And they become involved with our school even when it was labeled an at-risk school.

Steve: It helps when the teacher impresses on the student that their assessment includes this conference with the parent. The students do have power; they are somebody. When they tell their parents, "I really need you to come to the conference," moms and dads will usually show up.

Sharon: You need to make a commitment that you are going to bring parents in and that school will be a comfortable place for them. We even made sure that we had other parents who spoke Spanish at school so that our Hispanic families felt more comfortable when they arrived.

Leslie: If you make an honest effort to get in touch with parents, all but maybe one or two in your class will come in. That's pretty good.

Sharon: Community and partnership, again. You need to put them up front at the beginning of the year. A phone call every month to parents helps to continue the partnership.

Steve: I never realized how important phone calls are to parents. If you think you can teach without calling parents, you are fooling yourself.

The teachers and principal (Sharon) involved in this discussion have focused on how important parents are to their children's success in school settings. Clearly, the people in this conversation are committed to involving parents in setting academic goals for their children. They even, as Sharon says, "go out into the neighborhood" to bring parents into the school.

The participants mentioned at-risk schools. A school is labeled *at-risk* when many of the students—because of low socioeconomic status, for instance—are deemed at risk of failing to succeed in school. Often schools use the number of children who qualify for free lunch as a determiner.

This label, as is usually the case with labels in general, can result in troubling stereotyping and a presupposition that the problem is within the student. In many cases, the use of labels lowers academic expectations for students. Cheek, Flippo, and Lindsey (1997, p. 365) argue that the at-risk label has "no educational relevance." To designate a child at-risk does not provide any insight into the child's literacy development but focuses only on what children do not possess, their deficits. A better term is *children of promise,* which was gleaned from the work of Heath and Mangiola (1991), who suggest that educators abandon the deficit notion and focus on the interesting differences between children's home and school cultures.

Teachers must remember that demographic information applies the at-risk label, not individual children. The principal in the above discussion is clearly trying to move beyond the at-risk label and secure successful ways to interact with students and parents so that all of their students will be successful learners.

Within this chapter, we will consider many aspects of diversity. We will explore language, cultural, racial, socioeconomic, and academic diversity. Figure 8.1 presents an overview of children who might qualify as at-risk. As you scan this chart, you will notice that it includes children who are not achieving to their potential because of inappropriate or poor instruction. Each aspect of diversity will be important for you to consider as you contemplate teaching your first classroom of students. Diversity in the classroom is a *strength* of the classroom, not a problem to be remedied.

Guide Questions for Chapter 8

- What is important to understand about a student learning a second language?

- What principles can guide a teacher who is instructing a student learning English as a second language?

- How can the assessment process determine a student's language strengths?

- What is important to understand about a student whose culture, race, or socio-economic status does not represent a middle-class background?

- How can teachers become familiar with a child's cultural, racial, or socioeconomic status?

- How does a teacher bridge the home and school environments?

- How might a teacher make the classroom environment more culturally sensitive?

- How can teachers support the learning needs of students within the classroom?

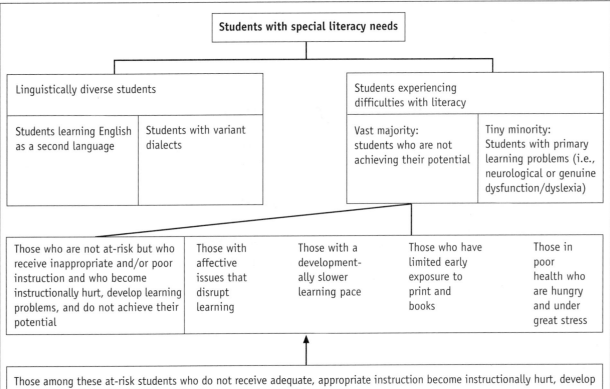

Figure 8.1
Overview of Potentially
At-Risk Students *Source:*
Adapted from Templeton
(1995, p. 585).

Language Diversity

The following is a conversation recorded by Vivian Paley (1981, pp. 116–117) after she initiated a discussion about languages with her kindergarten students. See if you can discover how the children resolve the issue of why there are so many different languages.

Teacher: Why are there so many different languages?

Lisa: Because some people don't know these other languages.

Kim: They can't talk the way we talk.

Eddie: Maybe when people are born they choose the language they want to know and then they go to a special place to learn it. I mean their mother chooses.

Andy: Like a child could tell his mother and father to take him to a place where they can learn French if they are French.

Warren: God gives people all the sounds. Then you can tell you're in a different place because it sounds different.

Wally: When you're little you try to think of what the name of something is and people tell you.

Eddie: Oh, yeah. Your mother tells you. You come out of her stomach and she talks English to you and she tells you the name for everything.

Deana: If you live in a different country, there's a different language there. Wherever you were born you talk in that language.

Warren: Wherever your mother was born.

Teacher: Your mother was born in China, Warren, but you speak English.

Deana: Because he never lived in China.

Warren: I'm going to go to Chinese school on Saturdays when I'm six.

Eddie: Someone has to teach you. My brother didn't know one word when he was born. Not even his name.

Earl: When I was little I said "ca-see."

Rose: What does that mean?

Earl: "Take me in the car." Now I know every word.

Rose: Me too.

Teacher: Akemi was born in Japan and she speaks Japanese. How are you learning English words now, Akemi?

Akemi: I listen to everybody.

The children in Paley's classroom took her abstract question of "Why are there so many languages?" and reconfigured it to one more within their experiences. This was their way of exploring how we learn language. Other keys to acquiring language include hearing people speak that language and learning the correct names for things.

You may be wondering why we discuss language diversity in a book that focuses on assessment and instruction. Ovando (1993) informs us that between 1970 and 1980 the United States became increasingly multiracial, multicultural, and multilingual. During these years, the United States increased in population by 11.6 percent. Within this 11.6 percent growth rate, Hispanics "increased by 61 percent, Native Americans by 71 percent, and Asian Americans by 141 percent" (p. 225). Olsen (1991) states that during the 1989–90 school year 5 percent of kindergarten through twelfth-grade students were classified as non–English-speaking or limited English proficient.

By the year 2020, Rossi and Stringfield (1995, p. 71) tell us, "the majority of students in America's public schools will be living in circumstances traditionally regarded as placing them at risk of educational failure. Many will be poorly housed, undernourished, subject to the effects of others' abuse of drugs, and provided with few positive adult role models." Additionally, most current projections expect that five million students will be from non–English-speaking backgrounds. Clearly, schools will be increasingly working with students from a variety of cultural, socioeconomic, and language backgrounds. The majority of children for whom English is a second language will study in mainstream classrooms with no additional support for acquiring English and subject knowledge (Freeman & Freeman, 1994). In other words, you will most likely be the primary teacher for children learning English as a second language.

When you begin teaching a child whose first language is not English, you will try to determine the child's facility with English and most likely with the first language as well. Along with considering the child's abilities with English, you need to discover if the child has just arrived in the United States. Children who are new to this country must become familiar not only with the new language, but with the American culture as it is represented in their new community. For instance, a child who has just arrived in a community from a home country at war will have to adjust to the new school as the war experiences move to the background of concern. Such a child might also have had fragmented learning experiences in the native country (Igoa, 1995). Other children may come to school not from the circumstances of a war-torn country but from the life of a migrant worker. These children are often jostled from one school to another as their parents move from crop to crop. Exploring the family circumstances will help you understand the child. Just looking at language facility alone will not provide a rich enough picture to understand the literacy learning of a child.

Learning a New Language

Often, students who are learning English as a second language pick up their first English expressions on the playground or in other social situations (Cummins, 1981). This makes sense, when you consider that this social language best serves students' needs. Children also need to learn academic language. Miramontes and Commins (1991) indicate that academic language takes five to seven years to develop, but school environments rarely recognize this long period of time. Educators tend to expect that students will become fluent in speaking and thinking in a new language within a year or two.

It is also important to consider the child's age at enrollment in an American school. Collier (1987) examined the test scores of immigrants after they completed an English as a second language (ESL) program at their school. Students who were between eight and eleven years old took four years to reach the fiftieth percentile on national standard achievement tests. They arrived at this performance level the fastest of any age of immigrant students because most of them were at grade level in their own country before coming to the United States. Younger students, ages five to seven, took five to eight years to reach this testing criteria because they were less advanced academically in the country of their birth before coming to the United States. The students at the greatest risk for success in American schools were those who were twelve or older. Few of them ever moved beyond the fortieth percentile on achievement tests even after four or five years of instruction. The older students faced the most hurdles in learning as they were expected to learn both a new language and the sophisticated, abstract concepts that were the routine curriculum of middle and high schools.

The Requirements of a New Language

Most of us tend to consider learning new vocabulary and syntax or grammar as the most important aspects of learning a new language. Although vocabulary and grammar are certainly important, a language consists of more than these components. Language develops within a culture and provides the means to communicate values, thoughts, opinions, and attitudes. Each language contains its own specific and unique nuances that allow these sophisticated exchanges between individuals. Words, phrases, gestures, voice inflections, and other elements are often idiosyncratic to a language and provide important clues to meaning.

To competently communicate with others, a person must possess knowledge of the language's phonology, morphology, syntax, and lexicon of a language. **Phonology** refers to learning the pronunciation of the words. **Morphology** includes the study of the structure of related words. **Syntax** involves the study of the order of words and how sentences are formed. Finally, the **lexicon** of a language is its vocabulary.

When we consider these dimensions of a language, we begin to perceive the complexity of mastering speaking, reading, and writing in a new language. As if these aspects of a new language were not enough of a challenge, Ovando (1993) adds five culture-related domains that students must also master before they are truly competent at communicating in a new language. These include

1. *Discourse*: **Discourse** relates to how language is organized beyond the sentence level—how paragraphs and longer pieces of writing are typically organized.

2. *Appropriateness*: Appropriateness relates to how we communicate in various settings. For example, conversation between a teacher and a student differs in form and organization from conversation between two students.

3. *Paralinguistics*: **Paralinguistics** involves studying the signs, gestures, and facial expressions that parallel oral communication—how language is communicated nonverbally.

4. *Pragmatics*: **Pragmatics** is concerned with how paralinguistics, discourse, and appropriateness interrelate. Speakers must learn, for example, how to take turns, listen, pace speech, and so on and to recognize the roles a speaker may take on in different situations.

5. *Cognitive-academic language proficiency*: Speakers must learn to gear their speech to learning abstract concepts.

By considering these dimensions of language, Ovando (1993, p. 216) helps us to understand that "language acquisition is a complicated, subtle, and culture-specific process." As teachers, we need to realize what children face in the complexity of learning a new language. Our students must acquire more than English vocabulary; learning a new language is a sophisticated, complicated process that requires time and patience.

A Typical Process of Learning a Second Language

Tough (1985) provides a framework for teachers to consider when they work with children learning English as a second language. At first, children will need a period of time to become *adjusted* to and *attuned* to the school environment and the new language. During this initial time in a classroom, a child may watch what is happening but be unwilling to participate or to try to speak in the new language. Krashen (1982) calls this time the silent period—a time when students look closely at the physical gestures of the teacher and listen closely to understand what is being said. A child who is beginning to feel comfortable in the new school setting will begin to use English for *self-help*. This child will ask for needed materials, start calling students by name, and ask to leave the class for the restroom. Following this development, the child will begin to use English to *join into activities*, to comment on what he or she is doing, and to ask about what other children are doing. The language uses up to this point are based in the here and now. The next step in learning English involves thinking more abstractly and using English to *find out about the world*. Children begin to form questions that they would like answered. At this phase of development, children need support in figuring out, for instance, how to explain a process, form a comparison, or make a prediction. The final phase involves using English to *extend learning*. Here language needs resemble those of children for whom English is a first language. For example, teachers may need to explain a complicated word or concept.

Tough's framework provides guidance for teachers who teach primarily in English, not the child's first language. Children, whether they are in a **bilingual** program that provides academic instruction in their first language or in an ESL program, will need support in their mainstream classroom as they move through the various levels of English acquisition.

You can find many ways to ensure that your classroom supports rather than hinders success for children learning English as a second language. Freeman and Freeman (1994) provide seven principles to support students as they acquire a second language:

1. Lessons should move from whole to part.

2. Lessons should involve students in active construction of knowledge.

3. Lessons should have current meaning and purpose for the students.

4. Lessons should engage groups of students in social interaction.

5. Lessons should develop both oral and written language.

6. Lessons should take place in the first language to build concepts and facilitate the acquisition of English.

7. Lessons should show faith in the learner in order to expand students' potential.

Freeman and Freeman consider these learning principles appropriate for all learning in a classroom. Indeed, you have already explored most of these principles. Some teachers express concern about principle six, which says lessons should take place in the student's first language. Although the idea makes sense, in fact few of us can do so. What we can do, however, is try to locate speakers of a student's first language to facilitate communication and to provide materials written in a student's first language. The student's first language will determine whether these tasks are easy or difficult to achieve. In many communities Spanish speakers and materials are easy to come by. You may have trouble finding speakers or materials in less frequently heard languages. Another helpful strategy is to match families new to the United States with other family members or members of their community or church who can ease communication for parents who struggle with English. It is important to discover and keep a list of these important people who can help you with communication in another language.

Assessment for Students Whose First Language Is Not English

Learning About a Student's Background

The most important part of assessment, particularly for students who do not speak English as a first language, is to understand a student's academic and personal background. As we mentioned earlier in this chapter, you need to know if the student is a recent immigrant or has been in the United States for a considerable period of time. The family's living conditions can provide useful information, too. Often, new immigrants move in with friends or relatives and the housing situation becomes quite crowded. Circumstances like these can make it difficult for a child to complete homework assignments or even to stay healthy.

In addition to the child's home background, you will also want to discover if the child can read and write in the first language. Children who are literate in a first language can use this knowledge in learning a second language. Classroom success should come easier and more quickly for them. Children who cannot read or write in their first language will need to learn about literacy as they learn a new language and will take considerably longer to match this success. Certainly, learning to read and write as you learn a new language creates a greater challenge. Knowing a student's literacy in a first language will help you set expectations for that in your class.

The best way to secure this information is to interview the parents and child, preferably in the home. You will need to prepare for this meeting by securing a person who can speak both the home language and English. Many school districts have lists of people who can serve in this capacity. Although this interview process may seem cumbersome and time consuming, it will provide you with important information about the student.

Learning About a Student's Ability to Read and Write in English

When you understand a student's home and language background, it is time to explore his or her facility in English. You can learn a lot about a student's speaking ability by observing and recording if and how the student communicates on the playground and in small classroom groups. Wong-Fillmore (1982) found that students in predominantly English-speaking classrooms acquire English faster than those in classrooms of children who speak the same first language. Students whose peers speak the same first language feel less need to communicate in the new language.

As a teacher, you will most likely want to compare your student's abilities to communicate in the first language and in English. In the best of circumstances, a student will maintain first language skills while acquiring a second language. Wong-Fillmore (1991) warns that students who lose skill in their home language suffer a huge disadvantage. These students have fewer and less varied conversations with their parents, and this loss of communication can lessen the family's role in the socialization of their child. Both schools and families should respect and encourage the child to speak the first language while gaining skills in English. The goal is to accomplish true bilingualism—students who can communicate fully in two or more languages. The accomplishment of true bilingualism may create an interesting tension as you support students in talking to same-language peers while also providing numerous opportunities for them to work with English-speaking peers.

The assessment strategies discussed in other chapters will help you explore the reading and writing abilities of a student who is learning English as a second language. An individual reading inventory (IRI) will help you assess an instructional level for reading in English. You can also ask the student to read from a book that the class will be reading in a literature study group. Be sure to consider the student's comprehension as well as pronunciation. A student may be able to pronounce the words but not possess the background knowledge to understand a story. Most stories read in American schools reflect American mainstream concepts and themes. So you may need to supply additional knowledge or ask peers to help. Students who have heard or read many stories in their first language may

····· TAKING A ·····
CLOSER LOOK

Learning a Second Language

The following includes some interesting characteristics of Spanish and Asian languages that may affect English communication.

Spanish-Influenced English

1. Students may have difficulty adjusting to eight English consonants not present in Spanish (*v, j, z, sh, ng, zh* (as in measure), *th* (them), *r*).
2. Students may substitute long vowels for short.
3. Students may omit verb endings.
4. Students may use double negatives, which are common in Spanish.

Asian-Influenced English

1. Students may use different syntax. They may ask for pepper and salt rather than salt and pepper.
2. Students may be confused about the meanings of words. The Thai word *fit* means that something is the wrong size.
3. Students may be reluctant to follow the teacher's directions. It is not proper, for example, for boys and girls to hold hands (Farris, 1997).

need to become familiar with Western storytelling's rather linear structure. Just as we might at first dislike stories from other cultures because we read them with our American expectations for story structure, so it is for students as they become familiar with Western stories.

You can discover a student's writing ability by asking the student to write in a journal. This informal writing assessment will most likely be part of your everyday instruction. A qualitative spelling inventory will discover how this student is representing words. Hudelson (1984) states that assessing a student's writing provides a window to her or his stage of language development. Students use pronunciation and knowledge from their first language as they write words in English. A child whose first language is Spanish may write the word *stop* in English as *ESTOP* based on sounds and writing from Spanish. Do not worry if aspects of a first language appear in the student's reading and writing of a second language. As a student develops skills in English, the characteristics from the first language will dissipate and disappear.

In a school in San Francisco, a city known for its language diversity, a group of students composed *Got Me a Story to Tell,* a book that provides information about themselves as well as their first language (Yee & Kokin, 1987). In Figure 8.2, taken from the appendices to *Got Me a Story to Tell,* the students share aspects of their language that they consider important for others to understand. For instance, Wilfredo tells us that in Spanish words are always spelled the way they sound. Camelia informs us that there are many Chinese dialects, hers being

Figure 8.2
Wilfredo Talks About the
Spanish Language
Source: Yee and Kokin
(1987).

APPENDIX: WILFREDO

SPANISH WORDS

Spanish words are always spelled just the way they sound.

Some Spanish words have accent marks in them. The accent mark tells you which syllable to say in a stronger way.

Here are some words from the story.

SPANISH	PRONUNCIATION	MEANING
abuelita	ah-booeh-leé-tah	grandmother
buena suerte	booeh´-nah sooehŕ-teh	Good luck
¿Cómo estás?	co´-mo es-tahś	How are you?
Estoy bien.	es-toý be-ehn	I am fine.
¿Cómo te llamas?	co´-mo teh yaĥ-mahs	What's your name?
Me llamo Wilfredo.	meh yaĥ-mo weel-freĥ-do	My name is Wilfredo.
Buenos días	booeh-noce deé-ahs	Good morning.
compañera	cohm-pah-nyeĥ-rah	good friend, comrade (female)
compañero	cohm-pah-nyeĥ-ro	good friend, comrade (male)
gracias	graĥ-seeahs	thank you

Cantonese. Her language is also tonal; raising and lowering your voice appropriately will help or hinder communication. Finally, Ruel shares the history of his language, Tagalog. Many dialects and languages are spoken in his home country of the Philippines.

You, too, may want students who are fluent in other languages to create guides that help classmates begin to understand the nuances of their language. This type of reflection will need to wait, however, until students have sufficient knowledge of English to make these comparisons.

Figure 8.2
Continued

APPENDIX: RUEL

TAGALOG WORDS

The Philippines is a country of many languages. It has been ruled by Spain and the United States during different periods, so a visitor can hear both Spanish and English spoken there.

The national language is based on Tagalog. There are about 87 different languages and dialects spoken in the Philippines.

Here are some Tagalog words.

TAGALOG WORDS	PRONUNCIATION	MEANING
lumpia	loom pyá	egg roll with meat and vegetables
adobo	ah doé bo	meat dish
pancit	pahń seet	noodle dish
kutsinta	koot siń ta	sticky flour cake
kalabaw	kah lah bow´	water buffalo
Nanay	Nah´ nigh	Mother
Tatay	tah´ tie	Father
Kumusta ka?	koo moos´ tah ka	How are you?
Mabuti pô,	mah boo´ tee po,	Fine, thank you.
*salamat.**	sah la´ mat	
mabuhay	mah boo´ high	welcome
Anong sarap!	ah nong´ sah rup´	It's delicious!

*Pô is used when talking to an older person or a person of authority.

Instruction for Students Whose First Language Is Not English

When you have determined a student's phase of English literacy development, you are ready to provide instruction. Most of the following strategies work best for beginning readers and writers. For students who are farther along, con-

Figure 8.2 Continued

APPENDIX: CAMELIA

CHINESE WORDS

There are many different Chinese languages. Camelia's family speaks Cantonese.

A person who is learning to speak Chinese has to learn to hear and say different tones. The same sound "see" can mean six different things. It all depends on how you raise or lower your voice.

Here are some words that might be fun to learn. Remember the tones are very important in Chinese. We wrote these words in English for you. They come close to the Chinese words, but are not exact.

ENGLISH SOUNDS	MEANING	CHINESE WRITING
Bah Ba	Father	爸爸
pung yau	friend	朋友
Nee ho ma?	Hi, how are you?	你好嗎?
Hoh ho. Nee na?	Fine. And you?	好好. 你呢?
Doe jay.	Thank you.	多謝
dim sum	meat and sweet pastries	點心
Poh Po	Your mother's mother	婆婆
Goong Goong	Your mother's father	公公

sider the recommendations for instruction for transitional and intermediate readers in Chapters 9 and 10.

Instruction That Supports Both Languages

The first instructional strategies and materials that we will discuss support the first language as the student learns a second language. Their goal is to let the student know that maintaining the home language is valuable and as important as learning English (Cummins, 1986).

Freeman and Freeman (1993) describe five strategies that support the first language of students. You need not be able to speak each student's home language to include these strategies in your classroom, although in some situations, you may want another student or adult to provide an English translation:

1. *Include environmental print written in the student's first language in the classroom.* The evidence of environmental print in the first language supports the student's first language and provides material that the student can read successfully. Encourage the student to write messages in the student's first language and post them.

2. *Supply the school and classroom libraries with books, magazines, and newspapers written in languages other than English.* Students can use these as research and resource materials for classroom activities. They can also bring these materials home so that their parents can read to them. These materials are easier to acquire now. Publishers are translating popular books into other languages, and some are publishing directly in other languages. Figure 8.3 shows a page from *Dragolía* (Cowley, 1987), the Spanish version of *The Jigaree* (Cowley, 1983). Texts translated into languages other than Spanish may be more difficult to secure. You may need to work with university professors of foreign languages or other language experts to provide translations.

3. *Encourage bilingual students to publish books and share their stories in their home language.* When students are allowed to write in their first language as well as English, they experience success and are willing to write more. Although you may not be able to read the story in a child's first language, older brothers or sisters, parents, friends, or others might provide a translation. In a bilingual classroom that worked simultaneously with the books *The Jigaree* and *Dragolía,* the Spanish-dominant students wrote their version in Spanish while the English-dominant students wrote theirs in English. Figure 8.4 shows two examples in which the teacher wrote what the children wrote or tried to write for their illustrations. In the final copy of each book, the teacher's writing was recorded along with the child's.

4. *Have bilingual students read and write with aides, parents, or other students who speak their first language.* Children, especially beginning readers and writers, need to hear stories read in their primary language. If you cannot read in the child's first language, locate people who can. Hearing stories in different languages will enrich the literacy experiences of all your students.

5. *Use videotapes produced professionally or by the students to support academic learning and self-esteem.* Students can create videotapes that are in English and their primary language. For instance, one group of students may videotape a play in English and another group can share the same play in their primary language. The class can serve as an audience for both plays and be enriched through both presentations.

Instruction That Supports the Learning of English

Bilingual instruction includes both supporting a child's first language and promoting English learning. Educational strategies focus primarily on beginning

Figure 8.3
Dragolía
Source: Cowley (1987).

¡Pedalea, Dragolía,
pedalea tras de mí!
Con tus patas grandes

readers and writers because even students beyond first or second grade most often enter English language instruction at the beginning developmental phase. If you teach older students, your goal will be to find materials that support them as beginning readers and writers while also engaging their interests. Language experience activities work well with older students as they can record their thoughts and ideas and then use them as a reading text.

Figure 8.4
Children's Versions of
Dragolía *Source:*
Barone (1995).

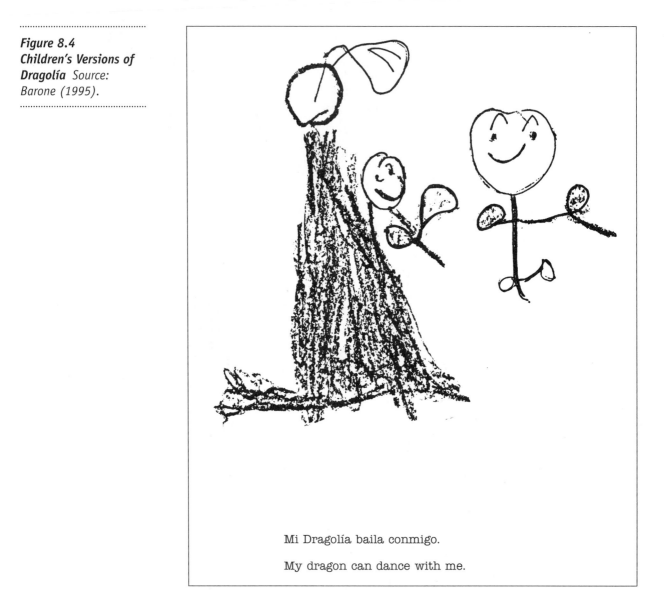

Mi Dragolía baila conmigo.

My dragon can dance with me.

If the student in your class who is learning English as a second language is beyond the beginning phase of reading and writing, your task will be to help him or her capture the abstract concepts that come up in class discussions and assignments.

Miramontes and Commins (1991, p. 85) encourage us to remember that as we work with children learning English as a second language we should focus on "what students *can* rather than *can't* do" so that "children's existing strategies and knowledge are recognized and accepted, becoming the basis for extending learning."

*Figure 8.4
Continued*

Mi Dragolía monta a bicicleta conmigo.

My dragon can ride a bike with me.

The following strategies are gleaned from a variety of experts. Although recommended for students learning English as a second language, they also support learning for your entire classroom. These broad-based strategies tie generally to classroom organization and instruction, and not specifically to discoveries made during the assessment process.

1. *Establish literacy routines.* By establishing systematic classroom routines, children learn what to expect in behavior, responsibilities, and learning. For example, if the school day begins with an exploration of the calendar, children will know where they are expected to sit, how they should respond, who will assume leadership (teacher or a student), and what the content of the discussion will be (Perez & Torres-Guzman, 1992).

2. *Provide time where children can talk.* One of the best ways to help a child speak and understand a new language is to allow plenty of time for children to talk. Show and tell, peer response groups, author's chair, or cooperative groups all make good talking times (Lindfors, 1989).

3. *Establish a daily story time.* All children benefit from a regularly scheduled time where the teacher reads stories and other texts to students. For children learning English as a second language, this is time to become familiar with American mainstream stories and concepts. Additionally, the child becomes familiar with vocabulary that infrequently occurs in oral conversation. Allen (1989) recommends that teachers first introduce concept books to children; the illustrations help carefully guide the student to the meaning. Predictable text is

Students talk together before participating in a play based on a story they are reading.

the next recommended step because students can glean meaning from repeated phrases and illustrations that closely match text.

4. *Use language experience as a strategy.* Language experience is highly recommended as a strategy for students learning English as a second language. In language experience activities children communicate predominantly in English;

the teacher writes out this talk, which the student then uses as reading material. When the language experience discussion relates to a real object, cooking experience, or science experiment, the children should have a lot to say that is grounded in the current situation. Through this process, the child makes learning connections between abstract words and the real event (Dixon & Nessel, 1983; Rigg, 1989). Children also see how the words spoken in English match to their printed form.

5. *Provide opportunities for children to write.* Children who are learning English as a second language need many opportunities to express themselves in writing. They should also be encouraged to write in the language that is most comfortable for them. When they choose to write in English, the teacher should focus on the content of the message and look to any interesting errors as ways to observe and document their growth in the new language (Edelsky, 1986). Teachers encourage these children in journal writing, story writing, report writing, writing class books and dialogue journals, and so on.

In dialogue journals, the student and teacher carry on a written discussion about a book or other topic. The teacher's responses help the student negotiate meaning and, partly because of the nonthreatening nature of the journal, students tend to write longer entries that have more conventional elements (Flores & Garcia, 1984; Reyes, 1991; Staton, Shuy, Peyton & Reed, 1988).

6. *Provide thematic instruction.* One of the most difficult tasks these children face is to acquire content knowledge as they are learning English. Often, as teachers, we share a concept with a child once and then assume the child will always understand and remember it. Children learning English as a second language need the freedom to rediscuss a topic or theme and come to a gradual and more permanent understanding of the concept (Perez & Torres-Guzman, 1992).

Study and topical themes allow students to focus on a central question and locate information in a variety of materials, from books to videos. As they search for meaningful answers to the central question, they are gaining essential vocabulary (Freeman & Freeman, 1994).

Second language learning is a complex field of education. As a teacher, you will draw on ideas and classroom strategies presented here and elsewhere as you investigate ways to support the learning of all of your students. In the next section, we will consider other aspects of diversity such as cultural, racial, and socioeconomic diversity, and their influences on literacy education.

Cultural, Racial, and Socioeconomic Diversity

In the previous section, Paley's students talked about speaking and learning another language. In her book, *White Teacher* (Paley, 1979), Paley describes her transition in understanding how to interact with children of color. At first she tried to be color blind—to ignore a child's skin color—but the children would not let her hold this neutral stance. She recalls the following (p. 8):

Valerie said to Fred, "Go 'way. Don't want you for a partner. I want someone white."

Bilingual students read and write with students whose first language is English.

We made pudding, vanilla and chocolate. Daniel said, "Valerie and Fred have to eat chocolate. That's their color."

We were looking at a set of pictures, part of a social studies curriculum. A playground fight was pictured. Joanne said, "The poor boy is helping the other boy." All the children wore jeans and T-shirts, but the 'poor boy' was black.

Keith and Fred became friends. One day Keith said, "Fred, the front of your hands is clean but the rest of you is dirty." Fred answered, "I ain't dirty." Keith looked worried. "Not really dirty. Just colored darkish." Fred looked at his skin and said, "I'm sunburned." Keith looked happy. "That's right."

Clearly, in this class in the late 1970s the white children and their teacher had little contact with children of color. Paley was concerned about how best to react to and resolve these explicit addresses to color. She was unsure of what to say to children or how to intercede in such incidents. Although Paley's concerns were important and not unlike concerns today, we are better served by taking a broader look that encompasses race, socioeconomic status, culture, religion, and so on. Each of us belongs to many groups that contribute to our identity and affect our personal development (Banks & Banks, 1993). Figure 8.5 shows some of the major groups that help to define an individual's personality. The groups do not necessarily exert equal influence on a child. For some, race may contribute the most influence; for others, religion or gender may be the most powerful influence.

Discussions of diversity have their own set of terms that are important to understand:

Culture: "**Culture** consists of knowledge, concepts, and values shared by group members through systems of communication. Culture also consists of the shared beliefs, symbols, and interpretations within a human group" (Banks & Banks, 1993, p. 8).

Gender: In addition to its use as a sexual classification of people, "**gender** consists of the socially and psychologically appropriate behavior for males and females sanctioned and expected within a society" (Banks & Banks, 1993, p. 17).

Race: "**Race** is a socially determined category that is related to physical characteristics in a complex way" (Banks & Banks, 1993, p. 18). This definition may seem surprising; however, the criteria for racial membership

Figure 8.5
Multiple Group
Memberships Source:
Banks and Banks (1993)

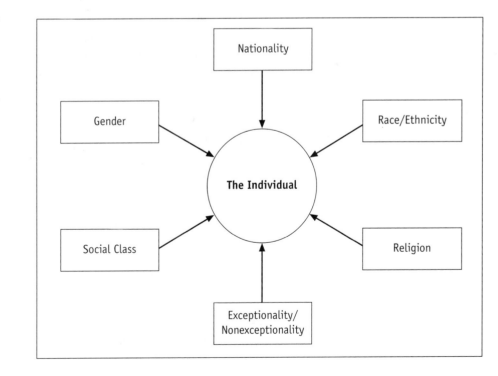

varies among cultures. For instance, in the United States, if a person has any ancestor who was classified as African American, that person is considered African American, even if he or she has no distinguishing African-American characteristics.

Social class: Social class is a complex term to define because societies continue to redefine it. Historically, characteristics that have defined low socioeconomic status in the United States, such as divorce rates and single heads of household, are now also considered characteristics of the middle class. The indicators that most often determine membership in the lower, middle, or upper class are income, education, occupation, lifestyle, and values (Banks & Banks, 1993).

The goal of teaching is to help all children learn, regardless of color or wealth. But growing evidence that children of color and children of poverty are experiencing difficulty learning in schools makes it imperative that we address the strengths and needs of these children directly (Allington & Walmsley, 1995; Au, 1993; Delpit, 1995). Schools have historically failed to meet the needs of these students and even to make them feel welcome. Schools have often failed to support students in their home cultures while showing them how to succeed in the mainstream culture (Delpit, 1995). To complicate this situation, more minority and poor children are coming to school, and the teaching force is becoming more middle-class and white. This situation means that minority and low-income children will more rarely, if ever, have a teacher who reflects their race or social status (Rossi, 1994). As you ponder this situation consider the following quotes about the realities these children face in school.

It is the children of poverty who are most likely to have literacy-learning difficulties (Allington, 1991, p. 237).

Children from working-class, poor, and minority ethnic families continued to do worse than children from rich and middle-class families on tests and examinations, were more likely to be held back in grade, to drop out of school earlier, and were much less likely to enter college or university (Connell, 1994, p. 129).

Schools with high concentrations of poor children routinely schedule significantly less classroom literacy instruction than schools with few poor children (Allington, 1991, p. 237).

The proportion of students of color projected for the twenty-first century is one-third of our school population, with many inner-city schools having well over 50 percent minority populations. At the same time, combined rates of retention, dropout, and those labeled at-risk for school failure will reach at least one-third, particularly in the inner city where failure rates may be 50 percent or more (Bartoli, 1995, p. 30).

In middle-class areas, youth programs are often viewed as opportunities to encourage and develop children's talent. In poor areas, youth programs are frequently thought of as interventions to discourage involvement with drugs and crime (Montgomery & Rossi, 1994, p. 7).

Gifted classes are still disproportionally white, whereas classes for the mentally retarded and emotionally disturbed are disproportionally African American (Sleeter & Grant, 1994, p. 27).

In many elementary schools, a disproportionate number of students from diverse backgrounds end up in the bottom reading group (Au, 1993, p. 11).

This sampling of quotes about children of poverty and color indicates the seriousness of the situation in schools. Let us consider what can change this picture from such a bleak one to a more optimistic one.

Assessment of Students with Diverse Backgrounds

Learning About a Student's Background

Knowing about each student's personal and academic background will help you understand each student and plan instruction. As you gain more knowledge about your students, you must simultaneously explore what you personally believe about children who come from cultures different from yours. Morrow (1995), among others, cautions us to explore our assumptions about children who come from culturally diverse backgrounds. We may be assuming that

- Parents of cultural backgrounds other than our own do not value literacy and therefore do not support the learning that occurs in schools.

- Existing school practices are adequate for all children to acquire literacy; home factors determine who does well in school.

Much evidence counters the first belief. Some families leave their home country and come to America just to give their children the ability to get ahead. The majority of these families value literacy as the key to their children becoming successful and upwardly mobile (Chall & Snow, 1982; Delgado-Gaitan, 1987; Goldenberg, 1984). Taylor and Dorsey-Gaines (1988) found that families living at the poverty level engaged in a variety of literacy events. These families were surrounded with print, although the print rarely contained books for children.

The second assumption, too, is heavily countered by research. Urzua (1986) studied the home and school contexts of children from Southeast Asia. Her study sheds a troubling light on what educators consider the key to children's success in school—being read to in the home. One child in her study lived in a home with few reading materials and parents who could not read; another child lived in a home with abundant reading materials and parents who could support literacy development. Counter to what we would typically expect, the child in the home with few materials did well in school while the other child did not. The first child was fortunate to be in a classroom where the teacher valued writing and the search for meaning within books. In the second child's classroom, the children worked in workbooks and writing consisted of copying. Extend this example to consider what would become of a child who comes from a literacy impoverished home into a class where children get little authentic reading and writing exposure. The classroom literacy context is critical for the literacy development of such a child.

Heath (1983) found results similar to Urzua's study. Heath studied children coming from three different communities and their success or lack of success at school. Her communities varied in composition and included poor white, poor African-American, and middle-class families. In their homes, she observed a variety of literacy events. As these children entered school, the middle-class children fared best. Heath's analysis was that literacy practices in these homes best matched the expectations of the school. She asserts that for all children to get good educations, schools must accommodate family and community literacy practices that vary from the mainstream.

As these research endeavors make clear, our understanding of literacy events in the home can help us build a literacy bridge between the home and school. Teachers can encourage children to share with the class important literacy events that occur at home. In this way, both the teacher and the children will broaden their concepts of literacy.

As a teacher, you can further build bridges between home and school with scheduled visits with the parents and children in their homes. This more positive relationship with the parents will increase your knowledge of home literacy events.

In Dyson's (1993) study of an urban primary classroom she discovered that children were most successful when the teacher allowed for a *permeable curriculum,* a curriculum that allowed the home culture to enter the school and the school culture to enter the home. She described this curriculum as "fluid and fuzzy"; the child's social world and language are interconnected in school and home or neighborhood events (p. 14). As she observed the children during writing workshop, she noted how their writing often served as a bridge between the home and school culture. Children would write about home situations, their thoughts about school, or versions of favorite television shows. As the students wrote and talked, their teachers began to understand and respect these children. They also saw the importance of blurring the boundaries between home and school.

Learning About Literacy

In assessing the literacy strengths of children from different cultural or poor socioeconomic environments, you would conduct informal assessment as discussed in previous chapters. You would ask children to write, spell, and read, and if working with a young child, you would most likely check to see if the child has a concept of word in print. As you determine a child's literacy abilities, focus most carefully on each child's strengths. Remember, many children from different cultures or from poor socioeconomic situations may lack experiences common to children in middle-class families. They will have a multitude of experiences with literacy, although they may have had few experiences listening to storybooks. They may not understand how a story is constructed or some of the language connected with stories, but they do have a rich background that includes talking, drawing, playing, storytelling, and some knowledge of print (Dyson, 1993). These experiences are the foundation on which you as a teacher will build as you help these children to a more formal understanding of literacy.

In the past, educators assessed and described these children as though they were deficient. Teachers would create lists of what these children could not do and even described some of them as disadvantaged. As soon as a teacher views a child as deficient, it becomes difficult to see that child's strengths and to have high expectations for that child's academic growth.

Educators now look beyond deficit explanations and consider differences among children (Miramontes & Commins, 1991). You can understand why so many teachers and researchers of literacy are finding it critical to become as familiar with a student's home as they are with the student's classroom. Only in learning about these two contexts can a teacher or researcher begin to understand a child's literacy strengths.

Some teachers worry when a child comes to school speaking a dialect different from the mainstream dialect. It is important for you as a teacher to support the child's dialect as you model the mainstream dialect, much as you would do with a child learning a second language (Delpit, 1995; Dyson, 1993). You may even encourage the child to help you understand the dialect by making it a study focus. In some schools children have created dictionaries that explain some of the idioms of their dialect. Figure 8.6 shows an example of such an explicit look at language from the book *Got Me a Story to Tell* (Yee & Kokin, 1987). In Figure 8.6, Deltrea helps us to understand some of the idioms and vocabulary from African-American dialect. As you can see, many of these phrases and words have come into more general use and are commonly heard in a variety of communication settings. In general, African-American English possesses many characteristics of Southern dialect, although African-American English is often viewed as culturally or socially inferior. Within African-American English, the *r* sound is frequently omitted, as are final *t* and *l* sounds. Nonstandard verb forms are common, such as *was* for *were* and *is* for *are* (Farris, 1997).

Although it is important to support the home language or dialect, you will be doing students a disservice and potentially harming their future aspirations, if you do not help them learn the mainstream language or dialect (Delpit, 1995). Whether children are speaking the mainstream dialect or learning English as their second language, they must be in control of their home speech and the mainstream speech. You will help children learn the mainstream dialect by modeling your own speech and by reading books. Talking about language that they discover in books provides children an opportunity to study the similarities and differences explicitly. For example, Nikola-Lisa (1995) writes about ways that authors use specific features of African-American language in books. His discussion would provide students with many opportunities to explore books looking for distinct characteristics of language. For example, in the book *Flossie and the Fox,* McKissack (1986) uses three characters to represent three different voices. The narrator uses a conversational tone, Big Mama and Flossie use rural dialect, and Mr. Fox uses formal language. The following lines from the book show these language differences:

Suddenly, Fox was beside her. "I have the proof," he said. "See, I have thick, luxurious fur. Feel for yourself."

Figure 8.6
Deltrea Talks About Black English Source: Yee and Kokin (1987).

APPENDIX: DELTREA

BLACK ENGLISH

Black people can usually speak two kinds of English—a standard English and a Black English, which we also call "Black Dialect." It is a language which comes from the rich culture and experiences of Afro-Americans. Today, many popular phrases and words have been taken from the Black Dialect.

Here are some words you might like to learn. You probably know some of them already.

1. He sho' has a *raggedy* coat. (old, ugly, or used looking)
2. Her rabbit coat sho' is *bad*. (nice, stylish)
3. Shawna wears some bad *rags*. (clothes)
4. Marvin's got a new *hog*. (Cadillac)
5. Wanda has got a bad *crib*. (house or apartment)
6. I gotta *split*. (go, leave)
7. Kevin sho' is *fine*. (good-looking)
8. She's *greasin' on* all my cookies. (eating up)
9. I don't wanna do it, *dig it?* (understand)
10. Don't be *messin' with my mind*. (confusing)
11. If you wanna go, it's *cool*. (all right, okay)
12. I gotta see *The Man*. (person in charge, usually a white man)

Fox leaned over for Flossie to rub his back.
"Ummm. Feels like rabbit fur to me," she say to Fox. "Shucks! You aine no fox. You a rabbit, all the time trying to fool me."

Children enjoy playing roles that include a change of dialect. In these situations, they will gain practice in switching dialects and becoming familiar with the appropriate contexts for each dialect.

Instruction for Students with Diverse Backgrounds

As you might have guessed, instruction for students who do not come from middle-class homes shares similarities with instruction for other students. For instance, all kinds of students need time for reading and writing, and all kinds of students should take part in deciding what they read and write. You will need to determine each student's literacy development and match instruction to it so that each student can experience success.

As a teacher, you can do much to make your classroom culturally sensitive with respect to literacy instruction and thus to provide a comfortable environment to support the learning of all of your students. Neuman and Roskos (1994) discuss ways to bridge between the home and school environments and to therefore provide culturally responsive classrooms:

- *Acknowledge and appreciate the home culture.* Encourage children to bring objects and share stories and events in the classroom during a sharing time.

- *Promote collaboration among children and between children and adults as they learn through social interaction.* Organize children in groups to take advantage of diversity so that children and teachers learn new knowledge or reconfigure previous knowledge.

- *Share the same standards of achievement.* Expect all children to enhance their literacy knowledge.

These suggestions should seem familiar: we discussed similar recommendations for students learning English as a second language. Some specific strategies will enhance the learning of all of your students as you create a culturally sensitive classroom.

Book Selection

In addition to providing appropriate instruction matched to developmental phase, make sure that all students are represented among the books you choose to read in class. We have seen teachers who never think about the book characters that children see on a daily basis. They select quality literature to share with their students, but no children of color appear in the stories. Although in the past it was difficult to find books that accurately represented children from other cultures, racial backgrounds, or socioeconomic levels, many well-written books are currently available. *Kaleidoscope* (1994) is a good example of a resource book that identifies and provides annotated bibliographies of books that focus on multicultural issues.

Other resources are available that will help you find to meet the academic and social needs of all of your students. One of these is a journal called *Booklinks* (50 East Huron St., Chicago, IL 60611). This journal presents collections of books by a variety of topics and themes. *Teaching Tolerance* is a free journal that focuses on helping teachers and students develop tolerance, understanding, and respect for all individuals and groups of people (400 Washington Ave., Montgomery, AL 36104).

····· TAKING A ·····
CLOSER LOOK

Criteria for Multicultural Book Selection

1. Select a variety of books that show diversity within and across cultures.
2. Select books that provide a variety of perspectives on issues and events.
3. Search for books that are considered currently correct in the information provided. Also, screen books for what they might leave out in the discussion of an event or issue.
4. When considering an individual book, think about
   a. *The author's point of view:* Is the author paternalistic about characters who are of non–Western peoples?
   b. *Characters:* Are people of color presented as individuals?
   c. *Language:* Is the story free of offensive terms?
   d. *Character speech:* Does the dialogue represent the characters and not make them appear inferior?
   e. *Author's background:* Is there evidence that this is a credible presentation?
   f. Consider the story's effect on a child and the child's self-esteem.

Source: Harris (1993).

Cooperative Groups

Cooperative groupings of students help students learn about each other as they study. As students work in these groups, they become more comfortable sharing their ideas and beliefs. They may be willing to talk about how a character was treated unfairly even when another student voices another opinion. Through the careful modeling of teachers, students learn to maintain respect for a person sharing an idea as they value and question the idea.

In cooperative groups, students learn a considerable amount of information about themselves and how they learn as they explore the topic under study. They develop a repertoire of strategies to use as they learn such as notemaking, generating and exploring questions, learning from mistakes, learning to value collaboration, and so on (Bartoli, 1995).

Other Recommendations

Delpit (1995) offers some additional recommendations for working with children of color. Valuing the reading and writing processes is not always enough. Some students, she insists, need direct, explicit instruction to understand the conventions that apply to reading and writing within middle-class settings. She

····· TAKING A ·····
CLOSER LOOK   **Stereotypes**

How does television influence our perceptions of other people?

1. Ask students to close their eyes for a moment and imagine a lawyer, then a police officer, then a doctor, then a criminal. Ask them to raise their hands if they saw either a female lawyer, an Asian-American police officer, a Latino doctor, or a white criminal. Explain that stereotypes operate so subtly sometimes that we don't even notice them. Offer a definition of stereotypes: "a generalized assumption about a whole group of people based on inadequate or oversimplified facts."

2. List the following "types of people" on the board, and ask students to assign each a race or nationality based on stereotypes. Have them fill in details about how each type of person dresses, how they talk, where they live, and what they value most in life.

   chemistry professor

   rap musician

   gang member

   bank president

   hair stylist

   political terrorist

   Now ask students to imagine the rap musician matching the description of the chemistry professor or the hair stylist fitting the description of the political terrorist. Discuss why it seems easy to think in terms of stereotypes and what harm stereotypes can do when they are applied to entire groups of people.

3. Remind students that, on the average, they spend more time in front of the television than they do in school. Have them name characters from their favorite shows who either fit or contradict a common stereotype. How might what they see on television influence their perceptions of other people?

Source: Aronson (1994, p. 31).

suggests that teachers not assume that all children will acquire this knowledge through exposure to reading and writing alone. She also recommends that teachers really understand the strengths of their students in settings other than school. In one vivid example, she talks about Howard, a seven-year-old whose teachers believed he needed special education support because he was unable to complete the simplest reading and math worksheets. When the teacher visited his home, she found that his mother had cerebral palsy and routinely used drugs. Howard, as a result, was responsible for getting his brother and sisters dressed and fed in the morning and doing the family laundry and shopping. This teacher returned to school with a changed opinion of Howard.

Finally, many authors—including Delpit (1995), Rossi (1994), and Allen, Michalove, and Shockly (1993)—remind us of the importance of making families know that they are welcome in our schools. Often, parents who represent different cultural, racial, or socioeconomic backgrounds from those typically associated with schools are reluctant to come and visit.

Students Who Require Additional Academic Support

Our third category under diversity focuses on children who require additional academic support to be successful literacy learners. Bartoli (1995, p. 29) informs us that "Over the past decade in American education the number of students given labels of reading and learning disability or deficiency—for example, LD, ADD, remedial, Chapter 1—has tripled, and the number of those failing or at risk for failure who eventually drop out of school has risen sharply as well." This group also is often disproportionately minority and poor (Rossi, 1994).

Assessment for Students Who Require Additional Academic Support

Your assessment of student literacy strengths is no different for a child who requires additional academic support. In fact, unless a previous teacher has documented such a need, you will begin your first informal assessment unaware of which, if any, of your students will require additional support. Even if a student has been documented as requiring additional academic support, you will want to conduct your own informal assessment to make sure that you have a current view of a child's literacy strengths. You will certainly need to perform an IRI and spelling and writing assessment. Depending on what you learn in small-group IRI assessment, you may want to continue the IRI process individually. In this way you can better determine how the child attempts to figure out unknown words, if he or she reads to acquire meaning or reads just to get to the end of a passage, and so on. You will also know the instructional and independent reading levels so that you can adapt grade level materials if necessary. The spelling assessment will show you how this child represents words, which will help you plan word study activities.

Be sure to find out what this student thinks about reading and writing. Some children who have difficulty learning to read and write find ways to avoid these activities in the classroom. This behavior is understandable. Few of us readily join into activities that we find especially difficult, especially when the whole classroom is watching. You will need to be sensitive to this student's feelings as you foster a supportive community of learners within your classroom.

Communication with the families of academically challenged students is particularly important so that they can furnish background on this student's academic history. Taylor's book *Learning Denied* (1991) vividly portrays how a student can suffer in a school setting when the parents and the school work in opposition. Taylor describes how a young boy named Patrick was constantly given formal tests in school and how the academic support given never really helped him develop as a reader and writer. The missing element in all of the testing and instruction was any real collaborative discussion with the parents. Patrick's life as a student might have been quite different had there been any open discussion between parents and school personnel.

Careful and consistent follow-up assessment is essential with children who find learning to read and write difficult. If you are working with a young child in first or second grade, you may be the first teacher to ponder additional academic support. You will want to carefully record the discoveries you made in assessment and the instruction you provide this child. After several months of supportive instruction, you will be better able to determine if this child needs additional support. The key here is to match appropriate instruction to the child's literacy development.

Unfortunately, some teachers teach to the whole class and disregard individual children's literacy development. In such circumstances, a child who fails to meet the grade-level literacy criteria will likely have difficulty with the assigned tasks. But if you have been providing instruction that best reflects the child's literacy knowledge, the child will be able to build on this knowledge and expand current understandings. With some students you may notice such slow progress that you are worried about future development. At this point, a teacher usually calls in a multidisciplinary team. A multidisciplinary team consists of a variety of experts who use multiple measures to view and assess the child. The team can help provide a broader focus in considering this child's future instruction and may make suggestions as to alternative instruction, formal testing, and other choices. If the team suggests formal testing, a school psychologist will be called in to conduct this assessment. The psychologist selects from a variety of individually administered tests, based on the perceived needs of the child. Following this assessment, the team and the parents and any other concerned parties meet to determine whether the child needs additional academic support and what that support may entail. Sometimes students are placed in settings other than the mainstream classroom. For a discussion of these settings and possible interventions, see Chapters 13 and 14.

Teachers who carefully conduct informal assessment with children, who document and interpret their discoveries, and who continue this assessment through their teaching have much to bring to these discussions. The knowledge that they share balances the information of other professionals and parents. Their academic experiences with the child help to frame possible additional educational experiences for the child.

When students are already in support programs, the mainstream teacher's informal assessment provides evidence of a child's growth. This new information is useful in revising an **individual educational plan** (IEP) for this student. See Chapter 13 for details about IEPs. Certainly this new knowledge will allow the teachers to know when this child has reached a literacy benchmark.

····· TAKING A ·····
CLOSER LOOK   **The Dilemma of Retention**

Teachers often worry about a student who has not quite accomplished grade-level academic goals. They want to prevent any student from suffering a year of frustration and failure. The most common reasons for retention include pressures of teacher accountability, development of more homogeneous classrooms, and student immaturity (Bossing & Brien, 1980). Although teachers consider retention only for serious reasons and in the best interest of the child, the benefits of retention are not supported in research studies.

Each year, approximately 6 percent of students are retained (Shephard & Smith, 1990). Retention has a long-standing history in the United States. In 1909, about one-third of first graders were retained (Ayres, 1909). Today, school districts have widely varied policies about retention. Some have a policy of no retention, whereas others retain as many as a quarter of their students (Allington & McGill-Franzen, 1991). Some school districts use developmental classes in place of formal retention. However, if the child repeats the grade, this additional year has resulted in a retention.

The question remains: Does retention benefit the student? Bossing and Brien (1980), Byrnes and Yamamoto (1986), and Shephard and Smith (1989) document no noticeable improvement in the academic or social performance of these students. Other research (Bossing & Brien, 1980) also shows a high correlation between retention and dropping out of school.

So does retention work? The answer is probably not. But the practice continues, probably, as Doyle suggests, because it seems to make sense; he calls it "conventional wisdom" (1989, p. 217). Educators and parents continue the practice, though it is not supported in the research, because it seems to make practical sense.

So if not retention, what other choices does a teacher have for students who are not working at grade level? The most successful teachers develop a treasure chest of ideas for working with students who represent a wide array of literacy abilities. Start yours by taking a moment to list strategies that you are familiar with that would support learners who are not at grade level literacy. Scan this chapter again and add to your list. As you continue your education and teaching career, you will find additional specific suggestions in research articles. You can revisit this list on occasion to ensure that you are working with all of your students.

Instruction for Students Who Require Additional Academic Support

In this section we discuss particularly effective overall ways that you as a classroom teacher can organize and structure your instruction for students who require extra support. See Chapter 13 for specific recommendations and activities that might be identified in an IEP.

One problem that has been frequently documented is that when students leave the room for additional instruction, they often find it hard to reenter the mainstream classroom and refocus on what is currently happening. Establishing classroom routines can help. By returning to the same academic routine, the child will quickly know what to expect and adjust more quickly. If the routine changes from day to day, then you might assign another student to reacclimate this student. This discussion between two students can ease the transition, and you will not have to stop and restart your instruction.

Make a special effort to create a permeable curriculum between the two classrooms. Your students need to know that what occurs in the mainstream and additional support classroom can be valued in either setting. You must master the art of hiding your frustration when a student must leave in the middle of a discussion, art project, or science experiment. Consider the feelings of the student, who must leave this engaging activity. As a teacher, careful planning will help you limit these situations by making sure that most long and involved instructional activities can come to closure before the student has to leave. This same type of planning will smooth transitions when the reading specialist or special education teacher works with students within your classroom.

Besides these general recommendations, carefully consider your curriculum to ensure that *all* of your students can be successful and challenged. The following specific strategies support learning for all students and in particular for those students who require additional academic support. These strategies go beyond those merely matching literacy development to instruction.

Providing Open-Ended Assignments

Teachers are becoming more comfortable with creating more open-ended assignments. Typically, teachers expect students to produce products that are constrained and focused on correct answers. For example, children might fill in the blanks on a worksheet or locate the main idea of a story. Now that we understand that children, like all readers, respond to what they read in a variety of ways, teachers are willing to consider diverse responses. Open-ended assignments can allow students to write about what they read. Their discussions might address the plot, characters, author, illustrator, or what the story made them think about. Then teachers can respond to writing content and appreciate the variety of responses rather than bemoan the fact that they are all so different (Stires, 1991).

Taping Text

Teachers, parents, or other students can tape narrative or expository material that students are expected to read on their own when this material is clearly at their frustration level. By using the taped copy of the material, the student can participate in the discussion and activities engaged in by her or his peers and is not penalized in sharing and learning academic knowledge as he or she builds literacy competency.

Peer Reading and Writing

Within a classroom, teachers can pair up students so that a more competent reader and writer can provide support to a student not as far along in development. Both students can read or work on a piece of writing together with each student providing support when the other needs it. One student might help another get ideas down on paper, while the other student can help with revision or editing. These situations have academic and social benefits for both students (Good & Brophy, 1994). Peer reading and writing work effectively in classrooms where working together and supporting each other are part of the class ethic. In these classrooms, students provide informal support to other students without the need for teacher structuring.

Cross-Age Tutoring

Cross-age tutoring is a variation on the idea of peer tutoring. In this type of tutoring, teachers match older and younger students together to work on reading and writing. Researchers (Bajtelsmit & Naab, 1994; Heath & Mangiola, 1991; Leland & Fitzpatrick, 1993; Schneider & Barone, 1996) have identified several benefits of cross-age tutoring—increased enthusiasm for reading and writing, increased student responsibility and empowerment, and improved reading and writing abilities. These pairings take a bit more effort than peer tutoring; teachers must work together and coordinate the details of the project. Students really benefit from this effort, however, especially older students who find learning to read and write difficult. In these situations they get to be the expert and experience success as a reader and writer.

Theme Units

This type of instructional organization is particularly important for students who are struggling with reading and writing. When you provide these students with numerous opportunities to explore a topic or theme, their understanding develops, and they feel that they are contributing to the exploration. In thematic units, teachers routinely provide both nonprint materials and materials at various reading levels, which legitimizes both the easier and nonprint materials.

Conclusion and Study Notes

Throughout this chapter we explored issues of diversity. We began the chapter looking at language diversity and the challenges to teachers and students as they work together to foster literacy. We then explored cultural, racial, and socioeconomic influences. We considered diversity that arises when students need additional academic support to be successful learners. Although each of these areas was dealt with separately for simplicity's sake, children can cross these categories or be connected to them all. It is not uncommon for a child who is learning English as a second language to also represent a minority culture, be poor, and have difficulty learning to read and write. In the same way, assessment and instruction suggestions certainly overlap among the categories. For example, we talked about cross-age tutoring for children who need additional academic support, but this strategy would have merit with all the students that you teach.

Working with the children described in this chapter can be an exciting opportunity. Getting to know families and children can help you develop as a person and as a teacher. The contexts of home and school can become blurred in exciting and authentic ways so that parents and children will become comfortable and successful in both settings.

In this chapter we have considered the following main points:

- The at-risk label is placed on children and schools for conditions that children were born into. These labels are acquired by children and schools through the general demographic data that fits the majority of children who are enrolled in a school.

- Children who are learning English as a second language first learn English that is used in social situations. It may take them between five and seven years to learn academic English.

- The goal of instructional strategies for children learning English as a second language is to let students know that the home language is valued and seen as important as they are learning English.

- It is the responsibility of the schools, not the responsibility of the home, to accommodate family and community literacy practices that vary from the mainstream.

- Children from nonmainstream backgrounds are most successful when the teacher allows for a permeable curriculum: a curriculum that allows the home culture to enter the school and the school culture to enter the home.

- Even if a student has been documented as requiring additional academic support, you will want to conduct your own informal assessment to make sure that you have a current view of a child's literacy strengths. In class, you will also want to make accommodations so that these students can be successful learners.

Key Terms

phonology

morphology

syntax

lexicon

discourse

paralinguistics

pragmatics

bilingual

culture

gender

race

social class

individualized educational plan

Follow-Up Activities

1. Visit a school that is known for its language diversity. Talk to classroom teachers about how they work with these students. Talk to ESL or bilingual teachers about the programs they have established and the goals they have created for students.

2. Visit a library and explore the multicultural picture books and novels. Look at older books and more current books. Think about the topics and themes and how the characters are represented. What similarities and differences do you notice?

3. Look through catalogues for classroom reading materials. Did you notice any materials written in other languages? How useful would they be in a classroom?

4. Check out local sources for speakers of other languages. In what languages would you be able to find someone to support you?

5. Visit several academic support classrooms. Talk with teachers to find out how they work with students and other teachers. If you can locate a school dedicated to children with special needs, visit it. Find out what children learn in this school and what curricula are used.

9 Transitional Literacy Development

Conversation

Leslie: As a teacher, I need to know what my students know. And *they* need to know what they know. Children need to be aware of their own strengths and achievements so that they can set goals for their next piece of learning. This is really important for my fourth-, fifth-, and sixth-graders.

Diane: How do you and the kids figure out their strengths and goals?

Leslie: It's like jumping into the deep end. But getting in over our heads can be the way to figure out what we don't know but can figure out. Like when it looks like we may not be able to complete a project, someone in the class rises to the occasion and solves the problem. Then we learn something about a student's strengths that we didn't know before.

Carol: When students are doing projects together, how do you figure out what each student learned?

Leslie: I often check to see who learned what by having students write down the ten most important things they learned. When we first started this, the kids were really hesitant to write down anything. I had to help them a bit. I told them, "If you say that we learned about volcanoes, that doesn't tell me much. If you say there are three kinds of volcanoes and then write about them, then I know what you learned, and so do you."

Joann: I saw a teacher walk around with a clipboard and take notes about what the students were doing and saying as they worked. She wanted to know all the way through a project what the students were thinking and what was confusing them.

She said one student was having trouble reading about electricity, so she had the student write down what she thought she knew. Then the student went back to reading to see what she learned.

Mark: When we watch and observe, and write notes and put them in students' files—those are called anecdotal notes, right? I think I'm beginning to see how instruction and assessment go together.

Kathy: It might be faster to give a multiple-choice test, but I can see how you can learn a lot more this way. It's really different from the way teachers figured out what I knew about something.

Steve: When I was a student-teacher, the second-grade kids made decisions, which I applauded. So I tried teaching that way. In conferences I showed parents both the grade book and the decisions students made about their learning. We talked about both and really looked at how their child grew.

Mark: What did you show them about student decisions?

Steve: At first I saved papers, but I wasn't sure why. Then I started to save good work that my sixth-graders wanted to take home but were willing to save to show their parents. Sometimes, too, kids came to me with work they wanted to save. Those kids showed me that they were interested in their work. It took a while, though. They had to trust me first.

Sarah: I remember a teacher telling me that her students wouldn't write at first. It took about a month before her students wrote without worrying about spelling and just got ideas down.

Steve: It is hard to know what your students know until you are sure that they trust you to take a chance with learning. They find it hard to make a mistake when they're not sure what the teacher will do.

These students and new teachers have much to say about assessing students' knowledge, teaching, and trust. Leslie believes in teaching that encourages students to get involved with projects. This type of learning–teaching organization is certainly more difficult to assess than more traditional types of learning. She has solved that problem by letting students share their new knowledge. She has also learned that this more complex learning structure encourages students to take on parts of the project that require their particular expertise. As the conversation continues, the participants start to see links between this type of instruction and assessment. They note how students can take leadership in this process and through this leadership come to understand their own and each others' academic strengths.

In this chapter, we will consider students who are now in a transitional literacy development phase. These students have moved beyond beginning concepts of reading and writing and are able to more flexibly consider reading and writing. We will consider how instruction now can extend beyond and build upon the instruction that was appropriate for beginning readers and writers.

Guide Questions for Chapter 9

- What literacy characteristics are most often associated with transitional readers and writers?

- What aspects of literacy learning are considered important for students who are transitional readers and writers? How would you assess these aspects?

- What instruction would support growth in fluency and growth in silent reading?

- What instruction would support students' extended meaning of text and students' reading of nonfiction material?

- What instructional concerns should teachers focus on in teaching writing to transitional readers and writers?

Who Are Transitional Readers and Writers?

Although transitional readers and writers develop at any grade level, students usually arrive at this phase within the second or third grades (see Table 9.1). Transitional readers and writers have begun to acquire more mature literacy behaviors. They begin to prefer to read silently (Barrs et al., 1989; Routman, 1988) and to read and write more fluently, and many of their invented spellings

Table 9.1
Overview of Transitional Readers and Writers

Reading

Silent reading predominates
Approaching fluency in oral and silent reading
Response (retellings, summaries, or analysis) to literature and meaning
  construction

Writing

Approaching fluency
Focus on meaning

Spelling and Orthographic Knowledge

Within-word pattern

- Abstract and relational
- Long and irregular vowels in single syllable words
- Spelling examples: bed—bed; chain—chane, chain; battle—batel, batle; commotion—cumshn; reversible—revresebl

are conventional (Templeton, 1995). These students are more fluent and flexible in their approach to reading and writing, and they require less adult support. Transitional students move beyond narrative books and explore nonfiction books more systematically. Their orthographic knowledge allows them to easily read most single-syllable words and to spend their remaining cognitive energy on comprehending and understanding what they are reading or writing.

Three Important Issues of the Transitional Phase

Students at this phase of development are consolidating information about reading and writing. At the same time, they are tentatively experimenting with reading longer books and new genres of literature. In writing, they are also exploring other forms to represent their ideas, and their writing tends to be longer and more complex (Graves, 1994).

Exploration into new genres in reading and writing is the first important issue for students in this phase. As they move beyond their areas of competence, they experience the risk of not feeling as successful and self-assured. Many of their early attempts at writing a chapter book, for instance, may end in failure (Calkins, 1986). For example, peers may find that important story elements are missing. Students need to learn persistence as they strive for success with their new literacy endeavors. Persistence and determination may be new to students, especially if they have been feeling competent in their earlier reading and writing endeavors. Teachers and students need to create a classroom environment that identifies and supports the new challenges and frustrations that children face.

A second issue is that students no longer show the rapid growth of the emergent and beginning reader and writer phases. This is a time of more subtle and complex learning. Students and teachers expend a lot of energy consolidating previous knowledge and mastering more complex learning skills. For example, students are expected to read chapter books that may take several days to read. They need to hold information from one reading session to another. Word study provides another example of this more complex learning: When students explored short vowels in single-syllable words, the relationship between the vowel, its sound, and its representation was pretty straightforward. Long-vowel patterns do not have this straightforward representation, and students must learn all of the possibilities of representing a long vowel in a single-syllable word.

A third issue involves the process of consolidating knowledge; students need time to become fluent readers and writers (Calkins, 1991; Routman, 1994). They may choose to reread a book several times so that they know they can do it well. Students often enjoy reading series books in which the characters remain the same and only the plot differs; they keep track of which books they have read by the number on the book's spine. Some of the currently popular book series are the *Goosebumps* books by Stine, the *Boxcar Children* series by Warner, and *The Babysitters' Club* by Martin. Parents and teachers sometimes get upset that children spend so much time reading these books and not wonderful, thought-provoking literature. Don't completely discount these worries, but notice, too, that these children are doing what adults do—reading books by a favorite author or in a favorite genre. Children will use this type of reading to become more comfortable and fluent readers and also to develop a love of reading.

In writing, you may see a similar process. Students tend to write stories that closely resemble their other stories. They find a successful formula and repeat it, much like the numbered books they have been reading.

■ Reading Instruction Integrated with Assessment

The instructional focus for transitional readers and writers shifts from knowledge of books and print and literal comprehension to fluency, inferential comprehension, silent reading, extended writing, and comprehension of nonfiction text. Instruction for transitional readers places a major emphasis on reading with students. Teachers use this time to teach new reading and comprehension skills and to prepare students for working independently as they develop into intermediate readers and writers.

Reading to Students

As students move into the transitional reading and writing phase, teachers expand the material they read to students to include genres other than narrative. Nonfiction or **expository text** is especially important (Doiron, 1994). This may be the first serious encounter with nonfiction for many students. As a teacher, you will encourage your students to consider how nonfiction texts differ from stories, particularly in how they are organized. Some students approach nonfiction text as though it should have a plot and characters (Vacca & Vacca, 1996). They also try to use a narrative reading strategy to read nonfiction material but find it does not help them understand the material. For instance, if a student skips a word in narrative material, he or she will most likely still comprehend the story. If a student reads *can* and skips *not* in nonfiction material, he or she may come away with an opposite understanding of the author's meaning. As you read nonfiction material to your students, they will model how important individual words can be.

Reading aloud to students, even after they have developed beyond beginning readers and writers, is important for many reasons. One of the most important is that reading aloud fosters positive attitudes about reading (Morrow, 1993). Students enjoy both the ritual of reading aloud and the discussions that often accompany read-aloud sessions. A second reason is that this process serves to enhance students' comprehension and sense of story structure as adults help students understand a text and see the value of personal connections to it (Morrow, 1993).

Jim Trelease (1989, p. 34) is perhaps the most vocal advocate for reading aloud to students. He believes that students "become better listeners and develop greater verbal skills. The more they hear other people's words, the greater becomes their desire to share their own through conversation and writing." Trelease focuses on reading fiction, but Beverly Kobrin (1988) extends reading to students to include nonfiction. Although she believes in the importance of reading stories to students, she asserts that children also find nonfiction exciting: "You do not have to read make-believe to entrance children. By their very nature, they are information sponges. They want to know about the real world" (p. 12). If you read poetry, fantasy, adventure, and other genres to your students, you will acquaint them with all of the possibilities of literature, and they will be more comfortable in choosing these genres for their own reading and writing endeavors.

Reading with Students

Teachers spend considerable time and effort helping students develop fluency, silent reading skills, and comprehension so that they can work independently as they grow as readers and writers (see Figure 9.1). This section focuses on strategies to support transitional readers and writers as they learn these skills.

Strategies to Facilitate Fluency

Harris and Hodges (1981) define **fluency** as expressing oneself "smoothly, easily, and readily, and having freedom from word identification problems" (p. 120). A fluent reader reads with accuracy and quickness and, if the reading is oral, with expression, too (Carver, 1989; Harris & Hodges, 1995). Beginning readers read in a word-by-word fashion; they are still spending considerable energy figuring out the words on a page (LaBerge & Samuels, 1974; Samuels, 1994). As students mature into transitional reading and writing, their rate of reading increases as they read more words automatically. Students who continue to hold on to a slow rate process text too slowly to get full comprehension. For instance, if they read at fifty words per minute or less, they have trouble remembering what they read at the beginning when they get to the end. This becomes a more serious problem as they move into longer text and chapter books.

Table 9.2 provides a framework for considering the reading rates appropriate to students reading narrative material. When students read nonfiction material, their rate will decrease as they read each word more carefully.

You can gather this information about a student's rate of reading when you time them as they read IRI passages. In general, students' oral reading rate as they pronounce each word will be slower than their silent rate. Rate students only on passages at independent or instructional levels. Passages at frustration level will be too difficult to read at a meaningful rate. You can compare students' reading rates to those on the chart. If a student's rates are significantly below those indicated, you will want to provide instruction to increase that student's fluency or rate of reading.

Following are several strategies to promote a student's fluency development. After you introduce these strategies, students can carry out most of them independently.

Rereadings or Repeated Readings

In rereadings or **repeated readings,** students reread the same text on numerous occasions to improve reading fluency. Repetitive reading need not be boring. You can find many ways to engage students in this process. Rasinski suggests that teachers model reading a book. After the teacher has finished reading the book, the student rereads the book modeling the teacher's fluent reading. Another example would be for students to

Figure 9.1
Observing Reading with
Transitional Students

Transitional Student Reading Checklist

Student's Interest and Attitude

_____ Involved with reading during SSR

_____ Shares interest in and excitement about books

_____ Brings books from home to school

_____ Selects a wide variety of books representing different genres

_____ Brings books from school to home

_____ Selects chapter books and completes them

Fluency

_____ Disfluent

_____ Some fluency

_____ Fluent

Reads Silently

_____ Reads silently

Construction of Meaning in Narrative Text

_____ Mainly retells or summarizes what is read

_____ Vacillates between retellings and summaries and inferential connections

_____ Predominantly makes inferential connections

Construction of Meaning in Expository Text

_____ Able to comprehend expository text

_____ Searches for information in text

_____ Varies rate of reading depending on purpose

N = Generally not observed
S = Sometimes observed
U = Usually observed

practice reading a book at their independent level to share with younger students. This exercise helps students see a real connection between rereading a book and sharing the book with a real audience (1988).

Other strategies to encourage rereading text might include *choral reading* (Rasinski, 1989) or tape-recorded text (Carbo, 1978). In choral reading, a group of students might read the same passage out loud together. This nudges the less fluent readers to increased fluency to keep up with the reading pace of more flu-

Table 9.2
Framework for
Rate of Reading

	Independent oral/silent	Instructional oral/silent	Frustration oral/silent
Beginning	60–80/	40–70/	20–35/
Transitional	80–130/90–140	70–120/70–120	40–60/40–60
Early Mature	130–140/140–250	120–150/120–200	≤80/≤100
Later Mature	140–160/250–500	150–160/200–250	≤100/≤120

ent readers. Choral reading usually involves a group of students, but students can work independently with tape-recorded text. The teacher or a student who is a fluent reader can tape record a text or section of text that the less fluent student can then read in time with the tape.

In either version of repeated reading, make sure that the reading material is easy or at an independent level. When you choose easy material, your student needn't spend time deciphering the words but can feel confidence and success in reading.

Timed Readings Timed readings are a variation of rereadings or repeated readings. Students read the same passage or poem over again until they reach their target reading rate. Students often keep charts to record their progress. Once they reach their goal with one passage or poem, they select another and the process continues. As students become more fluent on these passages, you should begin to notice increasingly fluent reading on unrehearsed passages.

To begin this process, you and a student choose a passage or poem that is about a hundred words or so in length, is at the student's instructional level, and is interesting to read. Construct a chart to record the student's progress. Time the student's first reading and record the rate on the chart. The student practices reading the passage at home or to peers in school, then again reads the passage and charts the score. This process is repeated until the student reaches the target goal. Often, this goal is 100 words in a minute.

Figure 9.2 is a chart that Sarah created to show her progress in reading the Silverstein poem *Sarah, Cynthia, Sylvia, Stout* (1974). You can see that within ten readings she had moved from a rate of 40 words per minute to 110 words per minute.

Readers' Theater Readers' theater is a simple form of dramatics well suited for the classroom. When students use this strategy, they read from a script and share a story with an audience (Sloyer, 1982). In order to prepare for this reading, students reread the script numerous times until they are able to read their part fluently. Rereading the text helps students develop fluency just as with

Figure 9.2
Sarah's Chart

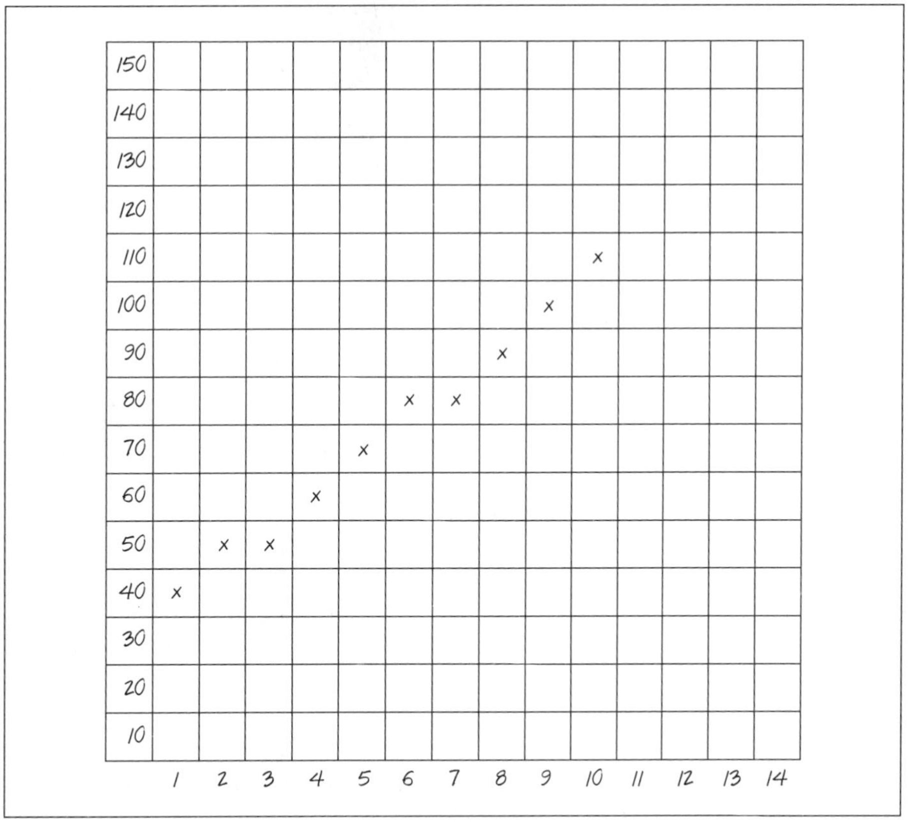

repeated readings. This performance requires no stage and minimal or no props or costumes.

Strategies to Facilitate Silent Reading

Beginning readers and writers, even when they are asked to read silently, read out loud. This strategy works well for beginning readers and writers; this aural feedback provides help with comprehension (Barrs, Ellis, Hester & Thomas, 1988; Gillet & Temple, 1994). However, if students fail to drop this strategy as they move into a transitional phase, their rate of reading slows down, and they do not develop a more mature reading style along with their peers.

Wilkinson found that students who read silently show some additional benefits in recall (1991). Students were more attentive and responsive in follow-up discussion. Wilkinson said that these effects varied depending on what happened before reading, during reading, and after reading.

You can observe if a student is truly reading silently when you administer an IRI. As the student is reading the silent passage, notice if you can hear the words pronounced. You can also observe this behavior during silent sustained reading. Remember to monitor the reading level of the materials. When reading becomes

····· TAKING A ·····
CLOSER LOOK   **The Issue of Word Calling**

Samuels called it "children barking at print" (1994)—the problem of children who can recognize words but fail to comprehend what they are reading. Stanovich describes it as "word calling." Stanovich noted that sometimes students who are having difficulty developing as readers and writers determine that reading is pronouncing words, not extracting meaning from text (1993).

Stanovich (1993) goes on to say that even when students are word calling, they are activating the meaning of each individual word. But because their attention is on phonics—the sound of the words—they do not collect the meanings of the individual words into comprehension of text.

If you have such students in your class, you will need to introduce strategies to develop comprehension such as opportunities to reread material and questions to answer. Moving students beyond word calling requires patience on the part of teachers and students. Students are often upset that they need to reread, for instance, because, according to their limited definition of reading, they believe that they are successful at processing text. You will need to help these students reach a new understanding about the purpose of reading—understanding text.

difficult or reaches a frustration level, students resort to more primitive reading behaviors, including mouthing the words and sometimes mumbling them out loud.

Most strategies are flexible: they improve reading in more than one critical area. Many strategies that help students feel comfortable with silent reading also serve to extend or deepen meaning.

K-W-L   K-W-L is a process for getting students engaged in the reading process before they start reading (Ogle, 1986). The initials stand for *know, want to learn,* and *learned.* In the K part, students record what they already know about a topic. Here you can discover your students' background knowledge and the understandings and misunderstandings they will be bringing to their reading. From this knowledge base, students ponder what they want to learn about this topic (W). Focused on these unanswered questions, students set about the task of reading so that they can extend their knowledge. When students have finished reading, they discuss what they have learned (L). The prereading activities get students better prepared to understand the reading content, and so to maintain their silent reading. The entire process teaches them how to set a purpose for reading and to reflect on what they have learned.

Focusing Questions   Without focus, students approach text as though they must learn everything in it. As a result, by the time they finish, they can't remember anything they read. Another strategy for helping your students to focus their reading comprehension is to provide them with broad-based guide questions before they begin to read. These questions should be similar to those you see at the beginning of each chapter in this book. Some teachers help students develop their own focusing questions by looking at the title of a chapter or section of text. For example, when a literature discussion group was reading *Ramona the Brave* (Cleary, 1975), it considered each chapter title as a focusing question. Group members decided that when they finished reading the chapter about Ramona's first day at school, they should be able to talk about Ramona's first day at school. This focus extended to the group discussion of the chapter and also helped students to read silently, as they knew ahead of time what was important to remember.

Strategies to Deepen and Widen the Construction of Meaning

Our comprehension goal for most beginning readers and writers is for them to understand the main elements of a story. We might ask them to retell a story or perhaps act it out to determine if they have this basic comprehension. As students move into the transitional phase, teachers remain concerned with literal comprehension, but they begin asking students to deepen and widen their comprehension and concentrate on some of the ideas that are inferred in reading. They support students in building connections between their own experiences and those that occur in a book.

You can measure your students' ability to look beyond literal meaning to those ideas that are not directly stated in a book but are inferred. One simple way is to note the type of questions students answer correctly on an IRI. Most IRIs indicate whether the question is literal or inferential.

Another way to discover this knowledge is to ask students to write about what they have just read. A student who retells or summarizes a story is focused on the literal. A student who writes about a personal connection or a connection to another book has extended beyond a literal comprehension of a story. Bear in mind, however, that students sometimes choose to respond in different ways on different days. For example, if this is the beginning of a story or the first time a story has been read, the student may choose to summarize or retell it. If the reading is a continuation of a story or a rereading, the student may write more personal connections (Barone, 1990). You can offset this variability by considering a student's writing over several days to determine an overall pattern of response.

The following written responses to *Bridge to Terabithia* (Patterson, 1977) demonstrate the differences between literal comprehension and interpretive understanding. Martha has written a literal retelling of what is happening in the book:

> Jesse has fallen in love with his music teacher. The Burks have one child. Jesse just met her. Her name is Leslie. In chapter 4, Jesse is in a race and made it to the finals, but he lets Leslie run and she won.

Nathan's writing is more interpretive of the story characters and events:

> I think Jesse has a mean family and should talk to them about it. He probably likes Leslie. I think Jesse is the fastest kid because he is smaller and lighter. I like the fourth chapter because the idea of Terabithia is neat. I don't think it's right to fight a girl over a couple of Twinkies. The book is sad.

Nathan could have made these personalized comments only if he understood the events in the book. He can form such thoughts because he has a literal comprehension of this story.

Beginning teachers often wonder how they can move students to these richer understandings of text. We offer some strategies here, but teachers who share their own inferential understandings directly with children help them see the importance of this type of response, especially in the classroom. Until students know that such personal interpretations are acceptable, they may be reluctant to share them.

Having Students Create and Identify Types of Questions about Reading (QAR) QAR—questions about reading—is a strategy developed by Raphael (1982) in which students determine the demands of a question before answering it. QARs teach children how to identify question types and to determine the appropriate sources of information to answer questions. Students who learn to analyze questions in this manner are better able to answer comprehension questions (Raphael, Wonnacott & Pearson, 1983).

Raphael identified four relationships between questions and answers (1986)—(1) right there, (2) think and search, (3) author and you, and (4) on your own. The following example of the QAR strategy begins with a brief paragraph and concludes with questions:

> Mary was riding her bike with her friends. She noticed that it was getting hotter and the sun seemed brighter than it had been a while ago. She told her friends that she needed to go home and she would be back later.
>
> 1. What was Mary doing?
> 2. What time of day was it?
> 3. Why did Mary go home?

Question 1 is a *right there* question or a **text-explicit question** and can be answered by reading directly from the text (Raphael, 1986). Question 2 is a *think and search* or **text-implicit question.** The answer is not directly stated in the text, and to answer it you would need to recall what time of day the sun gets hot and seems brighter. The last question is an *on your own* or **experience-based question.** You cannot find the answer in the text but would have to "read between the lines" and make associations with personal past experience. A simple reading experience like this one will enable you to identify a student's ability to think beyond the explicit lines of a story.

Raphael suggested that teachers apply four principles as they help students analyze and answer questions:

1. Give students immediate feedback about their categorization of a question.

2. Move from shorter to longer texts.

3. Begin with straightforward questions and then move to more complex ones.

4. Foster independence by beginning with small-group instruction and moving to independent practice.

Traditional students explore a book as they create questions for other students.

ReQuest Manzo (1969) designed **ReQuest,** a comprehension strategy, to help students (1) develop questions about the material they are reading, (2) adopt an inquiring, curious attitude about what they are reading, (3) develop purposes for reading, and (4) improve independent, silent reading comprehension. The first time you try this procedure you might start with one student and then move to small-group instruction. The teacher and student begin by silently reading the same text selection. When the reading is complete, they ask each other questions about the text. Manzo suggests at first providing the beginning of a question and letting the student finish it—for example, "Why did Leslie want . . . ?" Through this process, the teacher models forming good questions and determines the student's reasons for reading, and the student has a good opportunity to copy the model.

To prepare for this strategy (Tierney, Readence & Dishner, 1995), you need to

1. Find an appropriate reading selection.

2. Select a student and discuss this strategy together. Tell the student the purpose—to improve reading comprehension. Then describe how you will alternate turns asking each other questions.

3. Start reading the text until the first stopping point. Scaffold the student's formation of questions. Through the scaffolding process you will use the student's questions and help him or her develop more open-ended, text-implicit questions.

4. Let the student predict what the remainder of the text will be about.

5. Continue with silent reading.

6. Conduct a final discussion and any other appropriate activity.

Students find the opportunity to ask the teacher questions particularly appealing. One teacher asked students to develop questions that would "stump the teacher." As students read a story, they were to think of questions that the teacher would not be able to answer. The children really enjoyed the times when they stumped him, and they all would go back to the book to discover the answer. Through this process, the students learned how to form questions and how to find answers. "I don't know" became a rare answer in this class. If they didn't know, they now had strategies to return to the text to find out.

Reciprocal Teaching   Palincsar and Brown (1985, 1989) developed a strategy specifically for students who are having difficulty with comprehension. This strategy is similar to ReQuest in that teachers and students exchange roles and students increase in their involvement as the lesson continues. It extends the ReQuest procedure to include other important skills that enrich comprehension. **Reciprocal teaching** involves the modeling of questioning, summarizing, and predicting. The strategy has four steps:

1. Students predict from the title and illustrations what they think this text will be about.

2. Students create a question to answer as a purpose for reading a section of text.

3. After the section of text is read, students write a paragraph summarizing what it was about.

4. Students and teacher discuss this section of text. They may focus on vocabulary, in what ways the text was confusing, or any other pertinent issues.

To begin with, the teacher models leading the process. Gradually, students can take over the guiding role and work through the process with other students. The teacher moves into and out of the group occasionally to support or help the student in charge; however, the teacher is mostly an observer and the students have the active roles.

Although this procedure was developed for expository text, it can also work with narrative text. You might choose to use it as a connection for transitional readers and writers who are moving from narrative to exploring expository text.

Dialogical-Thinking Reading Lesson (D-TRL)   This structured lesson format was designed by Commeyras (1990) to teach critical thinking skills. Within this lesson, students are expected to think critically about moral, social, and political issues. The **dialogical-thinking reading lesson (D-TRL)** supports students in (1) revisiting text to validate and clarify information, (2) creating multiple interpretations, (3) supporting interpretations with text, and (4) evaluating of other possible interpretations. At first the teacher controls this lesson. As with other strategies, students pick up more responsibility as they become more comfortable with the process.

The D-TRL lesson has two basic parts. In the first part, students read silently on their own a selection about an age-appropriate issue that can be viewed from more than one perspective and that provides plenty of inspiration for discussion. Following reading, discussion begins with the students and teacher forming a central question that has two potential resolutions. Students then choose a resolution. They develop a list of supporting reasons that substantiate their decision and then evaluate each reason with respect to its truth and relevance. At the end of the discussion, students sum up the discussion and possibly draw a conclusion. During this process, the teacher records suggestions on the board or chart paper so that students can refer to them later.

Let's use the story of Jack and the beanstalk to model a D-TRL lesson. After the students have read a version of this story, the central question might be, "Was Jack fair?" Students might answer either yes or no for the following reasons:

Jack was fair.

1. He just wanted to get enough money to support his mother and himself. The giant had more than he needed.

2. The beanstalk was there, and all boys would want to climb it.

3. The giant was mean. He stole all these things from Jack.

Jack was not fair.

1. He stole from the giant.

2. He killed the giant.

3. He should have gotten a job to support his mother and himself.

The students then evaluate each reason as true, false, or "depends" and then decide how relevant the reason is. After this evaluation process, the students form a conclusion.

This type of lesson certainly fosters critical thinking. You may choose to work in small groups until you feel more comfortable with this type of discussion. When you and your students have experience with this structure, small groups can work on their own.

Strategies for Reading Longer Texts

Although transitional readers and writers continue to explore picture books, they also read chapter books. Many children are drawn to chapter books or novels because they have enjoyed hearing their teacher or parents read these to them. When they have heard a book, they will often want to read it on their own.

Students feel grown up when they read a chapter book, but they often lose interest. To informally assess your students' ability to read longer text, simply observe when students select a chapter book and if they finish on their own. You can provide supportive instruction for students who are constantly starting chapter books but never finishing them.

One clear way that you can support students in becoming familiar and comfortable with longer texts is by reading these books to them. As you continue reading, they are linking previous and current story events and so are learning to build the connections necessary to understand longer texts. Some students will choose to read the book independently. Because they are familiar with the story, they are successful with their independent reading. These successes may lead them to read stories you have not read with them.

The following strategies support students as they read longer books on their own. You can model most of the strategies in small group and then allow students to use the strategy independently.

Guided Reading-Thinking Activity (GRTA) The **guided reading-thinking activity (GRTA),** developed by Stauffer (1969), aims to (1) provide a format for teachers to provide systematic instruction, (2) improve comprehension, (3) facilitate students' reading through longer texts, and (4) engage students in reading.

You begin a GRTA by discussing a book cover and title with students. This discussion helps students build background for the story and prepare for reading. Record students' predictions of story content or events for future reference. Use this up-front time to discuss any potentially difficult vocabulary, but limit discussion to a few words crucial to comprehension. If you burden students with too many words and their meanings, your GRTA will lose its momentum. Following this discussion, offer a focusing question and allow students to silently read a section of the text that will allow them to answer this question. When they have finished, students can discuss answers to the focusing question. You might ask them to read the section of text where they found the answer. Repeat the whole procedure to the end of the reading.

As a variation on this strategy, some teachers ask students to brainstorm or form a written cluster about possible events that might happen within a chapter or story. For instance, when a group of students was reading *Dear Mr. Henshaw* (Cleary, 1983), their teacher asked them to cluster their thoughts about how it would feel to be lonely. They talked about personal feelings of loneliness before they considered the story character Leigh's feelings. Their focus for reading was to describe why Leigh was feeling lonely. Figure 9.3 shows the feelings cluster Mary did before reading a chapter in this book.

Another possible variation is to have students make a quick sketch in preparation for reading a section of text. One class was asked to draw the caravan that Danny lived in in the book *Danny, the Champion of the World* (Dahl, 1975). The students read the story and then compared Danny's caravan as described in the book to the illustrations that they drew before reading. Figure 9.4 shows Anti's drawing of the inside of Danny's caravan. Anti labeled all the elements in his drawing so that he would remember them clearly.

Figure 9.3
Mary's Cluster Composed
Before Reading *Source:*
Barone (1989).

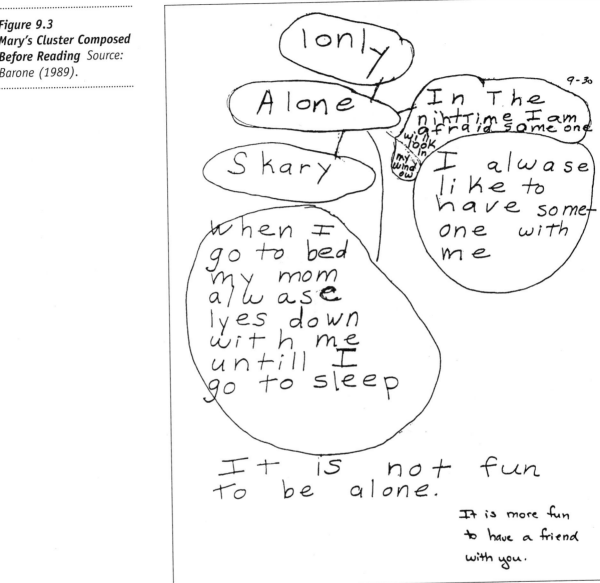

Whichever variation you choose, it is important to help children stay involved with text as they proceed through it. You may choose to start a book with a traditional form of the GRTA and then try other variations as you move through text.

Literature Logs or Dialogue Journals Staton (1980) and Atwell (1984) describe **literature logs** or **dialogue journals** as a place where students can freely write their reactions, feelings, or questions about a book that they are

Figure 9.4
Anti's Sketch Drawn
Before Reading *Source:*
Barone (1989).

reading. This is a good opportunity for you to respond in writing back to the student. Both you and the student should focus on the important issues related to the book, not on writing or spelling mechanics.

Staton (1987) offers some specific guidelines for teachers responding to student entries:

1. Focus on the content of the student response.

2. Support each student's ideas in writing a response.

3. Add thoughts in the response that are new or interesting to the student.

4. Write approximately the same amount as the student does.

5. Avoid comments such as "good job" or "fine work."

6. Ask few questions.

Conversing with students through these logs provides support on a daily basis as students read through longer text structures. One of the authors of this book supported her students in the transition to longer texts by having them write about their reading on a daily basis (Barone, 1990). The written responses connected with the dialogue between teacher and student provided the necessary support for students to become comfortable with chapter books. Figure 9.5 shows a literature log entry. Anna, a transitional reader and writer, wrote about her feelings about the ending of *Dear Mr. Henshaw.* She is concerned that this

Figure 9.5
Anna's Literature Log
Entry Source: Barone
(1989).

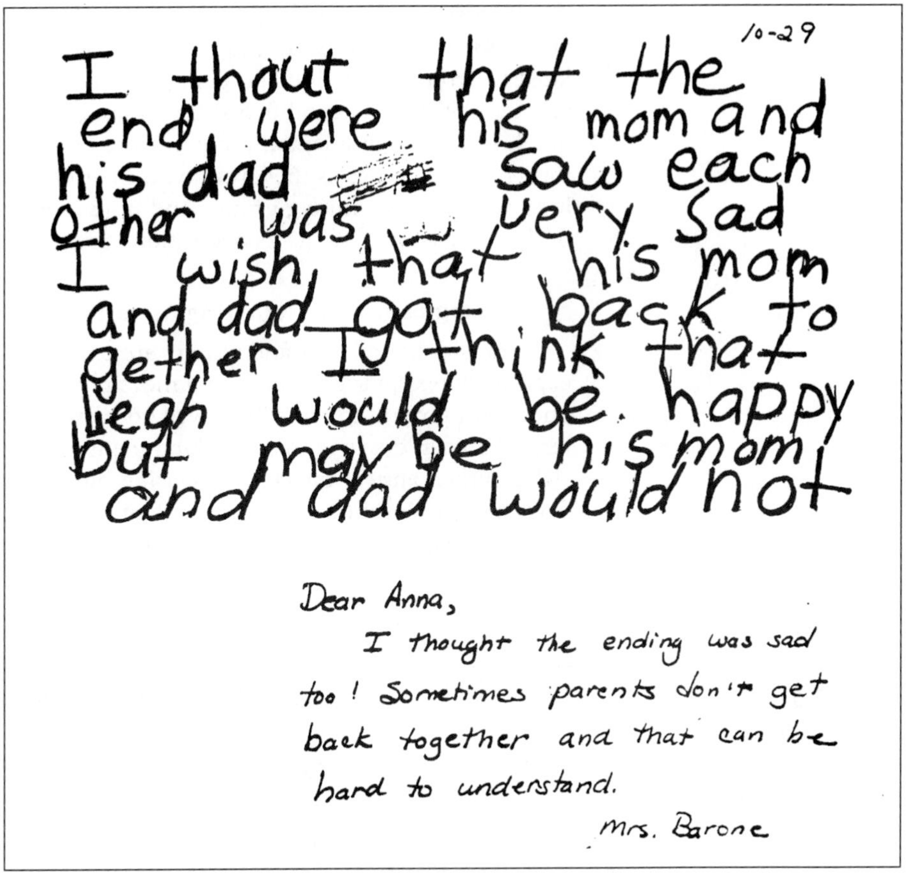

> 10-29
>
> I thout that the end were his mom and his dad ~~at~~ saw each other was very sad I wish that his mom and dad got back together I think that Leigh would be happy but maybe his mom and dad would not
>
> Dear Anna,
>   I thought the ending was sad too! Sometimes parents don't get back together and that can be hard to understand.
>   Mrs. Barone

book did not have what she considered a happy ending. Leigh's parents do not get back together at the end. Anna is able to consider this event from two viewpoints: those of the parents and those of Leigh. She knows that Leigh would be happy about a reconciliation, but she is not sure that the parents would feel the same way.

This type of open-ended writing clearly supports students' comprehension and understanding as they read through longer texts. It also provides a forum where teachers and students can have serious discussions about their reading and build bonds as members of a literate community.

Literature Groups Students in a literature group read and examine a book together. You might provide several books from which students can choose and then form literature groups among students who choose copies of the same book. Each group, with your guidance, determines a timeline for interaction with the book. Each day, the literature group meets to discuss its reading, perhaps looks at written comments, and then reads silently. As students get close to finishing the book, each literature group develops a culminating activity to share its book with the class.

Peterson and Eeds (1990) address the "grand conversations" that teachers and students have as they read through a book, and provide some guidelines related to group discussion and being a participating group member. Reutzel and Cooter (1991) have modified Peterson and Eeds's original checklist sheet. Figure 9.6 shows their adapted version. Note how this form helps students focus on their responsibilities as they work with their literature group. Such a checklist allows you to move among groups and note literacy behaviors as you simultaneously enjoy your students' conversations about books.

Strategies for Constructing Meaning in Nonfiction Material

Transitional readers and writers are expected to read nonfiction material or expository text in schoolwork on a more regular basis. This expectation makes it important for you to know how well your students comprehend nonfiction material. You can discover this by asking them to read a nonfiction passage from an IRI and then answer the comprehension questions. You can also select a passage from a grade-level text and ask students to read it and answer comprehension questions either into a tape recorder or through writing.

Figure 9.6
Record of Goal Completion for and Participation in Literature Response Groups

Literature Response Group Checklist

Name _____   Date _____

Author _____   Title _____

Preparation for Literature Study	Yes	No
Brought book to literature response group	_____	_____
Contributed to developing group reading goals	_____	_____
Completed work according to group goals	_____	_____
Read the assigned pages, chapters, etc.	_____	_____
Noted places to share (ones of interest, ones that were puzzling, etc.)	_____	_____
Completed group response assignments as they came to the day's discussion	_____	_____

Participation in the Literature Response Group	Weak	Good	Excellent
Participation in the discussion	_____	_____	_____
Quality of verbal responses	_____	_____	_____
Used text to support ideas	_____	_____	_____
Listened to others	_____	_____	_____

You also need to know if your students approach nonfiction material differently from narrative material. You can ask students about reading in a science book, for instance. If they start at the beginning and read straight through, then you know that they are not previewing the material. If they do not think of what they know about a topic before reading, you know that they are not attaching current reading to what they already know.

Do not expect too much with this assessment, especially with second- or third-grade children. Few of them will recognize the different challenges posed by nonfiction material. An older transitional reader, however, needs to know how to approach nonfiction material.

Unfortunately, not all students get direct instruction in how to read and comprehend nonfiction material. Many of those who don't, even students who have previously been considered good readers, develop reading problems. The following strategies provide some ways for you to help students understand the need for different reading strategies with nonfiction material. In addition to working directly with students, you can use these opportunities to share how you preview text, how you consider headings and subheadings, and how you discover the meaning of unknown words. This modeling is critical in encouraging students to own these strategies and use them independently to build comprehension and understanding.

Content Guided-Reading Thinking Activity (Content GRTA) With the **content GRTA** students decide what they know and don't know about a topic before they begin reading. In a content GRTA, unlike in a GRTA, students preview material to help them remember or build background knowledge that will improve comprehension (Gillet & Temple, 1994). The process of the content GRTA is as follows:

1. The teacher leads a discussion in which students are highly specific about what they know about the topic or what confuses them. Students may form predictions about what they will read or set questions that they want answered in their reading.

2. Students preview the text. They investigate illustrations, tables, bold print, and section titles. When the preview is complete, students discuss their discoveries. At this point, the students and teacher may consider unfamiliar vocabulary that will be important for comprehension.

3. Students read the text, section by section. Students turn section titles, if any, into questions that they can read the section and answer, along with any other important questions.

4. Students discuss their discoveries, and the process continues through the other sections of text.

In one class, the teacher was conducting a content GRTA as students read a book called *Extremely Weird: Endangered Species* (Lovett, 1992). This book was just one of several texts that students were examining as they participated in a theme unit about survival. The teacher began a discussion of tarantulas by asking students about what they knew about them and what they wanted to discover. One child wanted to know if tarantulas were poisonous. Another child wondered why they were considered endangered; he had seen lots of tarantulas at his ranch. At the end of the discussion, the students looked at the pictures and accompanying text they would be reading. Then they read the text. After they completed the reading, the teacher directed the students to return to their charts and to see if they had answered their questions. The students still weren't sure if tarantulas were poisonous. They thought that if people have them as pets they probably were not. One child decided that she would read some more in other books to answer this question.

This process is certainly more involved than simply reading text, but students really begin to understand nonfiction material when they study text in this more personally meaningful way. They often want more information about a topic and seek this information on their own.

Activating Prior Knowledge   The content GRTA demonstrates the importance of activating students' knowledge before they begin to read. Discussion of a topic before reading is one way to activate students' prior knowledge. Here are some other strategies:

1. *Anticipation guides.* Herber and Nelson (1986) described **anticipation guides** as a series of statements that students discuss before reading. Teachers develop anticipation guides—statements related to the major concepts—for students to consider before they begin to read nonfiction text. An anticipation guide for the tarantula text might look like this:

The most serious enemy of a tarantula is a wasp.

Red-knee tarantulas live in bushes and trees.

Red-knee tarantulas are endangered because people want them as pets.

Students discuss these questions and decide if they agree or disagree with each statement. They then read the text to confirm or disprove their decisions.

2. *List-group-label.* The **list-group-label** strategy provides a way to build students' vocabulary and to engage students' prior knowledge (Taba, 1967). In this strategy, either the teacher or students with the teacher create a list of words related to the topic. Students group the words and then provide a label for their grouping. A list of words for the tarantula passage might include

tarantula	tarantula wasp	enemy
red-knee tarantula	burrows	insects
endangered	exotic pet	three inches
invertebrate	farmer's plow	birds

Nonfiction Text Structure   Narrative text structure has a mostly consistent structure composed of a setting, initiating event, response, attempt, consequence, and reaction. Nonfiction, on the other hand, can be organized in a variety of ways. The most common nonfiction structures are (1) description, (2) collection,

Organizing Ideas

Miss Mayfield's second-grade class was exploring worms and snakes. The students had a range of books available for this investigation from picture books to encyclopedias. An early activity in this unit was the creation of a Venn diagram to organize what students already knew about worms and snakes. Miss Mayfield began this activity with a general whole-class discussion. As she added students' ideas to the diagram, students were expected to listen to their peers' ideas before adding their own.

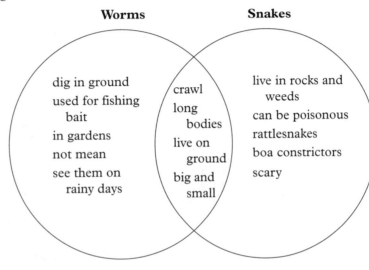

From this beginning, the class began a systematic study of worms and snakes. Miss Mayfield realized that they had some superficial knowledge of these creatures, but she also noted their enthusiasm for the topic as students continued to talk about worms and snakes even after the discussion. She could see that students would be interested in pursuing this inquiry.

(3) causation, (4) problem/solution, and (5) comparison (Meyer & Freedle, 1984). Students who understand the text structure they are reading will better comprehend the material. You can acquaint your students with the various structures by giving them an explanation of each and a brief example. Then select text that demonstrates each specific organization and help students recognize it. You can also provide graphic organizers to help students with this process.

If students were considering descriptive text, for example, they would note the topic and any descriptions of the topic. The tarantula text is a descriptive passage. Students might organize their information in the following way:

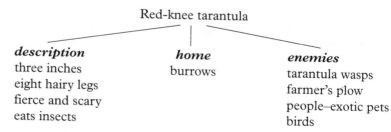

Red-knee tarantula

description	*home*	*enemies*
three inches	burrows	tarantula wasps
eight hairy legs		farmer's plow
fierce and scary		people–exotic pets
eats insects		birds

If students considered the whole book about endangered species, they would be investigating nonfiction text organized as a collection. Students could create a collection of several graphic organizers similar to the one developed for red-knee tarantulas.

Each text structure can be graphically organized to help students understand the content of the material they are reading. Students can also use these organizers to help explore the similarities and differences among various topics.

Reading Guides Teachers create **reading guides** to help students focus either on the process of reading nonfiction material or on the content. Reading guides also can be designed for students to work alone or with their peers. Wood, Lapp, and Flood (1992) have written a text that provides numerous reading guides for students. They created the textbook activity guide in Figure 9.7. This guide allows students to work with a partner and to use a variety of reading strategies. Such guides often let students monitor and record their comprehension as they read. These guides are more structured than other strategies discussed here. As a teacher, you need to think about your goals for a particular text and then structure a guide to match those goals.

Reading on Their Own: Cooperative and Independent Activities

Although reading to and reading with students are important to support students' literacy development, it is also critical that students have independent time to read.

Remember that the best way to grow as a reader is by reading. Students require daily time to read for pleasure, purpose, and interest. As they read, your students will gain reading experience, develop positive attitudes, gain knowledge in areas of interest, and learn about written language and the craft of writing narrative and expository text. Certainly, they should continue the practice of silent sustained reading (SSR) in addition to extended silent reading in their literature discussion groups and in reading in the content areas. These large blocks of time for silent reading allow students to develop into proficient readers. By providing this time, you are demonstrating to your students that good readers read a lot (Bertrand & Stice, 1995).

As you observe students during times of independent reading, note which strategies they are implementing independently. Sometimes you may want to sit next to a student and talk about reading. Here you can ask the student to share some of the reading content. Ask what the student does if he or she doesn't un-

Figure 9.7
Textbook Activity Guide
Source: Wood (1987,
pp. 20–21).

Figure 5
Textbook Activity Guide
(science—middle level)

Fossils

Names _____ Date(s) _____

Strategy Codes:
   RR - Read and retell in your own words
   DP - Read and discuss with partner
   PP - Predict with partner
   WR - Write a response on your own
 Skim - Read quickly for purpose stated and discuss with partner
  MOC - Organize information with a map, chart, or outline

Self-Monitoring Codes:
   _✓_   I understand this information.
   _?_   I'm not sure if I understand.
   _x_   I do not understand and I need to restudy.

1._____   PP   pp. 385–392. Survey the title, picture, charts, and headings. What do you expect to learn about this section?

2._____   WR   As you are reading, jot down three or more new words and definitions for your vocabulary collection.

3._____   RR   pp. 385–386, first three paragraphs

4._____   DP   pp. 386–387, next three paragraphs
            a. Describe several reasons why index or guide fossils are important.
            b. How can finding the right type of fossil help you to identify it?

5._____   MOC   Map pp. 387–389. Make an outline of the information.

1._____   2. _____   3. _____
  a. _____   a. _____   a. _____
  b. _____   b. _____   b. _____
  c. _____   c. _____   c. _____

6._____   Skim   p. 390, first three paragraphs
            Purpose: To understand the role of the following in the formation of
                     fossils
            ____ a. natural casts
            ____ b. trails and burrows
            ____ c. gastroliths

7._____   DP   pp. 390–391
            As an amateur fossil collector, describe
            a. where to find fossils
            b. what to use to find them
            c. how to prepare them for display

8._____   WR   p. 392, next to last paragraph
            Define *pseudofossil*. Jot down three other words that contain the
            prefix *pseudo*. Use the dictionary if necessary.

9._____   DP   Examine the fossil collection being passed around and list eight things
            you have learned by analyzing it.

derstand something he or she is reading. Use the opportunity to observe how the student is transferring your direct strategy instruction to independent practice.

■ *Writing Instruction Integrated with Assessment*

The best time to assess your transitional students is during writing workshop. The ten-minute writes we discussed previously will have shown you a lot about your students' writing skills. You will continue this type of assessment throughout the year.

Many teachers encourage their students to explore a variety of writing genres during this transitional time. After you have provided writing workshop mini-lessons to exploring genres other than the narrative story form, you can observe as children experiment with these forms in their own writing.

As you examine student writing products at each phase, focus on certain parts of the writing process (see Figure 9.8). You want to see your beginning readers and writers succeeding in producing many books. Transitional students

Figure 9.8
Observing Writing with
Transitional Students

Transitional Student Writing Checklist

Genres That Student Has Used in Writing

_____ Narrative, story

_____ Poetry

_____ Expository

Revision

_____ Adds to text

_____ Deletes text

_____ Rearranges text

Editing

_____ Able to correct spelling errors

_____ Able to correct punctuation

_____ Able to correct capitalization

_____ Able to correct grammar errors

N = Generally not observed
S = Sometimes observed
U = Usually observed

can write more easily, and you can expect more of them in revision and editing. Observe students as they move through the whole writing process, and note if they seriously revise their piece and become responsible for more of the editing. At this phase of development, you can expect that students will become more independent and responsible for drafting, revising, and editing.

Now that your students have examined various ways of organizing nonfiction text and explored other genres, encourage them to include these genres in their own writing. Most students will need encouragement as they experiment with these new genres. You can provide direct instruction in various genres and in revising and editing and can support students as they revise and edit independently and with the support of peers.

Writing with Students: Guided Writing Activities

Guided Instruction of Various Genres

In this section, we focus on the genres of expository (nonfiction) writing and poetry. As you might expect, you will need to provide plenty of modeling before your students become comfortable in writing in these new genres.

Expository Text Students can use the various nonfiction structural patterns and corresponding graphic organizers mentioned earlier to help them organize their own writing. They can select the best structure to reflect the content that they wish to share and then use this as a frame for their own writing.

Another strategy for helping students learn expository writing is to have them complete a six-sided cube (Tompkins, 1994). As students explore a topic, they read the directions for each side of the cube and then provide specific information. The directions for each side are as follows:

1. Describe it.

2. Compare it to other things you know.

3. Associate it to things it makes you think of.

4. Analyze what it is composed of.

5. Apply it by explaining what you can do with it.

6. Argue for or against it, using reasons you have discovered through your investigation.

This thinking before writing facilitates a student's writing about a topic from a variety of perspectives.

Poetry Transitional readers and writers often believe that all poetry must rhyme. One of your first tasks as a teacher will be to share with students poetry that does not use a rhyming structure. Temple (1989, p. 94) provides several lessons to help students believe that they are capable of writing poetry. Her lessons focus on "(a) interest in phrases that evoke mental imagery, (b) interest in sounds and rhythms of language, and (c) a careful economy of language." The two poetry forms that she recommends for exploration with students are *cinquain* and *diamante*. As an example of the cinquain, she had students discuss why they liked going to gym class. They talked about how they liked to play basketball. As they talked about basketball, she asked them to describe how their bodies feel when they run and jump in the game. Students offered words like *hot, sweaty, thirsty,* and so on. From this thinking, she showed them the form of a cinquain:

noun

adjective, adjective

three-word sentence

four participles

noun

Temple worked with the students as they created their whole-class poem:

Us

Sweaty, thirsty

Everybody likes gym

Jumping, crashing, running, smashing

Basketball

When the students realized that they could create a simple cinquain, they each composed their own. The students read their poems to each other so that they could enjoy each other's writing and see the variations of their poems.

The second form that Temple modeled was the diamante. The diamante is similarly arranged to the cinquain, except that it creates a contrast. The poem begins with a noun and ends with a contrasting noun:

noun

adjective, adjective

three-word sentence

participle, participle/participle, participle

three-word sentence

adjective, adjective

noun

Her students created the following class diamante poem after reading *Jack and the Beanstalk:*

Boy

hungry, poor

Sell the cow!

yelled at, chased out/climbing, sneaking

Grab the hen!

quick, rich

Jack

These forms are easy for students to write on their own. They can experiment with finding just the right word to describe their feelings, or they might explore the differences between frogs and toads and thus learn about content knowledge as they explore the writing of poetry. Children are easily successful with these forms and from this success are willing to experiment with more complex poetry writing.

Guided Instruction of Revision and Editing

When students are beginning readers and writers, they need many experiences with writing. As they move into the transitional phase of literacy development, it is time to expand this focus to revision and editing to prepare writing for an audience.

At first, students may think that *revision* means copying their writing over, thus making it neater. You need to help students understand that adding text, deleting text, and rearranging text are important steps in making it clearer for the reader. Calkins (1991, p. 83) advises that "drafts children produce, especially early in the year, will probably be like misshapen, gluey valentines, and we need to respond to them with the same warmth and trust." Students find the revision process difficult. They are, at first, more willing to add text than remove it, which they find a painful process and one to avoid (Tompkins, 1994).

One way to help students understand the nature of the revision process is to share with them a piece of your own writing. First, let students know that you would like them to help you with your writing. You can even pose a specific question about your writing. Then read them your piece as you display it on an overhead transparency. At first, ask them to comment on what they liked. Next, ask them where they were confused or what information they think should be added. Mark your writing based on their suggestions. Through this writing, you are modeling editing marks to show where text would be added or deleted.

In your next modeled lesson, you can ask a student to contribute a piece of writing. You would then repeat the same process using the student writing as the text to be revised. This type of repeated modeling encourages students in the revision process while it also teaches them to offer positive suggestions to their peers. Through this modeling, students are able to share this support when they are working independently, in pairs, or in small groups. When you move to using student writing, remember to be sensitive to the student as he or she watches the class constructively criticize his or her writing. Focusing on only one or two elements for revision will allow this process to remain positive.

Editing follows revision in preparing the writing for an audience. When the author is pleased with the writing content, it's time to edit the text for punctuation, grammar, and spelling. In the editing process, students proofread their writing with attention to form rather than meaning. Here again, the best way for students to become familiar with editing is through lessons modeled by the teacher. You can again share a piece of writing that requires editing. With your students, read through the piece at least three times. The first time, ask them to hunt for grammar errors such as subject/verb agreement, proper use of pronouns, and so on. On the next reading, look at punctuation and capitalization. On the third reading, focus on spelling.

As with revisions, you should model this process on numerous occasions with your writing and with student writing. Even with modeling, students will not find all the mechanical errors in their own papers. Working with peers will help them find errors they would otherwise miss.

Writing on Their Own: Cooperative and Independent Activities

As students take on more of the responsibility for the writing process, they learn how to be contributing partners in **peer response groups** and **peer editing groups.**

Peer Response Groups

When you have modeled how to revise text and the appropriate language and behavior to use with others in this process, students can perform these tasks independently. Most teachers usually partner students so that at least two students offer suggestions on revising each piece of writing. Many teachers use revision sheets so that students take the job of revising and helping with revision seriously. You may want to create a revision sheet something like the template shown in Figure 9.9.

Peer Editing Groups

Peer editing groups work in similar ways as peer response groups. Students seek out other students to help with the editing process once they have finished revising. Here again, teachers often ask that two students help with the editing process. You might choose to send an editing checklist (see Figure 9. 10) with the text to keep track of who edited what.

Student Assessment of Writing

Self-assessment lets students step back and reflect on the writing process and the writing they produced. Students may begin this self-assessment process by recalling how they decided on the topic for their writing, how well they did in sharing this information in a first draft, how they revised their writing, how carefully they edited, and how they shared their work.

Students then ponder this whole writing process and decide which part was the most successful or difficult. They consider why a certain step went well and

Figure 9.9
Revision Sheet

Peer Response Revision Sheet

Name _____

Title _____

Conference with Two Friends

    Name _____   Name _____

    Date _____   Date _____

What I Like

_____   _____

_____   _____

_____   _____

What Was Confusing

_____   _____

_____   _____

_____   _____

What Should Be Added

_____   _____

_____   _____

_____   _____

What I Did to Revise My Writing

_____

_____

_____

what they did in that step. For instance, some students may discover that they always have something to write about. They might recognize that their love for discovering new information makes this so. These students might also decide that editing is their most difficult task and realize that they are trying to edit for everything with only one reading of the text. This reflection lets them consider what they might do to make difficult parts of writing easier.

After students have considered the writing process, they focus on their writing product. They consider questions such as, "What pleases me most about this writing? What do I like about the way this writing is organized? What words really describe what I am trying to say?"

Students will make these kinds of assessments as they consider what pieces of writing to include in a portfolio and why. This same assessment allows students to determine what skills they need to work on in their next piece of writing.

Figure 9.10
Editing Checklist

Peer Editing Checklist

Name _____

Title _____

I have circled the words that might be misspelled.

Author _____

Editor 1 _____

Editor 2 _____

I have checked that all sentences end with a punctuation mark.

Author _____

Editor 1 _____

Editor 2 _____

I have checked that quotation marks are used.

Author _____

Editor 1 _____

Editor 2 _____

I have checked that the nouns and verbs in a sentence go together.

Author _____

Editor 1 _____

Editor 2 _____

I have checked all words that need capital letters.

Author _____

Editor 1 _____

Editor 2 _____

Word Study and Spelling Instruction Integrated with Assessment

Students have reached a transitional phase in orthographic knowledge when they begin to represent long vowel markers. Your observations from the qualitative spelling inventory, journal writing, and other forms of writing document this development. In their writing students might represent *BOAT* as *BOTE* or *MEAT* as *METE*. These students are now using two vowels to represent a long-vowel pattern. When these students write words or copy, they will do so in groups of letters; no longer do they only consider one letter at a time.

As students explore long-vowel patterns, they begin to understand the second principle of spelling, which is the *within-word principle:* they consider how letter patterns form sounds within a word (Templeton, 1991). Your goal for word study with transitional readers and writers is to help them stabilize their representations of long-vowel patterns (see Figure 9.11). They will build this knowledge of words on the alphabetic knowledge acquired during the beginning reader and writer phase.

The following sections share some ways for students to explore long-vowel patterns and focus on word meanings as well as spellings.

Word Study in the Within-Word Pattern Phase

Students at the within-word pattern phase of development focus their word study on long-vowel patterns within single-syllable words. They learn that long-vowel patterns are not linear like short-vowel patterns. They learn, for example, that the long sound of *e* can be represented in many different ways such as in *meat* or *feet*.

Identifying Words in Context

As students become more fluent readers and writers, they will find plenty of opportunities to examine interesting word forms in the stories and expository

*Figure 9.11
Observing Word Study
and Spelling with
Transitional Students*

Transitional Student Word Checklist

Words in Context

_____ Student uses context of text to figure out meaning of an unknown word

Word Sorts

_____ Student can explain *sort*

_____ Student is able to sort words accurately

_____ Student is able to sort words fluently

_____ Student is able to sort words independently in notebook

Spelling

_____ Student can find additional words that match pattern of words in spelling list

_____ Student has high accuracy of words correct on spelling test

_____ Student can spell words from list after the test

N = Generally not observed
S = Sometimes observed
U = Usually observed

text that they are reading. As students begin to explore long vowel words, they notice *homonyms* (such as *pail* and *pale*), which sound the same but are spelled differently and have different meanings, and *homophones* (such as *bat*), which sound the same, are spelled the same, and have a variety of meanings. These words, whose meanings are tied to spellings, are best studied in the context of real text.

Students enjoy discovering the etymology of homonyms to share with others as to why these pairs of words are spelled the way they are. *Answering Students' Questions about Words* (Tompkins & Yaden, 1986) answers student questions such as why homonyms sound the same and are spelled differently. The book explains that these words originated from two different languages. For example, *cell* comes from Latin *cella* and means a small room, while *sell* comes from Old English *sellan* and means to give or deliver. A few homonyms have developed from the same root. Both *muscle* and *mussel* originated from the Latin word *musculus*, which means "little mouse." Tompkins and Yaden state that "the Romans used metaphor in applying *musculus* to *muscles* and *mussels*" (p. 36). They compared the rippling of muscles to a little mouse running under the skin, and they thought that a shelled mussel looks like a mouse.

Students enjoy studying the etymology of homophones in the same way. Tompkins and Yaden (1986) use the word *toast* as an example. The meanings of *toast* come from the Latin *torrere*, "to bake." It is easy to see the connection to *toast* as bread that comes out of a toaster. It is harder to figure out how *toast*, as to salute someone, derived its meaning. One possible connection relates to the flavored toast eaten when drinking to the health or honor of someone or something.

Students, teachers, and parents enjoy exploring homonyms. Figure 9.12 shows a page from a student's word study notebook, which shows his list of all of the homonyms he and his parents could think of. When this assignment was finished, the teacher divided students into partnerships to discover the origins of the homonym pairs.

Word posters give students the creative enjoyment of displaying their found words in collections grouped around a theme. Students can create word posters of long vowel words, for example. They can expand these posters to include words related to a unit of study or to include a place where words can be added. The posters also help create an environment in which students are encouraged to think about words as an object of study.

Word Sorts and Word Study Notebooks

Teachers usually begin transitional readers and writers with an extensive exploration of long *a* pattern words. When students understand the possible ways to represent long *a* pattern and are becoming consistent in spelling these words, they are ready to explore other long-vowel patterns. These explorations are typically shorter in duration. To begin a study of long vowel *a*, you might ask your students to generate a list of words that have a long *a* sound, as in *cake*. The students can gather in small groups and begin to categorize the words. A group of seven transitional readers and writers generated the following list of long *a* words:

Figure 9.12
Homonym Page from
Student's Word Study
Notebook

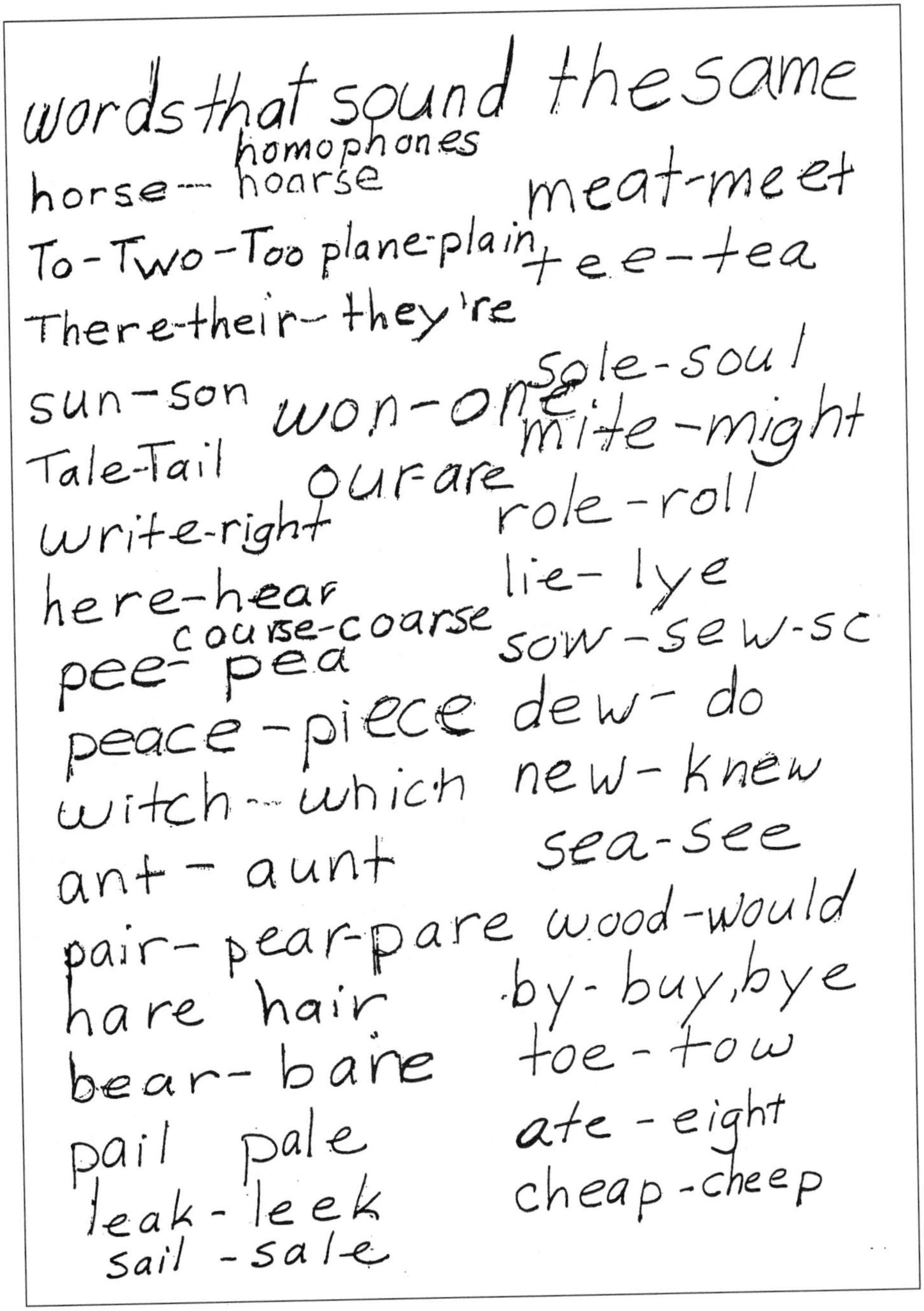

words that sound the same

homophones

horse — hoarse

To - Two - Too   plane - plain

meat - meet

tee - tea

There - their - they're

sun - son   won - one

sole - soul

Tale - Tail   our - are

mite - might

write - right

role - roll

here - hear

lie - lye

course - coarse

pee - pea   sow - sew - sc

peace - piece   dew - do

witch - which   new - knew

ant - aunt   sea - see

pair - pear - pare   wood - would

hare   hair   by - buy, bye

bear - bare   toe - tow

pail   pale   ate - eight

leak - leek   cheap - cheep

sail - sale

cape	bake	hail	mail
ape	bale	day	date
grape	sale	tail	sail

After they completed their list, they sorted the words into the following categories:

a-consonant-e (cake)	ai (sail)	ay (day)	words that sound alike
cape	hail	day	sale—sail
ape	tail		
grape	mail		
bake	sail		
bale			
sale			
date			

words that begin with b (bake)	words that end with l (mail)
bale	hail
bake	tail
	mail
	sail

Following this activity, the teacher asked the students to go back to their reading book and find additional words that had the *a* sound as in *cake*. They recorded these words in their word study notebooks. The following day, the students brought these words to their word study group and began sorting them. The students continued exploring the patterns of long *a* until the teacher, through her observations, could see that they were ready to explore another long vowel.

The students created their own categories in the above sorting activity, which is known as an **open sort.** The teacher could also have used a **closed sort,** in which he or she determined the categories and then asked students to find words that fit them.

Students in the transitional phase learn to be more systematic in the way they collect, sort, and reflect on word patterns. Students each have a spiral-bound word study notebook in which to record their sorts and revisit sorts for further classification or extension. The notebook helps students see how much they have learned to reach their current understandings.

You may be amazed at how contagious this process becomes. Students go home, find words that fit the patterns, and then bring their discoveries to school to add to their notebooks or posters.

Exploring Literature

In addition to the structured sort that was described above, you can encourage students to explore literature that is written to highlight word meanings and spelling patterns. Judith Viorst's book, *The Alphabet from Z to A with Much Confusion on the Way,* for example, teases children into exploring the sounds and spellings of letter patterns within words (1994). On the *Y* page she writes, "Y is for yew and for you, But it isn't for using." And on the *V* page she writes, "V is for vale and for veil, and (I cannot believe this!) for vane, vain, and vein! R is for—we're not at R yet. Now what is your hurry?" Clearly, after reading this book, children would have many words to explore.

Another exciting book that ties in well with word study is *One Sun* (McMillan, 1990). McMillan writes this book in what he calls terse verse. Each page contains a photograph of a happening at the beach and a two-word description. The first page begins with "sand hand." One page has a "snail trail" and lends itself to an exploration of long *a* words. This book could be used as a basis for further word study. You might ask your students to create their own book of terse verse.

In *Do Not Touch*, by Carrier (1988), each page has a foldout that reveals a part of a word. For example, one page states, "I never knew." When you open the page, the *new* part of *knew* is highlighted. On another page he writes, "Have a treat." When you unfold the page, you see *eat* coming out of the word treat. After reading this book, you might find ways for your students to explore words to see what smaller words are contained within them.

These books allow children to see the creative ways in which authors play with words. They serve as a model for word study and for students to create books in a similar format, thus providing a way for students to share word study with an audience.

Coordinating Spelling with Word Study

Students at the within-word pattern phase can be expected to study a list of words each week that reflects a long-vowel pattern. For example, during the first week of long vowel exploration, they could be expected to spell ten to fifteen words that use the *a*-consonant-*e* pattern, as in *cake*. Because the words are appropriate for these students to consider, they should have no difficulty learning these words for a Friday test and still be able to spell them on Monday. As the students systematically study other long *a* pattern words, they can study lists that include words with various patterns such as *cake, pail,* and *hay.*

Formal study, such as spelling lists, and informal study, such as word sorts and literature exploration, will help students learn to spell words accurately. They will learn to generalize their knowledge of long-vowel patterns to new words, as when they select among known patterns to figure out unfamiliar words. Through this type of thinking, children learn that spelling is a problem-solving endeavor, not a memorization task.

Conclusion and Study Notes

This chapter has shared the characteristics of transitional readers and writers. We have explored the literacy instruction and assessment that you as a teacher will explore with students at this phase of development, including nonfiction reading, silent reading, deepening and widening the construction of meaning, exploring a variety of writing genres, and long vowel word study.

As you work with transitional readers and writers, you will discover the excitement students feel as they become aware of their growing independence as readers and writers. Coupled with this new independence is some uneasiness as students begin to understand the new possibilities in reading and writing that are available to them.

In this chapter we have considered the following main points:

- Transitional students have moved beyond beginning concepts of reading and writing and are more flexible in their reading and writing.

- Exploration into new genres in reading and writing is important for transitional students.

- During the transitional phase, students consolidate previous knowledge and master more complex, subtle learning.

- Transitional students need reading and writing time to solidify these abilities.

- Teachers need to support transitional readers and writers as they develop fluency, as they move to silent reading, as their construction of meaning is deepened and widened, as they read longer texts, and as they explore nonfiction material.

- Transitional readers and writers experiment with writing expository texts and poetry.

- Transitional readers and writers seriously pursue revision and editing in their writing.

- Transitional readers and writers explore long-vowel patterns in word study.

Key Terms

fluency

expository text

repeated readings

timed reading

readers' theater

K-W-L

QARs

text-explicit question

text-implicit question

experience-based
 question

ReQuest

reciprocal teaching

dialogical-thinking reading
 lesson

guided reading-thinking
 strategy

literature logs

dialogue journals

content guided-thinking
 activity

anticipation guide

list-group-label

reading guides

peer response group

peer editing group

closed sort

open sort

word posters

Follow-Up Activities

1. Visit a third- or fourth-grade classroom. Ask the teacher if you might work with a group of four or five students. Give these students the qualitative spelling inventory. Look at and analyze the spelling of these students. Determine if any students can recognize within-word patterns.

2. Read a chapter from an intermediate novel to a group of fourth-graders. When you have finished reading, ask the students to write about what you have read. Talk to the students about their responses. Note if any of the responses are beyond a literal level of comprehension.

3. Create a poster exploring homonyms. Look up each word's etymology to see if you can discover why the words are spelled differently.

10 Intermediate and Advanced Literacy

Conversation

Assessment is integral to instruction. Diane and Tamara, who teach in multiage classrooms with fourth- through sixth-graders, discuss how they guide intermediate readers and writers to assess their work.

Donald: How do you assess while you teach?

Diane: I do a lot of one-on-one work with students. In one-on-one writing conferences, I say, "Tell me what you think is the best part of this piece," to students to assess their strengths. Then I'll say, "Show me what didn't work well and what you want to change, and where I can help you, so that we can make a plan." If a student says, "I made the ending go too fast. I don't like my ending," I answer, "Let's figure out how you might revise this piece to change the ending."

To understand their reading, I ask students to read to me in one-on-one conferences or with two or three students. I ask them to read with me for a few pages and then to read a few paragraphs to me. I listen to how they read. Are they hesitant? Do they stumble on a lot of words? Like the developmental spelling inventory, I do this oral reading three or four times a year.

Sometimes I sit back and watch the groups working at tables. A couple of weeks ago, I did a guided reading activity with a group. We worked together on a few words, and I showed students how to find meaning in words by comparing the word with what we already know.

Yesterday, the same group was sitting in the corner practicing what I had taught them. I was working with another group, but I was watching the group in the corner closely. They knew the lesson so well that they got the same book we were working with and taught the activity to another little boy. They were making meaning. I do a lot of this kind of kid-watching assessment.

Donald: How do you help students to see what they know?

Tamara: We encourage children to teach what they know to other children, particularly in mixed-age groups. Teaching consolidates what you know. A lot of people may think that if the children spend all their time teaching other kids, they're not learning anything. But when students read a chapter and then teach it to somebody who hasn't read it, they approach that material in a completely different way. In the process of organizing their thinking, setting priorities, and putting into language all the concepts that they've worked with, they find out what they know. As Diane said, you can observe kids and see how they teach somebody else. Sometimes they're perfectly confident, and other times they'll stop halfway through an explanation and say, "You know, I really don't know what to do right here." They're discovering what they know and don't know.

Diane and Tamara use conference time to sit beside students and learn about their development and their ability to function in the classroom. In this chapter we discuss intermediate and advanced readers and writers to see how independent students become. They will make use of the practices they acquire during these phases throughout their lives.

Guide Questions for Chapter 10

- What are the characteristics of intermediate and advanced readers and writers?
- What do students learn about studying and reading textbooks?
- How are intermediate and advanced writers involved in the writing process?
- What is the progression of word study during these phases?
- What is the meaning connection to spelling and vocabulary development?

Who Are Intermediate and Advanced Readers and Writers?

Students typically develop into intermediate readers in fourth through sixth grades, although some may not reach this phase until the secondary grades. As intermediate and advanced readers increase the volume of what they read, they widen their repertoire of reading styles. Intermediate and advanced readers and writers differ mostly in experience and depth of their knowledge of reading and writing styles and practices. Students as young as ten years old can be advanced readers. Table 10.1 shows that this learning has no endpoint. Readers continue to grow as they challenge themselves to read materials of greater linguistic and cognitive complexity.

Table 10.1
Overview of Intermediate and Advanced Readers and Writers

Reading

- Experience with different styles and genres
- Reading rates increase, and are flexible to purpose

Oral reading

- Expression and dramatic presence

Spelling and Orthographic Knowledge

1. Syllable juncture
   a. how syllables fit together
   b. external/inflectional: junctures and affixes
2. Derivational constancy
   a. morphological analysis
   b. internal/derivational: bases and roots

Spelling Examples

	Syllable juncture	Derivational constancy
bed	bed	bed
chain	chain	chain
battle	batel, battle	battle
commotion	comosion, commosion	commosion, commotion
reversible	reversble, reversable	reversable, reversible

Writing

- Experience with different writing styles and genres
- Building expression and voice

Written Response

- Analysis and generalization in responses

When you listen to intermediate readers, notice that they read most one- and two-syllable words accurately. Word recognition and spelling focus on poly-syllabic words, and students make connections between the way words are spelled and their meaning (Templeton, 1983). Students' instructional reading levels vary according to their familiarity with text concepts, vocabulary, and structure. When students are familiar with the material and presentation, they can read more easily, and their instructional level reaches a higher grade level. Conversely, when vocabulary, concepts, and genre are new, they find the text more difficult to read.

Reading rates for the instructional level over the course of the intermediate phase range from 85 words per minute for instructional-level material to 200 words per minute for easy materials. Advanced readers read slowly at 150 words per minute when materials are difficult but generally read at approximately 250 words per minute. They may read familiar and easy materials at rates between 350 and 500 words per minute.

Many intermediate readers enjoy reading entire series because with each successive book the reading becomes easier. They become acquainted with the characters—how they talk and what they are likely to do. Intermediate readers learn that writers and genres have distinct forms and styles of expression and vocabulary.

To develop a sense of the types of books intermediate readers read, visit an upper-elementary classroom and meet with several intermediate readers. Some may be reading easy series such as Beverly Cleary's Ramona books and Warner's Boxcar Children stories. More advanced intermediate students may be reading The Indian in the Cupboard series (Banks, 1981). Throughout the intermediate phase, students enjoy authors such as Jane Yolen and Judy Blume, who cover the entire range of intermediate-phase reading, from *Owl Moon* (Yolen, 1987) to *The Gift of Sarah Barker* (Yolen, 1992), and from *Fudge-a-mania* (Blume, 1990) to *Deenie* (Blume, 1991). As students become independent readers, teachers focus most on helping them understand and think about what they read (Newkirk, 1987). As they explore thematic studies, students acquire new purposes for reading. They develop a broader taste in reading and a broader repertoire of reading styles as they read different materials. Consider the different reading styles for the different texts outlined in Figure 10.1.

Intermediate writers want to make their writing more interactive and public (Rosenblatt, 1995). They experiment with different writing forms and with modeling of their various readings. Students build expression and voice in their writing by working to capture the way people talk. When intermediate students write

Figure 10.1
Literary Styles and Genre Schemes Source: Adapted from Templeton (1995).

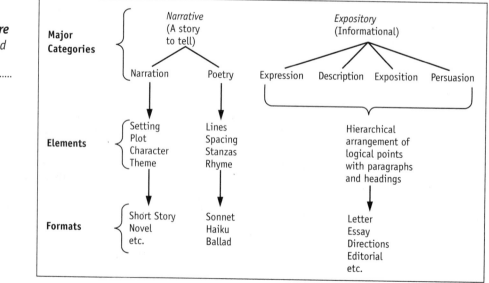

about what they read, they summarize events, analyze, and make generalizations. Their stories and reports are several pages long. They spend time on character development, and their stories may have a moral center and may come to a climax with a resolution.

In the writing process, intermediate writers develop competence in writing mechanics and may spend a good deal of time with rewriting and editing. At the beginning of this phase, their sentences may be quite lengthy and include plenty of connective *and*s and *and then*s. Eventually, they become more adept at writing more complicated sentences by embedding phrases and by using prepositional phrases.

Reading Instruction Integrated with Assessment

As a teacher, you will assess intermediate and advanced readers' knowledge of reading styles. You will use your discoveries to teach them as they broaden and deepen their interests and knowledge of reading styles and genres and develop lifelong reading styles to use in school and later at work.

Reading to Students

The amount of time students spend reading independently grows dramatically, and you may be tempted to stop reading aloud to them when they can read many books on their own. Yet reading aloud to students is an important teaching practice. By reading aloud to students you help them improve their vocabularies and their comprehension (Stahl, Richek & Vandevier, 1991). Reading to students nearly every day is still best. Some teachers prefer to read a chapter of a novel to small groups of students.

As you read aloud to students, they may comment that they have not been read to in a while. They may be unfamiliar with thinking and predicting before reading. Reading picture books to students is a fine way to show them how to think and interact in guided listening. Some students enjoy drawing while they listen, and sometimes drawings turn into responses. Students will readily accept the condition that while you read aloud, they must be active listeners and not distract others as they draw.

Book Talks

Teachers use book talks to introduce new books. A brief book talk may focus on a genre, an author, or a theme. Before the book talk, the teacher gathers as many reading materials as possible at different reading levels. The teacher says a few words about each book and guides students to books they may enjoy and be able to read. In these book talks, students can reciprocate by sharing their excitement about the books they know and enjoyed.

Listening to the Music of Language

Reading aloud is a time to introduce new story forms that contain new voices for students to hear. Folk tales often present a powerful opportunity for reading with expression and a special dialect. For example, Virginia Hamilton

(1985) and Julius Lester (1987, 1988, 1990, 1994) are two important children's authors who present the oral tradition of early African Americans. Virginia Hamilton, a prolific writer, has introduced many readers to folk tales, animal stories, and true tales. A favorite collection is *The People Could Fly* (Hamilton, 1985), which is accompanied by a tape of Hamilton and James Earl Jones reading many of the stories. Students love to hear Jones' deep, rich voice, and, after hearing these stories, they use his reading as a model for their expression.

Many authors and actors have given rich verbal expression to books, plays, and collections of stories on tape. By listening to these tapes, students experience oral reading as a dramatic art that is enjoyable to listen to and perform. These tapes lead to discussions of techniques for reading aloud to an audience. Show students how to mark texts for words to be read with special emphasis and how to make eye contact with the audience. Some students may be hesitant to read aloud; do not force them to read aloud if they are uncomfortable. Instead you may be able to interest them in dramatic readings by creating a reading chorus or by inviting them to read to younger children.

Poetry is written to be read aloud. As students listen to poetry, they concentrate on the sounds of language and how the poetry makes them feel. They learn to appreciate language in an aesthetic way that is important to their continued interest and growth as readers and writers.

Reading Informational Books

A detailed informational book such as Macaulay's *Pyramid* (1975) is perfect for a content guided-listening activity. Some informational or nonfiction books have specialized vocabulary and details that make them difficult to read to students. If you make copies or overheads of key figures and diagrams, students can better follow along as you read. After reading such an expository text aloud, make the book available in the classroom library (see Silverblank, 1992).

Reading with Students

Reading with students is usually a small-group activity. Working in small groups gives students a better chance to participate in discussions, which gives you a better understanding of their instructional levels, thinking, and comprehension. Whole-class reading activities may reduce to charting and brainstorming activities and brief reading sessions in textbooks.

During the first month of school, have conversations with students to assess their reading habits. Keep in mind the observation guidelines in Figure 10.2 as you observe which students have developed a repertoire of reading styles. Have them describe for you directly, in learning autobiographies, their experiences with these different reading styles.

Charting Ideas with Clusters, Webs, and Maps

Charting is an effective way for students to share ideas and for you to learn what students know about a topic. Teachers often use charting to introduce study techniques. For example, when your class begins a new chapter in a social

Figure 10.2
Observing Reading with
Intermediate Readers

Intermediate and Advanced Reader Checklist

Student's Interests and Attitudes

_____ Considers himself or herself a reader

_____ Reads for recreation: ___ No ___ Occasionally ___ Usually

_____ Reads independently in school and at home

_____ Completes the reading assigned in small-group reading sessions

_____ Participates in discussions of what he or she reads

_____ Enjoys a variety of genres

Construction of Meaning

_____ Reads to understand

_____ Stops to think and review when he or she does not understand

_____ Uses the information obtained in projects

_____ Summarizes what is read

_____ Analyzes what is read

_____ Finds favorite and interesting parts

_____ Responds in writing to what is read

_____ Shares responses in a small group

_____ Locates interesting vocabulary to study

Reading Activities the Student Engages In

_____ Creating clusters and webs in a small group

_____ Independent reading

_____ Partner reading

_____ Silently: ___ Slowly ___ Average rate ___ Quickly

_____ Dramatically: ___ Student is comfortable reading aloud to others

_____ Skimming

_____ Scanning

_____ Note taking from textbooks

_____ Finding and using reference materials available in class and school library

_____ Using the computer

What sort of support does the student need from the teacher?

N = Generally not observed

S = Sometimes observed

U = Usually observed

studies or science text, highlight key vocabulary terms by shaping them into a web or cluster to show relationships among concepts and terms.

Charts become more like outlines as students advance through the intermediate phase of development. Your charting gives students a model of how to condense what they read, a skill they will use when they take notes and outline texts. Date charts and post them around the room where students can copy them onto a single notebook page and return to them to refresh their memories at the beginning of discussions. Intermediate and advanced readers chart their ideas with Venn diagrams, color-coded webs to group common items, and compare/contrast several topics. They also benefit from the list-group-label activity discussed in Chapter 9. Students write fluently enough to volunteer as scribes for charting ideas, although some may be too shy to do so. Ask volunteers to spell the best they can and remind the rest of the group to encourage each other in their work. Students' invented spellings at this level usually are close enough to allow others to reread the charts.

Students use *story mapping* as a graphic means of summarizing and reflecting on the stories they read (Beck & McKeown, 1991; Davidson, 1982). As students draw maps of the events in a story, they hold the entire story in mind. When they share their maps, they share their interpretation of what they read, which gives you another view of their comprehension.

Guided Reading

Students benefit from continuing to read narrative texts in a GRTA *predict-read-confirm* cycle (Stauffer, 1980). Teachers usually spend twenty to thirty minutes on stories guided in this way. When you read stories too long to read in one sitting, students can work independently or with partners to finish reading and to prepare to discuss the story when they meet again. Intermediate and advanced readers can write their predictions; this individual work gives everyone in the group a chance to make predictions. Students also enjoy writing their predictions on chart paper, which you can post to remind students what they have read so far.

Response logs and double-entry drafts prepare students to discuss a story when they come back together as a group. In response logs, students find something in what they have read and respond to it (Tompkins, 1997). If they have difficulty thinking of responses, conduct some small-group sessions in which you model responses and in which other students talk about how they thought of their responses. Students in this intermediate phase write about how they relate to characters. They make generalizations about the characters and analyze their actions. Students may comment on the author's writing style and what they think of the genre. In the response log in Figure 10.3, for example, the student comments on the author providing background information from the previous book.

Students start double-entry drafts by writing one or two sentences from the text on the left side of the page. On the right side, students write their response to the quotation (Tompkins, 1997). Often they compare an event in the book with something that has happened to them or comment on events in the story

Figure 10.3
Examples of (a) a Response Log and (b) a Double-Entry Draft

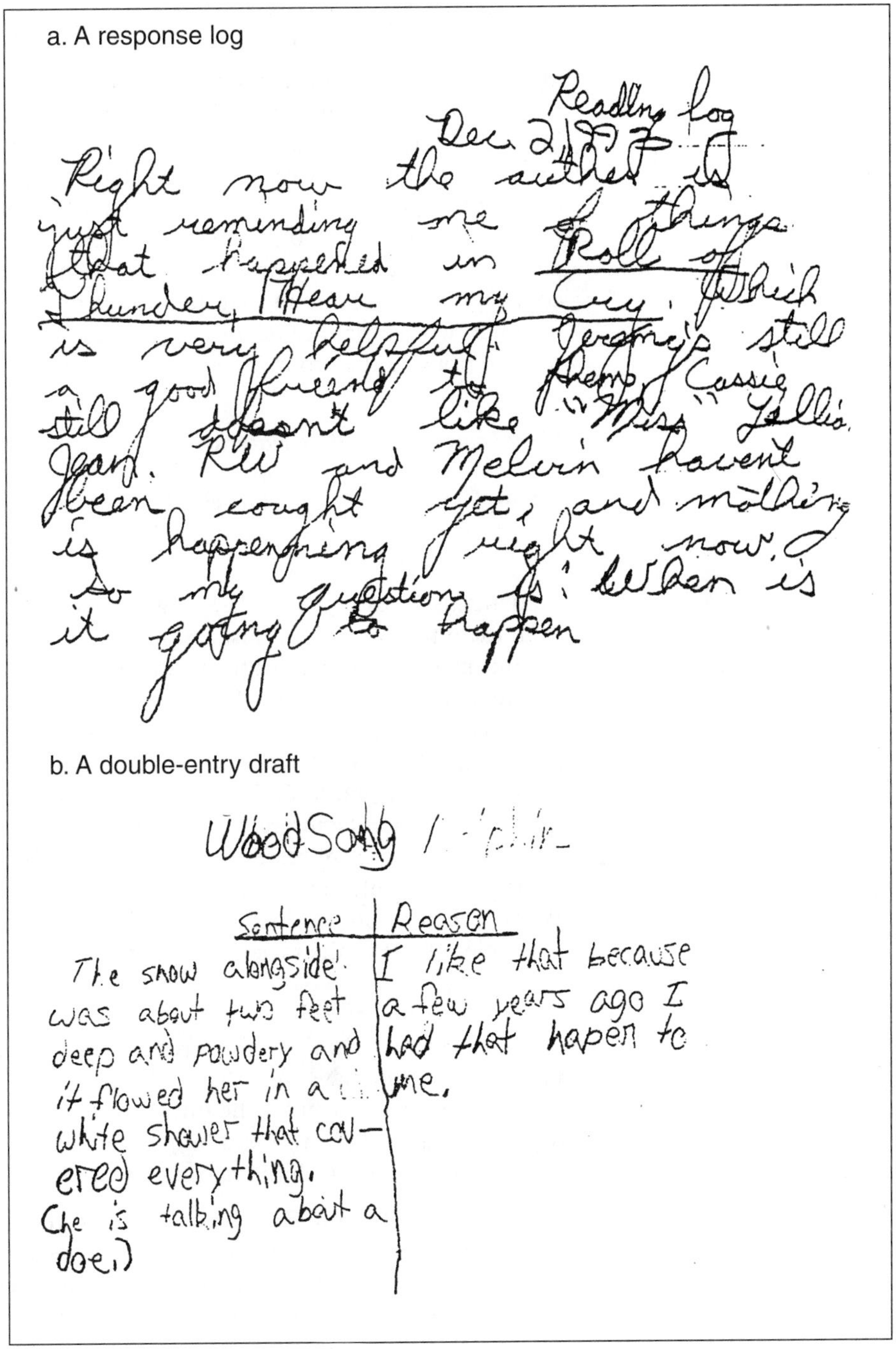

a. A response log

Reading log
Dec. 2 1997

Right now the auther is just reminding me of things that happened in Roll of Thunder, Hear my Cry. Which is very helpful. Jeremy's still a good friend to them. Cassie still doesn't like "Miss" Lillian Jean. RW and Melvin haven't bean cought yet, and nothing is happening right now. So my question is: When is it going to happen

b. A double-entry draft

WoodSong

Sentence	Reason
The snow alongside was about two feet deep and powdery and it flowed her in a white shower that covered everything. (She is talking about a doe.)	I like that because a few years ago I had that hapen to me.

that startled them. The double-entry draft in Figure 10.3 shows a student's response to an image in *Woodsong* (Paulson, 1991) and how this scene related to his life. Such reflections demonstrate that students understand what they read.

A good way to observe how carefully students are reading is to gather them into small-group guided reading sessions and teach them how to take notes on the chapter books they read. A **note-taking** technique that works well for students at this phase is to turn a notebook page sideways and make three columns (Bear & McIntosh, 1990). In the first column, list characters in order of appearance. In the second column, chronicle the main events in the book. The third column is reserved for special quotations or golden lines students want to remember, words that are new to them, and questions about the story that they want to bring to the group. The page will look like this:

Story Chart for Narrative Material

Major Characters	Key Events	Golden Lines, Questions, and Interesting Words

Students use these notes to keep track of story events and characters and read from them to begin group discussions of the chapter or chapters. Students can use this method throughout their schooling whenever they need to keep track of narratives or study for exams.

Guide students in reading content materials by using K-W-L (Ogle, 1986) and content GRTA (Stauffer, 1980; Templeton, 1995) activities for reflection as discussed in Chapter 9. Guided reading activities at the beginning of a thematic unit arouse students' interests and help them gather questions they want to answer. Good sources of readings to go along with textbook materials include selections from children's magazines such as *Discover* and *National Geographic World*. Because you conduct these readings in small groups, you may need only ten copies of a text: the saved funds can go toward buying other materials.

Strategic Reading

The saying, "Don't work harder, work smarter," characterizes **strategic reading.** Intermediate and advanced students are becoming more efficient and strategic readers. Consider the different reading styles that go with the writing forms in Figure 10.2, from reading textbooks and **scanning** an article for specific information to reading a poem or practicing a part for a play.

Study Skills and Routines Studying requires a range of reading styles from **skimming** at 1,000 words per minute to careful reading at fifty words per minute for note-taking. Special routines, such as techniques for getting information out of textbooks, are important study skills. Intermediate readers benefit from a series of lessons showing them specific study practices that lay the foundation for good study habits. Show students how to find information in expository materials and how to study their textbooks in preparation for tests. They will need both skills to make the most of further education and life (Gee, 1992). As you acquaint students with various study routines, see what **study skills** they have already acquired. See if they know their way around a textbook, if they know how to use an index, if they can follow the bold headings, and if they can summarize what they read.

Few of us are taught how to study a textbook. This instruction may be new to you, too. Start by having students share how they read chapters in their textbooks. Often students make the mistake of reading textbooks without skimming them first. When they are assigned a chapter, they read from beginning to end. Ask your students to consider what makes effective study practices. The results of such a brainstorming lesson are presented in Figure 10.4.

Note-taking is an effective way to study textbooks and class lectures. Intermediate readers start by practicing writing summary phrases of what they read. Model summarizing by using an overhead to outline in phrases what you read. When you show students how to take notes by using headings and listing major points, they will see that textbooks present information in a hierarchical structure from the most important points to details. When you give students practice in taking notes from oral presentations, they learn to note major ideas and to not write down every word a speaker says.

Teachers continue whole-class and small-group instruction in how to read textbooks throughout the intermediate and advanced phases. As part of the instruction, students follow a teacher-prepared set of directions as they read textbook chapters. Study guides pose questions for students to answer after reading a particular section. Students can apply the outlining process to any content text. As their skills improve, have them outline one or two sections of text on their own. A detailed study schedule is presented in Figure 10.5.

Such a schedule helps students learn to use textual aids such as graphs, tables, and the index. Step 13 is a new twist to outlining. Your students will need some support from you as they learn to read a section and then *close the book* to write a summary of what they read. This challenging step calls for active reading. As you review their work, see if they used their own words or simply copied from the book.

Taking Tests Most intermediate students have already learned how to take a standardized multiple-choice test. In the upper-elementary grades, however, both questions and language become more sophisticated and more complex. Show students how to rule out choices in multiple-choice tests, and show them that certain words in questions will guide them to particular answers.

Students learn how to answer essay questions when they practice reading the questions carefully and then webbing or outlining answers. You may want to conduct practice sessions and show students how to write within a specific time period. Be sure to make time for students to share papers so that they can learn from each other. Have them look for what they liked best and discuss how they came to organize their answers.

Social Aspects of Studying Students need to consider the social side of learning: how different teachers and subject areas place different demands on them as readers, writers, and studiers. They also need to see themselves as capable

*Figure 10.4
Students Brainstorm
Answers to the Question
What Do Effective
Readers Do?*

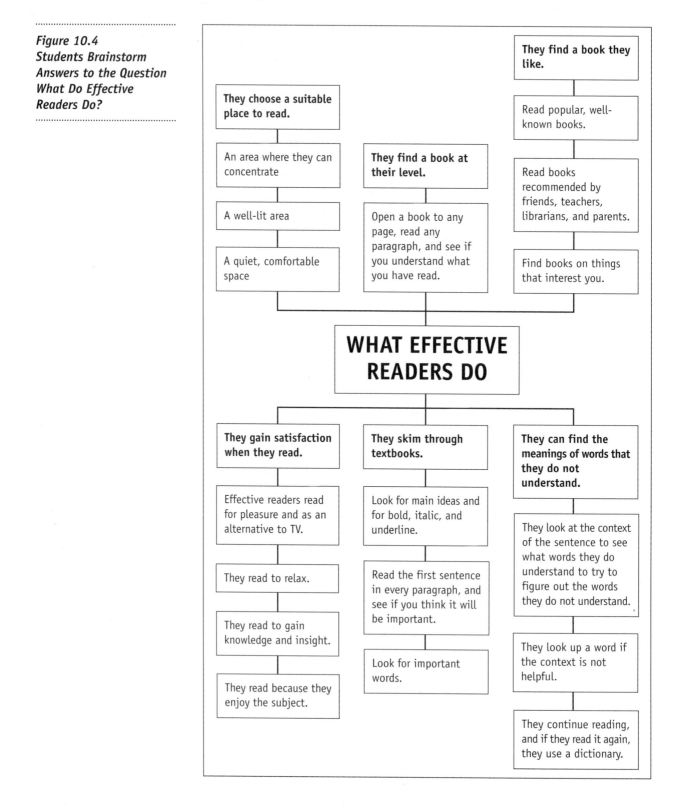

They find a book they like.

Read popular, well-known books.

Read books recommended by friends, teachers, librarians, and parents.

Find books on things that interest you.

They choose a suitable place to read.

An area where they can concentrate

A well-lit area

A quiet, comfortable space

They find a book at their level.

Open a book to any page, read any paragraph, and see if you understand what you have read.

WHAT EFFECTIVE READERS DO

They gain satisfaction when they read.

Effective readers read for pleasure and as an alternative to TV.

They read to relax.

They read to gain knowledge and insight.

They read because they enjoy the subject.

They skim through textbooks.

Look for main ideas and for bold, italic, and underline.

Read the first sentence in every paragraph, and see if you think it will be important.

Look for important words.

They can find the meanings of words that they do not understand.

They look at the context of the sentence to see what words they do understand to try to figure out the words they do not understand.

They look up a word if the context is not helpful.

They continue reading, and if they read it again, they use a dictionary.

Figure 10.5
How to Study a Chapter in a Textbook Source: Adapted from Gill and Bear (1988).

How to Study a Chapter

The following steps will help you study your textbooks and take notes. They will help you create a chapter outline that you can use for studying. You will be surprised by how much you remember if you follow these steps. (Note: There is nothing to write until step 11.)

1. Read the *chapter title*. What does it mean?
2. *Say to yourself what you think the chapter will be about and what you think it will include.*
3. Look at each *heading and subheading*. For each heading, say what you think will be included in this section.
4. Repeat step 2.
5. Look at the *exercises at the end of the chapter*. Say what you think the answers to the questions and exercises will be.
6. Repeat step 2.
7. With a pencil in your hand, *read the summary* or conclusion. Highlight important points by placing a star or Post-it note in the margin.
8. Repeat step 2.
9. Examine the *boxes, pictures, graphs, or charts* in the chapter. Say why each item is included.
10. Repeat step 2.
11. Now that the previewing is done, it's time to read and outline. *Write down the first heading*. Say to yourself again what you think it means.
12. With a pencil in hand start to *read the section*. As you read, look for the topic sentences; these tell you the main points of this section. When you come across an important sentence, place a star or Post-it in the margin to mark the spot. Read on. Highlight new topics. When you finish a section, go back and review the starred sentences. Erase stars that no longer seem to mark key ideas in this section.
    If a section is long (six to ten pages), read two or three pages, and then go to the next step.
13. *Close the book. Now write a summary of this section in outline format.* You can use a numbered outline, or you may just list main points using indents that denote hierarchy. For example:
    page 22: Acceleration
               roller coaster
               accelerated motion
               forces
                  change motion
                  force of gravity
    Be sure to note important terms in your outline. In science and math texts, reproduce simple diagrams and formulas in your outline. Use different colored pens to make notes for different systems.
14. Open the book and check your summary against the text. Underline or mark with a Post-it note important phrases in your outline. Close the book when you want to add something new to your outline.
15. Repeat steps 12 to 14 once if you do not understand a section. If you still do not understand a section, continue outlining and ask for assistance.
16. *Repeat steps 12 through 14* for each heading and section.

students. Teaching students to be aware of the social aspects of studying will help them motivate themselves to succeed. Discuss with your students their attitudes toward a class or subject and how their attitudes relate to their school success. Create an overhead that lists a few effective study practices, and brainstorm with students how they can work on each practice. Some of those practices might include studying with others, setting up a study schedule, finding a quiet place to study, rehearsing information through internal monologues, building a vision of what they want to achieve, and finding out what they need to do to earn a particular grade.

Finding Information

This is the *information age*. Information is critical to success in many professions, and we can find it in many places. Intermediate readers have little problem finding an abundance of information, but they need access to reference materials and information sources.

Exploring Libraries   Finding information is essential to thematic studies. With the help of teachers, librarians, and media and technology specialists, students learn where to find magazine articles, records, and documents. Teachers often work with librarians to arrange half-hour tours and meetings for small groups to explore sources of information.

At the beginning of the year, give students a survey that poses the question, Do you know your way around the library? As you develop exercises in which students search for information, focus on content studies. Have students work in pairs to hunt for information in the library and on the Internet. Students choose a topic and then find a book and a magazine article on the topic. They also list the bibliographic information. Students particularly enjoy researching for recent information about their favorite authors and contemporary personages such as singers and actors. Such contemporary searches familiarize students with indexes of magazine and newspaper articles.

Cruising the Information Superhighway   Telecommunications can be an important part of your literacy program. An incredible amount of information is available on the Internet and World Wide Web. Most schools have at least one computer and modem that connects the school to the Internet and World Wide Web. Students need to be online a half-hour every other day to become fully engaged in the Internet. If your school provides this experience, then regardless of their home circumstances, students will have the opportunity to communicate with other children, to publish their stories, and to search for information. Technology is changing rapidly, and you will see greater access for students with less hardware. Already, some students are cruising the Internet directly through their televisions without a separate computer.

Begin by assessing what your students know about computers, word processing, and telecommunications. In a survey, for example, ask students the following questions:

1. When do you use computers?

2. What kind of systems do you use: IBM compatible, Macintosh, DOS, Windows?

3. Do you know how to link to the Internet or the World Wide Web?

4. Describe how you use or want to use telecommunications:

   People I want to communicate with.

   Things I want to learn about.

5. What is the most interesting experience you have had communicating with someone on the computer? How far have you traveled through telecommunications?

Students often do well teaching each other what they know about computers. They like to work in pairs as they access the outside world via the Internet or the World Wide Web. As in all workshop settings, however, you will need to lay down ground rules. Students need to give each other space and independence at the computer and to give verbal advice without taking over the keyboard or mouse.

Other Sources of Information When your students have become familiar with school information resources, they are ready to consider where else they can go for information. Brainstorm with students how to find information, and perhaps select volunteers to seek information. Students usually suggest home or parents, another library, the phone book, or perhaps calling a reference librarian as sources of information. Make note of which sources of information students think of by themselves. Students can be quite resourceful when they are driven to find information for thematic studies and projects.

Reading on Their Own: Cooperative and Independent Reading Activities

Intermediate readers and writers learn to work cooperatively and independently for extended periods of time each day. Success in such projects and activities requires that students are comfortable with the responsibilities that go with student-guided work. In small-group meetings, observe students working cooperatively and guide them in ways to think and respond while they read. As students work in independent groups, sit in on a few meetings for updates on their progress and to assess the level of their cooperation and purpose.

Reading Workshops

Reading workshops take various forms: small groups of four to six students may choose to read a novel together in literature circles, or two students may decide to read a novel as partners. Workshops usually run approximately thirty minutes each day for intermediate readers. During this time, students read independently or with others (Atwell, 1987).

In partner reading, one person may read the book to another, which allows students of different functional and developmental levels to read together. As you walk around the room to observe partners, carry a notebook to make notes of what students are reading, who they are working with, and the level of their reading fluency. Many teachers carry a clipboard and make notes on sticky notes, which they transfer to student pages and records in their teacher portfolios.

In literature circles, students meet with partners who want to select and read the same book. These groups meet at least once or twice a week to read together silently and to share their responses. Students may decide to read chapters with a partner and to write daily in individual response logs. Each student must read the book at least at an instructional level to be able to respond to what they read. Provide copies of books that will work well with literature circles at various functional reading levels. As the groups form, meet with them to hear how they are progressing. Listen carefully for cooperation in the conversation patterns and to see if students are keeping up with the reading.

Nonfiction Trade Books

Libraries are a bountiful resource of nonfiction trade books for partner reading. Students bring back what they learn and share new information in small groups or with the whole class. Many thought-provoking passages can be read in ten minutes. Intermediate readers enjoy books such as *The Big Book of Tell Me Why* (Leokum, 1989), which covers a wide range of subjects including how things began, how creatures live, and how things are made. More difficult books such as *Why Do Clocks Run Clockwise? and Other Imponderables* (Feldman, 1987) work well for more advanced readers. Your students will enjoy culling information from one- and two-page explanations of questions such as, "Were diamonds always considered valuable? Did baseball really originate in America? What causes headaches? Why do sailors wear bell-bottom trousers? Why doesn't sugar spoil or get moldy? Why do surgeons wear blue or green when operating? What is the purpose of the white half-moons on the bases of our fingernails and toenails? Why do ants tend to congregate on sidewalks?" One question leads to another, and soon students are tantalized into exploring on their own.

Many nonfiction trade books are interactive and make great partner reading. *Earthsearch: A Kids' Geography Museum in a Book* (1990) and *The Explorabook* (1994), both by Cassidy, and *Material World* (Menzel, 1994) are three fascinating books to read with a partner for ten to fifteen minutes. Similar pieces are found in children's magazines such as *National Geographic World, Ranger Rick, 3-2-1 Contact,* and *Sports Illustrated for Kids. Magazines for Kids and Teens* by Stoll (1994) lists many children's magazines that are perfect for partner reading.

Student-Guided Reading Groups

After two or three months of watching you guide reading sessions, intermediate readers are ready to run their own groups. In student-guided reading groups, a pair of students prepares and conducts a guided-reading thinking activity (Bear & Invernizzi, 1984). The leaders choose a selection and prepare stopping points and open-ended questions to ask the rest of the group. First, they select a reading for the group. They may choose from their reading series or a magazine article that relates directly to a subject they are studying. They select materials that can be copied for the group and that can be read in thirty to forty minutes. After they meet with you to discuss their choice, the two leaders prepare for the student-guided reading lesson by reading the material carefully to find good places to stop and check predictions and to make new ones. If the group is reading expository materials, student leaders find good stopping points to chart what people have learned. Plan a final meeting with them before the lesson to review stopping points and to be sure they have written open-ended questions. Depending on the difficulty of the piece, the leaders may decide to read the selection to the group. Students usually do well at matching the difficulty of reading materials to their classmates' abilities.

After they run the group, leaders use the evaluation form in Figure 10.6 to assess their work. Each area is scored on a scale from one to five for a total of twenty points.

The *jigsaw method* is a good student-guided way for students to teach each other their texts (Slavin, 1986; Tierney, Readence & Dishner, 1990). Arrange students in small groups and divide the text into an equal number of sections. Have each group choose a section of material to study and become experts on. The first time you do this with your class, you may want to provide each group with *expert sheets*—questions for students to answer from their section. More experienced students can prepare a one-page summary of what they read. When students have become experts on their parts of the text, you make new groups comprised of an expert on each section of the book.

Jigsawing is a flexible routine. Jigsaw groups can outline their section of the chapter so that when all of the sections are put together students have a complete outline of the text to study. They learn a good deal about outlining by looking at how their classmates approached a similar task. In one adaptation, each expert group makes a presentation on their section: they make charts and overheads, write debates, and put on skits. As in any cooperative activity, it's good to have an evaluation time when students meet to discuss how they have contributed to their group's final product.

Figure 10.6
Self-Assessment of
Student-Guided Reading
Source: Adapted from Bear
and Invernizzi (1984).

Self-Assessment Checklist of Student-Guided Reading	
1. Preparation	_____ Were you well prepared?
2. Quality of the questions	_____ Did you ask thoughtful and inferential questions?
3. Where to ask	_____ Did you stop at good points to check predictions and to make new ones?
4. Probing	_____ Did you listen to the responses to the questions, and did you help group members to make good predictions?
5. Tact and politeness	_____ Did you manage the session using the ideas presented by the group members without being bossy or impolite?
6. Organization and teamwork	_____ Were you organized, and did you work together as a team?
7. Resolution	_____ Did you guide the group in a discussion of the work?

Score each objective on a scale from 5 to 0, where 5 represents excellent work and 0 represents failure. These points can be converted to a grade as needed.

Student Reflections: Show What You Know

Intermediate and advanced readers spend a good deal of time reading individually. Teachers often use sustained silent reading time to meet individually or with pairs of students to discuss their progress as readers. This means that within a week you can meet with fifteen or so students.

At the beginning of the year, or before you meet in individual conferences, ask students to complete a questionnaire in which they describe their reading habits and interests. Ask them to write about their favorite books, how often they read, how many novels they have read, how their reading habits have changed over the past year, and in what areas of reading they would like to improve.

Writing Instruction Integrated with Assessment

When professional writers talk about their craft, they are loud and clear about this point: to write well, one must read a great deal. Students must do plenty of reading and writing. Writing instruction is integrated with reading, and students use their own writings to practice what they learn about writing styles when they read. Guided practice in small groups leads to cooperative and independent writing activities. For example, writing workshop continues to be a favorite activity for intermediate and advanced writers. They also write regularly as part of content studies.

Writing with Students: Support Activities for Composing Together

Intermediate writers are familiar with the writing process. Writing together is a good way to find out what else students know about writing. You will discover what students have experienced and enjoyed if you have them share their work from the previous year in small groups or authors' chair. Use small-group discussions to develop a more detailed idea of what students know about each step of the writing process from prewriting to publication. Boost their recall by posting charts that summarize different parts of the writing process.

Free writes provide a sample to assess students' proficiency and development, as discussed in Chapters 4 and 5. Review the guidelines for evaluating composing skills in Table 4.6 for criteria by which to assess students' writing development. Students enter the intermediate phase with competency at least at a middle level in each area. Advanced writers meet the high-level criteria on this evaluation form.

To teach writing effectively, you will spend a good deal of time sitting beside students, and this implies some trust between you and your students. Your questions about their writing should not lead them to feel overly anxious about correctness or to use a death grip on their pencils. By the time they are intermediate readers, some students have had many unpleasant writing experiences in which their papers were embalmed with red ink (Graves, 1983). You will need plenty of tact and a trusting relationship to suggest that a student delete an entire section that took several hours to write.

Compare the information you gather in these writing activities to the observation guidelines in Figure 10.7. Note what aspects of the writing process your students understand and on what parts you want to offer guidance and modeling.

Guidelines to Ensure Meaning in Revising and Editing

Revising and editing become important parts of the writing process for intermediate and advanced writers. Help them bring order and strength to their writing by giving them a framework by which to evaluate it.

In ancient Rome, **Quintilian,** a teacher from Spain, taught Roman students how to make speeches. Quintilian presented a four-step process in preparing a speech (Murphy, 1987). Use this sequence to assess students' writing proficiency and to show them priorities in the writing process.

Figure 10.7
Observing While Writing
with Intermediate and
Advanced Writers

Intermediate and Advanced Writer Checklist

Familiarity with writing process ＿＿ Knowledgeable ＿＿ Some knowledge ＿＿ Little

Prewriting	＿＿＿ Finds subjects to write about
	＿＿＿ Brainstorms and makes notes before composing
Composing	＿＿＿ Works independently for 20 to 30 minutes
	＿＿＿ Composes with others
Revision	＿＿＿ Is open to ideas for revision
	＿＿＿ Asks others questions about their writing
Editing	＿＿＿ Makes corrections in spelling and writing mechanics
	＿＿＿ Refers to guide sheets for corrections

Postwriting ＿＿＿ Enjoys sharing writing ＿＿＿ Is interested in art work
＿＿＿ Finds places to publish ＿＿＿ Has effective meetings to
＿＿＿ Is careful in publishing or assess the writing
displaying

Does the student write with ＿＿＿ sincerity (have something to say)?
＿＿＿ clarity in language use?
＿＿＿ clarity in thought?
＿＿＿ correct mechanics?
＿＿＿ correct grammar?
＿＿＿ correct spelling?
＿＿＿ an interesting vocabulary?
＿＿＿ varied sentence structures?

N = Generally not observed
S = Sometimes observed
U = Usually observed

Sincerity: Did you have something to say?

Correctness: Did you write it correctly?

Clarity: Did you say it clearly?

Eloquence: Did you say it in an interesting way?

Start with evaluating writing *sincerity.* Students best understand sincerity as feeling that they have something to say. As you explore sincerity, observe how easy or hard it is for students to think of a topic. Sharing ideas is the best way to help them think about choices of topic. Start with the required curriculum and explore students' interests within these topics.

Evaluating *clarity* is simply deciding if what is written makes sense. Writing that lacks clarity most likely lacks information. Authors have trouble judging clarity because they are so close to what they have written. It's best to have students evaluate clarity in pairs and small groups by sharing their writing and making comments. Students focus their comments on two things: (1) specific comments on what they liked about the writing and (2) one comment on a particular part that was not clear or that they did not understand. By asking each other one question about the writing, group members guide each other back into the text for revision.

Correctness has to do with the mechanics of writing. This is a time to edit for punctuation, grammar, and spelling. Students use editing checklists, dictionaries, and spell checks on word processors. Ask students to circle or make margin notes as they work on correcting their writing. What they choose to work on shows you the edges of their learning, and you will see new competencies arise.

Developing *eloquence,* the final step in the process, can mean a great deal to students as they develop styles of writing. Because intermediate writers work to expand their writing, they often string together long sentences with simple conjunctions such as *and* and *then.* As they read each others' work, they find words, phrases, and sentences that strike them as eloquent. Help them see that shorter, leaner sentences usually sound best and make the best sense. Next, students examine their word choices. They can start by referring to thesauruses for synonyms to replace overused adjectives such as *good, pretty,* and *nice.*

Students' Knowledge of Writing Forms

Intermediate and advanced readers are open to many different writing forms. Most of their writings, however, have been stories, poems, and reports. They have had little experience with writing forms that are common in the world outside of school. Prod their understanding of writing's many uses by asking them to brainstorm different writing forms. Ask them to think of what they write and read at home and to conduct interviews to see what writing forms others use.

Remind students of the possibilities for writing by referring to a list of writing forms (Tchudi & Yates, 1983). The list can include all types of newspaper stories, booklets, interviews, comics, anecdotes and stories, plays, and science

····· TAKING A ·····
CLOSER LOOK   ## Weighing the Role of Mechanics in Writing

How important do you think correctness is in the writing process? The ability to write correctly is highly prized in some educational settings. To succeed in school, students need to know the mechanics of writing. But if you want students to take your ideas about their writing seriously and to take time to revise their writing, you must first give close attention to *what* students write and not *how* they write. Say to them, "We'll work on the mechanics and spelling later, but right now, let's look at what you are trying to say." The first goal is to establish a climate in which students can create something they are proud of and that is worthy of the time it takes to improve a piece of writing—to write correctly, neatly, with correct spelling and punctuation.

Teachers can become frustrated when time runs out on writing projects. Making mechanics too large a part of the writing process may leave even less time for composing. You will reduce the stress for yourself and students if you keep track of the writing schedule and give students feedback on how much time they have left to complete a finished product. Help them set priorities and manage their time. Look for a balance between creative work and working toward publication. Help them create a balance between the amount of time they spend composing and the amount of time they spend revising and editing. Establish a hierarchy of skills for students, and provide exercises that will show them how to look for specific features in their writing.

fiction. Encourage them to try different forms in their projects and units. For example, a student might write a letter to request information from a national conservation group.

Preparing for Required Writing Assessments

Students will take both teacher-made and district mandated writing tests throughout their schools careers, and they need to learn how to take short-answer and essay tests. As you plan instruction, first find out how and when your students are tested in writing and then schedule instruction to help them write well in these tests. Students usually take narrative writing tests two or three times in the elementary grades. The writing samples are scored by two readers who evaluate for factors such as clarity, expression, and organization. Obtain sample items for students to practice for this kind of test.

You can target mechanics in brief lessons with selected worksheets. Give your students some practice in punctuation by having them insert the punctuation in a paragraph or two that you have typed without punctuation. This gives them experience examining the sentence structure of well-written, interesting materials. Then have them return to rereading their own writing for these same features.

Writing on Their Own: Cooperative and Independent Activities

Teachers introduce skills for cooperative and independent writing in small-group guided writing activities. After that, students work in thirty-minute daily writing blocks and meet with the teacher for individual conferences. As you try these cooperative writing activities, you will see why students say that writing on their own is their favorite activity.

Writing Workshops

In many cases, you may meet with small groups for a month or two before you establish cooperative writing workshops. You want to be confident that students can work productively in a workshop setting. Students working with others accomplish more than they do alone, but workshop partnerships can change

Talking is essential to the writing process.

depending on the input students think they need (Stremmel & Ru, 1993). In workshops students may seek out others for different skills, choosing one student to work with while composing and then consulting on a design question with someone who has just made a pop-up book (cf. Palinscar, 1986; Rogoff, 1990). One writing workshop ground rule is that students must be working toward publication on a piece of writing.

Writing workshop is a good time for individual conferences. Students may schedule to meet with you when they reach a specific point in their writing, or, less formally, you can sit beside students who seem to be stuck or who have asked for your help. Graves suggests a hierarchy of questions to ask in writing conferences (1983):

1. How is it going?

2. Where are you in this draft?

3. What is the one thing you are trying to say in your writing?

The first question opens up conversation. Students may say that they are just fine, that they are busy writing. If they are unsure of what direction to take, the second question shows you where they left off. When students seem to be stuck, the last question helps them refocus.

Develop a repertoire of open-ended questions to encourage students to talk in conferences. Here are several questions that encourage reflection when students request your assistance (Nathan, Temple, Juntunen & Temple, 1989):

- Can you tell me about your piece of writing?

- Why did you choose this subject to write about?

- What kinds of changes have you made from your last draft?

- What problems did you have or are you having?

- What questions did your conference partner ask you?

- What questions do you want to ask me?

- Do you have more than one story here?

If there is room in your classroom, dedicate a table on the perimeter to writing materials and guides. Adapt the editing guide in Chapter 9 to meet your language arts curriculum goals, and supply the table with supplies and space for students to make covers for and to bind their publications.

Learning Logs

Intermediate-level students do about half of their writing in response to what they are learning. Some of this recording, summarizing, and questioning goes into *learning logs,* which they turn in at the end of each day. Learning logs provide a useful place to write free responses or specific responses to questions such as, "What does a leaf's color and shape mean?" In the math log in Figure 10.8, Brad demonstrates what he has learned about probability.

**Figure 10.8
Brad's Learning
Log on
Probability**

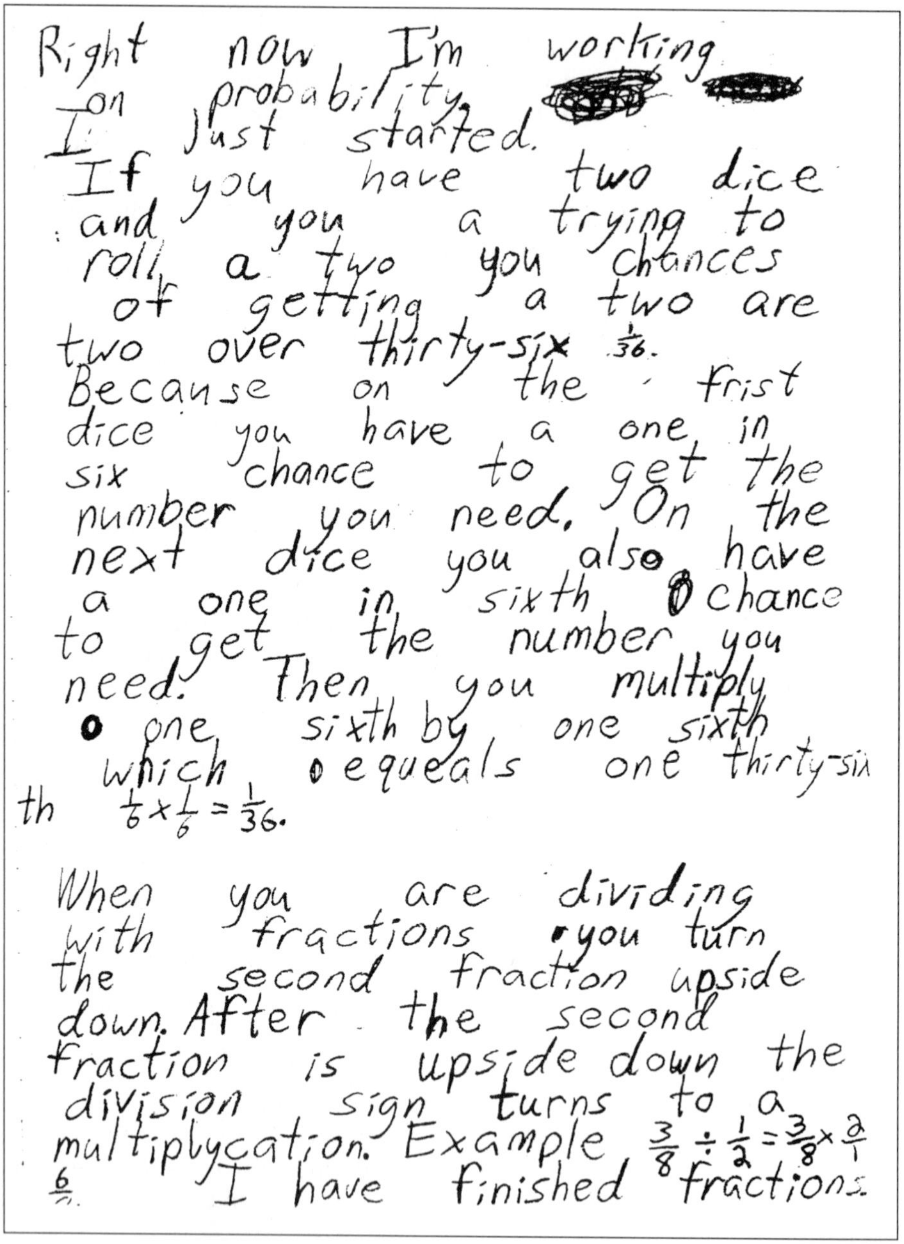

Right now I'm working on probability. ~~I~~ I just started. ⬛ ⬛
If you have two dice and you a trying to roll a two you chances of getting a two are two over thirty-six $\frac{2}{36}$.
Because on the frist dice you have a one in six chance to get the number you need. On the next dice you also have a one in sixth chance to get the number you need. Then you multiply one sixth by one sixth which equals one thirty-sixth $\frac{1}{6} \times \frac{1}{6} = \frac{1}{36}$.

When you are dividing with fractions you turn the second fraction upside down. After the second fraction is upside down the division sign turns to a multiplycation. Example $\frac{3}{8} \div \frac{1}{2} = \frac{3}{8} \times \frac{2}{1} = \frac{6}{2}$. I have finished fractions.

Word Study and Spelling Instruction Integrated with Assessment

Most intermediate readers and writers are in some part of the **syllable-juncture** phase of spelling development. During this time, students study the structure of polysyllabic words. As they enter into the **derivational-constancy**

STUDENT STUDY

Marika Shows What She Knows

Marika, a fourth-grader, has taken a piece of writing through the writing process. In Figure 10.9a she has evaluated her efforts by answering questions posed by her teacher. Her self-assessment was attached to the front of her second draft. Reflecting in this way leads students to place a personal value on their writing efforts before others evaluate their work. Although brief, Marika's reflection shows that she values her writing style.

Marika's teacher, Diane Olds, conducted a similar evaluation. She has found the form in Figure 10.9b useful in summarizing the process. Figures 10.9c through e show the rest of Marika's writing portfolio: her final draft, first draft with revisions, and her initial brainstorming web.

In her second draft, Marika dropped the opening sentence about plopping down on her friend's floor. The sentence showed great power of expression, but it was long. She replaced it with conversational phrasing that was also full of expression: "I mean, come on, was it crowded or was it." The invented spellings in Marika's writing indicate the word study that will be most beneficial. She knows how to spell single-syllable words and most two-syllable words. As you will see in the discussion below, an invented spelling like *ELLAGANE* for *elegant* gives some indication that she is in the syllable-juncture phase of spelling development.

Marika demonstrated sincerity—she could develop an idea to write about—and that she was familiar with revising and editing. Notice how she replaced the brief ending in the first draft with a more formal closing in which she generalized this experience to a broader view of buying presents. Using the guidelines from Chapter 4, it is clear that Marika is an intermediate writer. As her teacher could see in examining the fourth-grade curriculum and this piece, Marika has mastered most of the curricular goals for her grade level.

When you meet with students in individual conferences, start with the student's self-evaluation. Next, share your evaluation, beginning and ending with positive comments about the student's writing. Show specific changes you noted in first and second drafts.

Look first at the language and the power of the ideas and storytelling. Share with the student your pleasure in the freshness of first-draft writing and the ability to capture natural language patterns. Appreciate together what the student can do from one writing to the next. You can also compare drafts for significant changes that indicate developmental growth.

phase, vocabulary study is fully a part of their word study as they explore the **spelling-meaning** connection. Teachers and students alike enjoy learning interesting facts about **etymology**—the origins and history of words.

As you know from previous chapters, you assess students' orthographic knowledge—their knowledge of how words are spelled—by looking at their invented

*Figure 10.9
Marika's Writing
Portfolio
a) Marika's Reflec-
tions on Her
Writing*

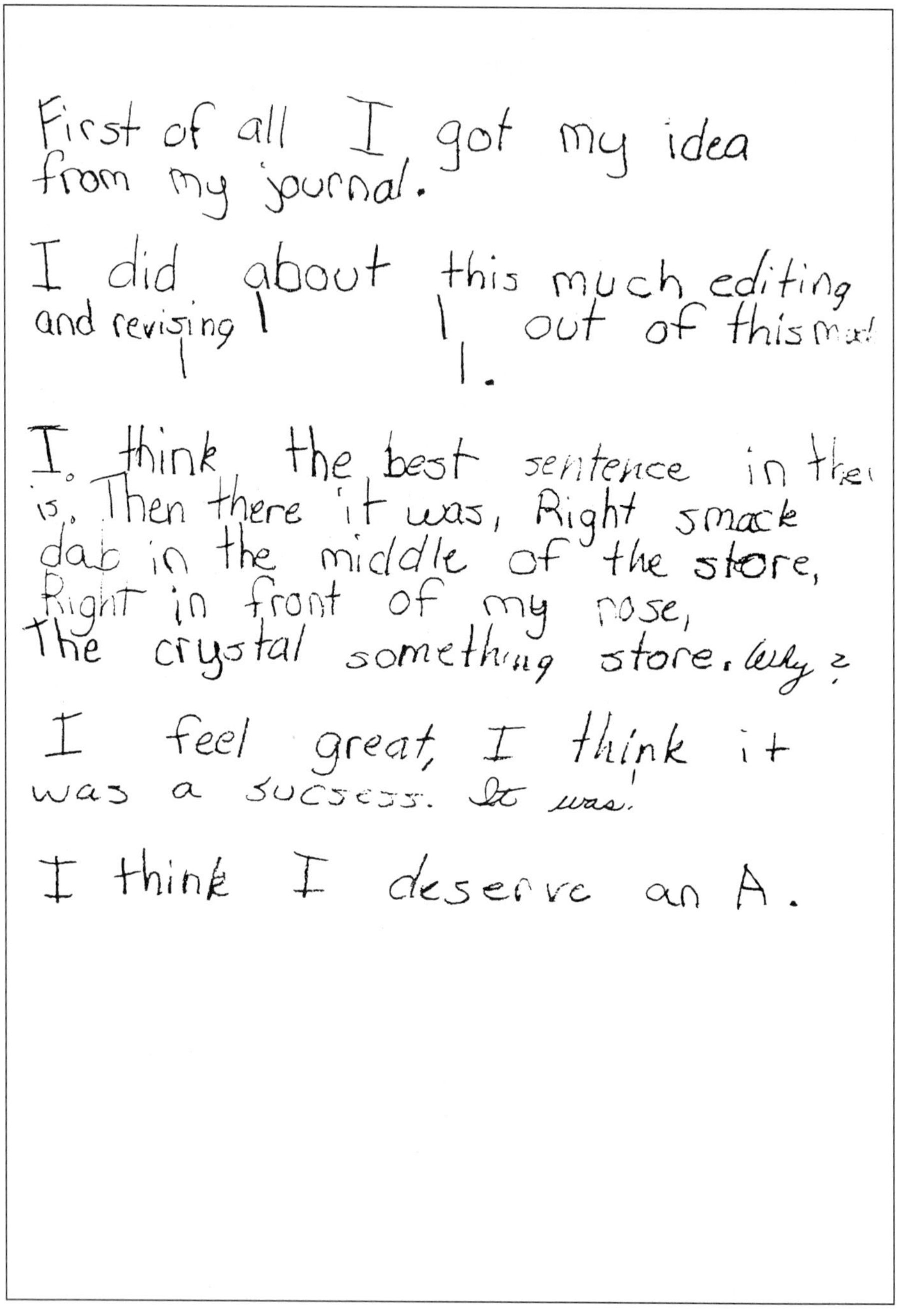

First of all I got my idea from my journal.

I did about this much editing and revising | | out of this much |.

I think the best sentence in the is, Then there it was, Right smack dab in the middle of the store, Right in front of my nose, The crystal something store. why?

I feel great, I think it was a sucsess. It was!

I think I deserve an A.

spelling in their writing or on a spelling inventory. Students experiment with **consonant doubling** as they move from within-word pattern into syllable-juncture spelling. Students at the beginning of the syllable-juncture phase spell most single-syllable words correctly and experiment with how two-syllable words fit together.

*Figure 10.9
Continued
b) Teacher's
Writing
Evaluation*

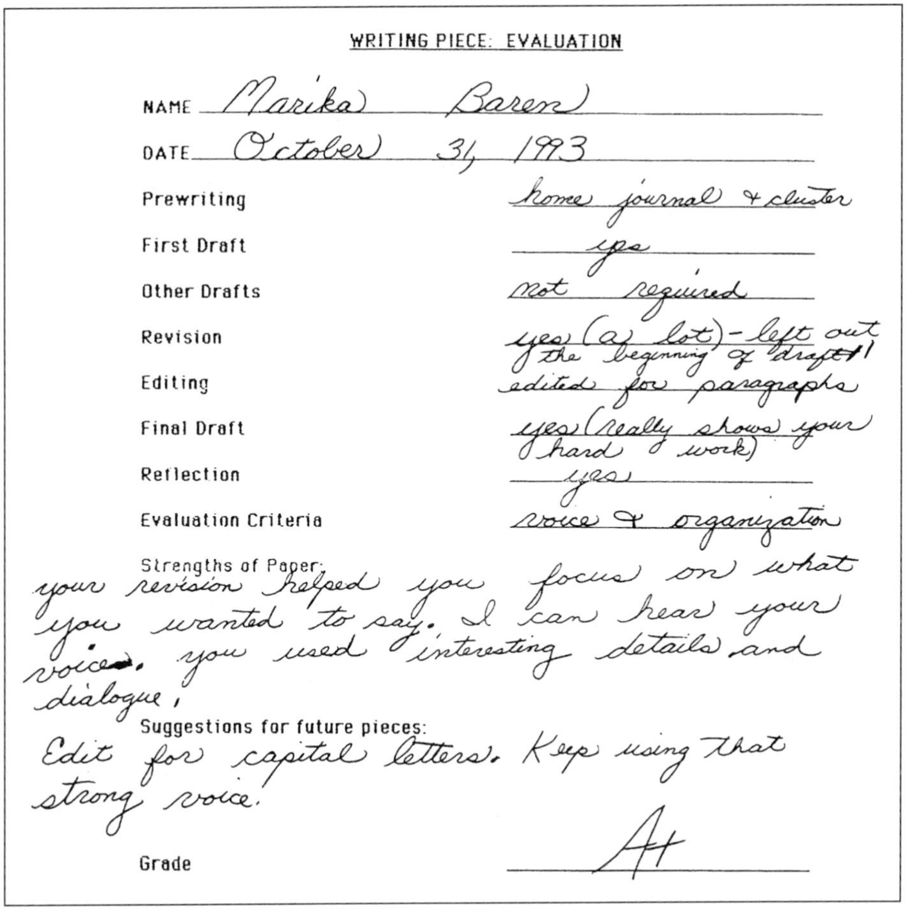

WRITING PIECE: EVALUATION

NAME *Marika Baren*

DATE *October 31, 1993*

Prewriting *home journal & cluster*

First Draft *yes*

Other Drafts *not required*

Revision *yes (a lot) – left out the beginning of draft 1*

Editing *edited for paragraphs*

Final Draft *yes (really shows your hard work)*

Reflection *yes*

Evaluation Criteria *voice & organization*

Strengths of Paper:
your revision helped you focus on what you wanted to say. I can hear your voice. you used interesting details and dialogue.

Suggestions for future pieces:
Edit for capital letters. Keep using that strong voice.

Grade *A+*

Using the error guide to the spelling assessment in Figure 4.8, focus on the last fifteen words of the twenty-five-word list. The progression tracks features from the beginning of the syllable-juncture phase through the derivational-constancy phase. Circle or write in the errors students make and estimate their spelling development. If you see clear differences in students' development within your class, organize word study groups by phase of development.

In addition to spelling phase, you will assess your students' use of orthographic knowledge during word study and spelling activities. As you read with students, observe how they examine words. In word study and spelling, see how students bring interest and meaning to their examinations of orthographic patterns. Figure 10.10 provides a list of word study and spelling behaviors by which to assess your intermediate students.

Word Study in the Syllable-Juncture Phase

Throughout this phase, students experiment with how two-syllable words combine. Word study in the syllable-juncture phase begins with easy suffixes

**Figure 10.9
Continued
c) Second
Draft, Page 1**

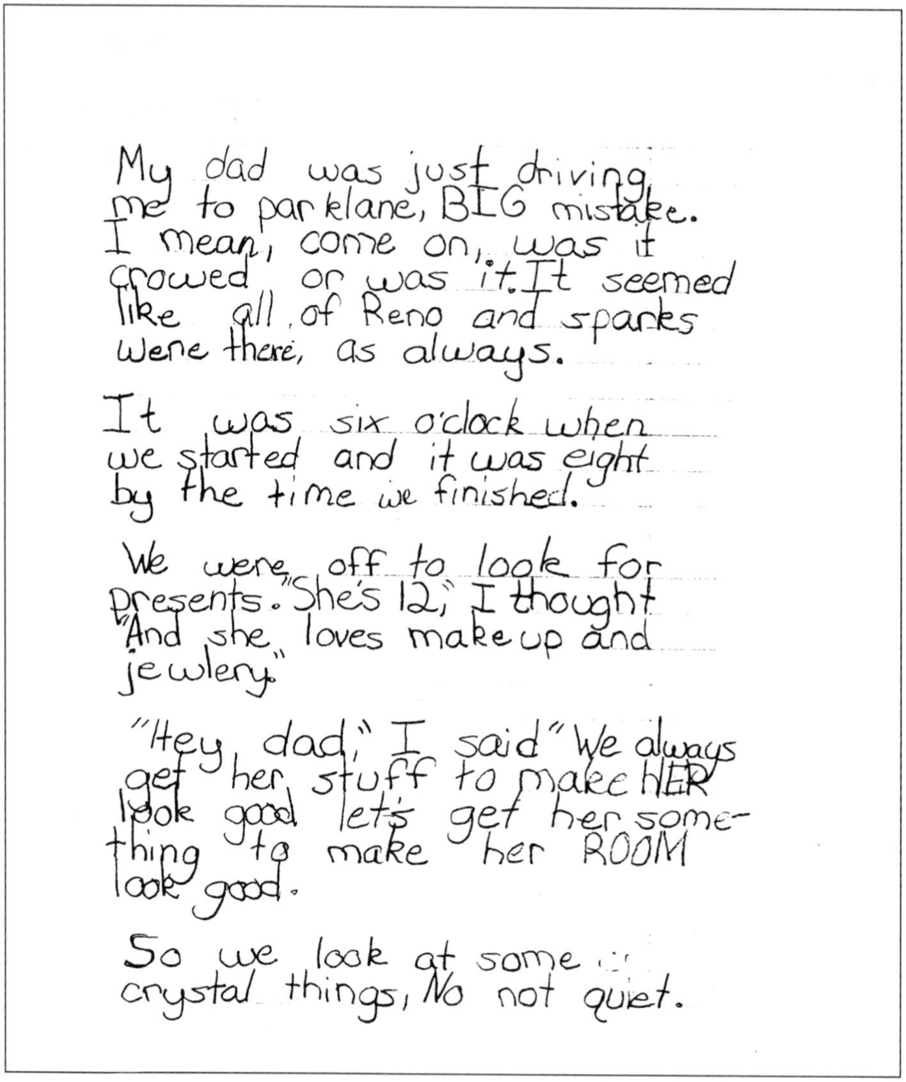

My dad was just driving me to parklane, BIG mistake. I mean, come on, was it crowed or was it. It seemed like all of Reno and sparks were there, as always.

It was six o'clock when we started and it was eight by the time we finished.

We were off to look for presents. "She's 12," I thought "And she loves make up and jewlery."

"Hey dad," I said "We always get her stuff to make HER look good lets get her something to make her ROOM look good.

So we look at some crystal things, No not quiet.

such as plural endings and then moves on to compound words. *The primary interest in the syllable-juncture phase is the doubling of consonants between syllables.* Students in the syllable-juncture phase learn that short vowels before the end of a syllable are usually followed by two consonants (*napkin* and *hopping*) (Bear, Invernizzi & Templeton, 1996; Henderson, 1990). The next major study is of open syllables and closed syllables. **Closed syllables** are short-vowel patterns that end in a consonant sound, as in **mess**age, **letter**, **man**age, and **bushel**. **Open syllables** are those that end with a long-vowel sound as in **labor**, **sea**son, **baby**, and **begin**. Students also study vowel and consonant patterns across syllables.

To begin with, have your students examine the most common patterns, the closed VCCV (**batted**, **sitting**, **planning**, **common**, **sister**, **picnic**, **party**, **twenty**,

Figure 10.9c
Continued
Second Draft,
Page 2

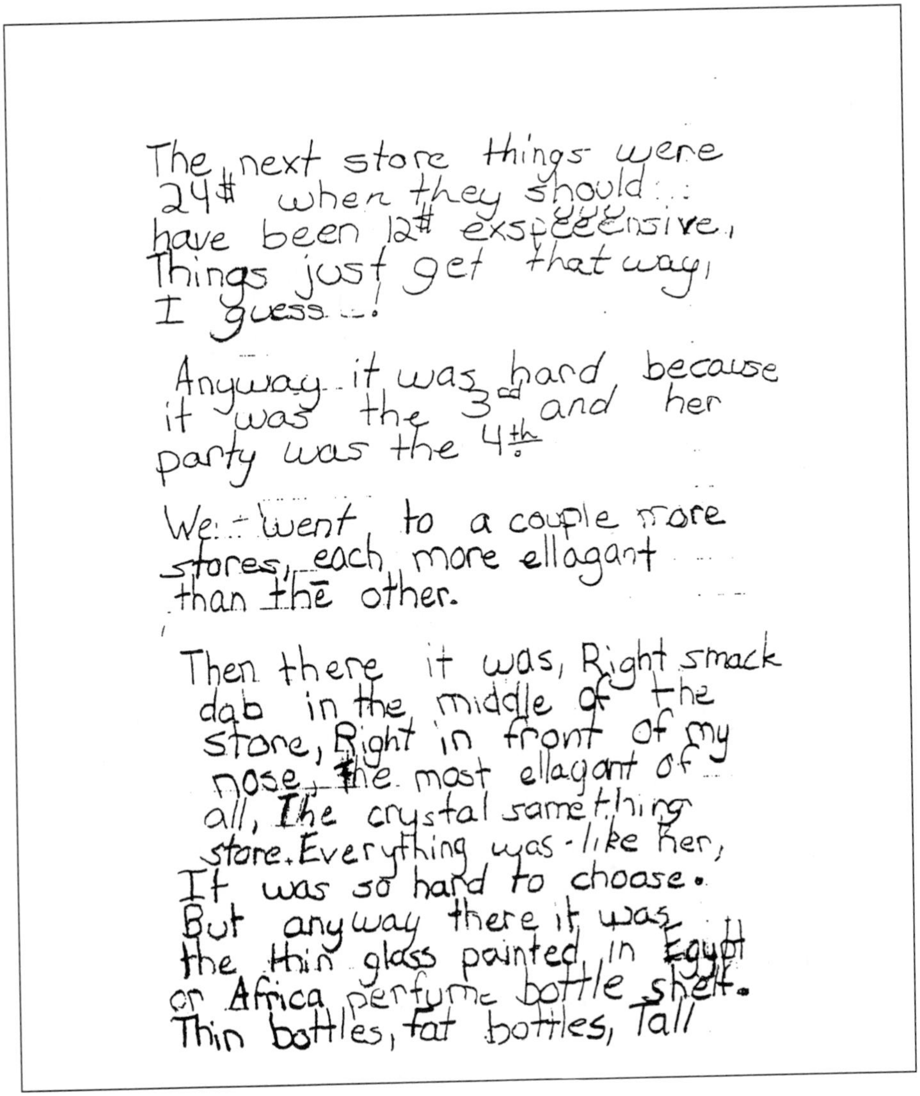

The next store things were 24¢ when they should have been 12¢ exspeeensive, Things just get that way, I guess...!

Anyway it was hard because it was the 3rd and her party was the 4th.

We went to a couple more stores, each more ellagant than the other.

Then there it was, Right smack dab in the middle of the store, Right in front of my nose, the most ellagant of all, The crystal same thing store. Everything was-like her, It was so hard to choose. But anyway there it was, the thin glass painted in Egypt or Africa perfume bottle shelf. Thin bottles, fat bottles, Tall

center, forbid, handle, window) and the open VCV (peanut, trading, beaches, ceiling, joking, liking, bacon, respect). In the course of examining the long and short vowels of open and closed syllables, draw their attention to **accented syllables** and how we spell word endings as in **puncture, bushel,** and **longer**. Finally, introduce your students to the meaning of simple prefixes and suffixes from un- and pre- to en-/em- and how they attach to their base words.

Guided Word Study in Reading

Upper-level word study helps students to expand their vocabularies and orthographic knowledge (Beck & McKeown, 1991). Throughout these two phases of spelling, word study connects closely with what students are reading and with

Figure 10.9c
Continued
Second Draft,
Page 3

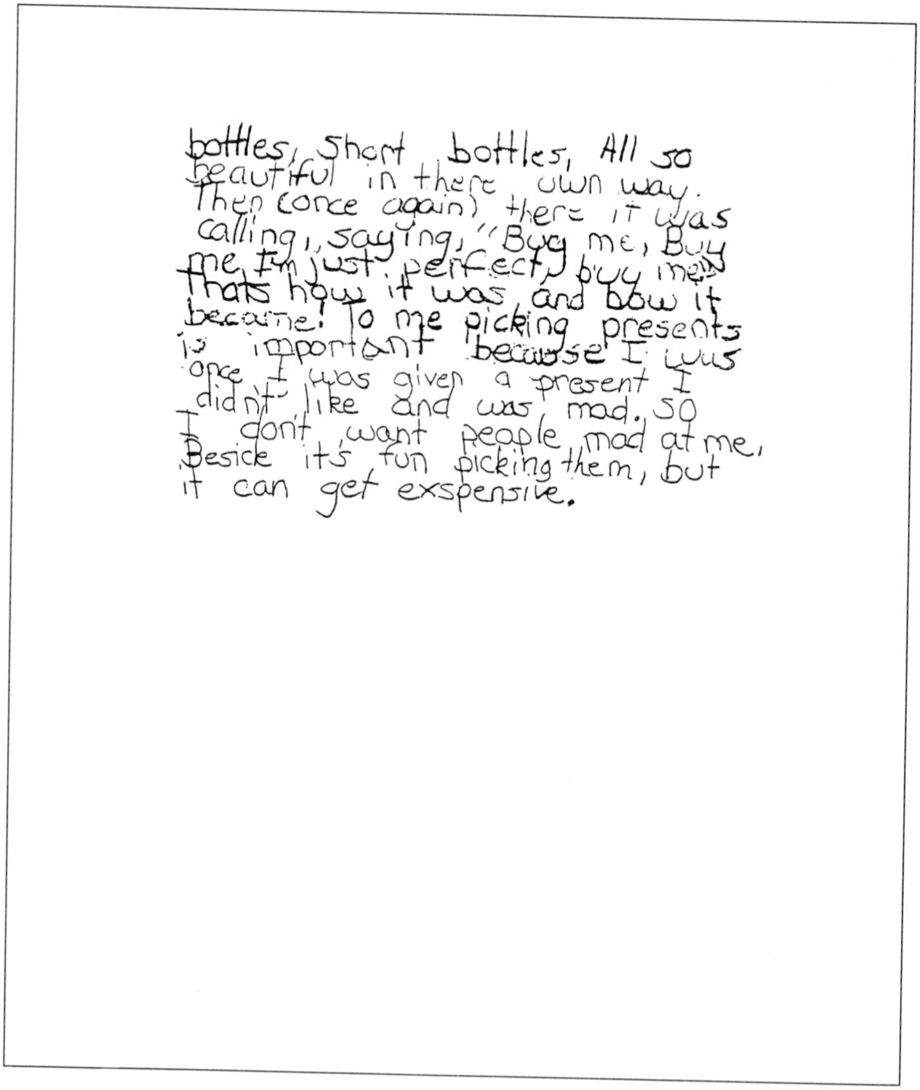

bottles, short bottles, All so beautiful in there own way. Then (once again) there it was calling, saying, "Buy me, Buy me, I'm just perfect, buy me." Thats how it was, and how it became! To me picking presents is important because I was once I was given a present I didn't like and was mad. So I don't want people mad at me, Beside it's fun picking them, but it can get exspensive.

their vocabulary and spelling studies. Word study in reading usually focuses on polysyllabic words. Gather students into small groups and guide them through strategies for interpreting words they cannot read or understand. As they read, observe how students cope with such a word: Do they pass over it? Do they stop to look up each word they do not know? How do they figure out a word? Have your students brainstorm ways to read and understand unfamiliar words. Remind them to be selective in their choice of which words to stop and analyze. For example, they may not need to stop for a detailed analysis of proper nouns, but they should stop when what they read does not make sense and when a word is unfamiliar or difficult to understand. Here are some strategies students can use to understand a word:

Figure 10.9
Continued
d) First
Draft, Page 1

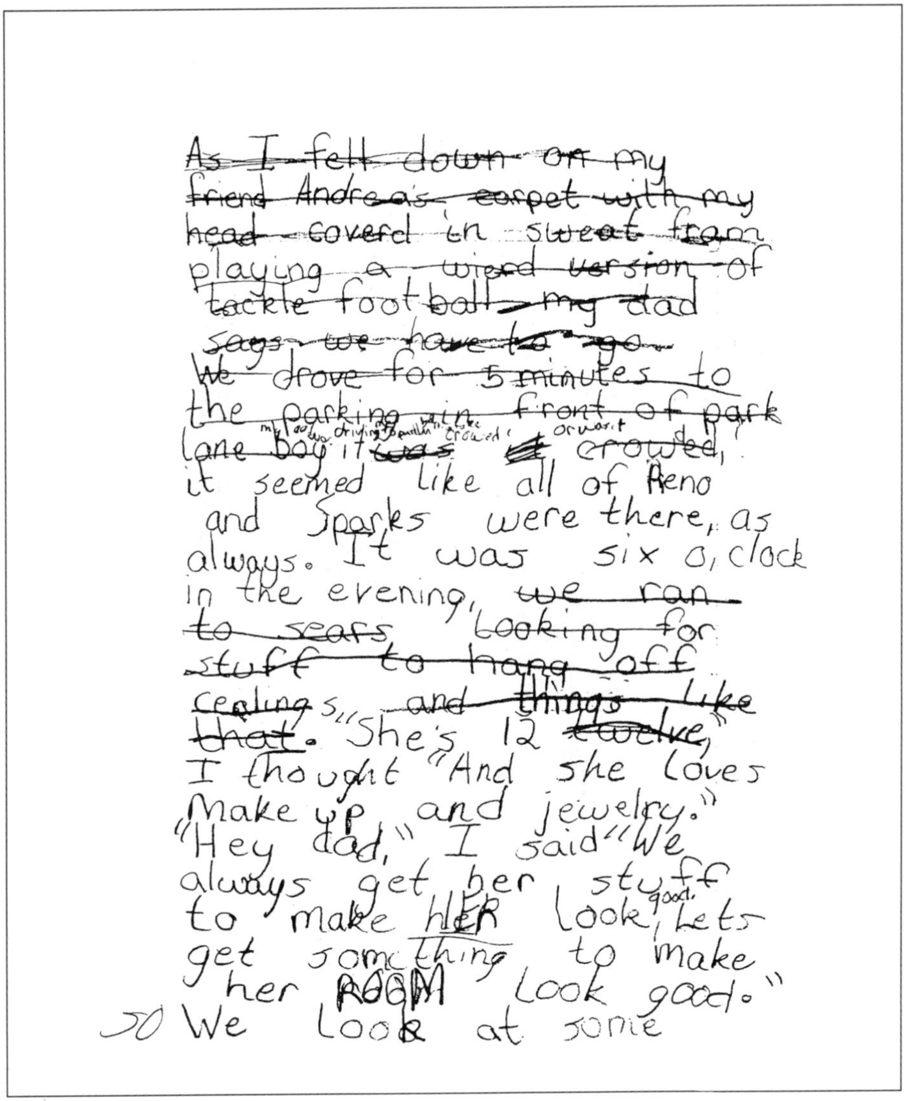

1. Think of a word that makes sense in that spot after reading the rest of the sentence or paragraph.

2. Sound it out.

3. Cover up the end of the word to see if the root word is familiar.

4. Break the word into syllables.

5. Think of a word that fits the spelling pattern.

Encourage your students' interest in words. Show them how to keep track of interesting or difficult words as they read by recording them in their word study

Figure 10.9d
Continued
First Draft,
Page 2

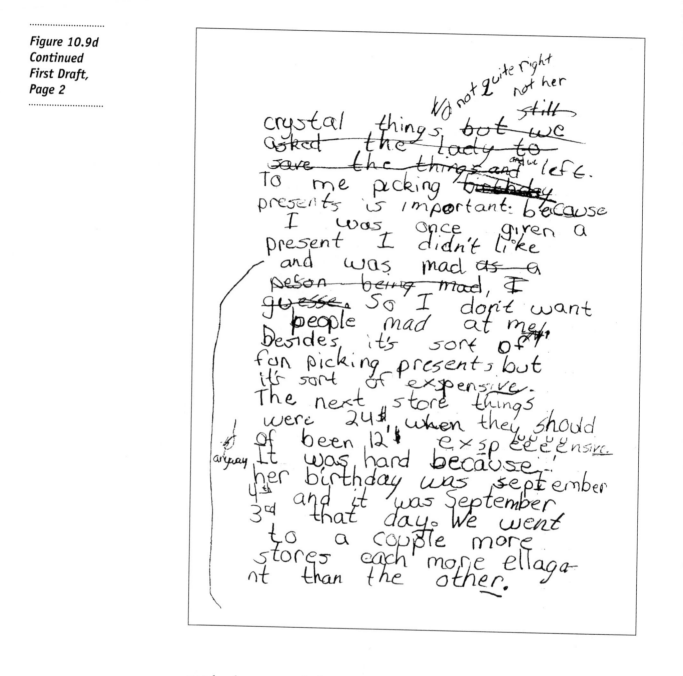

crystal things, ~~but~~ still we
~~asked the lady to~~
~~save the things and~~ left.
To me picking ~~birthday~~
presents is important: because
I was once given a
present I didn't like
and was mad ~~as a~~
~~peson being mad,~~ I
~~guesse.~~ So I don't want
people mad at me.
Besides, it's sort of
fun picking presents but
it's sort of expensive.
The next store things
were 24$, when they should
of been 12$ exspeeeensive.
It was hard because
her birthday was September
and it was September
3ʳᵈ that day. We went
to a couple more
stores each more ellaga-
nt than the other.

notebooks or on an index card or bookmark. Remind them to write the page number down so that they can return to study the word in context.

You can make word cards of the special vocabulary and key concepts that appear in bold print in textbooks. Have students meet in small groups or in pairs and sort these key term word cards into meaning categories. In one classroom,

Figure 10.9d
Continued
First Draft,
Page 3

Then there it was, right smack-dab in the middle of the store, right in front of my nose, the most ellagant of all, the crystal something store. Everything was just like her, It was so ooo hard to choose, but anyway there, it was the thin glass painted in egyt or africa perfume bottle shelf thin bottles, fat bottles, tall bottles, short bottles, all so beautifully painted. Then there it was, it was calling saying "Buy me, I'm just like her, buy me!" so thats how it was, and how it became. ~~she finished a eight~~ anyway at her party she loved it, I was so glad after all that ~~later~~ work

for example, a group of students in a science lesson created the category *light* and sorted the following words in that pile: *spectrum, rainbow, primary colors, rays,* and *white light* (Padak & Davidson, 1991).

Helping students become familiar with specialized vocabulary helps them also anticipate what is important in what they read. At the same time you gain a view into their background knowledge (Hammond, 1979). After reading the chapter, students can review these key terms with another semantic sort.

Figure 10.9
Continued
e) Initial
Brainstorming
Web

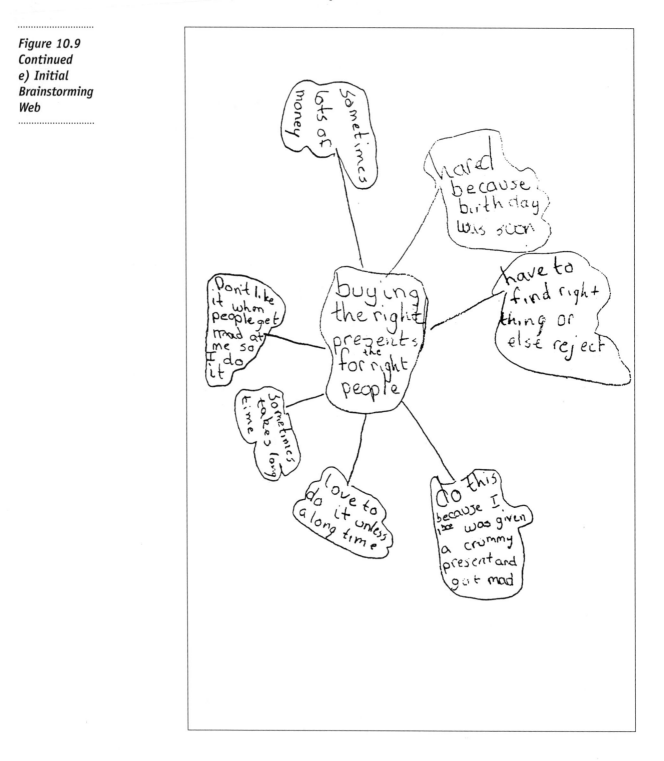

Figure 10.10
Observing Word Study
and Spelling among
Syllable-Juncture and
Derivational-Constancy
Spellers

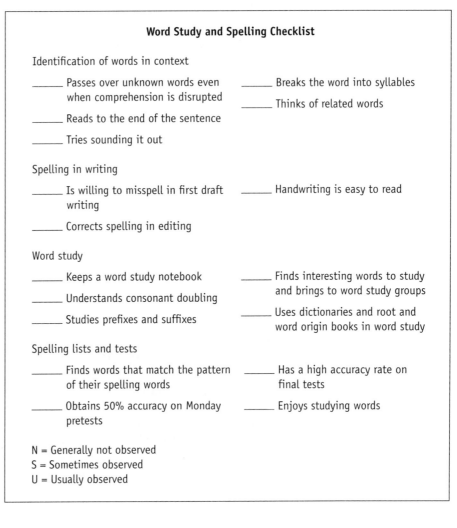

Word Study and Spelling Checklist

Identification of words in context

_____ Passes over unknown words even when comprehension is disrupted

_____ Reads to the end of the sentence

_____ Tries sounding it out

_____ Breaks the word into syllables

_____ Thinks of related words

Spelling in writing

_____ Is willing to misspell in first draft writing

_____ Corrects spelling in editing

_____ Handwriting is easy to read

Word study

_____ Keeps a word study notebook

_____ Understands consonant doubling

_____ Studies prefixes and suffixes

_____ Finds interesting words to study and brings to word study groups

_____ Uses dictionaries and root and word origin books in word study

Spelling lists and tests

_____ Finds words that match the pattern of their spelling words

_____ Obtains 50% accuracy on Monday pretests

_____ Has a high accuracy rate on final tests

_____ Enjoys studying words

N = Generally not observed
S = Sometimes observed
U = Usually observed

Word Sorts, Brainstorming, and Word Study Notebooks

Figure 10.11 shows an example of a word sort card sheet. After the cards are cut out, students read through them, set aside unknown words, and categorize the rest by orthographic pattern. Sorting the words in Figure 10.11 guides students to examine the principle of consonant doubling.

Conduct a word brainstorming session with chart paper on a table or chart stand, on an overhead, or on a white board. Ask your students to think of words that follow a particular pattern. Ask them, "Tell me words that have the accent on the first syllable, like *mi′nor.*" Have them keep a word study notebook or a folder to record lists of words they have categorized. Before coming to group or after a brainstorming session, students can collect words and organize them by category in the way you have demonstrated in small groups.

*Figure 10.11
A Word Study Sheet
to Cut Up for
Sorting*

	running	standing	diving
bumping	jumping	kicking	landing
stopping	sitting	slipping	flopping
saving	hiding	voting	naming
finding	shopping	swimming	boating
keeping	hoping	soaking	strolling

Word Study in the Derivational-Constancy Phase

Students begin to study suffixes toward the end of the syllable-juncture phase, and they see how suffixes can change a word from one part of speech to another (verb *convict* + *-ion* = *conviction,* a noun). As students examine common meanings between roots and bases, they see how words share meaning and how they differ in grammatical function. In the derivational phase students consider the meaning and spelling connection: *words related in meaning are often related in spelling as well, despite changes in sound* (Templeton, 1983).

Word study during the derivational-constancy phase follows a sequence that starts with changes in sound, as in consonant alternations (*music/musician*). Next, students study vowel alternations and consistencies in spelling despite changes in sound (*please/pleasant, reside/resident, local/locality*). Adding and subtracting syllables and looking at the changes leads to the study of Greek and Latin word elements.

Begin the study with **Greek prefixes** (*monopoly, bicycle*) and **Greek roots** (*telephone, thermometer*) and then study frequent **Latin roots** (*transport, predict, rupture*). Follow that with a look at Greek suffixes (*geologist, chlorine*) and finish with discussion of *absorbed* or *assimilated* prefixes, prefixes that have changed to complement the word that follows (*in* + *legal* = **il**legal).

Observation Guidelines for Setting Up Word Study Activities

Teachers use a variety of practices to assess students during small-group word study. These six guidelines are fundamental to word study assessment during this phase:

1. *Word study is matched to development and based on words students see in reading.* Look at your students' free writing and spelling inventories to determine their developmental level. Students need to be able to read the words they study, and they ought to be familiar with the word meanings. Show them that these words come from what they have been reading.

2. *Students can make accurate sorts.* Students find it difficult to examine orthographic patterns to make accurate sorts when they can't easily read the words. Go to an easier sort when necessary.

3. *Students are fluent in their work and ready to move on to a different sort.* Conversely, when students work slowly and with hesitancy, take a closer look at the difficulty of the material and categories.

4. *Students can add and subtract syllables and find patterns among words that share a common root.* Ask them to take off syllables at the front of words and at the end of words to see what is left. If they are unable to see the patterns, then go to a different feature for better success.

5. *Students can find interesting words for word study.* Ask them, "What words do you consider interesting and why?" They locate a variety of interesting words based on the following criteria:

- The word has an interesting meaning.

- They do not know the meaning.

- The word is difficult to pronounce.

- The word is fun to say.

- The word is hard to spell.

- The word sounds funny.

6. *Students know how to read dictionaries.* Some students have had little practice with dictionaries. Show them how to play games like "How many turns does it take to find the words that begin with an *m*?" In addition to dictionaries, students need word-origin books. Be sure to have available a few copies of several word study books. Here are several good ones:

Ayto, J. (1996). *Dictionary of word origins.* New York: Arcade Publishing.

Kennedy, J. (1996). *Word stems: A dictionary.* New York: Soho Press.

Schleifer, R. (1995). *Grow your vocabulary.* New York: Random House.

Shipley, J. (1945). *Dictionary of word origins.* New York: Dorset Press.

Word Study and Vocabulary Development

Students can collect and study words from their reading. Teachers often ask students to collect and study ten words a week and record their knowledge in word study notebooks or on index cards that they store in an envelope taped to the back of the word study notebooks.

In small groups, show students how to prepare their word study in the following way:

1. Find an interesting word and record the sentence.

2. Divide the word into parts by sound and meaning.

3. List related words and think what these parts mean.

4. Study the word in the dictionary and note interesting points.

Figure 10.12 presents four examples of student word studies. The first three word studies were prepared individually, and the fourth, a word study of *helicopter,* was a small-group effort. Notice how many scientific words the students found for *helicopter.*

Coordinating Spelling with Word Study

When you select spelling words, keep in mind the two phases of spelling development. Choose lists by their patterns to match students' development. Throughout both spelling phases students can use spelling words as key examples of spelling rules and also in word sorts.

Figure 10.12
Four Word Study
Examples

> *benevolent*
>
> *"We learned that there was one benevolent society that wanted to offer scholarships to graduates who go on to college."*
> *"Random Acts of Kindness" from the weekly magazine, p. 2*
>
> *bene = well*
> *vole = wish*
> *ent = a suffix used to form adjectives from nouns*
>
> | *bene* | *vol* | *ent* |
> |---|---|---|
> | *benefactor* | *volition* | *confident* |
> | *beneficial* | *voluntary* | *different* |
> | *benefit* | | *patient* |
> | *benevolence* | | |

> *compression*
>
> *"When the fuel-air mixture is incorrect, there is no ignition at the top of the compression stroke."*
> *How Engines Work, p. 8*
>
> *squeezing together in a small place*
>
> | *com* | *pres* | *sion* |
> |---|---|---|
> | *de* | *pres* | *sion* |
> | *im* | *pres* | *sion* |

Figure 10.12
Continued

helicopter

"An aircraft that derives its lift from blades that rotate about an approx. vertical central axis. [Fr. hélicoptère.]"
The American Heritage Dictionary, 3rd ed., 1994, p. 390

divide by sound:	heli	cop	ter
divide by meaning:	helic	o	pter
	helix (spiral)		ptero (winged thing)

Words with ptero (Greek, combining form for "winged thing"):
orthoptera—straight wings; cockroaches, crickets, grasshoppers; incomplete
          metamorphosis
pterographer—a writer on feathers or plumage
pterobranchiate—in zoology, a subsection of molluscoids
pterocarpous—in biology, having winged seeds or fruit
lepidoptera—wings covered with scales; butterflies and moths
hymenoptera—membrane; ants, wasps, bees
hemiptera—half

---

verisimilitude

"The dialogue of the passengers fit poorly with the verisimilitude of the journey by stagecoach."
The American Opportunity, p. 227

veri = truth
similis = like
tude = a suffix used to show condition or quality

veri	simili	tude
very	similar	attitude
verification	simulate	altitude
verify	simulation	
veritable	simplify	
	simple	
	simultaneous	

Syllable-Juncture Spellers

Focus your syllable-juncture spellers on learning how syllables combine. At the beginning of this phase, their spelling words should be a blend of two-syllable words and words that contain patterns from the late within-word phase. During a week-long lesson, focus on three or four patterns. Replace any words from the spelling lists that do not fit these patterns with additional examples of the patterns students are studying.

····· **TAKING A** ·····
CLOSER LOOK

Students' Role in Planning and Assessment

Students need to be "reachers" in learning (S. Hynds, quoted in Saks, 1995, p. 341)—to reach for new ideas and competencies. After students have studied thematic units that you have created, they can begin to reach by helping evaluate their work and plan units of study. Students find this greater choice in activity highly motivating.

In a fourth-grade classroom, Mrs. Erb asked her students to review the curricular goals and brainstorm ways they could study geography. They listed sixteen ways, including making maps, taking tests, asking parents, making posters, and doing presentations.

In her journal, Mrs. Erb wrote, "The next question was: 'How do we start?' This question really stumped them." When her students' organizational skills gave out, she helped them think of options for small-group projects that incorporated the curricular goals. Later, Mrs. Erb wrote that students were having a lot of fun and were "teaching themselves an incredible amount of information." The students continued to plan projects that matched their interests with the required curriculum.

Do not hesitate to choose words that complement other language studies. For example, toward the end of the syllable-juncture phase, students may look at a spelling word such as *fortunate* and brainstorm related words such as *fortune* and *fortunately*. They may, as part of their language studies, label words by parts of speech, in this case adjective, noun, and adverb, respectively.

Derivational-Constancy Spellers

Derivational-constancy spellers use spelling words to make the meaning connection. Select polysyllabic or multisyllabic words for them to examine for changes in spelling and sound that do not change meaning. Compile spelling lists that include plenty of word pairs that show how vowels change when syllables are added to a base word, such as *harmony/harmonious, impose/imposition,* and *narrate/narrative*.

You will increase your students' learning power and the connections they make between words and meaning if you link spelling with content studies. If students have words such as *flame* and *flammable* on their spelling lists, why not link them to a study of the chemical properties of substances that are flammable and inflammable?

Spelling words for students in the derivational-constancy phase serve as key words for further study in their word study notebooks. For example, the words *absent* and *abstention* serve as key words for studying the Latin prefix *ab-, away* (*abdicate, abduct, abject, absolute*). Using spelling words as key words, students can hunt in their textbooks for similar words and so link spelling words with thematic studies.

Conclusion and Study Notes

This chapter has explored ways to engage intermediate and advanced readers and writers in learning. Most of these students are in the upper-elementary grades. Developmentally, they are increasing their reading rate and expanding their knowledge of various genres and writing styles. In writing, the same widening of experience occurs as students learn to write with purpose. Through a process approach, intermediate students expand their repertoire of writing styles and genre to suit new purposes as they discover them.

Vocabulary and spelling are fully integrated into word study. Students concentrate on polysyllabic word study in which they make spelling and meaning connections between words and word parts. Teachers relate vocabulary to content area studies and help students find interesting words. They assess students as they conduct guided activities in small groups throughout reading, writing, and word study.

The final part of this chapter explored ways that reading and writing activities are incorporated into literature-based and thematic units of study.

- Intermediate readers enjoy reading series and have favorite genres they like to read.

- Advanced readers continue to advance in their reading interests, and they develop a repertoire of reading styles to use with different reading materials.

- Reading aloud to intermediate and advanced readers increases their interest in storytelling and the dramatic arts.

- There are many informational books for intermediate readers to use in their content studies.

- Guided reading activities include GRTAs, K-W-Ls, response logs, and double-entry drafts.

- Give students guided practice in studying, note-taking, and test taking.

- Survey students' experience finding information in libraries and throughout the Internet. Develop subject related lessons that familiarize students with various references.

- Revising and editing are regular parts of students' writing at this level. They follow revising and editing guides through successive drafts.

- Students need to keep sincerity and clarity as priorities in their writing.

- Students can generate a list of writing forms to consider.

- In writing conferences, teachers ask open-ended questions to encourage students to share their ideas and to reflect on their writing.

- During the syllable juncture phase of spelling, students examine how two-syllable words fit together. Word study at this phase begins with studying consonant doubling, and plural endings. They also study the long vowel, open syllable and compare it to the short vowel, closed syllable.

- Students make the meaning connection in their word study. For example, students learn the meanings of prefixes and suffixes.

- Advanced readers are most likely in the derivational constancy phase of spelling. During this phase they develop an understanding of roots, stems, and derivations of different words.

- In word study, students in the derivation constancy stage select words from their texts and use word study books that help them to understand the etymology of the words.

- Intermediate and advanced readers are learning to learn, and they take an active role in finding and selecting materials and activities for thematic and content units of study.

Key Terms

strategic reading	spelling-meaning connection
scanning and skimming	consonant doubling
study skills	closed and open syllables
note-taking	Greek and Latin roots
student-guided reading groups	etymology
Quintilian	accented syllables

Follow-Up Activities

1. Study word derivations using the word origin and root books mentioned in this chapter. Choose interesting words that you have come across in your reading.

2. Look through an elementary science or social studies textbook and make a semantic web of the key vocabulary in a chapter.

3. Interview a group of intermediate readers and find out what books they like to read. Discover what book series and authors are their favorites.

PART FOUR

Support for Readers Within and Beyond the Classroom

Contents

11 Understanding the Range of Reading and Writing Difficulties

12 Formal Literacy Testing and Measurement

13 Teaching Learners Who Experience Difficulties

14 Epilogue: Building a Community of Learners

11 Understanding the Range of Reading and Writing Difficulties

Randy: I'm worried about failures among my students. I don't want students to think they are failures because they fall behind the class at some point.

Kelly: There are two issues here: the kids' labels for each other and teachers' labels for kids.

Brian: Students know who is having difficulty. I don't have to point to children and say, "She can't read, and she can." They figure it out.

Lani: Parents become afraid that their kids will never catch up. A parent of a child I tutor said, "I want to know when my child will be at grade level." Grade level isn't as important as developmental level. I want parents to understand their children's development.

Lynn: Parents may believe their child is behind if the child's developmental level is different from other children at that age.

Diane: Most of the readers who are behind in our school are either learning disabled or in the ESL program, but those labels don't affect my responsibilities. Every child in my room is my responsibility—the learning-disabled child, the fully mainstreamed special education child, the ESL child, and the gifted child.

Amy: I agree with you, but how do we know we have a child with dyslexia in our classroom?

Suzy: Well, I don't think you can in first grade. First-graders who are on track with literacy learning make the kinds of errors that older children with dyslexia make.

Lani: One parent is worried that her first-grade child is dyslexic because she reverses letters. Several other family members have reading disabilities. I thought it was normal first-grade behavior to reverse *ps* and *bs*, but she's calling that dyslexia.

Amy: They're just learning their letters and sounds, and those letters look and sound alike.

Lynn: Teachers don't decide who's dyslexic and who isn't. If we suspect that a child is not making developmental progress, we start to work with others: parents, reading teachers, special education teachers, psychologists, speech and language specialists, counselors, the principal.

The difficulties that students can experience in learning to read and write involve their sense of their social, physical, and psychological worlds. All three worlds of experience influence those difficulties and our understanding of them. Randy talked about the students' *psychological world* when he expressed concern for students' self-esteem. The conversation addressed students' *physical world* when talk turned to understanding students who may have inherited some form of dyslexia. This chapter emphasizes the *social world* and the attitudes and motivations in the psychological world because these are the areas that teachers must assess daily as they present and plan instruction. With good instruction, most students who experience difficulties are capable of becoming successful readers and writers.

This chapter also includes a discussion of the terminology and the ways that educators describe students' difficulties and the fundamental information you need to talk to parents and educators about students' difficulties reading and writing.

Guide Questions for Chapter 11

Before you read this chapter, consider these questions:

- How does a teacher identify a difficulty?

- What are some of the difficulties students experience in learning to read and write?

- What is the continuum of reading difficulties that students may experience?

- What is a delay in learning?

- What is dyslexia?

- How do other learning difficulties affect students' literacy development?

The Developmental Continuum: A Model That Emphasizes Delay, Not Deficit or Difference

Students' **reading difficulties** are generally typified as deficits, differences, or delays (Valtin, 1978/1979). Nearly all students who are behind in their reading are experiencing delayed development. For that reason, professionals who work with students behind in their reading usually begin with a *delay* model. Unlike *difference* and *deficit models*, a delay model leads to a developmental approach to instruction. Most students who are delayed respond to the instructional practices presented in Chapters 6 through 10. They follow the same developmental sequence and respond to the same type of instruction as students who are not behind, and they have little need for an elaborate and separate series of teaching methods. Teachers turn to difference or deficit models only when developmental instruction does not seem to help a student to learn.

Some reading difficulties are attributed to *differences* in ways students learn that require special teaching methods. This is not the same as the unique personalities that all students possess that influence their approaches to literacy (Bussis, Chittenden, Amarel & Klausner, 1985). Such qualities do not interfere with learning to read and write. The clearest examples of true learning differences are found among students learning to read in a new language. As you learned in Chapter 9, students whose first language is not English approach reading and writing English differently from students whose primary language is English.

Some descriptions of reading and writing difficulties work from the hypothesis that students experience *deficits*. Often, a deficit is determined in the course of psychological testing similar to the tests discussed in the next chapter. Although even children who have severe learning difficulties follow the expected developmental sequence (Barone, 1995; Warner, 1994; Worthy & Invernizzi, 1990), children who have a **deficit** generally have a permanent neurologic or other severe physical disability that radically limits their growth and development. Few children who experience difficulties in reading are deficient, permanently disabled, or dyslexic. We will discuss the rare students whose performance does fail to fit on a **developmental continuum** and the accepted professional definitions of their reading disabilities later in this chapter.

Delayed learners learn to read in the same way as anyone else. Instead of focusing on deficits and disabilities, teachers concentrate on a continuum of achievement that builds on the developmental phases (Shaywitz, Escobar, Shaywitz, Fletcher & MaKuch, 1992). Each student is an individual, and each student who is behind has a set of factors that have contributed to the student's delays. The factors that contribute to learning delays are discussed throughout this chapter.

Some students are further behind in reading and spelling than teachers and parents would like them to be for their grade level, but they make steady progress throughout the year (Lipson & Wixson, 1986). The classroom teacher's task is to help such children be significantly less behind at the end of the year.

Figure 11.1 presents a developmental continuum for a third-grade classroom. The top line represents the continuum of possible student achievement levels. On the right end are students who mostly read at a third-grade instructional level, which corresponds roughly to the middle of the transitional phase of literacy development. Students who are *slightly behind* a third-grade level read second-grade material instructionally and may be in the transitional phase of development.

The two left categories on this continuum represent more serious issues. Students who are *somewhat behind* or *significantly behind* may be more than a year behind students achieving within the typical range. Students who are somewhat or significantly behind usually have a first-grade instructional reading level and

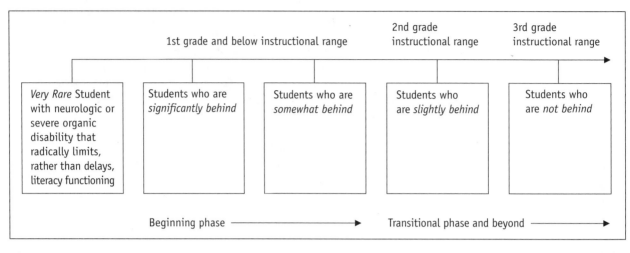

Figure 11.1
Developmental
Continuum for Third-
Grade Classroom

require support reading materials in instruction. Such students are usually in a different phase of development than the children who are either slightly below or at grade level.

In a class of twenty-eight students, a quarter to a third of the students may be slightly to significantly behind in reading. These eight or nine students would be spread out along the continuum in Figure 11.1. Third-grade students who are somewhat or significantly behind are in the beginning phase of literacy development. Though they experience a delay, they can still be taught in a developmental way. To progress, they need intensive support in reading instruction, often from literacy educators and special educators. There is no quick fix for students who are behind (Allington & Walmsley, 1995). They must spend plenty of time reading and writing before they achieve a grade and developmental level that will serve them in their intellectual pursuits.

It is also important to pay attention to the psychosocial dimension of students' learning (Lenneberg, 1967). Some students, especially those who are significantly behind, see themselves as stupid. They need successful reading experiences, developmental instruction, and warm support from teachers to overcome their feelings of inferiority.

One or two students in your classroom may have special learning needs that limit their academic achievement, including their ability to read and write. Students with severe difficulties such as mild mental handicaps and autism may progress in a developmental manner but fail to reach the intermediate and advanced phases.

■ *Recognizing a Student Who Is Experiencing Literacy Difficulties*

What guides a teacher's recognition that a student is having difficulty learning to read? Grade-level achievement and the developmental level provide a starting point for studying and understanding students' difficulties. Observation and assessment play important roles. At no other time in your teaching will you be more observant and clearer in your understanding of how students learn to read and write than when they experience difficulties. Teachers are drawn to students who are having difficulty learning to read or write.

Figure 11.2 outlines actions that you as a classroom teacher can take when you suspect that a student is having difficulty. These actions are part of the

Figure 11.2
A Classroom Teacher's Actions When a Literacy Difficulty Is Suspected: A Concept Map for Chapters 11 and 13

Observation, documentation, and interpretation	**A student is having difficulty with literacy.**
A child functioning differently from the typical range	When reading materials are geared to age or grade level, • Student experiences frustration. • Student does not learn from materials and instructional experiences. • Student is unable to read or write comfortably. *and/or* ↓ Student is clearly unhappy or uncomfortable with literacy experiences. *and/or* ↓
Signs to take a closer look	Student's listening comprehension reveals a capacity for understanding that is much higher than the level at which the child is reading. *and/or* ↓ One area of literacy (or of other learning) is considerably out of balance with other literacy behaviors.

Planning and evaluation	**Once this recognition occurs, the classroom teacher has two main goals:** ↓
	
	1. To understand and identify literacy difficulty and work with other teachers to
	  • Determine whether the child is within or outside of the developmental continuum (rule out rare possibility of dyslexia and other genuine organic limitations);
	  • Get special services as necessary and appropriate;
	  • As a classroom teacher, help resolve or address those causes you can;
	  • Better tailor instruction to the specific situation and needs of the student.
	2. To provide developmental instruction with interesting materials and activities.

integrated teaching and assessment process in which the teacher observes, documents, interprets, and evaluates and plans instruction. When you observe and document a student's difficulty you may see a child who is frustrated because she is functioning outside of the range of her peers. She may not be able to learn from classroom materials and literacy experiences. Use the assessments in Chapters 4 and 5 to take close looks at oral reading accuracy, word recognition, and reading comprehension in search of a fit between the reading materials and a student's reading.

Psychosocial difficulties emerge in a student's behavior and self-image (Roller, 1996). Some students with discipline problems are also significantly behind as readers and writers and show frustration in their work in school. Some are clearly unhappy or uncomfortable with reading and writing, particularly when reading materials beyond their instructional level. Even students who read at grade level may be considered slightly behind when they do not enjoy reading or writing. Keep close watch in your classroom for students who are unhappy reading and writing. Students with a negative attitude quickly fail to thrive.

Students who read grade-level materials at an instructional level might still be considered slightly behind if they show a much higher ability to listen and understand. Other students are considered slightly behind because they are significantly behind in one area. They may read well but write or spell significantly less well.

When you recognize a reading difficulty your goals are to (1) identify and understand the nature of the difficulty and (2) plan and provide instructional opportunities. Identification isn't about labeling children. It's an important part of the assessment process to help interpret your observations and documentation and explain them to others who will work with you to develop an effective instructional plan.

When everyone understands the underlying reasons for a student's difficulties, you will have the important task of tailoring instruction to the specific needs of the student. By understanding and identifying the nature of a student's difficulty, you can plan instruction that provides appropriate instructional opportunities at that student's developmental level. You may obtain special services outside of the classroom for students with severe organic or physical disabilities as well as those with serious related difficulties that put them significantly behind in reading or writing.

In the next section, we discuss in detail how to identify students' difficulties within and beyond the developmental continuum. Chapter 13 discusses methods of literacy instruction with students who experience either **developmental delays** or permanent difficulties.

Identifying and Understanding Sources of Students' Difficulties

To plan effective instruction that helps students be better readers and writers, you need to know what is causing them difficulty. We will first examine the reasons that a student who fits on the developmental continuum may have reading difficulties and then discuss the rare and special literacy needs of students whose difficulties truly limit their literacy achievement.

Special Literacy Needs Within the Developmental Continuum

Many students in your classes will have had life experiences that delay the pace of their development. These experiences won't prevent students from learning to read and write but can slow them down a little, some, or a lot.

Inexperience with Written Language

Inexperience with written language is a common difficulty. Preschool and kindergarten teachers often observe students' familiarity with written language in the way they play with books. Do they take the books down from the shelves? How do they flip through the pages? Teachers also watch how children hold and scribble with their crayons and pencils. They know that children who have books and have been read to at home are more likely to become readers. A thousand hours of listening to stories gives students the experience to develop an interest in literacy (Allington, 1994).

Inexperience with written language can come from generations of inexperience. For this reason, literacy programs in the primary grades encourage parents and children to read together at home (Edwards, 1995) as well as in before- and after-school programs. See Chapter 14 for a discussion of literacy programs. Written language activities differ across cultures. Look at where and how your students' families and communities use literacy. Set up learning experiences to complement reading, writing, and language activities at home.

Children reveal their experience with written language in their understanding of how stories are structured (Templeton, 1997). Assess their concept of story by asking them to retell a favorite story. Students with little book experience may describe a favorite cartoon or a movie, and when you ask specifically for a story they heard from a book, they may not come up with one. Look for a retelling that is more than a simple listing of events and includes not only a beginning, middle, and end but perhaps also other retelling strategies to comment on the story. Look for expression and detail in language. Students who have not been read to have a less well-developed concept of story than children who have been read to. Many third-grade beginning readers lack a well-developed concept of story. The best way to teach students about how written language is organized is to read to them.

Educational Interferences

Educational interferences block opportunities for development. One obvious interference is poor instruction. Plenty of other interferences have nothing to do with teaching or teachers but are broader and tie into the fabric of the communities in which students live. For example, you may work in one kindergarten where nearly all children are beginning readers by spring and in another where many first-graders are a year behind. Is it surprising that children who live with greater opportunities have a broader range of experiences and therefore know more about the world around them? Children who are around literacy grow up to be readers. The quality of a child's instruction and consistency in educational experiences can profoundly block or encourage learning.

Poor or Inappropriate Instruction   Poor instruction can also interfere with students' development (Henderson, 1981). Poor instruction is instruction that students find meaningless or too hard. The best way to avoid poor instruction is to know students' interests and what they know and to have a wide range of developmental activities for reading, writing, and word study. Learn about your students by developing projects with them and by setting up small-group activities that bring them together to discuss ideas and to make decisions about what they need to know and how they are going to find out (Walmsley, 1994).

Transience and Poverty   Transience is a common occurrence in many schools. Some have a transience rate of 50 percent. When families move around a lot, children have difficulty feeling comfortable with learning. Students who change schools two or more times a year rarely receive consistent instruction. Use the assessment activities in Chapter 4 and 5 to quickly learn about students who enter your classroom during the year.

Educational opportunities can be limited in any economic setting, and deprivation can occur at all economic levels. In comparing schools across socioeconomic levels, however, children who are poor often have fewer alternatives and options (Gutherie & Greaney, 1991; Kozol, 1991). At least one in four children currently lives in poverty (Connell, 1994); many of them lack books and computers at home and have fewer opportunities to read and write. This economic factor explains in part why poor children are overrepresented among children who have difficulty learning to read and write.

To assess how economic opportunities support learning, compare whole schools across several features: How many children qualify for free lunches and breakfasts? Which schools qualify for Title I funds? Compare standardized test scores by school and analyze the relationships among standardized test scores and physical, economic, and cultural opportunities. Some schools continue to expand their social and health services in order to provide support and consistency in children's lives (Dryfoos, 1996).

Maturational Delay and Slower Learning Pace

Students who experience a maturational delay develop in oral language and in writing at a slower rate than other students their age.

Parents of children with maturational delays often report that they, too, took a long time to learn to read. These children are just as bright as others but may appear less so because of their delay. The perception that these delayed children are less capable arises perhaps from the tendency to make large differences out of small ones, as when scores from yearly standardized group tests are interpreted individually or when all students in a grade level are expected to understand the same material with the same facility and effort (Stanovich, 1993/1994). Students with maturational delays may experience difficulties because they work at a frustration level so much of the time. When this happens regularly, they stop taking risks and suppress their interest in learning. If these children can retain a strong concept of themselves as readers and writers, they usually find their way to advanced reading and writing. When teachers keep them involved in developmental instruction, nearly all children make progress in learning to read and write.

Lack of Motivation and Self-esteem

Too much failure, too little help, or the wrong kind of instruction can lead to psychosocial difficulties such as lack of motivation and low self-esteem (Johnston & Winograd, 1985; Stanovich, 1986). Students lose their nerve when they worry that trying to read and write will lead to humiliation. Sometimes students cope with their difficulties by choosing to believe that they cannot learn to read. Consequently, they may give up on themselves as developing readers and writers.

Some older students who are significantly behind appear smug about their inability to read; this attitude is probably a defense. You cannot force them to be interested in reading and writing, but you can make sure that what you are asking them to do is developmentally appropriate. Keep reading to them, too, until they show an interest in learning to read. It does not take long to overcome this bravado in one-to-one and small-group tutoring, especially when you take time to understand their literacy development and find interesting reading materials to share.

Auditory and Vision Difficulties

Auditory Difficulties Students who have difficulty learning to read often have difficulty analyzing the phonology of the language (Perfetti, 1985; Vellutino, Scanlon, Sipay, Small, Pratt, Chen, & Denckla, 1996). They hear well, but have trouble analyzing language and connecting the sound to print. The sounds are not garbled, but they cannot easily identify the separate sounds and syllables in the speech stream.

Vision Difficulties Students must have fairly severe visual difficulties to affect their literacy development. Partially sighted students follow a normal developmental path in their learning but often must find reading alternatives such as technologies that allow them to feel the letters or Kurzweil machines that read texts aloud. Some computers also read aloud and enlarge text, and large-print books and magazines are especially useful.

Learning to read and write in Braille is difficult and time consuming. Partially sighted students who read Braille may not become recreational readers. Improved technologies have been an enormous help to readers with partial sight. Books on tape are an important resource to students with limited sight for reading.

When students complain about headaches or that they do not see well enough, or hold their books or their faces in an unusual position as they read, you should recommend an examination by an optometrist or ophthalmologist. The optometrist is a specialist who examines the acuity of students' vision, and the ophthalmologist is a medical doctor who examines eye health.

····· TAKING A ·····
CLOSER LOOK

What Do We Know About Vision and Reading Difficulties?

In your community, there may be optometrists and ophthalmologists who differ in their views of visual difficulties. There is some controversy about how vision plays a role in students learning and reading.

In a joint policy statement by the American Academy of Pediatrics, the American Association for Pediatric Ophthalmology and Strabismus, and the American Academy of Ophthalmology (1992), the concerns of these medical professionals are clearly presented. We have included an excerpt to show you their views of visual treatments for visual difficulties.

In a discussion of the role of the eyes in reading, they write:

> Decoding of retinal images occurs in the brain after visual signals are transmitted from the retina via the visual pathways. Unfortunately, however, it has become common practice among some to attribute reading difficulties to one or more subtle ocular or visual abnormalities. Although the eyes are obviously necessary for vision, the brain interprets visual symbols. Therefore, correcting subtle visual defects cannot alter the brain's processing of visual stimuli. Children with dyslexia or related learning disabilities have the same ocular health statistically as children without such conditions.[7] There is no peripheral eye defect that produces dyslexia

or other learning disabilities,[8-9] and there is no eye treatment that can cure dyslexia or associated learning disabilities.

In a section titled "Controversies," these medical eye care professionals are forthright in expressing their views about a variety of visual training programs:

> Eye defects, subtle or severe, do not cause reversal of letters, words, or numbers. No scientific evidence supports claims that the academic abilities of dyslexic or learning disabled children can be improved with treatment based on a) visual training, including muscle exercises, ocular pursuit, tracking exercises, or "training" glasses (with or without bifocals or prisms);[10-12] b) neurological organizational training (laterality training, crawling, balance board, perceptual training);[13-15] or c) tinted or colored lenses.[16-17] Some controversial methods of treatment result in a false sense of security that may delay or even prevent proper instruction or remediation. The expense of these methods is unwarranted, and they cannot be substituted for appropriate remedial educational measures. Claims of improved reading and learning after visual training, neurological organization training, or use of tinted or colored lenses are typically based upon poorly controlled studies that rely

Difficult reading can lead to behaviors that mimic vision problems. You may occasionally see students who hold books close to their faces as they read. This is usually a sign of stress and is related to the difficulty of the text, not to vision. Watch them read easier materials to see if they hold the book at a proper distance. Reading at a frustration level can give a student a headache, and some students complain of blurred vision after only fifteen minutes of reading. See if their symptoms subside after finding easier materials to read.

Developmental optometry is a field of optometry that uses *visual training* to improve reading. Advocates of this therapy claim that reading ability can be im-

(continued)

on anecdotal information or testimony. These studies are frequently carried out in combination with traditional educational remedial techniques.

References

7. Metzger RL, Werner DB: Use of visual training for reading disabilities: A review. *Pediatrics* 1984; 73:824–829.

8. Goldberg HK, Drash PW: The disabled reader. *J Pediatr Ophthalmol* 1968; 5:11–24.

9. Helveston EM, Weber JC, Miller K, et al: Visual function and academic performance. *Am J Ophthalmol* 1985; 99:346–355.

10. Levine MD: Reading disability: Do the eyes have it? *Pediatrics* 1984; 73:869–870.

11. Keough B, Pelland M: Vision training revisited. *J Learn Disabil* 1985; 18:228–236.

12. Beauchamp, GR: Optometric vision training. *Pediatrics* 1986; 77:121–124.

13. Cohen HJ, Birch HG, Taft LT: Some considerations for evaluating the Doman-Delacato "patterning method." *Pediatrics* 1970; 45:302–314.

14. Kavale K, Manson PD: One jumped off the balance beam: Meta-analysis of perceptual-motor training. *J Learn Disabil* 1983; 16:165–173.

15. Black JL, Collins DWK, DeRoach JN, et al: A detailed study of sequential saccadic eye movements for normal and poor reading children. *Percept Mot Skills* 1984; 59:423–434.

16. Solan HA: An appraisal of the Irlen technique of correcting reading disorders using tinted overlays and tinted lenses. *J Learn Disabil* 1990; 23:621–623.

17. Hoyt CS: Irlen lenses and reading difficulties. *J Learn Disabil* 1990; 23:624–626.

From an optometrist's perspective, you may want to refer to an article in *The Reading Teacher* in which two optometrists describe a variety of difficulties that they treat with visual training (Rouse & Ryan, 1984).

When a parent asks you for your opinion of visual difficulties and reading, you may want to share the latest statement by these and other professional groups. You can contact the professional organizations listed in Chapter 14 for policy statements on particular reading methods and difficulties. Suffice it to say, remedial methods must be studied carefully to see if and why they are effective.

proved through eye movement training and exercises (McCormick, 1995). Some evidence indicates that visual optometrics can reduce eye strain and that some students in visual tracking programs also make reading progress (Cohen, 1988). A review of the research, however, does not support using visual training to improve reading (American Academy of Ophthalmology, 1987; Kennedy, 1984; Olson, Kliegl & Davidson, 1983; Rayner, 1985). Some researchers do view visual differences as influencing reading. Perhaps they will eventually make a stronger case for their views (Willows, Kruk & Corcos, 1993). Visual accomodation, the ability to focus properly, and convergence, the ability to turn both eyes in for near point reading, are most useful in examining reading difficulties (Abrams, 1981). One does not need to be an expert in this area, but familiarity with the vision and vision programs and difficulties will help you guide parents to specialists for their opinions on particular eye exercises.

Strong relationships exist among different areas of child development. For example, kindergarten and first-grade children may show a link between smooth eye tracking and beginning reading, as when emergent readers lack a concept of word and also cannot yet follow pencil movement smoothly with their eyes. As the children mature, eye tracking becomes smoother and reading improves. This relationship merely reflects their overall development; it is not a causative relationship.

Learning Disabilities and Language-Processing Difficulties

Students considered learning disabled usually perform within the developmental continuum. Despite official definitions of **learning disabilities** that highlight organic reasons for students' difficulties, most learning-disabled students are not permanently limited in what they can achieve. Many students whom schools classify as learning disabled are significantly delayed, not halted, in their reading, and they continue to develop with appropriate developmental instruction (Abouzeid, 1992; Spear-Swerling & Sternberg, 1996; Vellutino et al., 1996).

Difficulties in language learning are a specific type of learning disability or learning difficulty. Students who have **language difficulties** are often delayed in their literacy development (Kamhi & Catts, 1991). It may take some time to determine that a child has a language difficulty. The process often requires a complete developmental and social history as well as time to see how the student responds to instruction. Evidence of a language difficulty can emerge from the results of tests administered by psychologists and speech and language specialists. Some language difficulties are not fully understood until difficulties arise in learning to read and write. Parents may report a brief history of ear infections or that the child was a little delayed in oral language development without knowing the true nature of a child's language difficulties.

Ear infections are a common medical difficulty that affect hearing and related language growth. Ear infections and fluid behind the ears can affect students' hearing in school, and ear infections early in life can affect students' oral language and literacy development (Kindig, 1995).

Researchers have begun to look carefully at specific aspects of language function that relate to reading difficulties. Students with relatively mild language difficulties usually have a good understanding of stories that are read to them, and their speaking, syntax, and pronunciation are adequate (Orlich et al., 1994). Students who are noticeably behind in language learning may or may not have speech and articulation difficulties. Their oral vocabularies may be smaller than other students' vocabularies, and they may have learned to talk later than siblings (Frith, 1981). You may hear parents of students with language difficulties comment that they are, or have been, the only ones who understood their children's language.

Students with noticeable delays in language development may have difficulty acquiring a concept of word. They may take longer to memorize a brief rhyme or a one-sentence dictation and to match what they have memorized with the text in front of them. Students with language difficulties may also experience difficulties developing phonemic awareness, word identification, and orthographic knowledge—knowledge of how words are spelled (Abouzeid, 1992). Students with mild language difficulties often have difficulty matching letter sounds with letter names, which also slows orthographic development. As a result, these students may be slower to acquire a sight-word vocabulary. They may be finishing second grade before they are solid beginning readers with sight vocabularies larger than fifty words. In word study, they may be just beginning to study and understand word families such as *bat, rat* or *red, bed.*

Students whose language difficulties relate to understanding orthography may find progress through transitional reading painfully slow. When the language difficulty is severe enough, the student may not progress much further than the transitional phase. It is not unusual for students with a language difficulty to have only 200 sight words by the end of third or fourth grade. Because they are in the within-word pattern of spelling, teachers follow the developmental progression by having students examine long-vowel patterns once they have a good understanding of short-vowel patterns. Transitional readers with language difficulties may remain somewhat disfluent and unable to read words quickly enough to read with a natural expression and fluency. They may still pause on common single-syllable words and may come to a stop when they read unfamiliar two- and three-syllable words. Furthermore, transitional readers with language difficulties may rely on inefficient strategies, partly because they read so much material at a frustration level. For example, they may become word callers. Concentrating on reading words, they forget to think while they read and are unable to read even familiar phrases such as *he said* or *for example* as phrases.

In word study, teachers sometimes ask transitional readers with a language delay to learn long-vowel patterns before they are ready. This can force students to merely memorize the patterns and the rules at a conscious level instead of internalizing them and so prevent students from applying the rules automatically. Students also can hold on too tightly to rules and word patterns that they apply at such a conscious level, which creates further stumbling blocks in reading.

Some students seem to reach a ceiling in learning to read at this transitional phase. Regardless of how much progress students may be able to make, they find it hard to remain patient in learning when they are in fifth grade and can achieve independent- or instructional-level reading only with easy *I Can Read* books. They need literacy activities different from those of classmates who have sight vocabularies well over 1,000 words. Help them maintain their motivation by deemphasizing grade-level textbooks and instead providing readable materials to supplement studies. Students in this phase of development can usually spell most single- and two-syllable words correctly with proofreading but may find three- and four-syllable words beyond their orthographic knowledge and become frustrated and lose motivation.

The cumulative effects of a mild language difficulty on oral vocabularies often show up in delayed middle school students. Beginning in middle school, most students learn new vocabulary more from reading than from speech. You can read to delayed students to help them acquire the vocabulary that other students learn by independent reading.

STUDENT STUDY

Why Can't Jack Read?

Jack Beetles was a fourth-grader and a beginning reader and writer. His story illustrates several possible causes of difficulties in learning to read and write. In spite of some indirect evidence of an organic or physical difficulty, Jack made steady progress in two years.

Jack came to a reading center for an individual assessment at the beginning of fourth grade. His family had just bought a home in a new neighborhood, and he was going to change schools. Jack's parents heard about the center through a friend and wanted some advice about grade placement and applications for special services if necessary. An informal reading inventory like those discussed in Chapter 4 showed, through Jack's expression and listening comprehension, that his language functioning was more than adequate. Jack certainly understood much better than he read; he showed a general weakness in the area of word recognition and spelling. The psychologist's report portrayed Jack as quite a bright and verbal boy.

After two sessions of careful work together and an extensive parent interview, it was difficult to know why Jack had not learned to read any better than he had. He was still learning about the CVC short-vowel patterns, and he had been stable for a year in his knowledge of initial and final consonants as well as most beginning consonant blends and digraphs. Jack was a reluctant writer, and his handwriting appeared sloppy for his age and coordination. He read and responded to instruction like any beginning reader. After listening to an informational text, he reread with accuracy and fluency a summarizing two-paragraph dictation. He collected sight words from his dictation, and he sorted pictures of short- and long-vowel

words into separate piles, which indicated that he had a good ability to discriminate among vowels.

Both parents were aware of Jack's difficulties and were hoping that things would improve. He had been enrolled in a private Montessori school and was receiving individual tutoring several times a week. In the parent interview, Ben, Jack's father, recalled that he may have had reading difficulties, and he was certain that his sister had difficulties. Jack had had ear infections and had drainage tubes placed in his ears by three years of age.

The parent interview and the psychologist's and teachers' reports shared consensus on certain indicators of emotional difficulties. Some of Jack's acting-out behaviors were likely associated with his lack of success learning to read and write. Other factors and behaviors also associated with difficulty in learning to read included ear infections, family history of difficulties, lack of word knowledge, and handwriting difficulties. Still, no one reason emerged why Jack had not learned to read. He showed no deviance in the quality of any of his literacy responses, but he was weak in word and orthographic knowledge. One hypothesis was that Jack may have had some organic learning difficulties that were compounded by his frustration.

During the summer, Jack attended a tutoring program in the reading center. After five weeks, it was apparent that he would respond to good instruction. Jack had not done much reading at his instructional level; he had a way of avoiding literacy at school and home. He needed support reading activities, word study, writing, and self-confidence in reading and writing.

Other Physical and Mental Health Complications

Students can experience a variety of difficulties that complicate the way they learn to read and write. Some may be **acquired difficulties** that stem from an

(continued)

The educators shared the following findings with Jack's parents in an interview and in a written report:

- Jack was significantly behind and needed two kinds of extensive help: (1) instruction to improve his reading and writing and (2) ways for him to succeed in school learning despite his difficulties reading and writing.

- No one could identify one absolute reason for Jack's difficulties.

- The educators who had worked with Jack were optimistic that he could progress and recommended that Jack receive some tutoring for a few months to see how he would progress.

We will take a closer look at Jack's instructional program in Chapter 13.

---

injury or from trauma before or at birth. Several of these physical and mental health complications are discussed here.

General Health Concerns Poor physical or mental health conditions can lead to developmental delays. Some children are seriously deprived of proper health care and fail to thrive (Boyer, 1987), but you may see them experience a physical growth spurt when they receive help. They may show similar growth in learning and literacy development as well.

Mild Mental Retardation Children with mild mental handicaps can also be considered developmentally delayed. This means they can be expected to develop in the same way as other students, but at a slower pace. Although they have a lower reading potential than students of average capacity, they can learn a good deal about reading and writing with sound developmental education paced to their learning rate.

ADD and Hyperactivity Some children with reading difficulties have an *attention deficit disorder (ADD)* or an *attention deficit disorder with hyperactivity (ADHD)*. ADD and ADHD are medical difficulties that must be assessed by a medical doctor. Unfortunately, these are difficult conditions to diagnose, and some children are misdiagnosed. Like children with severe reading difficulties, children who are properly diagnosed as having ADD or ADHD perform outside the continuum of attentional abilities.

It may be difficult to know which came first, the difficulty in learning or the attention deficit. As you observe a child, see if behaviors change in different instructional settings. You may find that developmental instruction lengthens a student's attention span and increases reading time. Students who make dramatic changes in reading and writing with developmental instruction and show otherwise acceptable behavior likely do not have an attention deficit but, rather, need developmental instruction.

Teachers, students and parents meet to discuss the student's development and instructional program.

Medications can affect a student's activity level in the classroom. For example, children diagnosed with ADD or ADHD may begin their medication at too high a dosage and, as a result, may appear tired. Ask parents or the school nurse to let you know when medications are introduced or adjusted. Medications such as Ritalin are frequently prescribed before other avenues are explored, and they are often administered without proper monitoring (Garber, Garber & Spizman, 1996; Hunt & Marshall, 1994). Parents and teachers must understand that these medications are designed to keep children from being overactive—not to make them attentive.

Some students may have further difficulty attending when, as beginning readers and writers, they laboriously spell out words sound by sound. Students who are distractible or who have trouble attending may have further problems attending to activities they find meaningless. Unfortunately, many typical school activities—memorizing spelling words, copying down homework, or memorizing multiplication tables—lack much meaning. You will succeed more often if you reconsider memorization tasks and supply these students with instruction that includes meaningful materials.

Extreme Emotional or Behavioral Disturbance Children with extreme emotional difficulties may account for 9 percent of the children who receive special services (U.S. Office of Special Education and Rehabilitative Services, 1992). With so much going on in their lives, they must make an extreme effort to concentrate on comprehending what they read. Give these students plenty of support by telling them about the stories they are going to read, by using creative dramatics to act out parts of a story, and by finding texts such as folk tales that have a clear structure. Read to them what they cannot read for themselves.

These considerations for students with special difficulties resemble what teachers do with any child. Students with special literacy needs experience a range of difficulties, but they follow the same sequence in their literacy development as other children. Chapter 13 discusses modifications in instruction for these students.

Students Beyond the Continuum

As shown in Figure 11.1, a few students have special literacy needs and do not perform within the continuum of development. These students have difficulties related to their physical capabilities that are usually indicated in their medical histories or in assessments of cognitive functioning. They include **dyslexia,** the most commonly known reading difficulty, and related language and learning difficulties.

Genuine Dyslexia

At some point in your teaching, when you are working with a student who is significantly behind, parents will likely ask you if their child is dyslexic. You, too, may wonder at times if a student who does not make progress is dyslexic.

Dyslexia has many definitions (Harris & Hodges, 1995). It is important to know how researchers define dyslexia and disabilities before you use their research information to guide your instruction and to help students and parents understand learning difficulties. Many research papers describe dyslexics much like students who are two or more years behind in their literacy achievement (Stanovich, 1988a). The definitions of dyslexia vary so remarkably that many educators avoid the term completely (McCormick, 1995). For example, many research papers describe students as dyslexic if they are two or more years behind in their literacy achievement, a definition that is too broad given our view that dyslexia is a rare occurrence (Stanovich, 1988a).

Research into dyslexia is exciting and encompasses many areas of study (Vellutino & Denckla, 1991). Brain-imaging research and genetic and familial studies are indicating that dyslexia may have specific correlates in the brain; dyslexics may be identified from gene analyses or brain-imaging (Duane & Gray, 1991; Gray & Kavanagh, 1985; Hynd & Hynd, 1984). Currently, when assessing for dyslexia we presume that congenital factors cause the difficulty. Medical histories and parent interviews may offer inferential evidence of physiological difficulty or congenital factors. These inferences and presumptions make assessment inexact. At best, based on recent research, we can say that dyslexia is off the continuum of development and reading difficulties described in Figure 11.1

::::: TAKING A :::::
CLOSER LOOK   **Dyslexia**

How do educators talk to parents about dyslexia? Few parents are familiar with the research literature or know the accepted professional definitions of dyslexia that educators and many allied professionals use. Many parents are aware only of the popular conceptions that give the impression that anyone with a reading difficulty is dyslexic (Harris & Hodges, 1981).

Parents sometimes tell teachers that another child in the family is dyslexic. This is of interest because dyslexia does sometimes run in families. When parents describe themselves or a child as dyslexic, you should listen and take notes. Although dyslexia is found in families, reading problems among children rarely stem from dyslexia but are instead caused by a combination of other factors. Most of the time the parents are equating a difficulty with a disability.

Make thorough notes, but leave the interpretation of what parents say until you know more about the student. It is unimportant at this point to have everyone agree on definitions or diagnoses. Share your understanding of dyslexia another time. You want parents to share information with you, and they may not if they sense that you do not agree with them. Avoid using the term by asking parents, "Tell me about your child's difficulties." The more specific their descriptions of a student's behavior, the better your ability to assess literacy development.

(Stanovich, 1988b). This conservative definition of dyslexia has an incidence rate of perhaps 3 percent or less (McCormick, 1995). For example, among 200 children who come to our university literacy center for tutoring each year, only a few are described as dyslexic. These children may have a permanent difficulty and may ultimately read no further than perhaps an early intermediate level. For learning and instruction, then, students with dyslexia need ways to compensate for this rare but real disability.

The assessment of dyslexia takes careful observation and teaching over time. No one test determines whether or not a child is dyslexic. Instead, teachers see how a student responds to developmental instruction over several months and then begin to gather other information that leads to such an assessment.

Here are two important points to remember about dyslexia: First, the accepted definition of dyslexia describes students who are disabled and are quite unlikely to read at an advanced level. Second, the positive side to this conservative definition is that dyslexia does not often occur. The vast majority of children who have reading difficulties and who are significantly behind in their achievement can make progress.

Alexia

Alexia is similar to dyslexia but much more severe. Alexia is a total inability to read, whereas dyslexia is a partial disability. Alexic children in elementary grades are quite rare. Usually, alexic children have language difficulties that are attributable to **traumatic brain injury,** and which result in the loss of previously acquired reading abilities.

Hyperlexia

Hyperlexia is an uncommon condition that jolts educators into rethinking how students learn to read. Hyperlexic students read words beautifully, often in a sing-song voice. But hyperlexic children have weak language skills and cannot demonstrate that they understand the stories they have read (Healy, 1982; Mehegan & Dreifus, 1972). At best, hyperlexic readers may understand most of the words and sentences, but their comprehension is not rich (Aaron, 1989) and they fail to reach the intermediate and advanced phases. Teachers can produce important progress in students' thinking and reading through a program of guided reading with clear and brief readings in a GRTA format (Worthy & Invernizzi, 1996).

Severe Language-Processing Difficulties

Children with severe language difficulties are usually identified before first grade. The results of tests administered by psychologists, early childhood specialists, and speech and language specialists often describe some difficulty of a physiological origin that may be acquired or genetic. For example, language difficulties may be traced to trauma at birth. Many children with severe language difficulties experience other learning difficulties. If a student has acquired the difficulty through a recent injury, ask specialists and prior teachers what progress the student made before and since the injury. A severe language difficulty is the most common difficulty of those beyond the continuum of reading development.

Literacy may not be a priority for students with the most severe language difficulties. Their literacy instruction must wait until their oral language skills can support literacy growth. For example, the student who cannot memorize a two-line rhyme will find it difficult to acquire a concept of word. Instruction with these students concentrates on oral language development.

Still, literacy can play a special role in instruction for students with severe language difficulties. As you will see in Chapter 13, language experience activities give a forum for expression and a vehicle for interaction with children with whom interaction may be difficult. So although literacy may not be a priority for students with severe language difficulties, you can use literacy to promote language use.

Permanent Hearing Impairments

Students with severe and profound hearing impairments cannot hear well enough to learn the oral language on which the writing system is based. Among school-age children, only .6 percent of the children have severe or profound hearing impairments and 4.5 percent have mild hearing losses (McCormick, 1995).

Children with severe and profound hearing losses usually learn to read in English as a second language. American Sign Language (ASL) combined with

····· TAKING A ·····
CLOSER LOOK

Teaching Children with Severe or Profound Hearing Loss

Literacy development of children with severe and profound hearing loss poses one of the greatest challenges to educators. When you understand the needs of these special students, you will see the importance of a strong language base in learning to read and write. Such an understanding also points out the need for students to have a strong first language. Consider the finding that the best readers among children with severe hearing losses are those whose parents are also hearing impaired and who use sign language (Birch & Stuckless, 1966; Geers & Moog, 1989). This subgroup may be better readers because they have a strong first language. Not unlike hearing individuals who learn a foreign language, they translate back and forth from their first language, albeit from a sign language to an oral language. Remember that few students with several years of high school foreign language study can read beyond a transitional level.

Each student's hearing loss is unique, and to understand a student's language development you will need to know something about the loss—when it occurred and how severe it is. The speech and language specialist can provide this information and show you how well the student can understand speech. You should also find out how well the student can hear with hearing aids.

Unless you are proficient in ASL, you may find it helpful to have a translator present when you begin to work with hearing-impaired children who use sign language, especially in discussions. Begin reading together with a brief oral reading to obtain a sense of the student's articulation and understanding of the phonology. Some students with hearing impairments become word callers. They can read the words and maybe answer several comprehension questions correctly, but they are unable to demonstrate a deep understanding of what they have learned. Their written responses are often limited to unorganized facts. Although writing samples reveal the student's use of grammar, you must be careful, in analyzing the writing, to differentiate among difficulties in speaking clearly, knowledge of language, and thinking.

Discuss with hearing-impaired students their comprehension of what they are reading so that you can help them with vocabulary and, through the discussion, model language structures. These discussions can be difficult when you are not sure what the students understand or may have said. As in all such cases where you have difficulty understanding a student, keep the door open for communication and use other forms of communication and demonstration to support your discussions. Guided reading-thinking activities, GRTAs, are important assessment tools with hearing-impaired students that focus on understanding the text.

You can learn a great deal about the student's orthographic knowledge and general knowledge of English by analyzing invented spelling and writing. Hearing-impaired children often are better spellers than they are readers because they have memorized the spellings. It is interesting that the invented spellings of many children with hearing impairments do not follow a developmental pattern. The explanation usually lies in what students actually hear. Many of their invented spellings are not based on letter–sound correspondences. Here are some samples of children's unusual invented spelling:

Invented	Actual
pitch	pencil
piage	practice
tepetone	telephone
andt	again
shae	short
siem	smile
elisha	elephant
aijonier	ashamed

(continued)

Quite a few students who have language difficulties had hearing problems during all or part of their childhood. When students have severe reading difficulties, teachers look for a history of ear infections and hearing tests. Teachers can refer a child who has had several years of ear infections to the school nurse or to an audiologist to test for hearing loss.

other language systems form the basis of these students' language and influence their writing syntax and the vocabulary they use and know. Furthermore, students with severe and profound hearing losses since birth may not have acquired facility in a first language. In such cases, the child develops a deficit from this lack of language experience in the critical period of language development from birth to age five.

Instructionally, many of the students with hearing impairments in public schools begin to reach a ceiling at the transitional phase. Some students who lack facility in a first language also lack the language development in vocabulary knowledge and sense of grammar to move beyond transitional or early intermediate phases of literacy development (Holt, 1994).

Students with mild to moderate hearing losses face some of the same difficulties in reading and writing. A teacher's first step is to find out when the loss occurred and how the loss affects the student's understanding of oral language.

How Understanding the Causes of Literacy Difficulties Helps the Classroom Teacher

Teachers work to understand a student's difficulties as a unique configuration of causes and needs. Based on those causes and needs, the teacher organizes literacy activities that provide instructional opportunities for the student to improve. An individual plan creates a path for instruction for a student that includes the teacher's recommendations for effective teaching. Teachers have three tasks when a literacy difficulty is identified:

1. Locate special services for those who need them,

2. Help address and resolve difficulties, and

3. Plan instruction for individual students.

Locate Special Services When Necessary and Appropriate

Students who are significantly behind will benefit from extra time reading and writing with the support of a teacher. Students who qualify for special education receive that support from the special education resource teacher. If the difficulty is not so severe, the student may qualify for other special programs such as working with Title I teachers or aides.

Students with permanent difficulties need services that help them become better readers and writers and also help them keep up with the other students in the classroom. Students who have limited literacy capabilities need to develop ways to understand the content curriculum—science, social studies, and math—in ways that are not literacy dependent. Chapter 13 discusses perseverance and coping strategies in detail. A special educator usually provides such support by reading tests and texts and by providing extra support for written assignments.

The first step to having a special educator teach a student in your classroom is having the student recommended for a formal evaluation by the child study team in your school. As the referring classroom teacher on a child study team, you assist in the evaluation by documenting the student's reading and writing behaviors. For example, teachers share writing samples and oral reading records to show how the student has progressed. Other members of the child study team administer a variety of tests, many of which are discussed in the next chapter.

A variety of other specialist services may be appropriate for a student including a reading specialist, a speech and language specialist, or a school counselor. As in special education, there is a process for referring children for special services. Some services may also be offered outside of school, such as private tutors, speech and language specialists, and counselors. A local college of education may have a university center that offers literacy assessments and tutoring year-round.

Addressing and Resolving Difficulties

Many difficulties can be addressed and resolved in the normal course of classroom events. Most of the students described in this chapter have spent too much time working at frustration levels. First, take a step backward in instruction to find activities that are easy for them. Motivate students by finding ways for them to be successful reading and writing.

A simple thing you can do to resolve a reading difficulty is to gather more content material that the student can read at an instructional level. Reduce the link between instruction and textbooks and related work sheets. Hunt for alternate reading materials and written assignments that are geared to the student's developmental level.

Talking to a student about a difficulty is often helpful. Just knowing that a teacher is going to offer encouragement produces a great deal of success. Some reading specialists and counselors start discussion groups for students to share ways they have overcome their difficulties. Ask your students who have difficulties to let you know when they are having problems with materials and assignments. As a team, you and the student can resolve immediate problems that arise by finding support from you or a peer, and the two of you can think of other ways to participate that are more appropriate given the student's developmental level or limiting condition.

A basic support for students with difficulties is more time to read and write. Have reading materials at a variety of reading levels available in the classroom and teach students how to support read with each other.

Plan Instruction to Meet Needs of Individual Students

Understanding the nature of a student's difficulties allows you to plan classroom instruction. When you know how far behind a student is in reading, you can teach the content in some other ways that avoid penalizing the student for being behind. Creating a realistic developmental time line for the student helps you predict how long to maintain certain instructional activities and keep them in the teaching cycle. For example, a second-grade classroom teacher will plan to maintain a small group of beginning readers who are behind to give them opportunities to read pattern books and create group and individual dictations.

Conclusion and Study Notes

This chapter has offered a perspective on teaching students with difficulties. In the opening conversation, Amy wanted to know how to identify a child with dyslexia. Given the definitions most often used by educators, dyslexia does not occur frequently. Most students who have reading difficulties are not dyslexic; they perform somewhere on the developmental continuum. In nearly all cases, teachers can help students progress according to their individual development as readers and writers. The next chapter addresses ways that students are tested for difficulties.

Here are some key points to remember in assessing and working with students with reading and writing difficulties:

- Students who are behind in reading need to be treated as capable learners who are delayed in development.

- The developmental continuum ranges from children who are developing as expected to children who are significantly behind and need additional instruction.

- A delay model shows how delayed students follow a common developmental sequence, but at a slower pace.

- A few students have rare physical difficulties that limit them in becoming proficient readers and writers.

- When a difficulty is recognized, the classroom teacher (1) works with other educators to learn more about the difficulty and to obtain special services and additional support in literacy instruction and (2) provides developmental instruction.

- Some students' difficulties can be attributed in part to the student's inexperience with written language.

- Home and educational situations can interfere with learning—for example, poverty, transience, and frustration-level instruction.

- Auditory difficulties can be part of language learning delays or difficulties.

- Visual difficulties are rarely the underlying reason why a child has problems learning to read and write.

- Students with language-learning disabilities also have difficulty learning to read and write.

- Dyslexia is a serious and rare form of reading difficulty that is presumed to have a neurologic base. Students with dyslexia are limited in their reading and writing achievement.

- Many people mistakenly equate any reading difficulty with dyslexia.

- Children who have severe and profound hearing losses have difficulties learning to read because they do not have a strong knowledge of the language they are trying to read. Furthermore, hearing-impaired learners have had trouble learning sound–letter connections.

Key Terms

deficits	acquired difficulties
developmental continuum	traumatic brain injury
reading difficulties	dyslexia
developmental delay	alexia
learning disability	hyperlexia
language difficulties	

Follow-Up Activities

1. If you know someone who had difficulty learning to read and was placed in special classes, ask that person to talk with you about the experience. Ask about the type of instruction received and what he or she learned.

2. Work in an elementary classroom for a week and try to identify students who are behind grade level in literacy achievement. Read and write with these children and discover where they are developmentally. Observe how well they read and understand assigned texts.

3. Visit children in the same grade in two schools in different parts of the community. Note any differences in levels of literacy development among the students.

4. Visit a special education class and identify special teaching methods. Look at the children's writing in their journals to see where they are developmentally. Did these writing samples supply any information about their language skills? Administer the spelling-by-stage assessment presented in Chapter 4. Do the students' spelling phases match their reading development?

5. Independently or as part of a small-group effort, interview two or three of the following specialists who study vision: an optometrist, an ophthalmologist, a vision specialist, a cognitive psychologist, an optician. Ask them about vision and learning to read. What visual factors do they believe make it difficult for some students to learn to read? Ask them what they know about dyslexia. Show them the following list of terms that are important to understanding visual difficulties. Would they include other terms in this list?

accommodation	convergence
accommodative spasm	crossed eyes
astigmatism	diplopia

farsightedness (hyperopia)   prism

legal blindness in your state   refraction

nearsightedness (myopia)   refractive error

farsightedness (hyperopia)   Snellen chart

legal blindness in your state   strabismus

nearsightedness (myopia)   visual training

ophthalmologist

12

Formal Literacy Testing and Measurement

Jane: We've talked about informally assessing our students, but what about standardized tests? Where do they fit in?

Mike: I was in a classroom last week where the teacher was worried about standardized tests. She practiced with her students how to answer the questions, and she hoped they'd do well.

Diane: Many teachers worry about standardized tests. This has become an even bigger concern now that teachers are using more literature-based curricula. They worry that the tests don't match how they teach their students.

Sharon: The teachers in my school worry about the tests, especially because ours is considered an at-risk school. Many of the children come from poor families. The state mandates that we test at certain grades so that we can compare student performance in this state to student performance nationwide. The issue is accountability. The state wants to make sure that we are doing a good job. As a staff, we have discussed the need for formal assessment and informal assessment. We are still not comfortable with the tests, but we make sure that the kids will do the best they can. We practice test-taking skills, and we try to make the kids comfortable. When the test results come back, we see if the scores follow any patterns. We would hate for all of our students to score low in one area, like math.

Mike: A teacher told me that her school had parent meetings where the parents and teachers looked at examples of test questions. Some of the parents were really surprised by the questions that were on the tests.

Gwen: I'll bet that after seeing some of the questions the parents began to understand why the teacher used informal assessment and portfolios. I like that idea of sharing the tests with the parents.

Todd: So each year some classes take standardized tests to see how they are doing. And if students are doing very well or having trouble, then I suppose a psychologist would test them individually.

Sharon: That's right. Although before a child is tested individually, usually a team works with the teacher and family, especially if the child is having trouble learning.

Joan: Okay, so some tests are given to groups of students. And then other tests are for individual students. Are all of these called standardized tests? Help! What is a standardized test?

The students, teachers, and principal in the above conversation are talking about some of the issues related to formal or standardized testing. They mention the concerns that teachers have in giving these tests, especially when their teaching methods do not match the format of the test. They also mention concerns about children who are considered at-risk because of their parents' economic situation. Some of them are puzzled about the differences between whole-class and individualized standardized testing and their purposes. This chapter considers standardized testing and its relationship to informal assessment.

Guide Questions for Chapter 12

- What are the essential characteristics of norm-referenced tests?

- What terms are used to report scores on norm-referenced tests?

- Compare the goals of a norm-referenced achievement test and a criterion-referenced test.

- Why are individual norm-referenced tests administered to students?

- What are the pros and cons of norm-referenced tests?

- In what ways are norm-referenced achievement tests changing to meet today's understandings of literacy?

▇ *Standardized or Norm-Referenced Tests*

Testing or assessment is an old concept. Bertrand (1991, p. 18) writes:

> In the Old Testament, Jephthah (Judges 12:5) ordered that all those that approached the Jordan fords unable to pronounce the word *shibboleth* should be killed. By doing so, he distinguished between his own men and those of the enemy, who could not say the sound *sh*. Thus, those who came with

the password pronounced as *sibboleth* failed a very effective early criterion-referenced achievement test and received immediate feedback.

Standardized or **norm-referenced tests** are formal measures of a skill or concept. In the above example, Jephthah had a pass-fail form of assessment—a clear, standardized criteria. Standardized or norm-referenced tests differ greatly from the informal assessment strategies discussed throughout this book. In informal assessment, the teacher interprets the results and qualitatively assesses the product or process of a student's learning. Formal assessment entails specific directions for administering the test and, usually, computer scoring that yields an exact numerical score (Rhodes & Shanklin, 1993). Students take norm-referenced tests throughout their schooling to determine how well they are performing in comparison to national or school district norms. In most of these situations, tests are administered to groups of students. You most likely took a norm-referenced test such as the SAT or ACT to gain college or university entry, one of the major uses of norm-referenced tests.

Formal norm-referenced tests are also administered to individuals. This type of test is usually given to students who show accelerated learning or consistent difficulty with learning. A school psychologist is often called in to administer individual intelligence tests, among other measures, and the results of these tests help decide the best instructional strategies or classroom placement to help the student learn (Gregory, 1996).

Norm-referenced tests may be achievement tests or diagnostic tests. **Achievement tests** measure past learning or achievement and usually contain several items to measure each learning task. **Diagnostic tests** assess specific knowledge about a subject. The test items are arranged to reflect increasing difficulty and to show growth of knowledge in an area and pinpoint areas where a student may be having difficulty (Gregory, 1996; Gronlund & Linn, 1990; Gillet & Temple, 1994).

Standardized tests are developed by testing publishers who administer them to large numbers of students of diverse ages, grades, and demographic groups to develop **norms** or standards for comparison (Rhodes & Shanklin, 1993). Test publishers determine statistically the average number of correct answers for each grade level. Questions are rewritten or changed until this criterion is reached. Governments and schools use the tests and scores to help make decisions about students, schools, or school systems (Bertrand, 1991). Individual scores are interpreted as the student's relative standing in a known group (Gronlund, 1985). For example, a student who scores at the 86th percentile on a particular test has outperformed 86 percent of the students taking the test in that norm-referenced group.

The importance often placed on these tests makes it important that you, as a teacher, can cogently discuss them with parents and other interested persons. In this chapter, we consider the vocabulary associated with these tests, their strengths and limitations, and balancing them with other forms of assessment.

Norm-Referenced Test Characteristics

The two most important characteristics of norm-referenced tests are their content validity and reliability (Gregory, 1996). These mean that a test such as the SAT or ACT must actually measure your achievement in the areas tested (content validity) and that if you took the test on several occasions, your scores would be similar (reliability).

Reliability

Reliability is a measure of how consistently a person will score on the test if he or she takes it several times (Gregory, 1996). When a test publisher is establishing norms, this characteristic is measured and reported in the test manual. You can check on a test or subtest's reliability in the manual, and you can also evaluate reliability by looking at the bands that are indicated on a test report. For instance, a subtest that has a wide band has more chance for a change in score on the next administration. Bands tend to be wider if a student scores in the middle ranges rather than at the highest or lowest levels of performance. In other words, a student who answers almost every question correctly should be able to do so at another testing time. Conversely, a student who answers few questions correctly is unlikely to do much better on a second testing. Salvia and Ysseldyke (1988) recommend that test reliability be at least .90 when used to make decisions about individuals.

Content Validity

Content validity indicates if the test is measuring what it is said to measure (Gregory, 1996). To establish validity, test publishers locate an adequate sample of questions that represent the content being measured. The characteristic of validity comes from an assumption that anything that exists in some quantity can be measured (Michaels & Karnes, 1950). This seems straightforward, but content validity can be difficult to attain. For example, many current reading achievement tests have been criticized because most of their subtests deal with skills such as sound-symbol relationships. Now that reading education emphasizes making meaning rather than decoding, critics have voiced their concerns about the validity of these tests for evaluating reading achievement.

Interpreting Norm-Referenced Test Results

Several weeks after students take norm-referenced achievement tests, schools receive profiles of results for the whole school, individual classes, and individual students. When the results come in, the school faculty meet as a group to talk about how students performed in comparison to other students in the school district and in the country. The faculty carefully analyze the scores for meaningful patterns. For instance, if all third-graders scored in the lower percentiles in vocabulary, the faculty might consider their students, their vocabulary curriculum, and the test itself and then develop a plan of action related to vocabulary learning. Teachers also analyze their classroom scores to develop a sense of how well their students are doing or where knowledge is lacking. Following from this more global analysis, teachers consider the results of each student so that they can share these results with parents.

····· **TAKING A** ·····
CLOSER LOOK Testing Terms

Achievement test A test that measures the extent to which a person has mastered a body of information or possesses a skill after instruction.

Criterion An indicator of the accepted value of outcome performance or a standard against which a measure is evaluated.

Criterion-referenced A test for which scores are interpreted by comparing the test taker's score to a specified performance level rather than to the scores of other people.

Developmental test An age-related, norm-referenced assessment of skills and behaviors that children have acquired (compared to children of the same chronological age). Sometimes such tests are inaccurately called *developmental screening tests*.

Diagnostic assessment Identification of a child who has special needs. In most cases, a multidisciplinary team of professionals assesses a child's specific areas of strength and weakness to determine the nature of the problems and to suggest causes as well as possible remedial strategies.

Intelligence test A series of tasks that yield a score indicative of cognitive functioning. Tasks typically require problem-solving and various intellectual operations such as conceiving, thinking, and reasoning. They may also reflect an earlier use of such intellectual functions (for example, informational, fact-based questions). They are standardized to the average performance of individuals who by independent criteria are of known degrees or levels of intelligence.

Norms Statistics or data that summarize the test performance of specified groups such as test takers of various ages or grades.

Norm-referenced A test for which scores are interpreted by comparing the test taker's performance to the performance of other people in a specified group.

Reliability The degree to which test scores are consistent, dependable, or repeatable; that is, the degree to which test scores can be attributed to actual differences in test takers' performance rather than to errors of measurement.

Score Any specific number resulting from the assessment of an individual.

Standardized test An instrument composed of empirically selected items that has definite instructions for use, adequately determined norms, and data on reliability and validity.

Utility The relative value or usefulness of an outcome as compared to other possible outcomes.

Validity The degree to which a test measures what it purports to measure.

Content validity Evidence of how well the content of a test relates to its intended purpose.

Criterion-related validity Evidence that demonstrates that test scores are systematically related to one or more outcome criteria.

Predictive validity Evidence of criterion-related validity in which scores on the criteria are observed at a later date; for example, the score on a test with predictive validity will predict future school performance.

Source: National Association for the Education of Young Children (1988).

Test Score Distributions

Norm-referenced tests are designed to reflect a **normal distribution** of scores (Gregory, 1996). The distribution **median** is the point that 50 percent of the scores will fall above and the other 50 percent will fall below. Norm-referenced tests are designed so that one-half of all students taking a particular grade-level test will score above the median and one-half will score below the median. Figure 12.1 shows a normal distribution curve.

You can see that 68 percent of the distribution falls in the average range (−1 to +1). Percentages drop in the *standard deviations* progressively farther away from the median. Test publishers report scores in many forms, but the most common are **percentiles** and **stanine** scores. On the normal curve, you can also see *Z scores* and *T scores,* which are usually reported and explained in test manuals.

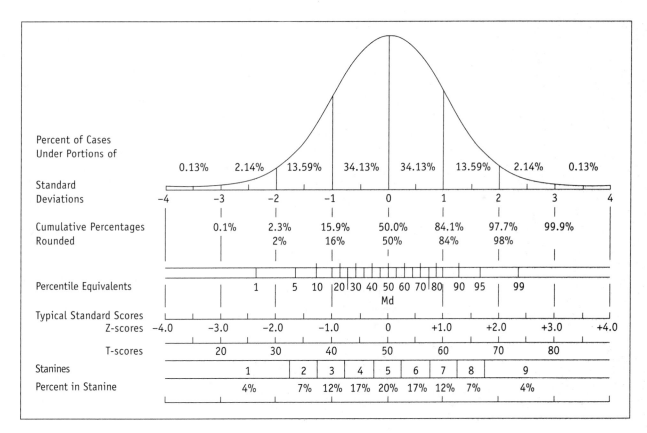

Figure 12.1
Normal Curve Graph
Source: Templeton (1995).

As you look at the normal curve, you may want to reacquaint yourself with many of the standards of measurement. Here are brief descriptions of these standards:

Median. The score at which half of the scores fall above and half fall below. On the normal curve this score is 50.

Raw score. A **raw score** is the actual number of correct answers achieved.

Percentiles. Raw scores are converted to percentiles so that comparisons can be made. Percentiles range from 1 to 99 with 1 being the lowest and 99 the highest.

Stanines. Stanines are similar to percentiles except that the distribution is divided into groups of nine. Stanines are broader than percentiles. Stanines range from 1 to 9 with 1 being the lowest and 9 the highest.

Grade equivalent scores do not appear on the normal curve in Figure 12.1. The International Reading Association (1991), along with others, has recommended that only percentiles and stanine scores be reported (Farr & Carey, 1986). Grade equivalent scores might indicate, for example, that a student scored at the 2.8 level on a test, indicating that the child performed at the second-grade, eight-month level. These scores are subject to parent and teacher misinterpretation. They give a false impression of specific curricular expectations for each month of a school year or that students' abilities can be measured this precisely. Further, it is possible for a first-grader who answered every question correctly in a test section to be scored in the 99th percentile, with a grade equivalent of 12. Some parents and teachers might then say that the child could perform at a twelfth-grade level. Although this score would demonstrate that the child did very well on this portion of the test, it would not follow that this child would be up to the reading challenges of twelfth-grade material.

An interesting phenomenon that has been described about norm-referenced test scores is called the **Lake Wobegon effect** (Foster, 1990; Gregory, 1996). Garrison Keillor, a writer and radio performer with a continuing monologue about a midwestern community called Lake Wobegon, described the community as a place where all the men were good looking, all the women were strong, and all the children were above average. Pikulski (1989) wrote about a West Virginian physician who found that 82 percent of the school districts and 32 states reported that their students scored above average. This effect is particularly interesting because norm-referenced tests are designed so that 50 percent of the students taking them score above the median and 50 percent score below. If the reporting school districts and states were correct, and students in large numbers were scoring above average, then the test publisher would be expected to adjust the test to return it to the correct parameters.

Looking At a Test Report

Figure 12.2 shows a student test report similar to those your students will receive. Although test publishers use different report forms, most provide similar

GRADE 2
STANFORD NORMS GR 2.5   LEVEL PRIM 2   FORM E

TESTS NUMBER OF ITEMS	RAW SCORE	NATL PR-S	LOCAL PR-S
WORD STUDY SKILLS 48	33	56-5	42-5
WORD READING 33	27	62-6	47-5
READING COMPREHENSION 40	33	70-6	57-5
VOCABULARY 35	23	54-5	33-4
LISTENING COMPREHENSION 30	19	42-5	22-3
SPELLING 30	16	57-5	41-5
CONCEPTS OF NUMBER 34	22	51-5	35-4
MATH COMPUTATION 38	20	27-4	27-4
MATH APPLICATIONS 36	29	81-7	72-6
ENVIRONMENT 27	24	95-8	92-8
READING 73	60	67-6	53-5
TOTAL READING 121	93	63-6	48-5
TOTAL LISTENING 65	42	49-5	26-4
TOTAL MATHEMATICS 108	71	53-5	42-5
COMPLETE BATTERY TOTAL 351	246	57-5	42-5

NATIONAL PERCENTILE BANDS
1 5 10 20 30 40 50 60 70 80 90

AGE   7 YRS   5 MOS

READING SKILLS GROUP: DEVELOPMENTAL

CONTENT CLUSTERS	RAW SCORE/NUMBER OF ITEMS	BELOW AVERAGE	AVERAGE	ABOVE AVERAGE
WORD STUDY SKILLS	33/48		✓	
Structural Analysis	12/12			✓
Phonetic Analysis - - Consonants	15/18		✓	
Phonetic Analysis - - Vowels	6/18		✓	
WORD READING	27/33		✓	
READING COMPREHENSION	33/40		✓	
VOCABULARY	23/35		✓	
LISTENING COMPREHENSION	19/30		✓	
Retention	12/15		✓	
Organization	7/15		✓	
SPELLING	16/30		✓	
Sight Words	5/6		✓	
Phonetic Principles	8/16		✓	
Structural Principles	3/8		✓	
CONCEPTS OF NUMBER	22/34		✓	
Whole Numbers	5/6		✓	
Place Value	7/15		✓	
Fractions	2/3		✓	
Operations and Properties	8/10		✓	
MATHEMATICS COMPUTATION	20/38		✓	
Addition with Whole Numbers	9/16	✓		
Subtraction with Whole Numbers	10/16		✓	
Multiplication with Whole Numbers	1/6	✓		
MATHEMATICS APPLICATIONS	29/36			✓
Problem Solving	12/15		✓	
Geometry/Measurement	13/15			✓
Graphs	4/6		✓	

WRITING TEST RESULTS:

CONTENT CLUSTERS	RAW SCORE/NUMBER OF ITEMS	BELOW AVERAGE	AVERAGE	ABOVE AVERAGE
ENVIRONMENT	24/27			
The Social Environment	12/14			
The Natural Environment	12/13			

Figure 12.2
Student Test Report

information. They report raw scores and the conversions of these scores to percentiles or stanines for ease of comparison. After reviewing this report, practice how you might interpret its information to the student's parents.

The notation at the top of the report, *Stanford norms Gr 2.5,* indicates that the student was compared to second-grade midyear norms. Tests generally provide norms for the beginning, middle, and end of the year. Look at the subtests this student took, and analyze the raw scores, the percentiles, and the stanines. Compare the band width for the listening subtest with that of the environment subtest. Notice that various subtest scores are combined to form total scores in reading, listening, and mathematics. For example, the combined scores of word study skills, word reading, and reading comprehension provide the total reading score. At the bottom of the report, the publishers have separated out the individual skills or concepts that were measured in each subtest. This shows how many items the student answered correctly in each subarea, such as sight words in spelling. Based on this numerical report, the student is ranked below average, average, or above average and then by developmental category: at grade level (developmental), above grade level (enrichment), or below grade level (remedial).

Most standardized achievement tests have numerous subtests and require a full week to administer. The subtests might include reading comprehension, word study skills, concepts of number, mathematics computation, mathematics application, spelling, language, social science, science, vocabulary, and listening comprehension. In word study skills, students are usually asked to answer questions similar to the one that follows.

1. Did the coach _____ you to throw the ball like that?

   A. learn

   B. learned

   C. taught

   D. teach

Students are expected to pick the one correct answer; there is no room for interpretation. Teachers find it frustrating when students begin to question the questions as they take the test. For example, one student came up during the test and asked about a math question. In this question, the student was expected to calculate the total amount of money spent on three items at the store. He said the question had no right answer because none of the answers had calculated tax.

Individual Testing

Teachers of students who are having difficulty learning or are accelerated at learning can recommend these students for individual testing. A psychologist will assemble tests that reflect the student's needs or difficulties. The tests may include diagnostic tests based on a specific identified learning difficulty or strength and usually include an individual intelligence test.

····· **TAKING A** ·····
CLOSER LOOK   ## First Grade Takes a Test

A vivid example of the stress that children suffer as they take tests is shared in Miriam Cohen's book (1980), *First Grade Takes a Test*. The story begins with the principal bringing the tests to the first grade. The teacher then directs the children to, "Read the questions carefully. Then take your pencil and fill in the box next to the right answer. You must work quickly. But do not worry, you can do it." After these directions, the children begin to work on the test. The first child to ask a question is George. He wants to talk about this question:

Rabbits eat _____.
❑ lettuce
❑ dog food
❑ sandwiches

George tells the teacher that rabbits eat carrots so that their teeth do not grow too long. He draws in a carrot so the people who made the test know the right answer.

Sammy has difficulty with this question about firemen:

What do firemen do?
❑ make bread
❑ put out fires
❑ sing

Sammy's friend has an uncle who is a fireman and who got his head stuck in a pipe. Sammy is confused because that is not an answer choice.

Other children have questions as they move through the test. When the time is over, many of them complain that they did not have enough time to finish. Some of them even comment about feeling stupid.

Diagnostic Norm-Referenced Tests

Diagnostic norm-referenced tests are usually administered to students who are having difficulty learning to read (Gillet & Temple, 1994). Some forms of these tests can be administered to groups, but they are usually administered individually. Diagnostic tests are used to support placement in programs such as Chapter 1 that provide additional literacy instruction for children.

Diagnostic tests differ from achievement tests in some important ways. These tests usually contain many subtests organized to determine a child's skills. The items are placed so that each item represents a graduated level of difficulty. By analyzing a child's responses on these tests, you should be able to see exactly where in a subject area that child is having difficulty (Gillet & Temple, 1994).

Diagnostic reading tests often begin by exploring a child's knowledge of letters and sound-symbol relationships. A subtest examines children's knowledge of word pronunciation. Some tests require children to read short passages and answer questions.

Although there are many diagnostic tests, especially in the area of reading, we consider the Woodcock Reading Mastery Test-Revised as an example (Woodcock, 1987). The Woodcock test has six individually administered subtests in its battery: visual-auditory learning, letter identification, word identification, word attack, word comprehension, and passage comprehension. These subtests measure student reading abilities from kindergarten through to adult levels. Many special education teachers and Chapter 1 teachers use this test, which takes about thirty to sixty minutes to administer and evaluates student reading readiness, basic skills, and comprehension. Student scores are norm-referenced.

Individual Intelligence Tests

Intelligence tests provide a score that is considered along with other assessment information in planning instruction and placement. The psychologist and the multidisciplinary team—a group that includes the child's parents and teacher and determines the best way to facilitate a child's learning—ponder this score as they seek to understand a student's reading difficulties. The team and psychologist might recommend additional supplementary classroom instruction, part-day placement in a support classroom, or full-day placement in a special education classroom. It is important to remember that students who have reading difficulties may achieve at any level on an intelligence test. However, reading achievement and intelligence scores do correlate in the higher grades (Gillet & Temple, 1994).

A frequently used individual intelligence test is the Weschler Intelligence Scale for Children-III (WISC-III). This most current revision of the Weschler Intelligence Scale has thirteen subtests that are balanced between verbal and performance abilities. The test is balanced in this way so that a student who is not proficient verbally can demonstrate an average intelligence score based on performance. The WISC-III is designed for students ages six to sixteen and is available in Spanish. Other tests are available for students younger or older (Gregory, 1996).

The scores from each of the subtests create a profile of the student's verbal intelligence, performance intelligence, and full-scale intelligence. The mean for an intelligence test is 100 and the standard deviation score is 15. Think back to the normal curve shown in Figure 12.1. With a standard deviation of 15, 68 percent of those taking this test would score between 85 and 115. The subtests include information (thirty items), similarities (nineteen items), arithmetic (twenty-four items), vocabulary (thirty items), comprehension (eighteen items), digit span (fifteen items), picture completion (thirty items), coding (fifty-nine items in A and 119 items in B), picture arrangement (fourteen items), block design (twelve items), object assembly (five items), symbol search (forty-five items in A and forty-five items in B), and mazes (ten items). Three of the tests are optional or supplemental: digit span (verbal) and mazes and symbol search (performance). A psychologist would administer these subtests only to gather additional information or if questioning the results on one subtest. Here are sample questions or items from each of the subtests:

Information

How many legs do you have?

What must you do to make water freeze?

What is the capital of France?

Similarities

In what way are a pencil and a crayon alike?

In what way are tea and coffee alike?

In what way are binoculars and a microscope alike?

Arithmetic

If I have one piece of candy and get another one, how may pieces will I have?

At 12 cents each, how much will 4 bars of soap cost?

If a suit sells for 1/2 of the regular price, what is the cost of a $120 suit?

Vocabulary

Define: ball, summer, poem, obstreperous.

Comprehension

Why do we wear shoes?

What is the thing to do if you see someone dropping his packages?

Why are we tried by a jury of our peers?

Digit Span

Report these digits forward:

1, 8–2, 7–9–8, 7–4–2–1

Report these digits backward:

6, 4–1, 9–5–9, 3–1–4–8

Picture Completion

Identify the missing part of a picture (for example, a car without a wheel, a dog without a leg, or a telephone without numerals).

Coding

A key is provided with numerals and symbols. Use this code to sequentially complete the coding task:

1	2	3	4	5
∠	∇	↑	≈	∃

2	1	4	2	5	3	4	1

Picture Arrangement

Place a series of pictures into a meaningful sequence.

Block Design

Reproduce designs using blocks:

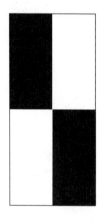

Object Assembly

Arrange pieces, similar to puzzle pieces, into a meaningful object.

Symbol Search

Decide if a symbol appears in an array:
↓   ∇ ⊗ ⇑   yes no

Mazes

Complete a series of mazes that range from relatively simple to more complex.

The test administrator reads all of the questions to the student, who is not expected to do any reading. When a student completes the entire battery, the scores from the information, comprehension, arithmetic, similarities, and vocabulary subtests are combined to form the verbal scale. Scores from picture completion, picture arrangement, block design, object assembly, and symbol search form the performance scale (Gillet & Temple, 1994).

As with other norm-referenced tests, it is important not to overinterpret these scores. They represent what a student did on a particular day with a particular psychologist. When the profiles are created from the raw scores, psychologists look for differences between performance and verbal scales and consider high and low performances on each subtest. They can determine from these results whether or not to recommend other tests or observations.

The WISC-III is never the sole criterion for deciding how to place or label a child. The multidisciplinary team, including parents, considers the results of this test and other measures in determining the strengths of a child and creating an optimal educational program (Kaufman, 1994).

The discovery that many intelligence test subtests correlated with one another led early researchers to consider the idea of general intelligence (Cattell, 1963; Spearman, 1927). Contemporary researchers have extended the idea of general intelligence to include *multiple intelligences models* (Gardner, 1983). Most understandings of intelligence were too narrow and should be broadened, according to Gardner, who described seven intelligences: linguistic intelligence, logical-mathematical intelligence, musical intelligence, spatial intelligence, bodily-kinesthetic intelligence, interpersonal intelligence, and intrapersonal intelligence. This more flexible view of intelligence changed the traditional use of one numeral to represent a person's intelligence. It extended our understandings of intelligence and the ways that students demonstrate their abilities in the classroom.

Criterion-Referenced Tests

Instead of comparing students to other students, as norm-referenced tests do, criterion-referenced tests look at whether a student has met an instructional or curricular goal. For example, if second-grade students are expected to spell single-syllable words with long-vowel patterns, a criterion-referenced test will include several items to test if students in the second grade have mastered this concept.

Criterion-referenced tests assess a student's knowledge of a particular skill. For example, the following item is from a criterion-referenced test that measures third-graders' knowledge of compound words. The students were asked to choose the word in each group that is a compound word:

1. A. complete

   B. picture

   C. listen

   D. sometime

A second example asks third-graders to choose the word that means more than one:

1. boy

   A. boys

   B. boyes

   C. boyis

   D. boyses

Each student's score reflects a percentage of items answered correctly for each subtest.

Criterion-referenced tests can be commercial or district-created. Commercial tests come with validity and reliability measures. When school district personnel create a criterion-referenced test, the first two years of use usually establish validity and reliability within the district (Gronlund & Linn, 1990).

One problem with criterion-referenced tests is that few of them engage students in authentic reading and writing endeavors. Before a school uses a commercial criterion-referenced test, educators need to examine the test carefully to determine if the skills measured reflect the school district's curricular expectations. If they choose to create their own, several years will pass before the test is normed and the results are dependable.

If the tests are closely tied to the curriculum and provide a measure of each student's knowledge, they provide a means for parents and students to see what aspects of the grade-level curriculum the students have mastered. The student report sheets are usually quite straightforward and help parents and teachers understand the skills that students have mastered. Here is a sample student's report:

Student Larry	**Grade** 4	**Year** 92/93
Total Math 91	**Total Reading 95**	**Total Writing 89**
Statistics problems 100	Vocabulary 96	Spelling 80
Geometry 100	Comprehension 94	Punctuation 100
Measurement 82	Study skills 83	Capitalization 78
Problem solving 100		Language 90
Fractions 50		Expression 100

These results indicate that the student has mastered most of the curricular goals for the fourth-grade year. He still needs work in fractions and capitalization. Each score is reported as a percentage that represents the actual number of questions the student answered correctly. No other forms of scoring are presented; the test considers only the student's mastery of the curriculum.

▨ *Formal Testing Within the Overall Assessment Framework*

These tests do serve a purpose, but their importance must be balanced with ongoing informal assessment and with other sources of information about student performance.

Flood and Lapp (1989) recommend using a comparison portfolio to put student evaluation in perspective for parents. Within this comparison portfolio are norm-referenced and criterion-referenced test scores, informal measures of assessment, writing samples, reading reports, self-assessments, and samples of materials used in the classroom. This type of portfolio shows parents how their child is progressing from a variety of perspectives rather than a single test score. This multidimensional quality reaffirms the importance of viewing learning through a variety of lenses.

Routman (1994), too, addresses the need to keep norm-referenced tests in perspective and part of a multidimensional view of students' learning. She describes evaluation as having five components:

- Observations of process and product as well as of collection of data,

- Recording of observations and data,

- Interpretation and analysis of observations and data,

- Reporting of information, and

- Application to teaching and learning.

Routman has adapted a profile from the work of Anthony, Johnson, Michelson, and Preece (1988). In her profile (see Figure 12.3), she constructs a grid that simultaneously looks at (1) the context of evaluation, (2) the structure of observation (observation or measurement), (3) contextualized or decontextualized measures, and (4) the product or process of evaluation. Contextualized measures are part of routine learning activities, such as proofreading exercises and dictations. Decontextualized measures—school, district, or state tests, for example—are not everyday occurrences in the classroom. The profile provides a multitude of ways to observe or measure children's literacy development. Most important, it places norm-referenced tests into a realistic perspective and shows how they inform teachers and parents about a child's literacy development.

In addition to the profile, Routman (1994) has created a framework for evaluating children's literacy. She surveys various aspects of literacy, such as oral reading or comprehension, and provides appropriate ways to assess this development through ongoing informal and formal assessment strategies. Figure 12.4 shows a revised version of her profile.

Although this framework includes only some of the possibilities for evaluation, it does demonstrate the various assessments that teachers conduct throughout the school year. It also suggests establishing numerous data points that reflect

Figure 12.3
Evaluation Data-
Gathering Profile *Source:*
Adapted from Anthony,
Johnson, Mickelson and
Preece (1988).

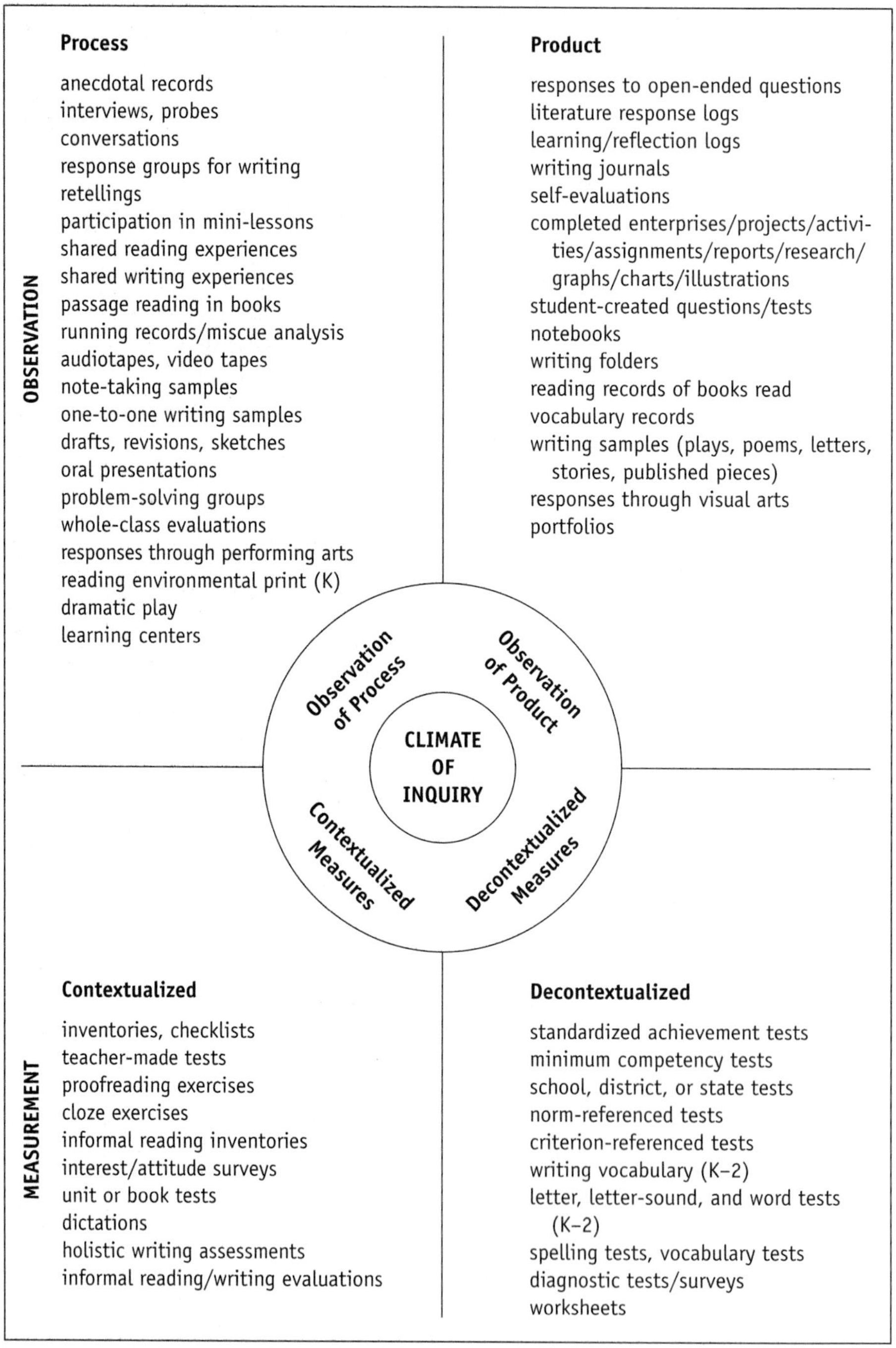

Process

anecdotal records
interviews, probes
conversations
response groups for writing
retellings
participation in mini-lessons
shared reading experiences
shared writing experiences
passage reading in books
running records/miscue analysis
audiotapes, video tapes
note-taking samples
one-to-one writing samples
drafts, revisions, sketches
oral presentations
problem-solving groups
whole-class evaluations
responses through performing arts
reading environmental print (K)
dramatic play
learning centers

Product

responses to open-ended questions
literature response logs
learning/reflection logs
writing journals
self-evaluations
completed enterprises/projects/activi-
   ties/assignments/reports/research/
   graphs/charts/illustrations
student-created questions/tests
notebooks
writing folders
reading records of books read
vocabulary records
writing samples (plays, poems, letters,
   stories, published pieces)
responses through visual arts
portfolios

OBSERVATION

Observation of Process
Observation of Product

CLIMATE OF INQUIRY

Contextualized Measures
Decontextualized Measures

MEASUREMENT

Contextualized

inventories, checklists
teacher-made tests
proofreading exercises
cloze exercises
informal reading inventories
interest/attitude surveys
unit or book tests
dictations
holistic writing assessments
informal reading/writing evaluations

Decontextualized

standardized achievement tests
minimum competency tests
school, district, or state tests
norm-referenced tests
criterion-referenced tests
writing vocabulary (K–2)
letter, letter-sound, and word tests
   (K–2)
spelling tests, vocabulary tests
diagnostic tests/surveys
worksheets

Figure 12.4
Framework for Literacy
Evaluation Source:
Adapted from Routman
(1994).

What Do I Want to Know?	How am I going to find out?		
	Informal and/or Ongoing		More Structured
Oral reading	One-to-one observation Paired reading	Shared reading Guided reading in group	Tape recordings Running records IRI
Spelling	Free writing Journal writing First-draft writing	Writing samples Journal writing Word study	Editing Weekly tests Developmental spelling assessment Standardized tests
Comprehension	Books child chooses Retellings	Group discussion Response logs Evidence to support ideas or opinions	Written tests Standardized tests
Reading-writing attitudes	Books chosen Text written Amount of reading and writing Interviews	Writing folder Responses in conferences Participation	Formal interview Records of books read or stories written
How a student views self as a reader or writer	Attitude survey	Reflection log Oral and written responses Portfolio choices	Self-evaluations

the processes and products involved in learning. Teachers use such a multidimensional perspective to make informed decisions about a child's literacy growth.

Pros and Cons of Norm-Referenced Tests and Measures

Some teachers, parents, and principals wholeheartedly support the use of norm-referenced tests, and others bemoan their use. You will most likely use them as a teacher. The following discussion considers both the pros and cons of norm-referenced testing.

Together a teacher, student, and parent explore a student's portfolio.

Pros

1. *Norm-referenced achievement tests facilitate state or school district policy making.* Most assessments of schools are conducted by insiders or personnel who work for the district. For example, a superintendent evaluates principals, and principals evaluate teachers. These evaluations rarely focus on instruction and curricular issues. Norm-referenced testing allows for an outside measure of student performance (Calfee, 1992). The results are standardized, and a school district can compare its results to those of other school districts and evaluate curricular priorities for students. For instance, if all students score low in comprehension, the school district may provide materials and instruction to teachers to help students progress in this area before the next testing cycle.

2. *Norm-referenced achievement tests tell the public whether students are meeting certain standards.* Test scores used to be a relatively private matter for schools, school districts, and parents. Many school districts now publish "report cards"

that include norm-referenced test scores. These report cards may print districtwide data or school-by-school results. Norm-referenced test scores have become important news items; newspapers often publish whole-school test scores (Rhodes & Shanklin, 1993). Some real estate agents even use norm-referenced test scores to recommend certain neighborhoods to families looking for a new home.

3. *Norm-referenced achievement tests can be used in curricular planning.* Schools face practical concerns in curricular evaluation and planning, and norm-referenced achievement tests are easy to administer and score (Tierney, Carter & Desai, 1991). Although norm-referenced tests are not designed to match instructional curriculum, they can help guide curricular planning. Teachers can look at their class profile and note any areas where students are excelling or having difficulty. Sometimes low test scores occur when students encounter a concept in a test before it is introduced into the curriculum. The teacher must decide if rescheduling this instruction makes sense to the curriculum as a whole and is best for the students. When a school district's students at a particular level score poorly in an area, experts may be recruited, and teachers may be coached to improve teaching and learning in this area.

4. *Norm-referenced achievement tests give parents and teachers feedback about how a student is doing in relation to other students in the district or country.* Some schools make norm-referenced test results the foremost reason for parent and teacher conferences. Parents come to expect this discussion with teachers (Calfee, 1992). Although this discussion is certainly important, teachers need to find many other opportunities for interaction.

Cons

1. *Norm-referenced testing consumes time that could be better used for classroom instruction.* Most teachers find norm-referenced standardized testing less useful than informal assessments. They are reluctant to give up the week that it takes to administer most norm-referenced achievement tests (Tierney, Carter & Desai, 1991). Teachers also express frustration when a school district requires them to administer more than one norm-referenced test in an academic year (Aronson & Farr, 1988).

2. *Few norm-referenced tests mirror the child-centered learning occurring in classrooms.* One of the most consistent criticisms of norm-referenced testing is that tests fail to match our current understandings of teaching and learning. Test publishers are responding to this criticism, and many norm-referenced achievement tests are being revised. One form of revision includes longer reading passages that better represent complete narratives or expository text. In some tests, students may be asked before reading the passage to answer a few questions that indicate background knowledge. This score is then factored into the evaluation of their answers. New questions go beyond literal comprehension to tap higher-order thinking. In these multiple-choice questions students can also mark an answer that might be possible (Rhodes & Shanklin, 1993). Some tests now assess students' interests or motivations in reading the content of a passage and ask students about their reading processes. For example, a student might be asked

about the literacy devices (for example, dialogue or character development) used within a passage (Vacca, Vacca & Gove, 1991).

Some new versions of norm-referenced tests also include sections where students actually write a story or passage. Students are given an example or prompt and then are free to explore that topic. This change in norm-referenced testing allows students to actually write rather than be evaluated on their writing skills by answering grammar-based multiple-choice questions. The drawback is that such questions require noncomputerized scoring, which is more labor intensive and expensive and can provide subjective results with low reliability among raters.

3. *Teachers often feel constrained to teach so that their students do well on the norm-referenced test, so that the test becomes the classroom curriculum.* In some schools test results are considered very important, and teachers tend to teach to the whole class. All children read the same book at the same time regardless of individual reading ability. They are expected to learn as one group, and even first-graders are not allowed to develop at their own pace (Roderick, 1995). In such settings the curriculum narrows, and teachers spend more time on drills for multiple-choice exams (Perrone, 1991). Perrone indicated that in such environments, "Children are encouraged to be more passive, more obedient to authority, and less enthusiastic about asking and answering open-ended questions" (p. 4).

Darling-Hammond and Wise (1985) found that teachers taught what was evaluated on the test and ignored other areas of the curriculum. They also noted that teachers taught the precise skills measured on the test, not the underlying concepts. Teachers used more multiple-choice tests than essay tests in their classrooms because these better reflected the testing format of the standardized tests they would administer to their students.

Other teachers worry that the holistic reading and writing strategies that they use in their classrooms will put their students at a disadvantage on the tests. Either they continue with the teaching and learning that they believe in and feel uncomfortable about the testing, or they abandon the strategies they prefer and move to a more skill-based curriculum that better matches test questions (Glaser & Brown, 1993).

4. *Students in lower-income settings tend to do worse on norm-referenced tests than students in middle-income settings.* Socioeconomic status accounts for most of the variance on a norm-referenced test. Students who come from affluent homes consistently do better on these tests (Vacca, Vacca & Gove, 1991). Although tests have been rewritten to avoid cultural bias, socioeconomic status is still an important factor in students' performance. African-American, Latino, Mexican-American, and Native American students are overrepresented among students who consistently find themselves at the bottom on educational assessments (Bartoli, 1995).

Allen, Michalove, and Shockley (1993) have described children in primary grades in low-socioeconomic schools as most at risk of failing to succeed academically. They concluded after several years of documented observation that "retention, ability grouping, compensatory classes, and state testing in theory are to provide a more appropriate education to each individual; in fact, they are disproportionately injurious to African-American children, males in particular" (p. 253). In the schools they observed, children were retained based on their results on norm-referenced standardized tests. As a result, some children were retained twice in the same grade level. Such use of norm-referenced testing, they found, hindered many low-income minority children in learning.

Weak performances by minority students on norm-referenced tests documented over time have led to complaints of cultural bias (Mullis & Jenkins, 1990). Test bias can occur when the test reflects the dominant culture's language and knowledge or when students lack familiarity with test-taking procedures. Despite efforts to counter cultural bias complaints through improving item selection (Garcia & Pearson, 1991), test publishers still face criticism.

5. *In schools that highly value norm-referenced testing, students are sometimes retained or placed in special education settings.* In many states, schools use retention in grade to give children who achieve low scores on a norm-referenced test an extra year to achieve the standard required (Allington & McGill-Franzen, 1995). Children who receive special education support also are not included in tested groups. In such schools, both retention and special education placements increase (Bartoli, 1995).

Conclusion and Study Notes

This chapter discussed standardized or norm-referenced tests. We have examined the characteristics of norm-referenced tests, including achievement tests, diagnostic norm-referenced tests, criterion-referenced tests, and individual tests such as the WISC-III. We also examined the vocabulary associated with norm-referenced testing.

In addition to considering the characteristics and purposes of norm-referenced testing, we explored ways to integrate norm-referenced testing with other informal ongoing modes of evaluation. The discussion ended with an exploration of the pros and cons associated with this type of evaluation.

We have considered the following main points:

- Standardized or norm-referenced tests are formal measures used to assess a skill or concept.

- In informal assessment, the teacher interprets the results and qualitatively assesses the product or process of a student's learning. Formal assessment provides specific directions for administering the test and scoring is most often done with computers and yields an exact numerical score.

- Reliability indicates consistency in scores if a person were to take the test several times.

- Content validity indicates if the test is measuring what it is said to measure.

- Diagnostic norm-referenced tests are usually administered to students who are having difficulty learning to read.

- Intelligence tests are used to determine a student's intelligence score, which is then considered along with other information in planning instruction and placement.

- Criterion-referenced tests assess whether a student has met an instructional or curricular goal.

- Formal testing must be balanced with informal ongoing assessment and other sources of information about student performance.

Key Terms

norm-referenced tests	utility
achievement tests	median
diagnostic tests	percentile
norms	stanine
reliability	raw score
validity	Lake Wobegon effect
normal distribution	

Follow-Up Activities

1. Use the test reports presented in this chapter to practice interpreting reported scores.

2. Visit a school principal and discuss that school's use of norm-referenced tests. Ask the principal to tell you how test results are shared with teachers and parents.

3. Go to the library and explore newspaper clippings that discuss test scores reported in a community. Are the scores reported accurately? What implications are drawn from these scores?

4. Ask a teacher to conduct a discussion about testing with students. What do the students say about these tests? How do they feel about them?

13 Teaching Learners Who Experience Difficulties

Conversation

Susan: How do I help a child in my class who is struggling with reading?

Tina: When I tutor, I take a child through the reading and writing processes and individualize a plan for her. But how can I do that with thirty kids in the room?

Doug: We need to individualize for each student and make assessment and learning less stressful for students.

Rora: Until you know where you're starting from with a student, it's hard for a teacher to be patient with or reduce the stress for the student.

Susan: How do students succeed when they can't read the textbooks? I did a practicum with a teacher who supplemented the textbooks, but she also insisted that students need to learn to read headings and to skim.

Doug: Until students catch up and can read textbooks independently, we have to adapt.

Rachael: I don't know how you could supplement everything. And how do you provide enough material for all of the different reading levels in a class?

Cathy: If you put the students in groups, they can share responsibilities. Sometimes kids who can't read are great at standing up in front of the group. Students can work in groups where they can support each other in learning.

Sharon: You can build groups that include students at various levels, and they can help each other out.

Rachael: But that risks bypassing slow readers who miss out on the practice they need.

Susan: They might miss out if you made that your entire program.

Kim: If they can't read what the other sixth-graders in class are reading, they're going to be constantly frustrated and no strategy will work.

Tina: Yes. So how do we help them catch up?

Amanda: You can find them different books, but is that going to be enough?

Kim: You can group them by reading ability, too.

Shari: In my school, we group students developmentally for some reading activities. We pick and choose materials out of the basal readers. We don't use social studies and science textbooks unless they match student levels. If I need some social studies and science materials for a group of students, we go to the library to find books. I also copy materials so that everyone in a group has a reading copy. We have silent reading time, which is one-on-one time when I can sit down with students. Writing workshop is another time when I work with students individually.

Rora: My fourth- through sixth-grade practicum classroom has two low groups of beginning readers who are behind and two other groups of intermediate readers.

Cathy: I observed a special education teacher who pulled students out of a third-grade class during reading time. Students wanted to work in her group.

Shari: My practice class had three or four reading groups. The special education teacher came into the classroom and worked with her students. They read big books, reread pattern books, and did word study. Sometimes the special education teacher led a group that included other students as well.

Diane: Our special education teacher, Title I teacher, and ESL teachers come into the room to work with students, but they are with us just a short time. I cannot accept that our struggling students are going to work with someone for thirty minutes a day but for the other five-and-a-half hours they would have no work that they could do.

Students need to experience dignity in what they do and read. In my fourth-through sixth-grade room I have three big baskets of simple reading books that range from almost wordless picture books up to beginning chapter books. The interesting thing is that not just the beginners read them. Some of the most competent readers in the room frequently pull things from the basket for sustained silent reading time.

We teach students to view the classroom as a community and to respect and value each other no matter who is a good reader, who is a good speller, or who is a good artist. Class meetings include lots of talk about not criticizing somebody who can't read. Students don't say, "Oh, look who went over and took the baby book out of the basket." You might see a child in my room reading *To Kill a Mockingbird* sitting next to a child struggling to read *Frog and Toad*.

Both Shari and Diane find ways for students at all reading levels to be active learners. This chapter explores two aspects of learning for students who struggle: *literacy instruction* and *perseverance*.

Some classrooms may have as many as twelve students who are behind. Within this group several students may be *significantly behind*—two or more years behind where they are expected to be reading. Among these students one or two students may experience a rare and severe difficulty in learning to read. The information in this chapter will help you to plan instructional programs and activities for students who are delayed as well as for students who have permanent or organic disabilities.

Guide Questions for Chapter 13

- How do teachers organize instruction for students who experience difficulties reading and writing?

- How do teachers create a developmental program for students who are somewhat or significantly behind to involve them in active classroom learning?

- What special programs serve students with special needs?

Planning Instruction for Students with Difficulties

Teachers need a clear sense of instructional direction for each student. The following discussion on educational planning concerns all children who have difficulties, including the 10 percent of school-age children who qualify for special education, those who qualify for Title I services, and those who have mild difficulty in learning to read and write. But planning individual programs is not the same as one-to-one teaching. Project work, independent work, and small-group activities and lessons form the foundation of classroom activities for students with difficulties.

Finding Ways for Students to Enjoy Reading and Writing

Even when you have a good sense of students' instructional levels and provide what you consider interesting reading material, some students with reading difficulties resist reading. You may offer support through choral reading and still some students will resist reading. This is true particularly for students in upper elementary grades; the further behind they are, the greater frustration they feel (Shaywitz, Holford, Holahan, Fletcher, Stuebing, Francis & Shaywitz, 1995; Stanovich, 1986). You may face an uphill battle to inspire students to enjoy literacy, but be patient. This chapter includes many suggestions to entice students to read, the most powerful of which is reading them good stories.

Planning for Change: Set Priorities and Understand What Can Be Achieved

Three planning strategies will help you make plans and set priorities (Payne, Mercer & Epstein, 1974). Ask these three questions to make and test plans that will accomplish your specific goals and objectives:

1. *Can we change the activity?* Can we change what the student does? Can we change how the student participates in an activity?

2. *Can we change the teacher?* What are the teacher's expectations? Would it help to change how the student is evaluated and graded?

3. *Can we change the student?* What changes will instruction bring in the student's literacy development? Can we show the student some different ways to complete assignments? What changes can we make to better motivate the student?

Focusing on these questions will help you develop activities and strategies that make sense. For each major activity, schedule a time line that includes regular meetings or phone calls to check on how the new activity is working. For example, if you work on a new homework procedure designed to lessen the homework load for a particular student, you should touch base with a parent and the student in a week or two to ask about noticeable change.

Considering Resources

As you plan for change, *consider resources.* Who among the personnel in your building has knowledge and materials that can help a student who has difficulties? When will other educators work with the student? Many people, programs, and specialists may participate in planning:

School-based participants: Consider special education teachers; reading and literacy specialists; Title I teachers and aides; previous teachers; ESL teachers; speech and language specialists; arts, music, computer, and gifted-and-talent teachers; and counselors, psychologists, nurses, and other health care professionals.

Caregivers: Consider any primary caregivers, including parents, siblings, and relatives.

Neighborhood support: Consider after-school and extracurricular programs, tutoring programs, private tutors, clubs, sports, or nonschool institutes.

Evaluate what part each can realistically be expected to play in the instructional program. Who will work with the child for a concentrated period of time?

Meeting to Plan

After evaluating resources, educators and parents meet to plan instruction. Part of being an effective planner is to be *proactive.* Proactive teachers think and act ahead to prevent problems from arising rather than dealing with problems only when they reach the critical point or when a child's misbehavior and frustration require caring. Proactive teachers make time to meet and to share information about assessments, teaching, and students' learning. Some of this work occurs in team meetings when teachers meet professionally as a group according to grade level, location, thematic studies, and content area. When difficulties become apparent, teachers and parents meet to discuss individual students and their learning and development.

Teachers sit beside students to instruct and assess.

As goals and objectives develop, evaluate the time line and make predictions in terms of phase of development about the student's progress. Make the predictions in the form of "if . . . then" statements: "If John continues to work in a small group each day and if he reads at his instructional level, does plenty of writing, and is engaged in word study at his developmental level, then we predict that he will be at *this* developmental level." Follow prediction making with a discussion of specific activities that address the goals and objectives. Other meetings scheduled at this time can include, for example, a brief appointment at two weeks to check in on a homework system and a longer progress-check meeting in two months.

Involve Other Educators and Allied Professionals

Many educators with specialized training work with students with difficulties. As you listen to various educators and allied professionals, think of ways to translate what they say to classroom practice. Ask group members to recall examples from instruction and assessments to help each other understand the student's strengths and needs.

By reading and listening to reports by specialists, you will learn how the child's social, physical, and psychological worlds relate to literacy development. The language specialist may talk about an early hearing impairment as related to a speech delay. The school history may reveal that the child has been in numerous schools, which may have affected achievement. When considering further testing, evaluate the dangers of overtesting and possible expenses to parents as well as research that supports the testing against the likelihood that the testing will inform instruction.

Involve Students in the Assessment Process

Students learn about taking responsibility for their learning when they are included in the planning process. They learn how they are being assessed, and they share their self-assessments. Students comment that they learn in these meetings that everyone is working to understand and help them. Work examples that students bring to an assessment meeting include samples of a journal, a writing folder, a learning log or response log, a personal reader, a word study notebook, or a word bank. If the meeting occurs after school, meet in the classroom where the student's materials are readily available.

You or another teacher can meet with the student prior to a child study meeting. This is a time to review the student's work since the last meeting and discuss which work demonstrates growth. You may then help the student develop goals to bring to the planning meeting. Students can also dictate or write about their goals and make lists of interests and project ideas.

Depending on the student, you may chose to interview the student about progress and goals either in the group meeting or individually. When the student attends a group meeting, guide the discussion to include the student. Ask what the student thinks about what is being said and allow plenty of response time. Table 13.1 presents questions that may guide a planning meeting.

Involve Parents in Planning

At your first meeting with a student's parents, listen and learn about the family and its history, viewpoints, dynamics, and any problems. Be sure to give parents plenty of time to talk. Ask open-ended questions that encourage them to reflect on their child's development and school history and how they view their child's work in your classroom.

Parents also have questions about you and fellow educators. They want to know who you are and what your philosophy of teaching is. They want to hear your impressions of their child. In addition, parents may come to meetings with recollections of their own difficulties learning in school. Keep in mind that your primary goals are to learn about the child and to ask parents to share what they want for their child and how they view the child's difficulties. Your guiding principle is to be an active listener; ask parents what they want to say and what questions they have. Parents may not know how to respond when you ask them about their goals for their children. They want their child to read better, but they may

Table 13.1
Questions to Help
Students Plan Instruction

What do you think you have learned and accomplished since our last meeting?

Can you share a few of your writing books?

Will you show us some of the books you have read recently?

How have we done in rereading dictations?

Do you have time for writing? Have you published and shared your writing recently?

What are you working on now?

What do you read during SSR?

What would you like to work on?

How are things going at your work area?

What sort of help do you need to get work done?

Are you able to read the texts?

Have you been turning assignments in?

What changes do you want to make?

What do you want us to work on?

not have any specific goals in mind. They may be waiting for you to tell them what the curriculum is, what difficulties there may be, and what they and the school should do next. Table 13.2 presents questions that can help you guide such a discussion.

In addition to general questions, you may want to ask some specific questions that relate to the future. These questions help parents consider reasonable goals for reading and writing at home. The literacy activities parents describe in these discussions become particularly important in later discussions of a difficulty. For example, a teacher may say to a parent, "Remember when we talked about your child guessing at words? Here is what her guesses tell us about her learning." Use examples parents provide to illustrate for them their child's development.

As the classroom teacher, you will likely explain achievement test scores and how they relate to the student's classroom achievement. This may occur at parent-teacher meeting days. Help parents keep a broad perspective by discussing the student's development as well. Use the developmental model in Chapter 3 to show parents their child's developmental path and the interrelationships between reading, writing, and spelling development. Show them specific reading and writing behaviors that they can look for within the developmental continuum.

Assess the Effectiveness of Instruction

Asking these questions will start you off on the right foot in assessment:

- Is the student enjoying her work?

- Is the student doing plenty of reading, writing, and word study at her independent and instructional levels?

Table 13.2
Questions to Consider
with Parents

General Questions
What are your goals for your child this year?
Will you describe your child's difficulties?
Why do you think your child is having difficulty?
What do you notice at home?
Does your child read or write at home?
Do you see evidence of your child's progress at home?
Has there been other testing that might be helpful to us?
Specific Questions
What would you like your child to read during the next few months?
How much time do you want to spend at home reading?
How much time do you think you can read together?
Do you want some advice on how to read with your child?
Do you have questions about spelling and writing in the assignments?

If the answers to both questions are yes, build on these successes. If the answers are no, plan steps to understand the student, to make new hypotheses about how she is learning, and to find materials that she will find worthwhile and motivating. This goes beyond asking the student what she would enjoy; it requires an exploration of topics and books and magazines that are at a proper functional level.

Develop Meaningful Goals and Objectives

The team uses input from educators, the student, and parents to develop a series of long- and short-term goals. The objectives should document whether or not the student is involved in plenty of work at an instructional level. When you meet to discuss and develop goals and objectives, consider these questions:

1. *Are the goals and objectives based on development?* Grade-level scores are inadequate criteria for measuring progress. As Warner (1995) points out, "Standardized, norm-referenced survey tests of achievement such as the KTEA should not be used to measure progress on a yearly basis, even though this practice is widespread in the schools. These tests lack sufficient reliability for that use. They are better used as part of the three-year mandatory reevaluation" (Warner, 1995, p. 2). Students' progress can be more meaningfully reported in terms of the phases of development outlined throughout this book. Figures 13.1 and 13.2 present individual and small-group report forms that can become part of students' cumulative records and provide assessment continuity from one grade to the next.

Figure 13.1
Summary of Literacy
Development by Phase
and Date

Seeley Elementary School

Student's name: _____   Date of birth: _____

Phases of Literacy Development	*Early*	*Middle*	*Late*
Emergent		9/8/94	
Beginning	10/10/94	1/15/95	
Transitional			
Intermediate			
Advanced			

Comments:

9/8/94	Barbara Kridel	
Date	Teacher's name	
10/10/94	Barbara Kridel	
Date	Teacher's name	
1/15/95	Barbara Kridel	
Date	Teacher's name	
Date	Teacher's name	
Date	Teacher's name	
Date	Teacher's name	

2. *Do the goals and objectives match the local curriculum?* For example, if fifth-grade students study United States history, fifth-grade students with severe difficulties will also need to learn the content that is a part of the social studies curriculum.

3. *Are the goals and objectives easily understood?* Goals and objectives need to be edited and revised for clarity. Use ordinary language to communicate best with educators, students, and parents (Warner, 1995).

4. *Do the objectives involve daily instructional activities?* Use daily instructional activities to measure the objectives you write. This makes it easier to observe the completion of an objective without time-consuming and unnecessary testing.

Special Services and Programs

As a classroom teacher, you may need to refer a child for special testing and possible inclusion in a special program. You may be asked to do so by parents who are wondering why their children are not doing better in school.

Qualifying for Special Services

Each school district offers special services to children who qualify for special education based on standards for eligibility determined by state and federal reg-

Name	Age in September	September Reading/ Writing	Spelling	January Reading/ Writing	Spelling	May Reading/ Writing	Spelling
Paula	7–3	Middle beginning	Middle letter name	Early transitional	Early within word pattern	Early intermediate	Early syllable juncture
Andrea	7–6	Early transitional	Early within word pattern	Late transitional	Late within word pattern	Early intermediate	Early syllable juncture
Leland	7–1	Late beginning	Middle letter name	Middle transitional	Middle within word pattern	Late transitional	Late within word pattern

Figure 13.2
Small-Group Profiles of
Literacy Development for
Teacher's Portfolio
....

ulations. Each school also has a process for gathering information and a child study team to determine eligibility once a referral has been made. In most school districts, students qualify for special educational services if they show a significant discrepancy between expected achievement and achievement test scores. After parents or guardians approve the testing, a school psychologist, a school nurse, the special education teacher, and perhaps a reading specialist conduct assessments.

Following the assessments, the child study team meets to review the results with parents. Team members discuss how the student qualifies or does not qualify for special services. Parents sometimes find these meetings intimidating; they may be the only noneducators present. Describe the process and information to them in nontechnical terms and include numerous examples of the student's work as illustrations.

If parents agree that they want their child involved in the special education program, the team works to create an individualized education plan (IEP). As IEP goals, objectives, and activities take shape, consider their reasonableness: Are they performable? Will you be able to provide the expected instruction in the classroom? Furthermore, the group must consider what support the student will need to succeed. This may be the time to consider alternative ways for the student to demonstrate knowledge and understanding of content material or to plan who will read the questions on a test to a student as needed.

IEPs describe instructional objectives in terms of instruction. The following Student Study presents long- and short-term goals, objectives, and support activities for Jack Beetles as he entered fourth grade at a new school. Notice that in this IEP, no special tests were given to monitor growth, and the activities took into account his developmental needs.

Inclusion, Integration, and Coordination

In the past, students who were referred to special programs were usually pulled out of the classroom to work in another room with a specialist. After examining the effectiveness of these referrals and pull-out programs (Allington, 1994; Kauffman, 1994; Morris, Ervin & Conrad, 1996), educators have begun to rethink special programs and the role of specialists in these programs (Walp & Walmsley, 1995; Walmsley & Allington, 1995). Educators are searching for a greater integration of instruction that provides students with consistent and supportive instruction across special programs and special teachers. As special educators and classroom teachers plan an IEP, they continue to search for the best way to blend methods and configure instruction.

Various factors influence the configuration of instruction, including the number of referred students in the classroom, room space, and scheduling issues that relate to when the special teacher can work with groups or individuals. Regardless of how they receive it, readers who are significantly behind need consistent and developmental instruction. Small-group instruction and opportunities for individual work with a teacher are critical elements in this regular experience.

Consistency in instruction may mean that the special educator or reading specialist visits the classroom daily to work with a small group of four or five students at a regular time and place. Many resource teachers become used to carrying materials in boxes on luggage carriers and carts. The reading specialist may come into the classroom to help collect dictations or to read with students. The Title I teacher may run GLTAs or GRTAs. Resource teachers also visit during writing workshops and help specific students with the writing process. By observing what goes on in the classroom, the special teacher better understands students' needs.

Sometimes the best method is to divide instructional responsibility for a student between the resource teacher and the classroom teacher. For example, the resource teacher may administer spelling tests and provide most of the word study activities or collect dictations that the student rereads during classroom SSR.

Many students worry about what they miss when they leave the classroom for special programs and may express their worry by unwillingness to go. When students work in special programs, classroom teachers are careful not to penalize them for missed work, especially by assigning all missed class work as homework or by introducing brand new concepts while they are away.

The classroom teacher and the specialists usually meet weekly to plan activities and special assignments that may require a bit more assistance. They use these brief planning meetings to brainstorm alternative ways to complete assignments, to update a student's personal reader, and to select some options for independent reading materials for the next two weeks.

STUDENT STUDY

Jack's Educational Plan

In Chapter 11, you learned that Jack was a bright student who was entering fourth grade. After the child study team met in October, it was determined that Jack qualified for special services. It was recommended that Jack receive regular assistance from the special education teacher, that he be referred to a program for gifted and talented students, and that he receive tutoring twice a week after school. In the area of counseling, the school counselor was available as needed, and the family was encouraged to consider some family counseling.

That first year, the special education teacher had several students from the fourth grade come to the resource room for small group and individual instruction. In the meeting to develop an IEP for Jack, the following goals, objectives, and activities were developed to begin in October and continue for a year. You can see that there are specific responsibilities to encourage Jack's participation in the assessment process.

Priority Annual Goal 1

As determined through informal assessment, Jack will be an active reader and will grow from a middle beginning reader to a transitional reader.

- *Objective 1.* With involvement in support reading activities, like individual dictations, Jack will read fluently to teacher satisfaction. Criteria are set at 90 words per minute (wpm) in repeated reading, with 97 percent accuracy. In January, Jack will reread several lengthy pattern books. By June, he will read simple chapter books at an instructional level—with good fluency (70 to 90 wpm) and good accuracy (≥92 percent).

- *Objective 2.* Given instructional reading and listening level materials, Jack will be actively involved in reading and listening activities that tap comprehension. Jack will comprehend material that he reads and listens to as measured by retelling, predictions in GRTAs and GLTAs, and written responses.

- *Objective 3.* Jack will be able to read the sight words in his word bank, with excellent accuracy (90 to 100 percent) and fluency. The number of words in his word bank should grow to 85 words.

Priority Annual Goal 2

As determined by informal assessment, Jack will increase his writing skills as a writer from a beginning to a late beginning level.

- *Objective 1.* Student will write in an extended fashion three times a week to student and teacher satisfaction. A journal format will be used. Fluency and interest will be observed.

- *Objective 2.* Jack will begin to reread what he has written for clarity and for response to student and teacher satisfaction.

- *Objective 3.* Clarity, spacing, and correctness will improve to teacher satisfaction. Correctness will include some punctuation and capitalization. Jack will be able to reread most of what he has written.

Priority Annual Goal 3

Jack will grow in his orthographic knowledge as evidenced in his spelling and word recognition. In reading, he will be able to read most single syllable words in context and many two-syllable words. In spelling, he will just enter the within-word pattern phase.

- *Objective 1.* Jack will sort pictures and single-syllable words by their short vowels with excellent accuracy and fluency. In picture sorts, Jack will sort by sound differences among short and long vowels.

- *Objective 2.* Jack will spell common word families correctly and many initial consonant

(continued)

blends and digraphs correctly. If there are to be spelling tests, given 20 words appropriate for students in the letter-name phase, Jack will spell words correctly with 90 percent accuracy.

Activities with the Special Education Teacher

- Collect individual content dictation once a week and schedule time to reread dictations daily.

- Begin word study on vowel families (*sat*, *sled*) and consonant blends and digraphs.

- Conduct developmental activities in small groups, including GRTAs and GLTAs, word study and spelling, review textbook assignments from the classroom, and work projects related to the content studies in the regular classroom.

- Schedule individual time (15 minutes two to three times a week) to develop coping strategies, read tests to Jack, do alternative assessment activities, and support work with assignments from the classroom.

An hour of instruction on a typical day with the special education teacher may include

Orientation at beginning and summary at the end (10 minutes)

Easy, independent-level reading (15 minutes)

Reviewing word bank (5 minutes)

Working in small-group GRTA (20 minutes)

Working on report for classroom (10 minutes)

Literacy Instruction for Students with Difficulties

Instructional programs require consistency in instruction over a long period of time. There is no quick fix for the reader who is significantly behind; rather, teachers plan instruction that is intellectually challenging and look for success over time. Students who are behind in their reading cannot languish in class, and yet some bright high school students with significant difficulties reading spend most of their time in special classes where they receive little intellectual challenge.

Do students who are behind require special instructional methods? Usually, no. The methods are much the same; the materials must be different. For example, a ten-year-old beginning reader who needs to practice repeated reading but who finds little of interest in *Brown Bear, Brown Bear* instead rereads individual dictations for repeated reading support.

Classroom instruction is organized in several ways. You will guide and direct some groups and partnerships, but student-directed groups will also work on projects related to thematic studies. Students work well with *proximal partners*—students who are close developmentally and benefit from working together. Within compatible zones of proximal development, the more advanced reader can practice reading and actually model literacy behaviors for the student who is slightly behind developmentally. For example, the less advanced student can watch the more advanced student do a picture sort for short vowels, which is a step beyond the level of the early beginning reader in the prephonemic phase of spelling. The student sees the next developmental step by watching the partner sort. When a more advanced student supports a less advanced student in rereading from a personal reader, the more advanced student gets more time reading at an independent level.

Many teachers work in small ability-related groups in which teachers and students read stories together and do some word study. Students also group by interest in content area studies and by how they can help each other. It is common to see one student in a partnership doing most of the writing while the other partner does some writing but takes responsibility for, say, the artwork.

When one or two students are well behind the others in reading, the teacher may avoid setting up either a fourth or fifth literacy instruction group by combining the behind students with another group but engaging them in different activities. In this way the teacher can make a little time to read with these students while the rest of the group is reading silently in a GRTA. When the larger group does a word sort, the teacher and two students work on a word sort at their developmental level. When the students work with the rest of the group, they need ways to avoid reading frustration-level materials.

The developmental-level instructional activities discussed in previous chapters, adjusted for interests, are appropriate for these students. The rest of this chapter discusses key instructional activities and considerations for working with students with difficulties. These activities and special considerations are grouped in five areas of literacy instruction: reading to, reading with, writing with, word study, and a miscellaneous category concerned with student **perseverance** and **coping.**

Start by Reading to Students

It may take some time before students who have had difficulties are ready to try reading *with* you, so build plenty of reading aloud *to* them into initial educational plans. Over time, begin to invite the student to participate by holding the book closer. For example, you might sit on the floor with a lower-elementary beginning reader and open a big book and point to words as you read. Read in a guided listening-thinking activity (GLTA) basic instructional cycle: *predict, listen, confirm.* Students become more confident as they see that their predictions are as fine as those of other students.

Books on tape make a good SSR activity. Students can follow along on the page as they listen. These tapes are found in libraries, bookstores, and even at video rental stores. Audiocassette players have become relatively inexpensive; you may be able to secure half a dozen cassette players for your class.

Reading with Students

Beginning and early transitional readers who are behind need plenty of support in their reading. You can use students' language and experiences to create reading materials and help them develop into recreational readers in the classroom.

Support Reading Activities

Support activities help students engage. They are used with most beginning readers and with transitional readers who are behind.

Group Experience Charts   Group experience charts work well with emergent and early beginning readers. The charts give them experience in reading easy texts. Children with difficulties may use unconventional language in their dictations. In general, avoid changing students' language when taking a dictation, although when a slight change does not decrease the student's accuracy in rereading you may clarify and expand the dictation by adding a word or two. The improved dictation shows the student some language patterns to use in later writing and speech. If you detect any hesitation, go back to the original language.

Patterns, Rhymes, and Chants   You can obtain extra mileage from an experience if you develop patterns, rhymes, and chants to accompany group experience charts. Older students like to use the rhymes as models for their dictated verses.

Individual Dictations   In addition to beginning readers, individual dictations serve older transitional readers in grades four through six who have a difficult time finding books of interest to read (Dixon & Nessel, 1983). Students reread their dictations two or three times daily, and older students in particular enjoy timed repeated-reading formats. Using either personal dictation or easy passages of 150 to 250 words, students reread their passages until they achieve a rate of approximately 100 words per minute (Morris, Ervin & Conrad, 1996; Samuels, 1979). When students regularly read dictations they experience fluency, they increase their sight vocabularies, and they advance their orthographic knowledge.

Content Dictations   **Content dictations** are integrated with classroom content studies. In these dictations students summarize and respond to material read to them either by a teacher, a student, or from tape. In addition to providing support reading materials at their instructional level, content dictations provide greater access to classroom activities; they encourage discussion and familiarize students with content-specific vocabulary. Content dictations develop from weekly news magazines as well as textbooks (Sharp, 1989). Figure 13.3 presents an example of a content dictation. Jenny, a sixth-grade transitional reader, dictated this summary of what she thought was important in an article she and a partner read for a unit of study titled "Web of Life." The teacher printed the dictation in a plain 18-point font to make the text easy to read.

Partners work best sitting side by side. The more advanced reader reads aloud, and the student who will dictate follows along as well as possible observing the key vocabulary and reviewing the figures and graphs. The reader stops at the end of a section or after enough new information has been introduced. Some readers can also take dictations, although you may need to show them how at first.

When the student can reread the dictation at a good rate and with accuracy, you or a reading partner can support the student in rereading the original text.

Figure 13.3
A Content Dictation
Based on a Science Unit
Reading

Jenny

Ecosystem

Ecosystems are where we live. We can't live without plants because they breathe out oxygen and we breathe it in. Animals who eat plants are herbivores and if they eat animals we call them carnivores.

Worms are decomposers. So are mushrooms.

When they burn down too many trees all the dirt washes away and they have to cook with manure for fuel.

Deer in the Grand Canyon grew too many and then there wasn't enough food because the animal that ate deer died.

Green plants use sunlight to make food.

The student also can add related texts written at an independent reading level to a personal reader. Class books of dictations and student writings based on field trips or special experiences or themes make good rereading material, too. Beginning and transitional readers find that these books provide enough support in vocabulary and familiarity to make for excellent instructional-level reading materials.

Developing Recreational Readers

As Diane Olds noted in the Conversation at the beginning of this chapter, it's easier to promote reading in the classroom when students feel accepted and know that their worth is not judged by their reading level. To accommodate students who experience difficulties, include in your classroom all kinds of books for students to read. No student who reads poorly should be deprived of information; each should have the opportunity to learn the same material through other forms or simply with easier books and a bit more support in reading them. The dignity Olds described comes when students are comfortable reading at their instructional levels.

Meet with students regularly in small groups or individually to discuss what they are reading. In the same manner as you conduct writing conferences, start with general questions: "Will you show me what you are reading? How is it going?" Ask the student to read you a paragraph or two, perhaps from the text they will read next. This is a good time to talk about selecting instructional-level materials. In choosing books for students, you may find that some upper-elementary students want to read enlarged print texts. They report a greater ease in reading.

Booklists can be a way to document what students have read and their reading growth. Transitional readers and intermediate readers who keep response logs of what they have read can reserve several pages at the front of the log for a reading list.

Teachers often arrange their classroom libraries by content area and color-code books by difficulty level. They include several monthly children's magazines. A listening area serves as a learning center or station in the classroom where students can listen to a story and follow along with the book, especially if it is a picture book. Unless the reader on the tape is reading slowly, most books on tape will be read too fluently for students with difficulties to follow along easily.

Reader's chair is an adaptation of author's chair. Reader's chair is a time when students share a favorite book they have read recently. Students meet with the teacher beforehand to share their choices and think with the teacher about what and how they might share. This may involve practice reading a memorable paragraph or two. Avoid at all costs, though—especially for students who are significantly behind—impromptu round-robin reading in which students are expected to read aloud before a group something they have not had a chance to read before.

Reading simple plays is a fun way students practice fluency and expression when they enter the transitional phase. If they have had a practice read-through, students enjoy participating in easy-to-read plays in small groups. Reader's theater books are full of easy materials (Bauer, 1990; Shepard, 1993).

Book clubs of three to six students give readers who are behind a sense of belonging to a group that reads a common book (Raphael, Goatley, McMahon & Woodman, 1995; Smith, 1988). In their club meetings, students talk informally about the book they are reading. Book clubs work best when all members can read the book at their instructional and independent levels. Although this may prove difficult for students significantly behind who cannot find readable books that challenge them intellectually, most students manage to find easy books that they can read as a group (Worthy, 1996). If you collaborate with other teachers to form book clubs, you will create a bigger pool of students from which to create book clubs among all kinds of readers.

The books you can secure in the numbers you need will dictate the size and number of your book clubs. Talk to other teachers who may have multiple copies of books to share. The only rule in selecting a book is that students have to be able to read the text with fair accuracy and good understanding. If students cannot read a text but want to be a part of a group, look for alternatives such as **books on tape** or partnered reading with a peer or other helper.

Magazines provide short-format stories and the support of attractive illustrations, which make them good materials for students with difficulties. It is easy for two students to sit together and thumb through a magazine. They can find articles to explore, and either the more capable student or you can read parts of the stories, particularly captions, to the behind reader. Magazines that complement content studies and nature and sport magazines that appeal to students of all ages are found in *Magazines for Kids and Teens* (Stoll, 1994).

Writing

How do you help students, especially those who are behind in their writing, see writing as worthwhile? Many students who have had difficulties learning to read and write have had unpleasant experiences writing. Some are almost phobic about it. They feel vulnerable when they write, as if their ideas, feelings, and life experiences, grammar, spelling, and punctuation are on the line and open to scrutiny.

In Chapter 10 we described the process of ensuring meaning in writing as following four steps: sincerity, clarity, correctness, and eloquence. Finding sincerity in writing is critical with students who are behind. Sincerity in writing returns to students who have lost interest in writing only after a good deal of daily practice and encouragement.

On the surface, school curricula are more concerned with teaching correct usage than with teaching and measuring sincerity. You can teach mechanics through lessons on punctuation and style, but be judicious about the time you spend working on mechanics in struggling students' independent writing. As is true for all writers, wait to work on matters of correctness until ideas are on the page and clearly presented.

Finding Ideas and Creating Interest

Students talk to find writing ideas. When a student is stuck, have a casual conversation about the subject. Verbal rehearsal is absolutely essential to the writing process. Having taken the first step of saying what they plan to write, they have more energy to focus on writing the words. When you express confidence in students' abilities to come up with ideas and support them over time, students begin to grow in their writing: When students have something to say, they write more, which leads them to learn more by writing and experimenting with language. They also try out ideas and care more about their writing, which encourages greater willingness to revise and edit for clarity and correctness.

When students talk, you build a sense of what they consider important. Take note when you hear a student become more animatedly verbal. You can point out these special topics of interest to a student: "I heard you talking about the basketball game you were in the other day. Is that something you would like to write about?" Ask students to use the first two pages of their journals or daily writing books to list subjects they may want to write about. Leading guided discussions in which students share their topics for writing may prompt other students to come up with ideas as well.

Encourage students to talk about their writing by asking them open-ended questions like those discussed in Chapter 10 regarding writing workshop. Following Graves' (1983) advice, begin with the most general question: "How is it going?" If you are lucky, students will begin to talk about what they are trying to write. If this general question does not start a dialogue, turn to more specific questions about what the student is writing, such as, "What part of your story are you working on now?"

Frequently respond to students when they write. These responses show students that teachers value what they have written and also begin dialogues about their ideas and writing. Be sure to comment on the ideas and respond to what the student has done well.

Support in Writing

Many writers who are behind have difficulty rereading what they have written. This is a good time to sit beside them as they write. As you sit together, ask the student to read words you cannot make out from the invented spelling. Briefly talk the student through some of the sounds in the word to create a more accurate invented spelling.

Your guidance and support add cohesion to their writing. When students are particularly reluctant, you may offer to take a dictation and, as they become more comfortable in composing, tell them, "You write for a while. I can pick up again after you write a few lines." As the student tires, you can resume taking dictation.

Addressing Correctness

Put correctness in proper perspective. If a child is writing with great hesitancy and with little detail, it seems pointless to focus on correctness. Forgive errors in spelling and proper mechanics until the student is writing enough to edit for correctness.

Ask students to suggest what they need to work on in their writing. Their choices give you an indication of the edge of their learning and what writing mechanics to work on in teacher-guided small-group lessons. Check sheets make good reminders to students of their priorities in revising and editing.

Writing workshops give students a chance to trade skills. Students who are less advanced in their writing may find a place of importance because of their ideas and advice or other talents they may share in art and design. In return, students help each other in writing mechanics.

The following Student Study discusses how Michael, a child who clearly had a learning disability, learned to write.

Word Study Activities

As for other students, word study is based on spelling development for students who have difficulties learning to read. Look for gradual growth in

STUDENT STUDY

Michael Learns to Write

Michael's story demonstrates that students with organic difficulties can make literacy progress if some motivational issues are addressed. Michael attended a university literacy center for several years—most intensely during the summers. During the first summer together, Michael grew from writing one-line stories with some trepidation to a three-page story about his camping trip.

After working together several hours over two days, meeting extensively with his parents, and looking at several years' worth of testing by school psychologists and special educators, we concluded that Michael had a language-based learning difficulty, which might be affecting his learning to read and write.

Michael came to the literacy center for an initial assessment in March of his fourth-grade year. He had already qualified for special services in special education. He had been working with a resource room teacher for a year. His performance on the informal inventory indicated that he was at a preprimer/primer instructional level. He had not yet reached independent-level reading with any material, and even first-grade material was at a frustration level for him. He was a middle beginning reader who had acquired some sight words but could read only half of the second-grade word list correctly.

During the first two days of working together, Michael made an individual dictation two paragraphs long. Michael could reread his typed dictation with good accuracy, but hesitation and deliberation made his rereading sound disfluent. His fluency increased with repeated reading.

Michael's spelling and word recognition were in synchrony: he could read many single-syllable words but had difficulty spelling them accurately. His invented spellings indicated some knowledge of complex vowel patterns, as in *TROTE* for *trout*. He asked if he had to write and wrote three words during this initial work together. His parents told us that Michael hated writing, and Michael said that he thought he was a "bad writer."

Michael showed some evidence of a specific language difficulty. The psychologist's testing revealed a mixed pattern of results with large differences among the subtest scores on the Wechsler Intelligence Scale for Children—III. Significant differences appeared between the verbal subtests and the performance subtests, and consistently higher scores on nonverbal subtests indicated strong nonverbal reasoning.

The scores on the individual subtests indicated that Michael's reasoning abilities were fine. Significantly lower scores on two verbal subtests indicated that he might find it difficult to learn vocabulary and verbal information, a difficulty related to language learning. Although such low scores could indicate that a student had not been exposed to the type of vocabulary and information items examined in this test, Michael seemed to have plenty of such activity and exposure, which raised questions about his language and vocabulary development. Michael's good reasoning abilities were confirmed in the listening comprehension part of the informal reading inventory. His difficulty learning verbal labels and facts was reflected in his performance on a test in which he had to give an opposite to the word called to him (for example, *good-bad*, *north-south*).

Michael's parents said that Michael had been viewed by some teachers at school as a difficult child to work with, and some teachers suspected that he had an attention deficit. Michael's mother believed that early on Michael had trouble re-

(continued)

sponding to and understanding language. She thought that during his first few years of life he often communicated through gestures. Michael's mother saw her son as dependent on her to keep channels of communication open. She also reported that Michael had a three-inch growth spurt in third grade.

Discussions with Michael's parents and two days of working with him revealed Michael as a sensitive person with more self-awareness and a little more anxiety than others. He was sensitive to the hurt of others, perhaps because of his own difficulties.

At first, Michael was a reluctant writer. Usually, he wrote one or two lines, and it was difficult to reread what he had written. Over a three-month period of working daily on writing in a small group, he became quite a writer. Figure 13.4 shows that Michael was writing with integrity and quantity. The invented spelling placed his level of orthographic development at the late letter-name phase. Michael would experience difficulties learning to read and write, but we were more hopeful that he would make progress if he maintained a good attitude, kept reading in instructional and meaningful material, and kept writing on a daily basis. As you read his story, notice the nice examples of letter-name invented spelling.

As do other children, those who struggle with language-learning disabilities learn in a developmental way (Abouzeid, 1992; Invernizzi & Worthy, 1989). Appropriate instruction helped Michael find integrity and helped his teachers understand his development.

students' abilities to sort words accurately and fluently. Guide their study by placing word study activities in classroom centers and color-coding them so students know which sorts to choose.

Some teachers wonder if older students who are beginning or transitional readers think picture sorts for vowel sounds are demeaning or too babyish. Teachers who have been using picture sorts for a while find that older students take these sorts seriously.

It is important to sort first by sound and then by orthographic pattern. Too often readers who are behind have memorized spelling rules that are beyond their developmental levels. Beware of being misled into overestimating a student's orthographic knowledge by the words and the spelling rules the student has memorized over the years. Their invented spelling and reading miscues will show you where they are unable to apply the rules with ease and accuracy. Sorting first by sound encourages students to analyze words first by their sounds and then by their orthographic patterns (Gaskins, Ehri, Cress, O'Hara & Donnelly, 1997). This is a classic example of having to take a step backward in instruction to find the point in students' performance where they can work with accuracy and speed.

Most students who have had difficulties reading and writing have had little success in spelling. They will learn more effectively if you discontinue spelling tests and have them instead practice word sorts and word study games (Bear, Invernizzi & Templeton, 1996). If you want to use spelling lists to reinforce familiar spelling patterns, be sure to use words that are at students' developmental

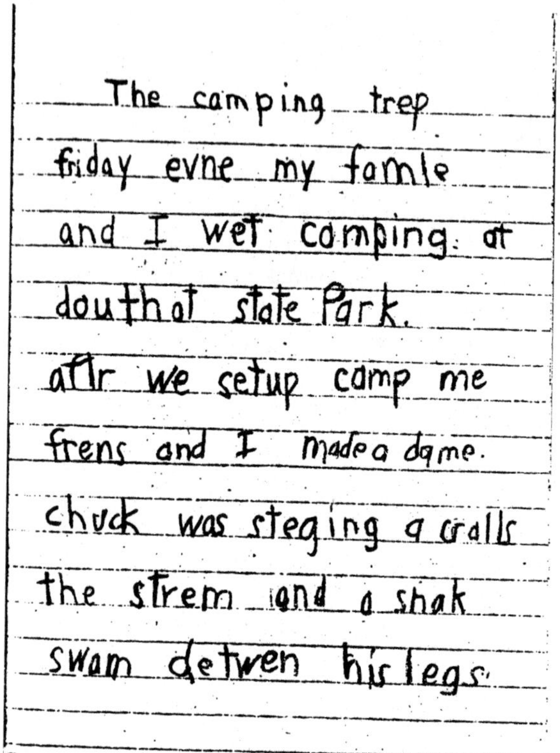

a

The camping trep
friday evne my famle
and I wet comping at
douthat state Park.
aftr we setup camp me
frens and I made a dame.
chuck was steging a cralls
the strem and a shak
swam detwen his legs

b

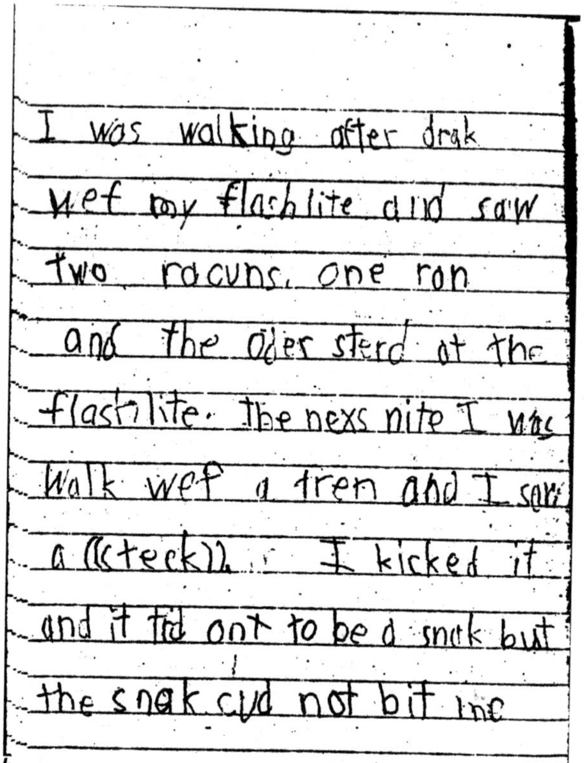

I was walking after drak
wef my flashlite and saw
two racuns. one ron
and the oder sterd at the
flastilite. The nexs nite I was
Walk wef a tren and I saw
a ((teck)). I kicked it
and it tid ont to be a snck but
the snak cud not bit me

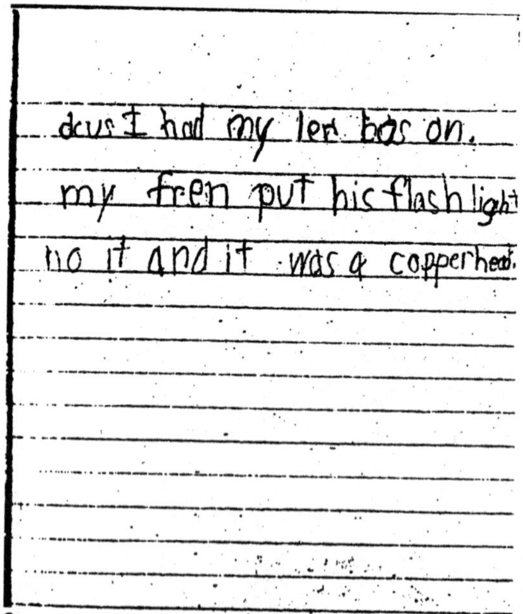

c

deus I had my ler bos on.
my fren put his flashlight
no it and it was a copperhed.

The Camping Trip

Friday evening my family and I went camping at Douthat State Park.

After we set up camp, my friends and I made a dam. Chuck was stepping across the stream and a snake swam between his legs.

I was walking after dark with my flashlight and saw two raccoons. One ran and the other stared at the flashlight. The next night I was walking with a friend and I saw a (stick). I kicked it, and it turned out to be a snake, but the snake could not bite me because I had my leather boots on. My friend put his flashlight on it, and it was a copperhead.

Figure 13.4
Michael's Camping Story
After Three Months of
Writing Instruction

levels and to focus on the patterns they are studying. On the pretest, students should be able to spell about half of the words correctly (Morris, Blanton, Blanton & Perney, 1995). You will be surprised how much more students learn when they are assigned instructional-level spelling lists.

As a result, you may have an additional spelling group to manage. Alleviate some of the work load by having a member of another spelling group call the words and by having students correct their own papers. Basal spellers a grade level or two back are a quick source of words that suit students' developmental levels. You may recall that beginning readers in the letter-name phase of spelling work with short-vowel words, students in the transitional phase examine long-vowel words, and students who are intermediate readers progress through the syllable-juncture phase by examining two-syllable words. Refer to the preceding chapters for more on the types of features to include in the spelling lists at each developmental level.

It works well for older readers in the beginning phase to begin word study notebooks earlier than usual. In this way they can engage in word study activities that look a good deal like those of more advanced students. Students write their sorts into word study notebooks and keep a list of their sight words in a special section. Some teachers ask older students to create a personal spelling dictionary in which they write words that they are unable to spell but use often in writing. This dictionary is a handy tool for editing.

Success in the Content Areas: Perseverance and Coping

Students need to be successful, active, and intellectually challenged, regardless of their reading levels. How can you help students who are as bright as anyone else to obtain information from encyclopedias or reference books that they cannot read? The first step is to examine the texts with students to see what, with a little persistence, they can read on their own. Students who have reading difficulties will find the text too difficult to read. You can help them by gathering a variety of materials on the subject from the school or public library from which they may glean enough readable materials to learn what they cannot learn from the conventional references.

Show students how the school library is organized and where to find informational books, biographies, fiction, and easy reference materials. Model for them how to ask for assistance—in this case, how to talk to the librarian—how to find a reference desk, and how to type in searches on the online catalogue. Have them survey the informational materials in their homes and in the classroom: almanacs, atlases, encyclopedias, software, online services, catalogs, and newspapers. Students like search games that require them to hunt through references and to ask reference librarians for help. Forewarn librarians before you plan such an exercise, however, so that they can prepare for the onslaught.

Most students can meet the challenge of learning to find and ask for information. Using telephone books is no easy trick and is not much different from using encyclopedias. Real-life materials give meaning to alphabetizing and looking for key words such as *automotive, florists, photographers,* and *printing.* Students feel as if they are on a giant scavenger hunt when they explore skills in real life. One question leads to another question, another interest, and another search.

Studying, Note-Taking, and Listening to Books on Tape

When students find materials, they still face the obstacles of reading the information and completing the writing assignment or requirement. Even beginning readers can learn to skim texts for general information and search for specific information. For students with reading difficulties, present orally the directions for how to read a chapter in the study guide in Chapter 10. Teach them how to study figures and tables and how to focus on the key vocabulary by reading the bold headings and looking for words within the text that are highlighted.

Within their limitations in writing quickly and accurately, give students practice taking notes. Have them write down key terms that they hear and anything the teacher writes on the blackboard or overhead. Students who have difficulty learning to read and write learn when it is appropriate to carry a piece of carbon paper and to ask a friend to use the carbon for an extra copy. They learn to borrow notes from classmates to photocopy.

Some educators may consider this a form of cheating, but students who are significantly behind in their reading are unable to take notes they need and have few alternatives. Some students also use tape recorders to record class notes. Tape recording can often contain extraneous noises and comments, however, and listening through the recording of an entire class to collect information is time consuming.

Books on tape play an important role in studying and coping in the regular classroom. Over time, you can develop a collection of taped textbooks for students. Because taping books is a time-consuming task, some teachers develop it into a project that involves other students, parents, and school volunteers. When volunteers make recordings, have them record a short trial passage to check the clarity of their reading.

An organization called Recording for the Blind and Dyslexic records textbooks on tape at little or no cost. This wonderful service has a large library of many commonly used textbooks already on tape. Students can contact Recording for the Blind and Dyslexic at 20 Roszel Road, Princeton, NJ 08540, telephone 800-221-1098 and 609-452-0606, Web site at www.rfbd.org, and info@rfbd.org. The Library of Congress also provides extensive services for the visually impaired, learning disabled, and dyslexic that are available through state or county libraries.

In the intermediate grades, both students with difficulties and teachers can gain enlightenment when they meet with other students to discuss learning. In these meetings, students who are behind in their reading realize that other students have problems, too, and they learn strategies for perseverance and coping from their peers. You or a counselor may schedule similar meetings for parents in which teachers discuss the curriculum and assignments and modifications made in testing and in classroom and homework assignments.

You provide an important service when you teach students how to be their own advocates—how to approach teachers at the beginning of the school year or when they have difficulty. In the upper elementary grades, rehearse with students how to discuss their needs with teachers—to ask teachers if they can borrow notes or to ask for help in making **adjustments in taking tests.** Teach intermediate students with difficulties how to find study partners and join study groups where they can listen to discussions of the text.

Alternative Ways for Students to Show What They Know

All students need alternative ways to show what they know. In Ms. Erb's fourth-grade class students listed ways to study geography (see Figure 13.5). Some of their ideas are conventional (take tests, worksheets), but eventually, students explored "do presentations" and "groups" in more detail. Out of this list, items 1, 3, 7, 8, 9, 11, 12, 14, and 16 are viable alternatives for students with difficulties.

Alternative test-taking strategies include reading aloud the test or, when less support is needed, making sure the student asks for troublesome questions to be read aloud. Providing extra time and a quiet place to work help students take their time to read the test. Resource teachers can assist in test taking that requires more time and assistance reading the questions. Sometimes tests are conducted orally.

Brainstorm with your students other ways they can show what they learned. Discuss some of the same options that the fourth-graders listed above. Show them activities developed by other students. You may suggest that they develop a demonstration, draw a comic strip to illustrate what they learned, create a play or a puppet play to dramatize concepts, paint a mural of a time line or a sequence in a story, or create a video. These alternative activities help students with difficulties find a community of sharing and inspiration to persevere in spite of their difficulties.

Special Instructional Methods

Many claims for success of special instructional methods lack the support of systematic study and research. Without research findings, teachers cannot know if a method will work elsewhere and if, in fact, it was the major factor in a student's growth. Claims for success often come from originators and teachers who

Figure 13.5
Student-Generated Ideas
for a Geography Unit

Ideas for a Geography Unit

1. make maps	5. take tests	9. learn at home	13. use encyclopedias
2. view movies	6. write reports	10. worksheets	14. watch filmstrips
3. do presentations	7. make models	11. groups	15. take quizzes
4. read books	8. ask parents	12. make posters	16. look at or make pictures

use the method and from students who believe they have benefited from the method. Nevertheless, educators need a broader level of understanding of special methods (Perfetti, 1982; Vellutino, 1979).

Before using a method, study the program to see if it works, why it works, and with whom it works. Maintain skepticism about special methods that do lack plenty of exercise reading and writing: they are the primary ingredients for the success of any program. Beware of the many methods for teaching readers who are behind that are expensive, ineffective, and actually destructive in their waste of people's resources, time, and hopes.

To illustrate the diversity of special programs, consider the many methods touted as treatments for dyslexia that focus on different parts of the body. One method asks students to stare at three pennies until vision is blurred to strengthen the eye muscles to improve reading. The Tomatis method (Tomatis, 1991) asks disabled readers as a first step in the instructional program to listen to sounds that simulate sounds they heard in the womb. Students have walked balance beams to improve their reading and have been prescribed motion sickness medications to correct reading problems (Levinson, 1994, 1980). Some chiropractors assert that physical adjustments alleviate reading problems. Geography may affect which special methods are used in your area. In California, the Lindamood method (Lindamood, Bell & Lindamood, 1992) and colored lenses (Irlen, 1991; Spafford, Grosser, Donatelle, Squillace & Dana, 1995) have some popularity.

All of these special programs are interesting and have their supporters. You may be surprised by their claims of effectiveness. In general, it is best to be skeptical of programs that are expensive and quick. Teachers who work with students with difficulties should look to the professional literature for descriptions and studies of specific methods. When a special program involves a medical type of treatment or therapy, refer those interested in the technique to other professionals such as reading researchers, ophthalmologists, and speech, language, and hearing specialists.

One group of modestly popular special methods is the **multisensory approach.** Although little systematic research supports their use, multisensory approaches have been in use for more than fifty years. Most of these approaches focus on teaching students to read words. The best-known multisensory approach is the Orton-Gillingham approach (Gillingham & Stillman, 1970; Moats, 1995). This approach is known as a **VAKT** approach—a visual, auditory, kinesthetic, tactile approach. The Orton-Gillingham approach uses a synthetic phonics approach as compared to the more common analytic approach. In this synthetic phonics approach, students see the word, sound it out, and feel the movement of the word as they trace it or write it in the air. Words and their phonetic elements are taught in a specific order.

The premise of this approach is that the multisensory information makes a greater impression and that this added input helps students to learn words. The major drawbacks to multisensory approaches are that the technique is not applied consistently each day and students do too little reading in meaningful materials to support what they may be learning about words. The Slingerland approach is a classroom adaptation of the Orton-Gillingham approach (Slinger-land, 1974) that uses reading materials in the classroom and shows students how to read rhythmically.

The **Fernald technique** is another well-known multisensory approach (Fernald, 1943; Stauffer, Abrams & Pikulski, 1978). It is similar to the Orton-Gillingham approach but uses an analytic phonics approach to work at the whole-word or single-syllable level. When students trace and sound out words, the syllables are sounded out together and not as individual sounds.

Like the Orton-Gillingham approach, children who use the Fernald method trace letters as they read an individual word. They focus on a single-syllable word from a dictation that they want to learn. With a crayon, the teacher writes the word on a piece of paper and then takes the student through the routine of tracing the word and saying the word until the student can write the word without tracing over the crayon.

The Fernald technique is the multisensory approach that is used in our literacy center—but with only a few children each year. These are students who have only a few words in their word banks and who have had extreme difficulty acquiring sight words from the readings in their personal readers. If they can have daily assistance, the Fernald technique helps them acquire sight words. Students no longer need the Fernald technique when they have acquired approximately fifty sight words and can learn words by rereading the selections in their personal readers.

Programs that work usually do so by matching the materials the students read to their developmental needs. Such instruction makes sense to students, and they will participate. If they do plenty of reading in material at their instructional and independent levels, they continue to develop. Special reading programs work in large part because they involve intense instruction over an extended period of time. Conversely, the downfall of many good methods and programs is lack of consistency over time. Reading and writing are habits. Exercised over a long period of time, at a level of play that is motivating and developmental, most students can learn to read and write quite well.

Conclusion and Study Notes

Many of the instructional activities from Chapters 7 through 10 are adaptable for students who experience difficulties reading and writing. This chapter has discussed assessment and presented many ways to plan instruction and make these adaptations given content studies and special needs. Here are some ways teachers provide developmental instruction to students with difficulties:

- When a difficulty is identified through informal work in the classroom, plan and consult with other educators to offer additional instruction and support for students.

- Involve parents and students in planning.

- Read to students who show reluctance or lack of interest in reading.

- For beginning readers, develop language experience activities to generate reading materials that are interesting and that students can read independently.

- Collect content dictations to bring the curriculum closer to students who are beginning- or early transitional-phase readers.

- Involve students with difficulties in book clubs to read instructional-level materials or partner them with a student who can read the book to provide added support.

- Provide reluctant writers with plenty of support. Start by having the student talk about topics and plans for writing.

- Develop word sorts and word study activities that look like activities done by other students. Gear the words and the patterns to the student's development.

- Teach perseverance and coping skills that will help students who are significantly behind or who have limiting difficulties succeed in school.

- Find alternative ways for students to show what they have learned that do not penalize students who are significantly behind or who are limited in their development.

Ultimately, you must keep two questions in mind: *Do the students enjoy reading and writing?* and *Are students doing plenty of reading, writing, and word study?* Students with difficulties learning to read and write often answer no to these questions. They feel stupid, and because they cannot read, they can drop further behind their peers. Finding yes answers to these questions is essential to motivating and teaching students who are behind in their reading. The adjustments you make to help students with difficulties master their curriculum and exercise their intelligence will contribute to their success in school.

Key Terms

perseverance and coping	multisensory approaches
adjustments in test taking	VAKT
content dictations	Fernald technique
books on tape	

Follow-Up Activities

1. Interview a classroom teacher to discover how the teacher works with students with difficulties. What adjustments does the teacher make in materials and assessments?

2. Visit with a special education teacher about how instruction is organized. Find out what difficulties students have and how the teacher teaches them to read and write. What special methods does the teacher use in class with students? Ask the teacher to describe the students' literacy development. Finally, find out how the special education teacher coordinates instruction with the classroom teacher. If possible, schedule another visit to ask the teacher about assessments, eligibility,

and educational planning. Conduct a similar interview with a school reading or literacy specialist. How does the specialist organize and coordinate instruction?

3. Call local and state libraries to discover how students can enroll in a books-on-tape program. Contact schools about volunteering with a teacher in the intermediate grades to record a book on tape.

4. Visit the learning center at your college or university. What services are available to students with learning difficulties? Refer to commercial telephone directories and social service directories for other resources and services.

14 Epilogue: Building a Community of Learners

Ken: When I substitute teach, I think about what we've learned about small-group instruction and readers' workshop. But I still see classrooms where the desks are in straight rows and the children receive only whole-class instruction. Most of the work they do is from dittos.

Tara: It sounds so boring! How do we make students so interested that they take work home?

Barbara: I'm wondering how to involve parents more. What's the parent connection? I'm working in an after-school tutoring program, and the kids aren't coming. Why aren't the parents making their children come for tutoring?

Lilly: That's the bigger issue: How do we involve parents more?

Sasha: I want to know more about literacy programs.

Martha: Here's another question: How do I stay in touch with new developments in teaching reading and writing?

These students are enthusiastic about beginning their teaching careers, but they still have some questions about starting integrated assessment and instruction, encouraging family participation, and staying current with literacy research. This epilogue addresses those issues.

Guide Questions for Chapter 14

- How do I involve parents in their children's literacy?
- How can we encourage more people to become involved in literacy in our school?
- How do I continue to grow as a professional?

Families, Schools, and Literacy

Teachers do not need to be neighbors and social friends of the families they work with, but they do need to understand the communities in which their students live. As a teacher, you will develop ways to become acquainted with students and ways to include families in literacy and learning. You will help your school create a climate that promotes literacy and learning. We begin by discussing these issues and listing the key ingredients of literacy-rich classrooms.

Including Families in Literacy and Learning

Families become involved in literacy and learning when students are highly motivated to complete an assignment or find information. Here are some ways that excite students and encourage communication between home and school.

Including Families in Thematic Studies

When you plan thematic studies, discuss with your students ways to involve others. Through their research students can explore talents, hobbies, and cultural and vocational interests. As they become involved in their thematic studies and project work, they begin to work on projects at home. Parents appreciate advance notice of upcoming activities that students will work on at home and projects that involve families or that require purchasing special materials.

Before a unit of study begins, write a brief letter home to introduce the theme. Invite parents to share in a variety of ways, from bringing in a collection of insects or rocks to inviting the class for a tour of their plant. In class, prepare subject-related questions that students can ask at home. These questions will help focus students as they go about gathering information.

Newsletters Home

Newsletters are another way to share with parents and families what is going on at school. Writing newsletters is a highly purposeful writing activity for students. They become interested in the activity and relish the opportunity to show parents what they have learned.

In their newsletters students may include a box that asks for volunteers or lists materials needed in the classroom. Some newsletters include activities for younger siblings such as word hunts, cartoons, connect-the-dots pictures, and riddles. *The Weekly News*, shown in Figure 14.1, is a summary of the important parts of each day as written by students and their teacher (Deschenes, Johnson, Poliquin, Potter & Steller, 1991).

Reading and Writing at Home

The best way to involve families in literacy is to ask them how they are already using and encouraging literacy and how they might like to become more involved (Rasinski & Fredericks, 1990, 1991). Ask parents what works at home and when they see their children reading and writing. Ask how the school might reflect their literacy goals. If parents become actively involved in making decisions about what they want to accomplish and the type of literacy program they prefer, they will better appreciate your help and advice (Comer & Hayes, 1991). You may find that the school's parent-teacher organization can help motivate parents in literacy learning.

Making Time for Literacy How families use reading and writing will depend on the parents' interests and experiences. There is no one quick way to involve families. Reading and writing are habits that must be nourished in many ways over a long period of time.

When you talk or write to parents about reading at home, share your ideas for building reading into family time. Encourage families to make time to read to children and to set aside time for individual or partner reading.

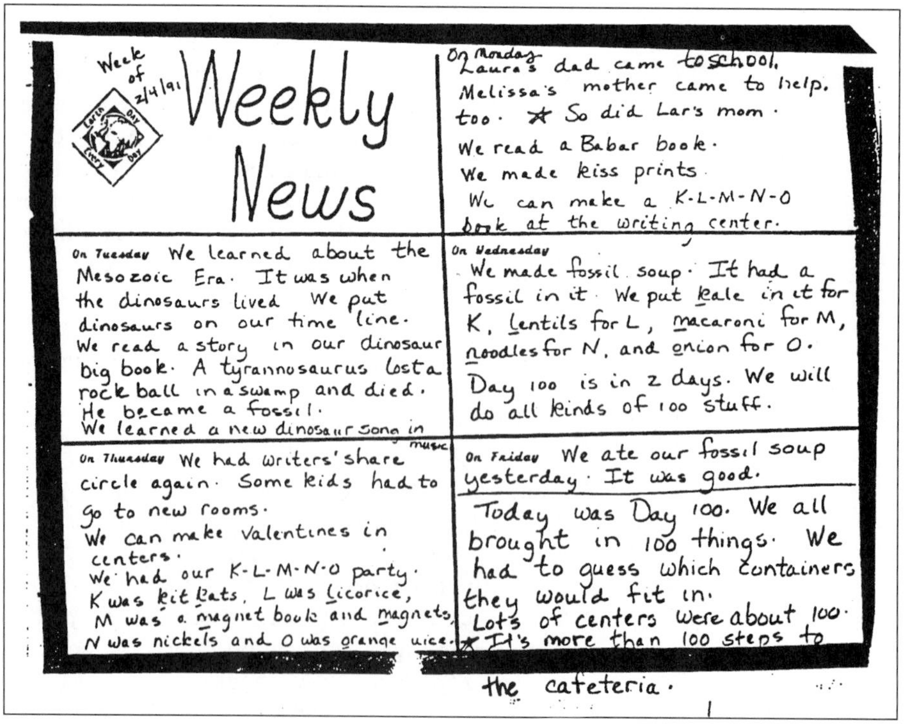
Week of 2/4/91

Weekly News

On Monday Laura's dad came to school. Melissa's mother came to help, too. ★ So did Lar's mom. We read a Babar book. We made kiss prints. We can make a K-L-M-N-O book at the writing center.

On Tuesday We learned about the Mesozoic Era. It was when the dinosaurs lived. We put dinosaurs on our time line. We read a story in our dinosaur big book. A tyrannosaurus lost a rock ball in a swamp and died. He became a fossil. We learned a new dinosaur song in music.

On Wednesday We made fossil soup. It had a fossil in it. We put kale in it for K, lentils for L, macaroni for M, noodles for N, and onion for O. Day 100 is in 2 days. We will do all kinds of 100 stuff.

On Thursday We had writers' share circle again. Some kids had to go to new rooms. We can make Valentines in centers. We had our K-L-M-N-O party. K was kit kats, L was licorice, M was a magnet book and magnets, N was nickels and O was orange uice.

On Friday We ate our fossil soup yesterday. It was good. Today was Day 100. We all brought in 100 things. We had to guess which containers they would fit in. Lots of centers were about 100. ★ It's more than 100 steps to the cafeteria.

Figure 14.1
Student Newsletter
Source: Adapted from Deschenes, Johnson, Poliquin, Potter & Steller (1991).

Send home information about book clubs and book order forms to encourage parents to buy books. Some families will not have books or writing materials around the house. You can help increase the number of books at home by locating sources of free or cheap books. Many service groups sponsor book drives and have books to give away. Yard sales and thrift stores have books at cheap prices. Grocery stores and department stores also offer inexpensive books that parents may purchase (Taylor & Strickland, 1986).

Home writing activities offer a wealth of literacy activities. Parents and children can write notes to family members, birthday and holiday greetings, shopping lists, menus, personal and business letters, answering machine messages, directions, captions for photograph albums, and dates on calendars (Pike, Compain & Mumper, 1994).

Libraries Libraries design programs to promote reading and library use for child-care workers and families. They offer special summer reading programs, storytelling festivals, dial-a-story programs, story reading times, and many other services.

Many libraries have available for two-week checkout kits, backpacks, and tote bags that are a self-contained unit of study. Some of them package dolls, musical instruments, books, and tapes in thematic tote bags, traveling suitcases, and backpacks to support study themes such as colors, frogs, lions, bears, all about me, music, and incredible edibles (Pike, Compain & Mumper, 1994).

Family Literacy Programs Some school systems, libraries, and adult literacy programs have developed family literacy projects and family learning centers to promote family literacy (Morrow, 1995; Morrow, Tracey & Maxwell, 1995). They instruct parents in how to be teachers at home, including book sharing, children's writing, creating home literacy centers, teaching the alphabet, and advice on how parents can help with homework (Shanahan, Mulhern & Rodriguez-Brown, 1995).

School as a Community for Learning

Three aspects by which we assess the effectiveness of schools and classroom instruction are resources in staff and materials, organization of instruction, and educators' knowledge and skills (Corcoran & Goertz, 1995). Let's examine the resources and teaching practices that have been found in literacy-rich classrooms and schools.

Literacy-Rich Classrooms

Key documented factors contribute to literacy-rich classrooms (Barone, 1994). Here is a list of such factors that support children's literacy development in classroom contexts:

1. *Classroom library available to children.* In addition to a school library, each classroom should have its own library. This library should be an attractive display that contains at least four books per child.

Children chatting about the exciting adventures they have had with learning.

2. *Daily sustained silent reading.* One way for children to really become involved with books is through a daily time during which they can read a book of their choice for pleasure. During silent sustained reading, children often choose to curl up in a comfortable spot in the room to read.

3. *Student work displayed.* Students feel like a part of the class when their work is displayed. They feel ownership or attachment to their learning environment.

4. *Daily reading to students by the teacher.* Teachers, even teachers of older students, find time each day to read to students. This helps familiarize young children with books and book language and is often a way to nudge older students to read books that they might never choose on their own.

5. *Student choice of reading materials.* Although teachers sometimes select the books their students will read, students also need opportunities to pick their own books. Choice of reading materials should occur outside of silent sustained reading as well as within it.

6. *Student choice of writing topic.* Students take ownership of their writing when they can write about topics they consider important. This does not exclude you from choosing the topic on occasion.

7. *Journal writing.* Students use a journal as a way to communicate with their teacher. Journals allow students to develop their fluency as writers and to build a trusting relationship with their teacher.

8. *Daily writing.* To become competent writers, students need numerous and consistent writing opportunities. Teachers often provide a daily writing workshop time so that students know that they can return to writing projects on a routine basis.

9. *Literature discussion groups.* Discussions enrich students' understandings of the books they are reading. In discussion groups, students can evaluate books and ideas and talk about points of agreement or disagreement.

10. *Written responses to literature.* In addition to talking about books, children should also write about the books they are reading. They may discover new insights or personal connections to books.

11. *Children involved in literacy projects.* Teachers extend a book experience by involving students in related projects such as big books or murals modeled on the book.

12. *Integrated reading and writing.* In literacy-rich classrooms, it is hard to distinguish when students are exploring reading or writing. Each of these is intertwined with the other as students use reading to generate writing and writing to extend reading.

13. *Thematically organized instruction.* Teachers pursue content in more depth by organizing their instruction around themes. Through this organization, they integrate all of the language arts to give students varied views of concepts.

14. *Children organized in flexible groupings.* Teachers informally and formally organize students to support instruction goals. Students might work alone, with a partner, in triads, in homogeneous groups, or in heterogeneous groups.

15. *Children working cooperatively.* Teachers support a cooperative ethic in the classroom. Students are encouraged to work productively with other students.

You have encountered the factors listed above throughout your study of this textbook. Now that they are familiar, read through the list one more time and think about how you might include each in your classroom. Visualize what your room might look like with your students working in a studio atmosphere as they learn to read and write.

Schoolwide Literacy Programs

Schoolwide literacy programs are designed to serve children across classrooms and grades. They give children extra practice in reading, writing, and word study. Most programs are designed to help children who are a little behind; others provide enrichment (Pikulski, 1994).

Title I Title I, a federally funded program, is common in schools that serve low-income children. Title I has been in the schools since 1965 and was designed to provide extra instruction in reading and mathematics. In most Title I programs children leave the regular classroom to work with a Title I teacher.

Reading Recovery Reading Recovery is a reading program from New Zealand that targets the lowest 20 percent of first-graders (Clay, 1985; Pinnell, Lyons, DeFord, Bryk & Seltzer, 1994). Students meet individually with a teacher for no more than thirty minutes daily for between twelve and twenty weeks. Each session includes five major activities:

1. Students reread familiar books.

2. The teacher observes independent reading.

3. The student writes with the teacher's help.

4. The teacher introduces a new book to the student.

5. The teacher guides the student through letter activities.

This program uses a variety of little books arranged by difficulty (Smith-Burke & Jaggar, 1994). These books resemble the pattern books we discussed in Chapter 7.

Success for All This is a comprehensive schoolwide program that features instruction in groups of fifteen to twenty students in a daily ninety-minute period. Components of the program include a listening comprehension program, the STAR program (story telling and retelling), and Beyond the Basics, the follow-up to the beginning reading program. Beyond the Basics is a cooperative and heterogeneous reading, writing, and language arts program of activities to accompany a basal reading series. Success for All includes process writing and writers' workshops in their Writing From the Heart program. It also contains a family literacy program component.

This program is in use in more than 300 schools, particularly in large school districts and low-income school settings. One of its strengths, according to the developers, is its staff development component (Slavin, 1996; Slavin, Madden, Karweit, Dolan & Wasik, 1996).

Literacy Programs with Tutors Many teachers set up tutorial writing clubs and homework groups as extensions of their classroom activities. Some programs accompany after-school child-care programs that meet at school. Many tutoring programs use students from neighboring middle and high schools and colleges and members of local service organizations as tutors (Hiebert & Taylor, 1994; Juel, 1994).

In these programs, trained tutors guide children in reading and writing. Some programs focus on students who have difficulty reading and writing, and others are more like extracurricular reading clubs. Some tutors meet with students during the school day, and others meet with children after school (Caserta-Henry, 1996; Invernizzi, Juel & Rosemary, 1997; Invernizzi, Johnston & Juel, 1995).

Growing as a Professional

Once you leave your college or university and begin your career as a teacher, you will want to keep growing as a professional. As you gain confidence through successful classroom experience, you will be ready to take on new challenges in your teaching and learning community. It's important, too, to keep up with the latest discoveries about literacy development and learning. Remember, you don't want interns or student teachers to complain that you lack the latest knowledge about learning. You will need energy and commitment to keep current and take new risks with teaching. The excitement of learning and teaching will keep you energized and motivated through this lifelong process.

Following are two broad categories that will help frame ways of growing as a professional. The first category explores self-initiated and implemented methods to extend your knowledge of teaching and learning. The second category of methods requires support from others to extend your knowledge of teaching and learning.

Extending Your Knowledge of Teaching and Learning on Your Own

Throughout this book we've maintained the importance of observing and reflecting on your students' learning and teaching. We have also advocated turning this same level of observation and reflection inward to your own teaching and learning. Here are several ways to practice this reflection.

Reflective Strategies

Journals We have often heard teachers comment about keeping a journal in which they record their thoughts or feelings about teaching and learning. At the end of most days, these teachers jot down important accomplishments, questions, and concerns triggered by their day in the classroom. Periodically, they comb through these journals to look for patterns. They might discover that they often complain about a particular student. Noticing several of these observations, a teacher might develop a plan to change the situations that cause problems for the student and frustration for the teacher. In such a journal you might notice that several students have asked to read a particular book and decide to form a literature discussion group centered on this book. The journal offers a systematic way to reflect on previous classroom learning situations and consider potential changes in teaching and learning.

Videotaping or Audiotaping Another strategy that allows for reflection on teaching and learning is to videotape or audiotape yourself as you interact with students. Later, you can view or listen in on yourself in the process of teaching. Note the quality and frequency of your talk compared to student talk. Reflect on your interaction with a student during reading and writing to see how you worked together.

Videotaping and audiotaping also allow you to observe the learning that is occurring in small groups while you are working with other students. You can review literature discussions or peer response groups, for instance, as another means to evaluate the strengths and needs of your students and yourself.

Reading Professional Books or Journal Articles An important way to keep abreast of developments in literacy is to read current professional books or journal articles. Visit your college or university bookstore and see what is required reading in other education classes. The university or college library has current articles and journals, or you may decide to subscribe to one of the journals that you find most valuable.

Trying New Strategies in Your Classroom

After you start teaching, you will read about new strategies to try in your classroom. We recommend that you try one new strategy at a time. If you try several all at once, you may wind up overwhelmed and your students frustrated with all of the changes. If the new strategy requires you to revamp your room or to dramatically change the way you teach or evaluate students, let your principal know what you are trying and enlist support for the process.

After you have implemented your new strategy for a while, stand back and decide if it is successful and contributes positively to your students' learning. Include your students in this evaluation: Have them talk or write about the strategy's success. For example, if you have your students tutor other students as a way to increase their reading and writing abilities, ask them what they think of this process. Remember that at first they will probably focus more on the difficulties; allow them several opportunities for reflections as this process becomes more familiar.

Extending Your Knowledge of Teaching and Learning with Support from Others

Although it is important to implement new ideas and strategies within your class and to reflect on your own teaching and the learning of your students, remember to include others in your process of professional growth. These outside partnerships can be as informal as working with another teacher and as formal as entering a graduate program.

Collaborating with Another Colleague

Working with another teacher can be a pleasant way to enrich your teaching. Often in these partnerships two teachers implement the same new strategy so that they can support one another during the process of change. Teachers also observe in each other's classrooms to learn from each other and to coach each other in new strategies. Such relationships offer teachers a peer to help with the often difficult process of change as well as a true collaborative, professional relationship. They also enhance the children's learning.

E-mail and Web sites have broadened and enhanced discussion among teachers. Groups are organized for multiaged schools, literacy, and student-centered work, to name just a few.

Joining Professional Organizations

Many groups of teachers have formed professional organizations to support teaching and learning. We recommend that you join at least one organization and become part of the professional community in a larger sense than within your own school. These organizations usually hold annual conferences where speakers share teaching strategies or research. Many organizations also publish books and journals that contain everything from practical advice to research articles. These organizations are most focused on literacy: The International Reading Association, 800 Barksdale Rd., Newark, DE 19714; National Council of Teachers of English, 1111 West Kenyon Rd., Urbana, IL 61801.

Attending Classes or Workshops

Teachers who have just finished a teacher education program may be reluctant to jump right into a graduate program, but one way to stay current is to attend classes offered by the university or the school district. When you are ready for further education, look for classes that focus on one topic that relates directly to your students and you. You might find a class on poetry and student poetry writing, or on portfolios, informal assessment, or other topics. These classes support you as you try new strategies in your classroom.

Working on Advanced Degrees

Many teachers embark on a graduate program to further their professional development. Graduate programs provide a systematic investigation of literacy that builds on prior knowledge and practical experience. Teachers make a more thorough investigation into their personal questions about literacy and enjoy the support of a community of learners that includes teaching colleagues and professors.

Teacher as Researcher

As you become an integral member of the profession, you may choose to address the questions that are most important to you by conducting research within your own classroom. Patterson, Santa, Short, and Smith (1993, p. 10) state that "reflection, inquiry, and action are interrelated in teacher research because teachers act as thinkers, learners, and practitioners throughout their studies." This multifaceted view of learning and teaching helps us all learn more about literacy. Your investigations will serve to enhance your joy and love of learning as you seek to understand the complexities involved in learning. You may succeed in having your work published and add to the knowledge of literacy development and learning. Then you will have come full circle and become not only a consumer of research but also a contributor.

The process of teaching and learning has no ending, and it never reaches completion. As a teacher, you will constantly and consistently evaluate your teaching and your students' learning. You will always be revising the teaching and learning community that you have cocreated with your students. This process will help you avoid burnout and instead be constantly revitalized as a teacher.

Conclusion and Study Notes

High-quality instruction is a combination of daily teaching practices and assessment techniques (Corcoran & Goertz, 1995; Newman, Marks & Gamoran, 1995). This thread has connected all the chapters in this book. Knowing that, and knowing the tools and techniques distilled in this book from the work of many fine educators, qualifies you, and, we hope, inspires you with the desire and confidence to sit beside students to understand and guide them in integrated assessment and instruction.

We thank you for letting us sit beside you as you read this book. We wish you great success in your teaching.

Glossary

accented syllables   A syllable in a polysyllabic word that is emphasized or stressed. Compare the accents in these homographs: **pre**sent and pre**sent**. Students in the syllable juncture phase examine accented syllables and then pay close attention to the unaccented syllables.

achievement tests   A test that measures the extent to which a person has mastery over a certain body of information or possesses a certain skill after instruction has taken place.

acquired difficulties   A student who has an acquired difficulty has often had some brain injury that interferes with reading, writing, or spelling.

adjustments in test taking   Teachers make adjustments in test taking activities for students who have difficulties learning to read and write who are somewhat or significantly behind. Giving the student more time, having the test read to the students, and altering the way students show their knowledge are ways in which teachers adjust tests for students with reading and writing difficulties.

aesthetic reading   Responses to books that are most focused on the personal aspects of the story; the personal connections.

alexia   Complete inability to read written texts, usually resulting in a loss of a previously acquired skill.

anticipation guide   Anticipation guides are developed by the teacher to be considered before students begin to read nonfiction text. They consist of a series of statements that students discuss before reading.

assessment   The assessment process is one of sitting beside students to guide their growth. Assessment is broader than teacher-made, end-of-the-chapter, or standardized tests. It involves observing students' growth in the normal course of classroom activities, projects, units of study, and special programs.

bilingual   A person who can read, write, and speak in at least two languages.

bilingualism   Students who can speak or understand two languages are bilingual; proficiency in the second language varies with the student's experience.

books on tape   Students who have difficulty reading their texts and assignments benefit from books on tape. The Library of Congress and Recordings for the Blind and Dyslexic develop materials on tape. There are also many commercial books on tape available in libraries and bookstores.

choral reading   Teachers and students read a text aloud together. Usually, teachers use choral reading as a support reading activity with beginning readers. Students choral read big books, experience charts, and familiar rhymes.

closed sort   Word sorts that classify words into predetermined categories.

closed syllables   Closed syllables are short vowels that close with a consonant sound. In polysyllabic words, a closed syllable is closed by two consonants (*pebble, travel*). Students examine closed syllables in the syllable juncture phase of spelling. (See open syllables.)

communicative speech   Language that is focused on communication.

concept of story   The knowledge students have of how stories are organized. This framework underlying concept of story includes students' knowledge of the structures of various types of stories.

concept of word   The ability to match spoken words to printed words as demonstrated by the ability to point to the words of a memorized text while reading. This demonstration must include one or more two-syllable words.

concept sort   Children sort pictures based on similarities.

consonant doubling   In polysyllabic words in English, consonants are doubled to show that the vowel is short *(pushing* and *bunny* are short vowels with double consonants; compare to *hotel* and *looked* where the consonants in the middle are not doubled). Students in the syllable juncture stage of spelling compare and contrast two-syllable words that double consonants and those that do not (*hop/hopping; time/timing*).

consonant-vowel-consonant   Consonant-vowel-consonant (CVC) spelling patterns are short vowel patterns studied by beginning readers in the letter name phase of spelling.

content dictations   Content dictations are individual dictations developed by students which summarize and discuss what they have learned from having a text read to them or in a classroom experience. This type of dictation is part of the language experience approach with older students who are beginning and early transitional readers. Rereading these dictations promotes fluency, vocabulary development, and involves the student in content area studies.

content guided-reading-thinking activity   The content GRTA is different from a GRTA in that students decide what they know and don't know about a topic before reading. Students preview the nonfiction material before reading it to build background knowledge.

coping   Coping strategies are used by students who have difficulty reading the assigned texts and in writing as well as one needs to do well in a course of study. These strategies include tape recording lectures, using books on tape, and finding alternative ways to show what one has learned.

culture   Culture consists of knowledge, concepts, and values shared by group members through systems of communication. Culture also consists of the shared beliefs, symbols, and interpretations within a human group.

deficits   Students who experience permanent difficulties that deprive them of an adequate level of functioning are said to experience a deficit. Learning will be limited by the deficit, and is not usually overcome. Rarely are a student's reading difficulties attributed to a deficit. (Compare to developmental delay.)

derivational constancy   The last phase of spelling development in which spellers learn about derivational relationships preserved in the spelling of words. *Derivational* refers to (1) the process by which new words are created from existing words and (2) the development of a word from its historical origin.

developmental continuum   There is continuum of development observed in the elementary classroom. Most students are reading at the expected instructional level for that grade level and time of year. Along this developmental continuum, some students are slightly behind, and others are somewhat behind, and a few students are significantly behind.

developmental delay   A student who experiences a developmental delay lags behind his or her classmates, and is behind where teachers and parents may expect the child to be. Developmental delays in reading are often related to delays in language learning, and physical maturation generally.

developmental descriptions   A student's literacy development is described in terms of phases of reading, writing, and spelling development.

diagnostic tests   An age-related, norm-referenced assessment of skills and behaviors that children have acquired (compared to children of the same chronological age). Sometimes such tests are inaccurately called developmental screening tests.

dialogical-thinking reading lesson   This format facilitates students' critical thinking. Students are expected to think critically about moral, social, and political issues related to what they are reading.

dialogue journals   Journals where students can freely write about their reactions, feelings, or questions about a book and the teacher writes in response to the content of the writing.

directionality of print   Children discover that print has directionality. In English, writing goes from the left to the right and from the top to bottom of a page.

discourse   The way language is organized beyond the sentence level. How paragraphs and longer pieces of writing are typically organized.

disfluency   A type of reading characterized by a slow reading rate, hesitancy, and lack of phrasing. The oral reading of beginning readers is often described as disfluent and word-by-word.

dyslexia   Dyslexia is a rare but definable reading disability. There is no one test to assess dyslexia; such an assessment requires a good deal of familiarity with the student and his or her learning. Either an acquired or inherited organic difficulty underlies dyslexia. A dyslexic's reading development is severely limited to, at best, a late transitional phase or a mid-fourth grade level. Many nonprofessionals and some professionals think that one in ten students are dyslexic. This view of dyslexia is more like what is called a significant type of reading difficulty.

efferent reading   Responses to books that are most focused on the elements of the story or the plot; the literal aspects of a story.

emergent literacy   Literacy development ranging from birth to beginning reading. This phase of literacy development corresponds to the prephonemic phases of word knowledge.

etymology   The study of the origin and historical development of words.

experienced-based question   To answer a question, it is necessary to move beyond the text and use personal past experience.

expository text   Nonfiction or informational text.

expressive mode   Readers enter the expressive mode when they take the materials in a text and compare and contrast them with their own lives. Students reenact materials in the expressive mode when materials are confusing and need to be interpreted in the context of their personal lives and experiences. (See participant role.)

factual comprehension questions   To check comprehension, a few factual questions are asked after students have read a graded passage in an informal reading inventory. Factual questions test relatively low levels of understanding.

Fernald technique   Grace Fernald was a reading educator during the first half of the twentieth century. She is known for having developed a multisensory or VAKT approach to teaching children to read. This technique complements the language experience approach as it makes use of the student's dictation. This approach includes an analytic phonics approach. It is a remedial technique that helps beginning readers who have very special difficulties acquire a sight vocabulary.

fluency   The ability to read words with accuracy and appropriate speed.

formal testing   Formal testing is testing that teachers or other experts administer to students to determine reading ability or intelligence for example. The results of these tests are based on right or wrong answers. Individual scores are interpreted against national norms.

frustration level   A student reading, writing, and spelling at a frustration level is reading, writing, and learning to spell with materials and assignments that are too difficult. Student's work is inaccurate and slow. The teacher replaces frustration level materials and assignments with instructional and independent level materials and activities.

full concept of word   A beginning reader who has a full or functional concept of word finger point reads a familiar text accurately, and when a teacher points to words in the middle of the text, the student can identify the word immediately. Students with a full concept of word are usually in the letter name phase of spelling, and they are able to reread two or three paragraph stories and dictations accurately.

functional descriptions of literacy   A functional description of literacy describes how a student reads particular materials. Grade levels are one type of functional description.

gender   Gender consists of the socially and psychologically appropriate behavior for males and females sanctioned and expected within a society.

generativity principle   The ability to represent new words by using a fixed amount of letters.

Greek and Latin roots   Many words contain roots that are traced to Greek and Latin words (**therm**ometer and dis**sect**, respectively).

group experience charts   Each child in a small group of beginning readers dictates one and two-sentence descriptions of a language experience. The teacher writes these sentences on a chart and rereads them with the children.

guided reading-thinking activity   An activity that provides a sense of students' involvement and comprehension of stories. Students predict what might happen in a story based on events that have already occurred.

hyperlexia   People with hyperlexia are able to read texts from an early age even though they have severe language and cognitive delays in development. This syndrome is quite rare. Students with hyperlexia read in a sing-song manner without comprehension.

independent level   An independent level is the level at which a student can read, write, and spell comfortably and easily. A student can work independently when the materials are at the student's independent level.

individual dictations   Beginning readers dictate a few sentences to three paragraphs describing a language experience. The teacher types the dictation and the students draw pictures to go with their individual dictations. These dictations are reread frequently to promote fluency and to help students develop their sight vocabularies.

individualized educational plan   An individualized instructional plan usually prepared for students who qualify for special education services.

inferential comprehension questions   Inferential questions are asked of students after they have read a passage in an informal reading inventory. Inferential questions test a student's ability to understand a text by fitting together information that is not explicitly stated in the text.

informal testing   Informal testing is testing that teachers administer to students to learn about students' abilities with reading for example. In informal testing, teachers can interpret the results and use these results as a basis for instruction. Teachers look for more than right and wrong answers.

instructional level   An instructional is the level at which a student can read, write, and spell with good accuracy and moderate fluency. A teacher's guidance is helpful when a student is involved in reading and writing activities at an instructional level.

integrated model of literacy   The only model of literacy that considers reading, writing, and spelling development and highlights the synchrony among these areas. Also called the synchrony model of literacy development.

interest inventory   An inventory or list of questions that allow you to become familiar with students' interests, both personal and school related.

interpretation   Teachers are negotiators when they explain student learning to others. In this role, teachers explain student work that has been observed and documented.

journals   Journals are kept by students as artists keep sketch books. Student write in them regularly and they usually record events in their lives. Students often choose their own topics for writing, and rarely are journals corrected.

K-W-L   A strategy to engage students in reading. In the K part, students list what they know about a topic. In the W part, students list what they would like to learn about a topic. In the L part, students list what they learned.

Lake Wobegon effect   The effect where more than 50 percent of school districts report the results of their standardized test scores as being above average.

language difficulties   Students who have difficulty processing in one of the language systems has a language difficulty. These language difficulties often make it difficult for students to learn to read, write, or spell. The language difficulties that are most often related to reading difficulties are in the phonological and orthographic language systems.

language experience approach   In this approach, children get to see their speech converted into print. Teachers use the oral discussion of students to form a story or text.

language experiences   These experiences are the basis for group and individual dictations from beginning readings. When a powerful experience is the basis for language, students create memorable language and build this language and experience into reading materials.

learning disability   Students with learning disabilities often have difficulties learning to read and write. This is often the case with students who have language related learning disabilities. While learning disabled students are often behind in their reading, they do learn how to read in much the same way as other learners.

lesson plan activities   Lesson plans in literacy involve a variety of activities that include reading to, reading with, writing with, and word study with students.

letter name   The third phase of spelling development when children start representing beginning, middle, and ending sounds of words with phonetically accurate letter choices. Often the selections are based on the sound of the letter name itself, rather than abstract letter-sound associations.

lexicon   The dictionary of words that a person possesses in his or her memory.

list-group-label   This strategy is used to engage students' prior knowledge. Students sort and classify vocabulary related to a unit of study.

literacy biography   A detailed description of a students' literacy history and current functioning. These biographies are used as part of a student's assessment.

literal comprehension questions   To check comprehension, literal questions are one type of question often asked of students after they have read a passage in an informal reading inventory. These questions test a student's ability to use the facts to answer questions that make direct use of the information in the text.

literature logs   Journals where students can freely write about their reactions, feelings, or questions about a book.

logs   Logs are records of what students learn and observe. Students may record their observations during and after a field trip in a learning log.

long vowels   Vowel sounds in words like the *a* in *cake*, *e* in *read*, *i* in *hide*, *o* in *coat*, and *u* in *blue*.

manner and point of articulation   The way sounds are articulated guides students as they spell. Some invented spellings are substitutions that are made with articulation in mind (*drive* spelled as *JRF*).

median   The score which half of the scores fall above and half fall below.

morphology   The study of structure and forms of words including derivation, inflection, and compounding.

multicultural   Classrooms are multicultural settings where students from a variety of cultures learn together daily. The multicultural nature of our schools makes it necessary to know how students' perceptions and manners are shaped by their experiences in their cultures at home.

multisensory approaches   Some reading educators use multisensory approaches to teach students with difficulties. These educators involve the student in kinesthetic and tactile experiences with letters and words. The Orton-Gillingham approach and the Fernald technique are two examples of multisensory approaches of teaching students about the structure of words and writing. There is the assumption that the greater the involvement of the other senses, the easier learning becomes.

no-book DRTA   An activity that helps teachers understand what students already know about a topic. Students would be asked to list everything that they think might be in a book. Once items are listed, students are asked to group them and provide a name for each group.

noncommunicative speech   Language that is created just for the pleasure of hearing it.

norm-referenced tests   Norm-referenced tests are formal measures used to assess a concept of skill. They include achievement and diagnostic tests. Students' scores are compared to other people's scores in a specified group.

normal distribution   A normal distribution assumes the median of a distribution is the point where 50 percent of the scores fall above and below it.

norms   Statistics or data that summarize the test performance of specified groups such as test takers of various ages or grades.

note taking   Students learn how to take notes while they read. In doing so, they rehearse what they are learning, and have a lasting record for studying. Note taking is also a skill that students practice while listening to a class lecture. Students learn how to write down the most salient information in a way that is efficient and complete.

observation   To observe means to perceive or notice and to watch attentively. Teachers use observation to focus in on the learning strengths and strategies that students use in their reading and writing.

open sort   A type of picture or word sort in which the categories for sorting are left open. Students sort pictures or words into groups based on their own judgment.

open syllables   Open syllables end with a long vowel (*table, fusion*). Students examine open syllables in the syllable juncture phase of spelling. (See closed syllables.)

oral reading accuracy   There are four types of oral reading errors that are counted as reading errors: omissions, substitutions, additions, and help from the teacher. Oral reading accuracy is obtained by dividing the numbers of words read correctly by the number of words in the passage. A 97 percent accuracy rate is often described as a criterion for independent level reading.

orthographic knowledge   Orthographic knowledge refers to the writing system of a language, specifically the correct sequence of letters, characters, or symbols.

paralinguistics   How language is communicated nonverbally. The signs, gestures, facial expressions that parallel oral communication.

participant role   When students read texts critically they are engaged in the participant role. Readers in the participant role interact with the text to learn specific information and to be persuaded. (Contrast with spectator role. See also transactional mode and expressive mode.)

pattern books   The language in pattern books repeat phrase and sentence patterns. These books are used with beginning readers for support in reading fluency.

peer editing group   Students work in groups with other students to offer suggestions for editing.

peer response group   Students work in groups with other students to offer suggestions for revision.

percentile   Raw scores are converted to percentiles so that comparisons can be made. Percentiles range from 1 to 99 with 1 being the lowest and 99 the highest.

perseverance   Perseverance is a personal quality that students who are significantly behind in their reading have as they find ways to complete classroom assignments in spite of their difficulties. By the end of sixth grade, students with severe and limiting reading difficulties need to be able to initiate conversations with teachers about alternative assignments for their learning.

personal readers   These individual books are composed of familiar reading materials that beginning readers reread regularly. Personal readers contain typed group experience charts, dictations, and copies of pattern books' rhymes.

phases of reading, writing, and spelling development   Students' literacy development has been described in terms of five phases of development: (1) emergent reading and writing and prephonemic spelling, (2) beginning reading and writing and semiphonemic and letter-name spelling, (3) transitional reading and writing and within-word pattern spelling, (4) intermediate reading and writing, and syllable juncture spelling, and (5) advanced reading and writing and derivational constancy spelling.

phases of spelling development   In learning to read and write, you can observe students' development by looking at students' spelling. Six phases of spelling development are described—prephonemic, semiphonemic, letter name, within word pattern, syllable juncture, and derivational constancy. See individual entries.

phonology   The study of speech sounds and their functions in a language.

planning and organization   After teachers have observed and interpreted the learning strengths and needs of their student, they plan instruction and organize learning events. Planning and organization can be long-term (yearly), monthly, weekly, and daily.

poetic mode   Poetry and fairy tales are written in the poetic mode. Generally, texts written in the poetic mode are fiction and emphasize the aesthetics in the presentation. (Compare to the transactional mode and the spectator role.)

portfolio   Portfolios serve as places to collect evidence of a student's literacy development. They may include artifacts collected by the student, teacher, or parents both at home or at school.

pragmatics   How paralinguistics, discourse, and appropriateness interrelate.

preconsonantal nasals   Nasals that occur before consonants, as in the words bump or pink. The vowel is nasalized as part of the air escapes through the nose during pronunciation.

predictable text   Predictable books that are written with rhythm, rhyme, and repetition in mind.

prephonemic   The first phase of spelling development before letter-sound correspondences are learned and coordinated with printed word boundaries. This spelling phase coincides with the emergent period of literacy development.

QARs   A strategy where students determine the demands of a question before answering it. Questions are (1) right there, (2) think and search, (3) author and you, and (4) on your own.

qualitative analysis of oral reading   In a qualitative analysis of oral reading, the teacher examines the student's miscues to see how the different language systems were used in reading. Miscues reflect a student's use of language systems, particularly the semantic, syntactic, and orthographic systems.

Quintilian   Quintilian was a teacher who lived in the first century. He taught Roman children rhetoric and literacy.

race   Race is a socially determined category that is related to physical characteristics in a complex way.

rationale for an activity   The rationale for an activity is a statement of how an activity matches students' literacy development and why the activity will be useful and interesting.

raw score   The actual number of right answers achieved.

readers theater   Readers theater is a simple form of dramatics that can be easily implemented in the classroom. Students read from a script or a story to an audience.

reading comprehension   In an informal assessment, teachers ask questions and have students retell what they read. A student's functional reading level is determined, in part, by how well the student has comprehended. A student who answers 70 percent of the comprehension questions correctly is probably reading materials at his or her instructional level.

reading difficulties   Students who do not read as well as they need or want to are said to experience a reading difficulty. These difficulties range in severity from a student with a rare neurologic disability to the student who is slightly behind.

reading guides   Guides that are structured by teachers to facilitate students' reading of nonfiction material. They focus on the content and the process of reading.

reading rate   Reading rates increase as student's literacy develops. Rate is usually described in terms of words per minute (words ÷ seconds × 60).

reading workshops   Reading workshop is often a whole class time when students read together. Students read independently or work with a partner during this period. Teachers help students create guidelines for reading together.

reciprocal teaching   A strategy that facilitates comprehension. Reciprocal teaching involves the modeling of questioning, summarizing, and predicting.

recurring principle   Children learn that a limited amount of letters appear in words again and again.

reliability   The degree to which test scores are consistent, dependable, or repeatable—that is, the degree to which test scores can be attributed to actual differences in test takers' performance rather than to errors of measurement.

repeated readings   Students reread a text numerous times. The goal of repeated readings is to improve fluency.

ReQuest   A strategy that facilitates comprehension. Students are expected to (1) develop questions about the material they are reading, (2) adopt an inquiring, curious attitude about what they are reading, (3) develop purposes for reading, and (4) improve independent, silent comprehension.

response logs   In response logs students focus their attention on what they have read and respond to one idea, one observation, or one passage. Often, students compare the text to their own experiences and their thoughts about what they thought would happen in a story.

retelling   Teachers analyze students' retellings to understand reading comprehension. In examining the quality of retellings, teachers look at the number of events or feelings recalled, how the students interpret the message, and how students use details or make inferences to substantiate ideas.

rhythm of language   The combination of speech and breathing creates the rhythm of language. The rhythm of language is structured at a phrase level.

rudimentary concept of word   A student who has a rudimentary concept of word is able to point accurately to the words of a familiar text, but when a teacher points to words in the middle of the text, the student is unable to read the word immediately. Students with a rudimentary concept of word are early beginning readers and are usually in the semiphonemic phase of spelling.

scanning   Scanning is a reading technique in which the reader looks through a designated area of a text for specific information about a topic. Scanning may begin with an index search that leads the reader to the relevant area(s) of the text. Intermediate and advanced readers develop scanning as an important reading style for informational texts. (See skimming.)

schemas   One way to describe the way information is organized in our minds.

semiphonemic   The second phase of spelling development when children start representing initial and final consonants. This spelling phase coincides with the beginning reading period of literacy development.

shared reading   Shared reading is a teaching practice conducted with small groups of beginning readers to guide them through a big book. Students make predictions about the story based on prior knowledge and picture cues, and the teacher uses the text to show students print conventions like punctuation, and uses the text for word study as when the teacher draws students' attention to orthographic patterns.

short vowels   Vowel sounds in words like the *a* in *hat*, *e* in *red*, *i* in *hit*, *o* in *pot*, and *u* in *hut*.

short-vowel word families   These families are made up of orthographic patterns that follow a CVC pattern and which rhyme; e.g., *-at*, *-id*, *-op*. Students in the letter name stage of spelling study these orthographic patterns.

skimming   To obtain an overview of a text, readers skim text quickly to understand the main ideas and the organization of the material. Students read headings, bold print, figures, and tables. This step precedes careful reading. Intermediate and advanced readers develop skimming as an important reading style for informational texts. (See scanning.)

social class   Social class is a complex term to define as societies. Historically, characteristics that defined the low socioeconomic status in the United States are now considered characteristics of the middle class. The indices that are most frequently used to determine membership in the low-, middle-, or upper class are income, education, occupation, lifestyle, and values.

spectator role   When students read fiction they are reading in the spectator role. While reading, the reality of the events are not questioned as long as they are clearly presented. Readers experience the emotional content of the writing, but, in a sense, watch as a spectator as the events of a story unfold. (Contrast with participant role.)

spelling assessments   Spelling assessments include an analysis of what words students spell correctly as well as the invented or temporary spellings. The results of a spelling assessment are usually expressed in terms of a phase of spelling development.

spelling-meaning connection   There is a powerful relationship between the spelling and the meaning of words. Students in the syllable juncture and derivational constancy phases of spelling study the meaning connection in the way words are spelled (e.g., syllable juncture students study prefixes and suffixes; derivational constancy students study roots: *sign, signature, signal*). (See etymology.)

stanine   Stanines are similar to percentiles except that the distribution is divided into groups of nine. Stanines are broader than percentiles. Stanines range from 1 to 9 with 1 being the lowest and 9 the highest.

strategic reading   Intermediate and advanced readers develop strategies which they use to read different materials for different purposes. Strategic readers ask themselves how they plan to read and learn the material before they read. Strategic readers also are careful to stop periodically to check their effectiveness as readers.

student-guided reading groups   Students work in pairs to organize and run a GRTA. After a few months of being involved in teacher-guided reading groups, intermediate readers learn to run their own reading groups. Partners select a text, find stopping points, and run a GRTA with their peers in a 30-minute reading session.

study skills   Study skills include the practices and strategies learners use to master the text they are reading for their particular needs. Study skills involve some sort of rehearsal of the materials through outlining, skimming, scanning, careful reading, reflection, and review.

support reading materials   These are materials that are written in a way that makes them memorable for rereading. Support materials combine repeating phrases, refrains, and rhyming patterns to provide support. Support materials are used by beginning readers.

syllable juncture   The fifth phase of spelling development, which coincides with intermediate or advanced reading. Syllable juncture spellers learn about the spelling changes that often take place at the point of transition from one syllable to the next.

synchrony   Occurring at the same time. Phases of spelling development are described in the context of reading and writing behaviors occurring at the same time.

syntax   The study of how sentences are formed and of the grammatical rules that govern their formation.

ten-minute write   Writing that is guided by a teacher as to topic and time as a way of evaluating students' writing.

text-explicit question   The answer to a question is right in the text.

text-implicit question   The answer to a question is not directly stated in the text.

timed reading   Timed readings are a variation of repeated readings. Students read the same passage or poem over again until they reach their target reading rate.

transactional mode   Informational or expository texts are written in this mode. When students read expository texts they interact with text, questioning its accuracy and utility. (See also participant role.)

traumatic brain injury   A trauma to the brain that results in permanent difficulties in processing information.

understanding   Understanding of what we read comes through an interactive process at many levels of language and thinking, and includes the orchestration of language and literacy, literal comprehension, and higher level thinking.

utility   The relative value of usefulness of an outcome as compared to other possible outcomes.

VAKT   VAKT stands for visual-auditory-kinesthetic-tactile, and describes a multisensory approach to teaching students who are significantly behind in learning to read and write. The Fernald and the Orton-Gillingham are VAKT approaches.

validity   The degree to which a test measures what it purports to measure.

vocabulary   The knowledge of the meaning and use of words determine one's vocabulary. A reading vocabulary is comprised of words students understand and can read.

vocabulary comprehension questions   To check comprehension, vocabulary questions are asked of students after they have read a passage in an informal reading inventory. These questions test a student's background knowledge and ability to use context to figure out the meaning of a word.

within-word pattern   The fourth phase of spelling development, which coincides with the transitional period of literacy development. Within-word pattern spellers have mastered the basic letter-sound correspondences of written English, and they grapple with letter sequences that function as a unit, especially long vowel patterns.

word bank   A collection of words that beginning readers know at sight and which they use in word study. These words are harvested from familiar texts like rhymes and individual dictations. The short term word bank contains words from the most recent text placed in the student's personal reader. The short term word bank is kept in a bag or envelope attached to the personal reader. The long term word bank is kept in a small container or file box.

word posters   Word posters are collections of words grouped around a theme.

word recognition in isolation   An informal measure of word recognition in isolation is part of many informal reading inventories. Students read words in isolation from graded word lists. A student's performance shows what words a student can read at sight as well as how the student analyzes words structurally.

writing workshops   Students write individually and/or collaboratively with partners. Writing workshops are held regularly in the elementary classroom to give students extended periods of time to go through all of the steps of the writing process.

Children's References

Recommended predictable books

Brown, M. (1957). *Goodnight moon.* New York: Harper & Row.

Carle, E. (1969). *The very hungry caterpillar.* Cleveland: Collins-World.

Fox, M. (1986). *Hattie and the fox.* New York: Bantam Doubleday Dell.

Galdone, P. (1975). *Henny penny.* New York: Houghton Mifflin.

Keats, E.J. (1972). *Over in the meadow.* New York: Four Winds.

Kent, J. (1971). *The fat cat.* New York: Scholastic.

Martin, B. (1967). *Brown bear, brown bear, what do you see?* New York: Holt, Rinehart, and Winston.

Mesler, J., & Cowley, J. (1980). *In a dark, dark wood.* New Zealand: Wright Group.

Seuling, B. (1976). *Teeny-tiny woman.* New York: Greenwillow.

Tafuri, N. (1984). *Have you seen my duckling?* New York: Greenwillow.

Recommended wordless books

Alexander, M. (1970). *Bobo's dream.* New York: Dial.

Day, A. (1985). *Good dog, Carl.* La Jolla, CA: Green Tiger.

DePaola, T. (1978). *Pancakes for breakfast.* San Diego: Harcourt Brace Jovanovich.

Hutchins, P. (1968). *Rosie's walk.* New York: Macmillan.

Martin, R. (1989). *Will's mammoth.* New York: Putnam.

Mayer, M. (1967). *A boy, a dog, and a frog.* New York: Dial.

Mayer, M. (1977). *Oops.* New York: Dial.

McCully, E. (1984). *Picnic.* New York: Harper & Row.

Turkle, B. (1976). *Deep in the forest.* New York: Dutton.

Wiesner, D. (1991) *Tuesday.* New York: Clarion.

Recommended alphabet books

Brent, I. (1993). *An alphabet of animals.* New York: Little, Brown.

Ehlert, L. (1989). *Eating the alphabet: Fruits and vegetables from A to Z.* New York: Harcourt Brace Jovanovich.

Emberly, E. (1978). *Ed Emberly's ABC.* New York: Little, Brown.

Hague, K. (1983). *Alphabears.* New York: Holt, Rinehart & Winston.

Hoban, T. (1982). *A, B, See.* New York: Greenwillow.

Hoban, T. (1987). *26 letters and 99 cents.* New York: Greenwillow.

Isadora, R. (1983). *City seen from A to Z.* New York: Greenwillow.

Kitchen, B. (1984). *Animal alphabet.* New York: Dial.

Lobel, A. (1981). *On market street.* New York: Greenwillow.

MacDonald, S. (1986). *Alphabatics.* New York: Bradbury.

Martin, B., & Archaumbault, J. (1989). *Chicka, chicka, boom, boom.* New York: Simon & Schuster.

Seuss, Dr. (1963). *Dr. Seuss's ABC.* New York: Random House.

Recommended concept books

Alberg, J., & Alberg, A. (1982). *The baby's catalogue.* New York: Little, Brown.

Anno, M. (1989). *Anno's faces.* New York: Philomel.

Barton, B. (1987). *Machines at work.* New York: Crowell.

Berenstain, S., & Berenstain, J. (1968). *Inside, outside, upside down.* New York: Random House.

Crews, D. (1978). *Freight train.* New York: Greenwillow.

Emberly, R. (1989). *City sounds.* New York: Little, Brown.

Hoban, T. (1972). *Push, pull, empty, full.* New York: Macmillan.

Pienkowski, J. (1975). *Shapes.* New York: Harvey House.

Robbins, K. (1983). *Tools.* New York: Four Winds.

Books cited in the text

Banks, L.R. (1981). *Indian in the cupboard.* New York: Doubleday.

Banks, L.R. (1986). *The return of the Indian.* New York: Avon.

Barrett, J. (1978). *Cloudy with a chance of meatballs.* New York: Macmillan.

Blume, J. (1990). *Fudge-a-mania.* New York: Dutton.

Blume, J. (1991). *Deenie.* New York: Dell.

Bolton, F. (1986). *Melting.* New York: Scholastic.

Brown, M. (1947). *Goodnight moon.* New York: Harper.

Carrier, L. (1988). *Do not touch.* Saxonville, MA: Picture Book Studio.

Cassidy, J. (1990). *Earthsearch: A kids' geography museum in a book.* Palo Alto, CA: Klutz.

Cassidy, J. (1994). *The explorabook.* Palo Alto, CA: Klutz.

Cauley, L. (1982). *The three little kittens.* New York: Putnam.

Cleary, B. (1975). *Ramona the brave.* New York: Morrow.

Cleary, B. (1981). *Ramona Quimby, age eight.* New York: Morrow.

Cleary, B. (1983). *Dear Mr. Henshaw.* New York: Morrow.

Cohen, M. (1980). *First grade takes a test.* New York: Dell Young Yearling.

Cole, J. (1992). *The magic schoolbus on the ocean floor.* New York: Scholastic.

Cowley, J. (1983). *Houses.* San Diego: Wright Group. Illustrations by Liz Fuller.

Cowley, J. (1983). *The jigaree.* Auckland, NZ: Shortland.

Cowley, J. (1986). *¡Vete!* Bothell, WA: Wright Group. Illustrations by Isabel Lowe.

Cowley, J. (1987). *Dragolia.* Auckland, NZ: Shortland.

Dahl, R. (1975). *Danny, the champion of the world.* New York: Knopf.

Feldman, D. (1987). *Why do clocks run clockwise? and other imponderables.* New York: Harper & Row.

Fox, M. (1986). *Hattie and the fox.* New York: Bradbury.

Goss, J., Harste, J., & Romney, S. (1981). *It didn't frighten me.* St. Petersburg, FL: Willowisp.

Hamilton, V. (1985). *The people could fly: American black folktales.* New York: Knopf.

Kundhardt, D. (1940). *Pat the bunny.* New York: Western.

Lee, D. (1975). *Alligator pie.* Boston: Houghton Mifflin.

Leokum, A. (1989). *The big book of tell me why.* New York: Purlieu.

Lester, J. (1968). *To be a slave.* New York: Dial.

Lester, J. (1987). *The tales of Uncle Remus: The adventures of Brer Rabbit.* New York: Dial.

Lester, J. (1988). *More tales of Uncle Remus: Further adventures of Brer Rabbit, his friends, enemies, and others.* New York: Dial.

Lester, J. (1990). *Further tales of Uncle Remus: The misadventures of Brer Rabbit, Brer Fox, Brer Wolf, the Doodang, and other creatures.* New York: Dial.

Lester, J. (1994). *The last tales of Uncle Remus.* New York: Dial.

Lovett, S. (1992). *Extremely weird: Endangered species.* Sante Fe, NM: Muir.

Macaulay, D. (1975). *Pyramid.* Boston: Houghton Mifflin.

Martin, B., Jr. (1967, 1983) *Brown bear, brown bear.* New York: Holt.

Martin, B., Jr., & Archambault, J. (1989). *Chicka chicka boom boom.* New York: Simon & Schuster.

McKissack, P. (1986). *Flossie and the fox.* New York: Dial.

McMillan, B. (1990). *One sun.* New York: Holiday House.

Menzel, P. (1994). *Material world.* Pasadena, CA: Sierra.

Parish, P. (1963). *Amelia Bedelia.* New York: Harper & Row. (And other books in the series.)

Patterson, K. (1977). *Bridge to Terabithia.* New York: Crowell.

Paulson, G. (1991). *Woodsong.* New York: Puffin.

Raffi. (1980). *The Raffi singable songbook.* New York: Crown.

Raffi. (1987). *Down by the bay.* New York: Crown.

Raffi. (1988). *Wheels on the bus.* New York: Crown.

Rylant, C., & Stevenson, S. (1991). *Henry Mudge and the bedtime thumps.* New York: Bradbury.

Scarry, R. (1984). *Richard Scarry's lowly worm bath book.* New York: Random House.

Seuss, Dr. (1984). *The butter battle book.* New York: Random House.

Shone, V. (1990). *Wheels.* New York: Scholastic.

Silverstein, S. (1974). *Where the sidewalk ends.* New York: Harper & Row.

Slier, D. (1985). *What do babies do?* New York: Random House.

Slobodkina, E. (1976). *Caps for sale.* New York: Scholastic.

Snyder, Z. (1967). *The Egypt game.* New York: Dell.

Stine, R.L. (1983). *Golden sword of Dragonwalk.* New York: Scholastic. (And other books in the Goosebumps series.)

Stone, V. (1990). *Wheels.* New York: Scholastic.

Viorst, J. (1972). *Alexander and the terrible, horrible, no good, very bad day.* New York: Atheneum.

Viorst, J. (1994). *The alphabet from Z to A with much confusion on the way.* New York: Atheneum.

Warner, G.C. (1988). *The boxcar children.* Niles, IL: Whitman.

Warner, G.C. (1992). *The boxcar children.* Cutchogue, NY: Buccaneer.

Wright, B. (1916). *The real Mother Goose.* New York: Rand McNally.

Yolen, J. (1987). *Owl moon.* New York: Putnam.

Yolen, J. (1992). *The gift of Sarah Barker.* New York: Puffin.

References

Commercial informal reading inventories

Bader, L. (1983). *Reading and language inventory.* New York: Macmillan.

Burns, P., & Roe, B. (1989). *Informal reading inventory* (3rd ed.). Boston: Houghton Mifflin.

Egleton, J. (1992). *Whole language evaluation: Reading, writing, and spelling for the intermediate grades.* Bothell, WA: Wright Group.

Flynt, E.S., & Cooter, Jr., R.B. (1993). *Reading inventory for the classroom.* Scottsdale, AZ: Gorsuch Scarisbrick.

Jeroski, S., Brownlie, F., & Kaser, L. (1990). *Reading and responding 4: Evaluation resources for your classroom.* Scarborough, Ont.: Nelson Canada.

Johns, J. (1981). *Advanced reading inventory.* Dubuque: Brown.

Johns, J. (1981). *Basic reading inventory.* Dubuque: Kendall/Hunt.

Leslie, L., & Caldwell, J. (1990). *Qualitative reading inventory.* New York: HarperCollins.

Rae, G., & Potter, T. (1981). *Informal reading diagnosis: A practical guide for the classroom teacher.* Englewood Cliffs, NJ: Prentice Hall.

Rakes, T., Choate, J., & Waller, G. (1983). *Individual evaluation procedures in reading.* Englewood Cliffs, NJ: Prentice Hall.

Rinsky, L., & Foussard, E. (1980). *The contemporary classroom reading inventory.* Dubuque: Gorsuch Scarisbrick.

Silvaroli, N. (1986). *Classroom reading inventory.* Dubuque: Brown.

Stieglitz, E. (1992). *The Stieglitz informal reading inventory.* Boston: Allyn and Bacon.

Warncke, E., & Shipman, D. (1984). *Group assessment in reading: Classroom teacher's handbook.* Englewood Cliffs, NJ: Prentice Hall.

Woods, M., & Moe, A. (1985). *Analytical reading inventory.* Columbus: Merrill.

Books and articles cited in the text

Aaron, P.G. (1989). *Dyslexia and hyperlexia: Diagnosis and management of developmental reading disabilities.* Boston: Kluwer.

Abouzeid, M. (1992). Stages of word knowledge in reading-disabled children. In S. Templeton & D. Bear (Eds.), *Development of orthographic knowledge and the foundations of literacy: A memorial Festschrift for Edmund H. Henderson* (pp. 279–306). Hillsdale, NJ: Erlbaum.

Abrams, J.C. (1981). The psychologist-educator views the relationship of vision to reading and related learning disabilities. *Journal of Learning Disabilities, 14,* 565–567.

Adams, M.J. (1990). *Beginning to read: Thinking and learning about print.* Cambridge, MA: MIT Press.

Allen, J., Shockley, B., & Michalove, B. (1993). *Engaging children: Community and chaos in the lives of young literacy learners.* Portsmouth, NH: Heinemann.

Allen, R.V. (1976). *Language experience in communication.* Boston: Houghton Mifflin.

Allen, V. (1989). Literature as a support to language acquisition. In P. Rigg & V. Allen (Eds.), *When they don't all speak English: Integrating the ESL student into the regular classroom* (pp. 55–64). Urbana, IL: National Council of Teachers of English.

Allington, R. (1983). The reading instruction provided readers of different reading abilities. *Elementary School Journal, 83,* 549–559.

Allington, R. (1991). Children who find learning to read difficult: School responses to diversity. In E. Hiebert (Ed.), *Literacy for a diverse society: Perspectives, practices, and policies* (pp. 237–252). New York: Teachers College.

Allington, R. (1994). Critical issues: What's special about special programs for children who find learning to read difficult? *Journal of Reading Behavior, 26,* 95–115.

Allington, R. (1994). The schools we have. The schools we need. *The Reading Teacher, 48* (1), 14–27.

Allington, R., & McGill-Franzen, A. (1991). *Educational reform and at-risk children: Exclusion, retention, transition, and special education in an era of increased accountability.* Final report to the U.S. Department of Education, Office of Educational Research and Improvement (Grant #R117E90143).

Allington, R., & McGill-Franzen, A. (1995). Flunking: Throwing good money after bad. In R. Allington & S. Walmsley (Eds.), *No quick fix: Rethinking literacy programs in America's elementary schools.* New York: Teachers College.

Allington, R., & Walmsley, S. (Eds.). (1995). *No quick fix: Rethinking literacy programs in America's elementary schools.* New York: Teachers College.

American Academy of Ophthalmology (1987). Policy statement: Learning disabilities, dyslexia, and vision. *Journal of Learning Disabilities, 20* (7), 412–413.

American Academy of Pediatrics, American Association for Pediatric Ophthalmology and Strabismus and the American Academy of Ophthalmology (March, 1992). *Policy Statement on Learning Disabilities, Dyslexia, and Vision.* San Francisco: American Academy of Ophthalmology.

Anderson, A., & Stokes, S. (1984). Social and institutional influences on the development and practice of literacy. In H. Goelman, A. Oberg & F. Smith (Eds.), *Awakening to literacy* (pp. 24–37). Portsmouth, NH: Heinemann.

Anderson, R.C., & Pearson, P.D. (1984). A schema-theoretic view of basic processes in reading comprehension. In P.D. Pearson, R. Barr, M. Kamil & P. Mosenthal (Eds.), *Handbook of reading research, Vol. I* (pp. 255–291). White Plains, New York: Longman.

Anderson, R.C., Hiebert, E.H., Scott, J.A., & Wilkinson, I.A.G. (1985). *Becoming a nation of readers: The report of the Commission on Reading.* Washington, DC: National Institute of Education.

Anthony, R., Johnson, T., Mickelson, N., & Preece, A. (1988, July). *Evaluation: A perspective for change.* Paper presented at the World Congress on Reading, International Reading Conference, Brisbane, Australia.

Applebee, A. (1978). *The child's concept of story: Ages 2 to 17.* Chicago: University of Chicago Press.

Applebee, A., Langer, J., & Mullis, I.V.S. (1987). *Learning to be literate in America: Reading, writing, and reasoning.* National Assessment of Educational Progress. Princeton, NJ: Educational Testing Service.

Aronson, D. (1994). Changing channels. *Teaching Tolerance, 3,* 28–35.

Aronson, E., & Farr, R. (1988). Issues of assessment. *Journal of Reading, 31,* 174–177.

Atwell, N. (1984). Writing and reading literature from the inside out. *Language Arts, 61,* 240–252.

Atwell, N. (1987). Building a dining room table: Dialogue journals about reading. In T. Fulweiler (Ed.), *The journal book* (pp. 157–170). Portsmouth, NH: Heinemann.

Atwell, N. (1987). *In the middle: Writing, reading and learning with adolescents.* Portsmouth, NH: Boynton/Cook.

Au, K. (1993). *Literacy instruction in multicultural settings.* Orlando, FL: Harcourt Brace Jovanovich.

Au, K.H., & Kawakami, A.J. (1984). Vygotskian perspectives on discussion processes in small-group reading-lessons. In P.L. Peterson, L.C. Wilkinson & M. Hallinan (Eds.), *The social contexts of instruction: Group organization and group process* (pp. 209–225). Orlando, FL: Academic.

Ayres, L. (1909). *Laggards in our schools.* New York: Russell Sage.

Bajtelsmit, L., & Naab, H. (1994). Partner writers: A shared reading and writing experience. *The Reading Teacher, 48,* 91–93.

Ballard, L. (1992). Portfolios and self-assessment. *English Journal, 81,* 46–48.

Banks, J., & Banks, C. (1993). *Multicultural education: Issues and perspectives* (2nd ed.). Boston: Allyn and Bacon.

Barone, D. (1989). Young children's written responses to literature: The relationship between written response and orthographic knowledge. In S. McCormick & J. Zutell (Eds.), *Cognitive and social perspectives for literacy research and instruction* (pp. 371–380). Chicago: National Reading Conference.

Barone, D. (1990). The written responses of young children: Beyond comprehension to story understanding. *The New Advocate, 3,* 49–56.

Barone, D. (1992). "That reminds me of": Using dialogue journals with young children. In C. Temple & P. Collins (Eds.), *Stories and readers: New perspectives on literature in the elementary classroom* (pp. 85–191). Norwood, MA: Gordon.

Barone, D. (1993). The butter battle book: Engaging children's thoughts about war. *Children's Literature in Education, 24* (2), 123–135.

Barone, D. (1994). The importance of classroom context: Literacy development of children prenatally exposed to crack/cocaine—Year two. *Research in the Teaching of English, 28,* 286–312.

Barone, D. (1995). Children prenatally exposed to crack or cocaine: Looking behind the label. *The Reading Teacher, 49,* 278.

Barrs, M., Ellis, S., Hester, H., & Thomas, A. (1989). *The primary language record.* Portsmouth, NH: Heinemann.

Bartoli, J. (1995). *Unequal opportunity: Learning to read in the U.S.A.* New York: Teachers College.

Bauer, C.F. (1990). *Reader's theater: Plays and poems to read aloud.* Bronx, NY: Wilson.

Bear, D. (1989). Why beginning reading must be word-by-word. *Visible Language, 23,* 353–367.

Bear, D. (1991a). Copying fluency and orthographic development. *Visible Language, 25* (1), 40–53.

Bear, D. (1991b). "Learning to fasten the seat of my union suit without looking around": The synchrony of literacy development. *Theory into Practice, 30* (3), 149–157.

Bear, D. (1992). The prosody of oral reading and stage of word knowledge. In S. Templeton & D. Bear (Eds.), *Development of orthographic knowledge and the foundations of literacy: A memorial Festschrift for Edmund H. Henderson* (pp. 137–189). Hillsdale, NJ: Erlbaum.

Bear, D., & Barone, D. (1989). Using children's spelling to group for word study and directed reading in the primary classroom. *Reading Psychology, 10,* (3) 275–292.

Bear, D., & Invernizzi, M. (1984). Student-directed reading groups. *Journal of Reading, 28* (3), 248–252.

Bear, D., & McIntosh, M. (1990). Directed reading-thinking activities to promote reading and study habits in social studies. *Social Education, 54* (6), 385–388.

Bear, D., Invernizzi, M., & Templeton, S. (1996). *Words their way: Word study for phonics, vocabulary, and spelling instruction.* Upper Saddle River, NJ: Prentice Hall.

Bear, D., Templeton, S., & Warner, M. (1991). The development of a qualitative inventory of higher levels of orthographic knowledge. In J. Zutell & S. McCormick, (Eds.), *Learner factors/teacher factors: Issues in literacy research and instruction: Fortieth yearbook of the national reading conference* (pp. 105–110). Chicago: NRC.

Beck, I., & McKeown, M. (1991). Conditions of vocabulary acquisition. In R. Barr, M. Kamil, P. Mosenthal & P.D. Pearson (Eds.), *Handbook of reading research: Volume II* (pp. 789–814). New York: Longman.

Bereiter, C. (1980). Development in writing. In L. Gregg & E. Steinberg (Eds.), *Cognitive processes in writing.* Hillsdale, NJ: Erlbaum.

Bertrand, J. (1991). Student assessment and evaluation. In B. Harp (Ed.), *Assessment and evaluation in whole language programs* (pp. 17–34). Norwood, MA: Gordon.

Bertrand, J., & Stice, C. (Eds.). (1995). *Empowering children at risk of school failure: A better way.* Norwood, MA: Gordon.

Betts, E. (1957). *Foundations of reading instruction.* New York: American Book.

Biemiller, A. (1970). The development of the use of graphic and contextual information as children learn to read. *Reading Research Quarterly, 6,* I (Fall), 75–96.

Birch, J., & Stuckless, E. (1966). The relationship between early manual communication and the later achievement of the deaf. *American Annals of the Deaf, 3,* 444–452, 499–504.

Bloom, L., & Lahey, M. (1978). *Language development and language disorders.* New York: Wiley.

Bossing, L., & Brien, P. (1980). *A review of the elementary school promotion/retention dilemma.* Murray, KY: Murray State University. ERIC Document Reproduction Service No. ED 212 362.

Bouffler, C. (Ed.). (1993). *Literacy evaluation: Issues and practicalities.* Portsmouth, NH: Heinemann.

Boyer, E. (1987). Early schooling and the nation's future. *Educational Leadership, 44* (6), 4–6.

Britton, J. (1994). *Language and learning: The importance of speech in children's development* (2nd ed.). Portsmouth, NH: Heinemann.

Bromley, K.D. (1991). *Webbing with literature: Creating story maps with children's books.* Boston: Allyn and Bacon.

Bronfenbrenner, U. (1981). *The ecology of human development: Experiments by nature and design.* Cambridge, MA: Harvard University Press.

Brown, H., & Cambourne, B. (1987). *Read and retell: A strategy for the whole-language/natural learning classroom.* Portsmouth, NH: Heinemann.

Bussis, A., Chittenden, E., Amarel, M., & Klausner, E. (1985). *Inquiry into meaning: An investigation of learning to read.* Hillsdale, NJ: Erlbaum.

Byrnes, D., & Yamamoto, K. (1986). Views of grade repetition. *Journal of Research and Development in Education, 20,* 14–20.

Calfee, R. (1992). Authentic assessment of reading and writing in the elementary classroom. In M. Dreher & W. Slater (Eds.), *Elementary school literacy: Critical issues* (pp. 211–226). Norwood, MA: Gordon.

Calfee, R., & Perfumo, P. (1993). Student portfolios: Opportunities for a revolution in assessment. *Journal of Reading, 36,* 21–25.

Calkins, L. (1986). *The art of teaching writing.* Portsmouth, NH: Heinemann.

Calkins, L. (1991). *Living between the lines.* Portsmouth, NH: Heinemann.

Carbo, M. (1978). Teaching reading with talking books. *The Reading Teacher, 32,* 267–273.

Carver, R. (1989). Silent reading rates in grade equivalents. *Journal of Reading Behavior, 21,* 155–166.

Carver, R. (1992). *Reading rate: A review of research and theory.* New York: Academic.

Caserta-Henry, C. (1996). Reading buddies: A first grade intervention program. *The Reading Teacher, 49* (6), 500–503.

Cathey, S.S. (1991). *Emerging concept of word: Exploring young children's abilities to read rhythmic text.* Doctoral dissertation, University of Nevada, Reno. UMI #9220355.

Cattell, R. (1963). Theory of fluid and crystallized intelligence: A critical experiment. *Journal of Educational Psychology, 54,* 1–22.

Cazden, C. (1972). *Child language and education.* New York: Holt, Rinehart & Winston.

Cazden, C. (1986). Classroom discourse. In M. Wittrock (Ed.), *Handbook of research on teaching* (3rd ed.) (pp. 432–463). New York: Macmillan.

Chall, J. (1983). *Stages of reading development.* New York: McGraw-Hill.

Chall, J. (1983). Literacy: Trends and explanations. *Educational Researcher, 12,* 3–8.

Chall, J., & Snow, C. (1982). *Families and literacy: The contributions of out of school experiences to children's acquisition of literacy.* A final report to the National Institute of Education, Washington, DC.

Cheek, E., Flippo, R., & Lindsey, J. (1997). *Reading for success in elementary schools.* Madison, WI: Brown and Benchmark.

Chittenden, E., & Courtney, R. (1989). Assessment of young children's reading: Documentation as an alternative to testing. In D.S. Strickland & L. Morrow (Eds.), *Emerging literacy: Young children learn to read and write* (pp. 107–120). Newark, DE: International Reading Association.

Chomsky, N. (1965). *Aspects of a theory of syntax.* Cambridge, MA: MIT Press.

Clandinin, D., & Connelly, F. (1986). Rhythms in teaching: The narrative study of teachers' personal practical knowledge of classrooms. *Teacher and Teacher Education, 2,* 377–387.

Clark, M. (1976). *Young fluent readers.* London: Heinemann.

Clarke, L. (1988). Invented versus traditional spelling in first-graders' writings: Effects on learning to spell and read. *Research in the Teaching of English, 22,* 281–309.

Clay, M.M. (1972). *Concepts about print test, sand and stones.* Exeter, NH: Heinemann.

Clay, M.M. (1972). *Reading: The patterning of complex behavior.* Auckland, NZ: Heinemann.

Clay, M.M. (1975). *What did I write? Beginning writing behaviour.* Auckland, NZ: Heinemann.

Clay, M.M. (1979). *Reading: The patterning of complex behavior* (2nd ed.). Auckland, NZ: Heinemann.

Clay, M.M. (1985). *The early detection of reading difficulties* (3rd ed.). Portsmouth, NH: Heinemann.

Clay, M.M. (1991). *Becoming literate: The construction of inner control.* Portsmouth, NH: Heinemann.

Clay, M.M. (1992). Language policy and literacy learning. *Reading Today, 11* (2), 3.

Clifford, P., & Friesen, S.L. (1993). A curious plan: Managing on the twelfth. *Harvard Educational Review, 63,* 339–358.

Cohen, A.H. (1988). The efficacy of optometric vision therapy. *Journal of the American Optometric Association, 59,* 95–105.

Collier, V. (1987, April). *Age and rate of acquisition of cognitive-academic second language proficiency.* Paper presented at the annual meeting of the American Education Research Association, Washington, DC.

Collins, J. (1986). Differential instruction in reading groups. In J. Cook-Gumperz, (Ed.), *The social construction of literacy* (pp. 117–137). New York: Cambridge University Press.

Collins, P. (1992). Before, during, and after: Using drama to read deeply. In C. Temple & P. Collins (Eds.), *Stories and readers: New perspectives on literature in the elementary school* (pp. 141–156). Norwood, MA: Gordon.

Comer, J. (1988). Educating poor minority children. *Scientific American, 259,* 43–48.

Comer, J., & Hayes, N. (1991). Parent involvement in schools: An ecological approach. *The Elementary School Journal, 91,* 271–277.

Commeyras, M. (1990). Analyzing a critical-thinking reading lesson. *Teaching and Teacher Education, 6,* 201–214.

Connell, R.W. (1994). Poverty and education. *Harvard Educational Review, 64,* 125–149.

Cook-Gumperz, J. (1986). Literacy and schooling: An unchanging equation? In J. Cook-Gumperz (Ed.), *The social construction of literacy* (pp. 16–44). New York: Cambridge University Press.

Corcoran, T., & Goertz, M. (1995). Instructional capacity and high performance schools. *Educational Researcher, 24* (9), 27–31.

Cramer, R. (1982). Informal approaches to evaluating children's writing. In J. Pikulski & T. Shanahan (Eds.), *Approaches to the informal evaluation of reading* (pp. 80–93). Newark, DE: International Reading Association.

Crystal, D. (1987). *The Cambridge encyclopedia of language.* New York: Cambridge University Press.

Csikszentmihalyi, M. (1990). Literacy and intrinsic motivation. *Daedalus, 119,* 115–140.

Cummins, J. (1981). The role of primary language development in promoting educational success for language minority students. In J. Cummins (Ed.), *Schooling and language minority students: A theoretical framework.* Los Angeles: Evaluation, Dissemination, and Assessment Center, California State University, Los Angeles.

Cummins, J. (1984). Language proficiency, bilingualism and academic achievement. *Bilingualism and special education: Issues in assessment and pedagogy* (pp. 130–151). San Diego: College-Hill.

Cummins, J. (1986). Empowering minority students: A framework for intervention. *Harvard Educational Review, 56,* 18–36.

Darling-Hammond, L., & Wise, A. (1985). Beyond standardization: State standards and school improvement. *The Elementary School Journal, 85,* 315–336.

Davidson, J. (1982). The group mapping. *Journal of Reading, 26,* 52–56.

Delgado-Gaitan, C. (1987). Mexican adult literacy: New directions for immigrants. In S.R. Goldman & K. Trueba (Eds.), *Becoming literate in English as a second language* (pp. 9–32). Norwood, NJ: Ablex.

Delpit, L. (1995). *Other people's children: Cultural conflict in the classroom.* New York: New Press.

Deschenes, L., Johnson, K., Poliquin, R., Potter, L., & Steller, S. (September, 1991). Alternative methods of reporting and communicating with parents. In J. Potter (Ed.), *Conversations about assessment: Proceedings of an assessment exchange conference* (pp. 9–18). Gorham, ME: Center for Applied Research and Evaluation, University of Southern Maine.

Dewey, J. (1938). *Experience and education.* New York: Collier Books.

Dewey, J. (1966). *Democracy and education.* New York: Free Press.

Dixon, C., & Nessel, D. (1983). *Language experience approach to reading and writing: Language-experience reading for second language learners.* Hayward, CA: Alemany.

Doiron, R. (1994). Using nonfiction in a read-aloud program: Letting the facts speak for themselves. *The Reading Teacher, 47,* 616–624.

Doyle, R. (1989). The resistance of conventional wisdom to research evidence: The case of retention in grade. *Phi Delta Kappan, 70,* 215–220.

Dryfoos, J.G. (1996). Full-service schools. *Educational Leadership, 53* (7), 18–23.

Duane, D.D., & Gray, D.B. (Eds.). (1991). *The reading brain: The biological basis of dyslexia.* Parkton, MD: York.

Dunn, S., & Pamenter, L. (1987). *Butterscotch dreams: Chants for fun and learning.* Portsmouth, NH: Heinemann.

Dunn, S., & Pamenter, L. (1990). *Crackers and crumbs: Chants for whole language.* Portsmouth, NH: Heinemann.

Durkin, D. (1966). *Children who read early.* New York: Teachers College.

Dyson, A. (1987). The value of "time off task": Young children's spontaneous talk and deliberate text. *Harvard Educational Review, 57,* 396–420.

Dyson, A. (1989). Research currents: The space/time travels of story writers. *Language Arts, 66,* 330–340.

Dyson, A.H. (1993). *Social worlds of children learning to write in an urban primary school.* New York: Teachers College.

Eccles, J. (1975). *Facing reality: Philosophical adventures by a brain scientist.* New York: Springer-Verlag.

Edelsky, C. (1986). *Writing in a bilingual program: Habia una vez.* Norwood, NJ: Ablex.

Edwards, P.A. (1995). Empowering low-income mothers and fathers to share books with young children. *The Reading Teacher, 48* (7), 558–564.

Eeds, M., & Wells, D. (1989). Grand conversations: An exploration of meaning construction in literature study groups. *Research in the Teaching of English, 23,* 4–29.

Egan, K. (1987). Literacy and the oral foundations of education. *Harvard Educational Review, 57,* 445–472.

Ehri, L. (1987). Learning to read and spell words. *Journal of Reading Behavior, 19,* 5–31.

Ekwall, E. (1986). *Ekwall reading inventory.* Boston: Allyn and Bacon.

Farr, R., & Carey, R. (1986). *Reading: What can be measured?* Newark, DE: International Reading Association.

Farris, P. (1997). *Language arts: Process, product, and assessment.* Madison, WI: Brown and Benchmark.

Fernald, G. (1943). *Remedial techniques in basic school subjects.* New York: McGraw-Hill.

Fine, M. (1990). *Framing dropouts: Notes on the politics of an urban high school.* Albany: State University of New York.

Flood, J., & Lapp, D. (1989). Reporting reading progress: A comparison portfolio for parents. *The Reading Teacher, 42,* 508–514.

Flores, B., & Garcia, E. (1984). A collaborative learning and teaching experience using journal writing. *National Association for Bilingual Education Journal, 7,* 67–83.

Foster, C. (1990). Achievement lists put pressure on students and schools. *Christian Science Monitor,* May 24, p. 7.

Freeman, D., & Freeman, Y. (1993). Strategies for promoting the primary languages of all students. *The Reading Teacher, 46,* 18–25.

Freeman, D., & Freeman, Y. (1994). *Between worlds: Access to second language acquisition.* Portsmouth, NH: Heinemann.

Frith, U. (1981). Experimental approaches to developmental dyslexia. *Psychological Research, 43,* 97–109.

Froebel, F. (1974). *The education of man.* Clifton, NJ: Kelly.

Ganske, K.A. (1994). Developmental spelling analysis: A diagnostic measure for instruction and research. Doctoral dissertation, University of Virginia, Charlottesville. DAI, *55-05A,* 1230.

Garber, S.W., Garber, D.M., & Spizman, R.F. (1996). *Beyond Ritalin: Facts about medication and other strategies for helping children, adolescents, and adults with attention deficit disorders.* New York: Villard.

Garcia, G., & Pearson, P.D. (1991). The role of assessment in a diverse society. In E. Hiebert (Ed.), *Literacy for a diverse society* (pp. 253–278). New York: Teachers College.

Gardner, H. (1983). *Frames of mind: The theory of multiple intelligences.* New York: Basic Books.

Gardner, H. (1991). *The unschooled mind: How children think and how schools should teach.* New York: Basic Books.

Gaskins, I., Ehri, L., Cress, C., O'Hara, C., & Donnelly, K. (1997). Procedures for word learning: Making discoveries about words. *The Reading Teacher, 50* (4), 312–327.

Gee, J.P. (1989). Two styles of narrative construction and their linguistic and educational implications. *Discourse Processes, 12,* 287–307.

Gee, J.P. (1992). *The social mind: Language, ideology, and social practice.* New York: Bergin & Garvey.

Geers, A., & Moog, J. (1989). Factors predictive of the development of literacy in profoundly hearing-impaired adolescents. *Volta Review, 91* (2), 69–86.

Gibbs, J. (1987). *Tribes: A process for social development and cooperative learning.* Santa Rosa, CA: Center Source Publications.

Gill, C.H., & Scharer, P.L. (1996). "Why do they get it on Friday and misspell it on Monday?" Teachers inquiring about their students as spellers. *Language Arts, 73,* 89–96.

Gill, J., & Bear, D. (1988). No book, whole book, and chapter DR-TAs: Three study techniques. *Journal of Reading, 31,* 444–449.

Gill, T. (1992). The relationship between word recognition and spelling. In S. Templeton & D. Bear (Eds.), *Development of orthographic knowledge and the foundations of literacy: A memorial Festschrift for Edmund H. Henderson.* Hillsdale, IL: Erlbaum.

Gillet, J., & Temple, C. (1990). *Understanding reading problems* (3rd ed.). New York: HarperCollins.

Gillet, J., & Temple, C. (1994). *Understanding reading problems: Assessment and instruction* (4th ed.). New York: HarperCollins.

Gillingham, A., & Stillman, B. (1970). *Remedial training for children with specific disability in reading, spelling, and penmanship.* Cambridge, MA: Educator's Publishing Service.

Giroux, H. (1992). Educational leadership and the crisis of democratic government. *Educational Researcher, 21* (4), 4–11.

Glaser, S., & Brown, C. (1993). *Portfolios and beyond: Collaborative assessment in reading and writing.* Norwood, MA: Gordon.

Goffman, E. (1981). *Forms of talk.* Philadelphia: University of Pennsylvania Press.

Goldenberg, C.N. (1984, October). *Low-income parents' contributions to the reading achievement of their first-grade children.* Paper presented at the meeting of the Evaluation Network/Evaluation Research Society, San Francisco.

Goldenburg, C. (1992). The limits of expectations: A case for case knowledge about teacher expectancy effects. *American Educational Research Journal, 29,* 517–544.

Good, T., & Brophy, J. (1994). *Looking in classrooms* (6th ed.). New York: Harper Collins.

Goodman, K. (1969). Analyzing oral reading miscues: Applied psycholinguistics. *Reading Research Quarterly, 5,* 9–30.

Goodman, K., & Goodman, Y. (Eds.). (1989). *The whole language evaluation book.* Portsmouth, NH: Heinemann.

Goodman, Y., Watson, D., & Burke, C. (1987). *Reading miscue inventory: Alternative procedures.* Katonah, NY: Owen.

Goswami, D., & Stillman, P.R. (Eds.). (1987). *Reclaiming the classroom: Teacher research as an agency for change.* Upper Montclair, NJ: Boynton/Cook.

Graff, H.J. (1987). *The legacies of literacy.* Bloomington: Indiana State University.

Graves, D. (1983). *Writing: Teachers and children at work.* Portsmouth, NH: Heinemann.

Graves, D. (1991). *Building a literate classroom.* Portsmouth, NH: Heinemann.

Graves, D. (1994). *A fresh look at writing.* Portsmouth, NH: Heinemann.

Graves, D., & Hansen, J. (1983). The author's chair. *Language Arts, 60,* 176–183.

Gray, D.B., & Kavanagh, J.K. (Eds.). (1985). *Biobehavioral measures of dyslexia.* Parkton, MD: York.

Greenfield, P. (1984). A theory of the teacher in the learning activities of everyday life. In B. Rogoff & J. Lave (Eds.), *Everyday cognition: Its development in social context* (pp. 117–138). Cambridge, MA: Harvard University Press.

Gregory, R. (1996). *Psychological testing* (2nd ed.). Boston: Allyn and Bacon.

Gronlund, N. (1985). *Measurement and evaluation in teaching* (5th ed.). Belmont, CA: Macmillan.

Gronlund, N., & Linn, R. (1990). *Measurement and evaluation in teaching* (6th ed.). New York: Macmillan.

Grosjean, F. (1989). Neurolinguists, beware! The bilingual is not two monolinguals in one person. *Brain and Language, 36,* 3–15.

Gutherie, J.T., & Greaney, V. (1991). Literacy acts. In R. Barr, M.L. Kamil, P. Mosenthal & P.D. Pearson (Eds.), *Handbook of reading research, Vol. II* (pp. 68–96). New York: Longman.

Guthrie, J., Van Meter, V., McCann, A., Wigfield, A., Bennett, L., Poundstone, C., Rice, M., Faibisch, F., Hunt, B., & Mitchell, A. (1996). Growth of literacy engagement: Changes in motivations and strategies during concept-oriented reading instruction. *Reading Research Quarterly, 31,* 306–333.

Halliday, M. (1975). *Learning how to mean: Exploration in the development of language.* London: Arnold.

Hammond, D. (1979). Anticipation activity. Paper presented at the Great Lakes Regional Conference, Detroit, MI. Noted in Padak & Davidson (1991).

Hansen, J. (1969). The impact of the home literacy environment on reading attitude. *Elementary English, 46,* 17–24.

Hansen, J. (1992). Literacy portfolios: Helping students know themselves. *Educational Leadership, 49,* 66–68.

Harris, T., & Hodges, R. (Eds.). (1981). *A dictionary of reading and related terms.* Newark, DE: International Reading Association.

Harris, T., & Hodges, R. (Eds.). (1995). *The literacy dictionary.* Newark, DE: International Reading Association.

Harris, V. (Ed.). (1993). *Teaching multicultural literature in grades K–8.* Norwood, MA: Gordon.

Harste, J., Short, K., & Burke, C. (1989). *Creating classrooms for authors: The reading/writing connection.* Portsmouth, NH: Heinemann.

Harste, J., Woodward, V., & Burke, C. (1984) *Language stories and literacy lessons.* Portsmouth, NH: Heinemann.

Hart, S. (1982). Analyzing the social organization for reading in one elementary school. In G. Spindler (Ed.), *Doing the ethnography of schooling* (pp. 410–438). New York: Holt, Rinehart & Winston.

Havelock, E. (1976). *Origins of western literacy.* Toronto: Ontario Institute for Studies in Education.

Healy, J.M. (1982). The enigma of hyperlexia. *Reading Research Quarterly, 17,* 319–338.

Heath S.B. (1982). What no bedtime story means. *Language in Society, 11,* 49–76.

Heath, S., & Mangiola, L. (1991). *Children of promise: Literate activity in linguistically and culturally diverse classrooms.* Washington, DC: National Association for the Education of Young Children.

Heath, S.B. (1983). *Ways with words: Language, life, and work in communities and classrooms.* Cambridge: Cambridge University Press.

Heath, S.B. (1991). The sense of being literate: Historical and cross-cultural features. In R. Barr, M.L. Kamil, P.B. Mosenthal & P.D. Pearson (Eds.), *Handbook of reading research, Vol. 2* (pp. 3–25). New York: Longman.

Henderson, E. (1981). *Learning to read and spell: A child's knowledge of words.* DeKalb: Northern Illinois University Press.

Henderson, E. (1990). *Teaching spelling* (2nd ed.). Boston: Houghton Mifflin.

Henderson, E., & Templeton, S. (1986). A developmental perspective of formal spelling instruction through alphabet, pattern, and meaning. *Elementary School Journal, 86,* 305–316.

Herber, H., & Nelson, J. (1986). Questioning is not the answer. In E. Dishner, T. Bean, J. Readence & D. Moore (Eds.), *Reading in the content areas: Improving classroom instruction* (3rd ed.) (pp. 227–233). Dubuque, IA: Kendall/Hunt.

Hiebert, E. (1983). An examination of ability grouping for reading instruction. *Reading Research Quarterly, 18,* 231–255.

Hiebert, E., Valencia, S., & Afflerbach, P. (1994). Definitions and perspectives. In S. Valencia, E. Hiebert & P. Afflerbach (Eds.), *Authentic reading assessment: Practices and possibilities* (pp. 6–21). Newark, DE: International Reading Association.

Hiebert, E.H., & Taylor, B.M. (1994). *Getting reading right from the start: Effective early intervention.* Boston: Allyn & Bacon.

Holdaway, D. (1979). *The foundations of literacy.* Sydney: Ashton Scholastic.

Holt, J. (1994). Classroom attributes and achievement test scores for deaf and hard of hearing students. *American Annals of the Deaf, 39* (4), 430–437. ERIC No: EJ493086

Huey, E.B. (1968). *The psychology and pedagogy of reading.* Cambridge, MA: MIT Press.

Hunt, N., & Marshall, K. (1994). *Exceptional children and youth: An introduction to special education.* Boston: Houghton Mifflin.

Hynd, G.W., & Hynd, C.R. (1984). Dyslexia: Neuroanatomical/neurolinguistic perspectives. *Reading Research Quarterly, 19,* 482–495.

Igoa, C. (1995). *The inner world of the immigrant child.* New York: St. Martin's.

International Reading Association (1985). *Literacy development and pre-first grade.* Newark, DE: IRA.

International Reading Association (1991). Resolutions on literacy assessment. Newark, DE: Author.

Invernizzi, M. (In press.) The book buddy program. *The Reading Teacher, 50.*

Invernizzi, M., & Worthy, J. (1989). An orthographic comparison of the spelling errors of learning disabled and normal children across four grade levels of spelling achievement. *Reading Psychology, 10* (2), 173–188.

Invernizzi, M., Abouzeid, M., & Gill, T. (1994). Using students' invented spelling as a guide for spelling instruction that emphasizes word study. *Elementary School Journal, 95* (2), 155–167.

Invernizzi, M., Johnston, F., & Juel, C. (1995). *Handbook for book buddies.* Charlottesville, VA: University of Virginia.

Invernizzi, M., Juel, C., & Rosemary, C. A. (1997). A community volunteer tutorial that works. *The Reading Teacher, 50,* 304–311.

IRA/NCTE Joint Task Force on Assessment of Reading and Writing. (1994). *Standards for the assessment of reading and writing.* Newark, DE: International Reading Association.

Irlen, H. (1991). *Reading by the colors.* Garden City Park: Avery.

Jett–Simpson, M. (1978). Reading comprehension through creative dramatics. In J. Stewig & S. Sebesta (Eds.), *Using literature in the elementary school.* Urbana, IL: NCTE.

Johns, J., & Luhn, M. (1983). The informal reading inventory: 1910–1980. *Reading World, 23* (1), 6–15.

Johnson, D., & Johnson, R. (1984). *Structuring cooperative learning: Lesson plans for teachers.* New Brighton, MN: Interaction.

Johnson, D.W., & Johnson, R. (1982). *Joining together: Group theory and group skills* (2nd ed.). New Brighton, MN: Interaction.

Johnson, D.W., & Johnson, R.T. (1987). *Learning together and alone* (2nd ed.). Englewood Cliffs, NJ: Prentice Hall.

Johnston, P. (1983). *Reading comprehension assessment: A cognitive basis.* Newark, DE: International Reading Association.

Johnston, P. (1992). *Constructive evaluation of literate activity.* New York: Longman.

Johnston, P.H., & Winograd, P.N. (1985). Passive failure in reading. *Journal of Reading Behavior, 17,* 279–301.

Juel, C. (1991). Beginning reading. In B. Barr, M.L. Kamil, P. Mosenthal & P.D. Pearson (Eds.), *Handbook of reading research* (vol. 2) (pp. 759–788). New York: Longman.

Juel, C. (1994). At-risk university students tutoring at-risk elementary school children: What factors make it effective? In E.H. Hiebert & B.M. Taylor (Eds.), *Getting reading right from the start: Effective early intervention* (pp. 39–63). Boston: Allyn & Bacon.

Juel, C., & Leavell, J. (1988). Retention and nonretention of at-risk readers in first grade and their subsequent reading achievement. *Journal of Learning Disabilities, 21* (9), 571–580.

Kamhi, A.G., & Catts, H.W. (Eds.). (1991). *Reading disabilities: A developmental language perspective.* Boston: Allyn and Bacon.

Kauffman, J.M. (1994). Places of change: Special education's power and identity in an era of educational reform. *Journal of Learning Disabilities, 27,* 610–618.

Kaufman, A. (1994). *Intelligent testing with the WISC-III.* New York: Wiley.

Kennedy, A. (1984). *The psychology of reading.* London: Methuen.

Kindig, J.S. (1995). Otitis media: Its relationship with delayed reading and attention deficit disorder. DAI, *56-09A,* 3520.

Kobrin, B. (1988). *Eyeopeners: How to choose and use children's books about real people, places, and things.* New York: Penguin Books.

Koch, K. (1970). *Wishes, lies, and dreams.* New York: Harper & Row.

Kornhaber, M., & Gardner, H. (1993). *Varieties of excellence: Identifying and assessing children's talents.* New York: National Center for Restructuring Education, Teachers College, Columbia University.

Kozol, J. (1991). *Savage inequalities.* New York: Crown.

Krashen, S. (1982). *Principles and practice in second language acquisition.* New York: Pergamon.

Kuglemass, J. (1990). *The ecology of the Foxfire approach.* Unpublished paper.

LaBerge, D., & Samuels, S. (1974). Toward a theory of automatic information processing in reading. *Cognitive Psychology, 6,* 293–323.

Labov, W. (1972). The transformation of experience in narrative syntax. In W. Labov (Ed.), *Language in the inner city: Studies in the black English vernacular.* Philadelphia: University of Pennsylvania Press.

Langer, J., & Applebee, A. (1986). Reading and writing instruction: Toward a theory of teaching and learning. In E.Z. Rothkopf (Ed.), *Review of research in education* (pp. 171–194). Washington, DC: American Educational Research Association.

Lapp, D., & Flood, J. (1993). Are there "real" writers living in your classroom? Implementing a writer-centered classroom. *The Reading Teacher, 47,* 254–258.

Lashley, K.S. (1951). The problem of serial order in behavior. In L. Jeffress (Ed.), *Cerebral mechanisms in behavior.* New York: Wiley.

Lea, J. (1980). The association between rhythmic ability and language ability. In F.M. Jones (Ed.), *Language disability in children: Assessment and remediation* (pp. 217–230). Baltimore: University Park Press.

Leland, C., & Fitzpatrick, R. (1993). Cross-age reading: A strategy for helping poor readers. *The Reading Teacher, 46,* 362–369.

Lenneberg, E.H. (1967). *Biological foundations of language.* New York: Wiley.

Levinson, H.N. (1980). *A solution to the riddle of dyslexia.* New York: Springer-Verlag.

Levinson, H.N. (1994). *A scientific Watergate: Dyslexia: How and why countless millions are deprived of breakthrough medical treatment.* Great Neck, NY: Stonebridge.

Lindamood, C., Bell, N., & Lindamood, P. (1992). Issues in phonological awareness assessment. *Annals of Dyslexia, 42,* 242–259.

Lindfors, J. (1989). The classroom: A good environment for language learning. In P. Rigg & V. Allen (Eds.), *When they don't all speak English: Integrating the ESL student into the regular classroom* (pp. 39–54). Urbana: National Council of Teachers of English.

Lipman, D. (1994). *We all sing together: Creative activities for children to use with multicultural folk songs.* Phoenix: Oryx.

Lipson, M., & Wixson, K.K. (1986). Reading disability research: An interactionist perspective. *Review of Educational Research, 56,* 111–136.

Lipson, M., & Wixson, K.K. (1991). *Assessment of instruction of reading disability*. New York: HarperCollins.

Lovell, J. (1992). Reader response theory in the elementary classroom. In C. Temple & P. Collins (Eds.), *Stories and readers: New perspectives on literature in the elementary school* (pp. 15–31). Norwood, MA: Gordon.

Lundberg, I., & Hoien, T. (1991). Initial enabling knowledge and skills in reading acquisition: Print awareness and phonological segmentation. In D. Sawyer & B. Fox (Eds.), *Phonological awareness in reading: The evolution of current perspectives* (pp. 73–95). New York: Springer-Verlag.

Manzo, A. (1969). The ReQuest procedure. *Journal of Reading, 12,* 123–126.

Marsh, G., Friedman, M., Welsh, V., & Desberg, P. (1981). A cognitive-developmental theory of reading acquisition. In G.E. Mackinnon & T.G. Waller (Eds.), *Reading research: Advances in theory and practice, Vol. 3* (pp. 199–221). New York: Plenum.

Masonheimer, P., Drum, P., & Ehri, L. (1984). Does environmental print identification lead children into word reading? *Journal of Reading Behavior, 16,* 257–271.

McCormick, S. (1995). *Instructing students who have literacy problems*. Englewood Cliffs, NJ: Merrill.

McGee, L., & Richgels, D. (1985). Teaching expository text structure to elementary students. *The Reading Teacher, 38,* 739–748.

McGee, L., & Richgels, D. (1990). *Literacy's beginnings: Supporting young readers and writers*. Boston: Allyn and Bacon.

McGee, L., & Richgels, D. (1996). *Literacy's beginnings: Supporting young readers and writers* (2nd ed.). Boston: Allyn and Bacon.

McIntosh, M.E., & Bear, D. (1993). Directed reading-thinking activities to promote learning through reading in mathematics. *The Clearing House, 67,* 40–45.

McKeown, M.G., Beck, I.L., Omanson, R.C., & Pople, M.T. (1985). Some effects of the nature and frequency of vocabulary instruction on the knowledge and use of words. *Reading Research Quarterly, 20,* 522–535.

Mehegan, C.C., & Dreifus, R.E. (1972). Hyperlexia: Exceptional reading ability in brain-damaged children. *Neurology, 22,* 1105–1111.

Meyer, B., & Freedle, R. (1984). Effects of discourse type on recall. *American Educational Research Journal, 21,* 121–143.

Michaels, W., & Karnes, M. (1950). *Measuring educational achievement*. New York: McGraw-Hill.

Miramontes, O., & Commins, N. (1991). Redefining literacy and literacy contexts: Discovering a community of learners. In E. Hiebert (Ed.), *Literacy for a diverse society: Perspectives, practices, and policies* (pp. 75–90). New York: Teachers College.

Moats, L.C. (1995). *Spelling: Development, disability and instruction*. Baltimore, MD: York.

Moll, L.C., & Greenberg, J.B. (1990). Creating zones of possibilities: Combining social contexts for instruction. In L.C. Moll (Ed.), *Vygotsky and education: Instructional implications and applications of sociohistorical psychology* (pp. 319–348). Cambridge, MA: Cambridge University Press.

Montgomery, A., & Rossi, R. (1994). Becoming at risk of failure in America's schools. In R. Rossi (Ed.), *Schools and students at risk: Context and framework for positive change* (pp. 3–22). New York: Teachers College.

Morris, D. (1980). Beginning readers' concept of word. In E. Henderson & J. Beers (Eds.), *Developmental and cognitive aspects of learning to spell* (pp. 97–111). Newark, DE: International Reading Association.

Morris, D. (1981). Concept of word: A developmental phenomenon in the beginning reading and writing process. *Language Arts, 58,* 659–668.

Morris, D. (1982). "Word sort": A categorization strategy for improving word recognition ability. *Reading Psychology, 3,* 247–259.

Morris, D. (1983). Concept of word and phoneme awareness in the beginning reader. *Research in the Teaching of English, 17,* 359–373.

Morris, D. (1993). The relationship between children's concept of word in text and phoneme awareness in learning to read: A longitudinal study. *Research in the Teaching of English, 27,* 133–154.

Morris, D., Blanton, L., & Blanton, W.E. (1995). Teaching low-achieving spellers at their "instructional level." *The Elementary School Journal, 96,* 163–177.

Morris, D., Blanton, L., Blanton, W.E., & Perney, J. (1995). Spelling instruction and achievement in six elementary classrooms. *Elementary School Journal, 96,* 143–162.

Morris, D., Ervin, C., & Conrad, K. (1996). A case study of middle school reading disability. *The Reading Teacher, 49* (5), 368–377.

Morrow, L. (1983). Home and school correlates of early interest in literature. *Journal of Educational Research, 76,* 221–230, 339–344.

Morrow, L. (1992). *Literacy development in the early years: Helping children read and write* (2nd ed.). Boston: Allyn and Bacon.

Morrow, L., & Smith, J. (1990). The effects of group setting on interactive storybook reading. *Reading Research Quarterly, 21,* 330–346.

Morrow, L.M. (Ed.). (1995). *Family literacy.* Newark, DE: International Reading Association.

Morrow, L.M., Tracey, D.H., & Maxwell, C.M. (Eds.). (1995). *A survey of family literacy in the United States.* Newark, DE: International Reading Association.

Mosenthal, J., Daniels, P., & Mekkelsen, J. (1994). The portfolio-as-text: Literacy portfolios in preservice, undergraduate, teacher education. In D. Leu & C. Kinzer (Eds.), *Examining central issues in literacy research, theory, and practice: Forty-second yearbook of the National Reading Conference* (pp. 315–324). Chicago: National Reading Conference.

Mullis, I., & Jenkins, L. (1990). *The reading report card, 1971–88: Trends from the nation's report card.* Princeton, NJ: National Assessment of Educational Progress, ETS.

Murphy, J.J. (1987). *Quintilian on the teaching of speech and writing.* Carbondale: Southern Illinois University Press.

NAEYC (1988). NAEYC position statement on standardized testing of young children 3 through 8 years of age. *Young Children, 43,* 42–47.

Nathan, R., Temple, F., Juntunen, K., & Temple, C. (1989). *Classroom strategies that work: An elementary teacher's guide to process writing.* Portsmouth, NH: Heinemann.

National Coalition of Advocates for Students (1992). *The good common school.* Boston: National Coalition of Advocates for Students.

Neisser, U. (1976). *Cognition and reality: Principles and implications of cognitive psychology.* San Francisco: Freeman.

Nessel, D.D., & Jones, M.B. (1981). *The language experience approach to reading: A handbook for teachers.* New York: Teachers College.

Neuman, S., & Roskos, K. (1991). Peers as literacy informants: A description of young children's literacy conversations in play. *Early Childhood Research Quarterly, 6,* 233–248.

Neuman, S., & Roskos, K. (1994). Bridging home and school with a culturally responsive approach. *Childhood Education, 70,* 210–214.

Neuman, S.B., & Roskos, K.A. (1993). *Language and literacy learning the early years: An integrated approach.* Fort Worth, TX: Harcourt Brace Jovanovich.

Newkirk, T. (1987). On the inside where it counts. In J. Hansen, T. Newkirk & D. Graves (Eds.), *Breaking ground: Teachers relate reading and writing in the elementary school.* Portsmouth, NH: Heinemann.

Newman, F.M., Marks, H.M., & Gamoran, A. (1995). Authentic pedagogy: standards that boost student performance. *Issues in Restructuring, 8,* 1–4.

Nikola-Lisa, W. (1995). Varied voices: Representations of African-American language in children's picture books. *The New Advocate, 8,* 223–242.

Ninio, A., & Bruner. J. (1978). The achievement and antecedents of labeling. *Journal of Child Language, 5,* 1–5.

Noddings, N. (1992). *The challenge to care in schools: An alternative approach to education.* New York: Teachers College.

Ogle, D.M. (1986). K-W-L: A teaching model that develops active reading of expository text. *The Reading Teacher, 39,* 564–570.

Ohlhausen, M., & Jepson, M. (1992). Lessons from Goldilocks: "Somebody's been choosing my books but I can make my own choices now!" *New Advocate, 5,* 31–46.

Olsen, R. (1991). Results of a K–12 and adult ESL survey, 1991. *TESOL Quarterly, 1,* 4.

Olson, R.K., Kliegl, R., & Davidson, B.J. (1983). Dyslexic and normal readers' eye movements. *Human Perception and Performance, 9,* 816–825.

Orlich, D., Harder, R., & Callahan, R. (1994). *Teaching strategies.* Lexington, MA: Heath.

Ovando, C. (1993). Language diversity and education. In J. Banks & C. Banks (Eds.), *Multicultural education: Issues and perspectives* (pp. 215–236). Boston: Allyn and Bacon.

Padak, N.D., & Davidson, J.L. (1991). Instructional activities for comprehending science texts. In C.M. Santa & D.E. Alverman (Eds.), *Science learning: Processes and applications* (pp 76–85). Newark, DE: International Reading Association.

Paley, V. (1979). *White teacher.* Cambridge, MA: Harvard University Press.

Paley, V. (1981). *Wally's stories: Conversations in kindergarten.* Cambridge, MA: Harvard University Press.

Paley, V. (1990). *The boy who would be a helicopter: The uses of storytelling in the classroom.* Cambridge, MA: Harvard University Press.

Palincsar, A., & Brown, A. (1985). Reciprocal teaching: A means to a meaningful end. In J. Osborn, & R.J. Tierney (Eds.), *Reading education: Foundations for a literate America* (pp. 11–28). Lexington, MA: Lexington Books.

Palincsar, A., & Brown, A. (1989, March). Discourse as a mechanism for acquiring process and knowledge. Paper presented at the American Educational Research Association, March, San Francisco.

Palinscar, A.S. (1986). The role of dialogue in providing scaffolded instruction. *Educational Psychologist, 21,* 73–98.

Pappas, C.C., Kiefer, B.Z., Levstik, L.S. (1995). *An integrated language perspective in the elementary school: Theory into action* (2nd ed.). White Plains, NY: Longman.

Patterson, L., Santa, C., Short, K., & Smith, K. (Eds.). (1993). *Teachers are researchers: Reflection and action.* Newark, DE: International Reading Association.

Patton, M. (1990). *Qualitative evaluation and research methods* (2nd ed.). Newbury Park, CA: Sage.

Payne, J.S., Mercer, C.D., & Epstein, M.H. (1974). *Education and rehabilitation techniques.* New York: Human Science.

Pearson, P.D. (1994). Commentary to Weiss' article "California's New English-Language Arts Assessment." In S. Valencia, E. Hiebert & P. Afflerbach (Eds.), *Authentic reading assessment: Practices and possibilities* (pp. 218–227). Delaware: International Reading Association.

Pelligrini, A., Perlmutter, J., Galda, L., & Brophy, G. (1990). Joint bookreading between black Head Start children and their mothers. *Child Development, 61,* 443–453.

Perez, B., & Torres-Guzman, M. (1992). *Learning in two worlds: An integrated Spanish/English biliteracy approach.* New York: Longman.

Perfetti, C. (1982). Dyslexia: From dysverbia to Dramamine. *Contemporary Psychology, 27* (2), 104–105.

Perfetti, C. (1985). *Reading ability.* New York: Oxford University Press.

Perrone, V. (Ed.). (1991). *Expanding student assessment.* Alexandria, VA: Association for Supervision and Curriculum Development.

Peterson, R., & Eeds, M. (1990). *Grand conversations: Literature groups in action.* New York: Scholastic.

Piaget, J., & Inhelder, B. (1969). *The psychology of the child.* New York: Basic Books.

Pichert, J.W., & Anderson, E.C. (1977). Taking different perspectives on a story. *Journal of Educational Psychology, 69,* 309–315.

Pike, K., Compain, R., & Mumper, J. (1994). *New connections: An integrated approach to literacy.* New York: HarperCollins.

Pikulski, J. (1989). Questions and answers. *The Reading Teacher, 7,* 533.

Pikulski, J. (1994). Preventing reading failure: A review of five effective programs. *The Reading Teacher, 48,* 30–39.

Pinker, S. (1994). *The language instinct: How the mind creates language.* New York: Harper.

Pinnell, G.S., Lyons, C.A., DeFord, D.E., Bryk, A.S., & Seltzer, M. (1994). Comparing instructional models for the literacy education of high-risk first graders. *Reading Research Quarterly, 29,* 9–40.

Poplin, M. (1984). Summary rationalizations, apologies and farewell: What we don't know about the learning disabled. *Learning Disabilities Quarterly, 7,* 130–134.

Purcell-Gates, V. (1996). Stories, coupons, and the *TV Guide*: Relationships between home literacy experiences and emergent literacy knowledge. *Reading Research Quarterly, 31,* 406–429.

Raphael, T. (1982). Question-answering strategies for children. *The Reading Teacher, 36,* 186–190.

Raphael, T. (1986). Teaching question/answer relationships, revisited. *The Reading Teacher, 39,* 516–522.

Raphael, T., Goatley, V., McMahon, S., & Woodman, D. (1995). Promoting meaningful conversations in student book clubs. In N. Roser & M. Martínez (Eds.), *Book talk and beyond* (pp. 66–79). Newark, DE: International Reading Association.

Raphael, T., Wonnacott, C., & Pearson, P.D. (1983). *Increasing students' sensitivity to sources of information: An instructional study in questions-answering behavior.* Tech. Rep. No. 238. Urbana: University of Illinois, Center for the Study of Reading.

Rasinski, T. (1988). Making repeated reading a functional part of classroom reading instruction. *Reading Horizons, 28,* 250–254.

Rasinski, T. (1989). Fluency for everyone: Incorporating fluency instruction in the classroom. *The Reading Teacher, 42,* 690–693.

Rasinski, T., & Fredericks, A. (1990). The best reading advice for parents. *The Reading Teacher, 43,* 344–345.

Rasinski, T., & Fredericks, A. (1991). The second best reading advice for parents. *The Reading Teacher, 44,* 438–439.

Rayner, K. (1985). The role of eye movements in learning to read and reading disability. *RASE, 6,* 53–60.

Rayner, K., & Pollatsek, A. (1989). *The psychology of reading.* Englewood Cliffs, NJ: Prentice Hall.

Read, C. (1975). *Children's categorization of speech sounds in English.* Urbana: National Council of Teachers of English.

Read, C., & Schreiber, P. (1981). Why short subjects are harder to find than long ones. In L. Gleitman & E. Wanner (Eds.), *Psycholinguistics: The state of the art.* Cambridge, MA: Harvard University Press.

Reutzel, D., & Cooter, R. (1991). Organizing for effective instruction: The reading workshop. *The Reading Teacher, 44,* 548–555.

Reyes, M. de la Luz. (1991). A process approach to literacy instruction for Spanish-speaking students: In search of a best fit. In E. Hiebert (Ed.), *Literacy for a diverse society: Perspectives, practices, and policies* (pp. 157–171). New York: Teachers College.

Rhodes, L. (1979). I can read! Predictable books as resources for reading and writing instruction. *The Reading Teacher, 34,* 511–518.

Rhodes, L., & Shanklin, N. (1993). *Windows into literacy: Assessing learners K–8.* Portsmouth, NH: Heinemann.

Ricard, R., & Snow C. (1990). Language use in and out of context. *Journal of Applied Developmental Psychology, 11,* 251–266.

Rigg, P. (1989). Language experience approach: Reading naturally. In P. Rigg & V. Allen (Eds.), *When they don't all speak English: Integrating the ESL student into the regular classroom* (pp. 65–76). Urbana, IL: National Council of Teachers of English.

Roderick, M. (1995). Grade retention and school dropout: Policy debate and research questions. *Phi Delta Kappa Research Bulletin, 15,* 1–5.

Rogoff, B. (1990). *Apprentices in thinking: Cognitive development in social context.* New York: Oxford University Press.

Roller, C.M. (1996). *Variability not disability: Struggling readers in a workshop classroom.* Newark, DE: International Reading Association.

Rosenblatt, L. (1978). *The reader, the text, the poem: The transactional theory of the literary work*. Carbondale, IL: Southern Illinois University Press.

Rosenblatt, L.M. (1995). Continuing the conversation: A clarification. *Research in the Teaching of English, 29* (3), 349–354.

Rossi, R. (Ed.). (1994). *Schools and students at risk: Context and framework for positive change*. New York: Teachers College.

Rossi, R., & Stringfield, S. (1995). What we must do for students placed at risk. *Phi Delta Kappan, 77,* 73–76.

Rouse, M.W., & Ryan, J.B. (1984). Teacher's guide to vision problems. *The Reading Teacher, 38*(3), 306–318.

Routman, R. (1988). *Transitions from literature to literacy.* Portsmouth, NH: Heinemann.

Routman, R. (1994). *Invitations: Changing as teachers and learners K–12*. Portsmouth, NH: Heinemann.

Rusk, R., & Scotland, J. (1979). *Doctrines of great educators.* New York: St. Martin's.

Rybczynski, M., & Troy, A. (1995). Literacy-enriched play centers: Trying them out in "the real world." *Childhood Education, 72,* 7–12.

Sabin, E., Clemmer, E., O'Connell, D., & Kowal, S. (1979). A pausological approach to speech development. In A.W. Siegman & S. Feldstein (Eds.), *Of speech and time.* Hillsdale, NJ: Erlbaum.

Saks, A.L. (1995). Viewpoints: A symposium on the usefulness of literacy research. *Research in the Teaching of English, 29* (3), 326–348.

Salvia, J., & Ysseldyke, S. (1988). *Assessment in special and remedial education* (4th ed.). Boston: Houghton Mifflin.

Samuels, S. (1979). The method of repeated readings. *The Reading Teacher, 32,* 403–408.

Samuels, S. (1994). Word recognition. In R. Ruddell, M. Ruddell & H. Singer (Eds.), *Theoretical models and processes of reading* (4th ed.) (pp. 359–380). Newark, DE: International Reading Association.

Sarason, S.B. (1993). *You are thinking of teaching? Opportunities, problems, realities.* San Francisco: Jossey-Bass.

Schlagal, R. (1992). Patterns of orthographic development into the intermediate grades. In S. Templeton & D. Bear (Eds.), *Development of orthographic knowledge and the foundations of literacy: A memorial Festschrift for Edmund H. Henderson* (pp. 31–52). Hillsdale, NJ: Erlbaum.

Schlagal, R., & Schlagal, J. (1992). The integrated character of spelling: Teaching strategies for multiple purposes. *Language Arts, 69,* 418–424.

Schneider, R., & Barone, D. (1996). Cross-age tutoring. *Childhood Education, 73,* 136–143.

Scribner, S., & Cole, M. (1981). *The psychology of literacy.* Cambridge, MA: Harvard University Press.

Shanahan, T., Mulhern, M., & Rodriguez-Brown, F. (1995). Project FLAME: Lessons learned from a family literacy program for linguistic minority families. *The Reading Teacher, 48* (7), 586–593.

Shannon, P. (Ed.). (1992). *Becoming political: Readings and writings in the politics of literacy education.* Portsmouth, NH: Heinemann.

Sharp, S.J. (1989). Using content subject matter with LEA in middle school. *Journal of Reading, 108–112.*

Shaywitz, B.A., Holford, T.D., Holahan, J.M., Fletcher, J.M., Stuebing, K.K., Francis, D.J., & Shaywitz, S.E. (1995). A Matthew effect for IQ but not for reading: Results from a longitudinal study. *Reading Research Quarterly, 30* (4), 894–906.

Shaywitz, S.E., Escobar, M.D., Shaywitz, B.A., Fletcher, J.M., & Makuch, R.W. (1992). Evidence that dyslexia may represent the lower tail of a normal distribution of reading ability. *New England Journal of Medicine, 326,* 145–150.

Shepard, A. (1993). *Stories on stage.* Bronx, NY: Wilson.

Shephard, L., & Smith, M. (1990). Synthesis of research on grade retention. *Educational Leadership, 47,* 84–88.

Shephard, L., & Smith, M. (Eds.). (1989). *Flunking grades: Research and policies on retention.* Philadelphia: Falmer.

Siks, G.B. (1977) *Drama with children.* New York: Harper & Row.

Silverblank, F. (1992). *An annotated bibliography of historical fiction for the social studies, grades 5 through 12.* Dubuque, IA: Kendall/Hunt.

Simons, H.D., & Murphy, S. (1986). In J. Cook-Gumperz (Ed.), *The social construction of literacy* (pp. 185–206). New York: Cambridge University Press.

Slavin, R. (1986). *Using student team learning* (3rd ed.). Baltimore: John Hopkins University Press, Center for Research on Elementary and Middle Schools.

Slavin, R. (1990). *Cooperative learning.* Englewood Cliffs, NJ: Prentice Hall.

Slavin, R.E. (February, 1996). Neverstreaming: Preventing learning disabilities. *Educational Leadership, 4–7.*

Slavin, R.E., Madden, N.A., Karweit, N.L., Dolan, L., & Wasik, B.A. (1996). *Every child, every school: Success for all.* Newbury Park, CA: Corwin.

Sleeter, C., & Grant, C. (1994). *Making choices for multicultural education* (2nd ed.). New York: Merrill.

Slingerland, B.H. (1974). *A multi-sensory approach to language arts for specific language disability children.* Cambridge, MA: Educator's Publishing Service.

Sloyer, S. (1982). *Readers theatre: Story dramatization in the classroom.* Urbana: National Council of Teachers of English.

Smith, F. (1971). *Understanding reading.* New York: Holt, Rinehart, & Winston.

Smith, F. (1988). *Joining the literacy club.* Portsmouth, NH: Heinemann.

Smith-Burke, T.M., & Jaggar, A.M. (1994). Implementing Reading Recovery in New York. In E.H. Hiebert & B.M. Taylor (Eds.), *Getting reading right from the start: Effective early intervention* (pp. 63–84). Boston: Allyn & Bacon.

Snow, C., & Ninio, A. (1986). The contracts of literacy: What children learn from learning to read books. In W.H. Teale & E. Sulzby (Eds.), *Emergent literacy: Writing and reading* (pp.116–138). Exeter, NH: Heinemann.

Snow, C.E., Barnes, W.S., Chandler, J., Goodman, I.F., & Hemphill, L. (1991). *Unfulfilled expectations: Home and school influences on literacy.* Cambridge, MA: Harvard University Press.

Spafford, C.S., Grosser, G.S., Donatelle, J.R., Squillace, S.R., & Dana, J.P. (1995). Contrast sensitivity differences between proficient and disabled readers using colored lenses. *Journal of Learning Disabilities, 28* (4), 240–252.

Spear-Swerling, L.L., & Sternberg, R.J. (1996). *Off track: When poor readers become learning disabled.* Boulder, CO: Westview.

Spearman, C. (1927). *The abilities of man: Their nature and measurement.* New York: Macmillan.

Stahl, S., Richek, M., & Vandevier, R. (1991). Learning meaning vocabulary through listening: A sixth-grade replication. In J. Zutell & S. McCormick (Eds.), *Learner factors/teacher factors: issues in literacy research and instruction* (pp. 185–192). Chicago: National Reading Conference.

Stallman, A., & Pearson, P. (1990). Formal measures of early literacy. In L. Morrow & J. Smith (Eds.), *Assessment for instruction in early literacy* (pp. 7–45). Englewood Cliffs, NJ: Prentice Hall.

Stanovich, K. (1986). Matthew effects in reading: Some consequences of individual differences in the acquisition of literacy. *Reading Research Quarterly, 21,* 360–407.

Stanovich, K. (1988a). Explaining the difference between the dyslexic and the garden-variety poor reader: The phonological-core-variable-difference model. *Journal of Learning Disabilities, 21* (10), 590–604.

Stanovich, K. (1988b). The right and wrong places to look for the cognitive locus of reading disability. *Annals of Dyslexia, 38,* 154–177.

Stanovich, K. (1993). The language code: Issues in word recognition. In S. Smith & M. Smith (Eds.), *Reading across the life span* (pp. 111–135). New York: Springer-Verlag.

Stanovich, K.E. (1993/1994). Romance and reality. *The Reading Teacher, 47,* 280–291.

Staton, J. (1980). Writing and counseling: Using a dialogue journal. *Language Arts, 57,* 514–518.

Staton, J. (1987). The power of responding in dialogue journals. In T. Fulwiler (Ed.), *The journal book* (pp. 47–63). Portsmouth, NH: Heinemann.

Staton, J., Shuy, R., Peyton, J., & Reed, L. (1988). *Dialogue journal communications.* Norwood, NJ: Ablex.

Stauffer, R. (1969). *Directing reading maturity as a cognitive process.* New York: Harper & Row.

Stauffer, R., Abrams, J., & Pikulski, J. (1978). *Diagnosis, correction, and prevention of reading disabilities.* New York: Harper & Row.

Stauffer, R.G. (1980). *The language-experience approach to the teaching of reading* (2nd ed.). New York: Harper & Row.

Stayter, F.Z., & Johnston, P.H. (1990). In T. Shanahan (Ed.), *Reading and writing together: New perspectives for the classroom* (pp. 253–272). Norwood, MA: Gordon.

Stewart, R., & Paradis, E. (1994). Portfolios: Agents of change and empowerment in classrooms. In D. Leu & C. Kinzer (Eds.), *Examining central issues in literacy research, theory, and practice: Forty-second yearbook of the National Reading Conference* (pp. 109–116). Chicago: National Reading Conference.

Stewig, J.T. (1983). *Informal drama in the elementary language arts program.* New York: Teachers College.

Stires, S. (1991). *With promise: Redefining reading and writing for "special" students.* Portsmouth, NH: Heinemann.

Stoll, D.R. (Ed.). (1994). *Magazines for kids and teens.* Newark, DE: International Reading Association.

Stone, L., & Church, J. (1984). *Childhood and adolescence.* New York: Random House.

Stremmel, A.J., & Ru, V.R. (1993). Teaching in the zone of proximal development: Implications for responsive teaching practice. *Child and Youth Care Forum, 22* (5), 337–350.

Sulzby, E. (1985). Children's emergent reading of favorite storybooks: A developmental study. *Reading Research Quarterly, 20,* 458–481.

Swanson, H., & Cochran, K. (1991). Learning disabilities, distinctive encoding, and hemispheric resources. *Brain and Language, 40,* 202–230.

Swearingen, R., & Allen, D. (1996). *Classroom assessment of reading processes.* Boston: Houghton Mifflin.

Taba, H. (1967). *Teacher's handbook for elementary social studies.* Reading, MA: Addison-Wesley.

Taylor, D. (1983). *Family literacy.* Exeter, NH: Heinemann.

Taylor, D. (1991). *Learning denied.* Portsmouth, NH: Heinemann.

Taylor, D. (1993). *From the child's point of view.* Portsmouth, NH: Heinemann.

Taylor, D., & Dorsey-Gaines, C. (1988). *Growing up literate: Learning from inner-city families.* Portsmouth, NH: Heinemann.

Taylor, D., & Strickland, D.S. (1986) *Family storybook reading.* Portsmouth, NH: Heinemann.

Taylor, W.L., & Piché, D.M. (1991). *A report on shortchanging children: The impact of fiscal inequity on the education of students at risk.* Washington, DC: U.S. House of Representatives, Committee on Education and Labor.

Tchudi, S., & Yates, J. (1983). *Teaching writing in the content areas: High school.* Washington, D.C.: National Education Association.

Teale, W. (1978). Positive environments for learning to read: What studies of early readers tell us. *Language Arts, 55,* 922–932.

Teale, W. (1982). Toward a theory of how children learn to read and write naturally. *Language Arts, 59,* 555–570.

Teale, W. (1984). Reading to young children: Its significance for literacy development. In H. Goelman, A. Oberg & F. Smith (Eds.), *Awakening to literacy* (pp. 110–121). Exeter, NH: Heinemann.

Teale, W., & Sulzby, E. (Eds.). (1986). *Emergent literacy: Writing and reading.* Norwood, NJ: Ablex.

Temple, C., Nathan, R., Burris, N., & Temple, F. (1988). *The beginnings of writing.* Boston: Allyn and Bacon.

Temple, C., Nathan, R., Temple, F., & Burris, N. (1993). *The beginnings of writing* (3rd ed.). Boston: Allyn and Bacon.

Temple, F. (1989). Poetry. In R. Nathan, F. Temple, K. Juntunen & C. Temple (Eds.), *Classroom strategies that work: An elementary teacher's guide to process writing* (pp. 94–98). Portsmouth, NH: Heinemann.

Templeton, S. (1983). Using the spelling/meaning connection to develop word knowledge in older students. *Journal of Reading, 27* (1), 8–14.

Templeton, S. (1986). Synthesis of research on the learning and teaching of spelling. *Educational Leadership, 43* (6), 73–78.

Templeton, S. (1989). Tacit and explicit knowledge of derivational morphology: Foundations for a unified approach to spelling and vocabulary development in the intermediate grades and beyond. *Reading Psychology: An International Quarterly, 10,* 233–254.

Templeton, S. (1991). Teaching and learning the English spelling system: Reconceptualizing method and purpose. *The Elementary School Journal, 92,* 183–201.

Templeton, S. (1995). *Children's literacy: Contexts for meaningful learning.* Boston: Houghton Mifflin.

Templeton, S. (1997). *Teaching the integrated language arts* (2nd ed.). Boston: Houghton Mifflin.

Templeton, S., & Bear, D. (Eds.). (1992). *Development of orthographic knowledge and the foundations of literacy: A memorial Festschrift for Edmund H. Henderson.* Hillsdale, NJ: Erlbaum.

Tierney, R., Carter, M., & Desai, L. (1991). *Portfolio assessment in the reading-writing classroom.* Norwood, MA: Gordon.

Tierney, R., Readence, J., & Dishner, E. (1990). *Reading strategies and practices* (3rd ed.). Boston: Allyn & Bacon.

Tierney, R., Readence, J., & Dishner, E. (1995). *Reading strategies and practices: A compendium* (4th ed.). Boston: Allyn and Bacon.

Tomatis, A.A. (1991). *The conscious ear: My life of transformation through listening.* Barrytown, NY: Station Hill.

Tompkins, G. (1994). *Teaching writing: Balancing process and product* (2nd ed.). Englewood Cliffs, NJ: Merrill/Prentice Hall.

Tompkins, G. (1997). *Literacy for the twenty-first century: A balanced approach.* Upper Saddle River, NJ: Prentice Hall.

Tompkins, G., & Hoskisson, K. (1995). *Language arts: Content and teaching strategies* (3rd ed.). Englewood Cliffs, NJ: Merrill.

Tompkins, G., & Yaden, D. (1986). *Answering students' questions about words.* Urbana: ERIC and National Council of Teachers of English.

Tough, J. (1985). *Talk two: Children using English as a second language.* London: Onyx.

Trelease, J. (1989). *The new read-aloud handbook.* New York: Penguin Books.

Tudge, J. (1990). Vygotsky, the zone of proximal development, and peer collaboration: Implications for classroom practice. In L.C. Moll (Ed.), *Vygotsky and education: Instructional implications and applications of sociohistorical psychology* (pp. 155–222). Cambridge, MA: Cambridge University Press.

Tunmer, W. (1989). The role of language-related factors in reading disability. In D. Shankweiler & I.Y. Liberman (Eds.), *Phonology and reading disability: Solving the reading puzzle* (pp. 10–32). Ann Arbor: University of Michigan Press.

Tyack, D., & Tobin, W. (1994). The "grammar" of schooling: Why has it been so hard to change? *American Educational Research Journal, 31* (3), 453–479.

U.S. Bureau of the Census. (1992). *Poverty in the United States: 1991.* Washington, DC: Government Printing Office.

U.S. Office of Special Education and Rehabilitative Services. (1992). *Fourteenth annual report to Congress on the implementation of the Individuals with Disabilities Education Act.* Washington, DC: U.S. Government Printing Office.

Ueland, B. (1992). *Strength to your sword arm: Selected writings by Brenda Ueland.* Duluth: Holy Cow.

Urzua, C. (1986). A children's story. In P. Rigg & D.S. Enright (Eds.), *Children and ESL: Integrating perspectives* (pp. 93–112). Washington, DC: Teachers of English to Speakers of Other Languages.

Vacca, J., Vacca, R., & Gove, M. (1991). *Reading and learning to read* (2nd ed.). New York: HarperCollins.

Vacca, R., & Vacca, J. (1996). *Content area reading* (5th ed.). New York: HarperCollins.

Valencia, S., Hiebert, E., & Afflerbach, J. (Eds.). (1994). *Authentic reading assessment: Practices and possibilities.* Newark, DE: International Reading Association.

Valencia, S., Pearson, P., Peters, C., & Wixson, K. (1989). Theory and practice in statewide reading assessment: Closing the gap. *Educational Leadership, 46,* 57–63.

Valtin, R. (1978/1979). Dyslexia: Deficit in reading or deficit in research? *Reading Research Quarterly, 14,* 201–221.

Vellutino, F.R. (1979). *Dyslexia: Theory and research.* Cambridge, MA: MIT Press.

Vellutino, F.R., & Denckla, M.B. (1991). Cognitive and neuropsychological foundations of word identification in poor and normally developing readers. In R. Barr et al. (Eds.), *Handbook of reading research* (vol. 2, pp. 571–608). White Plains: Longman.

Vellutino, F.R., Scanlon, D.M., Sipay, E.R., Small, S.G., Pratt, A., Chen, R., & Denckla, M.B. (1996). Cognitive profiles of difficult-to-remediate and readily remediated poor readers: Early intervention as a vehicle for distinguishing between cognitive and experiential deficits as basic causes of specific reading disability. *Journal of Educational Psychology, 88* (4), 601–638.

Venezky, R.L. (1991). The development of literacy in the industrialized nations of the west. In R. Barr, M.L. Kamil, P.B. Mosenthal & P.D. Pearson (Eds.), *Handbook of reading research, Vol. 2* (pp. 46–67). New York: Longman.

Vygotsky, L. (1978). In M. Cole, V. John-Steiner, S. Scribner & E. Souberman (Eds.), *Mind in society: The development of higher psychological processes.* Cambridge, MA: Harvard University Press.

Vygotsky, L. (1987). Thinking and speech. In R. Rieber & A. Carton (Eds.), *The collected works of L.S. Vygotsky, Vol. 1* (pp. 39–241). New York: Plenum.

Walmsley, S. (1994). *Children exploring their world: Theme teaching in elementary school.* Portsmouth, NH: Heinemann.

Walmsley, S., & Allington, R. (1995). Redefining and reforming instructional support programs for at-risk students. In R.L. Allington & S.A. Walmsley (Eds.), *No quick fix: Rethinking literacy programs in America's elementary schools* (pp. 19–44). New York: Teachers College.

Walp, T.P., & Walmsley, S. (1995). Scoring well on tests or becoming genuinely literate: Rethinking remediation in a small rural school. In R.L. Allington & S.A. Walmsley (Eds.), *No quick fix: Rethinking literacy programs in America's elementary schools* (pp. 177–196). New York: Teachers College.

Walsh, D., Price, G., & Gillingham, M. (1986). The crucial but fleeting skill of alphabet knowledge. *Reading Research Quarterly, 23,* 108–122.

Warner, M. (1994). Special education bureaucracy and the dilemma of modernism. *Holistic Education Review, 7,* 51–61.

Warner, M. (1995). Writing IEPs. Unpublished paper, University of Nevada, Reno.

Weaver, C. (1988). *Reading process and practice.* Portsmouth, NH: Heinemann.

Wells, D. (1995). Leading grand conversations. In N. Roser & M. Martinez (Eds.), *Book talk and beyond: Children and teachers respond to literature* (pp. 132–139). Newark, DE: International Reading Association.

Wells, G. (1986). The language experience of five-year-old children at home and at school. In J. Cook-Gumperz, (Ed.), *The social construction of literacy* (pp. 69–93). New York: Cambridge University Press.

Whiteford, P., Bradbury, B., & Saunders, P. (1989). Inequality and deprivation among families with children: An exploratory study. In D. Edgar, D. Keane, & P. McDonald (Eds.), *Child poverty* (pp. 20–49). Sydney: Allen & Unwin.

Wilkinson, I. (1991). A micro-experimental analysis of silent reading in small-group guided reading lessons. Doctoral dissertation, University of Illinois at Urbana-Champaign.

Willows, D.M., Kruk, R.S., & Corcos, E. (Eds.). (1993). *Visual processes in reading and reading disabilities.* Hillsdale, NJ: Erlbaum.

Wong-Fillmore, L. (1982). Instructional language as linguistic input: Second language learning in classrooms. In L.C. Wilkinson (Ed.), *Communicating in the classroom* (pp. 283–296). New York: Academic.

Wong-Fillmore, L. (1991). Language and cultural issues in early education. In S.L. Kagan (Ed.), *The care and education of America's young children: Obstacles and opportunities: The Ninetieth Yearbook of the National Society for the Study of Education* (pp. 3–49). Chicago: University of Chicago Press.

Wood, G. (1992). *Schools that work: America's most innovative public education programs.* New York: NAL-Dutton.

Wood, K.D. (1987). Helping students comprehend their textbooks. *Middle School Journal 18,* (2), 20–21.

Woodcock, R. (1987). *Woodcock reading mastery tests, revised.* Circle Pines, MN: American Guidance Service.

Worthy, J. (1996). A matter of interest: Literature that hooks reluctant readers and keeps them reading. *The Reading Teacher, 50* (3), 204–212.

Worthy, M.J., & Invernizzi, M. (1990). Spelling errors of normal and disabled students on achievement levels one through four: Instructional implications. *Annals of Dyslexia, 40,* 138–151.

Worthy, M.J., & Invernizzi, M. (1996). Hyperlexia: A study in the search for meaning. *Journal of Reading Behavior, 27* (4), 585–603.

Yee, S., & Kokin, L. (1987). *Got me a story to tell: A multi-ethnic book: five children tell about their lives.* San Francisco: St. John's Educational Threshold Center.

Page 11: Definition of *observe*. Copyright © 1996 by Houghton Mifflin Company. Adapted by reprinted by permission from *The American Heritage Dictionary of the English Language, Third Edition.*

Page 55: Excerpt from "The Wheels on the Bus." Text copyright © 1988 Troubador Learning, a division of Troubador Records, Ltd. Illustrations copyright © Sylvie Wickstrom. All rights reserved. Used by permission. Published by Crown Publishers, Inc., a Random House Company, 225 Park Avenue South, New York, New York, 10003.

Page 73: Excerpt from "Crackers and Crumbs" © 1990 Sonja Dunn from her book, *Crackers and Crumbs: Chants for Whole Language.* Reprinted with permission. Pembroke Publishers, Ltd., 538 Hood Road, Markham, Ontario L3R 3K9, Canada.

Page 74: Excerpt in "Taking a Closer Look" from John Holt, *Learning All the Time*, p. 13, Addison Wesley, 1989. © 1989 Holt Associates. Reprinted by permission of Addison-Wesley Longman, Inc.

Page 83: Figure 3.6 adapted from D. Barone (1990), The written response of young children: Beyond comprehension to story understanding, *The New Advocate*, 3, 49–56, p. 52.

Page 100: Figure 4.1, *top*—from Cynthia Rylant, *Henry and Mudge and the Bedtime Thumps*, illustrated by Suçie Stevenson. Reprinted with the permission of Simon & Schuster Books for Young Readers, an imprint of Simon & Schuster Children's Publishing Division. Text copyright © 1991 by Cynthia Rylant. Illustrations copyright © 1991 by Suçie Stevenson; *bottom*—cover and text from Peggy Parish, *Good Work, Amelia Bedelia*, illustrated by Lynn Sweat. Copyright © 1976. Reprinted by permission of Greenwillow Books, a division of William Morrow, Inc.

Page 101: Figure 4.1 (continued) from Judy Blume, *Fudge-a-Mania*. Copyright © 1990. Reprinted by permission of Dell Books, a division of Bantam Doubleday, Dell Publishing Group, Inc.

Page 121: Figure 4.3 adapted from *Words Their Way* by Bear/Templeton/ Invernizzi/Johnson, © 1996. Reprinted by permission of Prentice-Hall, Inc., Upper Saddle River, NJ.

Page 122: Table 4.5 adapted from *Words Their Way* by Bear/Templeton/ Invernizzi/Johnson, © 1996. Reprinted by permission of Prentice-Hall, Inc., Upper Saddle River, NJ.

Page 125: Figure 4.4 adapted from Ronald Cramer, Guidelines for evaluating composing, in *Approaches to the Informal Evaluation of Reading*, John J. Pikulski and Timothy Shanadan, editors, chart from pp. 91–93. Reprinted by permission of the International Reading Association and the author.

Pages 194–195: Excerpt reprinted with the permission of Simon & Schuster Books for Young Readers, an imprint of Simon & Schuster Children's Publishing Division from *Hattie and the Fox by Mem Fox*. Text copyright © Mem Fox.

Page 203: Figure 6.14 from Venice Stone, *Wheels*. Copyright © 1990 by Venice Stone. Published by Cartwheel Books by arrangement with Orchard Books. Reprinted by permission of Scholastic, Inc. Cartwheel Books is a registered trademark of Scholastic, Inc.

Page 237: Excerpt from "Alligator Pie" reprinted from *Alligator Pie* (Macmillan of Canada, 1974). Copyright © 1974 by Dennis Lee. With permission of the author.

Page 267: Figure 8.1 adapted from Shane Templeton, *Children's Literacy: Contexts for Meaningful Learning.* Copyright © 1995 by Houghton Mifflin Company. Used with permission.

Page 275: Figure 8.2 from S. Yee & L. Kokin (1987), *Got Me a Story to Tell: A Multi-Ethnic Book—Five Children Tell About Their Lives.* San Francisco: St. John's Educational Threshold Center. Reprinted with permission.

Page 279: Figure 8.3 from Joy Cowley, *Dragolia.* Reprinted with permission of Shortland Publications, Limited.

Page 285: Figure 8.5 adapted from *Multicultural Education: Issues and Perspective* (2nd ed.) by J. Banks and C. Banks, 1993, p. 14. Reprinted with permission from Allyn and Bacon and the authors.

Page 290: Figure 8.6 from S. Yee & L. Kokin (1987), *Got Me a Story to Tell: A Multi-ethnic Book—Five Children Tell About Their Lives.* San Francisco: St. John's Educational Threshold Center. Reprinted with permission.

Page 325: Figure 9.7 from K. D. Wood (1987), "Helping Students Comprehend Their Textbooks" from *Middle School Journal, 18*, 20–21. Used with permission from the National Middle School Association.

Page 351: Figure 10.5 adapted from Bear and Gill (1988), *Journal of Reading* (February), 448–449. Reprinted with permission from the International Reading Association.

Page 355: Figure 10.6 adapted from Bear and Invernizzi (1984), Student-directed reading groups, *Journal of*

Name Index

Aaron, P. G., 401
Abouzeid, M., 244, 394, 395, 451
Abrams, J. C., 393, 457
Adams, M. J., 68, 201, 235, 244
Afflerbach, P., 5, 8
Alexander and the Terrible, Horrible, No Good, Very Bad Day (Viorst), 177
Allen, J., 294, 428
Allen, R. V., 197
Allen, V., 281
Allington, R., 38, 178, 286, 296, 386, 389, 429, 441
Alphabet from Z to A . . . , The (Viorst), 336
Amarel, M., 385
American Academy of Ophthalmology, 392, 393
American Academy of Pediatrics, 392
American Association for Pediatric Ophthalmology and Strabismus, 392
American Heritage Dictionary, The, 11
Anderson, A., 178
Anderson, E. C., 44
Anderson, R. C., 4, 222
Answering Students' Questions About Words (Tompkins & Yaden), 334
Anthony, R., 423, 424
Applebee, A., 37, 39, 46, 69
Aronson, D., 293
Aronson, E., 427
Atwell, N., 16, 23, 94, 151, 221, 317, 353
Au, K. H., 10, 38, 286, 287
Ayres, L., 296
Ayto, J., 375

Babysitters' Club, The (Martin), 304
Bajtelsmit, L., 298
Ballard, L., 5
Banks, J. and C., 285, 286
Banks, L. R., 342
Barnes, W. S., 38
Barone, D., 70–78 passim, 82–87 passim, 114, 120, 123, 151, 157, 188, 234, 249, 253, 280, 298, 311, 317, 318, 319, 385, 463
Barrett, J., 227
Barrs, M., 303, 309
Bartoli, J., 286, 292, 294, 428, 429
Bauer, C. F., 447
Bear, D., 4, 47, 56, 72, 86, 102, 117–123 passim, 208, 215, 224, 239, 241, 244, 249, 342, 348–356 passim, 439, 451
Beck, I. L., 346, 367
Bell, N., 456
Bennett, L., 10
Bereiter, C., 89
Bertrand, J., 324, 409, 410
Betts, E., 96
Biemiller, A., 117, 118, 242
Big Book of Tell Me Why, The (Leokum), 354
Birch, J., 402
Blanton, L. and W. E., 102, 244, 453
Bloom, L., 32
Blume, J., 101, 342
Bolton, F., 228
Booklinks (journal), 291
Bossing, L., 296
Bouffler, C., 5
Boxcar Children series (Warner), 98, 304, 342

Boyer, E., 397
Bradbury, B., 38
Bridge to Terabithia (Patterson), 311
Brien, P., 296
Britton, J., 44
Bromley, K. D., 212
Bronfenbrenner, U., 27, 30, 39
Brophy, G., 178
Brophy, J., 298
Brown, A., 314
Brown, C., 428
Brown, H., 114, 150
Brown, M. W., 68, 176
Brown Bear, Brown Bear (Martin), 69, 194, 217, 224
Bruner, J., 18
Bryk, A. S., 466
Burke, C., 19, 68, 70, 149, 179, 228
Burns, P., 109, 114
Burris, N., 19
Bussis, A., 385
Butter Battle Book, The (Seuss), 87
Byrnes, D., 296

Calfee, R., 5, 426, 427
Calkins, L., 23, 80, 84, 85, 228, 304, 329
Cambourne, B., 114, 150
Cameron, A., 82
Caps for Sale (Slobodkina), 75
Carbo, M., 307
Carey, R., 414
Carrier, L., 337
Carter, M., 5, 156, 161, 427
Carver, R., 72, 81, 87, 306
Caserta-Henry, C., 466
Cassidy, J., 354

Cathey, S. S., 54
Cattell, R., 421
Catts, H. W., 394
Cauley, L., 176
Cazden, C., 21, 178
Chall, J., 37, 72, 287
Chandler, J., 38
Cheek, E., 266
Chen, R., 391
Chittenden, E., 24, 385
Chomsky, C., 21
Church, J., 175
Clandinin, D., 172
Clark, M., 18
Clarke, L., 72
Clay, M. M., 19, 21, 35, 67, 68, 173–
    183 *passim,* 466
Cleary, B., 82, 311, 316, 342
Clemmer, E., 118
Clifford, P., 211
Cloudy with a Chance of Meatballs
    (Barrett), 227
Cohen, A. H., 393
Cohen, M., 417
Cole, J., 82
Collier, V., 270
Collins, J., 39
Collins, P., 151
Comer, J., 9, 462
Commeyras, M., 314
Commins, N., 269, 280, 289
Compain, R., 463
Concepts about Print Test (Clay), 182
Connell, R. W., 38, 57, 286, 390
Connelly, F., 172
Conrad, K., 441, 445
Cook-Gumperz, J., 41, 42
Cooter, R. B. Jr., 320
Corcoran, T., 463, 469
Corcos, E., 393
Courtney, R., 24
Cowley, J., 217, 278
Cramer, R., 123, 124, 127
Cress, C., 451
Crystal, D., 54
Csikszentmihalyi, M., 13
Cummins, J., 47, 269, 278

Dahl, R., 101, 151, 316
Dana, J. P., 456

Daniels, P., 156
Danny, the Champion of the World
    (Dahl), 151, 316
Darling-Hammond, L., 428
Davidson, B. J., 393
Davidson, J., 346
Davidson, J. L., 371
Dear Mr. Henshaw (Cleary), 316, 319
Deenie (Blume), 342
DeFord, D. E., 466
Delgado-Gaitan, C., 287
Delpit, L., 286, 289, 292, 294
Denckla, M. B., 391, 399
Desai, L., 5, 156, 161, 427
Desberg, P., 19
Deschenes, L., 462
Dewey, J., 9, 21
Discover magazine, 348
Dishner, E., 313, 355
Dixon, C., 283, 445
Doiron, R., 305
Dolan, L., 466
Donatelle, J. R., 456
Donnelly, K., 451
Do Not Touch (Carrier), 337
Dorsey-Gaines, C., 287
Down by the Bay (Raffi), 217, 220,
    224
Doyle, R., 296
Dragolia (Cowley), 278, 279–281
Dreifus, R. E., 401
Drum, P., 178
Dryfoos, J. G., 390
Duane, D. D., 399
Dunn, S., 73, 217
Durkin, D., 18, 67
Dyson, A. H., 9, 29, 40, 79, 150, 288,
    289

Earthsearch (Cassidy), 354
Eating the Alphabet (Ehlert), 176
Eccles, J., 27
Edelsky, C., 283
Edwards, P. A., 389
Eeds, M., 151, 320
Egan, K., 36, 54
Ehlert, L., 176
Ehri, L., 68, 178, 451
Ellis, S., 309
Epstein, M. H., 433

Ervin, C., 441, 445
Escobar, M. D., 385
Explorabook, The (Cassidy), 354
Extremely Weird (Lovett), 321
Eyeopeners (Kobrin), 210

Faibisch, F., 10
Farr, R., 414, 427
Farris, P., 274, 289
Feldman, D., 354
Fernald, G., 457
Fine, M., 9
First Grade Takes a Test (Cohen), 417
Fitzpatrick, R., 298
Fletcher, J. M., 385, 433
Flippo, R., 266
Flood, J., 228, 324, 423
Flores, B., 283
Flossie and the Fox (McKissick), 289
Foster, C., 414
Fox, M., 194
Francis, D. J., 433
Fredericks, A., 462
Freedle, R., 323
Freeman, D. and Y., 269, 272, 278,
    283
Friedman, M., 19
Friesen, S. L., 211
Frith, U., 394
Froebel, F., 21
Fudge-a-Mania (Blume), 101, 342

Galda, L., 178
Gamoran, A., 469
Ganske, K. A., 102, 120
Garber, S. W. and D. M., 398
Garcia, E., 283
Garcia, G., 429
Gardner, H., 9, 13, 52, 421
Gaskins, I., 451
Gee, J. P., 33, 348
Geers, A., 402
Gibbs, J., 40
Gibson, J. J., 41, 47
Gift of Sarah Barker, The (Yolen), 342
Gill, C. H., 245
Gill, J., 4, 351
Gill, T., 66, 244
Gillet, J., 203, 309, 321, 410, 417,
    418, 421

Gillingham, A., 456
Gillingham, M., 72
Giroux, H., 39
Glaser, S., 428
Goatley, V., 447
Goertz, M., 463, 469
Goffman, E., 33
Goldenberg, C. N., 287
Goldenburg, C., 9
Good, T., 298
Goodman, I. F., 38
Goodman, K., 12, 19
Goodman, Y., 12, 19, 149
Goodnight Moon (Brown), 68, 176
Good Work, Amelia Bedelia (Parish), 98, 100
Goosebumps books (Stine), 98, 304
Goss, J., 218
Goswami, D., 16
Got Me a Story to Tell (Yee & Kokin), 274, 289
Gove, M., 428
Graff, H. J., 36
Graham Lecture (1994), 38
Grant, C., 287
Graves, D., 94, 228, 231, 304, 356, 361, 449
Gray, D. B., 399
Greaney, V., 390
Greenberg, J. B., 40
Greenfield, P., 178
Gregory, R., 410, 411, 413, 414, 418
Gronlund, N., 410, 422
Grosjean, F., 34
Grosser, G. S., 456
Gutherie, J. T., 390
Guthrie, J., 10

Halliday, M., 21
Hamilton, V., 343–344
Hammond, D., 371
Hansen, J., 9, 18, 231
Harris, T., 306, 399, 400
Harris, V., 292
Harste, J., 19, 68, 70, 179, 194, 218, 228
Hart, S., 178
Hattie and the Fox (Fox), 194–197
Havelock, E., 53, 54
Hayes, N., 462

Healy, J. M., 401
Heath, S. B,, 9, 16, 18, 27, 43, 175, 178, 266, 288, 298
Hemphill, L., 38
Henderson, E., 9, 15, 20, 58, 63, 66, 75, 80, 83, 102, 218, 240, 366, 390
Henry and Mudge (Rylant), 100
Herber, H., 322
Hester, H., 309
Hiebert, E. H., 5, 8, 178, 222, 466
Hodges, R., 306, 399, 400
Hoien, T., 235
Holahan, J. M., 433
Holdaway, D., 18, 67, 196
Holford, T. D., 433
Holt, J., 74, 403
Hoskisson, K., 196, 213
Houses (Cowley), 217, 224
Hudelson, 274
Huey, E. B., 32
Hunt, B., 10
Hunt, N., 398
Hynd, G. W. and C. R., 399
Hynds, S., 378

I Can Read books, 395
Igoa, C., 269
Indian in the Cupboard series (Banks), 342
Inhelder, B., 21
International Reading Association (IRA), 35, 174, 414, 469
Invernizzi, M., 86, 102, 120, 121, 215, 239, 241, 244, 354, 355, 366, 385, 401, 439, 451, 466
IRA/NCTE Joint Task Force on Assessment, 12, 23
Irlen, H., 456
It Didn't Frighten Me (Goss et al.), 218

Jaggar, A. M., 466
James and the Giant Peach (Dahl), 101
Jenkins, L., 429
Jepson, M., 149
Jett-Simpson, M., 451
Jigaree, The. See Dragolia
Johns, J., 96, 108

Johnson, D. W. and R. T., 21, 40
Johnson, K., 462
Johnson, T., 423, 424
Johnston, F., 466
Johnston, P. H., 8, 12, 149, 391
Jones, James Earl, 344
Jones, M. B., 238
Juel, C., 47, 207, 466
Julian series (Cameron), 82
Juntunen, K., 361

Kaleidoscope (resource book), 291
Karnes, M., 411
Karweit, N. L., 466
Kauffman, J. M., 441
Kaufman, A., 421
Kavanagh, J. K., 399
Kawakami, A. J., 10, 38
Keifer, B. Z., 212
Keillor, G., 414
Kennedy, A., 393
Kennedy, J., 375
Kiefer, B. Z., 212
Kindig, J. S., 394
Klausner, E., 385
Kliegl, R., 393
Kobrin, B., 210, 305
Koch, K., 225
Kokin, L., 274, 275, 289, 290
Kornhaber, M., 9, 13, 52
Kowal, S., 118
Kozol, J., 37, 38, 390
Krashen, S., 271
Kruk, R. S., 393
Kuglemass, J., 27, 30
Kundhardt, D., 67

LaBerge, D., 306
Labov, W., 32
Lahey, M., 32
Langer, J., 37, 39
Lapp, D., 228, 324, 423
Lashley, K. S., 53
Lea, J., 53
Learning Denied (Taylor), 294
Leavell, J., 47
Lee, E., 240
Leland, C., 298
Lenneberg, E. H., 53, 386
Leokum, A., 354
Lester, J., 344

Levinson, H. N., 456
Levstik, L. S., 212
Library of Congress, 454
Lindamood, C. and P., 456
Lindfors, J., 281
Lindsey, J., 266
Linn, R., 410, 422
Lipman, D., 217
Lipson, M., 118, 385
Lovell, J., 151, 152
Lovett, S., 321
Luhn, M., 96, 108
Lundberg, I., 235
Lyons, C. A., 466

Macaulay, D., 344
McCann, A., 10
McCormick, S., 389, 393, 399, 400, 401
McGee, L., 85, 176, 188, 201
McGill-Franzen, A., 296, 429
McIntosh, M. E., 5, 348
McKeown, M. G., 215, 346, 367
McKissick, P., 289
McMahon, S., 447
McMillan, B., 337
Madden, N. A., 466
Magazines for Kids and Teens (Stoll), 354
Magic School Bus series (Cole), 82
Makuch, R. W., 385
Mangiola, L., 266, 298
Manzo, A., 313
Marks, H. M., 469
Marsh, G., 19
Marshall, K., 398
Martin, B. Jr., 69, 217
Martin, R., 304
Masonheimer, P., 178
Material World (Menzel), 354
Maxwell, C. M., 463
Mehegan, C. C., 401
Mekkelsen, J., 156
Melting (Bolton), 228
Menzel, P., 354
Mercer, C. D., 433
Meyer, B., 323
Michaels, W., 411
Michalove, B., 294, 428
Mickelson, N., 423, 424

Miramontes, O., 269, 280, 289
Mitchell, A., 10
Moats, L. C., 456
Moll, L. C., 40
Montgomery, A., 286
Moog, J., 402
Morris, D., 69, 73, 102, 179, 190, 240, 244, 441, 445, 453
Morrow, L. M., 8, 14, 18, 66, 67, 175, 176, 196, 197, 201, 209, 287, 305, 463
Mosenthal, J., 156
Mulhern, M., 463
Mullis, I. V. S., 37, 429
Mumper, J., 463
Murphy, J. J., 357
Murphy, S., 34, 41

Naab, H., 298
NAEYC (National Association for the Education of Young Children), 412
Nathan, R., 19, 224, 361
National Coalition of Advocates for Students, 23
National Geographic World, 348, 354
Neisser, U., 4, 29, 44
Nelson, J., 322
Nessel, D. D., 238, 283, 445
Neuman, S. B., 108, 194, 199, 291
Newkirk, T., 80, 342
Newman, F. M., 469
New Read-Aloud Handbook, The (Trelease), 210
Nikola-Lisa, W., 289
Ninio, A., 18, 177
Noddings, N., 10, 40

O'Connell, D., 118
Ogle, D. M., 310, 348
O'Hara, C., 451
Ohlhausen, M., 149
Oh Mister Sun (Raffi), 217
Olds, D., 363, 446, 447
Olsen, R., 269
Olson, R. K., 393
One Sun (McMillan), 337
Orlich, D., 396
Ovando, C., 269, 270, 271
Owl Moon (Yolen), 342

Padak, N. D., 371
Paley, V., 151, 197, 268, 283–284
Palincsar, A. S., 10, 314, 361
Pamenter, L., 73, 217
Pappas, C. C., 212
Paradis, E., 156
Parish, P., 100
Patterson, L., 311, 469
Pat the Bunny (Kundhardt), 67
Patton, M., 9
Paulson, G., 348
Payne, J. S., 433
Pearson, P. D., 4, 17, 21, 312, 429
Pelligrini, A., 178
People Could Fly, The (Hamilton), 344
Perez, B., 281, 283
Perfetti, C., 73, 207, 391, 456
Perfumo, P., 5
Perlmutter, J., 178
Perney, J., 244, 453
Perrone, V., 428
Pestalozzi, 21
Peters, C., 21
Peterson, R., 320
Peyton, J., 283
Piaget, J., 21, 41
Piché, D. M., 37
Pichert, J. W., 44
Pike, K., 463
Pikulski, J., 414, 457, 465
Pinker, S., 175
Pinnell, G. S., 466
Poliquin, R., 462
Pollatsek, A., 54
Poundstone, C., 10
Pratt, A., 391
Preece, A., 423, 424
Price, G., 72
Purcell-Gates, V., 178
Pyramid (Macauley), 344

Raffi, 217, 220
Ramona series (Cleary), 82, 311, 342
Ranger Rick magazine, 354
Raphael, T., 4, 312, 447
Rasinski, T., 306, 307, 462
Rayner, K., 54, 393
Read, C., 53, 76, 77
Readence, J., 313, 355

Reading Teacher, The (Rouse & Ryan), 393
Real Mother Goose, The (Wright), 176
Recording for the Blind and Dyslexic, 454
Reed, L., 283
Reutzel, D., 320
Reyes, M. de la Luz, 283
Rhodes, L., 196, 410, 427
Ricard, R., 42
Rice, M., 10
Richek, M., 343
Richgels, D., 85, 176, 188, 201
Rigg, P., 283
Roderick, M., 428
Rodriguez-Brown, F., 463
Roe, B., 109, 114
Rogoff, B., 10, 361
Roller, C. M., 388
Romney, S., 218
Rosemary, C. A., 466
Rosenblatt, L. M., 151, 342
Roskos, K., 108, 194, 199, 291
Rossi, R., 269, 286, 294
Rouse, M. W., 393
Routman, R., 303, 304, 423, 425
Ru, V. R., 39, 40, 361
Rusk, R., 21
Ryan, J. B., 393
Rybczynski, M., 187
Rylant, C., 100

Sabin, E., 118
Saks, A. L., 378
Salvia, J., 411
Samuels, S., 306, 310, 445
Sand and Stones (Clay), 183
Santa, C., 469
Sarah, Cynthia, Sylvia, Stout (Silverstein), 308
Sarason, S. B., 16
Saunders, P., 38
Scanlon, D. M., 391
Scarry, R., 67
Scharer, P. L., 245
Schlagal, J., 240
Schlagal, R., 102, 120, 240
Schleifer, R., 375
Schneider, R., 298
Schreiber, P., 53

Scotland, J., 21
Scott, J. A., 222
Seltzer, M., 466
Seuss, Dr., 87
Shanahan, T., 463
Shanklin, N., 410, 427
Shannon, P., 37
Sharp, S. J., 445
Shaywitz, B. A. and S. E., 385, 433
Shepard, A., 447
Shephard, L., 296
Shipley, J., 375
Shockley, B., 294, 428
Shone, V., 203
Short, K., 228, 469
Shuy, R., 283
Siks, G. B., 210
Silverblank, F., 344
Silverstein, S., 308
Simons, H. D., 33, 41
Sipay, E. R., 391
Slavin, R. E., 22, 355, 466
Sleeter, C., 287
Slier, D., 176
Slingerland, B. H., 457
Slobodkina, E., 75
Sloyer, S., 308
Small, S. G., 391
Smith, F., 18, 447
Smith, J., 196
Smith, K., 469
Smith, M., 296
Smith-Burke, T. M., 466
Snow, C. E., 38, 42, 177, 287
Spafford, C. S., 456
Spearman, C., 421
Spear-Swerling, L. L., 394
Spizman, R. F., 398
Sports Illustrated for Kids, 354
Squillace, S. R., 456
Stahl, S., 343
Stallman, A., 21
Stanovich, K., 310, 390, 391, 399, 400, 433
Staton, J., 283, 317, 318
Stauffer, R., 142, 197, 212, 316, 346, 348, 457
Stayter, F. Z., 8
Steller, S., 462
Sternberg, R. J., 394

Stewart, R., 156
Stewig, J. T., 210
Stice, C., 324
Stillman, B., 456
Stillman, P. R., 16
Stine, R. L., 304
Stires, S., 297
Stokes, S., 178
Stone, L., 175
Story Box Series, The, 217
Stremmel, A. J., 39, 40, 361
Strickland, D. S., 463
Stringfield, S., 269
Stuckless, E., 402
Stuebing, K. K., 433
Sulzby, E., 69, 173, 183

Taba, H., 322
Taylor, B. M., 466
Taylor, D., 5, 49, 67, 154, 287, 294–295, 463
Taylor, W. L., 37
Tchudi, S., 358
Teaching Tolerance (journal), 291
Teale, W., 18, 67, 173
Temple, C., 19, 203, 224, 309, 321, 361, 410, 417, 418, 421
Temple, F., 19, 224, 327, 328, 361
Templeton, S., 58, 66, 72, 75, 77, 83, 86, 88, 102, 120, 121, 211, 215, 239–245 *passim*, 267, 304, 333, 341, 342, 348, 366, 374, 389, 413, 439, 451
Textbook Activity Guide, 325
Thomas, A., 309
Three Little Kittens, The (Cauley), 176
3–2–1 Contact magazine, 354
Tierney, R., 5, 156, 161, 313, 355, 427
Tobin, W., 40
Tomatis, A. A., 456
Tompkins, G., 196, 213, 327, 329, 334, 346
Torres-Guzman, M., 281, 283
Tough, J., 271
Tracey, D. H., 463
Trelease, J., 210, 305
Troy, A., 187
Tudge, J., 50
Tunmer, W., 47
Tyack, D., 40

Ueland, B., 9
Urzua, C., 287, 288
U.S. Bureau of the Census, 57
U.S. Department of Education, 39
U.S. Office of Special Education and
    Rehabilitative Services, 399

Vacca, J. and R., 305, 428
Valencia, S., 5, 8, 21
Valtin, R., 384
Vandevier, R., 343
Van Meter, V., 10
Vellutino, F. R., 391, 394, 399, 456
Venezky, R. L., 37
¡Vete! (Cowley), 217
Viorst, J., 177, 336
Vygotsky, L., 9–10, 21, 40

Walmsley, S., 286, 386, 390, 441
Walp, T. P., 441
Walsh, D., 72

Warner, G. C., 304, 342, 438, 439
Warner, M., 120, 385
Wasik, B. A., 466
Watson, D., 149
Weaver, C., 72
Wells, D., 151, 153
Wells, G., 33, 39
Welsh, V., 19
West, R., 38
What Do Babies Do? (Slier), 176
Wheels (Shone), 203
Whiteford, P., 38
White Teacher (Paley), 283
Why Do Clocks Run Clockwise? (Feldman), 354
Wigfield, A., 10
Wilkinson, L. A. G., 222, 309
Willows, D. M., 393
Winograd, P. N., 391
Wise, A., 428
Wishes, Lies, and Dreams (Koch), 225

Wixson, K. K., 21, 118, 385
Wong-Fillmore, L., 273
Wonnacott, C., 312
Wood, K. D., 325
Wood, 324
Woodcock, R., 418
Woodman, D., 447
Woodsong (Paulson), 348
Woodward, V., 19, 68, 70, 179
Worthy, M. J., 385, 401, 447, 451
Wright, B., 176
Wright Group, 183

Yaden, D., 334
Yamamoto, K., 296
Yates, J., 358
Yee, S., 274, 275, 289, 290
Yolen, J., 342
Ysseldyke, S., 411

Subject Index

Abilities and talents
  recognized, 9, 52
  teaching above or below, 20
Achievement test, 412, 416, 438
Acquired learning difficulties, 396–397
Acting out. *See* Drama activities
ACT test, 410, 411
ADD, ADHD (attention deficit disorder/with hyperactivity), 397–398
Advanced literacy. *See* Intermediate and advanced literacy
Aesthetic stance, 151. *See also* Response to literature
African Americans, 286, 287, 288, 428
  dialect of, 289–290
  oral tradition of, 344
Age of child. *See* Children
Alexia, 400–401
Aliteracy, 86
Alphabet books, choice of, 201
Alphabetic principle, 72
Alphabetizing, 241
American Sign Language (ASL), 401, 402
Anticipation guides, 322
Appropriateness of language, 270
Art activities. *See* Drama activities; Drawing
Articulation, manner and point of, 76
Asian Americans, 269, 287
Aspectual reading, 185
Assess, definition of, 11
Assessment
  activities of, 12–14
  of book knowledge, 182–185
  diagnostic, 412

DRTA and, 4
follow-up, 295
formal, *see* Tests and testing
four components of, 7, 12–14, 24
getting started, 106
individual, 93–137
informal, 6, 94–103, 140–141, 295, 299 (*see also* Portfolios)
informal, of emergent knowledge, 179–204
informal, qualitative inventories, 104–137
of instruction, 437–438
instruction integrated with, 7, 8–9, 24, 171–205
instruction in reading integrated with, 209–224, 305–326, 343–356
instruction in word study and spelling integrated with, 235–245, 332–337, 362–378
instruction in writing integrated with, 224–235, 326–332, 356–362
introductory interview, 106–108
motivating effect of, 10
of non-English-speaking students, 272–276
pulling information together, 154–159
reason for, 6, 94–95
seven key themes of, 8–10
seven perspectives of, 5–6
sharing results with parents and student, 132–135, 427
small-group, 145–153
special times for, 16–17, 24

of spelling, 120, 121–122, 127, 146
of students with diverse backgrounds, 288–290
summaries and profile guides of, 127–133
whole-class, 141–145
of writing, by student, 330–331
of writing, preparation for, 359
See also Evaluation
Assignments, open-ended, 297
At-risk schools and students, 266, 267, 294, 299
Attitude, 47–50
  and motivation, 49–50
Audiotaping, 106, 467
Auditory difficulties, 391, 394, 401–403
Australia, 38
Author's chair, 231, 356, 447
Autobiographies, student, 141–142

Beginning literacy, 71–80, 103, 104, 105, 109, 207–247
  beginning readers and writers identified, 207–208
  beginning readers discussed and interviewed, 256, 257, 259
  checklists (beginning reader, writer, speller), 215, 225, 237
  reading with students, 212–216
  response to literature, 221–222
  students reading and writing on their own, 221–224, 232–235
  support activities for, 212, 222–232
  teacher reading and writing with students, 212–216, 224–232

Behavioral problems, 399
Beyond the Basics program, 466
Big books, 196, 211, 216
Bilingualism, 34–36, 273. *See also*
    Language
Biographies (as teaching tool), 46
Black English, 290. *See also* Language
    (dialects)
Book clubs, 447–448, 463
Books
    alphabet, choice of, 201
    awareness of, 67
    big, 196, 211, 216
    children's choice of, 81–82, 149,
        264, 464
    children's knowledge of, 176–177,
        182–185
    choice of, for reading to students,
        210–211
    concept of book assessment, 184
    emergent reader response to,
        200–201
    at home, 463
    multicultural, selection of,
        291–292
    pattern, 217–218
    professional, 467–468
    shared book experience, 196, 201,
        465
    talking about, 151–152 (*see also*
        Response to literature)
    on tape, 444, 447, 448, 454
    wordless, 196–197
    word study, 375
    See also Reading
Book talks, 343
Brainstorming
    to find information, 353
    in planning curriculum, 14, 378
    to show what students know, 455
    word study, 242, 243, 368, 373,
        378
    in writing stories, 158, 164, 212,
        228, 229, 372
Breath groups, 54. *See also* Speech

Center activities, 217
Chants as reading aid, 445
Chapter I program, 465
Charting ideas, 212, 344, 346

Checklists
    beginning reader, writer, speller,
        215, 225, 237
    intermediate and advanced reader,
        writer, speller, 345, 355, 357,
        373
    literature response group, 319,
        320
    peer editing, 332
    transitional reader, writer, speller,
        307, 326, 333
Child abuse, reporting, 59
Child labor laws, 36
Children
    age of, and development of liter-
        acy, 173–174, 270
    choice and knowledge of books,
        81–82, 149, 176–177, 182–185,
        264, 464
    cross-age tutoring, 298
    journals kept by, *see* Journals
    literacy learning as viewed by,
        249–264
    poor and transient, 390
    young, language development in,
        53–54, 175–176
    See also Preschoolers; Students
Children of promise, 266
China, literacy in, 36
Chinese language, 274–275, 277
Choral reading. *See* Reading
Classrooms, literacy-rich, 463–465
Closed sorts, 203, 336
Closed syllables, 366–367
Clustering ideas, 212, 346
Cognition, 41–47
    metacognitive strategies (reflec-
        tion), 12, 14, 46–47, 356
    See also Thinking
Cognitive-academic language profi-
    ciency, 271
Common sense, 18, 22
Community connections, 40, 141,
    196, 219
    integration of, 58
    and students with learning difficul-
        ties, 434
    See also Parents
Comprehension. *See* Reading com-
    prehension; Understanding

Comprehension questions, 114–115,
    119
    question strategies, 310–314
Computer use, 56, 59, 352–353, 468
Concept of book, assessment of, 184
Concept of story, 45–46, 47
    lack of, 389
Concept of word, 69, 73–75, 79–80, 89
    difficulty in acquiring, 394, 401
    rudimentary and full, 207–208
Concept of word in print, 179, 189–
    192
Concept sorts, 202–204
Consonant doubling, 364, 366, 373
Consonant pictures and blends,
    240–241
Consonant-vowel-consonant (CVC)
    pattern, 243
Construction of meaning, 42–47,
    311–324
    fiction, 311–320
    nonfiction, 320–324
    See also Reading comprehension
Construction of story, reader's under-
    standing of, 69–70, 76, 82, 87
Content dictations, 445–446
Content-guided activity. *See* GLTA;
    GRTA
Content validity of test, 411, 412
Context
    identifying words in, 238–239,
        333–334
    shared, 41–42
    word study in, 242
Contextual expressions, 99
Cooperative groups (students), 232–
    233, 292, 324, 330–332, 360–
    361, 465
Criterion defined, 412
Criterion-referenced test, 10, 412,
    421–422
Criterion-related validity of test, 412
Critical thinking. *See* Thinking
Cross-age tutoring, 298
Cultural diversity (multiculturalism),
    34–36, 174, 269, 283–297
    book selection, 291–292
Culture defined, 285
Cumulative sequence in predictable
    book, 196

Curriculum
    brainstorming in planning, 14, 378
    permeable ("fluid and fuzzy"),
        288, 297, 299
    preschool and kindergarten, 173,
        180–181
    teachers pressured to cover, 38, 39
    test influence on, 427, 428
CVC (consonant-vowel-consonant)
        pattern, 243

DEAR (drop everything and read)
        time, 222
DED (double-entry draft) frame-
        work, 82, 346–348
Deficit, learning, 385
Derivational constancy phase, 87,
        88–89, 362–363, 373, 378
    word study in, 374–376
Development, integration of, 58
Developmental continuum, 384–386,
        451
    delay in, 385–386
    special literary needs within,
        389–399
    special literacy needs beyond,
        399–403
Developmental expressions, 95, 103–
        104, 127
Developmental test, 412
Diagnosis, definition of, 11
Diagnostic assessment, 412
Diagnostic tests, 410, 417–421
Dialects. See Language
Dialogical-thinking reading lesson
        (D-TRL), 314–316
Dialogue journals, 317–319. See also
        Journals
Dictation cycle, 218–220
    content dictations, 445–446
    individual dictations, 218–220,
        445
Dictionaries, 375
    dialect, created by children, 289
Digraphs, 240–241
Directionality of print, 178–179
Discourse, 270
Diversity. See Cultural diversity;
        Racial diversity; Socioeconomic
        diversity

Documentation
    as component of assessment
        process, 7, 12–13, 24, 154–159
    definition of, 11
    different ways of, 13
    of ideas, 212
    interpretation of, 14
Double-entry draft. See DED
Drama activities, 45, 151, 308–309
Drawing (as response to literature),
        151, 152, 343
Drawing pictures of words, 241
Drop-out rates, 37, 38, 286
DRTA (no-book directed reading
        thinking activity), 4, 46
    on assessment, 6
    creating your own, 5
Dyslexia, 187, 399–400
    treatments for, 456

Editing. See Writing
Education
    disparity of, 37
    funding for, 30, 37–38, 465
    interferences in, 389–390
    See also Instruction
Efferent stance, 151. See also Re-
        sponse to literature
Egocentrism, 42
Emergent literacy, 66–71, 72, 73, 80,
        103–105, 109, 171–205
    emergent readers and writers iden-
        tified, 173–174
    emergent readers discussed and in-
        terviewed, 254, 255
    informal assessment of, 179–204
    integrated instruction for, 194–204
    opposed to reading readiness, 66, 89
    spelling and orthography, 70, 173
Emotional disturbance, 399
English as second language (ESL),
        34–35, 60, 182, 269–283, 289,
        299
    Asian-influenced, 274
    for deaf children, 401
    instruction, 276–283
    learning process, 271–272
    Spanish-influenced, 274
    student's ability, 273–275
    student's background, 272–273

Environment. See Learning
        environment
Environmental print. See Print
Etymology, 363
Evaluation
    definition of, 11
    grading as part of, 14
    and planning, as component of as-
        sessment process, 7, 14–15, 24,
        140, 159–165
    portfolios used for, 161–164, 423
    self-evaluation by student, 14–15,
        161–162, 330–331, 355
    self-evaluation by teacher, 15–16,
        163–164
    of writing, 124–127, 365
Experience, worlds of. See Worlds of
        experience
Experience-based question, 312
Expository (nonfiction) texts, 45
    constructing meaning in, 320–324
    listening to, 211–212, 344
    reading, 305–306, 314, 320–324,
        354
    writing, 84, 327
Expressive mode, 45
Eye movements (in reading), 54–55
Eye problems. See Visual difficulties

Factual comprehensive questions, 114
Families, 461–463
    family literacy programs, 463
    See also Parents
Feedback
    to parents and teachers, 427
    to students, 52, 153, 232
Fernald technique, 457
Fiction. See Poetic mode
Fingerpointing (while reading), 72,
        116, 118
Fixation (in eye movement), 54–55
Fluency defined, 306. See also
        Reading
Focusing questions, 310–311
Formal assessment. See Tests and
        testing
Freewriting, 120. See also Writing
Frustration level, 96–109 passim, 115,
        117, 297, 306, 310
    avoidance of, 113

maturational delay and, 391
and vision problems, 392
See also Functional levels
Full concept of word, 207–208. *See
also* Concept of word
Functional levels, 95–103
comprehension questions, 115, 119
criteria for, 97
listening, 119
oral reading accuracy, 117, 119
spelling and writing, 99, 102, 103,
124, 127
word recognition, 109
See also Frustration level

Gender defined, 285
Generativity principle (in writing), 179
GLTA (guided listening-thinking ac-
tivity), 142–147, 211, 441
content, 344
small-group, 146–147, 148
students with learning problems,
444
whole-class, 142–145
Goals, student, 52
learning difficulties and, 438–439
planning for, 142
Goldilocks plan, 149
Grading, 6, 14
grade levels, 163–164, 438
and functional levels, 98–99
See also Evaluation
Greek prefixes and roots, 374
Group experience charts, 218, 445
Groupings, flexibility of, 465. *See also*
Cooperative groups (students);
Reading groups
GRTA (guided reading-thinking activity), 145, 146–147, 316–317,
402, 441
content, 321–324, 348
for hyperlexics, 401
predict-read-confirm cycle, 346
small-group, 145, 146–147, 148
Guided instruction of revision and
editing, 329–330
Guided listening-thinking activity,
Guided reading-thinking activity.
See GLTA; GRTA
Gutenberg Bible, 36

Hands-on learning, 21
Handwriting, 57–58
physical aspects of, 55
Health
physical, 53, 57, 397, 398
psychological/mental, 48–50,
397–399
reporting concerns about, 59
"Heaps" (in child's understanding of
story), 69
Hearing problems, 391, 394, 401–403
Hispanics, 269, 428
Holistic approach, 185, 428
Home. *See* Families; Parents
Homonyms and homophones, 334
Hyperactivity, 397–398
Hyperlexia, 401

Ideas
charting and clustering (web), 212,
344, 346, 372
documentation of, 212
finding (for writing), 448
organizing, 323
Illiteracy
cause of, 35
functional, 37
See also Literacy; Literacy, development of
Independent activities in read- and
writing. *See* Reading; Writing
Independent level, 96–103 *passim*,
109, 115, 117, 119
for repeated reading, 308
See also Functional levels
Independent reading, 185
Individual dictations, 218–220, 445
Individual educational plan (IEP),
295, 440–441
Inferential comprehension questions,
114
Informal assessments. *See* Assessment
Informal reading inventory. *See* IRI
Information, how to find, 352–353
Instruction
assessment of, 437–438
integration of, *see* Integration
in physical world, 57–59
planning, 134–135
poor or inappropriate, 390

in psychological world, 50, 52
scaffolded, 18–19, 314
special methods, 455–457
students with difficulties, 433–459
thematically organized, 465
See also Education
Instructional level, 96–103 *passim*,
109, 115, 117, 119. *See also*
Functional levels
Integration
of assessment and instruction, 7,
8–9, 24, 209–245, 264
five applications of concept of, 58
of instruction for emergent, 194–
204
integrated or synchrony model of
literacy, 62–64, 66, 89
of learning-difficulty student in
classroom, 441
of reading and writing, 465
Intelligence tests, 6, 412
individual, 418–421
Interest interview, 142
Intermediate and advanced literacy,
85–89, 103, 104, 105, 339–380
advanced readers discussed and interviewed, 261–263
checklists (reader, writer, word study
and speller), 345, 355, 357, 373
overview of, 341
readers and writers identified,
340–343
reading speed, 87, 341–342
spelling, 87–88, 362–378
students reading and writing on
their own, 353–356, 360–362
writing styles of, 127
writing with students, 356–359
Interpretation
as component of assessment
process, 7, 13–14, 24
definition of, 11
Interview
"getting to know you," 106–108
interest, 142
learning, 142
schedule, 107
Inventories
commercial informal reading, 109,
111, 112, 114

(Inventories, *cont.*)
elementary qualitative spelling, 121
informal reading, *see* IRI
spelling, 121, 157, 158, 163, 364
teacher-made, 112
IRI (informal reading inventory),
108–119, 130, 133, 145, 147–
148, 157, 158, 162
how to administer, 148
for non-English-speaking student,
273
and rate of reading, 306
and silent reading, 309
for student needing additional support, 294

Jigsaw method (group reading), 355
Journals, 45, 234, 250, 465
dialogue, 317–319
journal entries, 49–50, 77, 142,
157–158, 161
learning logs, 234, 361–362
preschool, 185–186, 200
response logs, 234, 346–347
teacher's personal log, 164, 467

Kindergarten. *See* Preschoolers
Koran, the, 36
KTEA test, 438
K-W-L (know, want to learn,
learned), 310, 348

Lake Wobegon effect, 414
Language
bilingualism, 34–35, 273
bilingual program, 271, 278–283
biology of, 53–54
as center of worlds of experience,
27–28
children's, assessment of, 57
children's development of, 53–54,
175–176
Chinese, 274–275, 277
dialects, 32, 115, 117, 176,
289–290
diversity of, 35, 60, 268–283
ecology of, 29–36
English, *see* English as second language (ESL)
five systems of, 125–126

health, and development of, 53–54
home talk vs. school talk, 33
informal inventory of, 133
new, requirements of, 270–272
rhythm of, 53–54
Spanish, 217, 274, 275
special role of, 41–42
spoken or oral, *see* Speech
student's first, 278
systems of (orthographic, syntactic,
semantic, pragmatic, prosodic),
124–126
Tagalog, 276
written, *see* Writing; Written language
See also Vocabulary
Language experience approach, 197–
199, 218
combined with shared reading, 220
for non-English-speaking students,
282–283
Language processing difficulties,
394–396, 401
Latinos, 428
Latin roots, 374, 378
Learning at home, 32–34
Learning difficulties, 384–405,
431–459
acquired, 396–397
addressing and resolving, 404–405
auditory, 391, 394, 401–403
community and other educators/
professionals involved with, 434,
435–436
developmental continuum, 384–
386, 389–403, 451
identifying the source, 398–403
and inclusion in classroom, 441
literacy instruction for, 433–459
parents involved in planning for,
434, 436–437, 440
physical and mental problems, 294,
396–399
planning instruction for, 433–443
reading, 384–405
recognition of, 386–388
and recreational reading, 446–448
special needs, 389–404
special services and programs,
403–404, 439–441

student perseverance and coping,
444, 453–455
students involved in planning for,
436
understanding the cause, 403–405
visual, 391–394
writing, 385, 398, 448–453
Learning disabilities, 394–396
Learning environment
literacy-rich, 18
parents and, *see* Parents
student partnerships in, 40–41,
232–233, 264
Learning logs. *See* Journals
Learning to read and write (basic
principles), 18–21
Lesson plan, 134, 135. *See also* Planning
Letter knowledge, 201–204
Letter-name spelling, 72, 76–79, 122,
123, 235
and word study, 242–243, 244–245
Letter reversals in writing and reading, 48
Letter-writing
by students, 234
by teacher to parents, 141
Lexicon, 270. *See also* Vocabulary
Libraries
exploration of, 352, 453, 463
school and classroom, 463
Lindamood method, 456
Listening comprehension, 119. *See
also* Understanding
Listening to exposition, 211–212,
344
Listening to stories, 68–69, 343–344
guided (GLTA), 142–147, 211
List-group-label strategy, 322, 346
Literacy
and aliteracy, 86
in ancient Europe and China, 36
assessment of, 93–137, 288–289,
294–295, 299
authentic activities, 179
construction of meaning in, 42–47,
311–324
development of, *see* Literacy, development of, *below*
essential elements of, 26–60

and freedom, 37
how to describe (fundamental and
    development expressions),
    95–104
and illiteracy, 35
and instruction for students with
    difficulties, 433–459
integrated model of, 62–64, 66, 89
literacy-rich classrooms, 463–465
mind, language, and, 41–42
perception in, 47
social importance and history of,
    36–38
three worlds of experience, 27–59
in the United States, 37–38
See also Reading; Writing
Literacy, development of
age of child and, 173–174, 270
basic principles of, 18–21
beginning phase, 71–80, 103, 104,
    105, 109, 207–247
children's views of, 249–264
"cracking the code," 72
difficulties in, 384–405
documentation of, 13
ecology (social world) of, 29–36
emergent phase, 66–73, 80, 89,
    103, 104, 105, 109, 171–205
families included in, 461–463
four guidelines for teaching and
    learning, 17–23
functional levels of, 94–103, 106,
    109
integration of, 9, 58, 62, 65, 264
intermediate and advanced phase,
    85–89, 103, 104, 105
knowledge of, 65
teachers' views of, 249–264
See also Literacy; Reading; Writing
Literacy biography, 154–156
Literature
exploring (transitional reader),
    336–337, 338
response to, *see* Response to litera-
    ture
Literature discussion groups, 319–
    320, 465
Literature logs, 317. *See also*
    Journals
Long vowels. *See* Vowels

Magazines, 448
Management skills, development of,
    18, 22–23
Manner and point of articulation, 76
Maturational delay, 390–391
"Maturing functions," 10
Mayfield, Francine, 250
Median score, 413, 414
Medications, effect of, 398
Metacognitive strategies. *See* Cogni-
    tion
Mental health, 397–399
Mental retardation, 397
Mexican-Americans, 428
Miscues (reading errors), 117, 451
Mispronunciations, 115
Monologue and dual or collective
    monologue, 175. *See also* Speech
Morphology, 270
Motivation
assessment and instruction as
    means of, 10
attitude and, 49–50
how to build, 50, 52–53
lack of, 391
in learning to read and write, 49–
    50, 51
psychological health and, 48–49
Multiculturalism. *See* Cultural
    diversity
Multidisciplinary team, 295, 421
Multisensory approach, 456–457

Narrative text. *See* Poetic mode
    (fiction)
National Council of Teachers of Eng-
    lish, 469
Native Americans, 269, 428
Newsletters, 461–462
New strategies, 468
No-book directed reading thinking
    activity. *See* DRTA
Noncommunicative speech, 175
Non-English-speaking students. *See*
    Students
Nonfiction. *See* Expository (non-fic-
    tion) texts
Normal distribution of test scores, 413
Norm-referenced (standardized)
    tests, 164, 409–416

characteristics (reliability, validity),
    411, 412
definition of, 412
diagnostic, 417–421
interpreting results, 411–416
pros and cons of, 425–429
See also Tests and testing
Norms, 410, 412
Notebooks, word study, 335–336, 373
Note-taking, 348, 349, 454
Nursery rhymes, 190–191

Observation
as component of assessment
    process, 7, 12, 24, 141–153
definition of, 11
developing skills of, 12
Open-ended assignments, 297
Open sorts, 203, 336
Open syllables, 366–367
Oral language. *See* Speech
Oral reading (reading aloud), 36
beginners, 72, 222
teacher, 52, 68–69, 194–197, 209–
    212, 305–306, 343–344, 464
teacher, and GLTA, 142–147, 211
teacher, to non-English-speaking
    student, 278
teacher, one-on-one, 182, 183
teacher, to student with learning
    problem, 395, 444
teacher, to transitional students,
    305–306
teacher and students together,
    213–214
Oral reading accuracy, 115–117, 119
how to mark, 116
qualitative analysis of, 94
Orthographic knowledge, 47, 66, 89
difficulty in developing, 395
emergent level, 70, 173
and handwriting, 55
integrated model, 63–64
intermediate and advanced level,
    87–89
summary sheet assessing, 130, 133
transitional level, 82, 303, 304
word recognition as test of, 108–
    109, 110
See also Spelling

Orthographic system of language, 125
Orton-Gillingham approach, 456, 457
Outlining, 349

Paralinguistics, 271
Parents
  of child with learning difficulty, 434, 436–437, 440
  culturally diverse, 35, 287
  gap between school and, 39–40
  involved in learning process, 9, 140, 192, 219, 264, 265–266
  meeting with, 434–435, 436–437, 440
  newsletters to, 461–462
  non-English-speaking, 35
  and reading and writing at home, 32–33, 67, 196, 222–224, 287–288, 462–463
  sharing assessment/test results with, 132–135, 427
  sharing child's accomplishments with, 20
  teacher's relationship with, 141, 288, 294
Participant role, 45
Partnerships, student. See Students
Passage selection and length (in assessing reading), 109–113
Patterns
  consonant-vowel-consonant (CVC), 243
  long-vowel, 337, 395
  reading, 445
  sequential, in predictable text, 196
  short-vowel, 243, 244
  VCCV and VCV, 366–367
  within-word (spelling), 82–83, 122, 123, 333–337
Pattern stories, 216, 217–218
Pattern writing activities, 224–227
Peer reading and writing, 298
  editing checklist, 332
  revision sheet, 331
  student response to, 159, 160, 330
  See also Students (partnerships of)
Penmanship. See Handwriting
Percentile scores, 413, 414

Perception, visual, 48
Perception in literacy, 47
Personal readers, 215–216
Personal writing, 45. See also Journals
Petrulli, Adine
  classroom of, 250–253
  discusses students, 254–256
Phonemic awareness, 201
  difficulty in developing, 395
  prephonemic, 70
  semiphonemic, 75–76, 122, 123, 208, 235–241, 244
Phonology, 270
Physical world, 52–59
  biology of language, 53–54
  health, 53, 57, 397, 398
  and learning difficulties, 396–397
  physical acts of reading and writing, 54–56
  suggestions for effective instruction in, 57–59
Pictures and picture cards, 239–241, 242–243
  difference between illustrations and print, child's recognition of, 183
  picture sorts, 451
Planning
  for change, 433–434
  curriculum, 427
  evaluation and, see Evaluation
  Goldilocks plan, 149
  and goal setting, 142
  for instruction, 134–135, 165–166
  lesson plan, 134, 135
  to meet special needs, 405, 433–443
Play, as important part of learning, 21
Play centers, writing in, 199
Poetic mode (fiction), 45, 46
  construction of meaning in, 311–320
  evaluation of skills in narrative writing, 124, 126
Poetry, 344
  writing, 327–329
Portfolios, 156–159
  exemplar, 157–159
  student-centered, 156–157, 192–193

teacher-centered, 156
using for evaluation, 161–164, 423
  See also Summaries and Profile guides
Postwriting, 231–232
Poverty. See Socioeconomic diversity
Pragmatics, 271
Pragmatic system of language, 126
Preconsonantal nasal, 79
Predictable text, 183, 194–196, 211, 281–282, 314, 346
Predictive validity of test, 412
Prephonemic. See Phonemic awareness
Preprofessionals Skills Test (PPST), 103
Preschoolers, 179–181, 194, 197
  awareness of book, 67
  curriculum for, 173, 180–181
  journals of, 185–186, 200
  knowledge of print, 68, 178–179, 183, 185–192
  non-English-speaking, 269
Prewriting, 228–229. See also Writing
Print
  concept of word in, 179, 189–192
  differences between illustrations and, child's recognition of, 183
  directionality of, 178–179
  environmental, 68, 278
  preschooler's knowledge of, 68, 178–179, 183, 185–192
Prior knowledge of subject, 322
Professional development network, 41
Professional organizations, 468
Profile guides, 127–132
Profile sheets, 154, 423, 440
Prosodic system of language, 126
Psychological world, 28, 41–52
  attitude and sense of self, 47–50
  constructing meaning in literacy, 42–47
  and learning difficulties, 397–398
  mind, language, and literacy, 41–42
  perception in literacy, 47
  psychological health and, 48–50, 397–399
  suggestions for effective instruction in, 50, 52

QAR (questions about reading), 312
Qualitative analysis of child's oral
    reading, 94
Questions
    comprehension, 114–115, 119
    experience-based, 312
    focusing, 310–311
    question strategies, 310–314
    about reader (QAR), 312
    text-explicit and -implicit, 312
Quintilian (teacher in Rome), 357

Race defined, 285–286
Racial diversity, 283–294
Rationale for activity, 135
Raw score, 414
Reader's chair, 447
Readers' theater, 308–309, 447. *See
    also* Drama activities
Reading
    aloud, *see* Oral reading
    beginners, *see* Beginning literacy
    behaviors and development, 6
    choices, 81–82, 149, 264, 464
    choral, 212, 213–215, 307–308
    comprehension of, *see* Reading
        comprehension
    and concept of story, 45–46, 47
    conventional, 69
    difficulty in, 384–405, 431–448
    early experiences, 69 (*see also*
        Preschoolers)
    effective, 350
    emergent readers, *see* Emergent lit-
        eracy
    environmental print, *see* Print
    expression in, 117–118, 119
    eye movements in, 54–55
    fingerpointing in, 72, 116, 118
    fluency/disfluency of, 72–73, 81,
        117–118, 119, 306–309
    functional and grade levels of, 96–
        99, 115, 117, 119, 297, 306–
        307, 310, 391
    guided, 346–348
    at home, 222–224, 287–288, 462–
        463
    independent, 185
    independent activities, 222–224,
        324

informal inventory of, *see* IRI
instruction integrated with assess-
    ment, 209–224, 305–326, 343–
    356
integrated model of, 63–64
integrated with writing, 465
intermediate and advanced, *see* In-
    termediate and advanced literacy
to learn, 86
learning to read by, 18–21, 222–224
letter reversals in, 48
and meaning construction, 69–70,
    75, 82, 87
as most sophisticated mental activ-
    ity, 42
motivation in learning, 49–50, 51
nonfiction, 305–306, 314, 320–
    324, 354
oral, *see* Oral reading (reading
    aloud)
passage selection and length (in as-
    sessment), 109–113
peer, 298
physical act of, 54–55
questions about, 312–314
rate of, *see* Reading rate (speed)
recreational, 446–448
repeated, 306–308
and response to literature, 69–70,
    75, 82, 87, 150–153, 200–201
shared, 216–218
shared book experience, 196, 201
silent, 81, 86, 309–310
silent, lip movement (LM) in, 116,
    118
silent sustained (SSR), 72, 222,
    233, 309, 324, 444, 464
strategic, 348–352
by students, 197, 221–224
by students, on their own, 324–
    326, 353–356
with students, 52, 212–216, 306–
    324, 344–353
with students with learning prob-
    lems, 444–448
support activities, 212, 222–224,
    445–448
synchrony between spelling and,
    111
taping text as aid in, 297, 307–308

teacher's professional, 467–468
timed, 308
transitional readers, *see* Transitional
    literacy
word-by-word (WxW), 73, 116, 306
word study in, 367–376
workshops, 149–153, 221, 353–354
See also Books; Print
Reading comprehension, 37, 109
    questions for (factual, vocabulary,
        inferential), 114
    question strategies, 310–314
    retelling as test of, 112, 113–115,
        149–150, 311
    story mapping and, 346
    word calling vs., 310
    See also Construction of meaning;
        Understanding
Reading groups, student-guided,
    354–355
Reading guides, 323
Reading level (RL), 37, 112
Reading pauses, 54, 115
Reading rate (speed), 54–55
    beginners, 74
    how to measure, 117
    intermediate and advanced, 87,
        341–342
    rereading and, 445
    for studying, 348
    transitional, 306, 308
Reading readiness, 66, 89
Reading Recovery program, 466
Reciprocal teaching, 314
Recurring principle (in writing), 179
Reflection. *See* Cognition (metacog-
    nitive strategies)
Refusal to read, 89, 185
Reliability of test, 411, 412
Repetition
    in noncommunicative speech, 175
    in predictable book, 196
ReQuest, 313–314
Research by teacher, 469
Resources, 434. *See also* Community
    connections; Special services
Response to literature, 69–70, 75, 82,
    87
    creative and cooperative (of begin-
        ners), 221–222

(Response to literature, *cont.*)
  through drama, art, writing, and
    talk, 150–153, 343
  emergent, 200–201
  group checklist, 319, 320
  response logs, 234, 346–347
  written, 465
Response to work of peers, 158, 160
Responsibility of student, 10, 22, 58
Responsibility of teacher (integrated
    with student), 58
Retelling, to test understanding, 112,
    113–115, 149–150
Retention, 296
Revision (rewriting). *See* Writing
Rhythm and rhymes
  easy rhymes, 217
  nursery rhymes, 190–191
  in predictable text, 196
  rhymes as reading aid, 445
  rhythm of language (speech en-
    velopes or breath groups), 53–54
Ritalin, 398
Routine, establishment of, 23
Rudimentary concept of word, 207–
    208. *See also* Concept of word

SAT test, 410, 411. *See also* Tests and
    testing
Scaffolded instruction, 18–19, 314
Scanning, 348. *See also* Reading rate
    (speed)
Schemas, 44–45
Schneider, Becky
  classroom of, 249–253
  discusses students, 257–263
School as community for learning,
    463–466
  literacy-rich classrooms, 463–465
  schoolwide programs, 465–466
School time, 30–31
Scores. *See* Test scores
Scribbling, 70, 185, 200
  importance of, 19
Self-concept of student, 47–51
Self-esteem, lack of, 391
Self-evaluation
  student, 14–15, 161–162, 330–331
  teacher, 15–16, 163–164
Semantic system of language, 126

Semiphonemic. *See* Phonemic aware-
    ness
Sequential pattern in predictable
    text, 196
Shared book experience, 196, 201,
    465
Shared context, 41–42
Shared reading, 216–218
  combined with language experi-
    ence materials, 220
Short vowels, 77–78, 79, 82–83, 242
  short-vowel patterns, 243, 244
  short-vowel word families, 242
Skimming, 348. *See also* Reading rate
    (speed)
Slingerland approach, 456–457
Small-group assessment, 145–153,
    356
  GLTA and GRTA in, 145, 146–
    147, 148
  instructional events as means of,
    148–153
Social context as important part of
    learning, 21
Social world, 28, 29–41
  ecology of language and literacy
    learning, 29–36
  social aspects of studying, 349, 352
  social class defined, 286
  social importance and history of
    literacy, 36–38
  suggestions for effective instruction
    in, 38–41
Socioeconomic diversity, 283–294
  poverty, 56–57, 288
  and test results, 428–429
  transience, 390
Sorting activities
  concept sorts, 202–204
  closed and open sorts, 203, 336
  picture sorts, 451
  See also Word sorts
Spanish, 274–275
  -influenced English, 274
  -language pattern books, 217
  WISC-III available in, 418
Special services and programs for
    students with learning difficul-
    ties, 403–404, 439–441
Spectator role, 45

Speech (spoken or oral language), 36,
    42
  communicative, 175–176
  noncommunicative, 175
  oral language repertoires, 32
  rhythms of (speech envelopes or
    breath groups), 54
Spelling
  assessment of, 120, 121–122, 127
  assessment of, spelling by stage,
    146
  beginning level, 229, 237
  checklists, 237, 333, 373
  derivational constancy phase, 87,
    88–89, 362–363, 373–376, 378
  emergent level, 70, 172
  functional levels, 99, 102
  instruction integrated with assess-
    ment, 235–245, 332–337, 362–
    378
  integrated model of, 63–64
  intermediate and advanced level,
    87–88, 362–378
  invented, 58, 120, 229, 303, 346,
    363–364, 451
  invented by deaf student, 402
  inventory, 121, 157, 158, 163, 364
  learning difficulties in, 451, 453
  letter-name, 72, 76–79, 122, 123,
    235, 242–243, 244–245
  prephonemic and semiphonemic,
    see Phonemic awareness
  syllable-juncture phase, 87, 88,
    122, 123, 362, 364–373, 377
  synchrony between reading and,
    111
  transitional level, 82–83, 303
  within-word pattern, 82–83, 122,
    123, 333–337
  word study coordinated with, 243–
    244, 337, 376–377
  See also Orthographic knowledge
Spelling-meaning connection, 363
SSR (sustained silent reading), 72,
    222, 233, 309, 324, 464
  books on tape along with, 444
SSW (sustained silent writing), 233–
    234
Standardized test, 164, 412. *See also*
    Norm-referenced tests

Stanine scores, 413, 414
STAR program, 466
Stereotypes, 266, 293
Stories
    acting out, 45, 151
    concept of story, 45–46, 47
    listening to, 68–69
    listening to, for non-English-speaking students, 281–282
    pattern, 216, 217–218
    student response to, *see* Response to literature
Story mapping, story chart, 346, 348
Storytelling, 197–199
    Western, 274
Students
    abilities and talents recognized, 9, 52
    additional academic support for, 294–298
    age of, 173–74, 270
    at-risk, 266, 267, 294, 299
    autobiographies of, 141–142
    background of diverse, 272–273, 287–288
    at beginning of school year, 140
    beginning readers and writers, *see* Beginning literacy
    cooperative groups of, 232–233, 292, 324, 330–332, 360–361, 465 (*see also* partnerships of, *below*)
    diversity of, 10–11, 267–300
    emergent, *see* Emergent literacy
    feedback to, 52, 153, 232
    first language of, 278
    getting to know them, 142–145
    goals of, 52, 142, 438–439
    handwriting of, 55, 57–58
    health and safety of, 59
    input of, into assessment process, 11–12, 378
    integration with teacher roles and responsibilities, 58
    intermediate and advanced, *see* Intermediate and advanced literacy
    involved in integrated process, 9, 11–12
    and language, assessment and knowledge of, 57, 175–176

    with learning problems, *see* Learning difficulties
    literacy learning as viewed by, 249–264
    multicultural and multiracial, 34–36, 269, 283–297
    non-English-speaking, 34, 269–270, 271–273, 278
    partnerships of, 40–41, 221, 232–233, 264, 298, 360–361, 443–444
    portfolios centered on, 156–157, 192–193
    prior knowledge of, 322
    reading and writing by, *see* Reading; Writing
    reading groups guided by, 354–355
    reading material chosen by, *see* Reading
    response of, to literature, *see* Response to literature
    response of, to peers' work, 159, 160, 330
    responsibility of, 10, 22, 58
    retention of, 296
    self-concept of, 47–51
    self-evaluation by, 14–15, 161–162, 330–331, 355
    sharing results with, 132–135
    with special needs, 267, 294–298
    teacher reading to and with, *see* Oral reading (reading aloud)
    three worlds of experience of, 27–59
    in transitional stage, *see* Transitional literacy
    troubled, 52, 388, 391
    work displayed, 464
    See also Children; Preschoolers
Studying
    how to study a chapter, 351
    social aspects of, 349, 352
    by students with learning difficulties, 454–455
    study skills, 349
    "study smart," 47
Subject areas, integration of, 58
Success for All program, 466
Summaries and Profile guides, 127–133

Support, additional academic, 294–298
Support activities
    reading, 212, 222–224, 445–448
    for teacher, 468–469
    writing, 224–232, 356–359, 449
Syllable juncture phase, 87, 88, 122, 123, 362, 364–365, 377
    word study in, 365–373
Synchrony, 62, 65
    between reading and spelling, 111
    See also Integration
Syntactic system of language, 125
Syntax, 270

Tagalog words, 276
Talk. *See* Language; Speech
Talking about books, 151–52. *See also* Response to literature
Tape, books on, 444, 447, 448, 454
Taping
    class notes, 454
    text, 297, 307–308
    See also Videotapes
Teacher(s)
    at beginning of school year, 140, 141
    -centered portfolio, 156
    ESL (English as a Second Language), 60
    and growing as professional, 466–469
    integration with student roles and responsibilities, 58
    involved in integrated process, 9
    literacy learning as viewed by, 249–264
    as model, 52, 306
    observation by, 12 (*See also* Observation)
    -parent relationships, 141, 288, 294
    personal log of, 164, 467
    pressured by curriculum, 38, 39
    reading to and with students, *see* Oral reading (reading aloud)
    as researcher, 469
    resource, 441
    self-evaluation by, 15–16, 163–164
    special, 441

(Teacher(s), *cont.*)
support activities for, 468–469
vigor of, 22
workshops for, 469
Teacher-made inventories, 112
Teacher-made tests, 11, 164
Teaching
"Big T" and "little t," 38–39
developmental, 52
four guidelines for, 17–23, 24
is not telling, 17, 21–22
and learning not the same, 20
reciprocal, 314
Television, 108
Telling vs. teaching, 21–22
Tests and testing
achievement, 412, 416, 438
alternative strategies, 455
of comprehension, *see* Reading
comprehension
criterion-referenced, 10, 412,
421–422
developmental, 412
diagnostic, 410, 417–421
end-of-year, 6
fairness of, 10–11
formal, 6, 295, 423–429
grading, 6, 14
how to take, 349
individual, 416–421
intelligence, 6, 412, 418–421
informal, 6
placement, 11
reliability of, 411, 412
standardized, 412 (*see also* Norm-
referenced [standardized] tests)
teacher-made, 11, 164
terms describing, 412
validity of, 411, 412
See also Assessment; Inventories
Test scores, 412
distribution of, 413–416
inadequacy of, 438
Textbook Activity Guide, 325
Text-explicit and text-implicit questions, 312
Theme units, 298
Thinking
critical, 43
critical, D-TRL and, 314–315

DRTA, 4, 5, 6, 46
schemas for, 44
See also Cognition
Three worlds of experience. *See*
Worlds of experience
Title I, 404, 433, 441
Tomatis method, 456
Transactional mode, 44, 45
Transience, 390
Transitional literacy, 80–85, 103,
104, 105, 303–338
checklists (reader, writer, word
study and speller), 307, 326,
333
and exploring literature, 336–337,
338
language difficulties and, 395
overview of, 303
readers and writers identified,
303–305
reading speed, 306, 308
reading with students, 306–324
students reading and writing on
their own, 324–326, 330–332
three important issues of, 304–305
transitional readers discussed and
interviewed, 258, 260
writing with students, 327–330
Traumatic brain injury, 401
Tutoring, 466
cross-age, 298

Understanding, 37
levels or types of, 42–43
listening comprehension, 119
of story construction, 69–70, 75,
82, 87
See also Reading comprehension
United States
literacy rate, 37–38
population, 269
Utility of test outcome, 412

VAKT approach, 456
Validity of test, 411, 412
VCCV and VCV patterns, 366–367
Videotapes, 467
for non-English-speaking students,
278
Vigor and common sense, 18, 22

Vision difficulties, 391–394
and visual training, 392–393
Visual perception, 48
Vocabulary
lexicon of language, 270
list-group-label strategy in building, 322
mixed, 35
sight, expansion of, 81, 85, 395
sight, slow development of, 395
special, word cards for, 370–371
word study and, 375–376
See also Language
Vocabulary comprehension questions, 114
Vowels (long and short), 76–79, 82–
83
differentiating between, 242–243
long vowel sounds and patterns,
334, 337, 395
picture sorts for, 451
sorting for word families, 242–243

Web of ideas, 212, 346, 372
Wechsler Intelligence Scale for Chil-
dren-III (WISC-III), 418, 421,
450
Whitney Elementary School (Las
(Vegas), 250–253
Whole-class assessment, 141–145
guided listening-thinking activity
(GLTA), 142–145
instructional events as means of,
148–153
profile sheets, 154
Within-word pattern. *See* Spelling
Woodcock Reading Mastery Test,
418
Word bank, 239, 241, 243
Word calling, 310
Word cards (for special vocabulary),
370–371
Word concept. *See* Concept of word;
Concept of word in print
Word knowledge. *See* Orthographic
knowledge
Word posters, 334
Word recognition in isolation, 108–
109, 110, 111. *See also* Ortho-
graphic knowledge

Words
  in context, identifying, 238–239, 333–334
  pictures of, *see* Picture cards and pictures
  sight, 239
  space between, *see* Writing
Word sorts, 239–241, 242–243, 334–336, 371, 373, 374
  for learning difficulties, 451
Word study
  activities for student with learning problems, 449–453
  brainstorming in, 242, 243, 368, 373, 378
  checklist, 373
  in context, 242
  in derivational constancy phase, 374–376
  games, 241, 243, 451
  guided, in reading, 367–373
  guidelines for setting up activities, 374–375
  integrated with assessment, 235–245, 332–337, 362–378
  in letter-name phase, 242–243, 244–245
  notebooks, 335–336, 373
  principles of, 244
  semiphonemic phase, 235–241
  small-group, 153
  spelling coordinated with, 243–244, 337, 376–377
  in syllable-juncture phase, 365–373
  and vocabulary development, 375–376
Word study books, 375
Workshops
  reading, 149–153, 221, 353–354
  for teacher, 469
  writing, 153, 233, 360–361
Worlds of experience, 27–59
  physical, 52–59
  psychological, 28, 41–52
  social, 28, 29–41

Writing
  beginning writers, 79–80, 207–208, 224–235
  behaviors and development, 6
  daily, 465
  developmental expression of, 127
  different forms of, 358–359 (*see also* Poetry)
  difficulty in, 385, 398, 448–453
  editing, 231, 330, 357–358
  editing checklist, 332
  emergent writers, 173–174 (*see also* Emergent literacy)
  in English as second language, 274, 283
  evaluation of, 123–126, 365
  expository (nonfiction, transactional mode), 45, 84, 125, 127, 211–212, 327
  fiction (poetic mode), 45, 46
  functional levels, 99, 102, 103, 127
  at home, 462–463
  independent activities, 233–235, 330–331, 360–361
  informal inventory of, 133
  instruction integrated with assessment, 224–235, 326–332, 356–362
  integrated model of, 63–64
  integrated with reading, 465
  intermediate and advanced, 85, 89, 127, 356–362
  journal-keeping, *see* Journals
  language use in, 124–126
  learning to write by, 18–21
  letter reversals in, 48
  letter-writing, 234
  mechanics of, 359, 448, 449
  metacognitive strategies in, 47
  as most sophisticated mental activity, 42
  motivation in learning to write, 49–50
  newsletters, 461–462

  narrative, evaluating skills in, 124, 126
  peer, 298
  personal (expressive mode), 45
  physical act of, 55–56
  in play centers, 199
  poetry, 327–329
  postwriting, 231–232
  preparing for assessment of, 359
  prewriting, 228–229
  recurring and generativity principles, 179
  religion and, 36
  as response to literature, 151
  rewriting, 231, 329, 357–358
  space between words, 80, 179, 193, 230
  stories, brainstorming in, *see* Brainstorming
  by students (choice of topic), 464
  by students (on their own), 330–332, 360–362
  support activities for, 224–232, 356–359, 449
  sustained silent (SSW), 233–234
  ten-minute assessment, 143–145
  together (freewriting), 52, 120, 122–123, 224–232, 327–330, 356–359
  transitional writers, 80, 83–85, 303, 327–330
  workshops, 153, 233, 360–361
  See also Handwriting; Scribbling; Written language
Writing from the Heart program, 466
Written language
  development of, 36, 42
  inexperience with, 389
  orthography of, 47
  schemas in, 44–45
  speech rhythms in, 54
  See also Language; Writing

Zone of proximal development, 21, 41